Criminal Law

Principles and Cases
Third Edition

West's Criminal Justice Series

Bennett & Hess *Criminal Investigation*

Blonien & Greenfield *California Law Manual for the Administration of Justice*

Burns *Corrections: Organization and Administration*

Cromwell & Keefer *Police-Community Relations, Second Edition*

Cromwell, Killinger, Kerper, Walker *Probation & Parole in the Criminal Justice System, Second Edition*

Cromwell, Killinger, Sarri & Solomon *Juvenile Delinquency: Readings*

Dix & Sharlot *Cases and Materials on Basic Criminal Law, Second Edition*

Dowling *Teaching Materials on Criminal Procedure*

Faust & Brantingham *Juvenile Justice Philosophy: Readings, Cases and Comments, Second Edition*

Felkenes *Michigan Criminal Justice Law Manual*

Ferdico *Criminal Procedure for the Law Enforcement Officer, Third Edition*

Ferguson *The Nature of Vice Control in the Administration of Justice*

Ferguson *Readings on Concepts of Criminal Law*

Gaines & Ricks *Readings on Police Organization and Management*

Gardner *Law of Criminal Evidence*

Gardner *Criminal Law, Third Edition*

Hess & Wrobleski *Introduction to Private Security*

Imwinkelried, et al *Criminal Evidence*

Johnson *Elements of Criminal Due Process*

Johnson *An Introduction to the Juvenile Justice System*

Kenney & More *Principles of Investigation*

Kerper & Israel *Introduction to the Criminal Justice System, Second Edition*

Kerper & Kerper *Legal Rights of the Convicted*

Killinger & Cromwell *Corrections in the Community: Readings, Second Edition*

Killinger & Cromwell *Introduction to Corrections: Readings*

Killinger, Cromwell and Cromwell *Issues in Corrections and Administration*

Killinger, Cromwell and Wood *Penology: The Evolution of Corrections in America, Second Edition*

Klein *Law of Evidence for Police, Second Edition*

LaFave *Principles of Criminal Law*

Leonard *Fundamentals of Law Enforcement: Problems and Issues*

Lewis *Criminal Procedure: The Supreme Court's View-Cases*

Maddex *Constitutional Law: Cases and Comments, Second Edition*

Markle *Criminal Investigation and Presentation of Evidence*

More *The American Police: Text and Readings*

More *Criminal Justice Management: Text and Readings*

More *Effective Police Administration, Second Edition*

Parker & Meier *Interpersonal Psych. for Law Enforcement and Corrections*

Perrine, et al *Administration of Justice: Principles and Procedures*

Roberg *Police Management and Organizational Behavior*

Roberg & Webb *Critical Issues in Corrections: Problems, Trends and Prospects*

Samaha *Criminal Law*

San Diego Police Department *Police Tactics in Hazardous Situations*

Schwartz & Goldstein *Law Enforcement Handbook, Second Edition*

Senna & Siegel *Juvenile Law: Cases and Comments*

Senna & Siegel *Introduction to Criminal Justice System, Third Edition*

Siegel *Criminology*

Siegel & Senna *Juvenile Delinquency: Theory, Practice and Law*

Smith & Berlin *Introduction to Probation and Parole, Second Edition*

Souryal *Police Administration and Management*

Sutor *Police Operations: Tactical Approaches to Crimes in Progress*

Vetter & Territo *Crime & Justice in America: A Human Perspective*

Wadman, Paxman & Bentley *Law Enforcement Supervision: A Case Study Approach*

Wrobleski & Hess *Introduction to Law Enforcement and Criminal Justice*

Criminal Law
Principles and Cases
Third Edition

Thomas J. Gardner
Member of the Wisconsin Bar and
Practicing Attorney
Police Science Instructor,
Milwaukee Area Technical College
Former Assistant District Attorney

West Publishing Company
St. Paul New York Los Angeles San Francisco

Copyediting: Barbara Hodgson
Interior Design: Mary Foster
Artwork: Century Design
Cover Design: Lucy Lesiak Design

Library of Congress Cataloging in Publication Data

Gardner, Thomas J., 1921–
    Criminal law.

    Includes index.
    1. Criminal law—United States—Cases. I. Title.
KF9218.G36 1985   345.73   84–17273
ISBN 0–314–85237–9   347.305

2nd Reprint—1987

Explanatory Note

The author has attempted to present the general principles of criminal law in this textbook. However, because of the variance in state statutes and court decisions from state to state, it is recommended that students and officers consult with their legal advisers before assuming that principles of law applicable in other jurisdictions exist in their states.

*To Tom C. and his
beautiful sisters.*

Summary of Contents

Table of Contents

Introduction

Despotism has been defined as the anarchy of lawless rulers, and anarchy as the despotism of lawless crowds. The forty men who met at the Philadelphia Convention in 1787 feared both extremes as they wrote a proposed new constitution for their society which was in crisis because of severe economic, political and foreign problems.

The Constitution that emerged from the Philadelphia Convention continues to be used today as the supreme law of the land. Its vitality is attributed to the fact that it permits a balance to be maintained between individual liberties and the collective needs of the society; between personal freedoms and the need for public order; and between the right to different lifestyles and the need for some degree of uniformity.

This Constitution and the system of government established under it have served the American people well for more than 190 years. It is not a perfect system of government because there never has been and never will be an absolutely perfect government in this world. Under this system Americans have emerged from the ten years of the severe depression of the 1930s and the four years of intense war in the early 1940s to become the most prosperous and affluent people in the world. Americans are also the freest people in the world as they enjoy more personal, economic, social and political freedom than any other people in the world.

Rational men since the early Greek philosophers have recognized that personal freedoms are never absolute. The personal freedoms of one person end when his or her activities come into conflict with the rights and freedoms of other persons or are contrary to the over-all needs and good of the society as expressed by the statutes and laws. The cliche that "your freedom extends as far as the end of my nose" is sometimes used to express the limited concept of freedom. Therefore, in a democratic society, government must regulate conduct to a limited extent, by use of criminal and civil laws, to ensure the rights and freedoms of the society as a whole.

Only a responsible society may be free. Persons in the society must generally respect the rights and dignities of their fellow men. They must also recognize their obligations and duties toward the society as a whole. In a democracy, this means bowing to the will of the majority upon occasion, because in a democracy as in a marriage, the individual does not always get his or her own way if the marriage or the democracy is to survive.

The 18th-century member of British Parliament, Edmund Burke, expressed this requirement of responsibility in a democracy in this way:

> Men are qualified for civil liberty in exact proportion to their own disposition to put moral chains upon their own appetites. Society cannot exist unless a controlling power upon will and appetite be placed somewhere and the less of it there is within, the more there is without. It is ordained in the external constitution of things that men of intemperate minds cannot be free. Their passions forge their fetters.

Personal freedoms and rights may be infringed on in many ways. The elderly persons who do not venture out of their homes at night because of the fear of being criminally assaulted have had their personal freedoms infringed on. The victims of a crime have had their rights infringed on. There is always the possibility in a democracy that the government (or one of the agencies of government) will abuse the power and authority vested in it and will infringe upon the liberties and rights of the people. Overseas, totalitarianism in the form of Fascist, Nazi and Communist governments have presented severe threats to the free people of the world.

The struggle for freedom and liberty goes on constantly in all democracies. American history is a record of this struggle and of the efforts to define the rights of the individual. Criminal law is a study of the authority of government to regulate conduct within constitutional limitations so that maximum freedoms and liberties may be enjoyed by all.

Thomas J. Gardner

Criminal Law

Principles and Cases
Third Edition

Part One

Basic Concepts of
Criminal Law

Chapter 1

Criminal Law Generally

A. INTRODUCTION TO CRIMINAL LAW

Does the United States Have a Serious Crime Problem?

The United States does have a serious crime problem. The problem has existed for some time. Detroit had hoped for a drop in crime, but instead, because the major crime rate was up 14 percent in 1983, a teenage curfew had to be imposed to break up a wave of violent street crime. Miami has been fighting a crime rate that is up 165 percent from the early 1970s.

Illinois Governor James R. Thompson, cochairman of the National Violent Crime Task Force, stated:

> The threat of violent crime has reached epidemic proportions. The statistics have gone off the charts; and it does not require a litany of shocking examples to recognize that each crime statistic represents a victimized human being, a shattered life, or a broken family. The time has come to take a unified approach to the problem of violent crime. The magnitude of the threat to our domestic tranquillity requires a consensus reaction.

> * * *

> Violent crime is exacting a fearful toll in the communities of our nation. Millions of our fellow citizens are being held hostage by their fear of crime and violence. Though violent crime can strike anyone, it most frequently affects the poor, the old, and the residents of the inner cities—precisely those persons who are least able to protect themselves. Even those who can afford a suburban residence or a privately guarded city apartment often find themselves defenseless on the streets.[1]

Countries in the free world[2] have always sought to ensure freedom through a system of laws that would protect the basic rights of individuals within their societies. Although public order is primarily a function of state governments and municipalities, domestic tranquillity cannot be achieved without the public's cooperation.

As a first step toward seeking public order, laws are enacted. Laws are rules created by government for the orderly functioning of an organized society. Criminal laws are rules of conduct that forbid specific acts or, in some instances, require certain acts. Criminal laws are distinguished from civil laws primarily because violations of criminal laws can be punished by imprisonment or other severe penalties.

The Goals of a Democracy

Through a system of laws, a democracy seeks to translate its basic principles and ideals into achievable goals. One of these goals is that of achieving public order and domestic tranquillity. To achieve these goals and remain a nation of laws requires a fine tuning in the balancing of the rights of individuals with the compelling needs of the society as a whole.

Criminal justice systems operate most successfully in democracies in which the majority of the people believe that the system and the laws are fair and that the system can operate efficiently and effectively.[3]

Laws Should Be the Will of the People

In a democracy, laws should be a product of the will of the people. Laws are enacted by the duly constituted representatives of the people. They are enforced, administered, and interpreted by civil servants and elected officials in other branches of government. In the United States, those branches are:

1. *The legislative branch.* Laws (including criminal laws) are enacted by the legislative branch. The chief executive officer participates in the legislative process by signing or vetoing proposed laws.

Government Regulation of Conduct

Government may regulate conduct by means of:

1. Civil offenses created by statutes or ordinances that usually punish specifically forbidden conduct only by fines or forfeiture (for example, speeding is ordinarily a civil offense punishable by a fine and forfeiture of points)

2. Criminal offenses that may be punished by imprisonment

---

2. *The executive branch.* Agencies within the executive branch of government administer and enforce laws. Law enforcement agencies are found within the executive branch of government and are charged with the enforcement of criminal laws, in addition to performing other duties.

3. *The judicial branch.* Persons who are charged with crimes have a right to be tried before a judge or a jury in a court in the judicial branch of government. Fact finders (jury or judge) determine the ultimate issues in cases presented before them. The issue of guilt or innocence is dealt with by the jury (if the case is tried before a jury). Judges in the United States have the power of judicial review in determining the constitutionality of laws or ordinances.

Public policy and laws are determined through democratic political processes. Debates as to what the law should or should not be take place constantly in democracies. Law enforcement officers do not make laws. Their traditional tasks are to enforce laws and maintain public order. They are also called on to provide a wide range of other public services, such as dealing with family disputes, coping with community tensions, guiding community crime prevention efforts, and providing aid in time of emergencies or disasters.[4]

Public and Private Law

Laws can be classified as either private or public laws. Private laws deal with relationships between individuals in which the government has only an indirect interest. Included in this group are such laws as the law of domestic relations (marriage, divorce, etc.), contract law, real estate law, and the law of private inheritance.

The government has a more direct interest in public laws and, in most instances, has specific responsibilities. Some examples of public law are public health laws (purity of foods and drugs, sanitation, etc.), vehicular and traffic laws, laws of criminal procedure, and criminal laws.

In early England, such offenses as robbery, theft, and murder were classified as private laws because it was believed that these offenses affected only the individual victims and did not directly affect the state. Victims or their families or clans would usually retaliate with violence if they knew who the offender was. They also had the alternative of bringing legal action against the offender. During the reign of Henry II (1154–89), English law first recognized that crime was more than a personal affair between the victim and the perpetrator, and that punishment should not be left largely to private enforcement. Today, criminal law is public law in both England and the United States, since it is recognized that crimes are offenses not only against the victim, but also against society. Criminal actions in the United States are brought only by the government, whereas the victim of the crime (or the heirs) may initiate a civil action against the offender. English law, however, has carried over some of the old concept; thus if the government decides not to initiate a criminal action, the victim may retain a private attorney and initiate both a criminal and a civil action.

The Subfields of Criminal Law

Law is a means to an end. To have an orderly society, there must be rules (law) controlling and governing the limits of individual behavior. American criminal law is made up of a number of subfields. *Substantive criminal law,* with which this book concerns itself, is one of those subfields. It concerns the conduct, acts, and omissions that have been designated as crimes. The acts (or omissions) plus the mental state and other essential elements are the ingredients that constitute a crime.

Criminal procedure is another subfield of criminal law. It consists of the steps that governmental agencies follow from the criminal incident through punishment of the offender. Other courses of study dealing with criminal procedure are criminal investigation, criminal evidence, and arrest, search, and seizure.

Criminology and criminalistics are fields that are separate from but related to substantive criminal law. *Criminology* is the sociological study of (a) the causes of crime, (b) the control of crime, and (c) the conditions under which criminal law developed. *Criminalistics* is the professional and scientific discipline directed to the recognition, identification, individualization, and evaluation of physical evidence by application of the natural sciences. Criminology is a branch of sociology; criminalistics is the application of science to criminal investigation and encompasses forensic science.[5]

Substantive Criminal Law

Substantive criminal law is an important branch of public law. It defines the standards of conduct that the society and the community require for the protection of the community as a whole. It establishes the standards necessary to preserve public order and to protect property rights. It protects the right of individual privacy and the right to move about freely without fear of molestation. It does this primarily by defining conduct that is unacceptable and therefore punishable.

In ancient times and on the frontiers in America, people had to protect themselves and thus moved about armed with weapons. If the law could not (or would not) punish an offender, the victim or family and friends would take on the punishment of the offender. Such retaliations could trigger blood feuds that went on for years between families and clans.

With the establishment of a system of laws and the growth of public confidence in the ability of the criminal justice system to preserve ordered liberty, people have generally ceased taking the law into their own hands. Public confidence that government, as an agent of the people, has the ability and the desire to maintain public order is an indispensable ingredient of a successful criminal justice system.

Legal Wrongs

Legal wrongs are either civil or criminal. A *civil wrong* is a private wrong (such as a tort or a contract violation) done to a person or property; a *criminal wrong* is a wrong in which the state and the public have declared an interest. Ordinarily, when a private wrong occurs, only the injured party or the party's representative may seek civil redress in a civil court of law. In almost every large American community there are two or three times as many civil courts, hearing civil cases in which private wrongs are alleged, as there are criminal courts, hearing cases involving public wrongs. In cases of public wrong, the state may either begin a criminal action in a criminal court or take the alleged public wrong into a civil court, as is done occasionally in obscenity, antitrust, or consumer fraud cases.

Distinction Between a Crime and a Tort

A *tort* is a civil wrong done to a person or to his or her property. The law of torts is the closest of the civil private laws to that of criminal law.

Legislative Designations of Crime

Reasons a Legislative Body Might Designate Specific Conduct as Criminal	*Reasons a Legislative Body Might Not Designate Specific Conduct as Criminal*
• To protect the public from violent or dangerous conduct	• It is not within the power of the government to prohibit such conduct.
• To protect public health	• The conduct in question is constitutionally protected.
• To maintain public order	• There is no demand by influential public or private groups or individuals for the regulation of such conduct.
• To protect the right of privacy of individuals	
• To protect public morality	• It would not be economically feasible to enforce a law criminalizing such conduct.
• Because there appears to be no other way in which to promote a desired public policy	• It would not be politically popular to pass a law criminalizing such conduct.

Often the same wrong may constitute both a tort and a crime. For example, battery, rape, theft, criminal libel, and criminal damage to property are all torts and also crimes. Both civil actions by the injured parties and criminal actions by the state may be brought against the offenders. The offenders may be convicted of the crime in a criminal court and then in a civil court found to be civilly liable and ordered to pay compensatory and punitive damages to the victims for the torts that were committed.

A man who has thrown rocks at the windows of a private building, breaking ten windows and injuring one of the occupants before he is stopped, has committed both crimes and torts. Not only may a criminal action be brought against him for his conduct, but civil tort actions may also be brought against him by the person who was injured and by the person whose property was damaged. However, a man who has seriously injured another person in an automobile accident, in which the police and a prosecutor determine that there was neither a criminal violation nor criminal negligence, cannot properly be charged with a crime. In this case, only a civil action may be brought by the injured person or his or her representative. If the defendant were found to be civilly liable, this would then be an example of a tort that was not also a crime.

B. THE CRIMINAL LAW AND THE MORAL LAW

Criminal laws reflect the moral and ethical beliefs of the society. Murder, for example, is considered morally wrong, and most people would not murder another person even if it were not forbidden by all American jurisdictions. Murder, then, is forbidden not only by the criminal law, but also by the moral law. This moral or ethical commitment to the law is known as the "law behind the law." The importance of the "law behind the law" lies in the fact that it compels most people to conform to standards necessary for public order regardless of whether a police officer is watching them or not. Public order is not possible without the "law behind the law," as there are not enough police to enforce criminal law without this moral and ethical backing. Without moral or ethical commitments, who would watch the watchman or who would "police the police"?

The standards set by moral laws are generally higher than those set by criminal laws. Moral law attempts to perfect personal character, whereas criminal law, in general, is aimed at misbehavior that falls substantially below the norms of the community. Criminal conduct is ordinarily unjustifiable and inexcusable.

Criminal law alone cannot bring all conduct into conformity with the standards expected by the community. Society uses many sanctions besides criminal law to encourage and coerce people to behave properly. A person with a good job and savings knows that a substantial money judgment could be obtained against him if he assaults, rapes, or libels other people. A man who beats his wife could end up in a divorce court instead of a criminal court. A person who is rude, abusive, and vulgar will lose friends and

Distinguishing Crime, Tort, and Moral Wrong	
Type of Wrong	*Court Determining Wrong*
Crime A public wrong against society	Criminal court
Tort A private wrong against an individual or individuals	Civil court
Moral wrong Violation of a moral or religious code	No punishment unless the moral wrong is also a crime or tort
A crime may also be a tort and a moral wrong.	For example, murder is a crime, a tort, and also a moral wrong.

social standing. An employee who cannot get along with other people or who punches another employee in the face could be fired by the employer. Suspension of a driver's license and the revocation of a tavern license are other examples of sanctions used to regulate behavior.

Criminal codes do not include all the general moral concepts of society. The issue of which moral concepts should be embodied in a criminal code is primarily a political question, although courts may override lawmakers when constitutional issues are involved. For example, to many Americans, abortion is a moral wrong, but the U.S. Supreme Court has ruled on the constitutional limitations of the states' and the federal government's power to criminally forbid abortion in *Roe v. Wade* [6] (see Chapter 13). This decision, like any other U.S. Supreme Court decision, could be vacated and set aside by an amendment to the U.S. Constitution that would give the federal and state governments full power to legislate in this area. Whether such an amendment would have sufficient support to be proposed and ratified is a political question for the Congress and the state legislative bodies.

The Eighteenth Amendment is an example of another dilemma that every democratic society faces. What social and governmental controls should be used to regulate the manufacture, sale, and consumption of alcohol? In 1918–19 a substantial number of Americans believed that consumption of intoxicating liquors was immoral and caused considerable social harm. They mustered sufficient political support to propose and ratify the Eighteenth Amendment forbidding the manufacture, sale, and consumption of intoxicating liquors except for limited uses. However, a significant number of Americans did not see anything morally wrong with having a glass of beer or a highball, thus creating a market for contraband, which the underworld readily supplied. The lesson learned from this situation was that if a significant number of people oppose and will not comply with a criminal law, enforcement of such law can run into serious difficulties.

Why a Person Would Or Would Not Commit a Crime

Why a Person Would Not Commit a Crime	*Why a Person Would Commit a Crime*
Moral or ethical commitment to obey the law ("law behind the law")	Neither moral nor ethical restraints are sufficient
Fear of arrest and punishment	Belief that he or she can get away without detection, arrest, and punishment
Social and peer pressures, of friends, associates, family, and community	Peer pressure
Fear of embarrassment to self, family, and friends	Because of belief that detection can be avoided, there is no embarrassment
Lack of motive or compelling drive to commit crime (no compelling desire to steal, murder, assault, rape, etc.)	Strong compelling desire or motive to achieve illegal objective (narcotic addiction, for example, provides motive for person who would probably not otherwise commit crime)
Lack of opportunity, or lack of capacity or skill to commit crime	Opportunity presents itself and person has capacity and skill
Fear of economic sanction: • loss of job, promotion • lawsuit and damages • loss of license, such as driver's license, tavern, lawyer, doctor, nurse, etc.	Crime can be a quick, easy way of obtaining money, drugs, power, or other objectives. Even if caught, the odds are good that the person will not go to prison. No more than three felonies out of a hundred result in imprisonment for the offender.

Consider the following examples that further illustrate other moral dilemmas:

Example 1: In 1983, a young woman entered a crowded New Bedford, Massachusetts tavern to purchase cigarettes. Men in the bar grabbed her and commenced gang-raping her. While she was being sexually assaulted, other tavern patrons watched and some cheered. No one came to her aid nor did anyone call the police. If this incident occurred in your state, could any of the witnesses be charged with a criminal offense?

Example 2: In 1964, Kitty Genovese was murdered in New York City in an attack that lasted some 35 minutes. More than 38 persons were in nearby apartments, with most witnessing the attack. Had the police been called immediately, or had someone come to her assistance, Kitty Genovese could have been saved. If this incident occurred in your state, could any of the witnesses be charged with a criminal offense?

The Principle That There Can Be *"No Punishment Without a Law for It"*

A basic principle of both English and American law is that no one can be lawfully punished for his or her conduct (or omission) unless that conduct has been clearly made a crime by statutory or common law of that jurisdiction. The Latin maxim *Nulla poena sine lege* ("no punishment without a law for it") long ago established this principle.

When Failure To Act Is a Crime: Crimes of Omission

Statute number of the offense in your state. (If not a crime, indicate status of this conduct in your state.)

1. Failure to remain at the scene of a vehicular accident in which a person was involved. (Also list other responsibilities of the person required in your state.) _____

2. Failure to aid an officer when requested to do so _____

3. Failure to report the death of a child _____

4. Failure to report the location of a human corpse _____

5. Failure by parent, guardian, etc. to provide adequate food, clothing, shelter, medical care, supervision, etc. for a child in their care when harm results or might result _____

6. Failure by parent, guardian, etc. to come to the aid of a child in their care when such aid would not place the adult in any serious danger _____

7. Failure to leave or withdraw when ordered by a public official who has declared that an unlawful assembly exists _____

8. Failure to "move on" or to leave a place when properly and lawfully ordered to do so by a law enforcement officer _____

9. Failure to properly identify oneself and explain one's conduct when properly and lawfully ordered to do so by a law enforcement officer (see sec. 250.6 Loitering or Prowling of the Model Penal Code) _____

10. Failure to submit to a breathalyzer test (or other similar test) when properly and lawfully requested to do so by a law enforcement officer _____

11. Failure to obey a proper and legal order of a court (see Chapter 21, on contempt) _____

12. Homicide by omission (see the Ford Pinto case in Chapter 5) _____

Although it is impossible for the state to enumerate in detail each act (or omission) that the legislature seeks to forbid, the criminal statute may describe generally the act or acts forbidden (or required). However, the criminal statute must be directed at a defined evil (or wrong) and must be written clearly enough to provide notice as to what acts are forbidden (or required).

Therefore, in view of the principle that there can be "no punishment without a law for it," the following questions must be asked before any person is arrested, charged with a crime, or convicted: *What has the person done that violates the statutes or common law of your state? Was the person legally (not morally) obligated to act and did he fail to perform his legal (not moral) duty?*

In view of these principles, did the witnesses in Examples 1 and 2 commit acts in violation of criminal laws in your jurisdiction? The answer is no, as none of their acts was unlawful. The next questions to be asked are *Was the person legally (not just morally) obligated to come to the assistance of the person in trouble? Was the person obligated to do something? Did the person cause or participate in the death (or murder) by the decision not to intervene?* Parents are legally obligated to help their children. The common law requires that husbands come to the assistance of their wives. Unless your state has a statute imposing an obligation on bystanders to come to the assistance of people in distress, there is no legal duty.

Civil Liability of Witnesses to Crimes

Witnesses to crimes are not criminally liable unless they perform acts that make them parties to the crime (see Chapter 4, Criminal Liability).

Are witnesses civilly liable for failure to act or to render aid in some form? The general rule of law is that there is no civil liability.[7] Public and private organizations, however, must exercise ordinary care in providing adequate security for customers, tenants, and others who are lawfully on their premises. This relationship creates a duty to aid and protect.

Because the tavern employees in Example 1 did not come to the aid of the woman being sexually assaulted, the tavern is civilly liable to the woman. A civil lawsuit was filed for this breach of duty to the woman, who was a customer and lawfully on the premises.[8]

C. CLASSIFICATION OF CRIMES

Many acts have been designated as criminal offenses in the United States. The President's Commission on Crime reported in 1966 in *The Challenge of Crime in a Free Society* (p. 18) that

---

"Good Samaritan" Laws

Broadly defined, "Good Samaritan" laws include statutes that fall into the following categories:

1. Practically all states have enacted "Good Samaritan" laws that encourage doctors and other health practitioners to aid injured or ill strangers. Such statutes do not encourage acts of heroism or impose a duty to aid, but rather they eliminate fear of malpractice suits that had discouraged doctors and others from rendering assistance to those who had been injured or were ill.

2. Some European countries impose on their citizens a duty to come to the aid of another and to rescue if this can be done without danger or peril to the person. Few states have enacted such statutes. Vermont is one of the exceptions. Failure to come to the aid of another when such aid "can be rendered without danger or peril to himself" is punishable by a fine up to $100 in Vermont.

3. Another form of a "Good Samaritan" law is a statute passed by Maryland in 1982: "Any person witnessing a violent assault upon the person of another may lawfully aid the person being assaulted by assisting in that person's defense" (Art. 27, Sec. 12A). This statute and others authorizing force in self-defense or the defense of another *do not impose a duty* to come to the assistance of another. See the 1982 case of *Alexander v. State* in Chapter 6, in which a prisoner in a Maryland penitentiary saw two guards subduing another prisoner and intervened to help the other prisoner.

the federal government alone has designated more than 2,800 offenses as crimes and noted that "a much larger number of State and local" offenses exist.

The large number of crimes in the United States may be classified as follows:

1. According to their sources, as statutory, common law, administrative, or constitutional crimes (see Chapter 2)

2. As felonies or misdemeanors, which determines the method in which they are tried and, in many states, affects the law of arrest for such offenses (see the following material)

3. According to the harm or wrong that occurs (see your state criminal code for classifications of crime, such as "crimes against the person," "crimes against property," etc.)

Felony and Misdemeanor

The felony–misdemeanor classification is the most common classification used for crimes. In old English common law, crimes were classified as either treason, felony, or misdemeanor. Treason was the most serious of the three, with the lands of the traitor being forfeited to the king on conviction. The felon's land might also be for-

feited, but usually he did not meet so horrible a death as the traitor. Ironically, under early English common law, those who were charged with a misdemeanor could call witnesses in their favor and have the assistance of counsel, whereas those who were charged with a felony did not have these rights.

As the years went by the classification of treason faded away because people were rarely charged with the crime. In 1967, the English Parliament decided that the distinction between felonies and misdemeanors had become so blurred that all distinctions between the two classes were abolished by the Criminal Law Act of 1967. The English now use the classification of arrestable and nonarrestable offenses. An English police officer has no power to arrest for the latter without a warrant, which limits the arrest authority of British police. But British officers have considerably more search authority than do American officers.

For procedural purposes, England now classifies crimes as summary and indictable offenses. *Summary offenses* are minor criminal charges tried before a magistrate having summary jurisdiction. A number of offenses that were previously felonies were made summary offenses. There is no right to a jury trial for a summary

---

Arrests for Criminal Offenses

In 1982, an estimated 12.1 million arrests were made for criminal offenses. The under-25 age group accounted for 53 percent of arrests nationally. The top 10 offenses for which arrests were made in this group are:

1.	Driving under the influence	1,778,400
2.	Larceny/theft	1,368,100
3.	Drunkenness (decriminalized in some states)	1,262,100
4.	Disorderly conduct	895,500
5.	Burglary	527,100
6.	Liquor law violations	501,300
7.	Marijuana violations	455,600
8.	Fraud	334,400
9.	Vandalism	245,700
10.	Weapon violations	193,500

Males accounted for 84 percent of all arrests and 90 percent of violent crimes. The offense that females were most often arrested was larceny/theft.

Note: Four of the top six offenses are alcohol-related offenses.
Source: FBI Uniform Crime Report, 1982

offense. Serious offenses, which are now referred to as *indictable offenses,* are all tried before a jury. This is possible because English jury procedures are much faster than those used in impaneling a jury in the United States. The distinction between serious and minor crimes is maintained in England, but the main distinction today lies in the right to have the offense tried with or without a jury.

The automatic forfeiture of the land of an offender was never used as a punishment for serious offenses in the United States, and treason was never used as a classification separate from felonies and misdemeanors. The classification of minor crimes as misdemeanors and serious crimes as felonies has always been used in the United States, and it has been the responsibility of legislatures to determine which crimes are misdemeanors and which are felonies. The legislatures have added many new felonies to the original list of common law felonies. Most of these new felonies are offenses not known at common law, but there are instances of common law misdemeanors becoming statutory felonies.

Effect of the Felony–Misdemeanor Classification Today

In the United States, whether a crime is a felony or a misdemeanor is important for the following reasons:

1. Public policy has made a felony a more serious offense than a misdemeanor. Imprisonment in a state prison and a longer term of imprisonment could be imposed for a felony. A felony conviction on a person's record could seriously affect his or her entering any of the professional fields. It would prevent employment with any law enforcement agency. It would prevent the obtaining of a commission with the U.S. armed forces. It might affect credit rating or ability to adopt a child. A misdemeanor conviction would not ordinarily have these effects.[9]

2. Law enforcement officers in states using the "in-presence" requirement for misdemeanor arrests may not make an arrest for a misdemeanor not committed in their presence. An arrest for a felony may be made if the officer has reasonable

grounds to believe that the person has committed the felony, regardless of whether or not the offense was committed in the officer's presence.

Example: An officer in a state using the "in-presence" requirement is sent to a department store, where the store security man tells him that he saw X shoplift a $25 item. Because the offense is a misdemeanor and did not occur in the officer's presence, the officer ordinarily may not make an arrest.

In the example given the officer would obtain the identification of the person and then "order the person in," that is, instruct him to report to the office of a prosecuting attorney at a given time. If the officer has reasonable grounds to believe that the person (a) will not report in as required, or (b) will cause injury to himself or others unless immediately arrested, or (c) will cause damage to property, the officer may then make an immediate arrest if the officer's jurisdiction uses these circumstances as exceptions to the "in-presence" requirement rule.

3. A person charged with a felony has a right to a preliminary hearing (or a "presentment or indictment of a grand jury").[10] The person must also be tried by a court having jurisdiction to hear felony cases. The person charged with a misdemeanor must be tried by a court having jurisdiction to hear and decide misdemeanor cases.

4. In most states, citizens would have no authority to make an arrest for a misdemeanor under their "citizen arrest" power unless the law of the state permitted an arrest for a breach of the peace committed in the citizen's presence. However, a citizen may generally arrest for a felony committed in his or her presence unless the statutes or common law of the state (or jurisdiction) provide otherwise.

Crimes of Commission as Distinguished from Crimes of Omission

The majority of criminal laws specifically punish certain acts of commission. These criminal laws forbid the commission of specific acts. Within each criminal code are a few laws by which the state imposes on a person an obligation and a duty to act under certain circumstances. A motorist who is involved in an accident is obligated to stop, render assistance, and identify himself or herself. Failure to comply with these demands of the law would be a crime of omission.

Before an officer makes an arrest or a prosecutor issues a criminal complaint, each must ask (a) what did the person do that violated the law or (b) what duty did the person fail to perform that he or she was legally obligated to?

White-collar Crimes

Such crimes as murder, rape, robbery, auto theft, battery, and larceny are ordinarily classified as "street crimes." Crimes that do not involve direct physical violence but yet are crimes of personal or corporate gain may be classified as "economic crimes," "business crimes," or "commercial crimes."

The term *white-collar crime* was originated in the 1930s by sociologist Edwin H. Sutherland to indicate the nonviolent crimes of personal enrichment committed by people in their work or occupation or, occasionally, in defrauding other people or governmental agencies. These crimes may be committed in offices, banks, financial institutions—anywhere money, securities, or anything of value is handled by white-collar employees and supervisors. Cheating, dishonesty, and corruption can also be found among blue-collar workers in factories, industrial plants, and other employment situations. Professor Sutherland originally intended the term white-collar crime more as a classification of offenders than as a classification of offenses. However, the term seems to be used today more as a classification of offenses.

Victimless Crimes

The term *victimless crimes* is used to designate crimes that do not have a victim in the sense that murder, robbery, rape, battery, and theft do.

Examples of Victimless Crimes Used by Many or All States

Drug violations

Public drunkenness * (decriminalized by many states)

Prostitution

Gambling (many forms of gambling now legalized)

Obscenity offenses involving consenting adults

Fortune telling

Dueling (both parties consent but can result in victim)

Loan sharking (when both parties voluntarily enter agreement)

Examples of Victimless Crimes That Have Been Abolished by Many States

Fornication
Adultery
Homosexual relations
Cohabitation
} Between consenting adults in a nonpublic place

Examples of Victimless Crimes That Have Been Declared Unconstitutional

Use of contraceptives (even by married couples)—*Griswold v. Connecticut,* 381 U.S. 479 (1965)

Possession of or reading obscene material in privacy of one's home—*Stanley v. Georgia,* 394 U.S. 557 (1969)

California made drug addiction a crime in and of itself—*Robinson v. California,* 370 U.S. 660 (1962)

* More arrests are made every year in the United States for public drunkenness than for any other offense.

Most victims of reported crimes are cooperative with the police and anxious that the offender be apprehended. The victimless crime is a crime committed by two or more persons, both of whom readily participate in the crime. Such offenses include narcotics violations, gambling, prostitution, homosexual acts, and liquor violations. For example, X sells heroin to Y (an addict) in X's apartment. No one else is present. The transaction is a crime, but the offense is unlikely to come to the attention of the police because there is no victim and neither X nor Y have any intention of disclosing their criminal act. (See Chapter 20 in which material from the Criminal Justice Standards and Goals Report is quoted, stating that the "nature of some victimless crimes makes them excellent targets for organized crime.")

The National Advisory Committee on Criminal Justice Standards and Goals also advises that "states and localities should exercise caution in considering the legalization or decriminalization of so-called 'victimless crimes' . . . because there is insufficient evidence that legalization or decriminalization of such crimes will materially reduce the income of organized crime."

D. GENERAL LIMITATIONS ON CRIMINAL LAWS

Ex Post Facto Laws

Article I, Sections 9 and 10 of the U.S. Constitution prohibit federal and state governments from enacting ex post facto laws. Most state constitutions also forbid such laws. Ex post facto (after the fact) restrictions apply only to criminal laws. Therefore, a state legislature may pass a new tax law and make it retroactive. Taxpayers would not like this and political reactions could result in the defeat of elected officials, but such a law would not involve constitutional violations.

The ex post facto limitation restricts the following: (a) creating a criminal law and making it retroactive so as to make conduct before the enactment of the law a criminal violation; (b) laws that aggravate a crime retroactively (for example, making a misdemeanor a felony as of a date six months before the enactment of the

legislation); (c) laws that increase the punishment for a crime retroactively; and (d) laws that alter the legal rules of evidence and permit conviction on less or different testimony than the law required at the time of the commission of the offense.

An ex post facto law is, then, a retroactive criminal law that works to the detriment of the defendant charged with an offense. However, a retroactive law that benefits a defendant is not forbidden. For example, a state legislature may pass a retroactive law that reduces a felony to a misdemeanor. In such case, the defendant would not challenge the validity of the law.

In the 1977 case of *Dobbert v. Florida*,[11] the U.S. Supreme Court reviewed the ex post facto cases that had come before that Court over the years. In the *Dobbert* case the defendant was sentenced to death under a Florida statute that was revised after the defendant's crimes to afford more, not less, protection. The penalty of death was part of the statute before the crimes and was retained in the statute after the crimes were committed. The Supreme Court affirmed the defendant's conviction, as the new statute provided him with more, rather than less, judicial protection than did the old statute.

Bill of Attainder

Article I, Sections 9 and 10 also forbid Congress and the states from enacting any bill of attainder. A *bill of attainder* is a legislative act that inflicts punishment without a judicial trial. In 1965, the U.S. Supreme Court stated the history of the bill of attainder, in *United States v. Brown:*

> The bill of attainder, a parliamentary act sentencing to death one or more specific persons, was a device often resorted to in sixteenth, seventeenth and eighteenth century England for dealing with persons who had attempted, or threatened to attempt, to overthrow the government. In addition to the death sentence, attainder generally carried with it a "corruption of blood" which meant that the attainted party's heirs could not inherit his property. The "bill of pains and penalties" was identical to the bill of attainder, except that it prescribed a penalty short of death e.g. banishment, deprivation of the right to vote, or exclusion of the designated party's sons from Parliament. Most bills of attainder and bills of pains and penalties named the parties to whom they were to apply; a few, however,

simply described them. While some left the designated parties a way of escaping the penalty, others did not. The use of bills of attainder and bills of pains and penalties was not limited to England. During the American Revolution, the legislatures of all thirteen States passed statutes directed against the Tories; among these statutes were a large number of bills of attainder and bills of pains and penalties.[12]

By forbidding bills of attainder, the Constitution limits legislatures to the task of rule making and gives to the courts the function of determining whether rules have been violated. In the *Brown* case, the defendant was a San Francisco longshoreman and an officer of his union. He was an open and avowed Communist and was charged and convicted of violating the Labor–Management Reporting and Disclosure Act of 1959, which made it a crime for a member of the Communist party to serve as an officer or an employee of a labor union. In a 5–4 decision, the Supreme Court held that the Reporting and Disclosure Act of 1959 was a bill of attainder, and stated that "Congress must accomplish such results by rules of general applicability. It cannot specify the people upon whom the sanction it prescribes is to be levied. Under our Constitution, Congress possesses full legislative authority, but the task of adjudication must be left to other tribunals."

Legislative bodies, however, have the power to punish for contempt for such acts as disrupting or immobilizing their vital legislative functions (see Chapter 21 and the 1972 U.S. Supreme Court case of *Groppi v. Leslie* in that chapter).

Void-for-Vagueness

In writing a criminal statute or ordinance, a legislative body must use clear and precise language that gives fair and adequate notice as to the conduct that is forbidden (or required). If the language of a statute or ordinance is vague, it may be held unconstitutional under the "void-for-vagueness" doctrine.

The void-for-vagueness test asks whether a statute or ordinance on its face "is so vague that men of common intelligence must guess at its meaning and differ as to its application."[13] A vague criminal statute or ordinance creates un-

certainty as to what the law requires and may have some or all the following results:

1. It may trap those who desire to be law-abiding by not providing fair notice of what is prohibited.[14]

2. It may cause arbitrary and discriminatory enforcement, since those who enforce and apply the law have no clear and explicit standards to guide them.[15]

3. When a vague statute "abut(s) upon sensitive areas of First Amendment freedoms, it operates to inhibit the exercise of (those) freedoms. Uncertain meaning inevitably leads citizens to steer far wider of the unlawful zone . . . than if the boundaries of the forbidden areas were clearly marked."[16]

Overbreadth

Criminal statutes and ordinances may also be held to be unconstitutional if the manner in which they are written violates the Overbreadth Doctrine. In 1967, the U.S. Supreme Court stated that overbreadth "offends the constitutional principle that a governmental purpose to control or prevent activities constitutionally subject to state regulation may not be achieved by means which sweep unnecessarily broadly and thereby invade the area of protected freedoms."[17]

A vague statute or ordinance may be overbroad if its uncertain boundaries leave open the possibility of punishment for protected conduct and thus lead people to avoid such protected activity in order to steer clear of violating the uncertain law.[18] However, a clear and precise statute may also be overbroad if it prohibits constitutionally protected conduct.

The void-for-vagueness test and the overbreadth test are separate and distinct. However, when First Amendment rights are at issue, the U.S. Supreme Court uses the two tests in a manner that makes them virtually one doctrine. From the cases, it can be stated that statutes and ordinances that regulate conduct must comply with the following requirements:

1. Fair and adequate notice must be given as to the conduct that is forbidden (or required).

2. A precise standard of conduct must be specified in terms of results that can reasonably be expected.

3. The statute or ordinance cannot permit or encourage arbitrary and discriminatory law enforcement that may result in erratic and arbitrary arrests and convictions.

4. The statute or ordinance cannot violate or infringe on rights that are secured or granted by the U.S. Constitution.

The following are some of the cases in which the Supreme Court has applied these doctrines:

COATES v. CITY OF CINCINNATI

Supreme Court of the United States (1971)

402 U.S. 611, 91 S. Ct. 1686

In this case, the Court declared unconstitutional a Cincinnati ordinance that made it illegal for three or more persons assembled on a city sidewalk to "annoy" those passing by. The Court stated:

Conduct that annoys some people does not annoy others. Thus, the ordinance is vague, not in the sense that it requires a person to conform his conduct to an imprecise but comprehensible normative standard, but rather in the sense that no conduct is specified at all.

PAPACHRISTOU v. CITY OF JACKSONVILLE

Supreme Court of the United States (1972)

405 U.S. 156, 92 S. Ct. 839

The Supreme Court held the following Jacksonville ordinance unconstitutionally vague:

Rogues and vagabonds, or dissolute persons who go about begging, common gamblers, . . . common drunkards, common night walkers, . . . lewd, wanton and lascivious persons, . . . common railers and brawlers, persons wandering or strolling around from place to place without any lawful purpose or object, habitual loafers, . . . shall be deemed vagrants.

"Status" Crimes

Criminal laws forbid persons from performing specific acts that have been determined to be harmful to others or to the society as a whole. In a few instances, criminal laws require certain acts. Under such criminal laws, persons may therefore be charged and convicted for what they have done or what they have failed to do.

But can a person be arrested and convicted for what he or she is—that is, a "status" or "chronic condition" that a person might voluntarily or involuntarily acquire? This question came before the U.S. Supreme Court in the 1962 case of *Robinson v. California*.[19] In that case, the defendant was convicted of violating a statute making it a criminal offense for a person to be addicted to the use of a narcotic.

In pointing out the many ways in which government may legitimately attack the evils of narcotic trafficking, the U.S. Supreme Court reversed the defendant's conviction. In holding that a state law that made "status" of narcotic addiction a criminal offense for which an offender might be prosecuted and imprisoned at any time, the Court held that such a criminal statute inflicted a "cruel and unusual punishment" in violation of the Eighth and Fourteenth Amendments of the U.S. Constitution. The Court stated that "even one day in prison would be a cruel and unusual punishment for the 'crime' of having a common cold."

In the 1968 case of *Powell v. Texas*,[20] the defendant was an alcoholic with approximately 100 arrests for acts of public intoxication. In this case, the defendant argued that since he was compelled to drink and since he could not control his "status," the state did not have the power to punish him for his acts of public intoxication. The U.S. Supreme Court, however, affirmed the defendant's conviction for public intoxication and would not extend the rule of law that had been established in the case of *Robinson v. California,* holding:

Traditional common-law concepts of personal accountability and essential considerations of federalism lead us to disagree with appellant. We are unable to conclude, on the state of this record or on the current state of medical knowledge, that chronic alcoholics in general, and Leroy Powell in particular, suffer from such an irresistible compulsion to drink and to get drunk in public that they are utterly unable to control their performance of either or both of these acts and thus cannot be deterred at all from public intoxication.

QUESTIONS AND PROBLEMS FOR CHAPTER 1

1. X and his wife, Y, were involved in an automobile accident in which X was not at fault in any way. However, their 10-year-old child was seriously injured. A doctor at the scene of the accident told X and Y that the child could be saved with immediate medical attention. However, because of their religious beliefs, X and Y refused to allow their child to be treated. The child died the next day. Could X and Y be charged? What could the charge be?

2. M is hired by a family that is going on vacation, to take care of their 90-year-old grandmother. M is to feed and give daily medication to the elderly woman, who cannot get out of bed. After three days on the job, M quits without notifying anyone and takes another job. The elderly woman dies because she did not receive medication or food and water for two days. Should M be charged with a criminal offense? Specify. (For a discussion of criminal imputability for negative acts, see pp. 591–610 of *Perkins on Criminal Law,* 2d ed. [Mineola, N.Y.: Foundation Press 1969].)

3. A five-year-old child is in sudden peril when a big wave hits him while in shallow water at the beach. Each of the following could have saved him with no risk to himself but all fail to come to the child's assistance. Indicate the legal liability of each and whether he can be charged in your state with the death of the child.
   a. the father of the child
   b. the lifeguard on duty

   c. a man who took pictures of the child's death

4. In a bad storm over your state, a plane lost most of its power 50 miles from the closest landing field. To lighten the load, the crew threw out baggage and other items. When this was not enough, the crew, in desperation, began to throw passengers off the plane. Had not 20 of the 40 passengers been thrown off, the pilot would not have been able to land the plane safely. Should the crew be congratulated for saving the plane, or charged with the deaths of the passengers who were killed?

5. Ten-year-old Johnnie is punished by his mother for eating all the cookies in the cookie jar. Which of the following instructions by the mother, given just before she left the house for an hour, would not violate the void-for-vagueness principle?
   a. "Be a good boy, Johnnie."
   b. "Don't do anything naughty, Johnnie."
   c. "Don't go into the cookie jar, Johnnie."
   d. "Don't eat anything and spoil your appetite because we are going to have dinner in an hour."
   e. c. and d. are correct

6. In the 1974 case of *Sumpter v. State,*[21] the defendant was convicted of the Indiana offense "of living in a house of ill fame." How should the following issues, which were presented to the Supreme Court of Indiana, be decided?
   a. The defendant argued that the use of the term "house of ill fame" is too imprecise

to adequately inform the defendant of the conduct forbidden by law. Is the Indiana statute void for vagueness?

b. The defendant argued that the statute imposes punishment for a "status" rather than overt criminal conduct. Is the statute unconstitutional because it imposes punishment for a "status"?

c. The defendant argued that the prostitution statute violated her First Amend-

ment rights in that Judeo-Christian ethics were given the force of criminal law. The defendant also argued that her right to equal protection of the laws was violated because the statute applied to women and not to men. How did the Indiana Supreme Court rule on these issues?

Chapter 2

Purposes, Scope, and Sources of Criminal Law

A. PURPOSES OF CRIMINAL LAW

Background of the American Criminal Justice System

People in all societies have the inherent right to protect their society and those living in that society from vicious acts that threaten either the society or the people. All societies in the history of the world have exercised this inherent right and have had either written or unwritten laws forbidding and punishing acts (or omissions) considered detrimental to the group or the individual.

From colonial days up through World War I, the criminal codes of the various American states were generally small and usually embodied only those crimes that were considered serious wrongs against the society. Because these criminal laws were used to define and enforce public morality, the traditional attitude of lawyers and judges was that a crime was essentially a moral wrong.

The United States in those days was primarily an agricultural society with a much more simple style of life than that of today. Since most people lived in rural areas or small towns, the criminal codes could confine themselves primarily with conduct that was considered a serious threat to society. In those days, religious institutions, the family, and social pressure from the neighborhood and the town were generally capable of regulating behavior in other respects.

The 1920s saw the beginnings of the rapid change of the United States from an agricultural society to an industrial society. This transformation, plus the unbelievable array of economic, social, and political changes that accompanied it, hastened the arrival of today's mass industrial society. With these changes, there was a lessening of the influence of American religious institutions, the community, and the home in molding and shaping behavior (particularly of youth) to the standards expected by society. To compensate for this change, criminal laws were passed in great profusion, and the burden of maintaining public order and safety was gradually shifted to the American justice system, causing it to strug- gle under an overload for the past 25 years. The American criminal justice system now bears the main burden of maintaining public order and safety.

General Purposes

The general purposes and objectives of American criminal law can best be expressed by the U.S. Constitution, which is the supreme law of the land. The Preamble to the Constitution states that the purposes of the Constitution (and government) are to "establish Justice, insure domestic Tranquility, . . . promote the general welfare and secure the Blessing of Liberty to ourselves and our Posterity." The U.S. Supreme Court has stated that the "most basic function of any government is to provide for the security of the individual and of his property."[1]

The U.S. District Court for the District of Columbia expressed the objective and purpose of criminal law in these terms in the first degree murder case of *United States v. Watson:*

> The object of the criminal law is to protect the public against depredations of a criminal. On the other hand, its purpose is also to prevent the conviction of the innocent, or the conviction of a person whose guilt is not established beyond a reasonable doubt. The Court must balance all these aims of the trial. This view was eloquently stated by Mr. Justice Cardozo in Snyder v. Commonwealth of Massachusetts, 291 U.S. 97, 122, 54 S. Ct. 330, 338, 78 L.Ed. 674: ". . . justice, though due to the accused, is due to the accuser also. The concept of fairness must not be strained till it is narrowed to a filament. We are to keep the balance true."[2]

Goals and Purposes of Criminal Law and the Criminal Justice System

1. To discourage and deter people from committing crimes

2. To protect society from dangerous and harmful people

3. To punish people who have committed crimes

4. To rehabilitate and reform people who have committed crimes

Criminal Law and the Right of Privacy

The criminal justice system and criminal law are essential in protecting the right of privacy that we treasure for ourselves and for our families. In discussing the right and the expectation of privacy, the U.S. Supreme Court wrote the following in 1967:—"The protection of a person's general right of privacy—his right to be let alone by other people—is, like the protection of his property and his very life, left largely to the law of the individual States." [3]

B. THE PERMISSIBLE SCOPE OF CRIMINAL LAWS IN THE UNITED STATES

Although criminal law and the criminal justice system are essential parts of the rule of law in a democracy that provides for basic freedoms, they are often used as instruments of suppression in a totalitarian state. Instead of ensuring freedom, criminal law in a dictatorship is often used to maintain the regime in power and to legalize a rule of terror and brute force. In a democracy, the criminal justice system and criminal law cannot master the people. They can be used only to serve the people. Therefore, there must be constitutional limits of the power of government to regulate the conduct of its citizens through the use of criminal law.

The Use of the Police Power to Maintain Public Order

Each state is responsible for the maintenance of public order and public safety within that state. To do this, the state must enact criminal laws

---

Development of Criminal Law in the United States

English criminal law as developed in the common law of England by English judges who adopted customs and usages

1st Stage in the American Colonies

Use of English common law as it came across the Atlantic with the early settlers

2nd Stage in the Independent American States Under the Articles of Confederation

Enactment of common law crimes into statutes and ordinances by newly created American legislative bodies

Continued use of other common law crimes in either their original or modified forms

3rd Stage with the Establishment of a Federal Form of Government Under the Present Constitution of the United States

Further definition of crimes by state legislatures with the creation of many new crimes in the past 50 years

Diminished use of common law crimes in all states with more than half the states abolishing common law crimes

In 1812, the U.S. Supreme Court held that federal courts had no authority to adopt common law crimes. Therefore, all federal criminal prosecutions "must be sustained by statutory authority."

and a criminal justice system under the "police power" of that state. The "police power" is an inherent power vested in each state. The Tenth Amendment of the U.S. Constitution provides that "the powers not delegated to the United States by the Constitution, nor prohibited by it to the States, are reserved to the States respectively or to the people."

The police power of the state is ordinarily defined as the power and the responsibility of the state to promote and provide for public health, safety, and morals. In the 1949 case of *Kovacs v. Cooper,* the Supreme Court stated:

> The police power of a state extends beyond health, morals and safety, and comprehends the duty, within constitutional limitations, to protect the well-being and tranquility of a community. A state or city may prohibit acts or things reasonably thought to bring evil or harm to its people.[4]

In the 1974 case of *Village of Belle Terre v. Boraas,* the Supreme Court sustained a zoning ordinance restricting land use to one-family dwellings, stating:

> The police power is not confined to elimination of filth, stench, and unhealthy places. It is ample to lay out zones where family values, youth values and the blessing of quiet seclusion, and clean air make the area a sanctuary for people.[5]

Limitations on the Use of the Police Power of the State to Regulate Conduct

In enacting criminal laws through the use of the police power, the state is regulating the conduct of citizens within the state by telling them what they may not do or what they must do. The state may not regulate conduct arbitrarily.

In enacting criminal law, the state must be able to show:

1. That there is a compelling public need to regulate the conduct the state seeks to regulate, and that the power to regulate is within the police power of the state. The U.S. Supreme Court held in *Lawton v. Steele* that "it must appear, first, that the interests of the public generally . . . require such interference; and, that the means . . . are not unduly oppressive upon individuals." [6]

2. That the law does not contravene the U.S. Constitution or infringe on any of the rights granted or secured by the U.S. Constitution or the constitution of that state.

3. That the language of the statute (or ordinance) clearly tells people what they are not to do (or what they must do) and that the law prohibits only the conduct that may be forbidden.

The following examples are used to illustrate these limitations. Suppose the following states create the following offenses as misdemeanors:

- State A enacts a law requiring that all people in the state go to a church of a specific religion every Sunday.
- State B enacts a law forbidding hula hooping and roller skating in that state.
- State C enacts a law forbidding the sale, use, or possession of any tobacco product.
- State D enacts a law requiring operators and passengers of motorcycles to wear protective headgear.

Not only would State A violate First Amendment rights to the freedom of religion by passage of a law of this nature, but also this statute is not within the police power of a state, as it serves no valid function of government. When the issue of the constitutionality of State B's law came before a court, State B would be asked why such a law was passed. State B would have to try to justify its law with arguments that public health, safety, or morals were involved. However, the law could not be justified because the sensitivities of a few people were disturbed by hula hooping and roller skating. There is no compelling public need for such a law, nor is it within the police power of the state to regulate this conduct. State C could show that its regulation is within the police power of the state because medical studies show that the use of tobacco products does affect peoples' health. A compelling public need for such a statute would have to be shown by State C to justify its regulation of this conduct. Enforcement of such a statute would be difficult, if not impossible.

Many states have passed statutes requiring motorcyclists and their passengers to wear protective head and eye gear. The issue of the constitutionality of these statutes has come before many state courts. The majority rule is that such statutes are a valid exercise of the police power of the state. The Wisconsin Supreme Court followed the majority rule in *Bisenius v. Karns* [7] and the issue was appealed to the U.S. Supreme Court, where the appeal was dismissed for want of a federal question.

Not all courts, however, have gone along with the majority rule. The Supreme Court of Illinois held in *People v. Fries* [8] that requiring operators and passengers to wear protective gear is beyond the police power of the state because the protection is for the person wearing the gear rather than for the public generally. A municipal court in Ohio ruled that there was no substantial relation to public health, safety, morals, or the general welfare, and that the statute was a denial of motorcyclists' liberty under the Fourteenth Amendment. The court stated that "included in man's 'liberty' is the freedom to be as foolish, foolhardy or reckless as he may wish, so long as others are not endangered thereby." [9]

C. SOURCES OF CRIMINAL LAW

Substantive criminal law can be found in the following sources, each of which will be discussed in the following pages:

1. Most criminal law is found in the statutes of each state and in the statutes of the federal government.

2. Criminal law can also be found in commercial, sanitation, health, financial, and tax administrative regulations that have criminal sanctions. These regulations are enacted by state and federal administrative and regulatory agencies.

3. A few sections of state constitutions and one section of the U.S. Constitution contain criminal law.

4. Criminal law, on rare occasions, can be found today in the common law of some states.

1. COMMON LAW CRIMES

As the common law was the first and earliest source of criminal laws, it is presented first. And because the historic source of American criminal law lies in the common law of England, it is necessary to review the development of criminal law in England and in the American colonies.

When the English kings gained control of the whole of England in the Middle Ages, royal judges began deciding civil and criminal cases throughout all of England, thus supporting the Crown by preserving the peace and dispensing justice. Few people in those days could read or write, and England was not yet a democracy. The king, the judges, and the ecclesiastical authorities played important roles not only in creating (sometimes inventing) criminal laws, but also in defining the elements and the scope of the criminal offenses. Judges became familiar with the general customs, usages, and moral concepts of the people and based judgments on them. In doing so, the judges determined which customs and moral concepts should prevail as law.

By the early 1600s, there were only a few criminal statutes, and the criminal law of England was made up primarily of the mandatory rules of conduct laid down by the English judges. In formulating the common law crimes of England, the royal judges believed that their decisions represented the best interests of the king and of the country as a whole. These decisions became the common law of England. As authoritative precedents, they were followed and applied in future cases wherever English common law was used and followed.

During this period of development of the criminal law in England, the English Parliament enacted a few criminal statutes, such as embezzlement, false pretense, and incest. The English ecclesiastical courts (religious courts) formulated and punished offenses that violated the moral code but that were not public offenses, such as private acts of fornication, adultery, and seduction.

The English settlers who began colonizing America in the early 1600s brought with them the English common law. This law formed the basis of the law in each of the individual colonies. Modifications and adjustments were made to meet the needs of the frontier life of each of the colonies. A great deal of discretion was vested in colonial governors, councils, and judges with respect to the enforcement and scope of offenses and with respect to the creation of new laws. However, for the most part, English common law crimes continued as the common law crimes in each of the colonies.

During the American Revolution and for some time after, there was a great deal of hostility toward the English in America, and this hostility extended to the common law. Justice Hugo L. Black of the U.S. Supreme Court referred to this situation in his 1958 dissenting opinion in *Green v. United States,* in which he stated:

> Those who formed the Constitution struck out anew free of previous shackles in an effort to obtain a better order of government more congenial to human liberty and welfare. It cannot be seriously claimed that they intended to adopt the common law wholesale. They accepted those portions of it which were adapted to this country and conformed to the ideals of its citizens and rejected the remainder. In truth, there was widespread hostility to the common law in general and profound opposition to its adoption into our jurisdiction from the commencement of the Revolutionary War until long after the Constitution was ratified.[10]

Many American lawyers and judges knew the value of many of the English common law principles, which at that point had been developing for more than 200 years. But the public wanted American law for Americans, and many changes were thus made by the new state legislative bodies, which transformed the English common law into statutory law.

Common Law Crimes in the United States

Most American states have used common law crimes (judge-made crimes) in their early histo-

ries. Some of these crimes were taken from English common law, whereas others were modified versions of English common law crimes. Others were defined by judges in those states.

In 1812, the case of *United States v. Hudson and Goodwin* [11] came before the U.S. Supreme Court. The defendants were charged with the common law crime of criminal libel because they wrote in a newspaper that the president of the United States and the Congress had secretly voted $2 million as a present to Napoleon Bonaparte. There was no federal statute making libel a crime, but criminal libel was a common law crime. The Supreme Court pointed out that state courts could punish a person for a violation of the common law crime of libel under their police power if they chose to adopt and incorporate the offense as part of the crimes of that state. But the Supreme Court held that federal courts had only that power and jurisdiction given to them by the U.S. Constitution and the Congress and had no power to adopt common law crimes. The rule that there are no federal common law crimes has been affirmed many times over the years. In 1949, Justice Robert H. Jackson wrote that "it is well and wisely settled that there can be no judge-made offenses against the United States and that every federal prosecution must be sustained by statutory authority." [12]

Today in the United States, almost half the states have abolished common law crime within their jurisdictions. In the states that have not abolished common law crimes, it is unusual for a person to be charged with a common law crime, because all state legislative bodies have enacted hundreds of statutory criminal offenses. A prosecutor who is charging a statutory offense is on much safer ground than he or she would be in charging a common law crime, which immediately leaves the charge vulnerable to attack. The following 1972 case illustrates the type of attack that may be made on common law crimes.

STATE v. PALENDRANO

Superior Court of New Jersey (1972)
120 N.J.Super. 336, 293 A.2d 747

The defendant (a woman) was indicted and charged in New Jersey with violating two statutory offenses and the common law crime of being a common scold. The defendant was found innocent of the two statutory offenses and made the following arguments against the common law crime of being a common scold:

1. *That a common scold [13] is no longer a crime in New Jersey.* The court agreed, stating, "Most, if not all of the elements of being a common scold are found in our present Disorderly Persons Act. To the extent that they are not found, such conduct is no longer an offense and is ignored by the law."

2. *That the charge is unconstitutionally vague and therefore unenforceable under the "due process" concepts of the Fourteenth Amendment of the U.S. Constitution.* The court agreed that the meaning of the term "common scold" has been all but lost over the years and thought that the average citizen should not be required to carry a pocket edition of Blackstone with him to ascertain what conduct was forbidden by law.

3. *That since only a woman can be a common scold the offense is a blatant violation of the equal protection requirement of the U.S. Constitution.* The Court agreed, stating that "the discrimination between the sexes is obvious. It is senseless. It is unconstitutional under the Equal Protection Clause."

Why Retain Common Law Crimes Today?

England retains and prosecutes a moderate number of common law crimes. However, it must be kept in mind that England, unlike the United States, has no written constitution, and that an act of Parliament is the supreme law of the land. English courts do not have the power to declare an act of Parliament unconstitutional. Nor does England use the federalist system of government under which a federal court system determines and imposes on state courts constitutional standards relating to criminal laws.

The English criminal justice system has operated remarkably well. This is probably one of the reasons why Parliament has not incorporated the remaining common law crimes of England into statutory form. Parliament also has apparently been satisfied with the judicial definition of these common law crimes and the limited number of prosecutions that charge common law crimes. There is no question of the constitutionality of such common law crimes in England, and the reasoning seems to be, "Why change that which is working well?"

Relatively few common law crimes exist today in the 20 or so American states that have not abolished common law crimes. Some argue that these common law crimes should be retained to fill any possible loopholes and gaps that might

exist in the statutory criminal codes of the states that have not abolished common law crimes. This argument, however, is weak in view of the results that occurred in the 1972 New Jersey "common scold" case.

Distinction Between Common Law Crimes and Common Law Rules of Criminal Procedure

Common law crimes are acts defined as crimes by judges; statutory crimes are crimes created and defined by a legislative body. Common law rules of criminal procedure are judge-made rules of criminal procedure having to do with such subjects as arrest, search, and seizure. There are also many statutory rules of criminal procedure that have been enacted by legislative bodies.

The abolition of common law crimes in about half the states does not mean that common law has been abolished. Abolishing common law crimes does not affect in any way the common law rules of criminal procedure or the civil common law rules that are used in civil courts. These rules remain in effect in all states unless the state legislative bodies pass laws changing them.

2. STATUTORY CRIMES

After the American Revolution, the new American state legislatures began converting common

Important Documents of the English-Speaking World

Magna Carta: 1215

A civil war in England forced King John to sign the Magna Carta (great document), which provided:

- No criminal "trial upon . . . simple accusation without producing credible witnesses to the truth therein."
- "No freeman shall be taken, imprisoned . . . except by lawful judgment of his peers or the law of the land."

Mayflower Compact: 1620

As the *Mayflower* rode at anchor off Cape Cod, some of the passengers threatened to go out on their own, without any framework of government. To avoid this threat of anarchy, the *Mayflower Compact* agreed that: "We . . . doe . . . solemnly and mutually . . . covenant and combine our selves together into a civil body politike for our better ordering and perservation . . . and by vertue hereof to enact . . . such just and equall lawes . . . unto which we promise all due submission and obedience."

English Bill of Rights: 1689

Because of the numerous attacks on personal liberty, the English Parliament forced King James II to abdicate and Parliament produced a Bill of Rights. This document served as a guide for Americans, as it provided that:

- "Suspending laws . . . without consent of Parliament is illegal."
- "Keeping a Standing Army within the Kingdom in Time of Peace unless it be with Consent of Parliament is against the law."
- "Election of Members of Parliament ought to be free."
- "Freedom of Speech . . . ought not to be impeached or questioned."

Declaration of Independence: July 4, 1776

After King George declared the American colonies to be in a state of rebellion and the English Parliament forbad all trade with the colonies, an eloquent statement of the American democratic creed was made in the *Declaration of Independence:*

> We hold these Truths to be self-evident, that all Men are created equal, that they are endowed by their Creator with certain unalienable Rights, that among these are Life, Liberty, and the Pursuit of Happiness.—That to secure these Rights, Governments are instituted among Men, deriving their just powers from the Consent of the Governed, that whenever any Form of Government becomes destructive of these Ends, it is the Right of the People to alter or to abolish it, and to institute new Government, laying its Foundation on such Principles, and organizing its Powers in such Form, as to them shall seem most likely to effect their Safety and Happiness.

U.S. Constitution: ratified 1788

Because of the failure to achieve a workable government under the Articles of Confederation, delegates from the American States met in Philadelphia in 1787. George Washington presided for months over the debates and arguments that led to the adoption and ratification of the Constitution used by the United States since that time.

law crimes to statutory form. Through the police power of the state, they had the power to amend, affirm, change, extend, abolish, modify, or alter any common law crime or rule. In many instances, state legislatures kept the common law crime intact by merely restating the law in statutory form. In other instances, legislatures created new crimes by forbidding and punishing conduct that was not a crime at common law. In still other instances, they redefined the common law crime by changing elements of the crime or removing common law limitations and extending the crime to cover conduct not included in the common law crime. If the common law punishment was considered too severe, changes were made in the degree or form of punishment. Attempts were made to clarify areas of doubt or uncertainty in common law crimes.

Practically all criminal laws that are enforced today are statutory laws enacted by legislative bodies. Most of today's statutory crimes were unknown at common law. Most of these criminal laws were enacted in the past 30 or 40 years to meet the problems of our mass industrial society.

3. ADMINISTRATIVE CRIMES

In 1911, the case of *United States v. Grimaud* [14] came before the U.S. Supreme Court. Congress had passed a statute authorizing the Secretary of Agriculture to make regulations concerning the use of government forests in order to preserve and maintain these areas as forest reserves. Violation of regulations created by the Secretary of Agriculture was made a criminal offense by the Congress. The defendant grazed his sheep on U.S. forest lands without first obtaining a permit as required under a regulation issued by the Secretary of Agriculture. As the federal courts were divided on the question of whether a violation of such regulation constituted a crime, the government appealed the case to the U.S. Supreme Court.

The Supreme Court held that Congress may constitutionally delegate to an administrative agency the power to make regulations that are enforced by criminal penalties established by that legislative body. The Court stated that the Secretary did not exercise the legislative power of declaring the penalty or fixing the punishment for grazing sheep without a permit, but the punishment is imposed by the act itself. The offense is not against the Secretary, but as the indictment properly concludes, "contrary to the laws of the United States and the peace and dignity thereof."

Today, it is well established that the Congress and most state legislatures may delegate to an administrative agency the power to make rules, and the legislature may provide by statute that such rules may be enforced by criminal penalties. In a few states, this procedure has been held to be unconstitutional. But in the majority of states, criminal laws may be created by the legislature establishing the framework and the administrative agency providing the specific regulation or rule within that framework. The delegation of such authority is constitutional in the majority of the states if:

1. the legislative act sets forth sufficient standards to guide the administrative agency and the act provides for criminal penalties for the violation of the administrative regulations created within the guidelines, and if

2. the administrative agency stays within the guidelines established by the legislative body in creating rules enforced by the criminal penalties; but

3. the rules of the administrative agency "must be explicit and unambiguous in order to sustain a criminal prosecution; they must adequately inform those who are subject to their terms what conduct will be considered evasive so as to bring the criminal penalties of the Act into operation" [15] and

4. the determination (adjudication) of whether there has been a violation of the "administrative crime" is made by a court with proper jurisdiction and is not made by the administrative agency.

Publication of Administrative Rules Having Criminal Sanctions

People who are subject to the criminal law cannot be presumed to know the law if information as to the contents of the law is not available to

Enactment and Requirements of Criminal Statutes

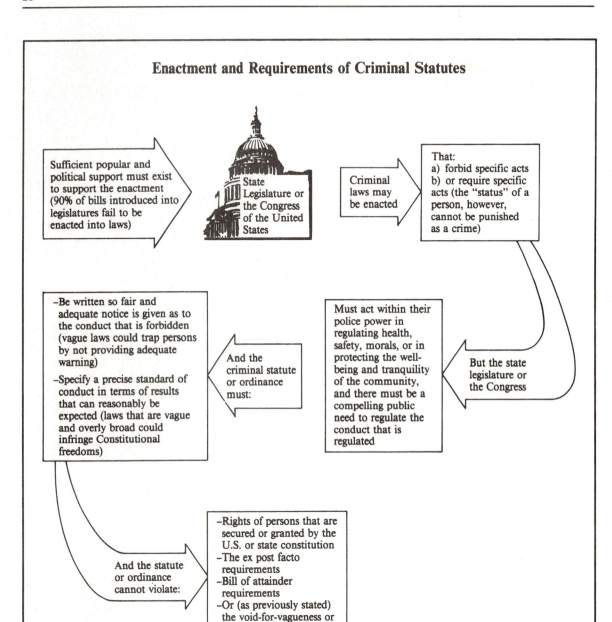

Sufficient popular and political support must exist to support the enactment (90% of bills introduced into legislatures fail to be enacted into laws)

State Legislature or the Congress of the United States

Criminal laws may be enacted

That:
a) forbid specific acts
b) or require specific acts (the "status" of a person, however, cannot be punished as a crime)

–Be written so fair and adequate notice is given as to the conduct that is forbidden (vague laws could trap persons by not providing adequate warning)

–Specify a precise standard of conduct in terms of results that can reasonably be expected (laws that are vague and overly broad could infringe Constitutional freedoms)

And the criminal statute or ordinance must:

Must act within their police power in regulating health, safety, morals, or in protecting the well-being and tranquility of the community, and there must be a compelling public need to regulate the conduct that is regulated

But the state legislature or the Congress

And the statute or ordinance cannot violate:

–Rights of persons that are secured or granted by the U.S. or state constitution
–The ex post facto requirements
–Bill of attainder requirements
–Or (as previously stated) the void-for-vagueness or overbreadth doctrines

Differentiation of Crimes				
Common law crimes	are	Custom, usage or moral values, and concepts of a community built up over a period of many years	plus	Adoption by judges of these customs or concepts in court decisions as crimes.
Statutory crimes	are	Enactment of bills by a legislative body	plus	Signing of the bills by the chief executive officer (governor or president).
Administrative crimes	are	Enactment of sufficient guidelines by a legislative body that are signed into law by the governor or president	plus	Authorized regulatory agencies create rules within the guidelines established by law.

them. This information is ordinarily available at public libraries or from governmental agencies on request. However, in 1933 and 1934, information as to administrative rules having criminal sanctions was sometimes not readily available from any source. The National Recovery Agency (NRA) and other New Deal agencies of the federal government were issuing regulations having criminal sanctions at an unprecedented rate because of the economic emergency that existed at the time. A committee of the American Bar Association (ABA) estimated that the NRA alone issued 2,998 orders in a one-year period and that these regulations were made known to the public through 5,991 press releases. Lawyers had to inform themselves of the law by reading the newspapers and hoping that the reporters had accurately reflected the facts. The ABA committee reported as follows:

> The total legislative output by, or in connection with, this one administrative agency staggers the imagination. Any calculation involves guess-work but a safe guess would be that the total exceeds 10,000 pages of 'law' in the period of one year. . . . Under these circumstances not only citizens but even lawyers are helpless in any effort to ascertain the law applicable to a given state of facts. The presumption of knowledge of the law becomes, to term it mildly, more than violent. Is it too much to expect that before these legislative enactments be given force and effect, they be subjected to simple formalities such as those suggested in the committee's conclusions? [16]

In 1935, the Federal Register Act was passed and in 1936 the Federal Register, designed for the publication of administrative orders and regulations, came into being.

4. CRIMINAL LAWS CREATED BY CONSTITUTIONS

The U.S. Constitution and state constitutions contain many provisions having to do with the rights of people within their jurisdictions, and they specify the criminal procedures that may or may not be used. They generally leave the definition of crimes to legislative bodies and the courts. The only sections of the U.S. Constitution that forbid or define conduct that is criminal are:

Article III, Section 3

(1) Treason against the United States, shall consist only in levying War against them, or in adhering to their Enemies, giving them Aid and Comfort. No Person shall be convicted of Treason unless on the Testimony of two Witnesses to the same overt Act, or on Confession in open Court.

(2) The Congress shall have Power to declare the Punishment of Treason.

Thirteenth Amendment

Section 1. Neither slavery nor involuntary servitude, except as a punishment for crime whereof the party shall have been duly convicted, shall exist within the United States, or any place subject to their jurisdiction.

Section 2. Congress shall have power to enforce this article by appropriate legislation.

State constitutions are usually considerably longer than the U.S. Constitution and contain more details. In addition to provisions having to do with treason and forbidding the holding of people in involuntary servitude, state constitutions may also forbid such conduct as dueling, cockfighting, and other offenses that concerned legislative bodies years ago.

5. INTERPRETATION OF CRIMINAL STATUTES

Criminal penalties were severe in the early history of the United States and England. The death penalty and long mandatory prison terms were common punishments for felonies. Because of the severity of these penalties, a rule of strict construction or strict interpretation of criminal laws came into existence. Under this rule, the courts would take the narrowest possible view in interpreting the offense and in determining the scope of the crime charged. Under the circumstances, this had a great deal of merit.

However, when state legislatures began reducing the number of mandatory sentences and reducing the severity of the punishment, many courts continued to use the rule of strict construction. This resulted in the occasional acquittal of offenders who had clearly violated the spirit and letter of the statutory law, but who were not successfully prosecuted because of the strict construction (interpretation) of the statute. Legislative bodies then began to attempt to anticipate every possible narrow interpretation that the courts might place on new statutes. As a result, the statutes became wordy and cumbersome.

In order to write criminal laws in simpler and clearer language, some legislative bodies began abolishing the "strict construction" rule by statute, so that they could avoid artificial and cumbersome language in proposed new criminal codes. Following are two examples of such statutes:

Texas: The provisions of this Code shall be liberally construed, so as to attain the objects intended by the

Legislature: The prevention, suppression and punishment of crime.[17]

New York: The general rule that a penal statute is to be strictly construed does not apply to this chapter, but the provisions herein must be construed according to the fair import of their terms to promote justice and effect the objects of the law.[18]

The Effect of Interpretation on Enforcement of Criminal Laws

A newly enacted criminal statute or ordinance must be read and interpreted by law enforcement officers having enforcement responsibility. Their interpretation of the statute or ordinance in most instances determines the initial scope of enforcement.

If, for example, a statute or ordinance applies only to conduct in a "public place," that phrase would need interpretation if it were not clearly defined in the legislation. After an individual officer or a law enforcement agency took some action based on the definition of a public place, a prosecutor might also have to interpret the phrase. The final definition of a public place would have to be made by the courts, unless the legislative body amended the statute or ordinance with a further clarification of the phrase.

Many criminal codes contain lists of definitions of words and phrases, in order to provide for uniform interpretations. In addition, many court decisions concern themselves with the interpretation of words and phrases. The task of interpreting words and phrases that have not been defined, however, remains for law enforcement officers and prosecutors. Their interpretation in many instances determines enforcement practices.

In determining what interpretations should be made of criminal statutes and ordinances, consideration should be given to the intent and expectation of the legislative body. For example, in many jurisdictions, most forms of gambling are illegal. However, the President's Commission on Crime points out that it is apparent that state legislatures "neither intend nor expect that such statutes be fully enforced." As a result, gambling statutes in most states are interpreted so as not to apply to friendly neighborhood poker games and other forms of social gambling.

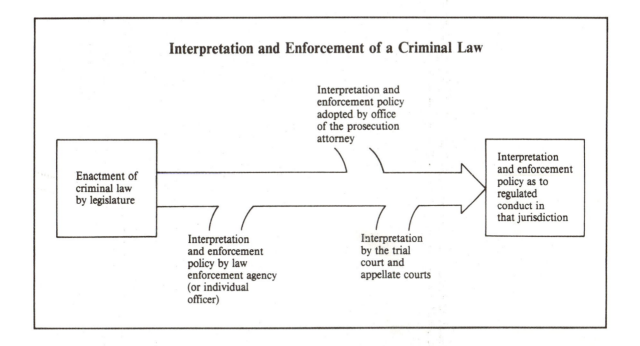

Interpretation and Enforcement of a Criminal Law

Interpretation and enforcement policy adopted by office of the prosecution attorney

Enactment of criminal law by legislature

Interpretation and enforcement policy as to regulated conduct in that jurisdiction

Interpretation and enforcement policy by law enforcement agency (or individual officer)

Interpretation by the trial court and appellate courts

QUESTIONS AND PROBLEMS FOR CHAPTER 2

1. Indicate whether the following conduct constitutes a crime in your jurisdiction. If so, what would be the specific charge? Also, indicate how you, as a law enforcement officer, would handle each situation.

   a. You are sent to a home in which a mother of two teenage daughters complains that the man who lives next door has set up a telescope on his second-floor rear porch and trains it on her daughters as they are sunbathing in their backyard.

   b. You are sent to a street on which two men are standing on a public sidewalk late at night watching a woman undress who has forgotten to pull down her bedroom shades.

   c. Same situation as b., except that the two men are standing in the woman's backyard.

   d. Same situation as b. You tell the two men standing on the sidewalk to move on, but they refuse, stating that they are not doing anything wrong and that they can stand on the sidewalk if they wish.

   e. You are sent to an apartment in which male residents are questioning a man they found standing in the backyard area of the apartment building. The man was not window peeping, but as it was midnight, the occupants of the apartment building are concerned. The man states that he was looking for a friend but can name no one who lives in the apartment building or in the neighborhood.

2. Do you think that criminal laws restrict personal freedom more than they protect personal freedom and the right of privacy? Give reasons for your answer.

3. How are criminal laws created in your state?

4. In 1976, it was reported that Denmark became the 17th country to make it an offense not to wear a seat belt while in a moving motor vehicle. Would American state governments have the power to impose this requirement through the use of the criminal laws of that jurisdiction? Give reasons for your answer.

Chapter 3

Essential Elements of a Crime

Since the development of common law and up until modern times, all crimes consisted of two essential elements: (1) the physical act or omission, and (2) a mental requirement known as criminal intent or purpose. Some writers refer to such crimes as "true crimes." Today, true crimes continue to make up a considerable number of crimes in any criminal code.

With the industrialization of the United States, modern legislative bodies began creating criminal laws that did not require the mental element essential to "true crimes." This relatively new type of crime is called a "strict liability" crime, or regulatory offense. Strict liability crimes can be found in criminal laws pertaining to traffic violations, narcotics, liquor, sanitation, hunting, and pure food laws. In strict liability crimes, the government does not have to prove intent or purpose and must show only that the accused performed the act (or omission) charged or brought about the results that are alleged and shown.

A. CRIMES REQUIRING PROOF OF MENTAL FAULT

Before a person may be convicted of a crime that requires proof of mental fault, the government must prove beyond a reasonable doubt:

1. *The external physical act:* That the conduct or act forbidden by the law of the jurisdiction was in fact committed by the defendant,

2. *The internal mental element:* That the act (or omission) was accompanied by a state of mind required by the criminal statute.

The Latin term *actus reus* (guilty act) is used by the courts and writers to describe the essential physical act, and the term *mens rea* (guilty mind) is used to describe the essential mental requirement. This mental requirement of criminal intent is embodied in criminal statutes in the following degrees:

- intentionally (the highest degree of mental fault)
- knowingly
- recklessly
- negligently

The U.S. Supreme Court has never created and announced a doctrine requiring proof of *mens rea* in all crimes and in all cases before an accused can be held accountable for his or her acts.[1] Therefore, the states are free to create criminal laws that do not require proof of *mens rea* or to create criminal laws requiring different degrees of mental fault or mental guilt. But if a degree of mental guilt is made an element of the crime by law, the prosecutor must then prove this essential element of the crime.

Necessity for the Concurrence of the Act and the Required Mental Element

A criminal intent without a criminal act is no crime. A person who possesses a certain criminal intent but does nothing to actually carry out the criminal intent has not committed a crime. To prove a true crime the state must show that the external physical act and the internal mental state essential to that crime occurred at the same time.

In some instances, an act without the required mental state (guilty mind) is no crime. A person incapable of entertaining the required criminal mind because of legal insanity has not committed a crime. Or, a student who picks up someone else's book or briefcase by mistake has performed a physical act, but if there is no guilty or criminal state of mind necessary for the crime of theft, there has been no crime committed. However, suppose that the student keeps the book or briefcase for two days and then, realizing the mistake, decides to keep the property. The taking and keeping of the property for two days has been a continuous act in the eyes of the law. The crime of theft occurred when the intent to deprive the true owner of permanent possession concurred with the act of taking and retaining possession.

Although the forbidden act and the guilty mind must concur, the results do not necessarily have to take place at the same time.

Example: While A is on vacation, X rigs a spring gun to A's front door (forbidden act),

---

Elements of Crime

Crimes may consist of combinations of the three human activities of thought, communication, and actions (or conduct).

Thoughts alone cannot be punished as crimes. However, thoughts could constitute the required mental element *(mens rea)* for verbal offenses or acts that have been designated as crimes.

Communications (words, etc.) may be offenses in themselves or may be combined with either thoughts or actions to constitute crimes. (See Chapter 10, The Limits of Free Speech.)

Human acts alone may constitute "strict liability" crimes, in which all that is required is that the state show that the defendant committed a forbidden act (or omission). When it is required that the state prove a specific mental element *(mens rea)*, the state must then prove the required intent, purpose, or knowledge that is an essential element of the crime.

---

setting it with the intention that A be killed when he opens the door (guilty mind). Two weeks after the spring gun is set in place, A returns from vacation and is shot and killed when he opens his door.

In the example given, the *actus reus* and the *mens rea* concurred, but the results did not occur until A opened the door two weeks after the act with intent to kill was performed.

The Forbidden Act or Omission *(Actus Reus)*

Most criminal laws forbid specific acts, and a few punish the failure to carry out a legal duty. The act forbidden or commanded by the law is set out in the definition of each particular offense, usually in terms of the harm or the wrong that occurs. In the crime of murder, it is the death of the victim caused by the defendant's forbidden act (or omission) that is the harm and the wrong. In the crime of larceny, it is the loss of personal or movable property caused by the defendant's wrongful taking and carrying away that is the harm and the wrong.

The manner in which the harm or wrong can be caused varies considerably. A murder can be committed by use of a gun, a knife, a blow, or poison or by any one of many different acts. The harm or the wrong done usually varies from crime to crime, but sometimes two crimes embody the same harm or wrong. All criminal homicides share the same harm or wrong, which is the death of a person. These crimes differ from one another primarily because of the differing states of mind of the offender at the time he or she causes the harm or wrong (the death of another person).

Actus Reus for Different Elements of Parties to a Crime

Chapter 4 explains the different categories of the criminal liability of parties to a crime. These categories are (a) the person who actually commits the crime, (b) the person who aided and assisted in the commission of the crime, and (c) the person who conspired in the planning of the crime.

Each of these categories have different *actus reus* elements.

Example: A hires B and C to murder X. A tells B and C how and where he wants X to be murdered. B is the vehicle driver and look-out while C commits the murder.

C's act in killing X is the *actus reus* of the direct commission of the crime. B's acts as aider and abetter are the *actus reus* of assistance. A jury could easily find that all three men (particularly A) conspired and agreed in the planning of the murder, which is the *actus reus* of agreement.

The state has the burden of proving beyond a reasonable doubt the *actus reus* element of every offense, and the jury must unanimously agree that the state has proved the *actus reus* elements before they may find a defendant guilty.

Because the *actus reus* element for each category is different, the jury must agree unanimously on which *actus reus* or which category the state has proven.

Innocent Acts That, If Done With Forbidden Intent, Are Crimes		
Innocent Acts	*Forbidden Intent*	*Resulting Crimes*
Possession of a tool or other instrumentality	To use such device to break into a depository or building and steal therefrom	Possession of burglarious tools
Traveling in interstate or foreign commerce	To avoid prosecution for a state felony, or to avoid giving testimony in such a prosecution	Fugitive felon or witness violation; 18 U.S.C.A. sec. 1073 & 1074(a)
Use of U.S. mail, telephone, or interstate wire facilities	To participate through racketeering in an enterprise	RICO violation; 18 U.S.C. sec. 1961–68
Transporting a female "through or across" the state of New Jersey	With the intent to engage in prostitution	N.J.S.A. 2A:133–12
Use of the U.S. mails	To advance a fraudulent scheme	Mail fraud; 18 U.S. C.A. sec. 1341
Use of a fictitious name or address	To further a fraudulent mail scheme	18 U.S.C.A. sec. 1342
Association with other people and even membership in an organization that advocates the overthrow of government by force or violence is not punishable . . .	Unless there is knowledge of the aim to use force or violence in the overthrow of government and there is shown to be an intent to bring it about	18 U.S.C.A. sec. 2385
Entering a train	If with intent "to commit any crime or offense against a person or property thereon"	18 U.S.C.A. sec. 1991
Going on "any military, naval, or Coast Guard reservation, post, fort, arsenal, yard, station, or installation . . .	For any purpose prohibited by law or lawful regulation"	18 U.S.C.A. sec. 1382
Teaching or demonstrating the use, application, or making of a firearm, explosive, or incendiary device, or a technique capable of causing injury or death	"Intending that the same will be unlawfully employed for use in, or in furtherance of, a civil disorder which may in any way or degree obstruct, delay, or adversely affect commerce," or the performance of any federally protected function	18 U.S.C.A. sec. 231(a) (1)
Travel in interstate or foreign commerce	With intent to incite a riot (statute requires an overt act, but such act could be a lawful act)	18 U.S.C.A. sec. 2101(a) (1)

The Guilty Mind (Mens Rea)

A cardinal principle of criminal law pertaining to "true crimes" was long ago expressed in Latin as *actus non facit reum nisi mens sit rea* (an act does not make a person guilty unless the mind is guilty).

The term *mens rea* also means evil intent, criminal purpose, and knowledge of the wrongfulness of conduct. It is also used to indicate the mental state required by the crime charged, whether that be specific intent to commit the crime, recklessness, guilty knowledge, malice, or criminal negligence.

Criminal liability usually requires "an evil-meaning mind (and) an evil-doing hand."[2] But the late Justice Robert H. Jackson complained of the "variety, disparity and confusion" of judicial definitions of the "requisite but elusive mental element" required in the proof of crimes. In 1970, the National Commission on Reform of Federal Criminal Laws complained of the "confused and inconsistent ad hoc approach" of federal courts to this problem and called for a new approach.

In the 1980 case of *United States v. Bailey,*[3] the U.S. Supreme Court pointed out that at "common law, crimes generally were classified as requiring either 'general intent' or 'specific intent.' This . . . distinction, however, has been the source of a good deal of confusion." Because of this problem, the Court pointed out that there has been a movement away from the common law classifications of *mens rea.* Citing Section 2.02 of the Model Penal Code and LaFave and Scott's book, *Criminal Law* (St. Paul: West Pub. Co., 1972), the Court suggested the following "in descending order of culpability: purpose, knowledge, recklessness, and negligence."

The following example illustrates situations in which the harm done is the same in all cases, but the mental element varies:

Example: X, a construction worker, is working on the fourth floor of a building under construction in the downtown area of a city. His conduct caused the death of W, who was hit on the head by a crowbar as he was walking on the sidewalk past the building.

1. X deliberately dropped the heavy crowbar so as to hit W on the head.

2. X did not want to kill anybody but wanted to see the people scatter when he dropped the crowbar to the sidewalk.

3. X threw the crowbar at another worker in a fight, but missed. The crowbar fell, killing W on the sidewalk below.

4. X came to work drunk and accidentally pushed the crowbar off the edge of the building.

5. Another worker called for the crowbar and X threw it to him, but the throw was bad and the crowbar hit W on the sidewalk below.

6. X was knocked unconscious when a crane collapsed, causing him to drop the crowbar, which hit and killed W.

In your jurisdiction, what degree of criminal liability should X be charged with in each example with respect to his conduct and mental state? As a jury could be the final judge in determining whether the "evil-meaning mind (and) evil-doing hand" existed, what arguments could a prosecutor and defense lawyer make to prove their cases?

See *United States v. Gypsum Co.,*[4] in which the U.S. Supreme Court stated that in the case of most crimes, "the limited distinction between knowledge and purpose has not been considered important."

In *United States v. Bailey,*[5] the Supreme Court stated that in a "general sense, 'purpose' corresponds loosely with the common-law concept of specific intent, while 'knowledge' corresponds loosely with the concept of 'general intent.' "

Proving the Criminal Intent or Criminal State of Mind

When criminal intent or another mental element is an essential element of a crime, the state has the burden of proving the required *mens rea.* Proof of the mental element may be made by:

1. Showing the acts of the defendant and the circumstances that existed at the time of the crime. As most people know what they are doing and also know the natural and probable consequences of their acts, a jury or judge may reasonably infer that the defendant intended the natural and probable consequences of his or her

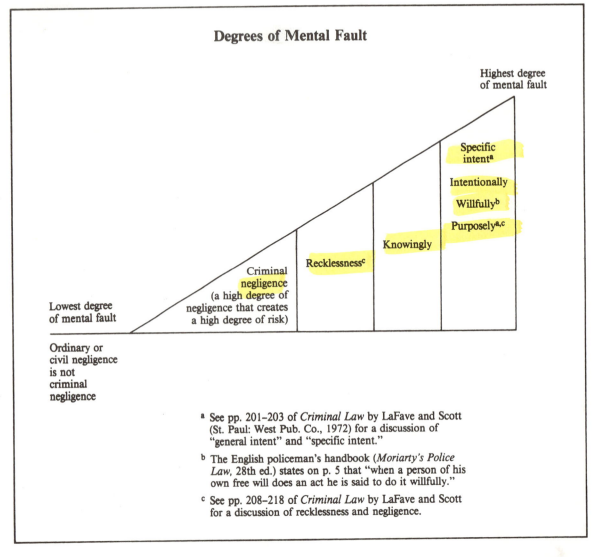

Degrees of Mental Fault

Highest degree of mental fault

Specific intent[a]

Intentionally

Willfully[b]

Purposely[a,c]

Knowingly

Recklessness[c]

Criminal negligence (a high degree of negligence that creates a high degree of risk)

Lowest degree of mental fault

Ordinary or civil negligence is not criminal negligence

[a] See pp. 201–203 of *Criminal Law* by LaFave and Scott (St. Paul: West Pub. Co., 1972) for a discussion of "general intent" and "specific intent."

[b] The English policeman's handbook (*Moriarty's Police Law*, 28th ed.) states on p. 5 that "when a person of his own free will does an act he is said to do it willfully."

[c] See pp. 208–218 of *Criminal Law* by LaFave and Scott for a discussion of recklessness and negligence.

deliberate acts.[6] Thus a person who pointed a loaded gun at another person and pulled the trigger knew what he or she was doing and desired the natural and probable consequences of the acts.

2. Producing evidence to show the statements of the defendant at the time of the crime as well as statements made after the crime. Statements of a defendant before or after a crime may be incriminating and may include admissions or a confession of guilt.

Only rarely is written evidence of intent or purpose of a defendant available to the state. The

following jury instruction on intent was approved by the Fifth Circuit Court of Appeals in the 1975 case of *United States v. Durham*:

It is reasonable to infer that a person ordinarily intends the natural and probable consequences of his knowing acts. The jury may draw the inference that the accused intended all of the consequences which one standing in like circumstances and possessing like knowledge should reasonably have expected to result from any intentional act or conscious omission. Any such inference drawn is entitled to be considered by the jury in determining whether or not the government has proved beyond a reasonable doubt that the defendant possessed the required criminal intent.[7]

Although it is reasonable to infer that a person ordinarily intends the natural and probable consequences of his or her knowing and deliberate acts, there is no inference that a person intends results that are not the natural, reasonable, or probable consequences of a voluntary act.

The Requirement of Scienter

"Scienter" is sometimes made an essential element of a crime that the state must prove beyond a reasonable doubt. *Scienter* is a legal term meaning a degree of knowledge that makes an individual legally responsible for the consequences of his or her acts. Scienter is alleged in a criminal complaint through charging that the accused person had sufficient knowledge to know that his or her act was unlawful. Examples of crimes in which state statutes most often require scienter are:

• in battery or assault to a law enforcement officer, knowledge that the victim is a law enforcement officer

• in refusing to aid a law enforcement officer, knowledge that the person requesting assistance was a law enforcement officer

• in obstructing a law enforcement officer, knowledge that the person obstructed was a law enforcement officer

• in receiving stolen property, knowledge that the property received was stolen property

• in possession of obscene material, knowledge of the nature of the material [8]

• in bribery of a public officer, knowledge that the person was a public official

• in harboring or aiding a felon, knowledge that the person aided was a felon

The following cases have appeared before the U.S. Supreme Court in recent years.

The Motive for Committing a Crime

Motive and intent are sometimes thought of as being one and the same. However, in the law there is a clear distinction between the two.

UNITED STATES v. FEOLA
Supreme Court of the United States (1975)
420 U.S. 671, 95 S. Ct. 1255

In most states, battery or assault to a law enforcement officer is a felony. However, most state statutes require proof of scienter—that the defendant knew that the person assaulted was a law enforcement officer. The defendants were convicted of conspiracy to assault federal officers in a heroin transaction with undercover federal narcotic agents. The defendants asserted that they did not know the men were federal officers, but as the federal criminal code does not require proof of this knowledge, their convictions were affirmed by the U.S. Supreme Court. The Court pointed out that the defendants may have been surprised when their victims turned out to be federal officers but that they knew from the beginning that the planned course of conduct was unlawful. The Court held:

A contrary conclusion would give insufficient protection to the agent enforcing an unpopular law, and none to the agent acting under cover.

FABRITZ v. TRAURIG
Review denied by U.S. Supreme Court (1978)
583 F.2d 697 (4th Cir.), 25 CrL 4105

The defendant, a 20-year-old mother, was found guilty of child abuse by a jury. The Maryland Court of Appeals found that the defendant's "failure to obtain medical attention" for her child "amounted to child abuse" and constituted "cruel and inhumane treatment." The mother had gone to her grandfather's funeral and left her child with friends for two or three days. When the defendant returned, the three-year-old child appeared normal but when the mother bathed the child, multiple severe bruises (later counted as 70) were discovered on the child's body. The child became ill but then seemed to improve and sat up and took liquids. However, the child's condition worsened, and the mother and a neighbor woman sat with the child. An ambulance was called, but the child died on the way to the hospital. The state agreed that the mother was totally ignorant of when or how the blows were inflicted on the child. A doctor testified that the child would have survived "had an operation been performed within at least twelve hours prior to death." The Federal Court of Appeals held that the conviction could not stand in absence of evidence that the mother knew that she was risking the child's life. Because the child died eight hours after the mother returned home, and the mother could not have saved the child, the conviction was reversed. The U.S. Supreme Court denied review and, in effect, affirmed the Federal Court of Appeal ruling that:

In these circumstances the conviction cannot stand—without even so much as a murmur of evidential justification.

As the Court said in Thompson v. Louisville: *"The ultimate question presented to us is whether the charges against petitioner were so totally devoid of evidentiary support as to render his conviction unconstitutional under the Due Process Clause of the Fourteenth Amendment. Decision of this question turns not on the sufficiency of the evidence, but on whether this conviction rests upon any evidence at all."* [9]

Intent is the mental purpose or design to commit a specific act (or omission), whereas motive is the cause, reason, inducement, or why an act is committed.

Example: A man entered a crowded tavern and when he saw the person he was looking for, he went up to the man and killed him by plunging a large knife into his body.

When this case was tried, the state easily proved intent to kill through the many eyewitnesses to the crime (that is, the jury easily inferred intent from the action of the defendant). But the state had no admissible evidence as to motive (why the defendant sought out the victim and killed him). However, the state had inadmissible hearsay evidence that the victim had sold the defendant a bad batch of heroin. The heroin caused the defendant to become ill. As soon as the defendant could get on his feet, he went out and killed the supplier of the heroin.

Intent is an essential element of many crimes and must be proved beyond reasonable doubt when required. Motive is not an element of any crime and the state does not have to show why a person committed a crime. To place the burden of proving motive on the state would make it unreasonably difficult to obtain a conviction in some cases.

Motive, however, is always relevant evidence that, if available to the state, can be used to show why the person committed the crime. In this sense, motive can be used to help prove intent or another degree of *mens rea,* in that it provides the trier of fact with more information and may remove doubt, thus answering the question "why." However, motive alone would not be sufficient to convict. But a person may be lawfully convicted even if there is no motive or if a motive cannot be shown.

Criminal homicides are committed for different motives, such as hatred, anger, greed, and revenge. However, homicide and other offenses may be committed for "good" motives. Robbing a bank to give the money to the poor and needy is still a crime, even if the stolen funds are used for a good purpose.

Newspapers sometimes give a great deal of publicity to mercy-killing cases (euthanasia). However, "(t)he mother who kills her imbecile and suffering child out of motives of compassion is just as guilty of murder as is the man who kills for gain, since each intentionally takes another human life." [10] Although motive is not relevant to the issue of guilt or innocence, it can be a factor in sentencing. The defendant who kills in a rape–murder case or in the course of a robbery could receive and serve a much longer sentence than a mercy-killing defendant, who killed because of love and compassion.

B. STRICT LIABILITY CRIMES

In enacting statutes to enforce rules having to do with traffic, liquor, purity of food, hunting, and narcotics offenses, modern legislative bodies often choose not to create "true crimes," but rather strict liability (or liability without mental fault) statutes.

Except for narcotic offenses, the penalties for strict liability offenses are usually lighter. The offenders are often not generally considered criminals in the true sense of the word, and the state is not required to carry the burden of proving criminal intent or other mental fault. The defendant is liable regardless of his or her state of mind at the time of the act.

The motor vehicle codes, hunting regulations, and the food and liquor laws of all states probably contain strict liability statutes. A bartender cannot ordinarily use as a defense the fact that the person to whom he sold liquor looked 22 when in fact the person was only 17. The driver of an overweight truck cannot argue that the company scales were faulty; nor can an adult male, in most, if not all, states, argue that he did not know the age of the 15-year-old girl with whom he had sexual intercourse.

UNITED STATES v. **MARVIN**
Review denied by U.S. Supreme Court (1983) 687 F.2d 1221 (8th Cr.), 33 CrL 4018

The defendant, who was a chiropractor, purchased $500 in food stamps for $200 cash. The food stamps were purchased from an undercover investigator who was seeking to find food-stamp fraud and abuse. The defendant was also charged as an aider and abettor in three other criminal counts in which he either arranged transactions or provided necessary money to purchase food stamps. The defendant was convicted of "knowingly" acquiring and possessing food stamps in violation of 7 U.S.C. 2024(b). The conviction for count 1 was reversed because the jury was not instructed that they had to find that the defendant "knowingly" violated the federal food stamp law. The finding, affirmed by the U.S. Supreme Court, held:

The government argues that purchase of food stamps is only a malum prohibitum, a crime unknown to the common law, a so-called "regulatory offense," as to which no mens rea need be shown. Certainly there are such offenses. Congress may make an act criminal without regard to the actor's state of mind. . . . "[C]ourts obviously must follow Congress' intent as to the required level of mental culpability for any particular offense." [11]

* * *

We hold that the defendant's requested instruction . . . should have been given. The jury should have been told that the government had to prove "that the defendant knowingly did an act which the law forbids." . . . This does not mean that the defendant must know, by chapter and verse, the precise law and regulation that forbid trafficking in food stamps for cash. But he must know that he was acting in violation of some law or regulation. Such a requirement places no unreasonable obstacle in the path of food-stamp prosecutions. Intent may often be inferred from circum-

stances, including, for example, purchases of stamps at a deep discount. Nor do we hold that the evidence here was insufficient to show the requisite intent. The fact remains, however, that under the instructions given the jury was permitted to convict, and could have done so, without finding that when defendant bought food stamps on the occasion charged in Count I, he knew he was doing something that the law had forbidden. The conviction on Count I must therefore be reversed.

C. PROXIMATE CAUSE OR CAUSATION

Crimes are defined in terms of conduct that is forbidden (or required) and the mental state existing at the time of the forbidden act (or omission). Crimes are also defined in terms of the harm done or the wrong that occurs. For example, X strikes W a hard blow on the face with intent to injure him. The following different results may occur:

1. For a week, W has a black eye that heals without any medical attention. (battery)

2. W loses his eye and has a scar on his face. (mayhem, unless the state statute requires a specific intent to maim)

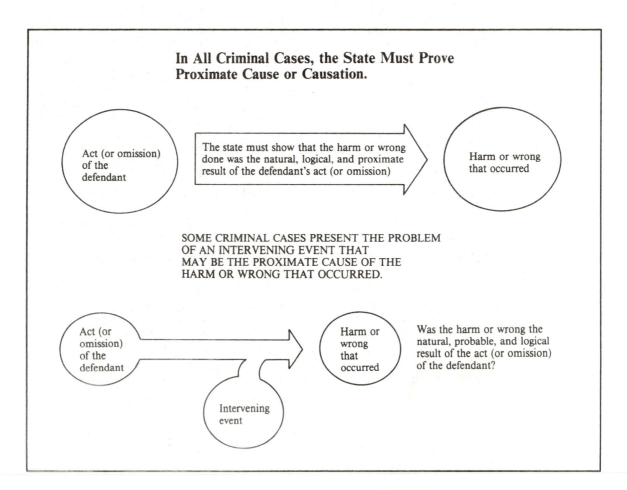

In All Criminal Cases, the State Must Prove Proximate Cause or Causation.

Act (or omission) of the defendant

The state must show that the harm or wrong done was the natural, logical, and proximate result of the defendant's act (or omission)

Harm or wrong that occurred

SOME CRIMINAL CASES PRESENT THE PROBLEM OF AN INTERVENING EVENT THAT MAY BE THE PROXIMATE CAUSE OF THE HARM OR WRONG THAT OCCURRED.

Act (or omission) of the defendant

Harm or wrong that occurred

Intervening event

Was the harm or wrong the natural, probable, and logical result of the act (or omission) of the defendant?

3. W is knocked unconscious and remains in a coma for days in a hospital. There is a great deal of bleeding but no disfiguration. (aggravated battery)

4. W is killed immediately when he falls backward and strikes his head against a hard object. (wrongful act manslaughter)

5. W's face is cut and bruised. He does not take care of the wound and an infection develops that causes W's death two weeks after the blow.

6. W's face is cut and bruised, and an ambulance is called to take him to a hospital. On the way to the hospital, the ambulance is involved in a traffic accident and W is killed.

Proximate cause (or causation) must be shown beyond a reasonable doubt by the state. The state must show that the unlawful and wrongful act of the defendant was the ordinary and probable cause of the harm or wrong that resulted. The harm or wrong must be the natural, logical, and proximate result of the unlawful act. In the first four examples, the causal relationship between X's wrongful act and the wrong and harm that occurred is apparent. However, in examples 5 and 6, there were intervening causes that brought about the death of W.[12] The following cases reflect state rulings on causation:

COMMONWEALTH v. CHEEKS

Supreme Court of Pennsylvania (1966)
423 Pa. 67, 223 A.2d 291

The defendant stabbed the victim in the stomach during a robbery. The wound was a nonfatal puncture about one inch in length, but the victim was uncooperative in the hospital and would not stay in bed. Four days after the injury, the victim's condition deteriorated and tubes had to be inserted to allow drainage of the gas and fluids. The victim pulled out the tubes while in delirium at least twice, as he had pulled out other tubes. The victim died seven days after the robbery. The defendant was convicted by a jury of first degree murder and, in affirming the conviction, the Supreme Court of Pennsylvania stated:

It is our studied conclusion that the question of causal connection was for the jury to resolve. The fact that the stabbing was not the immediate cause of death is not controlling. . . . (O)ne charged with homicide cannot escape liability merely because the blow he inflicted is not mortal, or the immediate cause of death. If his blow is the legal cause, i.e., if it started a chain of causation which led to the death, he is guilty of homicide.

In this case, the stabbing necessitated the operation; the operation was the direct cause of the stomach complication and abdominal distention; the insertion of the tubes was required to alleviate this condition and to save the victim's life. The fact that the victim, while in a weakened physical condition and disoriented mental state, pulled out the tubes and created the immediate situation, which resulted in his death, is not such an intervening and independent act sufficient to break the chain of causation or events between the stabbing and the death.[13]

WELCH v. STATE

Court of Criminal Appeals of Alabama (1970)
45 Ala. App. 657, 235 So.2d 906

The defendant fired a shotgun at his wife, hitting her in the lower right thigh. The victim was given no drug to offset blood coagulation and, two months after being shot, died when a blood clot formed in her left leg and then lodged in her lung.. In reversing the murder conviction, the appellate court stated:

The physician's expression (that the death was) "probably associated with it" is too vague to support a murder verdict. No testimony was given as to how blood clots form and circulate. No autopsy was made.

In a death as distinguished from a "killing" the prosecution must prove an absence of natural causes. That is, the first step is to prove the victim died because he was killed . . . .

Except as a literary expression "but for" is too imprecise for a rule of causation where proof beyond a reasonable doubt is axiomatic. Mankind might still be in Eden, but for Adam's biting an apple.

STATE v. NOSIS

Court of Appeals of Ohio
(1969)
22 Ohio App. 2d 16, 257
N.E.2d 414

The victim was a 65-year-old man who blew his horn several times when passing the defendant on a highway. This angered the defendant, who challenged the victim to a fight at the next stoplight. The victim's wife asked the defendant to leave her husband alone because he had a bad heart. However, the defendant followed the victim and his wife several miles to their suburban home, where he argued and made menacing gestures in the driveway, after being warned again of the victim's bad heart. When the wife went inside to call the sheriff, her husband collapsed and died less than an hour later of a heart attack. In charging the defendant with manslaughter, the prosecutor acknowledged that the defendant had not struck the deceased but argued that the defendant's threats and gestures amounted to an assault. Moreover, the defendant knew of the victim's heart condition. The prosecutor argued that the defendant could have reasonably anticipated that the threats were likely to result in death. In affirming the manslaughter conviction, the court stated:

Unlawful killing . . . may be established by proof of assault, or of menacing threats . . . which proximately caused death, when death could be reasonably anticipated by an ordinarily prudent person as likely to result from such conduct while possessed with knowledge of a heart ailment of the victim.

TERRY v. COMMONWEALTH

Supreme Court of Virginia
(1938)
171 Va. 505, 198 S.E. 911

The accused, while driving his car in an intoxicated condition, struck the rear end of another car so hard that it was forced across the intersection where it struck William Fox, a pedestrian. The blow broke Fox's left leg and rendered him temporarily unconscious. He was taken to the hospital that afternoon and examined carefully by Doctor R. F. Cline, who set the broken leg. The next day, Monday morning, Fox ate a good breakfast and seemed to be resting comfortably. Shortly after seven p.m. the Doctor again visited him and found that he had eaten a good dinner and was resting easily. At ten-thirty p.m., some three hours later, the doctor, in response to an emergency call from the hospital, returned and found that the patient was suffering from "acute pulmonary edema of the lungs." As a result of this disease he died Tuesday morning.

*   *   *

The normal procedure in such cases is for the Commonwealth to establish by competent evidence that death resulted from the injuries inflicted. Because a person dies within two days after receiving a severe injury, it does not necessarily follow that the injury was the proximate or efficient cause of death. The Commonwealth in this case relied solely on the testimony of the attending physician to supply the connecting link. This physician attended the deceased immediately after the injury and, while he said he did not make an intensive examination for internal injuries, he did make a very careful examination, and the only injury he found was a broken leg. He further stated that there were no other bruises on the body of the deceased; that the patient responded to treatment in a normal way, and that death was the result of a disease—that is, a sudden attack of acute pulmonary edema of the lungs. When pressed to state the cause of this disease, he said that the origin was unknown. Upon being asked, "Do perfectly well people have it?" he replied, "Yes, and young people can be seized with it. I have seen young people die right in bed . . . ."

Conviction of involuntary manslaughter reversed.

SEAGROVES v. STATE
Supreme Court of Tennessee (1955)
198 Tenn. 633, 281 S.W.2d 644

Where it appears that it is equally probable that death resulted from one cause as from another, and the defendant is not responsible for one of the causes, then any determination of the cause of death cannot be speculative and conjectural, and the evidence will be held insufficient to support a verdict of guilty.

DUNCAN v. STATE
Court of Appeals of Alabama (1942)
30 Ala. App. 356, 6 So.2d 450

If death was due solely and exclusively to natural cause, i.e., heart failure, with the blow in no way contributing to or accelerating it, then, under the indictment, there was no homicide, and at most (if the blow were wrongful) the defendant would only be guilty of some degree of assault.

STEVENS v. UNITED STATES
Court of Appeals of the District of Columbia (1969)
249 A.2d 514

(T)he causal connection must be proven beyond a reasonable doubt and not by mere conjecture and speculation.

The "Year-and-a-Day" Rule

The government must show proximate cause or causation in all criminal cases, since it is an essential element of any crime charged. Causation is related in some respects to the requirement of *corpus delicti* (proof that a crime was committed). However, the two requirements are separate and distinct. *Corpus delicti* will be discussed in Chapter 13.

Because of the nature of causation, most of the cases that have come before the courts have been criminal homicide cases. The "year and a day" rule is an ancient rule that places a time limit on causation in criminal homicide cases. Blackstone stated the rule as follows: "In order also to make the killing murder, it is requisite that the party die within a year and a day after the stroke received, or cause of death administered; in the computation of which the whole day upon which the hurt was done shall be reckoned the first." [14]

Some states (including California) have enlarged this rule to three years and a day. However, when a person seriously injures another person, he or she is taken into custody. A person who is held in police custody must be either charged with a crime or released. When a person is charged with a crime, the state must try the person within the "speedy trial" limit (see Chapter 7), which in many states is 90 or 100 days. The prosecutor must then charge attempted murder, aggravated assault (or battery) and go to trial on the lesser charge, as a defense lawyer is not likely to waive "speedy trial" and wait for the victim to die.

D. POSSESSION AS AN ESSENTIAL ELEMENT

The act of possession is an essential element of crimes such as carrying a concealed weapon, violations of the Uniform Controlled Substance Act (narcotics), and possession of burglarious tools and other contraband. *Actual possession* means that the object was either on the defendant's person or within reach and under his or her domination and control. It is immaterial that the defendant did not own the property, since ownership and possession are different concepts. It is possible for property to be possessed jointly by two or more persons at the same time.[15]

Constructive possession is used to indicate control over property and objects that the defendant does not have in actual possession. The object may be in his or her car parked two blocks away, in a desk drawer in the home or office, or in a suitcase stored somewhere for which he or she has a baggage claim check or key. Constructive possession would not be sufficient to sustain a conviction for carrying a concealed weapon, as a showing of actual possession is necessary. However, constructive possession would sustain a conviction for the possession of contraband, such as narcotics. The rules for the search of objects in a suspect's actual possession differ somewhat from the rules pertaining to the search for objects constructively possessed by a suspect.[16]

The mental element that must be proved in possession offenses is generally that of "intentionally" or "knowingly." These mental elements are usually easy to prove because a person with a loaded revolver or two pounds of marijuana in his or her pocket cannot argue convincingly that he or she did not know that the contraband was in actual possession. The intent to possess, then, is a state of mind existing at the time the person commits the offense. In seeking to determine the state of mind of the alleged offender in order to decide whether an intent existed, the jury or the court may base its decision on the defendant's acts, conduct, and other inferences that can be reasonably deducted from all the circumstances.

Possession is one of the rights of ownership of property. Criminal statutes do not require that ownership be proved. A person who possesses heroin may or may not be the owner of the heroin. Possession of personal property is presumptive evidence of ownership, and if the possession is accompanied by the exercise of complete acts of ownership for a considerable time, it is strong evidence of ownership. When objects

---

Essential Elements of a "True Crime"

The essential elements that the state must prove in showing that a "true crime" was committed are:

- the *act* element—the forbidden act (or failure to act)
- the *mental* element—the state of mind required for the crime (the guilty mind)
- the *harm* element—the wrong done (killing, physical injury, property damage, loss, etc.)
- the *cause* element—that the harm done was the natural and probable result of the wrongful act

Some crimes require proof of additional essential elements, such as scienter, possession (actual or constructive), etc.

Possession As an Essential Element

Possession may be: a. actual, or
b. constructive (not in actual possession)

Possession may be: a. in one person (sole), or
b. joint (in possession of more than one person)

Possession of a controlled substance may be:
a. of a "usable amount," or
b. of a "trace amount," or
c. within the body of the suspect (b. and c. depend on the law or court decisions within your state)
d. a combination of any of the above.

and articles are in a dwelling or a business place, they are deemed to be in the constructive possession of the person controlling the dwelling or business place—in the absence of evidence showing otherwise. Therefore, heroin found in an apartment that is searched under the authority of a search warrant is in the constructive possession of the person controlling and occupying the apartment unless the person can show otherwise.

The past criminal record of a defendant may sometimes be shown if the defendant takes the stand to testify in his or her own behalf. Past narcotic convictions could be shown if a defendant took the stand and argued that the heroin found in his apartment was not his and was not in his actual or constructive possession. The past convictions would reflect on the veracity of the defendant's testimony and also on the determination of whether he had actual or constructive possession of the heroin.

E. THE USE OF PRESUMPTIONS AND INFERENCES IN CRIMINAL LAW

Presumptions are used in criminal law. The first and earliest presumptions were common law presumptions created by courts. In modern times, most newly created presumptions are created by legislative bodies. The best-known presumption, and probably the oldest, is the presumption of innocence until proven guilty. The presumption of innocence until proven guilty is a rebuttable presumption (rebuttable presumptions may be overcome by evidence proving otherwise). The presumption of innocence may be overcome by evidence showing that a defendant is guilty beyond a reasonable doubt.

Some writers identify another form of presumption, called "conclusive presumption." A *conclusive presumption* is a statement of substantive law that cannot be overcome with evidence showing otherwise. There are few conclusive presumptions; probably the best known is the rule of law that a person under age seven has not reached the age of reason and therefore is not capable of committing a crime.

Functions of Presumptions

Presumptions are created to permit orderly civil and criminal trials. The Supreme Court of Pennsylvania [17] and the Supreme Court of Indiana [18] defined the function and legal significance of presumptions as follows:

A presumption of law is not evidence nor should it be weighed by the factfinder as though it had evidentiary value. Rather, a presumption is a rule of law enabling the party in whose favor it operates to take his case to the jury without presenting evidence of the fact presumed. It serves as a challenge for proof and indicates the party from whom such proof must be forthcoming. When the opponent of the presumption has met the burden of production thus imposed, however, the office of the presumption has been performed; the presumption is of no further effect and drops from the case.

Inferences Distinguished from Presumptions

A *presumption* is a deduction or conclusion that the law expressly directs that the trier of fact (jury or judge) *must* make. As most presumptions may be disputed, they may be outweighed or overcome with evidence showing otherwise. Unless presumptions are overcome with other evidence, judges and jurors *must* accept the presumption as true.

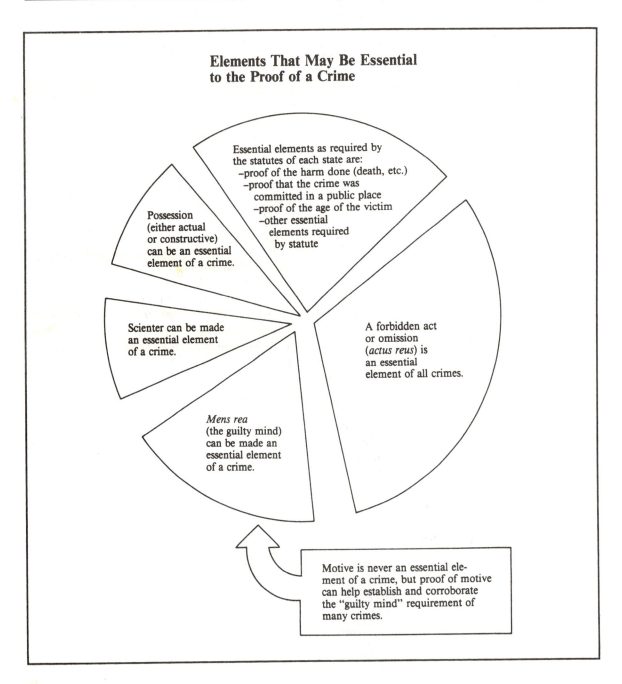

Elements That May Be Essential to the Proof of a Crime

Essential elements as required by the statutes of each state are:
–proof of the harm done (death, etc.)
–proof that the crime was committed in a public place
–proof of the age of the victim
–other essential elements required by statute

Possession (either actual or constructive) can be an essential element of a crime.

Scienter can be made an essential element of a crime.

A forbidden act or omission (*actus reus*) is an essential element of all crimes.

Mens rea (the guilty mind) can be made an essential element of a crime.

Motive is never an essential element of a crime, but proof of motive can help establish and corroborate the "guilty mind" requirement of many crimes.

An *inference* is a conclusion or deduction that a jury or a judge *may* make from a fact or a group of facts. For example, when evidence is presented showing that the defendant ran away or tried to conceal himself when a uniformed police officer approached, the jury or judge *may* draw an inference from these facts. If the defendant has no satisfactory explanation for his conduct, the inference that *may* (not *must*) be drawn is that this is evidence showing a guilty mind.

Requirement of Proof Beyond Reasonable Doubt in Criminal Cases

The courts have held that the state must prove all essential elements of a crime in a criminal trial. In the 1979 case of *Sandstrom v. Montana*,[19] the U.S. Supreme Court held that a jury instruction containing a conclusive or burden-shifting presumption as to intent violates a defendant's right to due process.

In the *Sandstrom* case, the trial court instructed the jury that "the law presumes that a person intends the ordinary consequences of his voluntary acts." The court held that when intent is an essential element of the crime, the giving of such an instruction is a constitutional error.

In the 1983 case of *Connecticut v. Johnson*,[20] the U.S. Supreme Court pointed out that a trial judge may not direct a jury to return a guilty verdict in a criminal case regardless of how overwhelming the evidence may appear. A conclusive or burden-shifting presumption on the issue of intent is the same as a directed verdict on that issue.

In the *Connecticut* case, the defendant was charged with attempted murder, robbery, kidnapping, and first degree sexual assault. The trial court instructed the jury that "a person's intention may be inferred from his conduct and every person is conclusively presumed to intend the natural and necessary consequence of his act." In holding that this instruction was constitutional error, the U.S. Supreme Court held:

> The conclusive presumption the jury was instructed to apply permitted the jury to convict respondent without

ever examining the evidence concerning an element of the crimes charged. Such an error deprived respondent of "constitutional rights so basic to a fair trial that their infraction can never be treated as harmless error."[21]

The Inference of Sanity in the Hinckley Case

In 1981, John Hinckley attempted to kill the president of the United States. In a wild shooting spree in Washington, D.C., Hinckley killed one person and seriously wounded others, including the president.

In his trial in a federal court in Washington, Hinckley and his attorneys entered pleas of not guilty and not guilty by reason of mental disease and defect. In federal courts, the government must carry the burden of showing a defendant (such as Hinckley) to be sane and normal. In the Hinckley case, the government was unable to carry this burden, and as a result, Hinckley was found by a jury to be not guilty by reason of mental disease and defect.

Many states do not follow the procedure used in the Hinckley case. In such states, there is an inference of sanity and an inference that the person is normal. A defendant using an insanity defense in these states has the burden of proving that he or she is so mentally diseased or defective that he or she was unable to formulate the mental intent to commit the crime. The U.S. Supreme Court under *Leland v. Oregon*[22] has ruled that states may continue today to require defendants to carry the burden of proving insanity.

QUESTIONS AND PROBLEMS FOR CHAPTER 3

1. A New York police officer made a lawful stop of a vehicle traveling at an excessive rate of speed. Four men were in the car and the officer smelled burnt marijuana coming from the vehicle. The officer then saw on the floor of the car an envelope marked "Supergold" which the officer associated with marijuana.[23] From the above information, there is sufficient evidence to arrest which of the following for possession of marijuana:
   a. the driver of the car, as the envelope of "Supergold" was on the floor near his feet
   b. the driver and the other man in the front seat, as the envelope of "Supergold" was on floor between them

c. as it can be inferred from the evidence that all the men possessed the marijuana, all four men may be arrested

d. the evidence is insufficient to arrest any of the men

2. Probable cause is necessary to make an arrest. To obtain a conviction in a criminal case, it is necessary that the evidence amount to proof beyond a reasonable doubt. From the information stated in Problem #1, answer a. through d. as whether the state of New York could prove possession of marijuana beyond a reasonable doubt.

3. An Arizona officer stopped a vehicle for excessive speed. The three male adults in the car had difficulty speaking English. None of the men had identification, and it was discovered that they were all traveling together in a stolen vehicle.[24] From the above information, which of the following may be arrested for the crime of operating a vehicle without the owner's consent?

a. only the person driving the vehicle at the time of the stop

b. all three of the men in the vehicle

c. none of the men may be arrested

4. X shoplifts in W's store. W sees X and attempts to apprehend him. X runs out of the store and down the street. After chasing X for a block, W has a heart attack and dies on the street. Can X be successfully charged with a homicide? Is this example any different than the *Nosis* case? In what ways?

5. At midnight, X gave his car keys to a friend whom X knew was drunk. X went to bed and his drunken friend went out with the car. In a head-on collision with another vehicle (the drunk was traveling in the wrong direction), both drivers were killed on an expressway. What can X be charged with in your state?[25]

Chapter 4

Criminal Liability

This chapter concerns itself with the question of criminal liability and the problem of whom besides the person (or persons) who actually committed the crime should be charged and punished. Criminal participation in which there is criminal liability may be classified as follows:

1. Violations of the preliminary or anticipatory crimes (also known as inchoate crimes). These crimes are preparatory and by their nature lead to the committing of a more serious offense

2. Parties to the principal offenses

3. Postcrime offenses, which are offenses committed after the principal offense and related to that offense

4. Offenses for which there is vicarious liability—that is, situations in which innocent parties (employers or corporations) may be held criminally liable for certain offenses of their employees

A. PRELIMINARY, ANTICIPATORY, OR INCHOATE CRIMES

When Is a Crime Committed?

Not all crimes are planned in advance. Some crimes are committed impulsively, the decision to commit the crime being made on the spur of the moment or almost spontaneously with the commission of the offense.

Nor are all crimes completed. In some instances, the person (or persons) who has carefully planned to commit a crime decides, for one reason or another, not to. Crimes are also not completed because of events that prevent their completion.

A person who plans in his mind to commit a crime has not yet violated any law. He or she may even in some instances express vocally his intention to commit a crime without committing an offense. However, in some instances, such a person may be subject to arrest or to detention for expressing such intentions. The following examples will illustrate this point.

Example 1: X works at a home for senior citizens and is angry with his employer. After four or five beers at a tavern, he states that he is going to siphon gasoline out of his car and set fire to the home.

Example 2: X, who has previously attempted to commit suicide, states that he is going home to kill his wife, his children, and himself.

Example 3: X states that he is going to embezzle money from his employer, who is not paying him enough.

In Examples 1 and 2, X is threatening the life and the safety of others (and his own life in Example 2). Example 3 is a property offense in which lives and safety are not involved. Officers in different jurisdictions might handle these situations in different ways. Possible courses of action are:

1. To take X into custody under the emergency detention laws of that jurisdiction, as he appears irresponsible and dangerous to himself or others (in Examples 1 and 2).

2. To arrest X for drunkenness or disorderly conduct if there is probable cause for such an arrest under the laws of that jurisdiction (in Examples 1 and 2).

3. To warn the intended victims and take protective steps to prevent X from carrying out his threats.

There are also some instances where the threat to commit a crime is a crime in itself.

Example: X angrily tells Y, "I am going to kill you." If such language constitutes "fighting words" and is one step away from violence, an officer may arrest X or order him into a prosecutor's office, if such action is justified under the statutes of that jurisdiction (see the *Chaplinsky* "fighting word" rule in Chapter 10).

Example: 18 U.S.C.A. Section 871 makes it a federal offense to do the following: "(a) Whoever knowingly and willfully . . . makes any such threat (to take the life or to inflict bodily harm) against the President, President-elect, Vice President or other officer next in the order of succession to the office of President, or Vice-President-elect, shall be fined not more than $1,000 or imprisoned not more than five years, or both."

Because of the apparent need to prevent serious social harm before it occurs, courts long ago created the three separate and distinct common law crimes of solicitation, conspiracy, and attempt. Although these offenses were crimes in themselves, each of these acts is preliminary or anticipatory to another more serious crime that the offender has in mind.

In considering the preliminary offenses, the following questions always arise: Where and when does noncriminal conduct become criminal conduct by a further act of the suspect? Which of the preliminary offenses, if any, has been violated by the suspect? When does the commission of the principal offense begin so as to allow the state to charge either the preliminary offense or the principal offense? Convictions of both preliminary and principal offenses are, in most instances, forbidden by statute or the double jeopardy principle.

1. SOLICITATION OR INCITEMENT

By the early 1800s, English and American courts had recognized solicitation as a misdemeanor under the common law. Solicitation may be defined as an attempt to get another person to commit a crime. It may also be described as an attempt to conspire to commit a crime. The solicitation does not have to be successful. The crime of solicitation is committed even if the person solicited refuses to cooperate and repudiates the proposal. It is also immaterial, in most instances, whether payment or reward is offered and whether it is accepted or refused. Evidence of the offer of payment or reward, however, can be important in proving solicitation.

From a practical point of view, two things are necessary for the successful prosecution of a charge of solicitation:

1. The cooperation of the person who was solicited

2. Evidence that supports and sustains (corroborates) the testimony of the cooperating state witness

The following example illustrates this point. A man (A) whose name was in the newspaper because he went into bankruptcy called the police and stated that a stranger (B) had telephoned him and asked him if he would like to make some money. When A said yes, B told him that he wanted his wife killed and would pay A to do the job. A realized that he was talking to someone with severe mental or emotional problems and pretended to be interested but said that the job would have to be done by a professional killer. A said that he had a contact with such a man, and after B gave A his name and telephone number, A called the police.

At this point, the police had a weak case to take into court, as a denial by B could raise a degree of doubt. Law enforcement officers also realized that the story A told them could be a fabrication or a hoax. For these reasons, they had to investigate further. This is ordinarily done by using an undercover officer. (Students occasionally ask if this would be entrapment; the answer is no. See the section on entrapment in Chapter 7.)

An undercover police officer telephoned B, pretending to be a hired killer from another city. A meeting was arranged and B again repeated his offer to pay to have his wife killed. When B paid money to the officer for the killing, the officer arrested B, who was charged with solicitation to commit murder under the statutes of that jurisdiction. The undercover officer was the complaining witness. His statements were corroborated by the money bearing B's fingerprints. Statements from A were also available as evidence.

In the circumstances set out above, a prosecutor would be unable to charge B criminally with solicitation to commit murder, if the state had abolished common law crimes and had neither a general solicitation statute nor a particularized statute making solicitation to commit murder a crime. Probably the only practical alternative left in such a jurisdiction would be either an emergency or civil detention action under the mental health statutes of that state.

The Model Penal Code Proposed Solicitation Statute

The present Federal Criminal Code (18 U.S.C.A. Section 2) and the proposed Federal Criminal

Code make solicitation a crime. Section 5.02 of the Model Penal Code proposes a general solicitation statute, part of which is as follows:

(1) *Definition of Solicitation.* A person is guilty of solicitation to commit a crime if with the purpose of promoting or facilitating its commission he commands, encourages or requests another person to engage in a specific conduct which would constitute such crime or an attempt to commit such crime or which would establish his complicity in its commission or attempted commission.

Although the Model Penal Code defines solicitation to include solicitation to commit any crime (misdemeanor or felony), most states with a general solicitation statute limit solicitation to the solicitation of a felony.

Of the few states that have comprehensive solicitation statutes, all but one limit solicitation to the solicitation of a felony. The Model Penal Code defines solicitation to include the solicitation to commit any crime, whether it be a misdemeanor or a felony.

2. CONSPIRACY

The crime of conspiracy is the oldest of the preliminary crimes. It received some legislative recognition as early as 1292, but it was not until the early 1600s that the crime of conspiracy was developed into an offense of wide scope, capable of extensive application by the English Court of the Star Chamber. This court was created in the late 1500s to try certain high crimes without a jury. Because of the ruthless methods supposedly used, the court is sometimes referred to as the "infamous Star Chamber."

Modern critics of the crime of conspiracy sometimes recall the ancient unsavory use of the crime of conspiracy, as did former Justice Robert H. Jackson in his concurring opinion in *Krulewitch v. United States:*

The crime comes down to us wrapped in vague but unpleasant connotations. It sounds historical undertones of treachery, secret plotting and violence on a scale that menaces social stability and the security of the state itself. "Privy conspiracy" ranks with sedition and rebellion in the Litany's prayer for deliverance. Conspiratorial movements do indeed lie back of the political assassination, the coup d'etat, the putsch, the revolution and seizure of power in modern times, as they have in all history.[1]

The federal government (18 U.S.C.A. Sec. 371) and probably all states have enacted statutes making conspiracy a crime in their jurisdictions. The reasoning behind such legislation generally is that when two or more persons plan a crime together (a) the extent of potential harm to the society is often increased considerably; (b) the possibility of the abandonment of the criminal plan is greatly reduced; (c) the chances of success in the criminal venture are greater than if only one individual were involved; and (d) their actions can be more difficult to detect than individual preparation to commit a crime.

The purpose, then, of criminal conspiracy statutes is to prevent and to punish criminal partnerships in crime and to stop, if possible, such criminal combinations of people before attempts to commit substantive crimes are made.

Although the statutes of each state define conspiracy within that state, the generally accepted common law definition of conspiracy is "a combination of two or more persons, by some concerted action, to accomplish some criminal or unlawful purpose, or to accomplish some purpose, not in itself criminal or unlawful, by criminal or unlawful means." [2]

Conspiracy Today

Conspiracy used to be known as the "darling of the prosecutor's nursery." [3] However, today the "new darling of the prosecutor's nursery" is the Federal RICO (Racketeer Influenced and Corrupt Organization Act) statute and the "little RICOs" that have been enacted in many states. (See Chapter 20 for a discussion of the RICO statutes.)

Conspiracy statutes have, in the past, been an important weapon in the fight against organized crime. In 1983, FBI Director William H. Webster testified that it was not until the 1980s that law enforcement agencies, prosecutors, and courts learned how to use RICO effectively. The RICO statutes have probably now become the most effective tool against organized crime with conspiracy being used when needed.

Enforcement agencies responsible for the policing of business practices have used conspiracy charges in antitrust, price-fixing, and restraint-of-trade cases. The common denominator found in all conspiracy cases is the government's allegation that the defendants, as a group, conspired to violate one or more of the criminal laws of that jurisdiction.

The Requirement of "Two or More" Guilty Persons

As conspiracy was looked on as a partnership in crime, the traditional view was that the state must prove the involvement of "two or more" guilty persons. If A and B were charged with conspiracy to murder and the jury found A guilty and B not guilty, the traditional view is that the conviction against A could not stand. The reasoning for the dismissal of the charge and conviction against A is that A could not conspire by himself and there would have to be "two or more" guilty persons for his conviction to stand.

The National Advisory Committee Report on Organized Crime referred to the requirement of "two or more" as an "antique conspiracy law." The American Law Institute Model Penal Code rejected the "bilateral" requirement of "two or more" in favor of the "unilateral approach."

In 1961, Illinois adopted the "unilateral approach," stating that the "two or more" requirement was "too technical and overlooked the realities of trials which involve differences in juries, contingent availability of witnesses, the varying ability of different prosecutors and defense attorneys, etc." [4] Section 8–2(b) of the Illinois Criminal Code states:

(b) Co-conspirators.

It shall not be a defense to conspiracy that the person or persons with whom the accused is alleged to have conspired:

1. Has not been prosecuted or convicted, or
2. Has been convicted of a different offense, or
3. Is not amenable to justice, or
4. Has been acquitted, or
5. Lacked the capacity to commit an offense.

After using the "two or more" requirement for many years, the U.S. Court of Military Appeals, in 1983, held in *United States v. Garcia* that when two coconspirators are tried separately on a conspiracy charge, the acquittal of one does not mean that the other conspirator must also be acquitted. In pointing out that more than 26 states have adopted the Model Penal Code "unilateral approach," the court held:

Our present system of judicial review is quite capable of considering the evidence against each and all the named conspirators, even when they are tried separately, and deciding the criminal responsibility of each without resort to a rule that must often result in a miscarriage of justice simply to avoid the possibility of a "wrong" verdict. . . . We do not now decide the question of whether inconsistent verdicts as to coconspirators in a *joint* trial may be treated separately.[5]

If One of the Two Parties Is Only Pretending to Have a Criminal Intent

If one of the two parties to a criminal plan is only pretending to go along with a criminal plan, when in fact he or she is an undercover police officer or a person cooperating with a law enforcement agency, conspiracy cannot be charged in states using the "two or more" requirement. However, in a state using the "unilateral approach," conspiracy could be charged. The following case reflects what is now the majority rule in the United States today:

STATE v. LAVARY
Superior Court of New Jersey
(1977)
152 N.J. Super. 413, 377 A.2d 1255

The New Jersey court ruled that a defendant can be convicted of conspiracy even though the person she conspired with was actually an undercover police officer. In affirming the defendant's conviction for conspiracy to commit atrocious assault and battery and to commit mayhem on a police officer, the New Jersey appellate court held:

The relevant Model Penal Code *section takes the approach that it is "immaterial to the guilt of a conspirator whose culpability has been established that the person or all of the persons with whom he conspired have not been or cannot be convicted."* Id., 305 Minn. at ——, 232 N.W.2d at 801–803.

The court there found the reasoning of those authorities persuasive and concluded that defendant was properly convicted of conspiracy.

Other jurisdictions have adopted this "unilateral" approach. In Saienni v. State, *Del., 346 A.2d 152 (Sup. Ct.1975), defendant argued on appeal he could not be guilty of conspiracy with a police informer and an undercover agent, both of whom had no intention of committing the crime. The court found the argument to be without merit.*

* * *

To hold otherwise here would mock justice, interfere with the interest of society in repressing crime, and lead to absurd results. This court finds, as evidenced by the proposed New Jersey Penal Code, *that a unilateral approach to the crime of conspiracy is appropriate and fully justified in New Jersey. This approach requires that the evaluation of guilt in New Jersey when conspiracy is charged be from the point of view of the individual actor. The court finds this interpretation fully consistent with modern New Jersey cases, not violative of any legislative directive and consistent with the increased danger and social harm inherent in the crime of conspiracy. The "intricacies and artificial distinctions" urged by defendant thwart rather than serve substantial justice and are hereby rejected. . . .*

For the above reasons, the motion to dismiss the indictment or grant judgment notwithstanding the verdict is denied.

Husband and Wife as Coconspirators

Under the old common law, a husband and wife were one person, with the wife being subject to the control and discipline of the husband (see the discussion on the defense of duress and coercion in Chapter 7). Because of this relationship, the common law rule held that *since* the husband and wife were one person, they could not conspire together and be charged as the two persons to a conspiracy.

This rule was adopted in the states, but in the few modern cases in which the issue has been presented before American courts, the courts have rejected the old common law rule. In the 1960 case of *United States v. Dege,*[6] the U.S. Supreme Court rejected the concept that a husband and wife are legally incapable of criminally conspiring with each other. In affirming the convictions of the husband and wife defendants for conspiring to illegally bring goods into the United States, the majority held:

> Considering that legitimate business enterprises between husband and wife have long been commonplace in our time, it would enthrone an unreality into a rule of law to suggest that man and wife are legally incapable of engaging in illicit enterprises and therefore, forsooth, do not engage in them.

This rule permits federal prosecutors to charge husband and wife with criminal conspiracy.

Charging Corporations with Conspiracy

A corporation may be charged with conspiracy along with those who are agents and usually officers of the corporation. The following 1911 case reflects the old "two or more guilty persons" requirement that is now the minority view in the United States:

UNITED STATES v. SANTA RITA STORES CO.

Supreme Court of New Mexico (1911)
16 N.M. 3, 113 P. 620

Two corporations and one man (Deegan) were charged with conspiracy to violate antitrust laws. Deegan was an agent for both corporations. In reversing the conviction, the court stated:

Undoubtedly, a conspiracy might be formed by two corporations acting through agents, yet there must be more than one person actually engaged in the formation of the conspiracy. In this case a conspiracy was not formed because of a lack of persons. Deegan could not conspire with himself; neither could two or more corporations conspire alone by means of Deegan. Had some other officer or agent of either corporation participated in, or had some knowledge of the scheme, then a conspiracy might have been formed between the two defendant corporations. The union of two or more persons, the conscious participation in the scheme of two or more minds, is indispensable to an unlawful combination, and it cannot be created by the action of one man alone.

The Wharton Rule

Some crimes cannot be committed alone. Examples of such crimes are dueling, bigamy, gambling, adultery, and incest. Part of the justification for the creation of the crime of conspiracy is that the criminal agreement presents danger to the society beyond that inherent in the crime that is planned. In the 1850 case of *Shannon v. Commonwealth,*[7] the court threw out a prosecution for conspiracy to commit adultery, in which the man and woman were defendants, stating, "nothing is more ridiculous."

The Wharton Rule [8] holds that when the state charges a conspiracy to commit a crime that requires at least two people to commit, the state must charge three or more persons to sustain the conspiracy charge. Therefore, in jurisdictions that follow the Wharton Rule, in order to charge conspiracy to gamble the state must charge at least three persons.

In the 1935 case of *Gebardi v. United States,* the U.S. Supreme Court reversed the conviction of a man and a woman who were convicted of conspiring to violate the Mann Act by planning to transport the woman defendant from one state to another for the purpose of engaging in sexual intercourse with the male defendant. The Court stated "that where it is impossible under any circumstances to commit the substantive offense without co-operative action, the preliminary agreement between the same parties to commit the offense is not an indictable conspiracy either at common law . . . or under the federal statute." [9]

Probably because of the organized crime problem in the Chicago area, Illinois is among the jurisdictions that have rejected the Wharton Rule. The Committee on the Revision of the Illinois Criminal Code Comments with respect to Section 8–2(a) of the Illinois Criminal Code are as follows:

The Committee felt that the Wharton Rule fails to take into account the preventive aspect of prosecuting conspiracies, that is, to discourage the more dangerous criminal activity of several persons by punishing the preliminary agreement to engage in such activity. That the criminal activity is of such nature as to inevitably require more than one person in its accomplishment seems the more reason to punish the preliminary agreement to undertake it.[10]

Section 5.04 of the Model Penal Code rejects the Wharton Rule. Although the federal statute making gambling a crime (18 U.S.C. Sec. 1955) requires "five or more persons," this represents, as the U.S. Supreme Court points out, "a legislative attempt to merge the conspiracy and the substantive offense into a single crime." [11]

Objective of the Conspiracy

Common law conspiracy is defined as "a combination of two or more persons . . . to accomplish some criminal or unlawful purpose." Under the common law, the unlawful act did not have to be criminal but could have been a tort or an act that violated public policy. The present general federal conspiracy statute (18 U.S.C.A. Sec. 371) prohibits not only conspiracy to commit a crime, but also any "offense against the United States, or to defraud the United States, or any agency thereof in any manner or for any purpose."

The tendency of modern conspiracy statutes is to limit the crime of conspiracy to criminal offenses. The proposed federal criminal code [12] (not yet enacted) limits the crime of conspiracy to "a crime or crimes." As the Federal Criminal Code is made up of more than 2,800 crimes, this gives considerable scope to future federal conspiracy charges.

3. ATTEMPT

In states that have statutorized a general solicitation crime, solicitation is infrequently charged. Attempt, however, is the most frequently charged of the three preliminary crimes. This difference exists because it is difficult for law enforcement agencies not only to detect criminal solicitation (other than prostitution and bribery), but also to obtain sufficient evidence with which to charge. On the other hand, people who attempt to commit a crime often expose to witnesses and possible victims their criminal intent and purpose by their acts. The near victim of a crime and other witnesses are more willing to disclose to the police what they have seen and heard than are those who are solicited by a friend or acquaintance to commit a crime.

In defining an attempt, the New York Criminal Code provides that "a person is guilty of an attempt to commit a crime when, with intent to commit a crime, he engages in conduct which tends to effect the commission of such crime." [13] But mere preparation to commit a crime is not an attempt. New York and other states require the state to show that the defendant performed acts that carried the "project forward within dangerous proximity of the criminal end to be attained." [14] Other courts ask whether the defendant's acts by themselves are unequivocal evidence of the criminal intent.

Attempt, like the other preparatory crimes, has its origins in early English law. Attempt charges were reportedly used as early as the 14th century. The modern doctrine of attempt had been formulated before the ratification of the U.S Constitution. Today, most states have enacted general attempt statutes that, with few exceptions, make the attempt to commit a felony or a misdemeanor a crime. Some states, however, limit the crime of attempt to felonies and only a few misdemeanors such as battery and misdemeanor theft.

What Acts by a Defendant Amount to an Attempt?

Courts and writers have spent a great deal of time with the most difficult problem in the area

---

Attempt Under the Federal Criminal Code

Although there is no comprehensive statutory definition of attempt in federal law, federal courts have rather uniformly adopted the standard set forth in Section 5.01 of the . . . Model Penal Code . . . that the requisite elements of attempt are:

1) an intent to engage in criminal conduct, and

2) conduct constituting a 'substantial step' towards the commission of the substantive offense which strongly corroborates the actor's criminal intent.

—*United States v. Joyce,*
693 F.2d 838 (8th Cir. 1982)

of attempt. When has a person who has an intent to commit a crime done enough to justify his or her arrest and conviction? Just how close to completing the crime must the defendant come before he or she can be successfully charged with attempt? Should the law emphasize what the defendant has done toward completing the crime or should the emphasis be on what remains to be done to complete the crime?

Statutes defining solicitation do not ordinarily require the showing of any overt act as an essential element of the crime. But from a practical point of view and in order to prove solicitation, there must be a showing of overt acts. In conspiracy, the overt act can be an act of mere preparation. A telephone call could suffice. But to prove attempt, the defendant must, in some jurisdictions, come within "dangerous proximity" of committing the crime, whereas in other states, the defendant must perform a substantial act toward the commission of the crime. At which step in the following example could a person be convicted of the crime of attempted burglary in your jurisdiction?

- *Step one:* X plans to burglarize a home and drives through a residential area looking for a residence to burglarize.
- *Step two:* At ten o'clock at night, X sees a dark house and parks his car a short distance away to observe the neighborhood.
- *Step three:* After he telephones the house and receives no answer, he rings the front and back doorbells of the residence.
- *Step four:* After trying the doors to see if one is unlocked, he tries the windows in an attempt to find one that is not locked from the inside.
- *Step five:* He sees an open window on the second floor and goes into the garage to look for a ladder.
- *Step six:* There is no ladder in the garage, so he tries other garages until he finds a ladder, which he "borrows" for a few minutes.
- *Step seven:* He places the ladder on the side of the house, under the open window.
- *Step eight:* He climbs the ladder.

- *Step nine:* He enters the house through the open second-floor window.

The Required Mental Element of Attempt

In charging an attempt, or any of the other preparatory crimes, the state must prove that the defendant intended to commit the intended crime and would have done so except that something occurred that prevented the act, or some fact came to his or her attention that caused a change of mind. For example, a police officer might arrive at the scene, or a man who is going to rape a woman might decide not to do so because he discovers that she is pregnant or he believes that she has a venereal disease. The trier of fact (a jury or judge) must determine from the defendant's act, conduct, and the circumstances that existed what the mental intent and purpose of the defendant was. Suppose that X in the example given were to argue that he placed the ladder alongside the house to get his cat off the roof, but no cat was seen on the roof. X's intentions would have to be determined by the jury or judge who would decide whether he is guilty of the crime of attempted burglary.

Is Failure to Complete the Criminal Act an Essential Element of Attempt?

Can a person be charged with attempted burglary, robbery, or rape and be convicted even when the evidence showed that the completed crime was committed? In the 1965 case of *People v. English,*[15] the New York Court of Appeals held that a conviction for attempted rape based on conduct amounting to a completed rape was invalid. However, the New York Penal Code was amended in 1967 and Section 110.00 (attempt to commit a crime) now permits a conviction for an attempt to commit a crime even when the evidence shows that the crime was completed. In 1961, the Illinois legislature amended Section 8–4 of the Illinois Criminal Code so that it is no longer necessary in that state to show that the attempt failed. The majority rule in the United States is that failure to complete a crime is not an essential element of the crime of attempt.[16]

Attempt Cases Illustrating State and Federal Rulings

MERRITT v. COMMONWEALTH
Court of Appeals of Virginia (1935)
164 Va. 653, 180 S.E. 395

The defendant was convicted of attempted murder and sentenced to eight years in the penitentiary for pointing a loaded pistol at another man within range of the revolver. The Supreme Court of Virginia reversed, stating:

The intent is the purpose formed in a man's mind, and is usually proved by his conduct, sometimes by his statements; the necessary intent constituting one element in an attempt is the intent in fact, as distinguished from an intent in law. From the act alleged, the law infers a general evil intent, on the principle that a man intends the probable and necessary consequences of his act. The act charged here is an assault. In order to raise this assault to a more substantive crime, it must be done with a specific intent to take life. This intent cannot be inferred from the act alleged. . . .

We cannot infer the specific intent to kill and murder from the allegation that the accused maliciously pointed the loaded pistol at Trull. From this allegation, a general evil purpose may be inferred, but not the specific design to kill.

PEOPLE v. PAYTON
Appellate Court of Illinois (1971)
2 Ill. App. 3d 693, 276 N.E.2d 775

The defendant fired a gun twice at a woman's husband and missed by only 18 inches at 100 feet. He alleged that he was only trying to scare the husband so that he would stay away from his estranged wife. The defendant's conviction for attempted murder was affirmed.

PEOPLE v. WELCH
Supreme Court of California (1972)
8 Cal. 3d 106, 104 Cal. Rptr. 217, 502 P.2d 225

The fact that the defendant discontinued his efforts to rape a woman when she told him that she had gonorrhea did not prevent his conviction for attempted rape, since all the elements of the crimes were proved.

BINDER v. ILLINOIS
Appellate Court of Illinois, First Division (1975)
18 Ill. App. 3d 960, 310 N.E.2d 661, *cert. denied,* 420 U.S. 947, 95 S. Ct. 1329, 16 CrL 4190

During a burglary stakeout, police officers observed the defendant try the doorknob on the side door of a garage, hit the door with his shoulder in an attempt to open it, and attempt to lift the overhead door of the garage. Also admitted for use was evidence that the defendant admitted that he tried to gain entry into the garage. This was held to be sufficient evidence to support the conviction for attempted burglary. The U.S. Supreme Court refused *certiorari.*

UNITED STATES v. JOYCE
United States Court of Appeals (1982)
693 F.2d 838 (8th Cir.)

In a "reverse sting operation," an undercover police officer let it be known that he had cocaine to sell. The defendant arrived in St. Louis with $22,000 to purchase a pound of cocaine. The undercover officer gave the defendant a sealed and wrapped package that he said contained cocaine. Without opening the package, the defendant immediately gave it back to the officer. The officer refused to open the package until the defendant produced the purchase money. The defendant would not produce the money until the package was opened. The defendant left without making a purchase. The defendant's jury conviction of attempting to possess cocaine with intent to distribute was reversed as the court held there was insufficient evidence to establish that the defendant engaged in conduct amounting to a "substantial step" toward committing the crime of possession with intent to distribute.

UNITED STATES v. MANDUJANO
Review denied by U.S. Supreme Court (1975)
499 F.2d 370 (5th Cir.) 419 U.S. 1114

Defendant was convicted of attempted distribution of heroin. A policeman, after extensive preliminary negotiations and efforts, contacted the defendant and paid him $650.00, which money was to have been used by Mandujano, the defendant, to go out and purchase heroin. The agent waited while the defendant made the effort. Later he returned and said that he was unable to locate his contact. He returned the money to the officer.

The Fifth Circuit held that the evidence was sufficient. In discussing the overt act element the court said: "The defendant must have engaged in conduct which constitutes a substantial step toward commission of the crime. A substantial step must be conduct strongly corroborative of the firmness of the defendant's criminal intent."

Impossibility as a Defense to an Attempt Charge

In the 1983 case of *State v. Lopez*, the defendant was charged with attempt to traffic in a controlled substance when he tried to sell a substance he mistakenly believed to be cocaine. The New Mexico Supreme Court rejected the defense of "impossibility" and affirmed the defendant's conviction, holding that:

> The defendant should be treated in accordance with the facts as he believes them to be. In the present case . . . Lopez demonstrated his readiness to violate the law. . . . When a defendant has done everything within his power to commit a crime, he has attempted to commit the crime. . . . Therefore, imposition of criminal liability is justified.[17]

In holding that a defendant can be convicted of attempt even when "completion is impossible," the New Mexico Supreme Court joined an increasing number of states that have rejected the distinctions between "legal" and "factual" impossibility.

Legal and factual impossibility can be defined and distinguished as follows:

1. In the defense of law known as *legal impossibility,* the completed act is not a crime even

though the defendant intended to commit a crime. In the 1906 case of *People v. Jaffe,*[18] the goods received by the defendant, who believed that they were stolen, were not stolen property. The court held that the defendant could not be convicted of the attempt to receive stolen property. In the 1939 case of *State v. Taylor,*[19] the defendant bribed a person, believing him to be a juror, when in fact the person was not a juror. The court held that the defendant could not be convicted of attempt to bribe a juror. Legal impossibility is therefore a complete defense to an attempt charge (but not to a conspiracy or solicitation charge). The mental purpose (*mens rea*) to commit a crime exists, but the completed act is not a crime. This defense, however, is only available in those states that continue to allow the defense. An increasing number of states are rejecting the defense.

2. The defense of fact known as *factual impossibility,* or physical impossibility, deals with situations in which, because of some physical or factual factor or situation unknown to the defendant, the crime attempted cannot be completed. An example of factual impossibility is found in the 1869 case of *Kunkle v. State,*[20] in which the victim was out of the range of the weapon that

the defendant used. In the 1966 case of *Osborn v. United States,*[21] the person who was offered a bribe by the defendant went to the police. The U.S. Supreme Court rejected the defense of impossibility, stating that "whatever continuing validity the doctrine of 'impossibility' with all of its subtleties, may continue to have in the law of criminal attempt, the body of the law is inapplicable here." When the criminal intent exists and the specific act that the defendant sought to complete is a crime, the defendant cannot argue impossibility just because he or she was unable to complete the crime. Factual impossibility is therefore not a defense to a charge of attempt.[22]

In addition to legal and factual impossibility, some courts also write of "inherent impossibility." The distinctions between these three forms of impossibility are sometimes difficult to determine. Court decisions vary considerably throughout the United States as to the application of the doctrine of impossibility. In 1967, the New York state legislature rejected impossibility defenses by the enactment of Section 110.10 of the New York Penal Code. The 1961 Committee Comment on the enactment of Section 8–4(b) of the Illinois Criminal Code is as follows:

It is the intent of section 8–4(b) to exclude both factual and legal impossibilities as defenses to prosecution for attempt. However, inherent impossibility (attempts to kill by witchcraft such as repeatedly stabbing a cloth dummy made to represent the person intended to be killed) is not intended to be excluded as a defense.[23]

Section 5.01 of the Model Penal Code eliminates the defenses of legal, factual, and inherent impossibility but proposes that (i)f the particular conduct charged . . . is so inherently unlikely to result or culminate in the commission of a crime . . . nor the actor presents a public danger . . . the Court shall exercise its power . . . to enter judgment and impose sentence for a crime of lower grade or degree, or, in extreme cases, may dismiss the prosecution.[24]

Renunciation or Abandonment of the Criminal Purpose

In attempt, conspiracy, and solicitation there is time for a person to change his or her mind and decide not to go ahead with the criminal project of completing the crime. The question of how far along the criminal enterprise had progressed and the reason for abandoning the project are important factors in determining whether the defense of abandonment should be accepted by a court.

Under the common law, abandonment would not be accepted as a defense if the defendant had performed required acts of the crime with criminal intent.[25] The status of this rule in the United States remains in doubt. Suppose a man places a ladder against the side of a dwelling, intending to enter and steal. At the last minute he changes his mind and walks away. Whether a man who voluntarily changed his mind under such circumstances could be convicted of attempted burglary might vary somewhat from state to state and from court to court. The question to be determined by a court or jury would be whether the conduct of the defendant before the abandonment amounted to attempted burglary. If the man discontinued his efforts to burglarize the dwelling because he heard someone coming or because he heard a dog barking inside the dwelling, his renunciation would not be considered voluntary.

Some of the states have abandonment and withdrawal statutes permitting the defense of abandonment under specific circumstances. Section 1001(3) of the proposed Federal Criminal Code provides that a voluntary and complete renunciation of the criminal effort is an affirmative defense to a charge of attempt. Section 5.01(4) of the Model Penal Code proposes the following withdrawal provision to a charge of criminal attempt:

(4) *Renunciation of Criminal Purpose.* When the actor's conduct would otherwise constitute an attempt under Subsection (1)(b) or (1)(c) of this Section, it is an affirmative defense that he abandoned his effort to commit the crime or otherwise prevented its commission, under circumstances manifesting a complete and voluntary renunciation of his criminal purpose. The establishment of such defense does not, however, affect the liability of an accomplice who did not join in such abandonment or prevention.

Within the meaning of this Article, renunciation of criminal purpose is not voluntary if it is motivated, in whole or in part, by circumstances, not present or

Preliminary, Anticipatory (or Inchoate) Crimes

	The crime consists of evidence showing:	*Other aspects of the crime*
Solicitation (the preparatory offense that is least often charged): The invitation to commit a crime	1. Requesting, encouraging, or commanding another person 2. to engage in a specific conduct that would constitute a crime (most states restrict general solicition to felonies) 3. or attempt to commit such crime	As there is generally no requirement for an overt act, the crime is complete when the solicitation is made. If the request to commit a crime is accepted, the solicitee can also be a coconspirator or an aider and abettor to an attempted or completed crime.
Conspiracy (the oldest of the preparatory offenses): The criminal partnership	1. An agreement between two or more persons (more than half the states now follow the Model Penal Code and do not require "two or more" guilty persons. In these states, proof of guilt of one person is sufficient.) 2. with specific intent 3. to commit a crime 4. or to obtain a legal goal by criminal acts 5. (half the states require proof that one or more of the parties acted to effect the object of the conspiracy)	A conspiracy is punishable whether or not it succeeds in its objective (*United States v. Rabinowich,* 238 U.S. 78). In federal courts and some states, convictions for both conspiracy and the completed crime are held not to violate double jeopardy. (*Pereira v. United States,* 347 U.S. 1, and *Iannelli v. United States,* 420 U.S. 770, 16 CrL 3127, 1975)
Attempt (the inchoate crime charged most often): An attempt often puts a possible victim in fear and apprehension. Many near victims can and do appear as witnesses in criminal trials.	1. That the defendant intended to commit the crime of which he or she is charged, and 2. that he or she did acts that (a) came within "dangerous proximity" of the criminal end or (b) are unequivocal evidence of the criminal intent, 3. and in some states, he or she would have committed the crime except for the intervention of another person or some other extraneous factor.	The American Law Institute Model Penal Code recommends the broadening of criminal liability for the crime of attempt (see Sec. 5.01[2] for a discussion of these proposals).

apparent at the inception of the actor's course of conduct, which increase the probability of detection or apprehension or which make more difficult the accomplishment of the criminal purpose. Renunciation is not complete if it is motivated by a decision to postpone the criminal conduct until a more advantageous time or to transfer the criminal effort to another but similar objective or victim.

In the 1970 case of *People v. Staples,*[26] the defendant admitted, in a written confession, that he had rented an office over a bank with intent to burglarize the bank. He brought in tools and equipment and had drilled partly through the floor over the bank. His defense was that he had abandoned the criminal project before the landlord became aware of what he was doing. The landlord turned over the defendant's tools and equipment to the police.

The defendant stated that when his wife came back from a trip, his "life as a bank robber seemed more and more absurd." In affirming his conviction for attempted burglary, the court held that the drilling was "the beginning of the breaking element." How would a prosecutor and a court in your state handle this if Staples himself had called the police in and disclosed his intention to abandon his criminal project?

B. PARTIES TO THE PRINCIPAL CRIME

Under the Common Law

The different degrees of criminal participation were recognized early in common law. Since many felonies were punishable by death, the common law courts categorized the various criminal roles of participation in order to distinguish the penalties that were to be applied. There were four common law categories:

1. A principal in the first degree was a person (or persons) who actually committed the crime.

2. A principal in the second degree was a person who was present at the commission of the crime, was not involved in the planning of the crime, but aided and abetted in the actual commission of the crime. This offender could not be tried under the common law until the actual perpetrator had been apprehended and convicted of the offense.

3. An accessory before the fact was a person who, knowing that a crime was to be committed, aided in the preparation for the crime but was not present at the time the crime was committed.

4. An accessory after the fact was a person who knew that the crime had been committed and gave aid or comfort to the person who committed the crime. Neither the accessory before the fact nor after the fact could be tried until after the conviction of the principal in the first degree.[27]

Criminal Liability in the United States Today

Today, most states[28] have done away with the four common law categories, and the majority of jurisdictions have by statute created only two categories of criminal liability:

1. All persons who knowingly are involved or connected in the commission of a crime either before or during its commission are known as principals (or parties to the crime) regardless of

their connection. This category is a combination of the common law principle in the first and second degree and the accessory before the fact. The existing federal statute (Sec. 2 of Title 18) reflects the usual criminal liability used today in the various states. This section reads as follows:

> Principals.
>
> (a) Whoever commits an offense against the United States or aids, abets, counsels, commands, induces or procures its commission, is punishable as a principal.
>
> (b) Whoever willfully causes an act to be done which if directly performed by him or another would be an offense against the United States, is punished as a principal.

2. The person or people who render aid to the criminal after he or she has committed the crime. Legislative bodies have statutorized criminal offenses in this category which were previously known to the common law as accessory after the fact. This category will be discussed in the section on post-crime offenses in this chapter.

Under the old common law, the degree of punishment varied considerably with the degree of criminal liability. The principal in the first degree would receive the death penalty for almost 200 offenses in England 150 years ago. The distinction between the principal in the first degree and the principal in the second degree was important under those circumstances. Today, probably all states make all principals (or parties to the crime) liable to the same degree of punishment.

The rule that neither the principal in the second degree nor the accessories before or after the fact could be forced to trial before the trial of the principal in the first degree has been abolished in most American jurisdictions. In states that have abolished the common law bar, any participant in a crime may be tried and convicted, even though the person who actually committed the crime has not been apprehended and tried or even identified.[29]

The Criminal Liability of Persons Involved in the Planning of a Crime

Mere knowledge of a contemplated crime or failure to disclose such information, without evidence of any further involvement in the crime,

---

Criminal Liability for a Completed Crime

Under the Old Common Law	Under Present Statutes
Principal in the first degree—person who actually committed a crime	All the following are equally liable:
Principal in the second degree—person who was a conspirator to the crime and was present at the commission of the crime whether he or she gave any assistance at that time or not	1. The person who commits the crime
	2. A party to a crime as a conspirator who advises, hires, counsels, or otherwise procures another to commit a crime
Accessory before the fact—person who was a conspirator to a felony (ordered, counseled, encouraged, etc.) but was not present at the commission of the offense	3. A party to a crime who intentionally and knowingly aids or abets the person who committed the crime
Accessory after the fact—person who knew that a crime was committed and gave aid or comfort to the person who committed the crime	Separate liability exists for the postcrime offenses, such as escape, refusal to aid an officer, obstructing, resisting, perjury, bribery, bail jumping, harboring a felon.

---

does not make a person liable as a party to that crime. However, the person who hires another to commit a crime or counsels, commands, induces, or procures the commission of the crime is punishable as a principal of the crime. Today, the "higher up" is regarded as more of a social menace than are the underlings. Under modern statutes, he or she can be punished just as severely as the person who actually committed the crime.

The mere association with persons who are planning or have committed a crime would not justify a conviction, but a person who consciously shares in any criminal act is liable whether or not there was an actual plan and conspiracy.[30]

If the circumstances show that there was a common design to commit an unlawful act to which all the parties assented, whatever is done in the furtherance of that design is the act of all the parties. To demonstrate a common design to commit a crime, it is necessary to show that there was an understanding between the parties. This does not mean that there has to be an expressed or formal agreement between the parties, but it does require that there be a meeting of the minds or a mutual understanding to accomplish a common criminal objective or to work together for a common criminal purpose.

Criminal Liability for the Conduct of Another

A person is criminally liable for the conduct of another if he or she solicits, aids, abets, agrees, or attempts to aid other persons in the planning or commission of an offense. The person is criminally liable if he or she causes another to perform the conduct when the other person is innocent of any wrongdoing. For example, a man would be criminally liable for sending commercial movers to pick up and deliver a baby grand piano that does not belong to him if he intends to steal the piano.

Under the "common design" rule, when persons have a common design to do an unlawful act, whatever is done in furtherance of the design or criminal plan is the act of all. The common design could be a conspiracy to commit a crime. Any member of the conspiracy is liable as a principal for any offense committed in furtherance of the conspiracy while he or she is a member of it. Latecomers cannot be convicted as principals for offenses that were committed before they joined the conspiracy or after they withdrew from the conspiracy.[31]

Aider and Abettor Cases [32]

UNITED STATES v. O'NEILL 729 F.2d 1440 (2d Cir.1983), *cert. denied,* —— U.S. ——, 34 CrL 4007	The fact that the defendants provided the following lawful goods and services to conspirators—fueled their plane, rented hangar space, stored ammunition and guns, falsely identified conspirators to outsiders, and offered to pay security guard $20,000 to disappear while the plane was being loaded—was sufficient to affirm their conviction for aiding and abetting.

UNITED STATES v. BUTTS 707 F.2d 1404, 33 CrL 2141 (3d Cir.1983)	Postal inspectors had probable cause to arrest Butts and Passanante and followed them to their car, in which another man, Morgan, was sitting. In holding that the officers had no authority to arrest Morgan, the court stated:

That arresting authorities had no reason to believe that Morgan knew about or was involved in the scheme involving the stolen checks. Morgan might have been sitting in the car simply because he had some unrelated and wholly lawful business with Butts or Passanante. Mere presence at a given location cannot in and of itself constitute probable cause to arrest.

STATE v. WALDEN Supreme Court of North Carolina (1982) 293 S.E.2d 780	Defendant was present while a man seriously injured her one-year-old son by beating him with a leather belt with a metal buckle. The mother was found guilty of assault on a theory of aiding and abetting solely on the grounds that she was present when her child was attacked and had a reasonable opportunity to prevent or attempt to prevent the attack but failed to do so. The Supreme Court of North Carolina affirmed the conviction, holding that the trial court properly instructed the jury as follows:

It is the duty of a parent to protect their children and to do whatever may be reasonably necessary for their care and their safety. A parent has a duty to protect their children and cannot stand passively by and refuse to do so when it is reasonably within their power to protect their children. A parent is bound to provide such reasonable care as necessary, under the circumstances facing them at that particular time. However, a parent is not required to do the impossible or the unreasonable in caring for their children.

Now a person is not guilty of a crime merely because she is present at the scene. To be guilty she must aid or actively encourage the person committing the crime, or in some way communicate to this person her intention to assist in its commission; or that she is present with the reasonable opportunity and duty to prevent the crime and fails to take reasonable steps to do so.

RAEL v. CADENA Supreme Court of New Mexico (1979) 93 N.M. 684, 604 P.2d 822	The defendant had not physically assisted in a battery but gave verbal encouragement to the assailant by yelling, "Kill him" and "Hit him more." In this *civil* action, the court found that liability did not require a finding of action in concert, nor even that the injury had directly resulted

from the encouragement. Citing Restatement Section 876(b), the court held:

It is clear, however, that in the United States, civil liability for assault and battery is not limited to the direct perpetrator, but extends to any person who by any means aids or encourages the act. Hargis v. Horrine, 230 Ark. 502, 323 S.W.2d 917 (1959); Ayer v. Robinson, 163 Cal.App. 2d 424, 329 P.2d 546 (1958); Guilbeau v. Guilbeau, 326 So.2d 654 (La. App. 1976); Duke v. Feldman, 245 Md. 454, 266 A.2d 345 (1967); Brink v. Purnell, 162 Mich. 147, 127 N.W. 322 (1910); 6 Am.Jur.2d Assault and Battery § 128 (1963); 6A C.J.S. Assault and Battery § 11 (1975); Annot., 72 A.L.R.2d 1229 (1960). According to the Restatement: "[f]or harm resulting to a third person from the tortious conduct of another, one is subject to liability if he

* * *

(b) knows that the other's conduct constitutes a breach of duty and gives substantial assistance or encouragement to the other so to conduct himself."–Restatement (Second) of Torts § 876 (1979)

Liability for Offenses Other Than the Planned and Intended Crime

When the evidence shows that there is a common design to commit an unlawful act to which all the defendants agreed, whatever is done in the furtherance of the criminal plan is the act of all if it is a natural and probable consequence of the intended crime. If guns are carried and a shot is fired by one member of the group, that shot is fired by all the defendants and all of them must answer for the results.[33]

In *People v. Jones,*[34] the California courts held that an accused who knew that his codefendants were armed was responsible for all the consequences when a night watchman was killed in a robbery. The defendant in the *Jones* case was unarmed.

The definition of the natural and probable consequences of the intended crime will vary somewhat from jury to jury and court to court. The following example illustrates the problem:

Example: X and Y conspire to burglarize a residence. X is the lookout and getaway driver while Y is in the house committing the burglary. Y commits the following additional crimes. Which of the following should X be charged with?

1. Y is surprised by the homeowner and, in his attempt to get away, kills the man.

2. Y is surprised by an 11-year-old boy who lives in the house and needlessly kills the boy.

3. In addition to stealing, Y comes on a woman in bed and rapes the woman.

4. After stealing from the house, Y sees a gallon of gasoline in the back hall of the house. He spills the gasoline around the house and burns it down.

Prosecutors could charge X with all the additional crimes, but whether X would be convicted would depend on whether the finder of fact determined that the additional acts were a natural and probable consequence of the burglary. It certainly could be argued in this case that X aided and assisted in all the crimes, because he was acting as look-out and the getaway driver. If X had hired Y to commit the burglary and X was not at the scene of the crime, his liability would be the same.

X's defense should be that some of the offenses are not the natural or probable consequence of the intended crime of burglary, and therefore he would not be criminally liable for those offenses. In all cases, X would be charged and convicted of the crime of burglary.

See the 1974 *Mumford v. Maryland* case. In that case, a rape and murder occurred during a burglary. The defendant (a 15-year-old girl) stated that she was elsewhere on the premises when the rape and murder occurred and that she did not know these crimes were being committed. In reversing her conviction for first-degree murder (felony murder) and ordering a new trial, the court stated: "There must be a direct causal connection between the homicide and the felony. Something more than mere coincidence in time and place between the two must be shown; otherwise, the felony-murder rule will not be applicable."

Theories as to the Origins of the Crime That Are Used in Charging and Prosecuting

When two or more defendants are charged with a crime (or crimes), there are two ways in which the offense could have originated. One origin of the crime involves a conspiracy, in which the parties planned the crime together and had an explicit or implicit understanding and meeting of the minds to commit the crime. The fact of the agreement imposes criminal liability on all the conspirators when the crime is committed by one member of the conspiracy. Liability is also imposed on all if one person commits another crime that is the natural and probable consequence of the agreed-upon crime. This liability is under the "conspiracy theory."

If there was no prior agreement or mutual understanding as to a criminal purpose, the crime would then be considered a spontaneous and impulsive act by the person who committed it. If the other defendant rendered either verbal or actual assistance, knowing that a crime was being committed, he or she was then aiding and abetting in the commission of the crime and is liable as a principal under the "complicity theory."

When two or more persons plead not guilty to a crime or crimes that they are alleged to have committed, they do not disclose to the police and the prosecutor the details of the history and the origins of the crime, even if they did commit it. Therefore, the state must proceed with the information that is available on one theory or the other (and sometimes on both theories).

In the 1894 case of *State v. Tally*,[35] a group of men in one town set out to kill a particular person who lived in another town. The friends of the victim, hearing of the plot against him, attempted to warn him by sending him a telegraph message. Another person, a judge, who also disliked the potential victim, directed the telegraph operator to destroy the message, telling him that it was unimportant. The man was killed and the judge was held liable for the

---

Criminal Liability for the Conduct of Another

A person is criminally liable for the conduct of another if he or she:

1. Has innocent people perform acts that, unknown to the innocent people, are crimes. *Example:* Having commercial movers take and carry away furniture or a piano that the person seeks to steal.

2. Knowingly becomes an aider and abettor to the crime of another. *Example:* Knowingly providing the means and transportation so that a person who has committed a crime may escape from the scene of the crime.

3. Conspires, hires, counsels, or otherwise procures another to commit a crime. Criminal liability when a "common design" extends to:
    a. the planned and intended crime (or crimes)
    b. crimes other than the planned and intended crime that are committed in the furtherance of the criminal plan, if such crimes are the natural and probable consequence of the intended crime

4. If, as a supervisor, employer, corporate officer, etc., the person has:
    a. "a positive duty to . . . . remedy violations . . . (and to) insure that violations will not occur." *United States v. Park,* 421 U.S. 658, 95 S. Ct. 1903 (1975).
    b. or, as required in *Vachon v. New Hampshire,* 414 U.S. 478, 94 S. Ct. 664 (1974), the person personally caused the forbidden act to be done.

> ### Scene of the Crime
>
> A person who was at the scene of a crime may be convicted for the crime if the state can prove beyond a reasonable doubt that:
>
> 1. he or she committed the crime, or
>
> 2. he or she intentionally aided and abetted the commission of the crime or that he or she was ready and willing to aid and abet the crime, and that the person who committed the crime knew this, or
>
> 3. that he or she was a party to the conspiracy to commit the crime and advised, hired, counseled, or otherwise procured the person to commit the crime, or
>
> 4. that vicarious liability exists for the acts of an employee, subordinate, etc.
>
> A person who was not at the scene of a crime may be convicted for the crime if the state can prove beyond a reasonable doubt that:
>
> 1. he or she was a party to the conspiracy to commit the crime and advised, hired, counseled, or otherwise procured the person to commit the crime, or
>
> 2. that vicarious liability exists for the acts of an employee, subordinate, etc.

murder under the "complicity theory," since, although he was not involved in the plans to murder the victim, he did render aid and assistance. The perpetrators of the crime were not aware of the assistance given by the judge until after they had committed the crime.

In the 1964 case of *State v. Nutley*,[36] two deputy sheriffs stopped a car from another state because they observed a discrepancy in the license plates. As the officers walked up to the car, one of the occupants shot and killed one of the officers. In the gunfight that followed between the remaining officer and the occupants of the car (each of whom was armed), the officer was wounded. All three men were convicted of first-degree murder and of attempted murder of the wounded officer. The Supreme Court of Wisconsin affirmed the convictions, stating that there was sufficient evidence to convict one of the defendants as the perpetrator of both crimes and the other defendants either under the "conspiracy theory" or under the "complicity theory." The court stated:

> It is not necessary that the aider and abettor enter into an agreement with the perpetrator to assist him in consummation of the crime. Nor is it necessary that the perpetrator be aware of the accomplice's efforts, in order to hold the accomplice liable for the substantive crime. . . .
>
> The rationale for the conspiracy theory recognizes that the fact of agreement materially reinforces the desire of the parties to carry out their portion of the division of criminal labor. Since each conspirator

psychologically reinforces the conduct of the overt perpetrator, each is justly held responsible for his substantive crime.

C. POSTCRIME OFFENSES

Today all states and the federal government have enacted many statutes meant to assist officers in performing their duty of investigating crimes and apprehending criminals. Some statutes punish people who knowingly give police false information with the intent to mislead them. Other statutes are designed to permit the proper and efficient functioning of the courts and the criminal justice system. Some of these offenses existed under the common law, whereas others have been created in modern times. Examples are:

• Refusing to aid an officer while such officer is doing any act in his or her official capacity

• Obstructing or resisting an officer while such officer is doing any act in his or her official capacity

• Obstructing justice

• Compounding a crime: the making of an agreement (for a consideration) to withhold evidence of, or to abstain from prosecuting, a crime of which the accused has knowledge. The elements of this offense are:

    a) the commission of a crime by another and the accused's knowledge of that crime.

b) an agreement or understanding to conceal, to withhold evidence of, or to abstain from prosecuting.

c) the receipt of a consideration (something of value, such as money or a promise). It has been held that it is not a crime for a victim to receive restitution, even when a wrong-doer hopes or thinks that the victim will drop the matter. (2 Wilkin, Crimes, Sec. 804, 1963)

• Misprision of a felony (failure to report or prosecute a known felon)

• Harboring or aiding felons
• Perjury
• Escape from custody
• Bribery of witnesses
• Bail jumping
• Communicating with jurors with intent to influence them

Are Material Witnesses Criminally Liable in Any Way?

A material witness is a witness who has material information regarding a crime. A person who

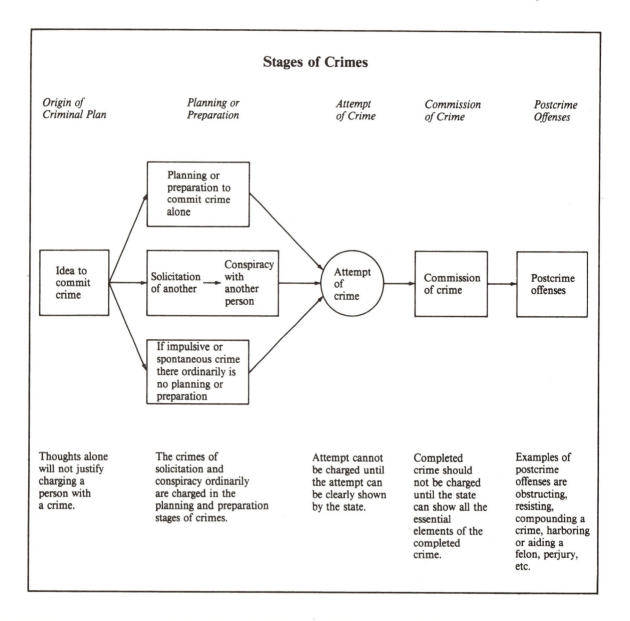

Stages of Crimes

Origin of Criminal Plan	*Planning or Preparation*	*Attempt of Crime*	*Commission of Crime*	*Postcrime Offenses*

Idea to commit crime → Planning or preparation to commit crime alone / Solicitation of another → Conspiracy with another person / If impulsive or spontaneous crime there ordinarily is no planning or preparation → Attempt of crime → Commission of crime → Postcrime offenses

Thoughts alone will not justify charging a person with a crime.	The crimes of solicitation and conspiracy ordinarily are charged in the planning and preparation stages of crimes.	Attempt cannot be charged until the attempt can be clearly shown by the state.	Completed crime should not be charged until the state can show all the essential elements of the completed crime.	Examples of postcrime offenses are obstructing, resisting, compounding a crime, harboring or aiding a felon, perjury, etc.

was in a business place at the time of an armed robbery and observed the robbers and the crime would be a material witness.

If the state cannot show probable cause that a material witness was a party to a crime, the material witness may not then be arrested. However, material witnesses may be reasonably detained to obtain their identity and to question them, as law enforcement officers have a legal duty and obligation to investigate criminal incidents.

Most material witnesses are cooperative and will honestly provide information that they have regarding a criminal incident. If it is shown that material witnesses provide false material information regarding a criminal incident to an investigating officer, the witness could be charged with obstructing and hindering a law enforcement officer in the performance of his (or her) duty. The following is an example of a cooperative witness:

Example: After the assassination of the Rev. Martin Luther King, Jr., a witness was able to identify James Earl Ray as the man rushing down the steps of the hotel from which the shots came. As Ray was not apprehended until many months after the shooting, police were concerned for the safety of the witness who was an older man living on a small pension. The man was cooperative and moved into the county jail in Memphis to assure his safety. He was free to come and go but was accompanied by officers when he left the jail for a walk or to have a beer. Because of the inconvenience of providing guards every day, the state of Tennessee went into court and asked that bail be set to assure the appearance of this cooperative witness at the trial of James Earl Ray (if and when he was apprehended). Bail was set at $10,000, and as the witness

did not have this amount of cash, he could not meet bail. He was then held in jail without any freedom to leave. Lawyers challenged this procedure and the statute authorizing it as a violation of due process. As a result, an apartment was rented and the witness lived there with 24-hour-a-day police protection until Ray was apprehended and went to trial.

The above example illustrates that unless there is probable cause to show that a witness has committed a crime, they can not be held. If a witness is uncooperative, they may be brought before a grand jury, coroner's inquest, "John Doe" proceedings, or court and questioned under oath. Under such circumstances, a witness would be compelled to answer questions. If the witness takes the Fifth Amendment, she or he could be granted witness immunity and then would face jail on contempt for failure to answer.

D. VICARIOUS LIABILITY

As discussed in Chapter 3, many recently enacted business, commercial, traffic, and health regulations are strict liability crimes. A strict liability offense forbids certain conduct or an omission and does not require the showing of any mental fault (*mens rea*). Proof that the person violated the statute is sufficient for a conviction.

Vicarious liability differs from strict liability. Vicarious liability punishes one person for the act of another (usually an employee). In vicarious liability, a mental fault is required, but the act or omission (*actus reus*) is sometimes dispensed with. This differs from a strict liability crime in which a mental fault is not required but an act or omission is. The following U.S. Supreme Court cases illustrate the law of vicarious liability.

DENNIS VACHON v.
NEW HAMPSHIRE

Supreme Court of the United States (1974)
414 U.S. 478, 94 S. Ct. 664, 14 CrL 4153

The defendant owned and operated the Head Shop in Manchester, New Hampshire. A 14-year-old girl walked into the shop and purchased for 25 cents a button inscribed "Copulation Not Masturbation." The defendant was convicted of contributing to the delinquency of a minor, which is a statutory offense in New Hampshire: "Anyone . . . who shall knowingly or wilfully encourage, aid, cause or abet or connive at, or who has knowingly or wilfully done any act to produce, promote or contribute to the delinquency of (a) child may be punished." [37]

The defendant was convicted in a trial at which the girl was the only witness for the state. The 14-year-old girl did not testify that the defendant sold her the buttom or that she even saw him in the store at the time of the sale. She testified that she could not identify the person who sold her the button. The defendant admitted that he "controlled the premises on July 26 [the date of the sale]." The majority of the U.S. Supreme Court reversed the defendant's conviction, holding:

Our independent examination of the trial record discloses that evidence is completely lacking that the appellant personally sold the girl the button or even that he was aware of the sale or present in the store at the time.

Dissenting opinion: The Chief Justice and two other justices dissented, stating that the majority were "rewriting . . . a state statute, in order to make it require a highly specific intent, and then turning around and saying that there was no evidence before the state courts to prove this kind of intent which we have said the statute requires." As no oral arguments were heard on this case, the dissenters asked that the case be set for oral argument.

UNITED STATES v. PARKS

Supreme Court of the United States (1975)
421 U.S. 658, 95 S. Ct. 1903

The defendant was the president of a retail food chain with 36,000 employees, 874 stores, and 16 warehouses. In 1970, federal inspectors advised officers of the corporation that unsanitary conditions were found in a warehouse. Twice in 1971, further unsanitary conditions were reported. In March of 1972, continued evidence of rodent activity and "rodent-contaminated lots of food items" were found. When the food corporation and Parks were charged with violations of the Federal Food, Drug and Cosmetic Act, the corporation pleaded guilty and Parks pleaded not guilty before a jury. In affirming Park's conviction, the U.S. Supreme Court held that the jury was properly instructed and that prior federal cases had demonstrated that the statute imposes on corporate officers "not only a positive duty to seek out and remedy violations when they occur but also, and primarily, a duty to implement measures that will insure that violations will not occur."

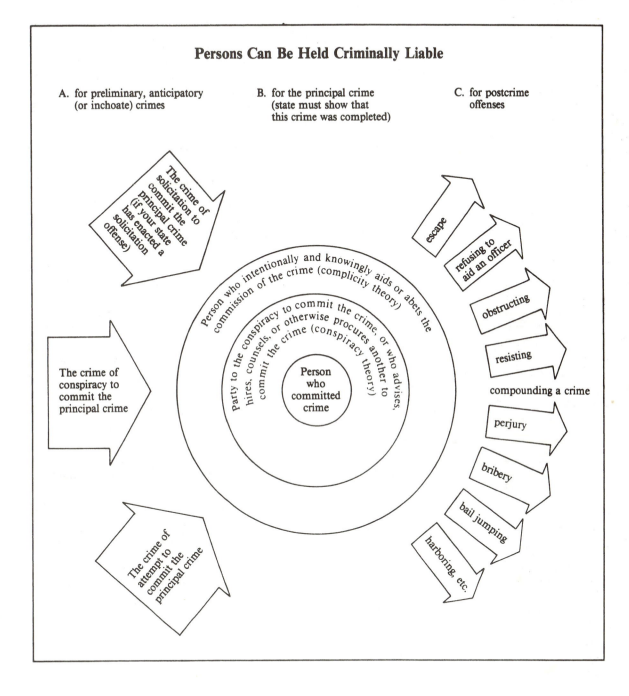

Persons Can Be Held Criminally Liable

A. for preliminary, anticipatory (or inchoate) crimes

B. for the principal crime (state must show that this crime was completed)

C. for postcrime offenses

The crime of solicitation to commit the principal crime (if your state has enacted a solicitation offense)

The crime of conspiracy to commit the principal crime

The crime of attempt to commit the principal crime

Person who intentionally and knowingly aids or abets the commission of the crime (complicity theory)

Party to the conspiracy to commit the crime, or who advises, hires, counsels, or otherwise procures another to commit the crime (conspiracy theory)

Person who committed crime

escape

refusing to aid an officer

obstructing

resisting

compounding a crime

perjury

bribery

bail jumping

harboring, etc.

QUESTIONS AND PROBLEMS FOR CHAPTER 4

1. The following situation occurred in Milwaukee: Two teenaged girls were walking toward a shopping center when a car containing two men in their twenties stopped. The men offered to give the girls a ride. When the girls refused, one of the men (the passenger) got out of the car and continued attempting to persuade the girls to ride with the men. When the man held one of the girls by her arm, she pulled away from him. The man then hit the girl a hard blow on her face, which sent her sprawling on the ground. The man immediately got back into the car and the driver quickly drove away. The other girl, however, observed the license of the vehicle and provided this information ·to the police when reporting the incident. When the investigating officers obtained the name and address of the owner of the vehicle, they went to that residence. The vehicle was parked in the driveway and a young man matching the description of the driver was identified as the owner of the vehicle. The man, at first, denied being at the scene of the crime. But after he realized that the girls could identify him, he told the following story. The owner and driver of the car said that he picked up a hitchhiker about his age and that the two men had stopped to pick up the girls. After the battery occurred, the driver said he drove his passenger a short distance and then dropped him off. He stated that he did not know the man's name and had never seen him before.

    a. Can the driver of the car be charged as party to the crime of battery?

    b. If so, on what theory and under what statute of your state?

    c. Is there sufficient evidence to obtain a conviction?

2. In 1984, CBS presented the TV movie *The Lost Honor of Kathryn Beck,* which is based on a book and German movie. Marlo Thomas plays Beck, who picks up a stranger at a party and takes him home for the night. After the man leaves in the morning, police burst in, search the apartment, and take Beck to police headquarters for questioning. The man is a terrorist wanted for felonies, and the police believe that Beck knows his whereabouts and is not disclosing such information. Beck has disclosed all the information that she has, but a police officer threatens to "salt her away as a material witness for the rest of her life."

    a. Based on the above statements, has Beck committed a crime for which she can be charged?

    b. Should the police hold her under such circumstances?

    c. Would a lawyer or prosecutor be able to secure her release on a writ of habeas corpus?

3. Complete the following statements:

    a. a person who was not at the scene of a crime may be charged and convicted of the crime if the state can show . . .

    b. a person who was at the scene of a crime may be charged and convicted of the crime if the state can show . . .

Chapter 5

Criminal Responsibility and the Capacity to Commit a Crime

A. ANCIENT CONCEPTS OF CRIMINAL RESPONSIBILITY

The law has undergone many changes over the centuries as to how criminal responsibility is determined and who has the capacity to commit a crime. At the time of the Norman Conquest of England (1066), for example, trial by ordeal and trial by battle were commonly used in the determination of criminal responsibility. A person who was of noble birth or titled could demand trial by battle if accused of a crime. If, in trial by battle, the suspect or accused came out second, it was then determined that he was guilty of the offense with which he was charged. However, the question of guilt or innocence could become moot, because the accused might be killed or badly injured.

In determining criminal responsibility in a trial by ordeal, the accused often would be required to take a pound weight of red-hot iron into his hands or to plunge his hand, up to the wrist, into boiling water. Ordeal by fire and ordeal by water were also used. Sir James Stephen described trial by ordeal in his *History of the Criminal Law of England,* published in 1883:

> It is unnecessary to give a minute account of the ceremonial of the ordeals. They were of various kinds. The general nature of all was the same. They were appeals to God to work a miracle in attestation of the innocence of the accused person. The handling of hot iron, plunging the hand or arm into boiling water unhurt, were the commonest. The ordeal of water was a very singular institution. Sinking was the sign of innocence, floating the sign of guilt. As any one would sink unless he understood how to float, and intentionally did so, it is difficult to see how anyone could ever be convicted by this means. Is it possible that this ordeal may have been an honourable form of suicide, like the Japanese happy despatch? In nearly every case the accused would sink. This would prove his innocence, indeed, but there would be no need to take him out. He would thus die honourably. If by accident he floated, he would be put to death disgracefully.[1]

Another form of superstition involved the concept that persons deliberately became witches or practiced witchcraft. Such persons were thought to be able to cause great social harm, such as crop failure, and to be able to cause serious injuries or bring illness and death to others.

Witchcraft first became a crime under the Roman Empire. During the 16th, 17th, and 18th centuries, thousands of persons were tried and put to death because it was believed that they were either witches or practiced witchcraft. Prosecution of such persons in the American colonies occurred in Massachusetts, Connecticut, and Virginia. These trials reached a high point in 1692, in Salem, Massachusetts, where 19 persons were executed as witches and 150 more were sent to prison. The Salem trials were the last American trials; the last English trial took place in 1712. In 1735, Scotland repealed all laws that made witchcraft a crime in that country.

Other Medieval Concepts

In the Middle Ages and later, animals were held criminally responsible for harm that they had done. They were tried in the same manner as human beings, except that domestic animals were taken before secular courts, whereas wild animals were required to face ecclesiastical (religious) courts. There were many animal trials at which horses, pigs, dogs, rats and even roosters were accused of such crimes as murder, battery, and destruction of crops. Some people believed that animals who committed such offenses were possessed by demons; others believed that the devil himself took the form of an animal.

In 1499, a bear that had been killing people in a German village was captured and brought to trial. The attorney appointed to defend the bear was allowed to argue for days that the animal had the right to be judged by a jury of its peers (that is, other bears). However, the animal was tried and convicted by human beings. It was sentenced to dangle from the public gallows until relatives of its victims stoned the animal to death. In 1694, a mare was convicted of criminal homicide in France and was burned to death. The court found that the horse was possessed by demons. As late as 1712, an Austrian court sentenced a dog to a year in the marketplace pillory, where humans were also confined. The dog had bitten a man in the leg.

Today, no industrial nation would hold that an animal had the mental capacity to formulate criminal intent. An animal that killed or seriously injured a human being would probably be destroyed in recognition of the possibility that it might again attack humans. Criminal responsibility, if any exists, would attach not to the vicious animal, but to its owner.

B. INFANCY AS AFFECTING CRIMINAL RESPONSIBILITY

Under the civil law, an infant (child) is a person who has not yet reached the age of majority, whether that age is 18, 19, 20, or 21 as determined by the law of each jurisdiction. Although infants, with some exceptions, are not able to enter into contracts, make wills, or vote, the law as to a child's criminal responsibility for his or her acts differs from the law governing the child's civil capacity.

The question of the criminal responsibility of children came before the courts in the Middle Ages, and by the 14th century, the common law had determined that children under the age of seven did not have the capacity to commit a crime. By that time, seven was established as the age of reason under ecclesiastical law and also as the age of responsibility under Roman civil law. In establishing the age of seven as the lowest age of criminal responsibility, the common law reasoned that a child under the age of seven did not have the mental capacity to formulate the intent to commit a crime and that, therefore, for children under seven, the threat of punishment would not serve as a deterrent against crime.

Most states continue to maintain this common law rule in the form of a conclusive presumption. The presumption is that children under the age of seven do not have the capacity to commit a crime. As the presumption is conclusive, evidence to the contrary may not be presented. Persons over the age of fourteen are inferred to be sane and capable of formulating the necessary mental frame of mind to commit a crime. Evidence showing otherwise, however, can be used to show incapacity.

Children between the ages of 7 and 14 are presumed to be without criminal capacity to commit a crime. This presumption, however, may be overcome by the presentation of evidence by the state showing that the child has the mental capacity and the ability to formulate the necessary criminal intent. British and American courts have held that the younger the child, the stronger must be the evidence of mental capacity. Testimony of doctors, psychiatrists, and other persons plus school records and reports are usually used to show that the child has physically, mentally, and emotionally reached an age of capacity at which he or she should be held responsible for his or her acts. The common law reasoning was that failure to punish particularly atrocious crimes committed by children between the ages of 7 and 14 would encourage other children to commit similar acts with no fear of punishment.

The Liability of Children Under State Statutes

All states have enacted statutes governing the jurisdiction of children's (juvenile) courts. These courts deal with children who are delinquent and in need of supervision or with children who are neglected and dependent. Delinquency is usually defined by statute as conduct by a child that, if committed by an adult, would be a violation of the criminal code of that state.

In the majority of states, children's courts have jurisdiction over persons under the age of 18. However other states set the children's court jurisdiction at an age above or below 18. State statutes usually also provide that juvenile courts may waive jurisdiction to the adult court of children 16 years of age or over, where public protection requires it, and the waiver is in the best interest of the child.

But what should be done with children under 16 who commit serious crimes? Should they remain in the juvenile system for treatment and released at age 18 or 19? Or should state statutes extend the length of juvenile commitment to age 21, or even to age 25? Or should the child be turned over to the adult system and sent to adult prison facilities?

These questions are being debated in many states. In 1984, a 14-year-old boy in Wisconsin pled no contest to killing a man, a woman and their 10-year-old son by repeatedly stabbing and shooting them. A few months later, an adult woman was kidnapped by a 14-year-old boy and an older youth. The woman was repeatedly raped, and tortured in her own car. She was then forced into the trunk of the vehicle and was driven to other neighborhoods where she was jeered at while she was put on display. Prior to this incident, the youths robbed two other women attending a church meeting.

C. THE INSANITY DEFENSE

No subject in criminal law has received as much attention and debate as the insanity defense. The questions of what degree of insanity, mental defect, or mental disease renders a person blameless for acts (or omissions) and what test or tests should be used in determining legal and moral liability have been debated for years.

A 1978 study shows that of the 2 million criminal cases in that year, only 1,600 defendants were acquitted (found not guilty) because of insanity. Less than .4 percent of defendants were able to use the defense successfully.

The insanity plea is seldom used in minor charges; it is most often used in murder cases and for other serious felony charges in which, in most instances, the evidence is so conclusive that the defendant has no other defense available to him.

John Hinckley's shooting of President Reagan, Mark Chapman's murder of John Lennon, the Son-of-Sam crimes are examples of cases that have brought the insanity defense to the public's attention. In these cases, defense lawyers used the plea as defensive tactics. It must be remembered that the state can also raise the issue of the sanity and competency of defendants.[2]

Stages in Criminal Proceedings When the Question of Insanity May be Raised

The question of insanity, mental disease, or defect may be raised at four separate stages of the criminal proceedings. A finding that the defendant is suffering from mental disease or defect will affect the proceeding differently, depending on which stage has been reached.

1. Insanity at the Time of the Criminal Incident If the defendant is found insane, mentally diseased, or defective at the time he or she committed the offense charged, then a judgment of not guilty because of insanity, mental disease,

or defect is entered and the defendant may never again be tried for that offense. The disposition of the case is then governed by the laws of that jurisdiction. In most states, the defendant is committed to a state mental institution for the criminally insane and held there until he or she is found to be sane, at which time the person may be eligible for release under the conditions provided for by the statutes of that jurisdiction.

2. Insanity (or Incompetency) at the Time of Trial A defendant who is insane, mentally diseased, or defective at the time of trial may not understand fully what is occurring and may not be of assistance to the defense attorney. When a court makes a finding that the defendant lacks competency to proceed with the trial, the proceedings must then be suspended and the defendant, in accordance with the statutes of that state, placed in an institution.

A defendant who has been found by a court to be incompetent to stand trial cannot be held indefinitely. In the 1972 case of *Jackson v. Indiana*,[3] the U.S. Supreme Court held that such defendants could not be held for longer than a "reasonable period of time" to determine whether they will regain their competency and capacity to stand trial. Some courts have held that a "reasonable period of time" is a period no longer than the maximum sentence for the crime or, at the longest, 18 months. After this period of time, the state must either:

• try the defendant, if he or she is found sane and capable of standing trial
• dismiss the charges
• if the defendant remains incompetent[4] and cannot be tried criminally, commence civil proceedings against the defendant for the purpose of committing him or her to a mental institution.

3. Insanity Just Prior to Execution Under the common law, if a person to be executed were found to be so disordered as not to understand the nature and purpose of the punishment about to be inflicted, the execution was stayed until such time as the person could understand what was about to occur. Blackstone, a great English writer and lawyer, stated that the reason for this rule was that if the condemned man were sane, he might offer some reason for the execution to be stayed. Probably all American jurisdictions that use the death penalty have adopted this rule, which was sustained by the majority of the U.S. Supreme Court in the 1958 case of *Caritativo v. California.*[5]

4. Insanity During Incarceration Within every prison population are persons who have used alcohol or drugs to excess or who have untreated venereal disease. These and other problems that manifest themselves while a prison term is being served can have a severe effect on the mental health of a prisoner and can result in his or her transfer to the mental ward of the prison hospital, in which the prisoner would serve the remainder of his or her term. If a mental disease, defect, or insanity exists at the time the prison terms ends, civil proceedings could then be initiated for the purpose of commitment to a mental institution. One study indicated that six times as many convicts became mentally ill while serving prison terms as persons found not guilty because of insanity, mental disease, or defect.

The M'Naghten Case and the "Right and Wrong" Test

It was not until the 1800s that English and American courts considered the question of whether insanity, mental disease, and mental defect should be factors in determining the criminal responsibilities of persons charged with crimes. The "right and wrong" test, which became the most widely used test to determine the question of legal insanity in the United States, was developed in 1843 in the aftermath of the famous English murder case of *Rex v. M'Naghten,* House of Lords, 1843.[6]

Daniel M'Naghten lived in London in the 1840s and believed that the British Home Secretary, Sir Robert Peel, was the head of a conspiracy to kill him. (Peel was the widely recognized founder of the British police, who thus received the nickname "Bobbies.") In 1843, M'Naghten shot and killed Edward Drummond, private secretary to Peel, because he mistook Drummond

for Peel. At his trial, the defense argued that M'Naghten was insane at the time of the shooting and that he should not be held responsible because his mental delusions had caused him to act as he did. The British jury agreed, and M'Naghten was found not guilty because of insanity.

The "right and wrong" test that emerged from the M'Naghten case became the prevailing standard and test for insanity in American courts. Under this test, the defendant is not legally responsible for his act if at the time he was "laboring under such a defect of reason, from diseases of the mind, as not to know the nature and quality of the act he was doing, or, if he did know it, that he did not know that what he was doing was wrong." The M'Naghten Rule established the burden of proof as follows:

> Every man is presumed to be sane and to possess a sufficient degree of reason to be responsible for his crimes, until the contrary be proved to (the jury's) satisfaction; and that to establish a defense on the ground of insanity, it must be clearly proved.

Other American Tests

Over the years, a few American jurisdictions adopted other tests than the M'Naghten right and wrong test. In 1871, the New Hampshire courts rejected the M'Naghten test and adopted the "New Hampshire test," but no other state has ever followed New Hampshire's lead.[7] In 1886, Alabama adopted the "irresistible impulse" test in *Parsons v. State.*[8] This test extended the M'Naghten Rule and held that, if it is found that the defendant had a mental disease that prevented him from controlling his conduct, even if he knew the difference between right and wrong, he should be found not guilty because of insanity. In practice, the "irresistible impulse" test often had the effect of freeing persons who had committed crimes of passion. An example of this is found in the novel *Anatomy of a Murder* by John Donaldson Voelker (under the alias Robert Traver). Voelker was a retired Supreme Court Justice of the state of Michigan when he wrote the story. Persons who have read the book or seen the movie made from the story know that in most states the issue before the court would have been that of self-defense or "heat-of-passion" manslaughter. Instead, the army officer in Voelker's story (based on an actual case) went free on the "irresistible impulse" defense.[9]

According to its critics, the principal fault of the M'Naghten test lies in its narrowness and its restricted application to only a small percentage of people who are mentally ill. In 1954, the "Durham product test" was adopted by the U.S. Court of Appeals for the District of Columbia in the case of *Durham v. United States.*[10] The court stated that "an accused is not criminally responsible if his unlawful act was the product of mental disease or defect." The Durham case established a test for insanity based on a substantial lack of mental capacity rather than a complete lack of capacity. It has been criticized on the grounds that it is too broad and places too much discretion in psychiatrists, rather than in the jury, for determining the legal issue of insanity. "Criminal responsibility is a legal not a medical question."[11]

The American Law Institute "Substantial Capacity" Test

About a year after the adoption of the Durham Rule by a few jurisdictions, the American Law Institute proposed still another test for determining criminal responsibility. In proposing the new rule, the following comment was made:

> No problem in the drafting of a penal code presents larger intrinsic difficulty than that of determining when individuals whose conduct would otherwise be criminal ought to be exculpated (freed of guilt) on the grounds that they were suffering from mental disease or defect when they acted as they did. What is involved specifically is the drawing of a line between the use of public agencies and public force to condemn the offender by conviction . . . the problem is to discriminate between the cases where a punitive-correctional disposition is appropriate and those in which a medical-custodial disposition is the only kind that the law should allow.

The final draft of the American Law Institute "substantial capacity" test is found in Section 4.01 of the 1962 Model Penal Code and states:

1. A person is not responsible for criminal conduct if at the time of such conduct as a result of mental disease or defect he lacks substantial capacity either to appreciate the criminality (wrongfulness) of his conduct or to conform his conduct to the requirement of law.

2. As used in this Article, the terms mental disease or defect do not include an abnormality manifested only by repeated criminal or otherwise antisocial conduct.

The Model Penal Code Test (or the A.L.I. "substantial capacity" test) is now reported to have been adopted by about half the states and also by the federal courts.

President Nixon's Proposed Test

did defendant know what he was doing,

Because a number of courts have indicated that complete abolition and throwing out of the insanity defense would violate "due process," many proposals have been made to change the defense by restricting or expanding it.

The U.S. Congress rejected President Nixon's 1973 proposal to restrict the insanity defense as follows:

> My new formulation would provide an insanity defense only if the defendant did not know what he was doing. . . . The only question considered germane in a murder case, for example, would be whether the defendant knew whether he was pulling the trigger of a gun. Questions such as the existence of a mental disease or defect would be reserved for consideration at the time of sentencing.

The "Guilty but Mentally Ill" Verdict [12]

Michigan was the first of at least eight states to enact, in 1975, statutes creating the alternative verdict of "guilty but mentally ill." The new statute was passed after several Michigan defendants committed additional murders after being acquitted and released after using the insanity defense.

In Illinois, Thomas Vanda killed a girl when he was 18. While undergoing psychiatric treatment in Chicago, he was released and killed another girl. He was found not guilty because of insanity. When doctors concluded that his psychosis had disappeared, he was again released over objections from the trial judge and his own defense attorney. In 1978, when he was 25 years

---

1984 Federal Crime Bill

Before adjourning in November, 1984, Congress passed a sweeping anti-crime bill which included the following changes:

Insanity Defense   The burden of proof in federal courts was shifted from the prosecution to the defense in insanity pleas.   A defendant using an insanity plea will now have to prove by clear and convincing evidence that he was insane at the time of the crime.   This follows the procedure used in most (if not all) states and makes it much more difficult for a defendant such as John Hinckley to be found not guilty because of insanity in a federal court.

Sentencing Reform   Early release on parole was eliminated and replaced by "determinate sentencing" which will require that more prisoners be forced to serve longer terms.   Also, a commission will be established to issue federal sentencing guidelines for federal judges.   It is hoped that the sentencing guidelines will end federal sentencing inequities.

Bail Reform   Federal judges may now consider the danger to the community presented by an accused in determining bail.   Any defendant deemed dangerous to a community may now be detained before trial.   Penalties for bail violations were also increased.

---

old, Thomas Vanda was again charged with murder.   The third victim was a 25-year-old woman.

Illinois enacted a "guilty but mentally ill" statute in 1981.   Governor James R. Thompson described the new statutory procedure as follows:

> Under this procedure, when an insanity defense is raised, the court, if the evidence permits, may instruct the jury on the alternative verdict of guilty but mentally ill.   When a person is not legally insane, he or she may be found guilty but mentally ill if, at the time of the offense, he or she suffered from a disorder of thought or mood that does not represent a condition amounting to insanity in the legal sense.
>
> When a guilty but mentally ill verdict is returned, the court may impose any sentence that could have been ordered for a conviction on the crime charged. However, the prison authorities must provide necessary psychiatric or psychological treatment to restore the offender to full capacity in an appropriate treatment setting.   If the mental illness is cured, the offender must be returned to prison to serve out his or her sentence.
>
> Insanity determinations under existing law deal in absolutes; a defendant must be found totally sane or totally insane.   This fails to reflect reality.   It does not allow the jury to consider the degree of an individual's mental impairment, the quality of the impairment, or the context in which the impairment is operative.   A mental impairment does not necessarily eradicate the state of mind required to make a person guilty of a crime, and the jury should be permitted to consider the gradations of a defendant's mental state.
>
> The guilty but mentally ill verdict does not abolish the insanity defense.   It simply recognizes that there are gradations in the degree of mental impairment; it

provides accountability, promotes treatment, and eliminates the need to manipulate the system.   Most importantly, it is designed to protect the public from violence inflicted by persons with mental ailments who previously slipped through the cracks in the criminal justice system.[13]

Opponents of the "guilty but mentally ill" verdict argue that it is nothing but a nice name for "guilty and going to prison."   The Alliance for Mentally Ill oppose such legislation "because it would stigmatize insane offenders with a criminal conviction, compounding the handicaps already faced by those persons in obtaining employment and social acceptance."[14]

Both the Supreme Court of Michigan[15] and the Supreme Court of Indiana[16] have affirmed the constitutionality of the "guilty but mentally ill" statutes in their states.   The Supreme Court of Michigan held in the 1982 case of *People v. Booth*[17] that an amnesiac ("forgetful") could enter a "guilty but mentally ill" plea under the Michigan statute.   Defendants in the *Booth* case had a loss of memory as to the crimes that were committed.   Both defendants were permitted to enter pleas of guilty but mentally ill.

Diminished Responsibility (or Capacity)

In 1957, the English Parliament introduced into law a new defense to the charge of murder known as "diminished responsibility."   This defense is separate and distinct from the defense of

Insanity and Competency

A defense of insanity is recognized by all but two states.

Two states—Montana and Idaho—have passed laws that abolish the insanity defense. In Idaho, however, psychiatric evidence is allowed on the issue of the intent to commit a crime.

In most states, a formal notice of an intent to rely on the insanity defense must be filed by defendants who wish to claim insanity as a defense. Such defendants enter a plea of not guilty at time of trial.

Competency to stand trial and the insanity defense are frequently confused.

The issue of insanity refers to the defendant's mental state at the time of the crime while the issue of competency concerns the ability of the defendant to assist in the preparation of his or her defense or to understand the proceedings. For example, a defendant may be found competent to stand trial but be found not guilty by reason of insanity.

Eight states provide a verdict of guilty but mentally ill.

In states in which this verdict is available, it is an alternative to (but does not preclude) a verdict of not guilty by reason of insanity.

According to the American Bar Association, since 1975, eight states have adopted the verdict of guilty but mentally ill; in chronological order, they are Michigan, Indiana, Illinois, Georgia, Kentucky, New Mexico, Delaware, and Alaska. Other states are considering adding such a verdict to those permitted by law.

Source: 1983 U.S. Department of Justice Report to the Nation on Crime.

---

insanity, in that partial forgiveness is possible, with a reduction of a charge from murder to manslaughter if an abnormal mental condition or mental disease is successfully shown to have existed at the time of the killing.

The English experience has shown that diminished responsibility has been pleaded with success in mercy-killing cases, as well as deserted-spouse or disappointed-lover cases when the killing occurred while the defendant was in a state of depression. Persons with chronic anxiety have also been able to use this new defense successfully. The English law was originally enacted because it was thought that defendants with mental conditions and abnormalities, such as those which would come under the M'Naghten test, would prefer a conviction for manslaughter rather than face the prospects of an indefinite or possibly lifelong confinement in a mental institution under an "acquittal" on the grounds of insanity.

A few states, including California, adopted the use of the defense of "diminished responsibility." In 1978, Dan White, a former San Francisco supervisor, concealed a gun and extra ammunition and entered City Hall, where he shot the

---

Incompetency

A person cannot stand trial in a court for a crime if he or she is incompetent. Competency can be defined as the ability to cooperate with one's attorney in one's defense combined with the awareness and understanding of the consequences of those proceedings.[20]

Capacity To Commit a Crime

A person cannot be found guilty of committing a crime if he or she lacked the capacity at the time of the crime to either appreciate the wrongfulness of the conduct, or to conform conduct to the requirements of the law. Criminal responsibility is a legal not a medical question. State courts use the M'Naghten test or the Model Penal Code "substantial capacity" test to determine a defendant's capacity to commit a crime.

Tests or Procedures Used to Determine Criminal Responsibility

Test or Procedure	Year When First Used	Type of Test	Extent of Use at Present Time
M'Naghten "right or wrong" test *½ courts*	1843	Based on ability of defendant to know the difference between right and wrong	Used by practically all American courts until the 1970s. Now used by only half the state courts.
Model Penal Code "substantial capacity" test	1955	Did defendant have the "substantial capacity" to (a) distinguish between right and wrong, or (b) to conform his conduct to the requirements of law?	Used by federal courts and many state courts. In federal courts, the prosecution must prove the defendant sane beyond a reasonable doubt. In the Hinckley case, the government could not carry this burden. Under *Leland v. Oregon,* 343 U.S. 790 (1952), states may continue today to require defendants to prove insanity.
Diminished capacity defense *partial forgiveness + States aint compelled to use this defense*	1957	*Only* partial forgiveness is possible if an abnormal mental or emotional condition is shown to have existed at the time of the crime (murder would be reduced to manslaughter).	Few states use this defense, since the "Twinkie Defense" was used in the slaying of San Francisco Mayor Moscone and Harvey Milk. States are not constitutionally compelled to recognize doctrine of diminished capacity. *Muench v. Israel,* 33 CrL 2506, 715 F.2d 1124 (7th Cir. 1983).
"Guilty but mentally ill" alternative verdict and plea *not insane — used by michigan*	1975	Defendant may be found "guilty but mentally ill" if all the following are found beyond a reasonable doubt: (a) defendant is guilty of offense, (b) defendant was mentally ill at time offense was committed, (c) defendant was not legally insane at time offense was committed.	Used in eight or more states with either the M'Naughten test or the "substantial capacity" test. States using "guilty but mentally ill" pleas are Michigan (1975), Indiana (1980), Illinois (1981), and New Mexico, Alaska, Georgia, Kentucky, and Delaware (1982).
Plea Bargaining		Such factors as emotional and mental conditions could be taken into consideration for plea bargaining.	Plea bargaining is used extensively in many state and federal courts (Hinckley offered to plea bargain and plea to lesser offenses but was turned down by the U.S. government).

Note: Tests that are no longer used in the United States include the "irresistible impulse" test and the "Durham product" test.

mayor of San Francisco six times. White then reloaded the gun, sought out Supervisor Harvey Milk (a leader of San Francisco's gay community), and executed him in the same manner.

As a defense to the charges of first-degree murder, White's attorney and a prominent psychiatrist presented a picture of a depressed defendant gorging himself on junk foods—Twinkies, Coca-Cola, chocolates—which depressed him further, causing him to consume even more junk foods. The jury accepted what is now called the "Twinkie Defense" and convicted White of two counts of manslaughter instead of murder.[18] The jury verdicts so enraged the San Francisco gay community that riots occurred protesting the results. In 1981, California abolished the use of the defense of diminished responsibility.[19] After five years in prison, Dan White was released in January 1984. His whereabouts were kept secret because of fear of retaliation from gays.

Can Compulsive Gambling Justify an Insanity Plea?

People with gambling fever could be suffering from a psychiatric disorder called pathologic, or compulsive, gambling. Most people who gamble regularly, however, do so in the hopes of striking it rich in a lottery, at the races, or at the craps or blackjack table.

In the 1982 case of *United States v. Lewellyn,*[21] the federal court found that there is no case authority holding that compulsive gambling can be used as an insanity defense. The defense attorney raised this argument in defense of his client charged with embezzlement.

Many times compulsive gambling is given as the reason for embezzlement or stolen funds. Accepting compulsive gambling as an insanity defense could set a dangerous precedent. In a state that allowed such a defense, thieves would claim kleptomania as a defense; arsonists could claim pyromania; perjurers could claim pathologic lying; drunk drivers could claim alcoholism, and prostitutes could claim nymphomania.

Many American cities have chapters of Gamblers Anonymous, where people with gambling problems may obtain help. With the growth of both legal and illegal gambling in the United States, the number of people needing assistance has grown. An increased number of people who are charged with embezzlement and theft argue that they are compulsive gamblers. If a court

---

American Psychiatric Association Formal Position on the Insanity Defense

After John Hinckley's acquittal on charges of shooting President Reagan and other persons, the American Psychiatric Association (APA), in 1983, issued their formal position on the insanity defense. The report, which was the first such position in the 138-year history of the APA, is of special interest because it is endorsed by those who provide most of the expert testimony in insanity cases. The report makes the following recommendations:

• That any revision of the insanity defense restrict the defense to "serious" mental disturbances generally diagnosed as psychoses. Persons with personality disorders, such as sociopaths, should be held responsible for their behavior.

• Psychiatrists should recognize the limits of their expertise and testify only as to medical opinions about a defendant's mental state and motivation.

• Psychiatrists should not testify as to "ultimate issues" as to whether a defendant was able to distinguish between right and wrong, appreciate the criminality of his behavior, or control his behavior.

• Insanity and criminal responsibility are legal and jury issues on which psychiatrists are unqualified to comment.

• Because psychiatrists lack the scientific expertise to make predictions as to future dangerousness, release should not be determined by psychiatrists alone. Release of a potentially violent patient should be viewed as a social decision rather than as a medical decision and should be made by a parole board. Such a decision should weigh not only medical opinion, but also the competing rights of society and the patient.

determines that they actually suffer from a mental disorder, this might be used as a justification for a lenient sentence.

Not only is there a question as to whether the person actually has a mental disorder, but there is also a question as to whether a defendant

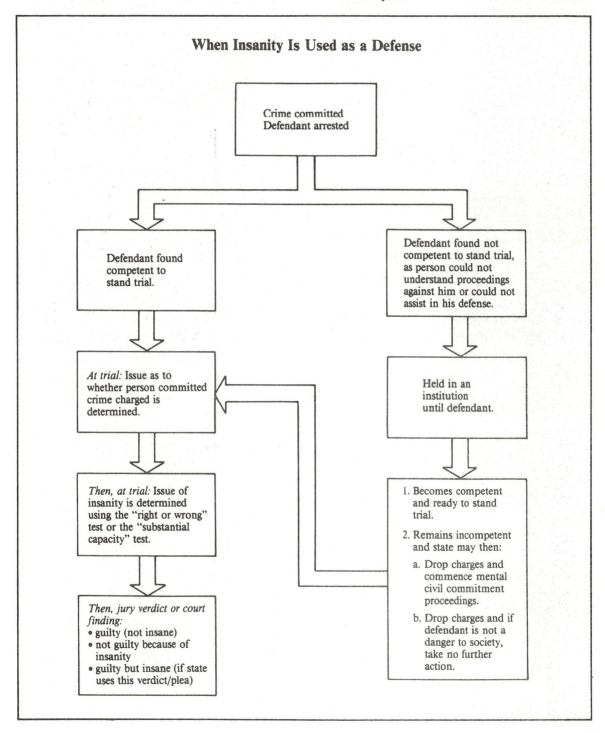

When Insanity Is Used as a Defense

Crime committed
Defendant arrested

Defendant found competent to stand trial.

Defendant found not competent to stand trial, as person could not understand proceedings against him or could not assist in his defense.

At trial: Issue as to whether person committed crime charged is determined.

Held in an institution until defendant.

Then, at trial: Issue of insanity is determined using the "right or wrong" test or the "substantial capacity" test.

1. Becomes competent and ready to stand trial.

2. Remains incompetent and state may then:

a. Drop charges and commence mental civil commitment proceedings.

b. Drop charges and if defendant is not a danger to society, take no further action.

Then, jury verdict or court finding:
• guilty (not insane)
• not guilty because of insanity
• guilty but insane (if state uses this verdict/plea)

actually lost all the stolen or embezzled money gambling. He or she may have some money stashed away in a secret account or hidden in a safe place. Such stolen or embezzled money should be returned to the victim.

Criminal Responsibility and the Capacity of Amnesia Victims and Deaf Mutes to Be Tried

Mental disease or defect is not the only condition that might leave defendants unable to assist in their own defense or unable to understand the nature of the proceedings against them. A physical handicap or a mental condition that does not amount to insanity might also cause a person to be incompetent to stand trial. "Competency can be defined generally as the ability to cooperate with one's attorney in one's defense and the awareness and understanding of the consequences of those proceedings." A person can be incompetent because of mental illness, mental retardation or a physical handicap (mental illness and mental retardation are two different things).

Amnesia is the total or partial loss of memory regarding past experiences. Brain injury, disease, mental disorder, shock, and the excessive use of alcohol or drugs are some of the many factors that can cause amnesia. Although amnesia victims ordinarily have no difficulty comprehending the nature of the criminal proceedings against them, they would not necessarily remember the facts that occurred at the time of the alleged crime.

In the case of *Thompson v. Alabama,*[22] the defendant could understand the crime charged and factual proceedings against her and could assist counsel in her defense. The court held that she was not rendered incompetent to stand trial by her alleged amnesia with respect to the commission of the alleged crime.

On the other hand, a total deaf-mute who could communicate only in a limited way, or not at all, might not be able to assist the attorney. He or she might not comprehend the nature of the criminal proceedings against him or her, even though he or she might remember in detail all the circumstances surrounding the crime charged.

Trial courts must determine the competency to proceed of deaf mutes and amnesia victims, as well as determining whether they understand the nature of the charges against them and whether they can assist their defense attorneys in defending against such charges. The 27-year-old defendant in the case of *Jackson v. Indiana,*[23] was charged with two separate crimes of robbery. He was mentally defective, with a mental level of a preschool child and could not read, write, or "otherwise communicate except through limited sign language." The trial court, on the advice of two psychiatrists, found that Jackson "lacked comprehension sufficient to make his defense" and ordered him committed to the Indiana Department of Mental Health until such time as that Department should certify to the court that the "defendant is sane." Arguing that Jackson's commitment under these circumstances amounted to a "life sentence," the defense appealed. The U.S. Supreme Court reversed and remanded the case stating:

> We hold . . . that a person charged by a State with a criminal offense who is committed solely on account of his incapacity to proceed to trial cannot be held more than the reasonable period of time necessary to determine whether there is a substantial probability that he will attain that capacity in the foreseeable future. If it is determined that this is not the case, then the State must either institute the customary civil commitment proceeding that would be required to commit indefinitely any other citizen, or release the defendant. Furthermore, even if it is determined that the defendant probably soon will be able to stand trial, his continued commitment must be justified by progress toward that goal. In light of differing state facilities and procedures and a lack of evidence in this record, we do not think it appropriate for us to attempt to prescribe arbitrary time limits. We note, however, that petitioner Jackson has now been confined for three and one-half years on a record that sufficiently established the lack of a substantial probability that he will even be able to participate fully in a trial.

D. THE CRIMINAL RESPONSIBILITY OF CORPORATIONS AND THE CAPACITY OF CORPORATIONS TO COMMIT CRIMES

A corporation is a legal entity created under the laws of a state or the federal government. Since a corporation is not a living person and must act through human beings, any crime committed in the corporate name must be committed by a person or persons in control of the corporation's affairs or in the employment of the corporation.

Sir William Blackstone wrote in his 18th-century Commentaries that "a corporation cannot commit treason or felony or other crime in its corporate capacity, though its members may in their distinct individual capacities." [24] Black-

stone's statement reflected the early common law thinking that since a corporation had no mind of its own, it could not formulate a criminal intent, and since it had no body, it could not be imprisoned or executed. The early common law view was understandable because there were relatively few corporations in those days, and there were other ways of handling crimes that were committed in the names of corporations. The corporate

Defenses Not Otherwise Covered in This Text

Defense	*Description of Defense*	*Present Status*
Automatism (unconsciousness)	Automatism is a state in which a person is capable of action but is not conscious of what he or she is doing. This defense is statutorized in some states, including California. Held to be an affirmative defense separate from insanity defense. *Fulcher v. State,* 633 P.2d 142 (Wyo.1981) 29 CrL 2556.	States adopting or statutorizing Sec. 2.01 Model Penal Code would hold as in *People v. Wilson,* 427 P.2d 820 (Cal. 1967). "Unconsciousness is a complete, not a partial defense to a criminal charge." See LaFave and Scott, *Criminal Law* (St. Paul: West Pub. Co., 1972), p. 337.
Premenstrual tension and syndrome	A form of emotional and physical distress that afflicts some women before their monthly periods. In certain cases, such stress is so severe that it seriously disrupts the women's lives. In 1982, Britain's Appeal Court held that it could not be used as a defense to a criminal charge but could be used in mitigation to lessen sentences.	No known American appellate case on the use of premenstrual syndrome as a defense in a criminal case.
Television intoxication	The 1978 case of *Zamora v. State,* 361 So.2d 776, 23 CrL 2490 (Fla. Dist. Ct. App. 1978), received national attention. Zamora was charged with first-degree murder, burglary, robbery, etc. His defense was that he was temporarily insane as a result of "involuntary subliminal television intoxication." The court proceedings were televised, and as Zamora was charged with the senseless slaying of an elderly woman, extensive coverage was given the case. Court held that insanity instructions were not necessary for the jury, as defense did not show insanity existed.	No other appellate case known. In 1978, Florida recognized a diminished capacity defense only when defendant's capacity was diminished to the point of inability to distinguish right from wrong. Defendant's attempt to come under this rule failed.
XYY chromosome defense	All persons have chromosomes. Some have either too few or too many, causing abnormalities. Some scientists believe that the abnormality of the supermale, or XYY in males, can cause such men to exhibit, antisocial or criminal conduct. Not recognized as a defense unless the requirements of the insanity test of the state are met.	See LaFave and Scott, *Criminal Law* (St. Paul: West Pub. Co., 1972), pp. 332–337 for cases and material on this subject.

officers (or employees) who committed the act (or acts) could be criminally charged. The corporation was civilly liable for the acts of its officers and employees and therefore civil suits for damages could be brought. And a corporation that had committed *ultra vires* acts (acts that are beyond the scope of the corporate charter or that violate the laws of the state) could have its corporate charter revoked by the state.

This old common law view changed as corporations became more numerous and as it became apparent that corporations should be made criminally responsible for some types of criminal acts. Today, corporations may be charged with many but not all crimes. It would be hard to imagine, for example, how a corporation could be charged and successfully convicted of rape. If a corporate employee, however, stole trade secrets from another, and his corporation, knowing of such theft, nevertheless used the stolen information for its benefit, the justification for charging the corporation with a criminal offense would be apparent.

Corporate criminal liability is a form of vicarious liability. That is, one person is punished for the act (or acts) of another. A corporation that is found to be criminally responsible for an act committed by even one employee of that corporation might be fined substantially for that offense. Through the fine, other employees and stockholders would suffer because of the vicarious liability of the corporation. In order to justify such criminal liability, there must be a showing that the corporation could have exercised control and precluded the act, or that there was authori-zation, consent, or knowledge of such act by persons in supervisory positions within the corporation.[25]

Corporate Homicide by Omission?

The 1979 case of *State of Indiana v. Ford Motor Co.*[26] received a great deal of newspaper attention. In finding that Ford was properly charged with reckless homicide, the Indiana Supreme Court held:

1. Federal law requires an automobile manufacturer to notify car owners of any safety-related defects and to remedy such defects.

2. The Ford Pinto had alleged defects in its design, yet Ford failed to provide notice of the defects and to correct the defects.

3. Deaths occurred in Indiana, allegedly as a result of the defects.

4. "A reckless homicide may result from either a positive act in violation of the [reckless homicide] statute that would amount to recklessness, or a reckless failure to perform an act which one was under a duty to perform."

5. "A commonsense reading of the Indiana [criminal code] discloses that a corporation can be prosecuted for any offense and can be convicted of that offense when the offense is committed by an agent acting within the scope of his authority."

The indictment against Ford was expressed in negative terms—charging an omission, rather than a positive reckless act.

QUESTIONS AND PROBLEMS FOR CHAPTER 5

1. What test for insanity (or mental disease or defect) is used in your state to determine criminal responsibility?

2. What disposition is made of a person found to be not guilty because of insanity (or mental disease or defect) in your state?

3. When and under what conditions may a person who has been found not guilty because of insanity (or mental disease or defect) be released from a mental institution in your state?

4. At what age does a child become criminally responsible as an adult in your state?

5. What is the jurisdiction of children's courts (or juvenile courts) in your state with respect to the age of children?

6. What are the statutes in your state with respect to the criminal responsibility and liability of corporations?

Chapter 6

Defenses That Seek to Justify the Use of Force

No person, whether a law enforcement officer or a private person, may use force against another unless lawful authority exists justifying the use of force. The burden of showing such authority is on the person using force.

A. SELF-DEFENSE AND THE DEFENSE OF OTHERS

Less Than Deadly Force

A person may threaten or intentionally use force against another for the purpose of preventing or terminating what he or she reasonably believes to be an *unlawful* interference with his or her person. Force must be *necessary* under the circumstances, and the person may use only such force or threat thereof as is *reasonable* to prevent or to terminate the interference.

The key words in determining the lawfulness of force in self-defense or the defense of another are:

- *unlawful.* The force or interference used against the person must be *unlawful*.

- *necessary.* Force must be *necessary* to protect the person or another from the use of *unlawful* force or interference by another.

- *reasonable.* The amount of force used in self-defense or defense of another must be *reasonable* under the circumstances that exist.

In determining what force is reasonable in self-defense, a court or a jury will take into account the size and age of the parties in relation to one another, the instruments or weapons used, and the aggressiveness of the assault made. Ordinarily, if fists were used in the attack and the parties were about the same size and strength, then fists and the strength of arms and body would be the maximum force that could be used in defense.

Example: A man who is attacked by another man about the same size and strength in a fistfight would not ordinarily be justified in viciously hitting his assailant with a baseball bat.

Example: A 70-year-old, 100-pound woman becomes angry at a 25-year-old, 200-pound man and begins to hit him with an umbrella. The man may defend himself by taking the umbrella

away from the woman, but because he has such physical control of the situation, the amount of force that he would be justified in using would end there.

Coming to the Aid of Another

A person may come to the aid of another and use *necessary* and *reasonable* force to defend the other person against *unlawful* force or interference. The person coming to the assistance or defense of another must reasonably believe that the facts are such that the third person would be privileged to act in self-defense, and must reasonably believe that his or her intervention is necessary for the protection against unlawful force or interference.

In the case of *People v. Young,*[1] Young intervened in a street struggle between three men. Young argued that he came to the assistance of the younger man, believing in good faith that the two older men were unlawfully assaulting the younger man. Young injured the kneecap of one of the men and struck the other about the head with his fist.

The two injured men were police officers in plain clothes making an arrest of the younger man. In affirming Young's conviction for battery, the Court of Appeals rejected the argument that Young was privileged to use such force under the circumstances, holding: "The weight of authority holds . . . that one who goes to the aid of a third person does so at his own peril."[2]

In the 1982 case of *Alexander v. State,*[3] the defendant, who was a prisoner, saw two guards subduing another prisoner. The defendant intervened, arguing that the two guards were violently attacking his friend and that the defendant acted to prevent injury.

At the defendant's trial for assaulting the guards, the judge instructed the jury that the defendant's right to defend the other prisoner was no greater than the prisoner's own right of self-defense. The defendant was therefore convicted.

A new trial was ordered by the Court of Appeals because Maryland had passed a "Good Samaritan" statute that changed the common law and encouraged persons to "get involved." This statute applied to all persons in Maryland and required that the jury determine whether the defendant believed that a violent assault was occurring and whether the defendant made a good faith attempt to defend his friend, the other prisoner.

The Use of Deadly Force in Self-defense or the Defense of Others

Deadly force is force that is likely to cause or is capable of causing death or serious bodily injury.

Firing a weapon at a person is the use of deadly force, whether the intent is to kill or to wound.

All persons (including law enforcement officers) may use deadly force, if necessary, to prevent imminent death or great bodily harm to themselves or others. The following civil case illustrates this rule of law:

MULLINS v. PENCE
Court of Appeals of Louisiana
(1974)
290 So.2d 803

When a belligerent customer in a bar refused to leave, the bartender called the police. Before the police arrived, the customer told the bartender that he was going to tear his arm off and beat him over the head with it. When the customer began climbing over the bar toward the bartender, the bartender pulled out a pistol and fired one shot into the customer (Mullins). When Mullins still did not retreat, the bartender (Pence) rapidly fired four more shots into Mullins. Mullins was six feet tall and weighed 215 pounds, whereas the bartender, a cripple, was five feet four inches tall and weighed 145 pounds. Mullins recovered and sued the bartender. In ruling in favor of the defendant bartender, the court quoted other Louisiana decisions, holding:

Of course, resort to the use of a dangerous weapon in order to repel a supposed attack upon defendant's person . . . cannot be countenanced as justifiable save in exceptional cases where the actor's fear of the danger is not only genuine but is founded on facts which would be likely to produce similar emotions in men of reasonable prudence. . . .

The trial court in this case seemed especially impressed with the belligerence of the plaintiff, the large difference in size and strength of the two parties confronting each other, an overt act made by the plaintiff toward Pence coupled with threats of serious bodily harm against the defendant, and the impossibility of retreat by Pence. Regarding the fact that five shots were actually fired into appellant, the trial court believed that Pence was reasonable in his fear following the first shot that the appellant was continuing in his act of aggression against him. Therefore, like the firing of the first shot, the appellee's action in firing the next series of shots was reasonable. We find no error in the trial court's application of the law to the facts in this case. For the above reasons, the trial court's judgment is affirmed, all costs to be paid by plaintiff-appellant.

Affirmed.

Loss of the Privilege of Self-defense by the Wrongdoer or Aggressor

The general rule in the United States is that the wrongdoer or aggressor loses and may not claim the defense of self-defense. If the victim is using lawful force, the victim may assert the privilege of self-defense. The defense of self-defense may be used only when lawful force is used to defend against unlawful force or interference.

How Do Victims of Violent Crime Protect Themselves?

- Rape victims are more likely than other violent crime victims to use force, try a verbal response, or attract attention, and they are less likely than the others to do nothing to protect themselves.

- Robbery victims are the least likely to try to talk themselves out of being victimized and the most likely to do nothing.

- Assault victims are the least likely to attract attention and the most likely to attempt some form of nonviolent evasion.

- Compared with simple assault victims, aggravated assault victims are more likely to use a weapon, less likely to try to talk themselves out of the incident, and less likely to do nothing to defend themselves. The fact that weapons are used more frequently by victims of aggravated assault than by victims of any other violent crime leads to the suspicion that some of these victims may have played a part in causing the incident.

Victim Response *	Percentage of Victims Responding, by Type of Crime *		
	Rape	Robbery	Assault
Weapons use			
Used or brandished gun or knife	1%	2%	2%
Physical force			
Used or tried physical force	33	23	23
Verbal response			
Threatened, argued, reasoned, etc. with offender	17	8	13
Attracting attention			
Tried to get help, attract attention, scare offender away	15	7	6
Nonviolent evasion			
Resisted without force, used evasive action	10	11	19
Other	5	4	7
No self-protective actions	19	45	30
Total	100% (873)	100% (5,868)	100% (24,876)

* Victim self-protective responses are listed in the table in order of assertiveness. If victims indicated that they took more than one type of action, only the most assertive action was used in the analysis.
Source: BJS National Crime Survey, 1973–79.

There are two situations, however, in which the aggressor or wrongdoer could regain his right and privilege of self-defense.

1. A wrongdoer (X) begins an encounter with the unlawful use of his fists or some nondeadly weapon. The victim, however, unlawfully uses deadly force, which, under the circumstances, is unnecessary and unreasonable. Now, X may use force in self-defense but is not privileged to resort to the use of force intended or likely to cause death unless (a) he has exhausted every means of escape (he has a duty to retreat) and (b) every means of avoiding death or great bodily harm to himself.

2. A wrongdoer may regain his right of self-defense if he (or she) withdraws in good faith from the fight and gives adequate notice to his victim as to his withdrawal. The wrongdoer has a duty to retreat, and his right to self-defense could be restored by retreating and giving notice (or attempting to).

The Privilege Not to Retreat, or the "Castle Doctrine"

A person who is violently assaulted in his own home by a trespasser or a person who has been invited into the home, has no duty to retreat (or flee) but may stand his ground and use such force as is necessary to defend himself.[4] The privilege not to retreat in one's home is known as the "castle doctrine."

The law has always recognized that a home is a person's castle and that the home is a special place of protection, security, and privacy that a person may lawfully protect from invasion.

A husband and wife have an equal right to be in their "castle," and neither has the legal right to eject the other. Because of this, some states hold that a "legal co-occupant" of a home, such as a husband or wife,[5] has a duty to retreat from the other instead of using deadly force. In the 1982 case of *State v. Bobbitt*,[6] a wife testified that she killed her husband in self-defense because he attacked her without provocation in their home. In affirming her conviction for manslaughter, the Supreme Court of Florida held that the jury was properly instructed that she had a duty to retreat before using deadly force. The court pointed out that fleeing would not leave her and others like her defenseless, since "a person placed in imminent danger of death or great bodily harm to himself by the wrongful attack of another has no duty to retreat if to do so would increase his own danger of death or great bodily harm."[7]

The "Battered Woman Syndrome" as a Form of Self-defense

Domestic homicides occur involving the killing of a spouse or other member of a household. When credible witnesses are available who provide information showing that the killing was necessary in self-defense, criminal charges generally will not be issued.

If, however, there are no witnesses to the killing and the only person alive to describe what occurred is the person who caused the killing, there may be reasons to believe that the killing was not in self-defense.

Women charged under such circumstances often use the "battered woman syndrome" as a form of self-defense. The defendant would have to take the witness stand to testify as to what she alleged occurred causing the killing. She would often have other witnesses who would testify as to a history of beatings and abuses inflicted on her by the deceased. Expert witnesses are also available to testify as to the syndromes associated with prolonged beatings and abuses on victims.

In the 1983 case of *People v. Minnis*,[8] the Illinois Appellate Court held that the trial court erred in refusing to allow an expert witness to testify as to the syndrome in the *Minnis* case, in which the defendant not only killed her husband,

but also dismembered his body. The court stated:

> It is true that in nearly all the reported cases the syndrome evidence has been utilized, if permitted, as a form of self-defense in a confrontational situation; i.e., the battered woman kills her batterer during or immediately after an attack. However, the instant case is not an ordinary one. We agree that defendant's testimony, if believed by the jury, clearly established that the force she used in throwing her husband off her body and in defending herself was reasonable under the circumstances, and thus expert testimony was unnecessary to explain it. However, her reasons for dismembering his body were very much at issue. The prosecutor used the dismemberment as substantive evidence to prove defendant's consciousness of guilt. A defendant clearly has the right to introduce evidence to rebut the State's evidence of consciousness of guilt.

> * * *

> The State's use of the dismemberment evidence rendered any explanation of it which would be consistent with innocence vital to the defendant's case.

The 1983 book *Manslaughter* (New York: Doubleday, 1983), by Steven Englund tells of another killing of a husband that received considerable attention. Jennifer Patri was charged with first-degree murder after she killed her husband and buried the battered body in her backyard. She testified in great detail as to years of beatings and abuse (including sexual abuse) by her husband and of the killing that she alleged occurred in self-defense. The jury found her guilty of manslaughter rather than first-degree murder. Instead of life, she received a 10-year sentence. After serving almost one-third of her sentence, she was paroled, in 1981.

B. THE USE OF FORCE IN THE DEFENSE OF PROPERTY

Less Than Deadly Force in the Defense of Property

A person is privileged to threaten or intentionally use force to protect property that is lawfully in his or her custody or care. No force may be used if verbal requests to terminate and stop such interference are complied with.

The interference with the property must be *unlawful.* Force may be used only when *necessary* to terminate the interference and the amount of force must be *reasonable* under the circumstances.

Example: Y, a store employee, observes X snatch merchandise and run out of the store. Y may use *necessary* and *reasonable* force to prevent the *unlawful* taking of merchandise by X.

Example: X snatches Mrs. Y's purse and runs off. Y, who observed the crime, would be justified in using necessary and reasonable force to recover the purse. Theft from the person (or robbery, if force is used) is a felony in most, if not all, states, which would authorize Y, in most states, to make a citizen's arrest. Force could also be used under these circumstances under the state law governing the use of force in making an arrest.

Deadly Force in the Defense of Property

Under the old common law used on the American frontier, deadly force was often used to protect property. A farmer who sought to prevent the theft of his horse, cattle, or farm equipment might use deadly force, if necessary, because law enforcement officers were seldom readily available.

Today, most, if not all, states forbid the use of deadly force in the defense of property. The reasons for the change in the law can be summarized as follows:

1. On the frontier, a horse and many other items of property were important for survival. Today, few items of property are vital to survival, as they can be replaced within a few days.

2. Today, many items of personal property (such as a car) are ordinarily insured against loss by theft. On the frontier, insurance was unknown and the loss of major or personal items could be a tragedy to a frontier family.

3. Today, thanks to modern communication and transportation, law enforcement agencies are readily available to assist persons confronted with theft.

The Use of Spring Guns and Mechanical Means for the Protection of Property

One cannot use deadly force to protect one's property. This maxim applies whether the owner is present or uses a remote control device. Some jurisdictions, such as Oregon, Wisconsin, and England, go so far as to punish separately the mere setting of a spring gun.

Example: A farmer who becomes exasperated because melons are being stolen from his melon patch is not justified in shooting the thieves with a shotgun. Neither can he set up a shotgun that is discharged when a thief brushes a wire attached to the trigger mechanism.

An interesting academic exercise, using several of the principles explained in this chapter, follows: X, believing that an animal is disturbing the blueberries in a remote corner of his property, sets a spring gun to eliminate the animal. Unknown to X, the disturbance is caused by Y, a stranger from a distant village, who stumbled on the patch, believing that the land was part of a public forest preserve. Y is killed when he inadvertently trips the spring trap. What, if anything, might X be charged with and what might his defenses be?

The common law in probably all states makes the user of such devices civilly liable for the wrongs that occur. The Restatement of Torts, Section 85, page 180, states:

> The value of human life and limb, not only to the individual concerned but also to society, so outweighs the interest of a possessor of land in excluding from it those whom he is not willing to admit thereto that a possessor of land has, as is stated in § 79, no privilege to use force intended or likely to cause death or serious harm against another whom the possessor sees about to enter his premises or meddle with his chattel, unless the intrusion threatens death or serious bodily harm to the occupiers or users of the premises. . . . A possessor of land cannot do indirectly and by a mechanical device that which, were he present, he could not do immediately and in person. Therefore, he cannot gain a privilege to install, for the purpose of protecting his land from intrusions harmless to the lives and limbs of the occupiers or users of it, a mechanical device whose only purpose is to inflict death or serious harm upon such as may intrude, by

giving notice of his intention to inflict, by mechanical means and indirectly, harm which he could not, even after request, inflict directly were he present.

The 1971 Iowa case of *Katko v. Briney* [9] received a great deal of attention when the plaintiff was awarded $30,000 in a civil judgment. The defendant in the civil suit had set up a shotgun trap in an unoccupied farmhouse that he and his wife owned because persons had broken into the house and had damaged property. The plaintiff broke into the unoccupied farmhouse seeking antique bottles and jars. When he opened a bedroom door, he detonated the shotgun and was hit in the right leg above the ankle bone. Much of his leg, including part of the tibia, was blown away. The court reviewed many cases throughout the United States holding persons who set such traps civilly liable.[10]

C. THE USE OF FORCE IN MAKING AN ARREST

Less Than Deadly Force in Making an Arrest

Force may not be used legally in making an arrest unless the arrest is a lawful, custodial arrest made in good faith. This does not mean that the arrested person must be found guilty of the charge; however, it does mean that probable cause (reasonable grounds to believe) must exist to authorize the arrest.

In most arrests, force is unnecessary because the person arrested complies with instructions and offers no resistance. If force should be necessary because of resistance or attempt to escape, the officer may use only such force as is reasonably believed necessary to:

1. detain the offender and to make the arrest
2. overcome any resistance by the offender
3. prevent an escape and retake the person if an escape occurs
4. protect the officer, others, and the prisoner, if necessary.

Defining the force that may be used in making an arrest, the Restatement of Torts 2d, Section

132 comment (a), states that if the officer (or citizen making a citizen's arrest):

is making or attempting to make an arrest for a criminal offense, he is acting for the protection of public interest and is permitted even a greater latitude than when he acts in self-defense, and he is not liable unless the means which he uses are clearly excessive.

The question of reasonable force came before a Florida court in the case of *City of Miami v. Albro*.[11] In that case, an arrestee's arm was broken as the arresting officer pushed him into the conveying squad car. The court stated:

In determining whether the officer applied excessive force in making the arrest, the jury should be instructed upon that issue. The limit of the force to be used by the police is set at the exercise of such force as reasonably appears necessary to carry out the duties imposed upon the officers by the public. . . . Whether the force used is reasonable is a question of fact to be determined in light of the circumstances of each particular case. In any case the officer can never use more force than reasonably appears to be necessary, or subject the person arrested to unnecessary risk of harm. If the officer exceeds the amount of force he is privileged to use under the circumstances, he is liable for only so much of the force as is excessive.

In 1973, a Wisconsin jury held that under the circumstances that existed (for example, size of the parties), the use of a blackjack in subduing a man arrested for a barroom fight was not unreasonable. In sustaining the jury finding, the Wisconsin Supreme Court stated that "the principle is clear that one who has police authority to maintain the peace has a privilege to use force, and the question then becomes simply whether the force was excessive in the accomplishment of the purpose." [12]

The Use of Deadly Force in Making an Arrest

The law regarding the privilege and right to use deadly force in making an arrest varies somewhat from state to state. Police departments also vary in the language they use to instruct their officers as to the use of deadly force and as to the restrictions placed on them. The International Association of Chiefs of Police recommends that

Uses of Deadly Force and Less Than Deadly Force

	Less Than Deadly Force	*Deadly Force*
In self-defense or the defense of others	"The use of (reasonable) force upon or toward another person is justified when the actor (reasonably) believes that such force is immediately necessary for the purpose of protecting himself or herself (or another) against the use of unlawful force by such other person on the present occasion." [a]	"The use of deadly force is not justified . . . unless such force is necessary to protect . . . against death, serious bodily harm, kidnapping, or sexual intercourse compelled by force or threat." [b]
In the defense of property	"Only such degree of force or threat thereof may intentionally be used as the actor reasonably believes is necessary to prevent or terminate the interference." [c]	Under the old common law, deadly force could be used in the defense of property. Many states, however, now forbid the use of intentional deadly force in the defense of property.
To apprehend a person who has committed a misdemeanor / To apprehend a fleeing felon	"When an officer is making or attempting to make an arrest for a criminal offense, he is acting for the protection of public interest and is permitted even a greater latitude than when he acts in self-defense, and he is not liable unless the means which he uses are clearly excessive." [d]	**NEVER** The International Association of Chiefs of Police recommends that deadly force be restricted to felons who, in the course of their crime, threaten the use of deadly force.
To stop a person for investigative purposes when only a "reasonable suspicion" exists	Only reasonable force under the circumstances that then exist.	**NEVER**
Disciplining children (corporal punishment)	Only parents and other persons having a status of *in loco parentis* to a child may use reasonable force "reasonably believed to be necessary for (the child's) proper control, training, or education." [e] Other persons (strangers, neighbors, etc.) may not discipline a child.	**NEVER**

a. Section 3.04(1) and 3.05(1) of the Model Penal Code.
b. Section 3.04(2)(b) of the Model Penal Code.
c. Section 939.49(1) of the Wisconsin Statutes.
d. Restatement of Torts, Section 132(a), as quoted by the Supreme Court of Wisconsin in *Wirsing v. Krzeminski*, 61 Wis. 2d 513, 213 N.W.2d 37 (1973).
e. Restatement of Torts, Section 147(2), as quoted by the U.S. Supreme Court in *Ingraham v. Wright*, 97 S. Ct. 481, 51 L.Ed.2d 711 (1977).

deadly force be restricted to the apprehension of perpetrators who, in the course of their crime, threaten the use of deadly force. In using deadly force when making an arrest:

1. The officer or person making a citizen's arrest must have probable cause to believe that a felony has been committed and that the person arrested committed it.

2. The arresting officer must give the defendant notice of his or her intention to arrest.

3. The defendant must either be fleeing or forcibly resisting.

4. The officer must have a reasonable belief that the use of force is necessary to make the arrest.

The following rules regarding deadly force are probably used by all states and law enforcement agencies:

1. Deadly force may never be used to make the arrest or to prevent the escape of a person who has committed a misdemeanor.

Example: Deadly force should not be used to stop a window peeper who is running away after being ordered to stop or to halt a shoplifter who has taken a $75 item and cannot be apprehended in any other way.

2. Deadly force should never be used on mere suspicion.

Example: In 1965, two New Orleans police officers fired at an automobile they were chasing because they suspected that the vehicle had been stolen. Mere suspicion does not justify the use of deadly force, and in Louisiana, deadly force cannot be used for the protection of property. Therefore, shooting the driver of the supposedly stolen vehicle was not justifiable homicide.[13]

Deadly Force and the "Fleeing Felon"

Under the old common law, deadly force could be used to apprehend a fleeing felon. However, there were few felonies under the old common law, and most of them (if not all) were punishable by death.

Today, there are many felonies in every state. Few of these felonies are punishable by death and many are not crimes that threaten violence or the use of deadly force.

The April 1984 issue of the *FBI Law Enforcement Bulletin* (pp. 30–31) points out that state

---

Determining the Lawfulness of the Use of Force

Initiator of Complaint	Where Tried *	Tests to Determine Lawfulness of Use of Force	Possible Result of Finding That Illegal or Unlawful Force Was Used
Victim, law enforcement officer, prosecutor, coroner or coroner's jury (or John Doe), or any combination of the above	In a criminal trial	See tests in chart on facing page (burden of proof on state is that of proof beyond reasonable doubt)	1. prison or jail 2. fine 3. other penalty 4. combination of above
Victim, or family and estate of victim and attorney representing them commence civil lawsuit	In either a state or federal civil trial	See tests in chart on facing page (burden of proof on plaintiff is preponderance of evidence, or clear and convincing evidence test)	Judgment for compensatory or punitive damages (employer is almost always also sued and could be liable for large money judgment)
Victim, or law enforcement agency, police and fire commission, or other employee	At place of employment to determine whether an employment rule was violated	Was an employment rule (for example, a police department regulation) violated? Test might be whether unnecessary or excessive force was used.	Dismissal, suspension, demotion, etc.

* Issue could be tried before any or all of the different courts and triers of fact listed. Serious violations would probably be tried before all.

legislatures have made the following changes to the common law fleeing felon rule:

a) Twelve states have adopted what is called the "modified" common law rule. This rule limits and restricts the use of deadly force to those felonies defined and identified as "dangerous" or "forcible" felonies or to situations where there is some threat to the officer or others if the apprehension is not made promptly. Within this group are Arkansas, Georgia, Illinois, New Jersey, New York, North Dakota, Oregon, Pennsylvania, Utah, Louisiana, South Carolina, and Vermont.

b) Seven states have adopted the Model Penal Code standard that permits the use of deadly force against fleeing felons when 1) the arrest is for a felony; *and* 2) the person effecting the arrest is a peace officer or is assisting a peace officer; *and* 3) the actor believes such force creates no substantial risk of injury to innocent persons; *and* 4) the actor believes that the felony included the use or threatened use of deadly force or there is a substantial risk that the suspect will cause death or serious bodily harm if apprehension is delayed. States adopting this standard are: Delaware, Hawaii, Kentucky, Maine, Nebraska, North Carolina, and Texas.

Most states have statutes forbidding the use of deadly force solely to prevent and defend against the loss of property. However, a few states have passed statutes authorizing the use of deadly force to apprehend fleeing felons who have committed any felony whether violent or nonviolent. The following case which has been appealed to the U.S. Supreme Court concerns a Tennessee fleeing felon statute which permitted the use of deadly force to apprehend all fleeing felons regardless of the severity of the crime:

GARNER v. MEMPHIS POLICE DEPARTMENT

U.S. Court of Appeals, Sixth Circuit (1983)
710 F.2d 240
Affirmed by the U.S. Supreme Court, — U.S. —, — S.Ct. —, 36 CrL 3233 (1985)

After committing a burglary, a 15-year-old youth fled from police officers with jewelry and $10 taken in the burglary. As the boy jumped over a fence, an officer shot him, believing that he would escape in the darkness. The officer had been taught that it was proper under Tennessee law to kill a fleeing felon rather than run the risk of allowing him to escape.

In a wrongful death civil suit, the officers were granted good faith immunity, as they relied on the statute. The federal court, however, found the state statute unconstitutional, as it authorized deadly force for all felonies, whether violent or nonviolent. The court held that the following guidelines should determine when deadly force can be used in fleeing felon situations:

Before taking a drastic measure of using deadly force as a last resort against a fleeing suspect, officers should have probable cause to believe not simply that the suspect has committed some felony, but that the suspect poses a threat to safety of the officers or a danger to the community if left at large; the officers may be justified in using deadly force if the suspect has committed a violent crime or if they have probable cause to believe that he is armed or that he will endanger the physical safety of others if not captured.

The U.S. Court of Appeals for the First Circuit reached the opposite conclusion in the case of *Conners v. McNulty.*[14] A Rhode Island statute authorized the "use of force dangerous to human life to make a lawful arrest for committing or attempting to commit a felony." Officers who shot and killed a Rhode Island burglar in compliance with the statute were found by a jury to be not civilly liable. The U.S. Court of Appeals affirmed the jury finding in 1983.

Does a Choke Hold Constitute Deadly Force? yes!

In 1982, the choke-hold case of *Lyons v. City of Los Angeles*[15] came before the U.S. Supreme

Court. Lyons alleged that after a traffic stop, Los Angeles police officers rendered him unconscious and damaged his larynx by applying a choke hold (either the "bar-arm control" hold, the "carotid-artery control" hold, or both).

Lyons alleged that there had been 17 deaths that were related to the use of the choke hold. As a result of the allegations, the Los Angeles chief of police prohibited the use of the bar-arm choke hold under any circumstances. The federal district court in Los Angeles issued a preliminary injunction against the use of choke holds under circumstances in which there is no threat to life or serious bodily injury. The U.S. Supreme Court held that federal courts did not have jurisdiction to grant the injunction that Lyons requested.

In 1983, at least 12 civil damage lawsuits were pending against the Los Angeles Police Department, alleging that persons were injured or died as a result of choke holds by officers. The plaintiff in the case of *Avery v. City of Los Angeles* (Sup.Ct., Los Angeles Co., 1983) received an award of $750,000 for injuries resulting from a choke hold. The family of a man who died as a result of a bar-arm choke hold received $500,000 in the case of *Nethery v. City of Chicago* (Cir.Ct., Cook Co., # 81 C2911, 1983).

An article entitled "Physiological Effects Resulting from Use of Neck Holds," in the July 1983 *FBI Law Enforcement Bulletin,* concludes:

> Because of the organs involved, neck holds must be considered potentially lethal whenever applied. Officers using this hold should have proper training in its use and effects. Police officers should have continual inservice training and practice in the use of the carotid sleeper. They should not use or be instructed in the use of the choke hold other than to demonstrate its potential lethal effect. Officers should recognize that death can result if the carotid sleeper is incorrectly applied.

Can Force Be Used to Resist an Unlawful Arrest? No!

Under the old common law, a person had a legal right to forcibly resist an unlawful arrest. This rule developed hundreds of years ago in England, when safeguards did not exist to protect a person

from unlawful arrest. Today, many safeguards exist, and the old rule has been changed by court decisions and statutes in many states. California Penal Code, Section 834a, and Connecticut Statute, Section 53a–23, are examples of such statutes. The Connecticut statute is as follows: "A person is not justified in using physical force to resist an arrest by a reasonably identifiable police officer, whether such arrest is legal or illegal."

Some states, however, retain the old rule. The Maryland Court of Appeals held that "one illegally arrested may use any reasonable means to effect his escape, even to the extent of using force." [16]

In a 1983 case, the Supreme Judicial Court of Massachusetts held that if an officer uses "excessive or unnecessary force to subdue the arrestee," then "regardless of whether the arrest is lawful or unlawful, the arrestee may defend himself by employing such force as reasonably appears to be necessary." But the court held that:

> In the absence of excessive or unnecessary force by an arresting officer, a person may not use force to resist an arrest by one who he knows or has good reason to believe is an authorized police officer, engaged in the performance of his duties, regardless of whether the arrest was unlawful in the circumstances. [17]

D. DOES THE USE OF HANDCUFFS AMOUNT TO EXCESSIVE OR UNREASONABLE FORCE? No

When an Arrest Is Made

Courts have generally upheld the use of handcuffs when an arrest is made. In the 1983 case of *Healy v. City of Brentwood,* the Missouri Court of Appeals, in pointing out that there is always an element of danger in making an arrest, held:

> Police officers face serious risks every time they carry out an arrest. Sometimes the most inoffensive appearing individuals turn out to be uncharacteristically violent. A police officer who is proceeding to convey any prisoner to a police headquarters in a police vehicle should not be faced with a civil lawsuit because he takes the precaution to handcuff the prisoner to prevent her from causing trouble on the way to headquarters. [18]

Healy was arrested after a computer check showed that she had an outstanding warrant for an unpaid fine. She did not resist the arrest by a female police officer. It was later discovered that the fine had been paid and that a mistake had been made. The St. Louis County Police Department encouraged the use of handcuffs in all arrests.

When an Investigative Stop Is Made

When circumstances warrant the use of handcuffs during an investigative stop, the court will sustain the preventive measure. In 1983, the Colorado Supreme Court cited *People v. Johnson*[19] in sustaining the use of handcuffs when police made an investigative stop in an attempt to apprehend armed robbers and murderers. The court held:

> The extended intrusion under the narrow circumstances of this case . . . is justified due to the fact that two armed robberies just occurred in a residential neighborhood, with the second robbery resulting in the death of one victim and serious injury to another. The suspects stopped by the police were reportedly armed with a sawed-off shotgun and other weapons, and the stop took place late at night in a deserted area. When weighed against the exigencies of the situation confronting the officers, it was not unreasonable to handcuff the defendant to ensure the safety of the officers.[20]

In Transporting Mental Patients

Some mental patients are elderly; others are small or weak; still others are strong and capable of committing desperate and dangerous acts. The question whether all or some mental patients can be handcuffed was presented to the Attorney General of Wisconsin. His opinion, dated 5 November, 1982, stated:

> Clearly, a police officer may use reasonable force to maintain custody over an individual facing an involuntary commitment hearing. But, if no force is necessary, then any force at all is unreasonable. Under the circumstances . . . I equate the use of physical restraints with the use of physical force. Therefore, the automatic or universal use of handcuffs or other restraints amounts to an unreasonable use of force where no restraint is required.

E. THE USE OF FORCE BY A PARENT OR PERSON *IN LOCO PARENTIS*

Parents, and persons who take the place of parents (*in loco parentis*), have a natural right to the custody, care, and control of their children. They have a duty to provide food, clothing, shelter, and medical care to the children and to educate and discipline them. A parent or a person *in loco parentis* may use a reasonable amount of force in disciplining a child. However, if the force is excessive, the parent or person *in loco parentis* may be charged criminally. How much force or discipline is reasonable would be determined in view of the child's age and sex; the physical, emotional, and mental condition of the child; the child's conduct that prompted the punishment; the degree of the force used or the methods used to inflict the punishment; and the resulting injury or the effect that the punishment had on the child.

Example: Compelling a young child to sit in scalding hot water or forcing a child to place his hands on a hot radiator would not be reasonable discipline under any circumstances and would be grounds to charge the parents criminally.

Who May Discipline a Child?

Besides the parents, any person taking the place of the parents and thus classified as *in loco parentis* may reasonably discipline a child in his or her care. This category includes legal guardians, foster parents, and public school teachers. In the 1977 case of *Ingraham v. Wright*,[21] the U.S. Supreme Court held that at common law, "teachers may impose reasonable but not excessive force to discipline a child." In reviewing the statutes that many states have passed with respect to the use of corporal punishment in public schools, the court pointed out that:

> Of the 23 States that have addressed the problem through legislation, 21 have authorized the moderate use of corporal punishment in public schools. Of these States only a few have elaborated on the common law test of reasonableness, typically providing for

approval or notification of the child's parents, or for infliction of punishment only by the principal or in the presence of an adult witness. Only two States, Massachusetts and New Jersey, have prohibited all corporal punishment in their public schools. Where the legislatures have not acted, the state courts have uniformly preserved the common law rule permitting teachers to use reasonable force in disciplining children in their charge.

Law enforcement officers, neighbors, and other adults who see children misbehave may not discipline a child (or children), although they may use reasonable force to prevent damage to property or injury to other persons or themselves. In Chapter 10, reference is made to an actual incident in which a 65-year-old man spanked an eight-year-old boy who made an obscene gesture to the man after the man reprimanded the boy for using vulgar language on a public street. The prosecutor did not charge the man with battery, as the boy's mother demanded, but the man was told that he had no right or privilege to discipline other people's children.

Reasonable force to maintain order (as distinguished from discipline) may be used by personnel on airplanes, ships, trains, or buses and by ushers for theaters, sporting events, and other public gatherings. A disorderly child or person may be ordered to leave if he or she is disturbing other persons or has failed to pay the fare or admission fee. The test, again, is that of reasonability. Did the provocation justify the action taken? Was the force reasonable under the circumstances? The Supreme Court of Minnesota held in 1885 that it was not reasonable to force a passenger off a moving train because he had not paid his fare.[22]

False Claims of Excessive or Unnecessary Force

Law enforcement officers and persons in private security are vulnerable to false claims that excessive or unnecessary force was used. To protect against such claims and lawsuits, the following precautions should be considered:

1. Write detailed and lengthy notes and reports as to the circumstances and the facts leading up to the event and the incident itself. Be sure to obtain the names and addresses of witnesses, as these people can be important in proving that proper and lawful procedures were used.

2. If there is any sign of injury or complaint of injury, immediately determine (if possible) the extent of injury. Confirm the injury (if possible), using one or more of the following methods:
   - examination by a qualified medical specialist
   - photographs of the injury
   - statements by the injured person as to the extent and limits of the injury
   - statements by witnesses as to their observations

3. If there are no injuries (or if injuries are minor), it is important that this fact be established by one or more of the following methods:
   - observations of witnesses
   - statement (or statements) of the person who might assert a future claim
   - refusal by the person to have medical or dental care
   - refusal by the person to submit to examination
   - refusal by the person to have photos taken

4. If there are injuries, it is important to determine the cause of the injuries, since the injuries may have:
   - existed before the incident or event
   - been caused by the person while they were fleeing or struggling
   - been self-inflicted after the incident
   - been caused by another person

QUESTIONS AND PROBLEMS FOR CHAPTER 6

Should the persons in the following actual cases be charged with a crime? Indicate what the charge should be (if any) in view of the laws of your jurisdiction and the material presented in this chapter. Give reasons for your answers, citing, wherever possible, statutes of your jurisdiction.

1. In Long Beach, California, a 19-year-old woman who was raped by two men invited them to a return date, at which time she killed one with a shotgun while the other man fled. The men had released the woman after raping her when she promised not to call the police and to agree to another meeting.

2. In Alexandria, Virginia, a 62-year-old retired army colonel was awakened just after midnight by someone rattling the chain lock on his bedroom door. When the noise stopped, the colonel took a pistol and went into the hall to investigate. In the dim light, he saw two men coming toward him from another room. He fired at them and fatally wounded two burglars. When police officers arrived, they found that the burglars were not armed and had in their possession only a large screwdriver and money taken from the house.

3. In Massachusetts, a divorced woman got into a quarrel with her fiancé. He threatened to kill her and her two young children. She ran to the basement of her home, where her children were watching television, and obtained her former husband's rifle. Five minutes after the quarrel, her fiancé came down the steps and the woman shot and killed him. Her fiancé had no weapons in his possession. (*Commonwealth v. Shaffer,* 326 N.E.2d 880 [1975]).

4. In Tennessee, a man caught a window peeper looking into his sister's window at night. The window peeper ran away, although he was ordered by the man to stay where he was. The man shot and killed the fleeing window peeper, who was also an adult male.

5. In Wisconsin, an older man was shocked by the vulgar language of three small boys. When he reprimanded the boys for their language, the oldest boy, who was eight, made an obscene gesture to the man with his finger, with words accompanying the gesture. The angry man chased the boy and gave the boy a spanking, which the man stated the boy deserved.

6. In Minnesota, the owner of a car chased a 28-year-old man who broke into his car and stole $150 in goods. The car owner shot the burglar in the foot, causing him to walk with a limp for the rest of his life. In Denver, Colorado, a store owner shot a fleeing burglar in the back, paralyzing him for life. The burglar, who was 14 years old, was on a beer-drinking spree with other boys and broke into the store to obtain more beer to continue the party.

7. A man observed two suspects breaking into a drugstore located across the street from his house. The man shot and injured both men. (*Commonwealth v. Klein,* 363 N.E.2d 1313, 21 CrL 2362 [Mass., 1977]).

8. When a speeder would not stop, a high-speed race took place. The speeding motorist was clocked at a speed of 103 mph. Police lights and sirens did not stop the speeder and she was forced off the highway. One of the officers opened the car door and repeatedly requested her to get out of the car. The woman was forcibly pulled from the car when she refused the repeated requests. In a civil lawsuit, she asks for money relief because of alleged neck and back injuries received when she was "yanked" out of the car. (*Clark v. Department of Public Safety,* 431 So.2d 83 [La. App., 1983]).

9. After the New York subway shooting of four youths, a New York grand jury re-

fused to charge Bernhard Goetz with attempted murder. However, a civil suit for millions of dollars was filed against Goetz. What arguments would the attorneys for the four youths make in alleging that the force used by Goetz was unlawful and excessive? What arguments would Goetz's attorneys make in defending him in the civil suit?

Chapter 7

Other Criminal Defenses

A. CRIMINAL DEFENSES GENERALLY

The ultimate burden of proving that a defendant committed the offense charged is always on the prosecution in a criminal case. All defendants are presumed innocent until proven guilty through evidence and witnesses produced and presented by the state.

The level of proof required is usually "beyond a reasonable doubt." This level of proof is the highest the law requires in any case. It means that the finder of fact must be convinced of the defendant's guilt to a moral certitude. It does not mean that the evidence must show that the defendant is guilty beyond *any* doubt; it means that he or she must be proven guilty beyond any *reasonable* doubt.

Because of the constitutional assumption of innocence, our system is deemed an accusatorial process. The accuser must bear the entire burden of sustaining the charge through competent evidence. The defendant does not have to do anything. Even if the defendant is guilty, he or she may opt to have the prosecution prove its case. The defendant does not have to remain silent or inactive. He or she may assert a number of defenses and still take advantage of the legal assumption of innocence.

Asserting Defenses by Motions

Defenses are raised by motions before, during, or after trial. The various motions that might be brought by the defense, in addition to the claim of innocence, generally fall into three main categories:

1. The court does not have jurisdiction (a) over the defendant or (b) over the offense (see Chapter 9, "Criminal Jurisdiction").
2. Evidence to be used against the defendant was allegedly obtained in an improper or an illegal manner.
3. The accused was compelled, privileged, or entrapped into committing the offense.

The defendant may properly use one of the defenses described in this chapter to justify his or her conduct.

Such motions may be classified as either procedural or substantive. *Procedural motions* attack the jurisdiction of the court by alleging that some formal defect has deprived the court of its authority to proceed (e.g., the complaint on which the charge is based is defective because it fails to allege a statutory element of the crime). These motions generally are "on the record," that is, no evidence is taken and the court is asked to review whatever is challenged on the record and determine if it is sufficient.

Substantive motions attack the manner in which evidence was obtained. The usual claim is that some portion of the evidence essential to a successful prosecution was obtained in an impermissible manner and must therefore be suppressed. One such motion is the charge that a defendant was not properly advised of his or her constitutional rights pursuant to the Miranda formula; the statement obtained from the defendant must thus be suppressed. Substantive motions usually require the taking of testimony by the court to determine whether or not the allegations raised by the motion are true.

Motions meant to attack the jurisdiction of the court or to suppress evidence are heard before the trial begins. The outcome of such motions could affect the continuation of the proceedings. The time and manner of the hearing of such motions are generally determined by the statutes or rules of evidence of a particular state. The court is generally given wide discretion to expand time limits in order to ensure that justice is done. Categories 1 and 2 above generally fall into the arena of substantive and procedural motions usually heard before trial.

Affirmative Defenses

The third category of motions may be placed under the heading of affirmative defenses. In an affirmative defense, the defendant, in effect, admits that he or she performed the acts charged but claims that he or she had a lawful excuse for doing so and thus is not guilty of a crime. When the defense chooses an affirmative defense, the defense has the obligation to submit proof that the affirmative defense is viable. The prosecution has the ultimate burden of supplying suffi-

---

Defenses and Defensive Tactics In Criminal Cases

1. Entering a plea of not guilty and (a) remaining silent or (b) taking the witness stand on one's own behalf

2. Entering a plea of not guilty because of mental disease or defect (with or without a plea of not guilty). See Chapter 5 for this defense.

3. Challenging the jurisdiction of the trial court. See Chapter 9 for different aspects of criminal jurisdiction.

4. Defense of infancy. See Chapter 5.

5. Attack on the criminal statute (see Chapter 1): (a) void-for-vagueness, (b) overbreadth, (c) status offense, (d) state cannot regulate the conduct that it seeks to regulate, (e) other constitutional grounds

6. Motions to dismiss (a) because of insufficiency of complaint or indictment or (b) because of insufficiency of evidence at the preliminary hearing

7. Motions to suppress (a) physical evidence, (b) admissions or confessions, (c) identification testimony or evidence

8. Challenge to procedural irregularities

9. Defense of immunity: (a) diplomatic immunity, (b) legislative immunity, (c) immunity granted by a court or legislative body

10. Defense of mistake or ignorance: (a) of fact, (b) of civil law, (c) of criminal law

11. Defense of intoxication or drug condition: (a) involuntarily acquired, (b) voluntarily acquired

12. The defense of duress, coercion, or compulsion: (a) where death results, (b) where the harm done is not death or serious injury

13. Necessity as a defense: (a) where death results, (b) where the harm to be avoided is greater than the harm done

14. Justification of the use of force: (a) in self-defense, (b) in the defense of property, (c) in arresting a person, (d) in arresting a person for a felony of violence, (e) by a law enforcement officer to make an investigative stop, (f) in disciplining children

15. Alibi as a defense

16. The defense that the defendant was acting under the authority, direction, or advice of another

17. The defense of double jeopardy

18. *Collateral estoppel* and *res judicata* as a defense

19. The defense of entrapment and frame-up

20. Lapse of time as a defense: (a) the speedy trial defense, (b) statute of limitations as a defense

21. Consent, contributory negligence, or condonation by the victim as a defense

---

cient evidence to find the defendant guilty beyond a reasonable doubt despite the affirmative defense claim. There is no shifting to the defense of the ultimate burden of proof—the defendant does not have to prove innocence but does bear the burden of persuading the jury that his or her claim is true. In other words, the defendant is not required to put any evidence before the jury. If he or she chooses to do so, however, it is the defendant's responsibility, if the claim is to be effective, to give the jury some basis to believe that claim. The defense can do this by presenting evidence through its own witnesses, or by cross-examining the prosecution's witnesses and drawing support for the defense allegation from them. In a case in which the defendant is charged with theft, for example, the defense may claim entrapment. By use of cross-examination, the defense may show that the police actually set up a defendant and, when he had the stolen property in his possession, arrested him. Or the defense may wait until the prosecution has put in its case, and then show through defense witnesses how the defendant was entrapped. Ordinarily, the defense would attempt to lay the groundwork through cross-examination, and then add evidence through defense witnesses to support the claim of entrapment. In any case, if the allegation is made, the responsibility of persuading the jury on the basis of the evidence falls on the defense. The prosecution must convince the jury that each element of the crime was committed by the defendant and that the claim of entrapment should not be accepted.

Motions attacking the jurisdiction of the court and those involving suppression of evidence because of the violation of some constitutional proscription or prosecutorial misconduct are not dealt with here. This chapter discusses those defenses that are generally considered affirmative defenses.

B. IMMUNITY AS A DEFENSE

Diplomatic Immunity

By reason of their positions, foreign diplomats stationed in the United States are immune from arrest and criminal prosecution. Most foreign diplomats are located in Washington, D.C., or in New York (United Nations), whereas consular officials may be found in Chicago, San Francisco, and other cities. According to "Procedures and Policies Relating to Diplomatic and Consular Officials," in the August 1973 issue of the *FBI Law Enforcement Bulletin*:

> Diplomatic immunity, a principle of international law, is broadly defined as the freedom from local jurisdiction accorded to duly accredited diplomatic officers, their families, and servants. Diplomatic officers should not be arrested or detained for any offense, and foreign career consular officers should not be arrested or detained except for the commission of a grave crime. Family members of diplomatic officers, their servants, and employees of a diplomatic mission are entitled to the same immunities under current U.S.

law (22 U.S.C. 252), if they are not nationals of or permanently resident in the receiving state.

> Associated with this personal diplomatic immunity is the inviolability enjoyed by the premises of the mission of the sending state and the private residence of a diplomatic agent, his property, papers, and correspondence.

* * *

> Consular officers are consuls general, deputy consuls general, consuls, and vice consuls. They are also official representatives of foreign governments. Consular officers are required to be treated with due respect, and all appropriate steps are to be taken to prevent any attack on their person, freedom, or dignity. They are entitled to limited immunities.

In New York City alone, police issue more than 250,000 parking tickets yearly to illegally parked diplomatic vehicles. Few of the tickets are paid.

Frustration and anger over diplomatic immunity has grown in the United States because of such incidents as:

• the injuring and killing of persons in American cities by the automobiles of foreign diplomats, with generally no compensation for the wrongs done

• occasional crimes being committed by family members of diplomats (in 1982, the son of the Brazilian ambassador shot a Washington, D.C., carpenter three times after drinking; in 1983, a relative of an Ethiopian delegate to the UN burglarized, sexually assaulted, and assaulted a 19-year-old New York art student). No criminal charges could be issued.

• diplomats and their families ignoring their bills, as they cannot be sued civilly

In 1983, the wife of a Soviet diplomat attached to the Russian UN Mission in New York was apprehended in Paramus, New Jersey, for shoplifting. As the woman did not have her diplomatic papers with her, she was held at the police station for 15 minutes until her identity could be confirmed by telephone.

After her release, the third secretary of the Soviet Mission went to Paramus, which is just over the George Washington Bridge, and demanded an apology from the chief of police. In the conversation between the two men, the police chief told the Soviet diplomat to "go pound salt." When the Soviet asked the police chief the meaning of this term, the police chief explained in graphic detail and the conversation ended.

Legislative Immunity

Article I, Section 6 of the U.S. Constitution provides that U.S. senators and representatives "shall in all cases except treason, felony and breach of the peace, be privileged from arrest during their attendance at the sessions of their respective houses, and in going to and returning from the same." Probably most state constitutions extend the same or similar privileges to state legislators while the state legislature is in session. Congressmen, senators, and state legislators thus have a limited degree of temporary immunity while their legislative bodies are in session. Charges, however, could be held until the legislative body adjourns.

Witness Immunity

Both the federal and state governments have enacted statutes that provide for the granting of immunity under specific circumstances. For instance, the Uniform Act for the Extradition of Witnesses provides that a person from another state who is summoned to testify under compul-

---

Immunity As a Defense

Type of Immunity	Source	Extent	Public Purpose
Diplomatic	Historically, diplomats in a foreign country are not subject to the civil or criminal laws of that country. Therefore, foreign diplomats in the United States are not subject to federal or state civil or criminal laws.	Total	Diplomatic immunity, it is hoped, guarantees that American diplomats in foreign countries will not be arrested.
Legislative	Many states have similar constitutional provisions to that found in Art. I, Sec. 6 of the U.S. Constitution, which provides that U.S. senators and congressmen "shall in all cases except treason, felony and breach of the peace, be privileged from arrest . . . at the sessions of their respective houses, and in going to and returning from the same."	Partial	Legislative immunity has existed since the birth of our republic. Its purpose was to prevent unnecessary harassment of legislators. As the question of legislative immunity seldom comes up, it is highly unlikely that the U.S. Constitution will be amended to change this form of immunity.
Witness *	Federal and state statutes authorize courts and legislative bodies to grant immunity in order to obtain testimony.	Specific types of crimes	This is sometimes the only way in which certain evidence and information can be obtained. A witness who has been granted immunity can no longer take the Fifth Amendment in refusing to answer, since his or her answers can no longer be used to incriminate him or her.

* Witness, immunity differs from testimonial privileges, such as husband–wife, physician–patient, lawyer–client, government–informer. A witness who has been granted immunity can be compelled to testify by jail threats. The person who has a privilege cannot be compelled to be put on a witness stand as a witness under most circumstances.

sion may be granted immunity from arrest for any pending criminal or civil wrong while in the state in response to such summons.

The most well-known grant of immunity occurs when a witness claims the Fifth Amendment privilege against self-incrimination. When this privilege is claimed, the court may be asked to compel the witness to testify and at the same time grant the witness immunity from prosecution for those matters on which he or she is compelled to give testimony. The theory is that if the information cannot be used against the witness in subsequent prosecution, there is no self-incrimination and the witness's protection under the Fifth Amendment is not violated. A grant of immunity by one level of government also bars any other level from prosecuting the witness and from using his or her answers as the basis for criminal proceedings. Such grants of immunity apply only to the extent allowed by state or federal law. If the law of the jurisdiction provides "transactional" immunity, the person granted immunity may not be prosecuted for the offense about which he or she was compelled to testify. If the jurisdiction provides "use" immunity, only the testimony that was compelled may

not be used against the witness. Any information that the authorities obtain through other means may be used to prosecute for the offense about which he or she was compelled to testify.

C. MISTAKE OR IGNORANCE OF FACT OR LAW AS A DEFENSE

Mistake or Ignorance of Fact [1]

A man walking out of a restaurant takes the wrong coat from the coatrack. A few minutes later, the true owner of the coat angrily complains to a police officer. The officer stops the man with the wrong coat blocks away and brings him back to the restaurant. Investigation shows that the man does have a coat similar to the coat that he walked away in. Is this a theft or has an honest mistake of fact been made?

The common law rule, statutorized in many states, is that an honest mistake or ignorance of fact is a defense if it negates the existence of a state of mind essential to the crime. Did the man take the coat with intent to deprive the owner of permanent possession of his coat? The following cases also illustrate this rule:

MORISSETTE v. UNITED STATES

Supreme Court of the United States (1952)
342 U.S. 246, 72 S. Ct. 240

The defendant had been deer hunting in northern Michigan on government property that had been used as a bombing range and was marked "Danger—Keep Out." However, the property was used extensively for hunting by people in the area. When the defendant failed to get a deer, he decided to salvage some of the spent bomb casings that had been lying around on the property for years. In broad daylight, he hauled out three truckloads and with much work realized a profit of $84. He was charged with and convicted of knowingly stealing and converting property of the United States. The trial judge would not allow the defense that the defendant believed that the property was abandoned, unwanted, and considered of no value to the government. After the trial court ruled that "this particular offense requires no element of criminal intent," the U.S. Supreme Court reversed the conviction, pointing out that criminal liability generally required an "evil-meaning mind (and) an evil-doing hand" and held:

Had the jury convicted on proper instructions it would be the end of the matter. But juries are not bound by what seems inescapable logic to judges. They might have concluded that the heaps of spent casings left in the hinterland to rust away presented an appearance of unwanted and aban-

doned junk, and that lack of any conscious deprivation of property or intentional injury was indicated by Morissette's good character, the openness of the taking, crushing and transporting of the casings, and the candor with which it was all admitted. They might have refused to brand Morissette as a thief. Had they done so, that too would have been the end of the matter.
Reversed.

CROWN v. TOLSON
23 Q.B.D. 168 (1889)

After the defendant was deserted by her husband, she was informed by persons she considered reliable that her husband had been lost at sea while on a ship bound from England to America. After waiting more than five years, during which time she believed herself a widow, she married again. Her first husband then reappeared and she was charged with bigamy.

The court held that she was not guilty of bigamy because she had believed, in good faith and on reasonable grounds, that her first husband was dead. The court stated:

At common law an honest and reasonable belief in the existence of circumstances, which, if true, would make the act for which a prisoner is indicted an innocent act has always been held to be a good defense.

The following three examples are found in the New York Criminal Code Annotated Practice Commentary to Section 15.20, *Effect of ignorance or mistake upon liability.*[2]

a) A police officer having a warrant for the arrest of A mistakenly arrests B, who resembles A, and holds him in a police station for an hour before ascertaining his mistake and releasing him. The officer is not guilty of "unlawful imprisonment" (sec. 135.05) because his mistake of fact "negatives a culpable mental state necessary for the commission of the offense," namely, "knowledge that the restriction is unlawful" (sec. 135.00(1)).

b) M has sexual intercourse with F, a mentally ill woman whose condition is not always apparent and is not known to or realized by M. Although M would be guilty of third degree rape if he had realized F's condition . . ., his unawareness thereof is, by statute, expressly made a defense to the charge (sec. 130.10).

c) During a heated argument between A and B, B, a man with a reputation for violence and rumored to carry a pistol on occasion, suddenly places his hand in his bulging pocket, and A strikes him in the face, breaking his nose. Although B did not have a pistol and was merely reaching for a cigarette, A is not guilty of assault . . . because his factual mistake was of a kind that supports a defense of justification (sec. 35.15(1)).

Therefore, the question of whether the defendant made an honest mistake of fact or was ignorant of the true facts and conditions is a question that must be determined by the trier of fact, whether a jury or a judge. The accused must show that he or she was honestly mistaken and that his or her conduct was prompted by this mistake or ignorance.

Strict Liability Statutes and the Defense of Mistake or Ignorance of Fact

Many modern statutes impose strict liability and forbid a prohibited act regardless of the person's state of mind. Ignorance or mistake of fact may not ordinarily be used as a defense with such strict liability statutes. Even in situations in which a well-grounded mistake of fact exists, the law and courts deem it necessary for the common good to require persons to ascertain the true facts at their peril or face the consequences of the law.

Strict criminal liability has been imposed on persons who failed to have a license or to comply with regulations when trafficking in drugs or firearms. Such acts, however, are not innocent acts. Courts have held that persons engaged in such dangerous activities may be held to the highest standards of care enforced by strict criminal liability.[3]

Other areas in which strict liability offenses are used are sale of liquor to minors, food and drug handling, traffic law violations, and sale of misbranded articles. The Supreme Court of Wisconsin pointed out in *State v. Collova* that:

> The persons to whom the regulations are directed are generally in a position to exercise such high degree of care; they will be encouraged to do so by the imposi-

tion of strict penal liability, and the penalties usually involved are such as to make the occasional punishment of one who has done everything that could have been done to avoid the violation a reasonable price to pay for the public benefit of the high standard of care that has been induced.[4]

Many states have statutes that provide that mistake or ignorance as to the age of a minor is no defense. Such cases could involve "statutory rape," selling liquor to a minor, and so on. The following case illustrates:

PENNSYLVANIA v. ROBINSON

Supreme Court of Pennsylvania, 438 A.2d 964, *appeal dismissed* by U.S. Supreme Ct., 31 CrL 4108 (1982)

The defendant was over 18 years of age when he had sexual intercourse with a child under 14 years of age in violation of Pennsylvania's "statutory rape" statute. The defendant argued that he made a reasonable mistake of fact as to the victim's age but was unable to use such a defense under Section 3102 of the Criminal Code, which states that "it is no defense that the actor did not know the age of the child, or reasonably believed the child to be the age of 14 years or older."

The Supreme Court of Pennsylvania held that the legislature may, in exercising its police power, pass a statute requiring that one 18 years of age or older who engages in sexual intercourse with a child under 18 years of age does so at his peril. The court ruled that due process does not require that a defendant be afforded the defense of mistake of age in "statutory rape" prosecutions. The U.S. Supreme Court dismissed the defendant's appeal.

Mistake or Ignorance of Criminal Law

The Latin maxim *Ignorantia legis neminem excusat* (Ignorance of the law excuses no one) may have caused Blackstone to change the phrase in his Commentaries (4 Bl.Comm. 27) to "Ignorance of the law which every one is bound to know, excuses no man." Blackstone's statement is a far better expression of the law, since courts will not allow a defendant who has committed an offense that is generally well known to the public to argue ignorance or mistake of that law. Serious offenses, such as murder, rape, robbery, and theft, are violations not only of the statutory law, but also of moral and ethical laws. Courts would not consider seriously a defense of mistake or ignorance of such laws. Nor would courts ordinarily permit a person charged with a traffic

violation in the state in which he or she is licensed to drive to argue ignorance of the traffic laws of that state. It is presumed that the holder of a license knows the traffic laws when the license is received or renewed.

But what of the hundreds of criminal laws that are not well known? The President's Commission on Law Enforcement and Administration of Justice reported in 1966, in *The Challenge of Crime in a Free Society* (p. 18), that the federal government alone has defined more than 2,800 crimes and has observed that the offenses that state and local governments have defined are even more numerous. If a man with little experience and training were to violate an insurance regulation or security exchange regulation that the general public would not be expected to know, could he plead ignorance of these criminal laws? The accused, of course, would have the burden of showing an honest ignorance of such law in order for his defense to be accepted. The following cases illustrate:

LAMBERT v. CALIFORNIA

Supreme Court of the United States (1957)
355 U.S. 225, 78 S. Ct. 240

The defendant was charged with and convicted of failing to register as required under a Los Angeles municipal ordinance that requires "any convicted person" who was in the city for longer than five days to register with local authorities. The defendant had been convicted of forgery and had lived in Los Angeles for longer than seven years without registering. In a 5/4 decision, the U.S. Supreme Court held that registration provision of the ordinance violated the due process requirement of the Fourteenth Amendment.

Justice William O. Douglas for the majority:

The rule that "ignorance of the law will not excuse" . . . is deep in our law, as is the principle that of all the powers of local government, the police power is "one of the least limitable." . . . On the other hand, due process places some limits on its exercise. Engrained in our concept of due process is the requirement of notice. Notice is sometimes essential so that the citizen has the chance to defend charges. Notice is required before property interests are disturbed, before assessments are made, before penalties are assessed. Notice is required in a myriad of situations where a penalty or forfeiture might be suffered for mere failure to act. . . .

This appellant on first becoming aware of her duty to register was given no opportunity to comply with the law and avoid its penalty, even though her default was entirely innocent. . . . Where a person did not know of the duty to register and where there was no proof of the probability of such knowledge, he may not be convicted consistently with due process. Were it otherwise, the evil would be as great as it is when the law is written too fine or in a language foreign to the community.

UNITED STATES v. PETERSEN

U.S. Court of Appeals, Ninth Circuit (1975)
513 F.2d 1133

In Petersen, the jury sent the trial judge a note after three days of deliberation and numerous clarifications on intent–motive. The note asked, "Is ignorance of the law any excuse?" The judge wrote across the note, in what he termed a "bold hand," "ignorance of the law is not an[y] excuse." The Ninth Circuit criticized the judge's action.

The Ninth Circuit suggested that within the circumstances of that case, the judge's note about the ignorance of the law was misleading.

UNITED STATES v. SCHILLECI

U.S. Court of Appeals, Fifth Circuit (1977)
545 F.2d 519

Wiretapping without court authority and in violation of the Federal Criminal Code, 18 U.S.C. 371, 2511, is a felony. The defendant in this case was a police chief who was convicted of three counts of conspiracy to wiretap.

Two illegal wiretaps were installed on a telephone in a tavern without a court order. The chief was present during the planning, but he argues that he took no active role in the decisions. The U.S. Court of Appeals ordered a new trial, holding that while ignorance of the law does not constitute an "excuse" for a crime, the defendant police chief was entitled to a jury instruction that the jury could consider his lack of knowledge "as evidence bearing on the credibility of his claim that he was not a knowing participant in the conspiracy or an active aider and abettor."

Mistake or Ignorance of Civil Law

Blackstone's maxim that "ignorance of the law which every one is bound to know excuses no man" also applies to civil law. The volume and complexity of civil law has increased considerably in recent years. An honest mistake of civil law could cause an unintentional violation of the criminal law. Take the example of a man with little education and knowledge of the law whose wife tells him that she is going to divorce him. She has a lawyer commence a divorce action, but the action is dropped after the service of the first papers. Several years later, the man, who honestly believes that his wife has divorced him, remarries and discovers that he has unintentionally violated the criminal law of bigamy. Could

he argue that his honest mistake of the civil law of divorce should be accepted as a defense to the charge of bigamy? The answer is yes, but the burden is on him to show that his conduct was prompted by an honest mistake of civil law.

D. INTOXICATION OR DRUGGED CONDITION AS A DEFENSE

Voluntary Intoxication or Drugged Condition

Under the common law, drunkenness was not a defense, but as Blackstone noted in his Commentaries, it was an aggravation of the offense rather than an excuse for any criminal misbehavior. The following 1894 New York case reflected the common law rule:

PEOPLE v. LEONARDI
Court of Appeals of New York
(1894)
143 N.Y. 360, 62 St. R. 352,
38 N.E. 372

At common law drunkenness was not only an excuse for crime, but evidence of intoxication while admissible, and to be considered in some cases, was yet generally of no avail. If a man made himself voluntarily drunk it was no excuse for any crime he might commit while he was so, and he had to take the responsibility of his own voluntary act. If the assault were unprovoked, the fact of intoxication would not be allowed to affect the legal character of the crime. The fact of intoxication was not to be permitted to be even considered by the jury upon the question of premeditation.

Today, the general rule remains the same. A defendant who voluntarily becomes intoxicated or drugged has no defense because of his or her intoxicated or drugged condition. There is one exception, however, and that is for specific intent crimes. New York Statute Section 15.25 states this exception, recognized by many states.[5] This

Statute provides that "intoxication is not, as such, a defense to a criminal charge; but in any prosecution for an offense, evidence of intoxication of the defendant may be offered by the defendant whenever it is relevant to negative an element of the crime charged." The following cases reflect the application of this rule:

PEOPLE v. GREEN
Appellate Court of Illinois
(1969)
105 Ill. App. 2d 345, 245
N.E.2d 506

An accused will not be convicted of murder but might be convicted of manslaughter if his voluntary intoxication was so extreme as to suspend entirely his power of reason rendering him incapable of any mental action unless intent to kill was formed before his intoxication.

COMMONWEALTH v.
BRIDGE
Supreme Court of Pennsylvania
(1981)
435 A.2d 151

The defendant was convicted of voluntary manslaughter and argued that voluntary intoxication negated his intent to kill. The court held the defendant's intoxication had nothing to do with the intent required for voluntary manslaughter, which is a homicide based on sudden provocation.

STATE v. HEDSTROM
Supreme Court of Wisconsin
(1982)
108 Wis. 2d 532, 322 N.W.2d
513

The court affirmed the use of a jury instruction requiring that accused be "utterly incapable of forming intent to kill" before intoxication could be used as a defense.

The drinking of alcoholic beverages or the use of drugs before the commission of the crime does not by itself establish intoxication or require the presentation of a jury instruction on intoxication. There must be a showing of intoxication so extreme that it would justify a jury finding that the defendant was incapable of formulating the necessary criminal state of mind. In such a case, the defendant may be convicted of a lesser included crime that does not require specific intent.

It is difficult to convince a jury that a defendant who was still functioning physically after using a large amount of drugs or alcohol was incapable of formulating the necessary criminal mind.

Involuntary Intoxication or Drugged Condition

Involuntary intoxication or drugged condition is a defense if the trier of fact (the jury or judge) believes the defendant's story, supported by credible evidence, that (a) he or she did not voluntarily take the drug or intoxicant and was tricked or forced into taking such substance and (b) the alcohol or drug rendered the defendant incapable of distinguishing between right and wrong with regard to the alleged criminal act at the time the

act was committed.[6] This would mean that the defendant was unable to form criminal intent but was physically able to commit the crime.

Insanity or Abnormality of Mind Caused by Alcohol or Drugs

Mere addiction to drugs or alcohol does not in itself constitute insanity. However, the prolonged or excessive use of alcohol and drugs can cause insanity and such conditions as delirium tremens. The insanity rules of the jurisdiction, whether the M'Naghten Rule or the American Law Institute Rule, would be used to determine the defendant's plea of not guilty because of insanity. If a jury or a judge found that the facts were such as to constitute temporary insanity, the defendant could be found not guilty because of insanity, but if the defendant were merely drunk or drugged, he or she should then be convicted.

In the 1978 case of *Commonwealth v. Sheehan*[7] the Massachusetts Supreme Judicial Court held that the "normal consequences of drug consumption" provide no basis for a claim that the defendant lacked criminal responsibility. The court noted that Massachusetts differs from most states because it does not recognize voluntary drunkenness as a factor negating specific intent.

Although the standards for determining insanity can vary somewhat from state to state, jury to jury, and court to court, alcohol and drugs affect different people in different ways. Weight, physical conditions, and individual factors can make a difference in the effect of the drug or alcohol. The strength and potency of drugs purchased on the street vary considerably and simply knowing the quantity consumed is not sufficient to measure its effect.

Drunkenness or Drugged Condition Induced with Intent to Commit a Crime

A finding that an intent to commit a crime was formed before the requisite degree of intoxication was reached would defeat the defense of voluntary or involuntary intoxication or drugged condition. Or, if there is a finding that such intoxicants or drugs were used to build up courage to commit the crime, these defenses would not stand. If it could be shown that the defendant was a habitual user of that particular drug or type of alcohol, it could then be argued that the defendant was well aware of the effect the drug or alcohol would ordinarily have on him or her.

E. DURESS OR COERCION (OR COMPULSION) AS A DEFENSE

In attempting to use the defense of duress or coercion, defendants must admit that they committed the offense charged but assert that they were forced to do so to avoid death or serious bodily injury to themselves or others. Defining duress and coercion in *People v. Sanders,* the court stated:

> In order for duress or fear produced by threats or menace to be a valid, legal excuse for doing anything, which otherwise would be criminal, the act must have been done under such threats or menaces as show that the life of the person threatened or menaced was in danger, or that there was reasonable cause to believe and actual belief that there was such danger. The danger must not be one of future violence, but of present and immediate violence at the time of the commission of the forbidden act. The danger of death at some future time in the absence of danger of death at the time of the commission of the offense will not

excuse. A person who aids and assists in the commission of the crime, or who commits a crime, is not relieved from criminality on account of fears excited by threats or menaces unless the danger be to life, nor unless that danger be present and immediate.[8]

A well-known case involving the defense of duress was that of Patricia Hearst. The question before the California jury was whether Hearst participated in the bank robbery voluntarily or under duress and coercion. The case was also unusual in that the jury could view movies of the actual robbery as it took place.

Duress or Coercion as Justification to Escape From Prison

In 1977, the Supreme Court of Delaware held that "intolerable conditions" were not justification for escape from prison because the defendants failed to give sufficient proof that such justification existed.[9] The court held that it was proper to employ the tests used by California courts in determining justification. The California tests, established in People v. Lovercamp,[10] hold that justification is available as a defense to the charge of escape from prison only when:

> (1) The prisoner is faced with a specific threat of death, forcible sexual attack or substantial bodily injury in the immediate future;
>
> (2) There is no time for a complaint to the authorities or there exists a history of futile complaints which make any result from such complaints illusory;
>
> (3) There is no time or opportunity to resort to the courts;
>
> (4) There is no evidence of force or violence used towards prison personnel or other "innocent" persons in the escape; and
>
> (5) The prisoner immediately reports to the proper authorities when he has attained a position of safety from the immediate threat.

In 1980, the U.S. Supreme Court ruled as follows in the escape case of *United States v. Bailey:*

> We therefore hold that, where a criminal defendant is charged with escape and claims that he is entitled to an instruction on the theory of duress or necessity, he must proffer evidence of a bona fide effort to surrender or return to custody as soon as the claimed duress or necessity had lost its coercive force. We have reviewed the evidence examined elaborately in the majority and dissenting opinions below, and find the case

not even close, even under respondents' versions of the facts, as to whether they either surrendered or offered to surrender at their earliest possible opportunity. Since we have determined that this is an indispensable element of the defense of duress or necessity, respondents were not entitled to any instruction on such a theory. Vague and necessarily self-serving statements of defendants or witnesses as to future good intentions or ambiguous conduct simply do not support a finding of this element of the defense.[11]

The Defense of Duress in a Charge of Murder

Under the common law, the defense of duress was not available to a defendant in a murder or treason charge. Blackstone stated that the reason for this was that a man under duress "ought rather to die himself than escape by the murder of an innocent."[12] This apparently is the common law today in England and in more than half the American states. About 20 states define the defense of duress by statute, and most do not allow the defense in murder cases (or sometimes in other serious crimes). In a few states, however, if the defense of duress is believed by a jury (or court) in a murder charge, this may reduce the charge of first-degree murder to manslaughter.[13]

Example: C has a gun and threatens to kill A unless A kills B. A believes that C will kill him, and to save his own life, A kills B. A would be charged with first-degree murder in most states, since the defense of duress would not be accepted. However, a few states would reduce the charge to manslaughter if duress and coercion could be proved. In all states, C would be charged with first-degree murder.

Coercion of Wives

Under the old common law, a woman who married lost practically all the few rights she had had before marriage. A husband could discipline his wife with a stick no bigger than the thickness of his thumb. He controlled any property she may have owned or inherited. Courts were reluctant to grant her a divorce, and if they did, the husband would probably receive custody of the children unless he was unfit. Until the 1920s, neither married nor single women could vote in most states, and few well-paying jobs were available to women before World War II.

Because of the control a husband exerted over his wife, there was a common-law rebuttable presumption holding that if a wife committed a crime in her husband's presence, the husband had coerced her into committing the crime. To successfully charge the wife, the state had to present evidence that would overcome the presumption of coercion by the husband. With the emancipation of women in recent decades, this presumption of coercion by the husband has been abolished in most, if not all, states. A married woman today may use the defense of coercion, but like everyone else, she has the burden of proving that she would not have committed the crime charged were it not for the threat of imminent death or serious bodily harm to herself or to another person.

F. NECESSITY AS A DEFENSE[14]

A person who, because of necessity, performs an act that otherwise would constitute a crime may use the justification of necessity as a defense, if the "harm or evil sought to be avoided by such conduct is greater than that sought to be prevented by the law defining the offense charged."[15]

Example: An airplane crashes at night in an isolated area. As it is very cold and rescue is not likely until daylight, the survivors break into a summer cottage and use the food and blankets in the cottage to comfort the injured and to sustain themselves until help arrives.

In the example given, the necessity of breaking into the cottage is obvious. The defense of necessity is justified when:

1. The conduct or act charged must have been done to prevent a significant harm or evil.

2. There must have been no adequate alternative and the consequences could not have been avoided.

3. The harm caused must not be greater than the harm avoided.

In the example given, the survivors would openly admit what they had done. The owner of the cottage would be assured of compensation for the damages.   Law enforcement officers and the prosecutor would not consider criminal charges and the matter would not receive further atten-

tion.   In the following cases, prosecutors did charge, even though defendants argued necessity to justify their conduct:

CLEVELAND v. MUNICIPALITY OF ANCHORAGE
Supreme Court of Alaska
(1981)
631 P.2d 1073, 29 CrL 2475

Four defendants were charged with and convicted of trespassing when they refused to leave an abortion clinic where they were attempting to disrupt abortions being performed there.   They argued the defense of necessity to prevent the "killing of unborn children".   The Supreme Court of Alaska held that the trial court was correct in refusing a jury instruction on necessity, holding that:

1. The defense would apply only if the defendants acted out of duress or to prevent "unlawful" harm to another.

2. The activity of the defendants was a "protest" rather than a lifesaving mission.

3. The defendants had lawful means and methods available to them.

4. The defendants' conduct intruded on the rights of the clinic and its patients.

5. Persons who, through civil disobedience, seek to disrupt abortions must face the consequence of their unlawful activities.

(See Chapter 12 for the law on abortions.)

STATE v. OLSEN
Wisconsin Court of Appeals
(1981)
99 Wis.2d 572, 299 N.W.2d 632

The four defendants formed a line blocking a road being used for a shipment of nuclear material, which defendants believed was unsafe.   They would not move when a sheriff requested them to move and were arrested and charged with disorderly conduct.   As defenses, the defendants argued "necessity," "self-defense," and "defense of others."[16]   The court held that none of the defenses was applicable to the defendants.

STATE v. MARLEY
Supreme Court of Hawaii
(1973)
509 P.2d 1095

The defendants were convicted of criminal trespass after they entered the Honeywell Corporation offices during the Vietnam War to protest and to stop the corporation's "war crimes."   The court held that the activities of the corporation were not unlawful.   Therefore, as the "harm" that defendants sought to stop was not unlawful and did not arise from a natural source, the defendants could not use the defense of necessity.

When Death Results from the Defendant's Attempt to Save Self or Others

The question of whether, under any circumstances, homicide would be justified to save the lives of others or of the defendant was presented in the following cases, which came before courts many years ago.

UNITED STATES v. HOLMES 26 Fed. Cas. 360 (1842)	The defendant was a member of the crew of a ship that sank, leaving him and many others in an overcrowded lifeboat. Because the ship's mate feared that the boat would sink, he ordered the male passengers thrown overboard, leaving the women and the ship's crew. The defendant assisted in throwing 16 of the men out of the boat to their deaths. A grand jury refused to indict him for murder, so he was charged with and convicted of manslaughter.
REX v. DUDLEY AND STEPHENS 14 Q.B.D. 273 (1884)	The defendants and another man and a boy were shipwrecked and adrift in an open boat for 18 days. After seven days without food or water, the defendants suggested that the men kill the boy, who was then very weak. When the other man refused, the defendants killed the boy and all the men fed on the boy's body. Four days later, they were rescued. The jury, by a special verdict, found that the men would probably have died within the four days had they not fed on the boy's body. The jury also found that the boy would probably have died before being rescued. However, the defendants were convicted of murder, with the sentence commuted to six months' imprisonment.

These two cases have been debated by judges, lawyers, and law students throughout the English-speaking world for years. Few persons urge that the doctrine of necessity be expanded to full forgiveness instead of the partial forgiveness of manslaughter used in both the cases given. In commenting on the problem, former U.S. Supreme Court Justice Benjamin N. Cardozo observed: "Where two or more are overtaken by a common disaster, there is no right on the part of one to save the lives of some, by killing of another. There is no rule of human jettison."[17]

The attitude of the British courts today is probably reflected by the 1971 case of *Southwark London Borough v. Williams:*

> the law regards with the deepest suspicion any remedies of self-help, and permits these remedies to be resorted to only in very special circumstances. The reason for such circumspection is clear—necessity can very easily become simply a mask for anarchy.[18]

Other Uses of the Defense of Necessity

Many different types of genuine emergencies can be justification for minor violations of the law. A man rushing a badly bleeding child to a hospital 20 miles away could, if the road conditions were good, exceed the speed limit. He would not be justified, however, in running down a pedestrian.

Arguments over whether extreme hunger justifies theft of food have to be resolved by looking at each incident separately. The man who had just spent all his money on gambling or whiskey would not be justified in stealing food. Nor would the man who broke into a fine restaurant because he did not like the food available to him at the Salvation Army or the Rescue Mission. The person who was directly responsible for creating an emergency would not be in as good a position to use the defense of necessity as would a person who had done nothing to cause the emergency.

G. ALIBI AS A CRIMINAL DEFENSE

In using the defense of alibi, the defendant is asserting that he or she physically could not have committed the crime because at the time the crime was committed, he or she was at another place.

Example: X is charged with robbery and has been identified by two witnesses and the victim as the man who robbed a liquor store. X uses the defense of alibi and argues that it was physically impossible for him to rob the store, since he was at his mother's home 100 miles away at the time of the robbery. His mother and his wife corroborate X's story, stating that they were there also.

Because an alibi can be easily fabricated, it must be carefully investigated. Many states have statutes requiring defendants who plan to use an alibi defense to serve notice on the prosecutor before trial.[19] These statutes are meant to safeguard against the wrongful use of alibis, as they give law enforcement agencies and prosecutors necessary notice and time to investigate the merits of the proposed alibi.

Alibi Notice Statutes

Alibi notice statutes require that defendants make disclosures regarding their cases. Such disclosure includes the place where the defendant claimed to have been at the time the crime was committed and the names and addresses of witnesses to the alibi, if known.

In the 1973 case of *Wardius v. Oregon*,[20] the U.S. Supreme Court held that when a defendant is compelled to disclose information regarding his or her case, the state must also make similar disclosures. The U.S. Supreme Court held:

> [In] the absence of a strong showing of state interests to the contrary, discovery must be a two-way street. The State may not insist that trials be run as a "search

for truth" so far as defense witnesses are concerned, while maintaining "poker game" secrecy for its own witnesses. It is fundamentally unfair to require a defendant to divulge the details of his own case while at the same time subjecting him to the hazard of surprise concerning refutation of the very pieces of evidence which he disclosed to the State.

Alibi notice statutes now require disclosure by prosecutors as well as defendants.

Determining the Validity of Alibi Defenses

An alibi presented to and believed by a jury constitutes a complete defense to the crime charged. Even if the alibi raises only a reasonable doubt in the mind of a jury, it becomes a good defense because the jury cannot convict if a reasonable doubt exists. If only two or three of the jurors believe the alibi, a "hung" jury may result. The burden is not on the defendant to show that he or she was not at the scene of the crime, but is on the state to show beyond reasonable doubt that the defendant was at the scene and did commit the crime. Charges of perjury, solicitation to commit perjury, or subornation of perjury have resulted when it has been shown that alibi witnesses testified falsely or that attempts were made to persuade persons to testify falsely.

Failure to Give Notice of Alibi and Names of Alibi Witnesses

The U.S. Supreme Court noted in 1983 that 35 states have statutes that permit trial judges in those states to prohibit a defendant from introducing testimony of an undisclosed alibi witness unless proper notice is given as required by statute. The following cases illustrate this rule:

TALIAFERRO v. MARYLAND
Supreme Court of the United States (1983)
461 U.S. 948, 33 CrL 4063

Without giving prior notice of alibi and the name of the alibi witness, the defendant in this case attempted on the second day of trial to call an alibi witness. The trial judge refused to grant a delay, as requested by the prosecutor, and would not permit the witness to testify. Defendant's conviction was affirmed and the Court denied review of the case.

ALICEA v. GAGNON
U.S. Court of Appeals, Seventh

The Wisconsin notice-of-alibi statute permitted excluding not only alibi witnesses, but also alibi testimony if proper notice were not given. This

Circuit (1982)
675 F.2d 913, 31 CrL 2065

would mean that a defendant taking the stand could not testify as to his alibi. Excluding the defendant's own testimony was held to be unconstitutional by the federal appeals court. If such alibi testimony would weaken a case, a continuance of the trial would be the remedy.

H. THE DEFENSE THAT THE DEFENDANT WAS ACTING UNDER THE AUTHORITY, DIRECTION OR ADVICE OF ANOTHER

A person who commits an act that is obviously criminal, such as arson or murder, and then attempts to use as a defense the fact that he or she was acting under the direction of a superior officer or on the advice of an attorney or another person would ordinarily be held fully liable for such an offense. The general rule is that one who performs a criminal act under the advice, direction, or order of another cannot use such a defense.

However, because there are hundreds of crimes not well known to the general public, the U.S. Supreme Court, in 1908, quoted with ap-

proval a jury instruction stating that when a person:

> fully and honestly lays all the facts before his counsel, and in good faith and honestly follows such advice, relying upon it and believing it to be correct, and only intends that his acts shall be lawful, he could not be convicted of crime which involves wilful and unlawful intent; even if such advice were an inaccurate construction of the law. But, on the other hand, no man can wilfully and knowingly violate the law, and excuse himself from consequences thereof by pleading that he followed the advice of counsel.[21]

In the 1975 case of *Toomey v. Tolin,*[22] it was held that following the advice of a legal adviser was a complete defense for law enforcement officers involved in a civil suit for false arrest and malicious prosecution. Other cases having to do with the interpretation and application of criminal laws are:[23]

COX v. LOUISIANA
Supreme Court of the United States (1965)
379 U.S. 559, 85 S. Ct. 476

Among other charges, the defendant was convicted of demonstrating "in or near" a courthouse in violation of a Louisiana law modeled after a 1949 federal statute. In a 5/4 decision, the U.S. Supreme Court reversed the conviction, stating:

The highest police officials of the city, in the presence of the Sheriff and Mayor, in effect, told the demonstrators that they could meet where they did, 101 feet from the courthouse steps, but could not meet closer to the courthouse. In effect, appellant was advised that a demonstration at the place it was held would not be one "near" the courthouse within the terms of the statute.

RALEY v. OHIO
Supreme Court of the United States (1957)
360 U.S. 423, 79 S. Ct. 1257

The U.S. Supreme Court held "that the Due Process Clause prevented conviction of persons for refusing to answer questions of a state investigating commission when they relied upon assurance of the commission, either express or implied, that they had a privilege under state law to refuse to answer, though in fact this privilege was not available to them." The Court stated that this "would be to sanction an indefensible sort of entrapment by the State—convicting a citizen for exercising a privilege which the State had clearly told him was available to him."

I. THE DEFENSE OF DOUBLE JEOPARDY

The Fifth Amendment of the U.S. Constitution provides that "no person . . . shall . . . for the same offense . . . be twice put in jeopardy of life or limb." In the 1978 case of *United States v. Scott,*[24] the U.S. Supreme Court, quoting other Supreme Court cases, held that the double jeopardy clause ensures:

> that the State with all its resources and power should not be allowed to make repeated attempts to convict an individual for an alleged offense, thereby subjecting him to embarrassment, expense and ordeal and compelling him to live in a continuing state of anxiety and insecurity, as well as enhancing the possibility that even though innocent he may be found guilty.[25]

Therefore, a person who has been acquitted by a judge or a jury may not be tried again, even if subsequent investigation reveals evidence that proves conclusively that the defendant is guilty. If the acquittal resulted from a finding of mental defect or illness at the time of the commission of the offense, the defendant cannot be retried even though sanity is recovered.

When Is a Defendant Placed in Jeopardy?

In the 1984 case of *Press-Enterprise Co. v. Superior Court,*[26] the U.S. Supreme Court pointed out that jeopardy attaches when a jury is sworn.[27] In a nonjury trial, the Court pointed out that jeopardy attaches when the first witness is sworn.[28]

Prosecution by Both State and Federal Governments

Since most crimes are crimes only against a state, only the state may prosecute for that crime. Some crimes, however, are offenses not only against the state, but also the federal government. The robbery of a federally insured bank or savings and loan association is an example.

The question of whether state and federal government may both prosecute for such offenses has come before the U.S. Supreme Court more than a dozen times. Justice Oliver Wendell Holmes, repeating the rule that both state and federal prosecution in such cases is not in violation of the Fifth Amendment, stated that the rule "is too plain to need more than a statement."[29] The reasoning is presented in the 1959 case of *Bartkus v. Illinois* as follows:

> Every citizen of the United States is also a citizen of a State or territory. He may be said to owe allegiance to two sovereigns, and may be liable to punishment for an infraction of the laws of either. The same act may be an offense or transgression of the law of both. That either or both may (if they see fit) punish such an offender cannot be doubted. Yet it cannot be truly averted that the offender has been twice punished for the same offense; but only that by one act he has committed two offenses, for each of which he is justly punishable. He could not plead the punishment by one in bar to a conviction by the other.[30]

In *Bartkus v. Illinois,* the defendant was tried in a federal court and acquitted of robbing a federally insured bank. He was then indicted by an Illinois grand jury and convicted on substantially the same evidence used in the federal court. The Illinois court sentenced him to life imprisonment under the Illinois Habitual Criminal Statute. The U.S. Supreme Court affirmed the conviction, holding that the second trial did not violate the Fifth Amendment of the U.S. Constitution.

However, since *Bartkus v. Illinois,* many states, including Illinois, have passed legislation that forbids prosecution after there has been prosecution in another jurisdiction for the same crime. In such states, it is the law of the state, and not the double jeopardy clause, that forbids prosecution after prosecution in another jurisdiction.

In 1978, Dan White was convicted of two counts of manslaughter by a California jury for the murders of San Francisco Mayor George

Moscone and Supervisor Harvey Milk (see "Twinkie Defense" in Chapter 5). Believing that the manslaughter convictions were inadequate, the governor of California, Mayor Dianne Feinstein, and California congressmen urged the U.S. Department of Justice to try White on charges of violating his victims' civil rights. Although the Justice Department had done this in previous cases, it decided not to prosecute in the White case, stating that in this case, it would not be an appropriate application of the law.

The U.S. Justice Department did charge a former autoworker with a federal civil rights violation for killing an Asian American man with a baseball bat in a Detroit suburb. After plea bargaining, the Michigan trial court had fined the former autoworker and placed him on probation. In 1984, a federal jury found the man guilty of the civil rights violation. The offense can be punished by a maximum penalty of life in prison.

Prosecution by Both a State and a Municipality for the "Same Offense"

Cities, counties, towns, villages, and other municipalities are created by states to assist in providing necessary governmental services. Because municipalities owe their existence to the state, they are not separate sovereigns and are only an arm of the state. In recognizing that the only sovereign in a state is the state government, the U.S. Supreme Court held in *Waller v. Florida* that:

> Political subdivisions of States—counties, cities or whatever—never were and never have been considered as sovereign entities. Rather, they have been traditionally regarded as subordinate governmental instrumentalities created by the State to assist in the carrying out of state governmental functions.[31]

States grant to municipalities the right to enact penal-type ordinances triable in municipal courts. A person who is tried for shoplifting in a municipal court (ordinance violation) cannot be tried again for the same offense in a state court (violation of state law). The prosecution for the municipal ordinance violation places a defendant in jeopardy and bars another prosecution under state statutes for the same offense.

Tests for Determining Double Jeopardy

The double jeopardy clause forbids multiple prosecutions and multiple punishments for the "same offense." A suspect, however, can generally be charged with as many "separate offenses" as have been committed. For example, a man who steals a car to use in the robbery of a bank may be charged with both offenses. If, during the robbery, he transports a hostage many miles, he may be charged with kidnapping. If he rapes and then kills the hostage, he may also be charged with these offenses.

The two tests used to determine whether double jeopardy has occurred are:

1. The *same evidence test,* which was used by English courts as early as 1796 and is used in federal courts and in the majority of state courts. This test was restated by the U.S. Supreme Court in *Brown v. Ohio:*

> The established test for determining whether two offenses are sufficiently distinguishable to permit the imposition of cumulative punishment was stated in Blockburger v. United States, 284 U.S. 299, 304, 52 S. Ct. 180, 182, 76 L.Ed. 306 (1932):
>
> "The applicable rule is that where the same act or transaction constitutes a violation of two distinct statutory provisions, the test to be applied to determine whether there are two offenses or only one, is whether each provision requires proof of an additional fact which the other does not. . . ."
>
> This test emphasizes the elements of the two crimes. "If each requires proof that the other does not, the *Blockburger* test would be satisfied, notwithstanding a substantial overlap in the proof offered to establish the crimes. . . ." Iannelli v. United States, 420 U.S. 770, 785 n. 17, 95 S. Ct. 1284, 1294, 43 L.Ed.2d 616 (1975).[32]

2. The *same transaction test,* which does not permit multiple prosecutions for different offenses unless they involve separate "transactions." Offenses are considered the same (a) if there is but one act or a single ultimate goal or (b) if there is but one motivating intent or one common design. Justice William J. Brennan, Jr. urging adoption of the same transaction test, criticized the same evidence test because it:

> does not enforce but virtually annuls the constitutional guarantee. For example, where a single criminal episode involves several victims, under the "same evidence" test a separate prosecution may be brought as

to each. . . . The "same evidence" test permits multiple prosecutions where a single transaction is divisible into chronologically discrete crimes. . . . Even a single criminal act may lead to multiple prosecutions if it is viewed from the perspectives of different statutes. . . . Given the tendency of modern criminal legislation to divide the phases of a criminal transaction into numerous separate crimes, the opportunities for multiple prosecutions for an essentially unitary criminal episode are frightening. And given our tradition of virtually unreviewable prosecutorial discretion concerning the initiation and scope of a criminal prosecution, the potentialities for abuse inherent in the "same evidence" test are simply intolerable.[33]

The 1978 case of *State v. Ramirez*[34] illustrates the differences in the application of the two rules. The defendant in the *Ramirez* case was observed shoplifting by a store employee. When the defendant noticed the employee following her, she threw away some of the merchandise and damaged several figurines. She then resisted arrest. The defendant was charged with and convicted in a municipal court of the ordinance violations of criminal damage to property and resisting or obstructing an officer. Later, she was charged in a state court with shoplifting.

The trial court hearing the shoplifting charge used the same transaction test to determine whether double jeopardy had occurred, and under that test dismissed the shoplifting charge against the defendant. However, the Wisconsin Supreme Court held that the same evidence test should have been used. As Wisconsin had no mandatory joinder rule requiring that all offenses arising out of the same incident be tried together, the court held that:

> the defendant would not be subjected to double jeopardy by virtue of prosecutions under both the state statute and municipal ordinance upon the facts as they appear in the record and that it was error to order that the information charging shoplifting be dismissed.

Other U.S. Supreme Court Rulings with Respect to Double Jeopardy

Some aspects of criminal charging are now regulated by state statutes. Other areas are controlled by court decisions. The following U.S. Supreme Court cases illustrate decisions which might be hard to reconcile:

MISSOURI v. HUNTER Supreme Court of the United States (1983) 459 U.S. 359, 103 S. Ct. 673	Although the double jeopardy clause forbids multiple punishment for same offense, it does not forbid the imposition, at the same trial, of convictions and punishments for two or more offenses that are specifically intended by the legislature to carry separate punishments. In the *Hunter* case, the defendant's conviction and punishment for robbery and armed criminal action was affirmed even though the offenses constituted the "same" crime.
WHALEN v. UNITED STATES Supreme Court of the United States (1980) 445 U.S. 684, 100 S. Ct. 1432	The imposition of consecutive sentences for felony–murder and for rape on which the felony–murder was based was held to be contrary to the intent of Congress. As the sentences violated the statutory sentencing scheme, they also were held by the Supreme Court to violate the double jeopardy clause.
SPRADLING v. TEXAS Appeal denied by Supreme Court of the United States (1982) 455 U.S. 971, 30 CrL 4218	Two women were killed by a hit-and-run automobile as they were walking together. The defendant later identified himself as the driver and two indictments were issued. One charged the defendant with failing to stop and render aid to one woman (a felony) and the second indictment with the second felony of failing to stop and aid the second woman. The

defendant was convicted under the first indictment but the jury suspended his sentence. When Texas sought to prosecute Spradling on the second indictment, his lawyer appealed claiming double jeopardy. His motion was denied and the Supreme Court denied appeal.

BALL v. UNITED STATES
Supreme Court of the United States (1896)
163 U.S. 662, 672

The court held: "It is elementary in our law that a person can be tried a second time for an offense when his prior conviction for that same offense has been set aside by his appeal."

In his article "Multiple Offenders and Multiple Offenses," published in the first edition of this text, Attorney Michael Ash observed that:

> the law on what constitutes "separate offenses" is neither consistent nor clear. To get a meaningful handle on this question, the reader will have to familiarize himself with statutes and state court rulings in the jurisdiction in which he is interested and especially with whether his jurisdiction follows the "same evidence" or the "same transaction" test. Even then many questions will remain.

Res Judicata and Collateral Estoppel as Part of the Double Jeopardy Guarantee

If Smith has a lawsuit against Jones, Smith is entitled to his day in court. However, if Smith loses his case, the controversy between the two persons has then been adjudicated and Smith cannot continue to commence new lawsuits based on the same issue. Should Smith commence a new lawsuit on the same issue against Jones, the lawyer for Jones could use *res judicata* (the issue has been decided) as a defense.

Collateral estoppel, an extension of the doctrine of *res judicata,* forbids retrying of factual issues that have already been determined. The doctrines of *res judicata* and *collateral estoppel* apply not only to civil cases, but as early as 1916 were also made applicable to criminal cases by the U.S. Supreme Court.[35] The following cases illustrate the application of *res judicata* and *collateral estoppel* in criminal cases:

ASHE v. SWENSON
Supreme Court of the United States (1970)
397 U.S. 436, 90 S. Ct. 1189

In 1960, six men playing poker in the basement of a house were surprised and robbed by three or four masked gunmen. The defendant was arrested and charged with six counts of robbery but was first brought to trial on the charge of robbing only one of the poker players. The jury found Ashe not guilty, after being instructed that the theft of "any money" would sustain a conviction. Six weeks later, Ashe was tried for the robbery of another of the poker players and this time convicted. The appeal was from the conviction. In reversing the conviction, the U.S. Supreme Court stated:

The question is not whether Missouri could validly charge the petitioner with six separate offenses for the robbery of the six poker players. It is not whether he could have received a total of six punishments if he had been convicted in a single trial of robbing the six victims. It is simply whether, after a jury determined by its verdict that the petitioner was not one of the robbers, the State could constitutionally hale him before a new jury to litigate that issue again. . . .

In this case the State in its brief has frankly conceded that following the petitioner's acquittal, it treated the first trial as no more than a dry run for the second prosecution: "No doubt the prosecutor felt the state had a provable case on the first charge and, when he lost, he did what every good attorney would do—he refined his presentation in light of the turn of events at the first trial." But this is precisely what the constitutional guarantee forbids.

STATE v. PROULX
Supreme Court of New Hampshire (1970)
110 N.H. 187, 263 A.2d 673

The defendant was charged with incest based on allegations that he had sexual intercourse with his daughter on four different specific days in 1967 and 1968. His entire defense was that no act of intercourse had taken place. After he was acquitted of these charges, the state then charged him with the rape of his daughter on four days different from those that figured in the first trial. The defendant argues that double jeopardy bars the second trial.

The Court held that the doctrine of *collateral estoppel,* not double jeopardy, barred the second prosecution.

Collateral estoppel which is an extension of the doctrine of res judicata bars relitigation of factual issues which have already been determined and, like the doctrine of double jeopardy, is designed to eliminate the expense, vexation, waste and possible inconsistent results of duplicatory litigation.

J. ENTRAPMENT, FRAME-UP AND "OUTRAGEOUS GOVERNMENT CONDUCT" AS DEFENSES

1. ENTRAPMENT

When the U.S. Supreme Court recognized entrapment as a defense for the first time, Justice Owen J. Roberts wrote in the 1932 case of *Sorrells v. United States* that "society is at war with the criminal classes, and courts have uniformly held that in waging this warfare, the forces of prevention and detection may use traps, decoys, and deception to obtain evidence of the commission of crime."[36] It has always been necessary for law enforcement agencies to determine whether offenses that would not ordinarily be reported to them by victims or witnesses are being committed within their jurisdiction.

In investigating possible narcotics, gambling, prostitution, homosexual, and liquor violations, it is often necessary for law enforcement officials to

set traps, make some inducements, and employ decoys to afford suspects an opportunity to commit the crime of which they are suspected. Officers and agents of the officers must often act in the capacity of willing victims. Some encouragement, some pretended willingness, some persuasion, some temptation, and some inducement may be made by law enforcement officers or their agents, but it is improper for officers to use excessive inducement, encouragement, or temptation, which is likely to cause persons to commit crimes they would not ordinarily be disposed to commit.

A defendant using the defense of entrapment admits that he or she has committed the crime but alleges that a law enforcement officer or an officer's agent has used improper methods to induce the act that would not have been done had it not been for the improper inducement or encouragement of the officer. In a frame-up defense, the defendant claims innocence and maintains that evidence was planted by the police. If it can be shown that the defendant was

---

Entrapment as a Defense in the De Lorean Case and Other Cases

Entrapment is an affirmative defense that must be raised by a defendant. The defendant must produce evidence showing:

1. that the government initiated, suggested, or proposed the crime and

2. that the defendant was not predisposed to commit the crime.

If the defense shows the above, one of the following two results will occur:

1. If entrapment is shown to have clearly occurred as a matter of law, the trial judge should dismiss the criminal charge.

2. If the defendant has raised a factual question as to whether entrapment occurred (as in the De Lorean case), the defendant is then entitled to a jury instruction on the issue, with the jury making the factual determination.

The issue of entrapment was raised in the five-month De Lorean trial ending in August 1984. Defense lawyers showed on lengthy cross-examination of government agents that potential evidence was destroyed, that investigative guidelines were violated, and that the agents failed to keep a proper rein on their paid informant. The agents admitted that they, not De Lorean, had been in charge during the drug transaction. When De Lorean backed out of the drug deal because of a lack of cash, it was government agents who called him back suggesting the use of collateral. When the government's chief prosecutor and the drug agents had drinks together, the defense presented the meeting as a boozy celebration of De Lorean's imminent arrest. Agents admitted that they speculated as to whether they would make the cover of *Time* magazine. De Lorean did not take the witness stand in his own defense, but the jury after seven days of deliberation found him not guilty of all eight criminal charges. See the series of articles entitled "Entrapment, Inducement, and the Use of Unwitting Middlemen" commencing in the December 1983 *FBI Law Enforcement Bulletin*. The series of articles, which continues in 1984, thoroughly discuss the law of entrapment, citing many court cases.

---

entrapped or framed, the result is a complete defense, and the charge must fall.

What Inducements Do Not Amount to Entrapment?

Courts throughout the United States have long recognized that it is proper for law enforcement officers (or their agents) to create ordinary opportunities for a person to commit an offense if the criminal intent or willingness originated in the mind of the defendant. The fact that the officer afforded the opportunity or the facility for the defendant to commit the crime in order to obtain evidence does not constitute entrapment. For example, a mere offer to purchase narcotics, obscene literature, or other contraband without further inducement is not entrapment. The tolerable degree of governmental participation in a criminal enterprise was defined in the following cases that came before the U.S. Supreme Court:

UNITED STATES v. RUSSELL

Supreme Court of the United States (1973)

411 U.S. 423, 93 S. Ct. 1637

An undercover agent for the Federal Bureau of Narcotics was assigned the task of locating the laboratory in the Pacific Northwest in which "speed" was being produced illegally. The agent contacted the defendant and other suspects and offered to supply them with an essential ingredient that was difficult to obtain but necessary. The government agent was shown the laboratory in which the "speed" was produced and was told that the defendants had been producing the drug for seven months. The essential drug was delivered with the agreement that the agent would receive half the finished batch of "speed" in payment. About a month after the government agent received "speed" from the defendants, he was informed that another batch was being made. He obtained a search warrant and the defendants were arrested and charged with the unlawful manufacture, sale, and delivery of "speed." Defendant Russell's sole defense was entrapment.   In holding that the participation of the narcotics agent was not entrapment, the Supreme Court stated:

The illicit manufacture of drugs is not a sporadic, isolated criminal incident, but a continuing, though illegal, business enterprise.   In order to obtain convictions for illegally manufacturing drugs, the gathering of evidence of past unlawful conduct frequently proves to be an all but impossible task.   Thus in drug-related offenses law enforcement personnel have turned to one of the only practicable means of detection: the infiltration of drug rings and a limited participation in their unlawful present practices.   Such infiltration is a recognized and permissible means of apprehension; if that be so, then the supply of some item of value that the drug ring requires must, as a general rule, also be permissible.   For an agent will not be taken into the confidence of the illegal entrepreneurs unless he has something of value to offer them.   Law enforcement tactics such as this can hardly be said to violate "fundamental fairness" or "shocking to the universal sense of justice."

HAMPTON v. UNITED STATES

Supreme Court of the United States (1976)
425 U.S. 484, 96 S. Ct. 1646

An informer arranged two separate unlawful heroin sales by the defendant to undercover law enforcement officers.   A government witness testified at the trial that the defendant supplied the heroin, but the defendant testified that he received the heroin that he sold to the agents from the informer.   The defendant also claimed that he believed the substance to be a "non-narcotic counterfeit drug which would give the same reaction as heroin."   The defendant requested that the jury be instructed that he be found not guilty if they found that the informer, acting as a government agent, supplied the heroin.   However, the trial court would not give the instruction and the jury convicted the defendant despite his claims.   On appeal to the U.S. Supreme Court, the defendant argued that the jury instruction should have been given, because when the government itself supplies narcotics, the defendant is a victim of illegal government entrapment.   In affirming the defendant's conviction, the Court held that a successful entrapment defense required that the defendant not have the criminal intention until implanted by the government agent.   With respect to conduct by law enforcement officers, the Court held:

In Russell *we held that the statutory defense of entrapment was not available where it was conceded that a government agent supplied a necessary ingredient in the manufacture of an illicit drug.   We reaffirmed the principle of* Sorrells v. United States, *287 U.S. 435 (1932), and* Sherman v. United States, *356 U.S. 369 (1958), that the entrapment defense "focus[es] on the intent or predisposition of the defendant to commit the crime,"* Russell, *supra, at 429, rather than upon the conduct of the Government's agents.   We ruled out the possibility that the defense of entrapment could ever be based upon governmental misconduct in a case, such as this one, where the predisposition of the defendant to commit the crime was established.*

* * *

The police conduct here no more deprived defendant of any right secured to him by the United States Constitution than did the police conduct in Russell *deprive Russell of any rights.*
Affirmed.

What Inducements Are Improper and Do Amount to Entrapment?

Although law enforcement officers or their agents may create the usual or ordinary opportunity for a defendant to commit a crime, they may not use excessive inducement, temptations, urg-ing, or solicitations to commit a crime. Persistent coaxing or appeals to sympathy, pity, and friendship caused the U.S. Supreme Court to hold that the procedures used in the following cases were improper and amounted to entrapment:

SORRELLS v. UNITED STATES
Supreme Court of the United States (1932)
287 U.S. 435, 53 S. Ct. 210

During prohibition, a federal prohibition officer became acquainted with the defendant. The officer passed himself off as a tourist and the two men discovered that they had served in the same U.S. Army division in World War I. After gaining the defendant's confidence by talking about war experiences, the federal agent asked for some liquor but was twice refused. After the third request, the defendant did go out and buy some illegal liquor for the officer. He was then arrested and prosecuted for violating the National Prohibition Act. In holding that the officer used improper inducements which amounted to entrapment, the Court quoted the decision in *Newman v. United States,* 299 F. 128 as follows:

It is well settled that decoys may be used to entrap criminals, and to present opportunity to one intending or willing to commit crime. But decoys are not permissible to ensnare the innocent and law-abiding into the commission of crime. When the criminal design originates, not with the accused, but is conceived in the mind of the government officers, and the accused is by persuasion, deceitful representation, or inducement lured into the commission of a criminal act, the government is estopped by sound public policy from prosecution therefor.

SHERMAN v. UNITED STATES
Supreme Court of the United States (1958)
356 U.S. 369, 78 S. Ct. 819

A government informant and the defendant met in a doctor's office where they were both being treated for narcotics addiction. After several accidental meetings, the informant asked the defendant for a source of narcotics, stating that he was not responding to treatments. The defendant tried to avoid the issue but the informant continued to ask for narcotics, stating that he was suffering. The defendant then, on several occasions, obtained a supply of narcotics which he shared with the informant. In holding that the informant "not only enticed the defendant into carrying out an illegal sale but also into returning to the habit of use" and that this was entrapment, the Court reversed the conviction of the defendant, stating:

The function of law enforcement is the prevention of crime and apprehension of criminals. Manifestly, that function does not include the manufacturing of crime. Criminal activity is such that stealth and strategy are necessary weapons in the arsenal of the police officer. However, "A different question is presented when the criminal design originates with the officials of the government, and they implant in the mind of an innocent person the disposition to commit the alleged offense and induce its commission in order that they may prosecute." 356 U.S. 372, quoting Sorrells v. United States, 287 U.S. at 442.

Tests Used to Determine When a Defendant Is Predisposed to Commit the Crime

In the 1973 case of *United States v. Russell,* the U.S. Supreme Court stated that, "this Court's opinions in Sorrells v. United States . . . and Sherman v. United States . . . held that the principal element in the defense of entrapment was the defendant's predisposition to commit the crime." The Supreme Court also pointed out that the entrapment defense was not of a constitutional dimension, and that Congress or any of the state legislatures may address themselves to the problem and "adopt any substantive definition of the defense that it may desire." Some states already have defined entrapment by statute, and more may do so in the future. Most states, however, use common law definitions of the defense of entrapment.[37] The jury instruction given by the court in the *Russell* case states this definition:

> Where a person has the willingness and the readiness to break the law, the mere fact that the Government Agent provides what appears to be a favorable opportunity is not entrapment and the jury should acquit the defendant if it had a . . . reasonable doubt whether the defendant had the previous intent or purpose to commit the offense . . . and did so only because he was induced or persuaded by some officer or agent of the Government.[38]

Therefore, the circumstances and the extent of government encouragement or participation would have to be considered by the trier of fact or law in determining the issue of entrapment. Most states and the federal courts use the "origin-of-intent" test or the "inducement test" in determining whether the defendant was predis-

posed to commit the crime charged. Under this test, the defendant's past criminal record is important as to the issue of whether entrapment did or did not exist. Therefore, a defendant who had several narcotics convictions would find it more difficult to show that he was not predisposed to commit further narcotics offenses if entrapment was used as a defense to a narcotics charge. The state would find it more difficult to show predisposition if a defendant had no criminal record and earned his or her living in a manner that would not suggest that he or she was predisposed to commit the crime charged.

In the *Sorrells* and *Sherman* cases, minority concurring opinions were written urging the adoption of what is known as the "objective." This test differs from the origin-of-intent test primarily in the fact that the state cannot present the past record of the defendant with respect to the issue of whether entrapment did or did not exist. In the minority concurring opinion in *Sherman v. United States,* the minority justices stated:

> A test that looks to the character and predisposition of the defendant rather than the conduct of the police loses sight of the underlying reason for the defense of entrapment. No matter what the defendant's past record and present inclinations to criminality, or the depths to which he has sunk in the estimation of society, certain police conduct to ensnare him into further crime is not to be tolerated by an advanced society.

In judging the defendant's conduct, the jury must determine whether his or her immediate and ready compliance with the inducement of the officer should be construed as indicating a prior disposition to commit the offense. If the defendant did not immediately comply with the inducement or showed reluctance to commit the crime, the jury would have to determine whether the reluctance was due to fear of detection or whether there existed a genuine reluctance on the part of the defendant to commit the crime charged.

2. "OUTRAGEOUS GOVERNMENT CONDUCT"

The Court of Appeals hearing the Abscam case of *United States v. Myers* noted that although "the defense of entrapment was available to all seven appellants, none except Lederer elected to assert the defense."[39]

The court pointed out that the defense of entrapment, as recognized in federal courts, "focuses on the state of mind of the defendant and precludes conviction only when government agents by their inducements prevail upon a person who was not predisposed to commit the type of crime charged."[40]

The Abscam defendants argued that the "methods used by government agents in developing the cases against them exceed an outer limit of fairness mandated by the Due Process Clause."[41] They argued that "the conduct of Abscam violated standards of due process because the Government's role in the investigation was excessive and fundamentally unfair."[42]

In alleging "outrageous government conduct," defendants referred to Justice Lewis F. Powell's statement in *Hampton v. United States* that "police overinvolvement in crime would have to reach a demonstrable level of outrageousness before it could bar conviction."[43] Reference was also made to "outrageous violation of physical integrity, e.g., *Rochin v. California,* 342 U.S. 165."[44]

The court recognized in both the *Myers* and *Williams* cases "the possibility that at some point deliberate governmental efforts to render ambiguous events over which agents can exercise considerable control would transgress due process limits of fundamental fairness."[45]

The court rejected the Abscam defendants' claims that due process was violated by the conduct of the government agents. It held that the evidence "reveals them [defendants] as unmistakably involved in a corrupt agreement to misuse public office for private gain,"[46] and that the "conduct of the investigation, though subject to some criticism, affords no basis for rejecting the convictions."[47]

Arguments by the defendants that the court would not accept were (a) that "the Government created the crimes";[48] (b) that the inducements offered to the defendants "were so excessive that a court should declare them to exceed limits . . . . in the Due Process Clause";[49] and (c) that government agents "coached" defendants into committing the crimes.[50]

3. THE FRAME-UP DEFENSE

In the 1983 case of *Moore v. United States,*[51] the defendant claimed that a police officer "planted" a gun on him when he was stopped and searched on a street in Washington, D.C. The Court pointed out that "this is not a case in which appellant denied any knowledge of the source of the item allegedly seized. Nor is this a case in which appellant did not allege he was illegally searched by police."

In the *Moore* case, the defendant alleged that he was framed when the officer "planted" the gun on him. The defense argued that as the defendant was not carrying a concealed weapon, he should not be convicted of carrying a concealed weapon.

In a frame-up defense, if a law enforcement officer is accused of "planting" the illegal contraband (gun, drugs, etc.), the officer is then accused of illegal acts. When a defendant claims that he did not know who placed the contraband in his pocket (or on his person) and that he does not know the source of the contraband, he is alleging that (a) he was framed by another person, and that (b) as he did not knowingly and intentionally possess the contraband, he should not be convicted as an essential element of the crime of possession cannot be shown.

A form of frame-up that would not be a defense is illustrated by the following example:

Example: A wife persuades her husband to commit a burglary and while the burglary is in process, the wife calls the police, who apprehend the husband.

Although the husband has been framed by the wife, he could not successfuly use this as a defense to either entrapment or frame-up. The husband could be convicted of burglary and the wife would also probably be charged as a party to the crime of burglary.

Sting and Scam Operations

In recent years, law enforcement agencies have used deception to obtain evidence against persons committing crimes. Sting and scam operations have received the most public attention and have been the most successful. The LEAA (Law Enforcement Assistance Administration) reported that it had funded some 54 sting operations in 39 locations from Maine to Hawaii in the period from 1978 to 1981. As a result, arrest warrants were issued for 4,448 persons on 8,439 charges. Such sting operations have helped solve hijackings; crack auto theft rings; solve such crimes as murder, assault, rape, burglary, and robbery; and have gathered invaluable criminal intelligence information on the inner workings of organized crime. Examples of some of these sting and scam operations that received public attention are:

Abscam—In this undercover FBI sting operation, FBI agents dressed as Arab sheiks and paid bribes to U.S. congressmen and other high officials suspected of engaging in such conduct. As a result of Abscam, seven members of the U.S. Congress, including one senator, were indicted and convicted of a series of offenses.

"The Store"—This undercover, antifencing sting operation attracted thieves, robbers, burglars, and con men in the San Francisco area, resulting in the arrest of 298 persons on charges ranging from burglary to auto theft.

Operation TARPIT ("Thieves And Receivers Put In a Trap")—Seven phony storefront operations were set up in Los Angeles County, which, after 22 months of operations, resulted in recovering $42 million in stolen property. A similar sting in Norfolk, Virginia recovered $16.4 million in stolen property and closed an operation that was cashing between $40,000 and $60,000 worth of bogus certified checks and money orders each day.

Operation Greylord *—Because of information that for "the right price, bagmen can fix the outcome of court cases in Chicago ranging from theft to divorce to traffic violations to murder," [†] a massive Abscam-type probe was commenced. The purpose was to uncover crooked attorneys, judges, and court personnel. With the assistance of a judge from southern Illinois, indictments were obtained for more than 20 persons, including a number of judges.

Operation Corkscrew—In order to determine whether some Cleveland judges were accepting bribes, FBI agents, in an Abscam-type sting operation, paid $85,000 to a court bailiff who had presented himself as a bagman arranging bribes. They ignored one small detail—obtaining pictures of the judges who the bailiff stated were accepting bribes. More than a year later, the FBI agents discovered the bailiff had used imposters to act as judges. The bungled sting did not disclose any crooked judges, but the bailiff and other persons who had pocketed the $85,000 were charged with criminal offenses.

Operation Hornet's Nest—Law enforcement officers in the Los Angeles area recovered $23.5 million in stolen goods and made 459 felony arrests in what is called the biggest sting operation conducted to date. The sting operation was funded with a $100,000 investment from the U.S. Justice Department and operated almost a year, in 1983, until the task force ran out of money. Property recovered included vehicles, guns, electronic and office equipment, and counterfeit and stolen credit cards.

Internal Revenue Stings—In addition to a giant computer network, undercover agents, use of informants, the IRS is using broad and sophisticated sting operations. In such operations, false documentation and laundered government money is used to infiltrate and penetrate businesses suspected of tax fraud.

* "Greylord" is a reference to the wigs worn by British judges.
† Statement by Illinois Judge Lockwood who worked with the FBI to uncover corrupt lawyers and judges.

K. THE RIGHT TO A SPEEDY TRIAL AS A DEFENSE

The Sixth Amendment of the U.S. Constitution provides that "in all criminal prosecutions, the accused shall enjoy the right to a speedy and public trial." Most defendants charged with a serious crime do not ordinarily wish either a speedy or public trial, but unless the right to a speedy trial is waived with the consent of the trial court, the constitutional mandate of a speedy trial must be complied with. Some states have enacted statutory requirements that specify the time period in which a defendant must be tried. These statutes do not necessarily incorporate constitutional standards and may use alternate remedies without violating the Sixth Amendment requirements.

In holding that right to a speedy trial commences when a person "is indicted, arrested, or otherwise officially accused," the U.S. Supreme Court held in *United States v. Marion* that:

> The protection of the Amendment is activated only when a criminal prosecution has begun and extends only to those persons who have been "accused" in the course of that prosecution. These provisions would seem to afford no protection to those not yet accused, nor would they seem to require the Government to discover, investigate, and accuse any person within any particular period of time.[52]

The Court stated that the purpose and "interests served by the Speedy Trial Clause" are as follows:

> Inordinate delay between arrest, indictment, and trial may impair a defendant's ability to present an effective defense. But the major evils protected against by the speedy trial guarantee exist quite apart from actual or possible prejudice to an accused's defense. To legally arrest and detain, the Government must assert probable cause to believe the arrestee has committed a crime. Arrest is a public act that may seriously interfere with the defendant's liberty, whether he is free on bail or not, and that may disrupt his employment, drain his financial resources, curtail his associations, subject him to public obloquy, and create anxiety in him, his family and his friends.[53]

In 1982, the widely publicized case of *United States v. MacDonald* [54] came before the U.S. Supreme Court. In 1970, Captain MacDonald's pregnant wife and two small daughters were brutally murdered in their home on the military reservation at Fort Bragg, North Carolina.

MacDonald, who is a physician, told a story of a bizarre and ritualistic murder by four intruders high on drugs. MacDonald was injured and clubbed into unconsciousness.

Because physical evidence at the murder scene contradicted MacDonald's story, he was charged by the Army with the three murders on May 1, 1970. After hearing 56 witnesses in a further investigation, the Army dismissed the charges on October 23, 1970. However, the U.S. Justice Department picked up the investigation in 1972, and in January 1975, a federal grand jury indicted MacDonald with the three murders.

MacDonald's attorney argued that MacDonald's right to a speedy trial had been violated, but the trial judge denied the motion and MacDonald was convicted in a jury trial of two counts of second-degree murder and one count of first-degree murder. He was sentenced to three consecutive terms of life imprisonment. The U.S. Supreme Court affirmed his convictions, holding that there were no speedy trial violations and stating: "Once the charges instituted by the Army were dismissed, MacDonald was legally and constitutionally in the same posture as though no charges had been made. He was free to go about his affairs, to practice his profession, and to continue with his life."

L. TIME (STATUTE OF LIMITATIONS) AS A DEFENSE

The old English common law adopted the doctrine that "no lapse bars the King"; therefore, statutes limiting the time for criminal prosecutions are rare in England.

However, criminal statutes of limitations appeared in America as early as 1652. The federal government adopted time limits for the prosecution of most federal crimes in 1790, and the majority of the states have enacted statutes of limitations for most crimes. Only South Carolina and Wyoming have no statutes of limitations.[55]

The speedy trial requirements are constitutional mandates and therefore are imposed on the states. Statutes of limitations on criminal prosecutions are optional legislative enactments. Reasons given for limitations on criminal prosecutions are:

> A limitation statute is designed to protect individuals from having to defend themselves against charges when the basic facts may have become obscured by the passage of time and to minimize the danger of official punishment because of acts in the far-distant past.[56]

> * * *

> The Speedy Trial Clause and the limitations statutes work in tandem to prevent pretrial delay: the statutory period insures against pre-accusation delays and the Sixth Amendment controls the post-indictment time span. . . . Both provisions shield defendants from endless anxiety about possible prosecution and from impairment of the ability to mount a defense. By encouraging speedy prosecution, they also afford society protection from unincarcerated offenders, and insure against a diminution of the deterrent value of immediate convictions, as well as the reduced capacity of the government to prove its case.[57]

Statutes of limitations generally permit a longer period for the prosecution of felonies than for the prosecution of misdemeanors. No time limit is generally placed on prosecution for murder. As discovery of some theft offenses could occur years after the theft, extensions of time are generally given based on the time of discovery of the offense.

The running of time under a criminal statute of limitation could be halted by:

• issuance of an arrest warrant or summons, an indictment, filing of information, or the commencement of prosecution

• statute requirement that the person must be a public resident of that state for the time to toll

M. CONSENT, CONTRIBUTORY NEGLIGENCE OR CONDONATION BY THE VICTIM AS A DEFENSE

Consent as a Defense

Lack of consent by the victim is an essential element of some crimes. Therefore in a rape or theft case, the defense that the victim consented to sexual intercourse or to the taking of the property may be used as a defense to the criminal charge. In a charge of statutory rape, the defendant may not use the defense of consent because

children under certain ages are deemed incapable of giving consent to such acts. Other crimes, such as murder, gambling, narcotics offenses, and prostitution, cannot be consented to by the persons involved because the enforcement of such offenses concerns announced public policy. These offenses are against the society rather than the individual and, even where there are victims involved, the consent of the victim would be no defense.

Consent is implied on a football field, in a boxing ring, and under other circumstances. A hard tackle on a football field or a knock-out punch in a boxing ring would not be batteries, since implied consent exists. Kissing a woman at a New Year's Eve party would not ordinarily be disorderly conduct or a battery, although a man who seized a strange woman on the street and kissed her could be charged with disorderly conduct and, in some instances, battery.

Many crimes are against the government, so the question arises whether a governmental official (such as a police officer) could consent to the offense. The answer is no, but the question comes up from time to time, usually having to do with the interpretation of the law. For example, see the U.S. Supreme Court case of *Cox v. Louisiana* in this chapter, in which the defendant was told by law enforcement officers that he and others could demonstrate up to 101 feet away from the courthouse but no closer. Was this consent to violate the law or was it an interpretation of the law forbidding demonstrating "near" the courthouse? The officers could not consent to the violation of the law, but they could interpret what they would consider "near" for enforcement purposes.

Contributory Negligence by the Victim as a Defense to a Criminal Charge

Contributory negligence may be used as a defense in a civil suit, but it may not be used as a defense in a criminal action. A defendant who is charged with manslaughter or reckless homicide may not use as a defense the fact that the victim was also negligent. This issue may be important with respect to whether the defendant's conduct was the proximate cause of the injury or death, and it may be important in determining whether the defendant was criminally negligent, but it may not be used as a defense in itself.

Condonation as a Defense

Condonation, or the forgiveness of the criminal act by the victim, is no defense. In *State v. Craig,*[58] the defendant's mother forgave his act of burning her barn. The barn was burned without her consent, which constituted arson. Condonation after the offense was committed was not permitted as a defense.

Although restitution to compensate the victim for the harm and injury that occurred as a result of the crime is no bar to criminal prosecution, it certainly may be taken into consideration by the court in sentencing as an indication that the defendant recognizes that what he or she did was wrong and seeks to make amends.

N. PRIVILEGE AS A DEFENSE

Should public officials and employees who act in good faith and in reasonable fulfillment of a duty of their public office have a defense of privilege under such circumstances? A few states have statutorized such a defense.

Probably because of the good sense and judgment of the parties involved, few cases have come into the courts. The following 1981 Wisconsin appellate case is one of them:

STATE v. SCHOENHEIDER
Wisconsin Court of Appeals (1981)
104 Wis. 2d 114, 310 N.W.2d 650

The defendant was the vice-president of a volunteer fire department. He testified that he was lying in bed when he heard sirens. After dressing quickly, he drove his car with flashing red lights to the scene of a traffic accident. In attempting to park his vehicle, he collided with the rear of a parked car.

A state trooper investigating the accident, arrested the defendant after a field sobriety test. A breathalyzer test showed 0.12 percent by weight of alcohol. Defendant was convicted of driving under the influence, despite his defense that he was acting in "good faith" in his capacity as a volunteer fire fighter. The court of appeals affirmed the conviction, holding that "the defendant had no apparent authority to engage in the conduct of driving while under the influence of an intoxicant."

QUESTIONS AND PROBLEMS FOR CHAPTER 7

Available answers for questions 1 to 10:

a. *This would be held to be entrapment.*

b. *This would be held to be a frame-up or a procedure that was illegal or improper.*

c. *The state cannot prove an essential element of the crime in this case.*

d. None *of the above defenses would bar or prevent prosecution by the state.*

1. An undercover police officer offers to purchase heroin from a suspected heroin pusher.

2. Unmarked police cars are used to enforce traffic laws.

3. The undercover officer used a false name and did not disclose that he was a police officer.

4. The defendant is not too intelligent and lets his girl friend talk him into committing the crime. He argues entrapment.

5. A police informant sold heroin to the defendant and then informed officers. The defendant was arrested and charged with the possession of the heroin that he had just purchased from the informant.

6. The evidence shows that the defendant did not know that heroin was in the

package he was delivering. The defendant is charged with possession of heroin.

7. Young, attractive women police officers dressed in modest clothing stand on street corners. Men who solicit them for prostitution are arrested.

8. A male police officer dresses as a woman and arrests a man who, thinking the officer is a woman, assaults him.

9. A plainclothes officer offers to pay a bartender two dollars for a fifty-cent beer after the closing hour of the tavern.

10. A police informant places heroin in the defendant's coat pocket. The informant tells the police that the defendant has heroin in his possession. When the defendant is arrested, he is not aware of the presence of the heroin in his pocket.

Select the correct answer for the following questions from these available answers:

a. *Is a statutory defense in your jurisdiction.*

b. *Is a common law defense in your jurisdiction (that is, the defense is recognized by the courts but is not found in the statutes of your jurisdiction).*

c. *Is* neither *a statutory nor common law defense so as to justify the conduct of a defendant.*

11. Self-defense and the defense of others

12. A worthy motive is used as a defense for committing a crime

13. Entrapment

14. An honest mistake of fact

15. An honest mistake of criminal law generally

16. An honest mistake of civil law

17. That the defendant was innocent of any criminal intent when charged with a crime requiring that the state show intent

18. Insanity at the time of the criminal incident

19. Involuntary intoxication or drugged condition

20. Voluntary intoxication or drugged condition

21. That the defendant was framed by another person and did not know that the package he was delivering contained heroin

22. Mistake as to the age of a minor as a defense to a criminal charge

23. Failure of the state to prove an essential element of the crime that the state has charged

24. The defendant challenges the constitutionality of the offense charged

25. The criminal statute is found to be constitutional and the defendant argues that he or she honestly believed (mistakenly) that the statute was invalid

26. The fact that the defendant's conduct is privileged, although otherwise criminal

27. The fact that the defendant believes that his or her act was the only means of preventing imminent death or serious bodily harm to self or another

28. Necessity as a criminal defense

29. Withdrawal from the plan to commit a crime as a defense

30. The defense that the other parties to the crime received no sentence of imprisonment (or lighter sentences than did the defendant)

31. The use of deadly force solely to protect property as a justification and defense to a charge of homicide

32. The defense that the statute of limitations for the crime charged had run out

33. The defendant used *excessive* force in defending self and uses this as a defense

34. The defendant used *reasonable* force under the circumstances in defending self and uses this as a defense

35. The defendant argues contributory negligence on the part of the victim as a defense

36. The defendant is charged with a battery and uses as a defense the abusive and

vulgar language ("fighting words") of the victim

37. The defendant is charged with battery of his wife and argues that a husband has the right to use force to discipline his wife

38. The defendant is charged with battery of a 12-year-old boy (no relative of defendant) and argues that he had the right to discipline the child for breaking a window in the defendant's home

39. The defendant uses as a defense the fact that the person who directly committed the crime was not convicted or was convicted of some lesser crime

40. The defendant is charged with attempted rape and presents as a defense medical evidence showing that he is sexually impotent (unable to complete the sex act)

Note: 1985 case affecting material on page 124 "Prosecution by Both a State and a Municipality for the 'Same Offense' "

In 1985 the case of *Fugate v. New Mexico,* —— U.S. ——, —— S.Ct. ——, 36 CrL 3229 was heard before the U.S. Supreme Court. Four U.S. Supreme Court justices affirmed a New Mexico Supreme Court decision holding that the defendant's conviction in a municipal court of driving while intoxicated and careless driving while intoxicated does not create a double jeopardy bar to his subsequent prosecution in a state criminal court for vehicle homicide based on the same incident. Four justices voted not to affirm the conviction and one justice took no part in the decision. The decision of the New Mexico Supreme Court was therefore affirmed by the equally divided Court with no written decision.

Chapter 8

Criminal Punishment

Punishment has always been part of all criminal offenses. The concepts of crime and punishment are inseparable. Criminal codes are called penal codes or penal laws in some states, indicating that violations of such laws are subject to punishment.

Crimes are classified in terms of their punishment. For example, Section 1.04 of the Model Penal Code states that an "offense . . . for which a sentence of . . . imprisonment is authorized, constitutes a crime." Section 1.04(2) of the Model Penal Code states that a "crime is a felony" if the punishment "is [imprisonment] in excess of one year."

Many states, in seeking to provide for more uniform punishments, use a classification system for penalties. There may be five classes of felonies (Class A through Class E), with each class having a statutory punishment. Misdemeanors are usually classified from Class A through Class C.

A. PUNISHMENTS USED IN EARLY ENGLAND

The criminal punishments used 200 years ago in England and Europe were severe. In England alone, more than 200 offenses were punishable by death. Condemned criminals were usually hanged, although occasionally they were beheaded, quartered, or drawn (dragged along the ground at the tail of a horse). Burning continued till 1790 to be the punishment inflicted on women for treason, high or petty (which later included not only the murder by a wife of her husband, and the murder of a master or mistress by a servant, but also several offenses against the coin). . . . In practice, women were strangled before they were burnt; this however, depended on the executioner. In one notorious case a woman was actually burnt alive for murdering her husband, the executioner being afraid to strangle her because he was caught by the fire.[1]

For lesser offenses, various forms of mutilations, such as cropping (clipping of the ears), blinding, amputation of the hand, and branding, were common. The whipping post and the pillory were often used, as were fines and imprisonment. The pillory is a frame erected on a post. The offender's head and hands are placed in the open holes and the top board is then moved into place, immobilizing the offender in a standing position.

Practices Used in England to Avoid Severe Penalties

Probably because of the severity of penalties, procedures developed in England by which severe penalties could be avoided. By usage and custom, the following came into practice:

1. **"Benefit of Clergy"** In the 12th century, a controversy arose as to whether priests accused of felonies should be tried by the royal courts or the ecclesiastical courts. It was decided that the royal courts could try priests but could not put them to death for the first felony conviction. This privilege was known as the "benefit of clergy," and by the end of the Middle Ages, it was extended to all laypeople who could read.

The test to determine which laypeople could claim the privilege of "benefit of clergy" was their ability to recite the first verse of Psalm 51: "Have mercy upon me, O God, after Thy great goodness." This came to be known as the "neck verse" because it saved the accused from hanging. The only punishment that could then be inflicted was imprisonment for one year and having an "M" branded on the brawn of the left thumb to prevent claiming of the privilege again. For many years, only three crimes were excluded from "benefit of clergy" (high treason, highway robbery, and the willful burning of a house), but in 1769, Blackstone noted that "among the variety of actions which men are daily liable to commit no less than 160 have been declared by Act of Parliament to be felonies without benefit of clergy."[2]

2. **The Law of Sanctuary** In very early times a criminal who took refuge in a church could not be taken from it, but was allowed to take before a coroner an oath of abjuration. That is to say, he admitted his guilt, and swore to leave the realm for life, at a place appointed for that purpose. In process of time abjuration became obsolete, but

various places came to be privileged, and 'sanctuary men' were allowed to live there under regulations, some of which were imposed by statute . . . In 1623 sanctuary was abolished absolutely but in a modified form sanctuaries continued apparently in defiance of the law for another century, so far at least as regards the execution of civil process.[3]

3. Transportation Persons convicted of crimes in England were pardoned if they agreed to be transported to a colony (first America and then Australia) for a number of years—usually seven. The first convicts were sent abroad in 1655. By the time of the American Revolution, some 2,000 convicts a year were being sent to the colonies. After the American Revolution, Australia became the principal place to which prisoners were sent under the condition of the pardon. Over the years, approximately 100,000 prisoners were sent to America, and an equal number sent to Australia.[4] Australia and other colonies objected strongly to the practice of transporting convicts, which was gradually abolished between 1853 and 1864. Penal servitude or imprisonment and hard labor on public works were substituted.[5]

Other penalties that could be imposed for treason or the conviction of a felony were forfeiture of property and corruption of blood. Forfeiture of land and property could be imposed on a person in addition to the death penalty. Corruption of blood affected the family of the defendant. There was no right of descent through a person whose blood was corrupted. This practice, abolished in England by the Forfeiture Act of 1870, was never used in the United States.

B. PUNISHMENTS USED IN EARLY AMERICA

Blackstone points out that English criminal law and punishments, before the American Revolution, were fairly civilized when compared with those of the rest of Europe. Justice Thurgood Marshall makes the following observations in comparing capital punishment in the American colonies with its use in England:

Capital punishment was not as common a penalty in the American Colonies. "The Capitall Lawes of New-

England," dating from 1636, were drawn by the Massachusetts Bay Colony and are the first written expression of capital offenses known to exist in this country. These laws make the following crimes capital offenses: idolatry, witchcraft, blasphemy, murder, assault in sudden anger, sodomy, buggery, adultery, statutory rape, rape, manstealing, perjury in a capital trial, and rebellion. Each crime is accompanied by a reference to the Old Testament to indicate its source. It is not known with any certainty exactly when, or even if, these laws were enacted as drafted; and, if so, just how vigorously these laws were enforced. We do know that the other Colonies had a variety of laws that spanned the spectrum of severity.

By the 18th century, the list of crimes became much less theocratic and much more secular. In the average colony, there were 12 capital crimes. This was far fewer than existed in England, and part of the reason was that there was a scarcity of labor in the Colonies.[6]

C. THE CONSTITUTIONAL LIMITATION ON PUNISHMENT

The Eighth Amendment of the U.S. Constitution, ratified in 1791 as part of the Bill of Rights, provides that "excessive bail shall not be required, nor excessive fines imposed, nor cruel and unusual punishments inflicted." Two members of Congress opposed passage of this amendment. One stated: What is meant by the term excessive bail? Who are to be the judges? What is understood by excessive fines? It lies with the court to determine. No cruel and unusual punishment is to be inflicted; it is sometimes necessary to hang a man, villains often deserve whipping, and perhaps having their ears cut off; but are we in future to be prevented from inflicting these punishments because they are cruel? If a more lenient mode of correcting vice and deterring others from the commission of it could be invented, it would be very prudent in the Legislature to adopt it; but until we have some security that this will be done, we ought not to be restrained from making necessary laws by any declaration of this kind.[7]

Justice William J. Brennan stated in 1972 that "the Cruel and Unusual Punishments Clause, like the other great clauses of the Constitution, is not susceptible of precise definition. Yet we know that the values and ideals it embodies are basic to our scheme of government. And we

---

Criminal Laws and Punishment

Through criminal laws, the criminal justice system seeks:
- to protect society
- to deter persons from committing crimes
- to rehabilitate persons who have committed crimes
- to punish persons who have committed crimes

Sentences for criminal offenses are most often determined by the:
- seriousness of the crime
- harm to the victim or society
- need to deter others
- need to protect society
- need to maintain supervision over the offender
- possibility of rehabilitation

---

know also that the Clause imposes upon this Court the duty, when the issue is properly pre-sented, to determine the constitutional validity of a challenged punishment, whatever that punishment may be."[8]

What Punishment Is Appropriate for a Particular Crime?

In the 1984 case of *Pulley v. Harris,* the U.S. Supreme Court defined the manner of evaluating the appropriateness of a punishment for a particular crime:

> Traditionally, "proportionality" has been used with reference to an abstract evaluation of the appropriateness of a sentence for a particular crime. Looking to the gravity of the offense and the severity of the penalty, to sentences imposed for other crimes, and to sentencing practices in other jurisdictions, this Court has occasionally struck down punishments as inherently disproportionate, and therefore cruel and unusual, when imposed for a particular crime or category of crime. See, *e.g., Solem v. Helm,* 463 U.S. 277 (1983); *Enmund v. Florida,* 458 U.S. 782 (1982); *Coker v. Georgia,* 433 U.S. 584 (1977). The death penalty is not in all cases a disproportionate penalty in this sense.[9]

Options Available to State Legislature Seeking to Achieve Public Order

Can add additional punishment if:
- the offender is a habitual criminal
- the offender used a dangerous weapon in committing the crime
- property taken or damaged is in excess of certain monetary amount

Can create an additional crime of the following conduct:
- conceals his or her identity while committing a crime
- resists or obstructs a law enforcement officer who is investigating the crime
- escapes from custody
- falsely identifies himself (or herself) to law enforcement officer during detention or arrest

Can make the conduct a more serious crime if a misdemeanor battery is committed:
- by a prisoner (can be charged as felony)
- to a law enforcement officer or fire fighter acting in official capacity
- to a witness or juror
- to a public officer

Can impose separate sentences for two offenses that constitute the same crime
See *Missouri v. Hunter,* 103 S. Ct. 673 (1983), in which defendant took part in an armed robbery and was convicted and punished for robbery in the first degree (10 years) and armed criminal conduct (15 years).

Cases That Illustrate the Constitutional Limitation on Punishment

WEEMS v. UNITED STATES Supreme Court of the United States (1910) 217 U.S. 349, 30 S. Ct. 550	The Supreme Court held in 1910 that 15 years at hard labor in ankle chains was excessive punishment for the crime of falsifying government records. This was the first time in the history of the Supreme Court that a legislatively established penalty was invalidated as being "cruel and unusual."
LOUISIANA EX REL. FRANCIS v. RESWEBER Supreme Court of the United States (1947) 329 U.S. 459, 67 S. Ct. 374	Because of an accidental failure of equipment, the defendant was not executed in the first attempt. The Court held that there was no intention to inflict unnecessary pain, and even though the defendant had been subjected to a current of electricity, this did not prevent the State from executing him in the second attempt. In *Furman,* the Court stated that "had the failure been intentional, however, the punishment would have been, like torture, so degrading and indecent as to amount to a refusal to accord the criminal human status."
ROBINSON v. CALIFORNIA Supreme Court of the United States (1962) 370 U.S. 660, 82 S. Ct. 1417	California enacted a law making narcotics addiction in itself a crime. The defendant received a 90-day sentence for being a narcotics addict. The Court held that a state may not punish a person for being "mentally ill, or a leper, or . . . afflicted with a venereal disease," or for being addicted to narcotics. "Even one day in prison would be a cruel and unusual punishment for the 'crime' of having a common cold."
TROP v. DULLES Supreme Court of the United States (1958) 356 U.S. 86, 78 S. Ct. 590	The citizenship of a convicted wartime deserter was taken away after he had already served three years at hard labor, forfeited all pay, and received a dishonorable discharge. In holding that the taking away of the citizenship of the defendant was a violation of the "cruel and unusual punishment" clause of the Eighth Amendment, the Court stated: "The basic concept underlying the (Clause) is nothing less than the dignity of man. While the State has the power to punish, the (Clause) stands to assure that this power be exercised within the limits of civilized standards."
WILKERSON v. UTAH Supreme Court of the United States (1879) 99 U.S. 130, 25 L.Ed. 345	In this case, the Court upheld death by shooting, on the grounds that such was a common method of execution. The Court stated: *Cruel and unusual punishments are forbidden by the Constitution, but the authorities referred to [treatises on military law] are quite sufficient to show that the punishment of shooting as a mode of executing the death penalty for the crime of murder in the first degree is not included in that category, within the meaning of the [Clause]. Soldiers convicted of desertion or other*

capital military offenses are in the great majority of cases sentenced to be shot, and the ceremony for such occasions is given in great fulness by the writers upon the subject of courts-martial.

ROBERTS v. LOUISIANA
Supreme Court of the United States (1977)
431 U.S. 633, 97 S. Ct. 1993

The Supreme Court held that the fact that the murder victim was a police officer performing his regular duties may be regarded as an aggravating circumstance. The Court held that there is a special interest in affording protection to those public servants who regularly risk their lives in order to safeguard other persons and property. However, a Louisiana statute that provided for a mandatory sentence of death for the crime of first-degree murder of a police officer and that did not allow consideration for particularized mitigating factors was held unconstitutional. The Supreme Court held that such a statute invites "jurors to disregard their oaths and choose a verdict for a lesser offense whenever they feel the death penalty is inappropriate."

WOODSON v. NORTH CAROLINA
Supreme Court of the United States (1976)
428 U.S. 280, 96 S. Ct. 2978

In holding a North Carolina death penalty statute unconstitutional because it provided for an automatic death penalty in all first-degree murder cases, the Court held that "the Eighth Amendment draws much of its meaning from 'the evolving standards of decency that mark the progress of a maturing society.'" The Court concluded that North Carolina's mandatory death penalty statute varied "markedly from contemporary standards."

COKER v. GEORGIA
Supreme Court of the United States (1977)
433 U.S. 584, 97 S. Ct. 2861

The defendant escaped from a Georgia prison where he had been serving sentences for murder, rape, kidnapping, and aggravated assault. While committing an armed robbery and another offense, he raped an adult woman. The defendant was convicted of rape, armed robbery, and other offenses and was sentenced to death on the rape charge. The U.S. Supreme Court reversed the sentence of death, holding: "That question, with respect to rape of an adult woman, is now before us. We have concluded that a sentence of death is grossly disproportionate and excessive punishment for the crime of rape and is therefore forbidden by the Eighth Amendment as cruel and unusual punishment."

D. CORPORAL PUNISHMENT

Corporal Punishment as Criminal Punishment

Corporal punishment was used as criminal punishment in the early history of the United States. Mutilations, such as cutting off ears and various types of branding, were discontinued many de-

cades ago. Whipping, however, continued in some American states into this century. The Eighth Circuit Court of Appeals observed that in 1968 only two states permitted the use of the strap as punishment. As a result of the Eighth Circuit Court's decision in the 1968 case of *Jackson v. Bishop,* whipping as a form of punishment was discontinued in the remaining two states. In the *Jackson* case, the Court held:

> We have no difficulty in reaching the conclusion that the use of the strap in the penitentiaries of Arkansas is punishment which, in this last third of the 20th century, runs afoul of the Eighth Amendment; that the strap's use, irrespective of any precautionary conditions which may be imposed, offends contemporary concepts of decency and human dignity and precepts of civilization which we profess to possess; and that it also violates those standards of good conscience and fundamental fairness enunciated by this court in the *Carey* and *Lee* cases.[10]

The Use of Corporal Punishment in Schools

In the 1977 case of *Ingraham v. Wright,* the U.S. Supreme Court held that:

> At common law a single principle has governed the use of corporal punishment since before the American Revolution: teachers may impose reasonable but not excessive force to discipline a child. . . . The prevalent rule in this country today privileges such force as a teacher or administrator "reasonably believes to be necessary for [the child's] proper control, training, or education." Restatement (Second) of Torts § 147(2); see *id.,* § 153(2) . . .
>
> Of the 23 States that have addressed the problem through legislation, 21 have authorized the moderate use of corporal punishment in public schools. Of these States only a few have elaborated on the common law test of reasonableness, typically providing for approval or notification of the child's parents, or for infliction of punishment only by the principal or in the presence of an adult witness. Only two States, Massachusetts and New Jersey, have prohibited all corporal punishment in their public schools. Where the legislatures have not acted, the state courts have uniformly preserved the common law rule permitting teachers to use reasonable force in disciplining children in their charge.[11]

In holding that the Eighth Amendment "cruel and unusual punishment" clause is not applicable to the use of corporal punishment for disciplinary purposes in the public schools, the Court held:

> The schoolchild has little need for the protection of the Eighth Amendment. Though attendance may not always be voluntary, the public school remains an open institution. Except perhaps when very young, the child is not physically restrained from leaving school during school hours; and at the end of the school day, the child is invariably free to return home. Even while at school, the child brings with him the support of family and friends and is rarely apart from teachers and other pupils who may witness and protest any instances of mistreatment.
>
> The openness of the public school and its supervision by the community afford significant safeguards against the kinds of abuses from which the Eighth Amendment protects the prisoner. In virtually every community where corporal punishment is permitted in the schools, these safeguards are reinforced by the legal constraints of the common law. Public school teachers and administrators are privileged at common law to inflict only such corporal punishment as is reasonably necessary for the proper education and discipline of the child; any punishment going beyond the privilege may result in both civil and criminal liability. . . . As long as the schools are open to public scrutiny, there is no reason to believe that the common law constraints will not effectively remedy and deter excesses such as those alleged in this case.
>
> We conclude that when public school teachers or administrators impose disciplinary corporal punishment, the Eighth Amendment is inapplicable. The pertinent constitutional question is whether the imposition is consonant with the requirements of due process.

E. CAPITAL PUNISHMENT

The death penalty was widely accepted at the time the U.S. Constitution and the Bill of Rights were ratified. The only reference to capital punishment in the Constitution is found in the Fifth Amendment, which reads: "No person shall be held to answer for a capital, or otherwise infamous crime, unless . . ."

In 1972, the Supreme Court handed down a decision in the death penalties cases of *Furman v. Georgia, Jackson v. Georgia,* and *Branch v. Texas.*[12] Each of the three defendants had been convicted and sentenced to death (Furman for murder, Jackson and Branch for rape). In a long, confusing decision with nine separate opinions and no true majority position, five of the justices held that in the three cases before them, the death penalty was cruel and unusual. Justices Marshall and Brennan concluded that the death penalty was totally impermissible. The Chief Justice and Justices Powell, Rehnquist, and Blackmun dissented in separate opinions.

The Position of the Majority in the *Furman* Case

The majority of five did not hold that capital punishment was in and of itself cruel and unusual. They held that the way in which the punishment was inflicted on the three defendants in the cases before the Court was cruel and unusual. They also argued that the death penalty was so seldom imposed that it was no longer a deterrent to crime and that when it was imposed, it was imposed in a discriminatory fashion. Justice Marshall wrote: "It also is evident that the burden of capital punishment falls upon the poor, the ignorant, and the underprivileged members of society. It is the poor, and the members of minority groups who are least able to voice their complaints against capital punishment." [13]

Not only did each of the five majority justices file a separate opinion in the *Furman* case, but each of the four dissenting justices also wrote separate opinions.

The Death Penalty After *Furman v. Georgia*

The 5/4 decision of *Furman v. Georgia* invalidated the death penalty statutes of 41 states as well as legislation enacted by Congress. The U.S. Supreme Court pointed out that after *Furman v. Georgia:*

> In response to that decision, roughly two-thirds of the States promptly redrafted their capital sentencing statutes in an effort to limit jury discretion and avoid arbitrary and inconsistent results. All of the new statutes provide for automatic appeal of death sentences. Most, such as Georgia's, require the reviewing court, to some extent at least, to determine whether, considering both the crime and the defendant, the sentence is disproportionate to that imposed in similar cases. Not every State has adopted such a procedure. In some States, such as Florida, the appellate court performs proportionality review despite the absence of a statutory requirement; in others, such as California and Texas, it does not. [14]

In 1976, the U.S. Supreme Court reviewed the new death penalty statutes of Georgia,[15] Florida,[16] and Texas.[17] In the 1984 California death penalty case of *Pulley v. Harris,*[18] the U.S. Supreme Court quoted their 1976 *Jurek v. Texas* decision in affirming the death penalty procedure used by California:

Texas' capital sentencing procedures, like those of Georgia and Florida, do not violate the Eighth and Fourteenth Amendments. By narrowing its definition of capital murder, Texas has essentially said that there must be at least one statutory aggravating circumstance in a first-degree murder case before a death sentence may even be considered. By authorizing the defense to bring before the jury at the separate sentencing hearing whatever mitigating circumstances relating to the individual defendant can be adduced, Texas has ensured that the sentencing jury will have adequate guidance to enable it to perform its sentencing function. By providing prompt judicial review of the jury's decision in a court with statewide jurisdiction, Texas has provided a means to promote the evenhanded, rational, and consistent imposition of death sentences under law. Because this system serves to assure that sentences of death will not be "wantonly" or "freakishly" imposed, it does not violate the Constitution.

Standards to Guide Sentencing Deliberations in Capital Punishment Cases

The death penalty differs from other penalties that may be imposed because of its severity and because it is irrevocable. In *Furman v. Georgia,* the U.S. Supreme Court held that the death penalty "could not be imposed under sentencing procedures that created a substantial risk that it would be inflicted in an arbitrary and capricious manner." [19]

In the 1976 case of *Gregg v. Georgia,*[20] the U.S. Supreme Court again held that the death penalty was not unconstitutionally "cruel and unusual" punishment. The Court pointed out that the use of the death penalty for murder "has a long history of acceptance both in the United States and in England" and that "it is apparent from the text of the Constitution that the existence of capital punishment was accepted by the Framers."

In the 1984 case of *Pulley v. Harris,* the U.S. Supreme Court reviewed the statutes and procedures used by California in considering the death penalty. Harris had deliberately and ruthlessly killed two teenage boys by gunfire in order to steal their car to use in a bank robbery. After killing the boys, Harris finished eating the hamburgers the boys had been eating. After considering California's statutory special circumstances,[21] the statutory list of relevant factors,[22] and the procedures used in California, the U.S. Supreme Court held:

> By requiring the jury to find at least one special circumstance beyond a reasonable doubt, the statute limits the death sentence to a small sub-class of capital-eligible cases. The statutory list of relevant factors, applied to defendants within this sub-class, "provide[s] jury guidance and lessen[s] the chance of arbitrary application of the death penalty," *Harris v. Pulley,* 692 F.2d, at 1194, "guarantee[ing] that the jury's discretion will be guided and its consideration deliberate," *id.,* at 1195. The jury's "discretion is suitably directed and limited so as to minimize the risk of wholly arbitrary and capricious action." *Gregg,* 428 U.S., at 189. Its decision is reviewed by the trial judge and the State Supreme Court. On its face, this system, without any requirement or practice of comparative proportionality review, cannot be successfully challenged under *Furman* and our subsequent cases.

F. IMPRISONMENT AS A PUNISHMENT

Under early Roman law, imprisonment was illegal as punishment and was used for detention only.[23] Imprisonment is as old as the law of England, but only rarely did statutes in early England provide for imprisonment as punishment for crime. Nearly every English court had its own particular prison, and the right of keeping a gaol (jail) in and for a particular district was given as a franchise that the king granted to particular persons, just as he granted other rights connected with the administration of justice in England. In addition to the franchise prisons, there was the Fleet, the prison of the Star Chamber and of the Court of Chancery.[24]

Because of the filthy, unsanitary conditions of the early English prisons and the corruption and brutality that arose from the franchise system, reform movements began in England as early as 1773. In that year, John Howard became sheriff of Bedfordshire. When he saw the disgraceful conditions in his jail, he proposed that salaried gaolers should replace the franchise system. The condition of American prisons has also been the subject of many reform movements, and the use of prisons for the purpose of punishment has been subject to much debate.

The Supreme Court stated in 1970 that "[a] State has wide latitude in fixing the punishment for state crime." [25] But a filthy, dirty prison or brutality within the prison can be held to be a violation of the Eighth Amendment "cruel and unusual punishment" clause.[26] The following Supreme Court cases have to do with the use of imprisonment as a punishment.

By the End of 1982, 37 States Had Death Penalty Laws in Effect

Of the more than 3,800 executions that have occurred since 1930—

- 86 percent were for murder
- 60 percent took place in the South
- 76 percent occurred before 1950
- More that 53 percent of those executed were black
- Less than 1 percent of those executed were female

In the 1972 landmark case of *Furman v. Georgia,* the U.S. Supreme Court ruled that the death penalty as applied in the various states often had been used in an arbitrary and capricious manner, thereby violating Eighth Amendment guarantees against cruel and unusual punishment. All of the more than 600 persons then living on death row eventually had their capital sentences removed. However, the numbers began to build up again as many states moved quickly to revise their capital punishment laws.

In 1977, the first execution in a decade was carried out in Utah. Two more executions followed in 1979 (one each in Florida and Nevada), one in 1981 (Indiana), and two in 1982 (Virginia and Texas). As of April 1983, one additional execution was conducted in Alabama.

Source: 1983 U.S. Department of Justice Report to the Nation on Crime

WILLIAMS v. ILLINOIS

Supreme Court of the United States (1970)
399 U.S. 235, 90 S. Ct. 2018

did more time than the maximum penalties
unfair to poor people.

The defendant was convicted in Illinois of petty theft and received the maximum sentence provided by state law: one year imprisonment and a $500 fine. The judgment of the court also provided that if at the end of the one-year sentence, the defendant could not pay the fine, he would "work off" the fine at the rate of five dollars per day. This provision was permitted by state law. The defendant showed that he was without funds and petitioned to be released at the end of the year so that he could get a job and pay the fine and court costs. The Supreme Court of Illinois rejected the petition and the Supreme Court of the United States reversed stating:

The mere fact that an indigent in a particular case may be imprisoned for a longer time than a non-indigent convicted of the same offense does not, of course, give rise to a violation of the Equal Protection Clause. Sentencing judges are vested with wide discretion in the exceedingly difficult task of determining the appropriate punishment in the countless variety of situations that appear. The Constitution permits qualitative differences in meting out punishment and there is no requirement that two persons convicted of the same offense receive identical sentences.

* * *

The State is not powerless to enforce judgments against those financially unable to pay a fine; indeed, a different result would amount to inverse discrimination since it would enable an indigent to avoid both the fine and imprisonment for nonpayment whereas other defendants must always suffer one or the other conviction.

It is unnecessary for us to canvass the numerous alternatives to which the State by legislative enactment—or judges within the scope of their authority—may resort in order to avoid imprisoning an indigent beyond the statutory maximum for involuntary nonpayment of a fine or court costs. Appellant has suggested several plans, some of which are already utilized in some States, while others resemble those proposed by various studies. The State is free to choose from among the variety of solutions already proposed and, of course, it may devise new ones.

* * *

We conclude that when the aggregate imprisonment exceeds the maximum period fixed by the statute and results directly from an involuntary nonpayment of a fine or court costs we are confronted with an impermissible discrimination that rests on ability to pay, and accordingly, we vacate the judgment below.

TATE v. SHORT

Supreme Court of the United States (1971)
401 U.S. 395, 91 S. Ct. 668

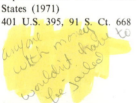
anyone with money wouldn't have to be jailed

The defendant accumulated fines of $425 on nine traffic offenses in Houston, Texas. The defendant showed that he was indigent, but he was required to satisfy the fines at the rate of five dollars per day by serving 85 days at a prison farm. In reversing the court order, the Supreme Court stated:

Our opinion in Williams *stated the premise of this conclusion in saying that "the Equal Protection Clause of the Fourteenth Amendment requires that the statutory ceiling placed on imprisonment for any substantive offense be the same for all defendants irrespective of their economic status." 399 U.S., at 244, 26 L.Ed.2d at 594. Since Texas has legislated a "fines only" policy for traffic offenses, that statutory ceiling cannot, consistently with the Equal Protection Clause, limit the punishment to payment of the fine if one is able to pay it, yet convert the fine into a prison term for an indigent defendant without the means to pay his fine. Imprisonment in such a case is not imposed to further any penal objective of the State. It is imposed to augment the State's revenues but obviously does not serve that purpose; the defendant cannot pay because he is indigent and his imprisonment, rather than aiding collection of the revenue, saddles the State with the cost of feeding and housing him for the period of his imprisonment.*

In footnote 19 of the Williams *case, the Court stated: "We wish to make clear that nothing in our decision today precludes imprisonment for willful refusal to pay a fine or court costs. See Ex parte Smith, 97 Utah 280, 92 P.2d 1098 (1939)." Therefore, a person who has money or an income may be imprisoned for refusal to pay either a fine or court costs.*

G. FORFEITURE AS A PUNISHMENT

The concept and use of forfeiture goes back to early English law. Seizing the property that was used to commit a crime is a strong deterrent to crime. Seizing the profits of crime is also a deterrent in crimes committed for profit.

Forfeiture was first used in custom violations, such as smuggling. In addition to the traditional criminal punishments of death and fines, the economic sanction of forfeiture was imposed with seizure of ships, implements, and the goods being smuggled.

Forfeiture not only punished the wrongdoer by depriving them of ships (or boats), implements, and goods, but it also rewarded the king and government who benefited from the use and sale of these items.

The concept of forfeiture came to America with English common law. It was used over the years in various forms. During the period when beer and other alcoholic beverage were contraband (Prohibition), forfeiture was used extensively to deter and discourage violations of the manufacture, sale, and use of illegal alcohol.

Federal statutes today authorize the forfeiture not only of contraband property, but also of instrumentalities used in narcotics, gambling, and untaxed alcohol and tobacco. For example, Section 55 of the Uniform Controlled Substance Act, which has been adopted by many states and the federal government, provides for forfeiture not only of controlled substances in violation of the law, but also of all raw material, all vehicles—"used, or intended for use"—weapons, records and books, all property, "including money" and profits. Section 55.5 of the act details forfeiture proceedings.

In 1980, Florida extended the use of forfeiture under the Florida Contraband Forfeiture Act, which permits the seizure and forfeiture of any instrumentality of a felony. Under this statute, the vehicle used by a burglar could be seized and forfeited; money used in any felony as well as items, such as a Rolex watch used by a drug trafficker to time his deliveries, may be seized and forfeited.

Cars, boats, and planes that have been seized under Florida statutes and the statutes of other states and the federal government are often used by law enforcement agencies in their work. Un-

Alternatives to Traditional Punishments

The American Correctional Association reported recidivism rates up to 44 percent in 1982 in some crimes. Recidivism was defined as re-arrest and conviction after three years of release from prison. Not only are the traditional punishments not working well, but also more than half the states and the District of Columbia are under court order to change violations in one or more of their prisons, largely related to overcrowding. The following are some of the alternatives to traditional punishments being used or considered (such alternatives are generally used only for nonviolent crimes):

Alternative	Description of Alternative	Probable Use
Antabuse	A chemical that makes a person ill if he or she drinks alcohol. Used when alcohol abuse is the root of the problem and cause of criminal conduct.	Person agrees to take voluntarily as condition of probation or parole, usually to avoid imprisonment.
"Chemical castration"	Use of a controversial drug, Dep-Provera, which does not eliminate sex drive but does diminish it. Possible side effects include fatigue, loss of hair, itching, headaches, weight gain, and symptoms resembling female menopause.	Voluntary use as a condition of probation or parole after some imprisonment or to avoid any imprisonment.
"Electronic shackles"	A device worn like an ankle bracelet that sends a constant radio signal to a receiver on the detainee's telephone. If the device is tampered with or if the wearer leaves home, the sheriff's office is automatically notified. Detainee is under "house arrest" or imprisoned at home.	Also used as a mixture of penalties tailored to the offender. Person must agree to "shackles" as condition of parole, probation, or work release program.
Community-service sentences	Tasks such as bookkeeping, painting, carpentry, electrical work, plumbing, etc. for churches, charities, elderly persons, public places, and even the victim's property. Particularly applicable when defendant has a skill or profession.	Also used with a mixture of punishments tailored to offender. Person must agree to services as a condition of parole, probation, or work release.
Voluntary commitment to drug or alcohol treatment	Many crimes are related to serious drug or alcohol problems. Treatment programs are not effective unless participant cooperates fully.	Could be used in a mixture of punishments believed to achieve the best results. Defendants would voluntarily commit themselves as a condition of probation or parole.
Denver boot	The boot is a $275 device that locks on the front wheel of a vehicle and renders the car immobile until the driver pays fines owed and police remove the clamp. Generally not used until five or more parking tickets are unpaid. Only 29 percent of parking tickets issued in Chicago are paid, with over $70 million owed in unpaid tickets. Court cases have upheld the use of the boot. (See *Baker v. City of Iowa City,* 260 N.W.2d 427 for case citations.)	Use of the boot frees law enforcement and court personnel for other tasks, cuts number of persons in jail, and brings in much needed funds. Use of the boot also increases the number of persons who voluntarily pay traffic and parking fines.
"Son of Sam" legislative bills	Some persons who commit crimes receive considerable public attention and receive money from interviews, books, films, and other money-making ventures. After committing murders in New York, "Son of Sam" was receiving money from such sources, causing the state of New York to enact a "Son of Sam" statute.	Such statutes give victims and the families of victims liens against such profits and monies. Such monies would be held in escrow until claims could be filed and verified.

der Florida's Forfeiture Act, municipalities cannot reduce the normal funding of their police agencies. Money obtained from forfeiture or the sale of goods is used to expand the ability of law enforcement agencies' capabilities to fight crime.

The Internal Revenue Service also seizes property of persons charged or convicted of crimes under tax liens. As persons involved in marijuana, cocaine, and other narcotics often make huge profits without paying proper taxes, tax liens may be filed against them. Property belonging to such persons may be seized. Such property could include homes, furniture, cars, stereo equipment, video games, gems, and real estate.

H. CAREER CRIMINALS AND THE REPEAT OFFENDER

Priority as to law enforcement is most often determined by the crime itself. High priority is most often given when crimes involve injury or death, or when important aspects of public interest are involved.

Attention is focused on the person committing the crime rather than on the crime when it is determined that the person is a career criminal or a repeater (or a habitual criminal). The career criminal or repeater has received special attention and priority since studies done between 1975 and 1978 showed that in Washington, D.C., 7 percent of the criminals committed 24 percent of the crimes. By taking such persons off the street, the incident of crimes can be considerably lessened.

Many cities and states have created career-criminal programs. Such programs ordinarily:

• operate under statutes providing additional and longer sentences for repeat offenders

• establish special career-criminal units in the offices of police and prosecutors that vigorously investigate frequently committed crimes (auto theft, for example) or crimes following patterns

• speed up prosecution if it is determined that the person is a career criminal or repeater (definitions of these offenses can be found in the state statute)

• discourage plea bargaining, which would lessen prison terms, unless the suspect incriminates associates

This concentration of resources on career criminals and repeaters is justified, because these offenders commit such a high proportion of crimes. One crime that receives the attention of many career-criminal programs is auto theft. In the early 1970s, when teenage "joy-riders" were responsible for stealing many cars, auto theft was a low-priority crime.

However, organized criminal groups moved into "chop-shop" operations and commenced stealing expensive cars in larger and larger numbers. This criminal operation is much more serious than the "joy-rider" who illegally uses a vehicle for a period of time before abandoning or returning it. As car thefts were committed more and more by repeat offenders, the offense became a high-priority crime in many cities.

Two repeater (recidivist) cases have come before the U.S. Supreme Court in recent years. The 1980 Texas case of *Rummel v. Estelle* [27] involved a defendant who received a life sentence under the Texas repeater statutes for three nonviolent crimes that netted the defendant a total of $230. The Court affirmed the sentence and conviction, holding that states were free to decide what punishment fit local crimes and that the sentence did not violate the Eighth Amendment. The following case was decided by the U.S. Supreme Court:

SOLEM v. HELM
Supreme Court of the United States (1983)
463 U.S. 277, 33 CrL 3220

Helm lived in South Dakota and had a serious problem with alcohol. By 1975, he had committed six nonviolent felonies. In 1979, he pleaded guilty to uttering a "no account" check for $100 (his seventh felony). Under the South Dakota recidivist statute, he was sentenced to life imprisonment. Unlike Texas, South Dakota statutes prevented the possibility of parole in such cases. Murderers and rapists were eligible for parole in South Dakota, but Helm would never be eligible for parole. In holding that the sentence violated the Eighth Amendment, the Supreme Court held:

The Constitution requires us to examine Helm's sentence to determine if it is proportionate to his crime. Applying objective criteria, we find that Helm has received the penultimate sentence for relatively minor criminal conduct. He has been treated more harshly than other criminals in the State who have committed more serious crimes. He has been treated more harshly than he would have been in any other jurisdiction, with the possible exception of a single State. We conclude that his sentence is significantly disproportionate to his crime, and is therefore prohibited by the Eighth Amendment.

A Small Group of Career Criminals Commit the Vast Majority of Crimes

Chronic offenders commit:

- 61 percent of all homicides
- 76 percent of all rapes
- 73 percent of all robberies
- 65 percent of all aggravated assaults

Chronic violent offenders start out and remain violent.

Prior criminal behavior is one of the best predictors of future criminality.

Relatively few offenders specialize.

Most criminals engage in several types of crime:

- Repeat offenders tend to switch between misdemeanors and felonies and between violent and property crimes, often engaging in related types of crime, such as property and drug offenses.
- It appears that juveniles, even more than adults, are generalists. This may be due partly to the random, unplanned nature of much juvenile crime.

Source: 1983 U.S. Department of Justice Report to the Nation on Crime

Chapter 9

Criminal Jurisdiction

The concept of jurisdiction has a number of aspects in criminal law. There must be jurisdiction (power and authority) to create a criminal law. Jurisdiction also has to do with the enforcement of criminal law. A city that hires a police force authorizes it to enforce the law. What is the extent of the jurisdiction of this authority? What is the authority of officers outside the municipality that employs them? Jurisdiction also has to do with the authority and power of a court to try a criminal case. Following are some of the questions this chapter deals with:

• Can a person be charged with and convicted of a crime that the state (or the federal government) does not have the jurisdiction to create?

• Can a person be tried by a court that does not have jurisdiction over the crime he or she is alleged to have committed?

• Can a person be tried for a crime before jurisdiction over his or her person is obtained (that is, before the person has been captured or has submitted voluntarily to the jurisdiction of the court)?

• If two American citizens were on the moon and one killed the other, would a court in the United States have jurisdiction and, if so, which court?

• What could be the authority for an officer to make an arrest outside his or her jurisdiction?

A. JURISDICTION TO LEGISLATE CRIMINAL LAWS

Most criminal laws enforced today come into existence by enactments of either state legislative bodies or the Congress of the United States. If these bodies are legislating within the scope of the power granted to them by their constitutions, they then have the jurisdiction and the power to create crimes. If they exceed their jurisdiction or their authority, the laws that they enact are invalid and persons cannot be tried and punished for violations of such laws. Note the following exaggerated example:

Example: Citizens in State X do not like the Nevada law legalizing prostitution in some parts of that state nor do they approve of Nevada's gambling laws. Pressure is put on the legislators in State X, and laws are passed making it a criminal offense for citizens of State X to go to Nevada to gamble or patronize the houses of prostitution.

State X does not have the jurisdiction or the authority to enact such laws, any more than the state of New York could pass a law forbidding murder in California. The jurisdiction and the police power to legislate with respect to prostitution and gambling in Nevada rests solely with the Nevada legislature, and the jurisdiction with respect to homicide in California is primarily within the jurisdiction of the California legislature.

B. JURISDICTION OVER THE OFFENSE CHARGED AND OVER THE PERSON

Jurisdiction over the Offense Charged

When a state or the federal government issues a criminal complaint and seeks to commence a criminal action, it must allege and prove that the court has jurisdiction not only over the offense (or offenses) charged, but also over the defendant's person. The Sixth Amendment of the U.S. Constitution provides that "in all criminal prosecutions, the accused shall enjoy the right to a speedy and public trial, by an impartial jury of the State and district wherein the crime shall have been committed, which district shall have been previously ascertained by law."

Therefore, a person charged with a crime has a right to demand that the criminal trial be held in the proper venue. Venue refers to the locality, particularly the county, in which the criminal act or acts charged are alleged to have occurred. In 22 Corpus Juris Secundum (Criminal Law), Section 173, the following statement is made: "Venue is not an element of the offense, and it has been said that persons obviously guilty of criminal acts cannot escape punishment through technical questions of venue." The following case illustrates the defense of lack of jurisdiction:

GARDNER v. STATE
Supreme Court of Arkansas
(1978)
569 S.W.2d 74, *review denied*
by U.S. Supreme Court 24 CrL
4196

The defendant was convicted of raping a 16-year-old girl in the backseat of a car driven from Foreman, Arkansas to Idabel, Oklahoma. On appeal, the defendant challenged the jurisdiction of the Arkansas courts, as the trip took the vehicle into Texas and then Oklahoma. The Supreme Court of Arkansas, in ruling that there was substantial evidence presented at the trial to conclude that the offense occurred in Arkansas, held:

It is not essential to a prosecution in this state that all the elements of crime charged take place in Arkansas. It has been said that it is generally accepted that if the requisite elements of the crime are committed in different jurisdictions, any state in which an essential part of the crime is committed may take jurisdiction.

As a moving vehicle can travel through two or more counties (or states) within a short time, most states have statutes that provide that if some acts material and essential to a crime occur in one county (or state) and some acts in another, the accused may be tried in either county (or state).

Venue and jurisdiction will not ordinarily be presumed in criminal cases but may be inferred from the evidence available in the case. For example, the body of a man who was shot is found. There are no eyewitnesses to the crime and there is no evidence showing that the body has been moved. From this evidence, probably all courts would conclude or infer that the crime occurred in the county and state in which the body was found.[1] The accused has a right to be tried in the county or state in which the crime occurred. Thus if prosecution has been in one venue but evidence is discovered that reveals the venue lies elsewhere, the venue must be changed.

Jurisdiction over the Person Charged with a Crime

Not only must the state show that the court has jurisdiction over the offense charged, but it must also show that jurisdiction over the person exists.

The fact that the accused is physically present in the court is usually sufficient to show jurisdiction over the person.[2] American courts cannot try a defendant in absentia (that is, without the accused being present) because of the defendant's Sixth Amendment rights "to be informed of the nature and cause of the accusation; to be confronted with the witnesses against him." The state must therefore have the defendant lawfully in custody. Or, the defendant voluntarily appears and submits to the jurisdiction of the court.

In minor offenses, when it is permitted by the statutes of a jurisdiction (usually with the permission of the court), the defendant may request and be granted the privilege of not appearing personally. Under these circumstances, the defendant is represented by an attorney and usually enters a plea of guilty or no contest (again with the permission of the court).

As a general rule, once a court has acquired jurisdiction of the accused and the charge against him or her, this jurisdiction continues until final disposition or determination of the case is made in the manner prescribed by law. If the defendant "jumps bail" or fails to appear as ordered, the jurisdiction of the court continues and the defendant is then liable for other charges.

In 1973, the case of *Taylor v. United States,*[3] came before the Supreme Court. The defendant, who was charged with selling cocaine, failed to return to court after a luncheon recess during his trial. After waiting that day for the defendant to appear, the trial judge continued with the case. The jury found the defendant guilty after being instructed that they were to draw no inference from the defendant's absence. The Supreme Court affirmed the conviction of the defendant.

Limits of Criminal Jurisdiction

At common law, prosecution for a crime could be commenced at any time. However, all states and the federal government have, by statutes, imposed time limitations for arrests and prosecutions of practically all crimes in the United States. Misdemeanors usually have a shorter statute of limitations than do felonies, whereas probably no state has placed a time limit on first-degree murder. State statutes usually provide that the running of the statute of limitations is stopped by the issuance of warrants or summonses. Many states do not include the time in which the wanted person was not a public resident of that state.

Practically all persons are subject to the jurisdiction of the state or the nation in which they reside or voluntarily enter. Persons going into Canada to fish or vacationers traveling in Mexico subject themselves to the laws of those nations and are subject to criminal prosecutions if they violate criminal laws. The exceptions, pointed out in Chapter 7 under "Immunity as a Defense," are persons with diplomatic passports and (under certain conditions) national and state legislators. All other persons are subject to the criminal laws of the jurisdiction in which they commit a crime.

Forcible Abduction as a Means of Obtaining Jurisdiction over the Person of a Defendant

Many American courts follow a century-old doctrine, holding that the manner in which jurisdiction is obtained over the person of a defendant does not impair the power to charge and try a defendant. This doctrine, known as the Ker-Frisbie rule, originated in the following cases: *

---

* It should be noted that the conduct of some of the officers or Pinkerton agent in the following cases would justify civil suits against them today by the defendants in the cases. Officers may not use unnecessary force or improperly kidnap persons to bring them into another jurisdiction.

KER v. ILLINOIS
Supreme Court of the United States (1886)
119 U.S. 436, 7 S. Ct. 225

The defendant who resided in South America, was indicted by an Illinois grand jury for larceny and embezzlement. On the request of the governor of Illinois, the president of the United States issued a warrant authorizing a Pinkerton agent to take custody of Ker from authorities in Peru. The agent did not serve the warrant or request Peruvian authorities to surrender Ker to him. Instead, he forcibly abducted Ker and placed him aboard an American ship. Ker was tried and convicted in Illinois. On appeal to the U.S. Supreme Court, it was held that Ker could be tried by the state of Illinois regardless of the methods used to obtain personal jurisdiction over him.[4]

FRISBEE v. COLLINS
Supreme Court of the United States (1952)
342 U.S. 519, 72 S. Ct. 509

A prisoner in a Michigan state prison complained in a habeas corpus petition to the federal courts that he had been kidnapped, handcuffed, and blackjacked in Chicago by Michigan law enforcement officers. He argued that his criminal conviction in Michigan violated due process and the Federal Kidnapping Act. The U.S. Supreme Court held that the Ker doctrine continued to be valid and that the Michigan courts had jurisdiction over the person of the defendant even if forcible abduction had been used. The Court held:

Due process of law is satisfied when one present in court is convicted of crime after being fairly appraised of charges against him and after a fair trial in accordance with constitutional procedural safeguards.

The U.S. Supreme Court continued to reaffirm the Ker–Frisbie rule in recent years.[5] In 1982, the case of *State v. Monje*[6] came before the Wisconsin Supreme Court. In that case, a Wisconsin police officer went into Illinois and arrested Monje, who was wanted for armed robbery in Wisconsin. The officer, however, brought Monje back into Wisconsin without complying with the Uniform Criminal Extradition Act. In affirming the Ker–Frisbie rule, it was held that: "This court has recognized that there is nothing in the constitution which prohibits a person from being tried even though the extradition process is totally ignored in removing him from an asylum state."

C. NATION-TO-NATION JURISDICTION OVER CRIMES

Nations long ago realized that the world could not afford criminal jurisdictional gaps between nations. An alarming situation would exist, for example, if a person could commit a murder in the middle of the Atlantic or Pacific Ocean and no nation would have criminal jurisdiction. Because of this, the jurisdiction of each nation was extended to follow its ships over the high seas. The English common law gave jurisdiction to English courts over crimes committed on British ships and over crimes committed by British subjects on foreign ships.

Today, statutes in both England and the United States give each country jurisdiction over crimes committed not only on ships, but also on aircraft controlled by each country. By virtue of the international convention ratified by the Tokyo Convention Act of 1967, the courts of any country in the world may try piracy (armed violence at sea committed on a surface ship or an aircraft), even though the piracy was not committed within that country's territorial waters.[7] In addition to piracy, international conventions of nations have sought the elimination of slave trading, war crimes, hijacking and sabotage of civil aircraft, genocide, and terrorism.

Because of the statutes giving many nations jurisdictions over crimes, situations could exist in which a number of nations could have concurrent jurisdiction (that is, the same crime could be tried in the courts of two or three nations).

Example: An American airline plane flies from the United States to England. While the plane is on the ground in England, one American kills another American passenger aboard the aircraft. The person committing the crime could be tried by either Great Britain or the United States (or both nations). In view of the fact that only Americans were involved and that the incident occurred on an American plane, the British would probably waive jurisdiction to the United States and the accused would be extradited for trial before a federal court in the United States.

Example: While a German ship is traveling from one American city to another on the Great Lakes, one crew member murders another crew member (neither man is American). If the ship were in American navigable waters at the time the incident occurred, the United States would have jurisdiction over the crime. One of the states may also have jurisdiction. But because Germany also has jurisdiction and Americans were not involved in the incident, jurisdiction would probably be waived to Germany.

Territorial Limitations as Affecting Criminal Jurisdiction

Each nation has established territorial limits in the oceans and the air space around it. These claims to the right of sovereignty in territorial waters range from 12 miles to 200 and even 500 miles out from shore. The following cases illustrate that such territorial limitations do not limit criminal jurisdiction:

UNITED STATES v. LEE

Supreme Court of the United States (1927)
274 U.S. 559, 47 S. Ct. 746

After the crew of a Coast Guard ship noticed that the defendant's boat alongside a foreign ship in "Rum Row," they observed 71 cases of illegal whiskey on the defendant's deck. The U.S. Supreme Court affirmed the seizure and the conviction of the defendant even though the seizure occurred beyond American territorial waters.

UNITED STATES v. LAYTON

U.S. District Court, Northern California (1981)
509 F.Supp. 212

Just before the killings and suicides at the People's Temple in Guyana, Congressman Leo Ryan was killed and other persons were wounded in a savage attack on them. The defendant, Larry Layton, was charged in the United States with the following crimes that occurred in South America: (a) conspiracy to murder a U.S. Congressman, (b) aiding and abetting his murder, (c) conspiracy to murder an internationally protected person, (d) aiding and abetting in this murder (these charges are under 18 U.S.C. Sec. 351 and Sec. 1117). The Court held that an "attack upon a member of Congress, wherever it occurs, equally threatens the free and proper functioning of government." The Court further stated:

Courts have generally inferred such jurisdiction for two types of statutes: (1) statutes which represent an effort by the government to protect itself against obstructions and frauds; and (2) statutes where the vulnerability of the United States outside its own territory to the occurrence of the prohibited conduct is sufficient because of the nature of the offense to infer reasonably that Congress meant to reach those extraterritorial offenses.

UNITED STATES v. RICARDO

United States Court of Appeals, Fifth Circuit (1980)
619 F.2d 1124

The defendants were convicted of conspiracy to import marijuana into the United States. The entire conspiracy took place abroad, with no overt acts in the United States.

BROWN v. UNITED STATES

United States Court of Appeals, Fourth Circuit (1976)
549 F.2d 954

The defendant was convicted of conspiracy to import heroin into the United States by the U.S. mails from West Germany.

UNITED STATES v. CONROY

United States Court of Appeals, Fifth Circuit (1979)
589 F.2d 1258, 24 CrL 2509

The Court held that, given probable cause or as a matter of necessity, the Coast Guard has authority to search an American vessel in waters governed by another country. The defendant in this case ran with 7,000 pounds of marijuana into Haitian waters when he was approached by a Coast Guard vessel. After receiving permission from the Haitian government, the Coast Guard searched the defendant's vessel.

In 1980, the U.S. Congress passed a statute (21 U.S.C. 955a) giving the federal government criminal jurisdiction over all stateless vessels on the high seas that are engaged in the distribution of controlled substances (illegal drugs). A stateless vessel would be a ship or boat not flying any national flag or flying the flags of two or more countries. If a vessel registered with a foreign country should engage in narcotic activity on the high seas, the United States has, in the past, requested permission of that country to board the vessel. Through these means, all ships, registered or not registered, can be boarded if there is probable cause to believe that the ship is involved in narcotic activity. The new federal statute was tested and affirmed in the 1982 case of *United States v. Marino-Garcia*.[8]

American courts have approached jurisdictional problems in much the same way as have British courts over the years. In 1879, the British Criminal Code Commissioners asked and answered the following question: "A shot is fired in one place which wounds a man in another place, who dies in a third place. In which of these places is the crime committed?" In 1879, the answer was "in each of the three places." In 1970, the British Law Commission's Working Paper No. 29 asked the same question and gave the same answer.

Many states have, by statute, extended criminal liability beyond their territorial jurisdiction so as to permit them to exercise criminal jurisdiction in situations illustrated by the following:

Example: X, who lives in Paris and has never been in the United States, wants Y, who lives in a city in your state, killed. X contacts a hired killer who lives in Chicago and contracts with him to have Y killed for $5,000. The hired gun goes to the city in which Y lives and kills him. The killer is apprehended and tells everything. Can a prosecuting officer in your state issue a criminal complaint and warrant against X and have him extradited to the United States to face the murder charge?

The Law of Nations

After the Nazi defeat in 1945, the Allied Nations tried many of the surviving military and civilian Nazi leaders before an international tribunal at Nuremberg, Germany. Some of the defendants were executed; others received jail sentences. Defense lawyers at the war crimes trials argued that the Nuremberg trials had no legal basis in international law and that the defendants were being charged under penal laws created after the act (ex post facto). The following are excerpts from the closing argument of Justice Robert H. Jackson, who represented the United States before the tribunal:

> No half-century ever witnessed slaughter on such a scale, such cruelties and inhumanities, such wholesale deportations of people into slavery, such annihilations of minorities. The terror of Torquemada pales before the Nazi inquisition. . . . Goaded by these facts, we have moved to redress the blight on the record of our era . . . . we should not overlook the unique and emergent character of this body as an International Military Tribunal. It is no part of the constitutional mechanism of internal justice of any of the Signatory nations. Germany has unconditionally surrendered, but no peace treaty has been signed or agreed upon. The Allies are still technically in a state of war with Germany, although the enemy's political and military institutions have collapsed. As a Military Tribunal, it is a continuation of the war effort of the Allied Nations. As an International Tribunal, it is not bound by the procedural and substantive refinements of our respective judicial or constitutional systems, nor will its rulings introduce precedents into any country's internal civil system of justice. As an International Military Tribunal, it rises above the provincial and transient and seeks guidance not only from International Law but also from the basic principles of jurisprudence which are assumptions of civilization and which long have found embodiment in the codes of all nations.

D. CRIMINAL JURISDICTION OF THE FEDERAL GOVERNMENT

Federal crimes fall into the following three classes:

1. Crimes affecting interstate commerce, over which the U.S. Constitution gives Congress exclusive power. The Mann Act, the Dyer Act, the Lindberg Act, and the Fugitive Felon Act are examples of this class of federal crimes.

2. Crimes committed in places beyond the jurisdiction of any state. These include crimes committed in the District of Columbia and crimes

committed overseas by the military or on American-controlled ships or aircraft.

3. Crimes that interfere with the activities of the federal government.[9] As the scope of the activities of the federal government is broad, this category of federal crimes is broad. It includes fraud by use of the U.S. mails, robbery of federally insured banks or savings and loan associations, violation of the federal income tax laws, and attempts to overthrow the U.S. government.

Federal jurisdiction over homicide is exercised in the following situations: [10]

• within the special maritime and territorial jurisdiction

• when death results from sabotage, or certain cases of reckless or negligent destruction of "federal" transportation facilities

• when the victim is the president of the United States, the vice-president, or successors to the office [11]

• when the victim is engaged in performing federal functions

• when the victim was killed "on account of the performance of his official duties"

• when death occurs in connection with a federally punishable bank robbery

• when the homicide occurred during an offense defined by the Civil Rights Act of 1968 (18 U.S.C.A. Sec. 245)

The proposed new Federal Criminal Code would extend federal jurisdiction to the following additional situations:

• when the death occurs in connection with any federally punishable robbery or burglary, for example, of a post office or under the Antiracketeering Act (18 U.S.C.A. Sec. 241)

• when death occurs in connection with any federally punishable obstruction of justice, such as intimidating witnesses and jurors (18 U.S.C.A. Sec. 1503 and Sec. 1505)

• when death occurs in connection with federally punishable conspiracies against civil rights (18 U.S.C.A. Sec. 241)

• when the death occurs in connection with any other federal offense

Federal Enclaves and the Assimilative Crimes Act of 1948

Federal enclaves are federally owned and controlled lands that can be found in all states. Military installations, such a army posts, naval yards, air force bases, coast guard stations, and marine bases, are enclaves if they are within the borders of states. National parks and forest lands and federal buildings, such as post offices, federal court buildings, and federal office buildings, are also enclaves. The federal government owns almost one-fourth of the land in the conti-

---

Areas of Federal and State Jurisdiction

The federal government has jurisdiction within the following three limited areas:
1. for the protection of interstate commerce
2. for the protection of the activities and interests of the federal government
3. for the protection of the rights of citizenship

In maintaining public order and public safety, states have broad jurisdiction within their police powers to:
1. provide for the safety of their people
2. provide for the health of their people
3. protect the morals of their people
4. "protect the well-being and tranquility of a community" by prohibiting "acts or things reasonably thought to bring evil or harm." (U.S. Supreme Court in *Kovacs v. Cooper*, 336 U.S. 77, 69 S. Ct. 448 [1949])

nental United States and has exclusive jurisdiction over much of this land.

Before 1948, some of the enclaves had a degree of autonomy, which created some problems throughout the United States. These problems had to do with the sale of liquor and the fact that gambling was permitted on many military bases. For example, slot machines were (and still are) illegal in Illinois but were available for use at the Great Lakes Naval Training Station and at Fort Sheridan army base, located in the Chicago area. Congress had passed criminal laws dealing with a few serious crimes committed in enclaves, but there was not a complete criminal code for the enclaves.

In 1948, Congress passed the Assimilative Crimes Act (18 U.S.C.A. Sec. 13), which incorporates, by reference, the state criminal law of the surrounding state in force at the time of the defendant's conduct. Therefore, if slot machines are illegal in the state of Illinois, they are also illegal on such federal enclaves as the Great Lakes Naval Training Station and Fort Sheridan, which are within the borders of the state of Illinois. In the case of *United States v. Sharpnack,*[12] the U.S. Supreme Court held that the Assimilative Crimes Act was constitutional. In that case, the defendant, who was a civilian, was convicted of committing sex crimes involving two boys at the Randolph Air Force Base, a federal enclave in Texas. In affirming the conviction, the Court stated:

There is no doubt that Congress may validly adopt a criminal code for each federal enclave. It certainly may do so by drafting new laws or by copying laws defining the criminal offenses in force throughout the State in which the enclave is situated. As a practical matter, it has to proceed largely on a wholesale basis. Its reason for adopting local laws is not so much because Congress has examined them individually as it is because the laws are already in force throughout the State in which the enclave is situated. The basic legislative decision made by Congress is its decision to conform the laws in the enclave to the local laws as to all offenses not punishable by any enactment of Congress. Whether Congress sets forth the assimilated laws in full or assimilates them by reference, the result is as definite and as ascertainable as are the state laws themselves.

The proposed Federal Criminal Code before Congress provides that the code itself define all the serious crimes and limit assimilated crimes to misdemeanors. This proposed change for criminal laws applicable to federal enclaves is designed "to minimize the consequences of the wholesale purchase of . . . grossly disparate existing state laws and penalties."

Indian Tribes Within the United States

In 1832, Chief Justice John Marshall stated, in *Worcester v. State of Georgia:* "The Indian nations had always been considered as distinct, independent, political communities, retaining their original natural rights, as the undisputed possessors of the soil, from time immemorial."[13]

In 1886, the U.S. Supreme Court stated, in *United States v. Kagama:*

They [the Indian tribes] were, and always have been regarded as having a semi-independent position when they preserved their tribal relations; not as states, not as nations, not as possessed of the full attributes of sovereignty, but as a separate people, with the power of regulating their internal and social relations, and thus far not brought under the laws of the Union or of the state within whose limits they reside. . . . These Indian tribes are the wards of the nation. . . . They owe no allegiance to the states, and receive from them no protection.[14]

In 1916, the Supreme Court stated, in *United States v. Quiver:*

At an early period it became the settled policy of Congress to permit the personal and domestic relations of the Indians with each other to be regulated and offenses by one Indian against the person or property of another Indian to be dealt with, according to their tribal customs and laws.[15]

In 1977, the Supreme Court stated, in *United States v. Antelope,* that:

In the present case we are dealing not with matters of tribal self-regulation, but with federal regulation of criminal conduct within Indian country implicating Indian interests. . . . Federal regulation of Indian affairs is not based upon impermissible classifications. Rather, such regulation is rooted in the unique status of Indians as "a separate people" with their own political institutions. Federal regulation of Indian tribes, therefore, is governance of *once-sovereign politi-*

cal communities; it is not to be viewed as legislation of a " 'racial' group consisting of 'Indians.' "   *Morton v. Mancari,* 417 U.S., at 553 n. 24.[16]

Criminal Jurisdiction of Indian Tribal Courts

In 1975 and again in 1977, the U.S. Supreme Court held that:

> Indian tribes are unique aggregations possessing attributes of sovereignty over both their members and their territory, *Worcester v. Georgia,* 6 Pet. 515, 557 (1832); they are "a separate people" possessing the power of regulating their internal and social relations. *United States v. Mazurie,* 419 U.S. 544, 557 (1975).[17]

Indians living on reservations and within "Indian country" are subject to the jurisdictions of Indian tribal courts.   The authority of Indian tribal courts to impose criminal penalties is limited by federal law (25 U.S.C. Sec. 1302[7]) to the petty misdemeanor ceilings of six months' imprisonment and a $500 fine.

Under the federal Major Crimes Act, U.S. federal courts have criminal jurisdiction for 14 serious crimes committed by Indians on Indian reservations and within "Indian country." [18]   In the 1973 case of *Keeble v. United States,*[19] the Supreme Court noted that the federal government has characterized the Major Crimes Act as "a carefully limited intrusion of federal power into the otherwise exclusive jurisdiction of the Indian tribes to punish Indians for crimes committed on Indian land."

Indians who leave "Indian country" and commit crimes in a state or another place are subject to the criminal jurisdiction of the state or place in which the crime was committed.   However, the state has jurisdiction over offenses committed on Indian reservations or within "Indian country" by persons who are non-Indian.[20]

E. THE MILITARY MARTIAL, AND WAR POWER JURISDICTION OF THE FEDERAL GOVERNMENT

Article I, Section 8 of the U.S. Constitution provides (in part) that:

> The Congress shall have power: . . . To define and punish Piracies and Felonies committed on the high Seas, and Offenses against the Law of Nations; To declare War . . . and make Rules concerning Captures on Land and Water; To raise and support Armies . . . ; To provide and maintain a Navy; To make Rules for the Government and Regulation of the land and naval Forces; To provide for calling forth the Militia to execute the Laws of the Union, suppress Insurrections and repel Invasions; . . . To make all Laws which shall be necessary and proper for carrying into Execution the foregoing Powers, and all other Powers vested by this Constitution in the Government of the United States, or in any Department or Officer thereof.

Article II of the U.S. Constitution provides in part that:

> Section 1. The executive Power shall be vested in a President of the United States of America. . . .
>
> Section 2. The President shall be Commander in Chief of the Army and Navy of the United States, and of the Militia of the several States, when called into the actual Service of the United States.

Jurisdiction of Military Courts

When a person enters the American military service, he or she becomes subject to the court-martial process for violations of the Uniform Code of Military Justice.[21] Over the years, hundreds of thousands of military personnel have been tried for many offenses, ranging from "military" crimes, such as desertion, unauthorized absences, willful disobedience of orders, and drunkenness on duty, to "civilian" crimes, such as rape, murder, and drug violations, that took place on leave. The question of the extent of the jurisdiction of the military courts came before the U.S. Supreme Court in the following case in 1969:

O'CALLAHAN v. PARKER

Supreme Court of the United States (1969)
395 U.S. 258, 89 S. Ct. 1683

In 1956, the defendant was a sergeant in the U.S. Army stationed near Honolulu. While on an evening pass and in civilian clothes, he had a few beers at a bar in Honolulu. He broke into the room of a young girl and assaulted and attempted to rape her. While fleeing from her room onto Waikiki Beach, he was apprehended by a hotel security officer who turned him over to the Honolulu city police. When the police determined that he was a member of the armed forces, they turned him over to the military police. He was charged with and convicted of, under the Uniform Code of Military Justice, attempted rape, housebreaking, and assault with intent to rape. The defendant was sentenced to 10 years imprisonment at hard labor and forfeiture of all pay and allowances, and was dishonorably discharged. While being confined at the penitentiary at Lewisburg, Pennsylvania, O'Callahan filed a petition for a writ of habeas corpus, alleging, among other things, that the military court-martial was without jurisdiction to try him for nonmilitary offenses committed while off-post and while on an evening pass. In holding that service personnel could not be tried by court-martial for offenses that were not service-connected, and that they were entitled to trial by civilian courts, the Court stated:

"In the present case petitioner was properly absent from his military base when he committed the crimes with which he is charged. There was no connection—not even the remotest one—between his military duties and the crimes in question. The crimes were not committed on a military post or enclave; nor was the person whom he attacked performing any duties relating to the military.

* * *

Civil courts were open. The offenses were committed within our territorial limits, not in the occupied zone of a foreign country. The offenses did not involve any question of the flouting of military authority, the security of a military post, or the integrity of military property.

We have accordingly decided that since petitioner's crimes were not service connected, he could not be tried by court-martial but rather was entitled to trial by the civilian courts.

Reversed.

When Is an Offense "Service Connected"?

In the 1975 case of *Schlesinger v. Councilman*,[22] Chief Justice Warren Burger pointed out that:

In *Relford v. United States Disciplinary Commandant*,[23] 401 U.S. 355, 365 (1971), this Court identified 12 factors that *O'Callahan v. Parker, supra,* held should be weighed in determining whether an offense is service connected:

"1. The serviceman's proper absence from the base.

"2. The crime's commission away from the base.

"3. Its commission at a place not under military control.

"4. Its commission within our territorial limits and not in an occupied zone of a foreign country.

"5. Its commission in peacetime and its being unrelated to authority stemming from the war power.

"6. The absence of any connection between the defendant's military duties and the crime.

"7. The victim's not being engaged in the performance of any duty relating to the military.

"8. The presence and availability of a civilian court in which the case can be prosecuted.

"9. The absence of any flouting of military authority.

"10. The absence of any threat to a military post.

"11. The absence of any violation of military property.

"12. The offense's being among those traditionally prosecuted in civilian courts." 401 U.S., *supra*, at 365.

In the 1983 case of *United States v. Lockwood*,[24] Lockwood was found to have stolen a wallet from another airman on the Sheppard Air Force Base. With identification from the stolen wallet, he then fraudulently obtained a loan in a city near the base. Lockwood was convicted by a military court of forgery and larceny. The U.S. Court of Military Appeals affirmed the convictions, holding both offenses to be service-connected, stating:

> The "practical reasons of dispatch" which have led to the military practice of joining all known offenses in a single trial also help support the conclusion that where related on-base and off-base offenses are involved, there is a military interest in having all the offenses tried by court-martial, so that they can be disposed of together without delay. The existence of this interest, in turn, helps provide a basis for finding service connection for the off-base offenses. . . .

> Additional reasons exist for finding service connection as to the forgery and larceny which took place off-base. . . . In the case at bar, appellant initiated his off-base offenses by a larceny commited at Sheppard Air Force Base. The Armed Services have an interest in punishing a crime which is initiated within a military enclave, even if the offense is consummated off-post.

> Since the Armed Services retain a property interest in a military identification card, appellant's use of Sage's card really involved the use of military property to commit a crime. Thus, his action could be considered a "flouting of military authority." Relford v. U.S., 401 U.S. at 365. Moreover, the Armed Services must protect reliance on the military identification card by those who deal with persons purporting to be members of the Armed Services.

Crimes Committed by American Military Service Persons While Stationed in Foreign Countries

American military personnel are stationed in many countries throughout the world. If a service person commits a crime while off-base, off-duty, and in a foreign country, he (or she) is subject to the jurisdiction of the laws of that country. Under the status of forces agreement that many countries have with the United States, the military person could be tried by the courts in that foreign country.[25] However, in many instances the prosecutor in the foreign country will waive jurisdiction and turn the offender over to the American military authorities for trial before a military court.

Examples of crimes that American service personnel were charged with are 1983, *Plaster v. United States*,[26] murder of a West German taxidriver and desertion; 1974, *United States v. Newvine*,[27] murder of a Mexican prostitute; 1971, *Bell v. Clark*,[28] rape of a German woman.

Because foreign countries want a continued American military presence, they will often waive criminal jurisdiction. Military courts would then be the only courts with jurisdiction. Foreign prosecutors are aware that military punishment would probably be more severe than civilian punishment.

Trial of American Citizens by Foreign Courts

Americans who commit crimes in foreign countries are subject to prosecution before foreign courts, whether they are military personnel or tourists. American civilians have been sentenced to serve long prison terms in Turkey, Mexico, and other countries for narcotics violations, a grim reminder that sentences in some countries are more severe than they are in the United States.

When an American citizen commits a crime in a foreign country, generally only the foreign country would have jurisdiction to try the crime.

The exception to this would be in cases in which the crime was a violation of the U.S. criminal code (for example, the killing of Congressman Leo Ryan in Guyana, South America).

Martial Law and the Use of Military Forces in the Continental United States

In attempting to define martial law in 1946, the U.S. Supreme Court made the following statements in the case of *Duncan v. Kahanamoku:*

> The term "martial law" carries no precise meaning. The Constitution does not refer to "martial law" at all and no Act of Congress has defined the term. It has been employed in various ways by different people and at different times. By some it has been identified as "military law" limited to members of, and those connected with, the armed forces. Others have said that the term does not imply a system of established rules but denotes simply some kind of day to day expression of a General's will dictated by what he considers the imperious necessity of the moment. . . . In 1857 the confusion as to the meaning of the phrase was so great that the Attorney General in an official opinion had this to say about it: "The Common Law authorities and commentators afford no clue to what martial law, as understood in England, really is. . . . In this Country it is still worse." . . . What was true in 1857 remains true today.[29]

Military forces have been used many times in the history of our country to maintain public order and to enforce laws. In 1787, the year in which the Constitution was formulated, the governor of the Massachusetts colony used the militia to cope with Shay's Rebellion. Federal troops were sent by President Washington into Pennsylvania to suppress the Whiskey Rebellion of 1794. Federal troops were used by President Lincoln to prevent the withdrawal of the southern states from the Union and to maintain public order. Federal troops remained in the South until the 1880s. During some of this time, mar-

tial law was in effect in the southern states in which federal troops remained.

Federal troops were used by President Eisenhower to secure compliance with Supreme Court school desegregation orders in Arkansas in 1957, and by President Kennedy in Mississippi in 1962 and in Alabama in 1963. In the 29-month period between January 1968 and the end of May 1970, National Guard troops were called up 324 times to cope with urban riots and disorders and unrest on college campuses.[30] In all the incidents in the 1950s, 1960s, and 1970s, troops and National Guard units provided additional manpower to civilian law enforcement agencies that had the primary responsibility for preserving public order. Persons arrested or taken into custody were brought before federal and state courts, where they were provided all their constitutional rights.

In any street confrontation, law enforcement officers at the scene represent the authority of the state at that time and place. Should they need assistance, the resources of their department are available to them. If their department cannot handle the problem, other departments may be called on for assistance or manpower from the state may be requested. If the state does not have the resources to handle the situation, assistance may be requested from the federal government. The federal government is obligated under Article IV, Section 4 of the U.S. Constitution to commit such force as may be necessary to restore public order.[31]

May Civilians Be Tried by Military Courts?

The question of whether civilians may be tried by military courts has come before the U.S. Supreme Court in the following cases:

DUNCAN v. KAHANAMOKU
Supreme Court of the United

After the attack on Pearl Harbor, in 1941, martial law was declared for the Territory of Hawaii by the territorial governor. Civil and criminal courts were forbidden to try cases and the military authorities took over the

States (1946)
327 U.S. 304, 66 S. Ct. 606

government of Hawaii. The Supreme Court reviewed two of the cases tried by military courts.

Petitioner in case No. 15 was a stockbroker convicted of embezzling stock eight months after Pearl Harbor. The offense was committed against another civilian. The military tribunal sentenced him to five years' imprisonment (later reduced to four).

Duncan (case No. 14) was a civilian shipfitter employed in the navy yard. He engaged in a brawl with two armed marine sentries at the yard and was sentenced to six months' imprisonment

In reversing the convictions and ruling that "military tribunals have no such standing," the Court quoted the case of *Dow v. Johnson,*[32] stating:

The military should always be kept in subjection to the laws of the country to which it belongs, and that he is no friend of the Republic who advocates the contrary. The established principle of every free people is, that the law shall alone govern; and to it the military must always yield.

KINSELLA v. UNITED STATES

Supreme Court of the United States (1960)
861 U.S. 234, 80 S. Ct. 297

Mrs. Dial was the wife of a soldier assigned to a tank battalion in Germany. The Dials and their three children lived in government housing quarters on a military base in Germany. Because of the death of one of their children, both of the Dials were charged with and convicted of involuntary manslaughter before a military court and both were sentenced to prison. Mrs. Dial challenged the jurisdiction of the court-martial to try her. The Court stated:

We therefore hold that Mrs. Dial is protected by the specific provisions of Article III and the Fifth and Sixth Amendments and that her prosecution and conviction by court-martial are not constitutionally permissible.

McELROY v. UNITED STATES EX REL. GUAGLIARDO

Supreme Court of the United States (1960)
361 U.S. 281, 80 S. Ct. 305

The Court, in applying the principles of *Kinsella*, held unconstitutional those provisions of the Uniform Code of Military Justice that subjected "persons . . . employed by . . . the armed forces outside the United States" to court-martial jurisdiction.

EX PARTE QUIRIN

Supreme Court of the United States (1942)
317 U.S. 1, 63 S. Ct. 1

The defendants were all Nazi spies who had received training at a sabotage school in Germany and then landed on beaches in Long Island and in Florida at night during World War II. While landing from submarines, they wore German marine infantry uniforms, which they buried before proceeding in civilian clothes to cities in the United States. The defendants were convicted in trials before military courts. The Supreme Court affirmed the convictions and the jurisdictions of the courts, stating:

By universal agreement and practice, the law of war draws a distinction between the armed forces and the peaceful populations of belligerent nations and also between those who are lawful and unlawful combatants. Lawful combatants are subject to capture and detention as prisoners of war by opposing military forces.   Unlawful combatants are likewise subject to capture and detention, but in addition they are subject to trial and punishment by military tribunals for acts which render their belligerency unlawful.   The spy who secretly and without uniform passes the military lines of a belligerent in time of war, seeking to gather military information and communicate it to the enemy, or an enemy combatant who without uniform comes secretly through the lines for the purpose of waging war by destruction of life or property, are familiar examples of belligerents who are generally deemed not to be entitled to the status of prisoners of war, but to be offenders against the law of war subject to trial and punishment by military tribunals . . .

The rule, then is that civilians may not be tried by military courts in the United States unless they are spies as described by the Supreme Court in *Ex Parte Quirin*.   In 1957, a famous Russian spy, Colonel Abel, was captured in New York City.   As it was not in time of war, Colonel Abel was tried before a federal district court in New York.[33]

Jurisdiction Arising from the General War Powers

Justice Oliver Wendell Holmes has been quoted as stating that when courts use the power of judicial review, they are not determining what the wisest and most prudent policy of government should have been or should be.   The Con-

---

General Jurisdiction Requirements

In order to charge a person with a crime, the state or federal government must:
- charge under a statute or ordinance that is constitutional on its face,
- charge in the county or place in which the crime is alleged to have occurred, and
- produce the person to be charged before the court that will try him or her.

Indians who commit crimes while *not* within their reservation or "Indian country" are subject to the jurisdiction of the state or government, just as non-Indians are.   Indians who commit crimes while on their reservation or within "Indian country" can be tried (a) by their tribal court and punished by not more than six months' imprisonment and/or $500 fine (25 U.S.C. Sec. 1302[7]), or (b) before a U.S. federal court for the 14 serious crimes under the Federal Major Crimes Act (18 U.S.C. Sec. 1153 and 3242).

Non-Indians charged with committing crimes against other non-Indians in "Indian country" are subject to prosecution under state law.   *United States v. McBratney,* 104 U.S. 621 (1881); *United States v. Antelope,* 430 U.S. 641, 97 S. Ct. 1395 (1977), footnote # 2.

U.S. military personnel may be tried by a military court if:
- the offense is a military crime or can be shown to be "service-connected," or
- the offense was committed on a military reservation, post, or property, or
- the offense was committed beyond the territorial limits of the United States and of American courts.

Persons who commit crimes on federal enclaves can be tried before:
- a federal court, using the criminal code of the surrounding state under the Assimilative Crimes Act (18 U.S.C. Sec. 13)
- a military court, if the person was a member of the U.S. armed services and the enclave was a military post or military reservation.

stitution gives the power to determine public policy to the legislative and executive branches of government. In judicial review, the courts determine only whether the act or policy is within the lawful scope of authority granted by the Constitution of the United States. Courts cannot be Monday-morning strategists, determining what the quarterback should have done in Saturday's game. Their function in judicial review is to determine only whether or not the "quarterback" acted within the rules.

In time of war or national emergency, the government must use its "war powers" to respond to the emergency. Former Chief Justice Charles E. Hughes wrote that the war power of the government is "the power to wage war successfully." Justice Felix Frankfurter wrote that "the validity of action under the war power must be judged wholly in the context of war. That action is not to be stigmatized as lawless because like action in times of peace would be lawless." [34] The question of the extent of the power of government to act in time of war was presented before the U.S. Supreme Court while World War II was still being fought.

KOREMATSU v. UNITED STATES

Supreme Court of the United States (1944)
323 U.S. 214, 65 S. Ct. 193

After the Japanese attack on Pearl Harbor in 1941, the president of the United States imposed a curfew and ordered all persons of Japanese ancestry in certain West Coast military areas to remain in their residences from 8 P.M. to 6 A.M. This action was sustained by the Supreme Court in the case of *Hirabayashi v. United States.* [35] In March of 1942, Congress enacted legislation authorizing the Executive Department to exclude persons of Japanese ancestry from military areas or zones designated by the Executive Department. Violation of such exclusionary order was made punishable by imprisonment for not more than one year. The defendant was convicted for violating the exclusion order. He was of Japanese ancestry and challenged the constitutionality of the law and the action taken. In sustaining the constitutionality of the law and the action of the Executive Department, the Court stated:

Like curfew, exclusion of those of Japanese origin was deemed necessary because of the presence of an unascertained number of disloyal members of the group, most of whom we have no doubt, were loyal to this country. It was because we could not reject the finding of the military authorities that it was impossible to bring about an immediate segregation of the disloyal from the loyal that we sustained the validity of the curfew order as applying to the whole group. In the instant case, temporary exclusion of the entire group was rested by the military on the same ground. . . . Approximately five thousand American citizens of Japanese ancestry refused to swear unqualified allegiance to the United States and to renounce allegiance to the Japanese Emperor, and several thousand evacuees requested repatriation to Japan.

"We uphold the exclusion order as of the time it was made and when the petitioner violated it. . . . In doing so, we are not unmindful of the hardships imposed by it upon a large group of American citizens. . . . But hardships are part of war, and war is an aggregation of hardships. All citizens alike, both in and out of uniform, feel the impact of war in greater or lesser measure. Citizenship has its responsibilities as well as its privileges, and in time of war the burden is always heavier.

Jurisdiction of Law Enforcement Officers

The jurisdiction of law enforcement officers:

- is limited to their municipality or county (in the case of deputy sheriffs) unless determined to be otherwise by state statute.

- may extend into other states, counties, or municipalities if authorized by hot (or fresh) pursuit statutes or common law authority. If an arrest is made in another state, the officer must comply with the Uniform Criminal Extradition Act and take the suspect before a judge in that state to commence extradition proceedings.

- may be extended to other counties or municipalities in their state under the authority of a state arrest or search warrant.

- may be supplemented by the statutory or common law authority to make a "citizen's arrest" in their state.

SUPPLEMENTARY READING FOR CHAPTER 9

Federal Crimes and Jurisdiction
by William J. Mulligan *

INTRODUCTION

The federal government, unlike the states, exercises no general police powers to regulate its citizenry. There is no federal criminal common law. Federal crimes are of statutory origin. They have not been passed down to us from the Magna Carta as interpreted by experience and reason.

Although our forefathers could have provided in the Constitution that the Congress had a general police power exclusive, superior or coextensive with that of the states, they did not do so. Instead they limited the powers of Congress and retained to the states and people powers not otherwise conferred on the federal government. Such restrictive grant of power to the federal government was the result of philosophical and political concern of the drafters against a strong centralized government.

The philosophic and political background was explained by the Supreme Court in an early case upholding the validity of the White Slave Act.[1] In Hoke v. United States, 227 U.S. 308, 322 (1913) the Court stated: "Our dual form of government has its perplexities, State and Nation having different spheres of jurisdiction, . . . but it must be kept in mind that we are one people; and the powers reserved to the States and those conferred on the Nation are adapted to be exercised, whether independently or concurrently, to promote the general welfare, material, and moral." In regulating or prohibiting commerce among the states, Congress is equally free to support state legislative policy or to devise a policy of its own. The Supreme Court stated that Congress "may exercise this authority in aid of the policy of the State, if it sees fit to do so. It is equally clear that the policy of Congress acting independently of the States may induce legislation without reference to the particular policy or law of any given State. Acting within the authority conferred by the Constitution it is for Congress to determine what legislation will attain its purposes. The control of Congress over interstate commerce is not to be limited by the State laws."[2]

The limited scope of federal criminal law may amaze the present day observer who even casually examines and compares the federal and state criminal offenses. Quantitatively there exist more federal crimes than state offenses. Yet federal jurisdictional requirements limit areas of federal law enforcement.

---

* William J. Mulligan is a former U.S. Attorney for the Eastern District of Wisconsin. Mr. Mulligan was assisted in the preparation of this article by Attorney David B. Bukey, also of the U.S. Attorney's office for the Eastern District of Wisconsin. The views expressed in this article do not necessarily reflect those of the U.S. Department of Justice.

Federal investigative and prosecutorial forces are restricted from entry into a matter of solely state concern. They may not enter into a matter unless a federal jurisdictional basis is established.

JURISDICTIONAL BASIS

Within the limited areas of federal jurisdiction, there are three primary bases of jurisdiction. They basically evolve from the nature and character of our federal system of government, i.e., a dual form of government with a national centralized government and its component states. Each of these primary bases is related to the nature and character of that government.

1. Protection of Federal Interest. The centralized national government has an inherent interest in protecting itself, its operations and interests. Implicit in this basis is the government's right to protect its officials, personnel, agencies, property or interests. Thus, the federal government may make criminal an assault upon or injury to the President, members of Congress, Judges, U.S. Attorneys and their assistants, and other federal agents.[3] It may make criminal the counterfeiting or forging of its currency, obligations and securities,[4] theft of its property,[5] theft from its mails,[6] fraud against the government or its agencies,[7] and fraud against its revenues.[8] The government can also uphold the integrity of its function and operations by prohibiting bribery of its officials,[9] conflicts of interest,[10] obstruction and interference with its judicial operations,[11] perjury in its courts or before a grand jury.[12] Similarly the government can prevent its services from being perverted to illicit ends, i.e., the use of the mails to defraud,[13] the use of the mails to extort,[14] the use of the mails to promote, manage, establish or carry on an illegal enterprise involving gambling, prostitution or narcotics.[15] Not only are the government's direct interests safeguarded, but the government's indirect interest in federally insured banks and savings and loan associations are protected. These include preventing the making of false statements to federal agencies or statements designed to defraud or mislead federal agencies.[16] The government's interests include the preservation of its navigable waters and the air in our environment.[17]

The federal government's interest in protecting its property has given rise to the area of assimilative crimes, i.e., the incorporation of state criminal laws in such areas as federal Indian and military reservations, federal enclaves and federal buildings.[18]

2. Protection of Commerce. The Founding Fathers initially held a rather limited view of protecting the federal government's interest in foreign and interstate commerce. Through the years the commerce clause has been liberally construed and expanded to include any effect upon interstate commerce.[19] This has given the federal government much greater power of a general police nature. It has become the basis for statutes prohibiting interstate transportation of stolen motor vehicles,[20] controlled substances,[21] gun control,[22] theft from interstate shipment[23] unlawful flight of a defendant, witness or prisoner to avoid prosecution, testimony or confinement,[24] hijacking of aircraft,[25] interstate transportation of pornography,[26] and extortion.[27]

3. Protection of Citizenship Rights. The Thirteenth, Fourteenth and Fifteenth Amendments to the United States Constitution adopted in 1866 serve as the basis for a series of federal criminal statutes prohibiting deprivation of rights of persons. Thus, when two or more persons combine to deprive any person of his or her rights, there is a violation of the federal criminal code.[28] When any person, acting under color of state law, such as a police officer, denies a person of his rights, it is a felony.[29] The latter area includes such practices as police brutality. It is also unlawful for anyone to move in interstate or foreign commerce to avoid prosecution, custody, testimony or confinement in connection with the damaging or destroying of any building, dwelling, synagogue, church, religious center or educational institution, public or private.[30]

DUAL PROSECUTION AND PROSECUTIVE DISCRETION

An examination of the areas of federal jurisdiction quickly demonstrates great overlapping with state criminal offenses. The robbery of a bank (whose deposits are insured by the Federal Deposit Insurance Corporation) is both a robbery punishable under state criminal laws and a federal crime punishable under 18 U.S.C.A. § 2113. Assuming the perpetrator is apprehended, should he be prosecuted by both state and federal authorities? Should the resources of both the state and federal criminal justice system be called into play? Should both the state and federal systems take the time and effort to process the case? Should both the state and federal systems expend the funds necessary to pay witness fees, jury fees and defense attorney fees? Generally, these questions are answered in the negative. In this era of crowded court calendars and limited budgets, such dual prosecutions would be improvident.

What then should determine whether the culprit is prosecuted in the state or federal system? Should it be simply the free enterprise system, i.e., that agency who has apprehended the villain?

In the case of a drug violation what are the determinative factors of state and federal prosecution? What type of drug is involved? What is the amount? What differences of proof are required by the different jurisdictions (e.g., which is most likely to uphold the search)? What is the past record of the defendant? What is the level of dealing—street level? Wholesaler? In which system is the defendant more likely to get an appropriate sentence?

These are some of the factors that must be weighed by the arresting officers and the prosecuting authorities in deciding whether to seek state or federal prosecution.

Although it has been held that prosecution by both state and federal authorities for offenses arising out of the same incident does not constitute double jeopardy,[31] there are some statutes which prohibit dual prosecution. For example, in the case of a theft or embezzlement from an interstate shipment of goods or chattels, Section 659 of Title 18, United States Code provides that a "judgment of conviction or acquittal on the merits under the laws of any state shall be a bar

to any prosecution under this section for the same act or acts."

AUTHORITY OF STATE OFFICER TO ARREST FOR FEDERAL OFFENSE

In the typical situation where a state officer makes an arrest and federal prosecution follows, there is no problem because the state officer originally acted to enforce state law. Thus, he arrests a person for the robbery of a state bank whose deposits are insured by the Federal Deposit Insurance Corporation. This single occurrence of bank robbery constitutes both a state and federal crime. Here there is no question of the state officer's arrest power. The problem arises when there is an arrest by a state officer for a federal offense when there is no state offense.

A state officer possesses the authority to arrest for a federal crime under the command of a warrant. The authority is found in 18 U.S.C.A. § 3041 which provides in pertinent part:

> For any offense against the United States, the offender may, by any justice or judge of the United States, or by any United States Magistrate, or by any Chancellor, judge of a supreme or superior court, Chief or first judge of common pleas, mayor of a city, justice of the peace, or other magistrate, of any state where the offender may be found, and at the expense of the United States, be arrested and imprisoned or released as provided in Chapter 207 of this title, as the case may be, for trial before such court of the United States as by law has cognizance of the offense.

This statute has been construed as permitting local law enforcement officers to execute a warrant of arrest for a federal violation.[32]

The state and federal courts have held that state officers have the power to apprehend federal offenders without a warrant. Most cases that have given detailed consideration to this issue have found as the basis the "supremacy" clause of the federal constitution.[33] It has been specifically held that state officers have the power and *duty* to enforce federal criminal law.[34] It has also been recognized that a state officer is an ordinary citizen and therefore possesses the power of arrest of a private citizen.[35]

SEARCHES BY STATE OFFICERS

At one time the United States Supreme Court ruled that evidence unreasonably obtained by state officers, who were not acting under a claim of federal authority, could be used in federal court since the Fourth Amendment was not directed to misconduct of such officials (the so-called "silver platter" doctrine).[36] The Supreme Court, however, in Wolf v. Colorado, 338 U.S. 25 (1949) held that the Fourth Amendment by virtue of the Fourteenth Amendment prohibited unreasonable searches and seizures by state officers. In Elkins v. United States, 364 U.S. 206 (1960), the silver platter doctrine was abolished, when the Court declared that evidence obtained by state officers during a search which, if conducted by federal officers, would have violated the Fourth Amendment was inadmissible in a federal criminal trial even when there was no participation by federal officers in the search and seizure.

FEDERAL–STATE COOPERATION IN OBTAINING CONFESSIONS

Although federal and state cooperation in obtaining a confession is commendable, there are several pitfalls. A confession is not voluntary if it is the product of any promise or inducement.[37] It may not be the fruit of the poisonous tree of prior illegality.[38] Nor may it be obtained during a period of unnecessary delay which occurred by the cooperative efforts of state and federal officers in bringing the defendant before a magistrate as required by Rule 5, Federal Rules of Criminal Procedure.[39]

FEDERAL OFFENSES OF PARTICULAR INTEREST

In the multitude of federal offenses, some are of particular and frequent interest to state law enforcement officers. In part this is due to the frequency of occurrence of these offenses and the similarity to state offenses. In other cases, federal statutory provisions provide valuable assistance to state officers in the enforcement of state criminal law. Some of these federal offenses will be briefly discussed.

1. *Interstate Transportation of Stolen Motor Vehicles.* Auto theft represents statistically a large area of criminal activity. Basically, this is a local matter or state offense. Frequently, however, the vehicle is taken from one state to another and sometimes thereafter is concealed. Such activity places a burden on local law enforcement in investigating the occurrence, recovering the vehicle and prosecuting of the offense when large distances become involved. Under federal law it is unlawful for any person to transport a vehicle in interstate or foreign commerce knowing the vehicle to have been stolen or thereafter to conceal such a vehicle, 18 U.S.C.A. §§ 2312, 2313. As a matter of policy, federal efforts are normally concentrated on car theft rings although efforts are frequently made to return car thieves, particulary juveniles.

2. *Interstate Transportation of Stolen Property.* Two common areas of criminal activity are prohibited by 18 U.S.C.A. § 2314. First, it is unlawful for anyone to transport in interstate or foreign commerce any goods, wares, merchandise, securities or money of the value of $5000 or more, knowing the same to have been stolen, converted or taken by fraud. Thus, stolen merchandise valued at $5000 or more may not be taken to another state for disposition. Second, it is unlawful for anyone with fraudulent intent to transport in interstate or foreign commerce any falsely made, forged, altered or counterfeit securities (which includes money orders and checks). There is no monetary requirement with respect to this latter offense.

3. *Thefts and Embezzlement from Interstate Shipments.* The purview of federal criminal law relating to thefts and embezzlements from interstate or foreign shipments of freight or property is extensive. It is set forth in 18 U.S.C.A. § 659. It protects pipeline systems, railroad cars, wagons, motortrucks, other vehicles, tank or storage facilities, stations, station houses, platforms, depots, steamboats, vessels, wharves, aircraft, air terminals, airports, baggage in the possession of common carriers. The federal protection is afforded even though the goods are at temporary rest until they reach their final destination.[40]

4. *Mail Thefts.* The theft of letters, cards, packages or matter from mail receptacles, mail boxes or carriers violates 18 U.S.C.A. § 1708. Separate provisions apply to thefts by postal employees.[41] Frequently, this type of criminal activity is coupled with the obtaining, forging and uttering of U.S. Treasury checks. The latter activities are prohibited by 18 U.S.C.A. § 495.

5. *Bank Robbery and Related Crimes.* Federal Reserve Banks, National Banks and other banks, savings and loan associations and credit unions, the deposits of which are insured by federal agencies are protected from robbery, larceny or burglary by 18 U.S.C.A. § 2113. There are some state banks and other financial institutions whose deposits are not insured and they are not afforded this federal protection.

6. *Kidnapping.* 18 U.S.C.A. § 1201 generally prohibits kidnapping or abduction of any person for reward or ransom, when wilful interstate transportation of the victim or use of the special maritime or territorial jurisdiction of the United States is involved. However, the statute expressly excludes abduction of a minor child by his or her parent, thus leaving this common byproduct of domestic disputes between estranged parents to local authorities. The federal kidnapping statute provides for imprisonment up to life.

7. *Wiretapping and Other Eavesdropping.* In 1968 legislation was enacted making it a federal offense for anyone to intercept, endeavor to intercept or procure any other person to intercept any wire or oral communication except in limited exceptions.[42] The legislation also prohibited wilfully using, endeavoring to use or procuring another to use any electronic, mechanical, or other device to interstate transportation of the victim or use of the special maritime cable or like connection used in wire communication, or when the device transmits communication by radio or interferes with the communication, or when the device has been transmitted by mail or transported in interstate commerce or is used on the premises of a business which affects interstate or foreign commerce or for obtaining information relating to such a business.[43] It is also unlawful to disclose or use the content of an illegal interception.[44] Manufacture, distribution, possession and advertising of intercepting devices is also illegal.[45]

Statutory exceptions are limited to certain court ordered wiretaps (based on federal or state enabling laws), certain activities of communications common carriers and employees of the Federal Communications Commission, foreign intelligence and national security matters.[46] An exception is also made in the case of a person acting under color of state law, e.g., a police officer, to intercept a wire or oral communication where he is a party to the communication or where one of the parties to the communication has given prior consent to the interception.[47] Persons not acting under color of law may intercept in similar circumstances unless the communication is intercepted for the purpose of committing any criminal or tortious act or for the purpose of committing any other injurious act.[48]

8. *Gambling.* Essentially gambling activities are regulated or prohibited by local and state legislation. Federal legislation, 18 U.S.C.A. § 1955, prohibits the conducting, financing, managing, supervising, directing or owning of all or a part of an illegal gambling business in violation of state or local law, involving five or more persons who conduct, finance, manage, supervise, direct or own all or part of such business which has been or remains in substantially continuous operation for a period in excess of thirty days or has a gross revenue of $2000 in any single day. 18 U.S.C.A. § 1084 prohibits the interstate or foreign transmission by wire communications facility of wagering information by one engaged in the business of betting or wagering. 18 U.S.C.A. § 1952 prohibits interstate or foreign travel or the use of the mails in aid of racketeering enterprises such as a business enterprise involving gambling. 18 U.S.C.A. § 1953 prohibits the interstate transportation of wagering paraphernalia. 18 U.S.C.A. § 1082 prohibits operation of a gambling establishment on a gambling ship.

9. *Narcotics and Other Controlled Substances.* Federal criminal law involving drugs is basically concerned with two areas of enforcement: the

importation of controlled substances into the United States from foreign countries and, secondly, the distribution or possession with intent to distribute of controlled substances within the United States. 21 U.S.C.A. § 811 establishes 6 schedules of controlled substances which may also be supplemented or modified (within appropriate limits) from time to time by the Drug Enforcement Administration, on the authority of the Attorney General. Penalties for controlled substance offenses vary with the schedule of the controlled substance involved and certain substances (such as heroin) which are classified as "narcotic drugs" involve even stiffer penalties. Since most controlled substance offenses overlap with state jurisdiction, federal officials will often defer smaller cases to local authorities so that their efforts can be directed against the higher echelons of drug traffic. 21 U.S.C.A. §§ 846 and 963 establish specific controlled substance conspiracy statutes, which do not require proof of specific overt acts and which are penalized according to the type of substance involved.

10. *Firearms.* The federal law regulating firearms is a complex series of statutes enacted by Congress, chiefly in 1968, as a compromise between those favoring stiffer gun control enforcement and those opposing any regulation in this area at all. The result is a law leaving the great bulk of firearms enforcement to state and local authorities, with regulations of dealers, restriction of certain types of dangerous weapons and regulation of sales to certain specified types of individuals remaining for the federal government. The law applies to both licensed firearms dealers and also to individuals. 18 U.S.C.A. § 922 prohibits dealers from selling firearms to out-of-state residents, to minors, to convicted felons, to persons under indictment, fugitives, or drug users and it is also illegal for such persons to purchase weapons. The law requires specific forms to be filled out by a dealer for each firearm sale, and requires certain information to be furnished by the transferee at that time. A common area of federal prosecution deals with the falsifying of such forms, for example, by convicted felons who attempt to purchase weapons. Another area of federal concern is unlicensed dealing in firearms

which also is made an offense under 18 U.S.C.A. § 922. Federal law provides for imprisonment up to 10 years for the use or carrying of a firearm to commit a felony, punishable under the laws of the United States, in addition to such other sentence as the individual may receive. Under present firearms law it is not illegal to possess or receive most types of firearms, however, certain more dangerous weapons are *per se* illegal unless specific transfer taxes are paid and unless registered with the Secretary of the Treasury.[49] These include machine guns and sawed-off shotguns, the unlawful possession of which is a major area of federal prosecution.

11. *Prostitution.* Prostitution activities are basically prohibited by state and local law. Federal concern in this area centers upon some interstate involvement. Thus, the White Slave Act, 18 U.S.C.A. § 2421 et seq. prohibits the interstate transportation of any woman or girl for purpose of prostitution, debauchery or any other immoral purpose, or with the intent and purpose to induce, entice or compel such woman or girl to become a prostitute or give herself up to debauchery or to engage in any other immoral practice. It is also unlawful to procure or obtain any ticket or tickets or any form of transportation or evidence of the right thereto, to be used by any woman or girl in interstate commerce in going to any place for the purpose of prostitution, debauchery or any other immoral purpose. 18 U.S.C.A. § 1952 prohibits travel in interstate or foreign commerce or the use of the mails in aid of prostitution offenses in violation of state or federal law.

12. *Unlawful Flight Statute.* The unlawful flight to avoid prosecution statute, 18 U.S.C.A. § 1073, or as it is sometimes referred to, the fugitive felon act, was basically enacted as a means of permitting federal investigative resources being used to locate state fugitives who may have fled from one state to another. The fugitive may either be a person seeking to avoid prosecution for a felony, a person seeking to avoid giving testimony in a felony case, or a person seeking to avoid custody or confinement on a felony matter. Although federal investigative agents may apprehend a person who has

traveled in interstate commerce for such purposes, actual prosecution must be personally approved in writing by the Attorney General of the United States or an Assistant Attorney General of the United States.

13. *Conspiracy.* The federal conspiracy statute, 18 U.S.C.A. § 371, is one of the most wide sweeping tools available to any federal prosecutor and thus is often either criticized or applauded, depending upon whether the person talking is defending or prosecuting a conspiracy charge. The law makes it illegal for 2 persons to "combine or conspire" either to commit any offense against the laws of the United States or to defraud the government of the United States. With the vast number of "laws of the United States" on the books, this obviously covers a lot of territory. A conspiracy may be defined as an agreement followed by the commission of an "overt act." Under conspiracy law the actual substantive crime need not have been completed for the conspiracy charge to be sustained and the overt act need not be an act criminal in nature. Another reason for federal prosecutors' favoring conspiracy charges is the generally more liberal evidentiary rules in that area which typically permit more evidence of a hearsay nature to be admitted at trial. For all of these reasons, federal conspiracy prosecutions are often used in selective significant areas of concern such as organized crime, white-collar crime, and political corruption.

14. *Racketeer Influenced and Corrupt Organizations.* One of the most devastating weapons available to federal law enforcement is Chapter 96 of Title 18 United States Code, 18 U.S.C.A. § 1961 et seq. 18 U.S.C.A. § 1962 makes it unlawful for any person who has received any income derived, directly or indirectly, from a pattern of racketeering activity to use or invest, directly or indirectly, any part of such income, in acquisition of any enterprise which is engaged in, or the activities of which affect, interstate or foreign commerce. Purchases of stock on the open market are excepted if the person or members of his immediate family or accomplices after such purchase do not own 1% aggregate of the securities in a clan or do not have power to elect

a director. It is also unlawful for any person through a pattern of racketeering activity to acquire or maintain, directly or indirectly, any interest in or control of any enterprise which is engaged in, or the activities of which affect, interstate or foreign commerce. It is also unlawful for anyone employed by or associated with such an enterprise to conduct or participate in the conduct of its affairs through a pattern of racketeering activity.

Racketeering activity is defined by 18 U.S.C.A. § 1961 to include state offenses involving murder, kidnapping, gambling, arson, robbery, bribery, extortion or dealing in narcotics or dangerous drugs, which are punishable by imprisonment for more than one year or federal felony offenses involving bribery, sports bribery, counterfeiting, theft from interstate shipment, embezzlement from pension and welfare funds, extortionate credit transactions, transmission of gambling information, mail fraud, wire fraud, obstruction of justice, of criminal investigation or of state or local law enforcement, relating to interference with commerce, robbery, or extortion, racketeering, interstate transportation of wagering paraphernalia, unlawful welfare fund payments, illegal gambling businesses, interstate transportation of stolen property, white slave traffic, certain labor law violations, bankruptcy fraud, securities fraud or dealing in narcotics or other dangerous drugs.

A pattern of racketeering activity requires at least two acts of racketeering activity, one of which occurred after October 15, 1970 and the last of which occurred within ten years.

The statute, 18 U.S.C.A. §§ 1963 and 1964 provides, in addition to criminal penalties, for the forfeiture of the enterprise to the United States and permits treble damage awards to those victimized. It is also possible to enjoin the participants from again engaging in such prohibited activities.

15. *Mail Fraud.* 18 U.S.C.A. § 1341 prohibits the use of the mails as part of a scheme or artifice to defraud. The gist of the mail fraud offense is the use of the mails by a defendant, but usually this element can be established through introduction into evidence of some correspon-

dence or other document sent through the mails at one point by a defendant or an agent. Traditionally the mail fraud statute has been aimed at con-men, dummy corporations, phony franchise schemes and other frauds upon the general public. However, the law has recently been used against corrupt public officials as well.

CONCLUSION

Federal criminal statutes, although subject to limited jurisdictional basis, serve as important force in complementing state and local law enforcement.

QUESTIONS AND PROBLEMS FOR CHAPTER 9

Using the following choices, indicate which court has jurisdiction in situations 1 to 13.

a. Only *a U.S. federal court would have jurisdiction*

b. Only *a military court or tribunal would have jurisdiction*

c. Only *your state courts or municipal courts would have jurisdiction*

d. Two *of the above courts would have jurisdiction (indicate which two)*

e. None *of the above courts would have jurisdiction*

1. A soldier on a weekend leave in your city gets drunk on Saturday night and breaks a store window. He is in civilian clothes. c

2. A substantial amount of evidence becomes available to the sheriff's department in your county showing that the soldier in question No. 1 committed a burglary that Saturday afternoon. Which jurisdiction can prosecute? c

3. The president of the United States is shot and killed while visiting your state. d - A & c

4. The governor of a neighboring state is shot and killed in your state. c

5. X, who lives in London, hires and pays Y, who lives in Mexico City, to go into your state and kill W. Y is apprehended after he kills W. Can Y be prosecuted, and where? d - c & mexico

6. Can an arrest warrant for X be issued and X extradited to your state for prosecution? Where can he be tried? c & where crim took place

7. M drives a car at high speed in your state while under the influence of alcohol. He is near your state border when he hits another vehicle. The impact carries both cars into a neighboring state, where the driver of the other car dies. The homicide charge against M would be in which court? both

8. An American soldier with a weekend pass and in civilian clothes commits a felony in Mexico. The Mexican authorities state that they will waive their jurisdiction to try the soldier. Where can he be tried in the United States? b

9. Same as No. 8 except that the man is a civilian. Can he be tried in the United States? No Mexico's jurisdiction

10. A spy captured in time of peace in the United States would be tried   A

11. A German national who is illegally in the United States is apprehended committing a burglary in your jurisdiction. c

12. A U.S. congressman kills his wife in your state and claims legislative immunity because Congress is in session. c

13. A man arrested in your state with $5,000 worth of heroin could be tried for this offense   c

Part Two

The Balancing of Constitutional Rights with the Need for Public Order

Chapter 10

The Limits of Free Speech

A. BELIEF—SPEECH—ACTION

Belief

As thought and belief are not subject to control by government, persons may entertain any thoughts on any subject. Because thought and belief, by themselves, do not infringe on the rights of other persons, the right to believe is an absolute right. As persons may not be punished for what they think, thoughts about committing a crime are not, by themselves, punishable by the state.

Speech

Speech and other forms of communication, however, are not absolute rights, for they can seriously clash with the rights of others. For example, a man who calls another man's wife or mother the most vile and vulgar names he can think of may not assert that this is within his constitutional freedom of speech. The U.S. Supreme Court has stated that the right of freedom of speech and other forms of communication "implies the existence of an organized society maintaining public order without which liberty itself would be lost in the excess of unrestrained abuses."[1] The Court has also stated that "the line between speech unconditionally guaranteed and speech which may be regulated, suppressed or punished is finely drawn."[2]

Human communications take many forms. Pure speech includes words spoken on a face-to-face basis or through the media of radio, television, or recording devices. Written communication includes newspapers, books, and magazines as well as signs or symbols carried or displayed in public. A certain gesture with a finger and the hand, which would be interpreted by many as obscene, is certainly a form of communication. Picketing, protest marches, boycotts, and the like are also forms of communication. (These forms are discussed in Chapter 11.)

Action

Speech is often the link between thought and action. Action, like speech, is not an absolute right, because it can interfere with the rights of others; a person has a right to swing his arm, but his right to swing his arm ends where another person's nose begins. Each state and the federal government have enacted criminal statutes forbidding certain conduct and, in some instances, requiring other conduct.

Example: A man may believe that the 55-mile-per-hour speed limit is unreasonable. He may state this belief in any form of communication available to him because this communication would not ordinarily present any "clear and present danger" to other persons. However, when the man actually violates the speed limit by action, he may then be punished.

Example: In an extreme case, a man may believe that he has the right to kill the president of the United States because he disagrees with his policies. However, beause of the "clear and present danger" that communication of this thought presents, the man may be arrested and convicted under 18 U.S.C., Section 871(a) of the Federal Code if he knowingly and willfully threatens the life of the president or encourages other persons to do so.[3]

B. TESTS USED TO DISTINGUISH SPEECH THAT IS UNCONDITIONALLY GUARANTEED FROM SPEECH THAT MAY BE REGULATED AND PUNISHED

The "Dangerous-Tendency" Test

The old common law test for determining which speech and communication could be regulated, suppressed, and punished was the "dangerous-tendency" test or the "bad-tendency" doctrine. The last major U.S. Supreme Court case in which this test was used was the 1925 case of *Gitlow v. New York,* in which the Court stated that a "state in the exercise of its police powers may punish those who abuse this freedom of speech by utterances inimical to the public welfare, tending to corrupt public morals, incite to crime, or disturb the public peace."[4]

The "Clear and Present Danger" Test

A fundamental concept of the U.S. Constitution is that no government has the authority to suppress and forbid speech and punish the speaker unless the connection between the speech and an illegal action is so close that the speech presents a "clear and present" danger. Justice Oliver Wendell Holmes announced the "clear and present danger" doctrine in the 1919 case of *Schenck v. United States,* in which he stated:

> The most stringent protection of free speech would not protect a man in falsely shouting "Fire" in a crowded theater, causing a panic. It would not even protect a man from an injunction against uttering words that may have all the effect of force. The question in every case is whether the words are used in such circumstances that are of such a nature as to create a clear and present danger that they will bring about the substantive evils that Congress has a right to protect. It is a question of proximity and degree. When a nation is at war many things that might be said in time of peace are such a hindrance to its efforts that their utterances will not be endured so long as men fight and that no court could regard them as protected by any constitutional right.[5]

First Amendment Rights as "Preferred Rights"

First Amendment freedoms are highly treasured by our society. The U.S. Supreme Court has classified them as having a "preferred position" and has stated in *Herndon v. Lowry,* that:

> The power of a state to abridge freedom of speech and of assembly is the exception rather than the rule and the penalizing even of utterances of a defined character must find its justification in a reasonable apprehension of danger to organized government. The judgment of the legislature is not unfettered. The limitation upon individual liberty must have appropriate relation to the safety of the state.[6]

However, Justice Felix Frankfurter wrote in regard to the phrase "the preferred position of freedom of speech": "I deem it a mischievous phrase, if it carries the thought which it may subtly imply, that any law touching communication is infected with presumptive invalidity."

Communications That May Be Restricted and Regulated by Government

The First Amendment of the Constitution provides that "Congress shall make no law . . . abridging the freedom of speech, or of the press." A small group of persons, including Justice Hugo Black, has argued that government should not restrict speech or communication in any way. These "absolutists" (as they are called) argue that the First Amendment should be interpreted literally and that freedom of speech and communication be absolute rather than limited.

However, most justices and people in democratic societies have believed otherwise. There have always been restrictions on speech and communications in the United States within constitutional limitations. Chief Justice Warren Burger stated in *Miller v. California* with regard to obscenity that "no amount of 'fatigue' should lead us to adopt a convenient 'institutional' rationale—an absolutist, 'anything goes' view of the First Amendment—because it will lighten our burden." [7]

The balance of this chapter outlines the general areas in which speech and communications are restricted by criminal and civil law or by other means.

C. THE INSULTING OR "FIGHTING WORD"

The "fighting word" test was first clearly presented by the U.S. Supreme Court in the 1942 case of *Chaplinsky v. New Hampshire.* The defendant in that case was arrested when he said to a city marshall on a public sidewalk, "You are a goddamned racketeer" and "a damned fascist and the whole government of Rochester are fascist or agents of fascists." The U.S. Supreme Court affirmed Chaplinsky's conviction under a New Hampshire opprobrious language statute because the New Hampshire courts had limited the statute to "fighting words." The U.S. Supreme Court stated:

> It is well understood that the right of free speech is not absolute at all times and under all circumstances.

There are certain well-defined and narrowly limited classes of speech, the prevention and punishment of which have never been thought to raise any Constitutional problem. These include the lewd and obscene, the profane, the libelous, and the insulting or "fighting" words—those which by their very utterance inflict injury or tend to incite an immediate breach of the peace. It has been well observed that such utterances are no essential part of any exposition of ideas, and are of such slight social value as a step to truth that any benefit that may be derived from them is clearly outweighed by the social interest in order and morality.[8]

In commenting on *Chaplinsky* in 1971, the U.S. Supreme Court, in *Gooding v. Wilson,*[9] quoted the Supreme Court of New Hampshire in *Chaplinsky* as follows:

> No words were forbidden except such as have a direct tendency to cause acts of violence by the person to whom, individually, the remark is addressed. . . .
>
> The test is what men of common intelligence would understand would be words likely to cause an average addressee to fight. . . . Derisive and annoying words can be taken as coming within the purview of the statute . . . only when they have this characteristic of plainly tending to excite the addressee to a breach of the peace. . . .
>
> The Statute, as construed, does no more than prohibit, the face-to-face words plainly likely to cause a breach of the peace by the addressee. 91 N.H. 310, 313, 320–321, 18 A.2d 754, 758, 762 (1941)

The Requirements for a "Fighting Word" Violation

The requirements for the "fighting word" violation are (a) that a valid criminal statute or ordinance exist in that jurisdiction which clearly and specifically prohibits such language likely to cause a breach of the peace by the person to whom it is addressed; (b) that such language is used and addressed to a person on a face-to-face basis and that the words and the manner in which they were used could cause the average person to respond with an act of violence.

The occasion, the manner, and the context in which the words were used do much to determine the offensiveness of the words. The words must be one step away from violence. The following examples illustrate two different situations:

Example: Two old friends who have not seen each other for a long time meet in a tavern with only themselves, the bartender, and an off-duty police officer present. One man joyfully exclaims to the other, "Joe, you old X#%_____." The bystanders are amused, and Joe is not offended by the language.

Example: A man walking down a street makes foul and insulting remarks to every girl and woman he meets, causing angry reactions. Persons complain to an officer, who hears him make such remarks.

In the first example, there would be no justification for an arrest, whereas in the second example, there would be ample justification for an arrest in jurisdictions having statutes or ordinances that forbid language or conduct tending to cause or provoke a disturbance or a breach of the peace.

The First Limitation on the "Fighting Word" Doctrine

In recent years, the U.S. Supreme Court has imposed two additional limitations on the "fighting word" doctrine. The first limitation was established in the 1970 case of *Cohen v. California.* In protest of the Vietnam War, Cohen wore a jacket bearing the words "Fuck the Draft" into the Los Angeles courthouse. In reversing Cohen's conviction for a "fighting word" violation, the U.S. Supreme Court held:

> This court has . . . held that the States are free to ban the simple use, without a demonstration of additional justifying circumstances of so-called "fighting words," those personally abusive epithets which, when addressed to the ordinary citizen, are, as a matter of common knowledge, inherently likely to provoke violent reaction. While the four-letter word displayed by Cohen in relation to the draft is not uncommonly employed in a personally provocative fashion, in this instance it was clearly not "directed to the person of the hearer." Cantwell v. Connecticut, 310 U.S. 296, 309, 60 S.Ct. 900 (1940) No individual actually or likely to be present could reasonably have regarded the

words on appellant's jacket as a direct personal insult. Nor do we have here an instance of the exercise of the State's police power to prevent a speaker from intentionally provoking a given group to hostile reaction. There is, as noted above, no showing that anyone who saw Cohen was in fact violently aroused or that appellant intended such a result. . . .

Persons confronted with Cohen's jacket were in quite a different posture than, say, those subjected to the raucous emissions of sound trucks blaring outside their residences. Those in the Los Angeles courthouse could effectively avoid further bombardment of their sensibilities simply by averting their eyes. . . .

We have been shown no evidence that substantial numbers of citizens are standing ready to strike out physically at whoever may assault their sensibilities with exerations like that uttered by Cohen. There may be some persons about with such lawless and violent proclivities, but that is an insufficient base upon which to erect, consistently with constitutional values, a governmental power to force persons who wish to ventilate their dissident views into avoiding particular forms of expression. . . .

Absent a more particularized and compelling reason for its actions, the State may not, consistently with the First and Fourteenth Amendments, make the simple public display here involved of this single four-letter expletive a criminal offense. Because this is the only arguably sustainable rationale for the conviction here at issue, the judgment below must be reversed.[10]

The *Cohen* case established two new concepts to be used in applying the "fighting word" doctrine:

1. The U.S. Supreme Court defended Cohen's use of the admittedly vulgar word "fuck." The Court refused to allow a state "to cleanse public debate to the point where it is grammatically palatable to the most squeamish among us" because the Court concluded that "one man's vulgarity is another's lyric."[11] This ruling makes it difficult to define any vulgar, profane, impolite, or other type of curses as "fighting words" in and of themselves.

2. The U.S. Supreme Court held in the *Cohen* case that people "in the Los Angeles courthouse could effectively avoid further bombardment of their sensibilities simply by averting their eyes." In the 1975 case of *Erznoznik v. City of Jacksonville,* the Supreme Court held that "the burden normally falls upon the viewer to avoid further bombardment of [his] sensibilities simply by averting [his] eyes."[12]

The following case illustrates the application of the principles found in the *Cohen* case:

VILLAGE OF SKOKIE v. NATIONAL SOCIALIST PARTY OF AMERICA

Supreme Court of Illinois (1978)
69 Ill. 2d 605, 14 Ill.Dec. 890, 373 N.E.2d 21

Nazis sought to march and demonstrate peacefully in the village of Skokie, Illinois, where more than half the 70,000 population are of "Jewish religion or Jewish ancestry." The village of Skokie attempted to prevent the march and demonstration, urging that the swastika and the storm-trooper uniforms amounted to "fighting words." The Supreme Court of Illinois ruled that the use of the swastika was entitled to First Amendment protection, holding:

The display of the swastika, as offensive to the principles of a free nation as the memories it recalls may be, is symbolic political speech intended to convey to the public the beliefs of those who display it. It does not, in our opinion, fall within the definition of "fighting words," and that doctrine cannot be used here to overcome the heavy presumption against the constitutional validity of a prior restraint.

Nor can we find that the swastika, while not representing fighting words, is nevertheless so offensive and peace threatening to the public that its display can be enjoined. We do not doubt that the sight of this symbol is abhorrent to the Jewish citizens of Skokie, and that the survivors of the Nazi persecutions, tormented by their recollections, may have strong feelings regarding its display. Yet it is entirely clear that this factor does not justify enjoining defendants' speech.

* * *

By placing the burden upon the viewer to avoid further bombardment, the Supreme Court has permitted speakers to justify the initial intrusion into the citizen's sensibilities.

We accordingly, albeit reluctantly, conclude that the display of the swastika cannot be enjoined under the fighting-words exception to free speech, nor can anticipation of a hostile audience justify the prior restraint. Furthermore, Cohen *and* Erznoznik *direct the citizens of Skokie that it is their burden to avoid the offensive symbol if they can do so without unreasonable inconvenience.*

The Second Limitation on the "Fighting Word" Doctrine

The second limitation to the "fighting word" doctrine resulted from the 1972 case of *Gooding v. Wilson.*[13] The new test appears to require the likelihood that "the person addressed would make an immediate violent response." Courts using this test would hold that evidence was necessary to show that the victim was aggravated to fight immediately, and that only being "insulting" is not sufficient for a "fighting word" conviction. Cases illustrating this limitation include:

ROSENFELD v. NEW JERSEY
Supreme Court of the United States (1972)
408 U.S. 901, 92 S. Ct. 2479

The defendant used the term motherfucker several times at a public school board meeting. Because the defendant's words were not directed toward any specific individual, and because physical violence on the part of the audience was unlikely, the U.S. Supreme Court vacated the defendant's conviction.

BROWN v. OKLAHOMA
Supreme Court of the United States (1972)
408 U.S. 914, 92 S. Ct. 2507

During a meeting at which no police officers were present, the defendant referred to police officers in general as "motherfucking fascist pigs" and to one officer in particular as that "black motherfucking pig." The Supreme Court vacated the defendant's conviction under a statute prohibiting obscene or lascivious language in a public place or in the presence of females.

DOWNS v. STATE
Court of Appeals of Maryland (1976)
278 Md. 610, 366 A.2d 41

In a crowded restaurant filled with a racially mixed crowd, the defendant stated in a loud voice to his friends that "all the goddamn policemen in this county are no fucking good, they're just after me" and "the fucking niggers in this county are no better than goddamn policemen." A state trooper who was in the restaurant went over to the defendant's table and told him that his talk was disruptive, and that he would be placed under arrest if he did not refrain from using such profane language. Downs replied, "You ain't bad enough to place me under arrest." When the trooper then arrested the defendant, a scuffle occurred. The defendant was charged with disorderly conduct ("fighting words"), resisting arrest, and assault and battery. On appeal, the Maryland Court of Appeals reversed the defendant's "fighting words" conviction, holding: [14]

We need not consider whether Downs' first remark, "All the goddamn policemen in this County are no fucking good, they're just after me," constituted "fighting" words because the state trooper, a possible addressee, was not aroused by the comment. We need only examine his second remark, "[T]he fucking niggers in this County are no better than goddamn policemen." Since Cohen v. California, . . . *apparently teaches that the use of the adjective "fucking" is not punishable in the absence of compelling reasons, the potentially punishable words are "[T]he niggers in this County are no better than goddamn policemen." This remark was made by Downs during a conversation with friends. There was no direct evidence that it was spoken to anyone other than the persons sitting in the booth with Downs. Even if there were, no evidence was adduced that anyone else, besides Trooper Taylor, heard this statement. Even if someone else did, there was no evidence that he or she was offended by it. And, even if someone were offended by it, there was no evidence that any person was so aroused as to respond in a violent manner. Thus, Downs' remarks were not the kind of personally abusive epithets which fall outside of the protection of the First Amendment under the rubric of "fighting" words. He engaged in protected speech. That his views might be offensive to someone who overhead him does not warrant a conviction for disorderly conduct.* Bachelar v. Maryland, *397 U.S. 564, 90 S. Ct. 1312, 25 L.Ed.2d 570 (1970). Accordingly, we hold that the trial judge erred in not granting Downs' motion for judgment of acquittal on the disorderly conduct charge, and that conviction must be reversed.*

CITY OF OAK PARK v. SMITH

Court of Appeals of Michigan (1978)
79 Mich. App. 757, 262 N.W.2d 900

When the defendant's careless driving almost caused an accident with an unmarked police car, the defendant gave the man in the other car "the finger," not knowing that he was a police officer. The Court of Appeals of Michigan reversed the defendant's conviction, holding that the gesture did not amount to a "fighting word" because the testimony of the officer "discloses that the officer, far from being aggravated to fight was only 'insulted.' " The Court, however, held the ordinance to be constitutional, stating:

In sustaining the Oak Park ordinance, this Court does not intend to condone or open the door to the gesture of "the finger" in all future occurrences. Defendant and the public are admonished that in other circumstances and conditions, such conduct is punishable under the ordinance. Given the right circumstances, the law may retaliate, not with its finger but with its long arm.

Abusive Language Addressed to Law Enforcement Officers

The unanimous decision of *Chaplinsky v. New Hampshire* has been affirmed many times by the U.S. Supreme Court since the establishment of the "fighting word" doctrine in 1942. In the *Chaplinsky* case, the defendant was convicted for addressing insulting and fighting language to a law enforcement officer. Most state courts have also applied the "fighting word" doctrine in this manner. The Supreme Court of Wisconsin reflected this reasoning in the 1965 case of *Lane v. Collins,* holding that:

> The underlying reason for disorderly conduct statutes and ordinances proscribing abusive language is that such language tends to provoke retaliatory conduct on the part of the person to whom it is addressed that amounts to breach of the peace. . . . The fact that the abusive language is directed to a policeman or other law enforcement officer and is not overheard by others does not prevent it from being a violation of such statute or ordinance.[15]

However, before convicting for a "fighting word" violation addressed to a police officer, some courts have imposed one of the following requirements:

• Florida courts require that it must be shown either that such language "had no significance than to arouse (a) crowd into action against the police officer"[16] or that public interest, such as preventing "the possibility of a riot erupting resulting in injury to innocent bystanders,"[17] exists.

• In Footnote #23 of the 1969 case of *Williams v. District of Columbia,* Federal Judge McGowan suggests that law enforcement officers caution persons and warn them before an arrest or "order in" for abusive language. Judge McGowan stated:

> A policeman's special powers and training and his constant exposure to situations where the norms of common speech are not distinguished by unvarying delicacy of expression, leave him less free to react as quickly as the private citizen to a purely verbal as-

sault. On a situation where he is both the victim of the provocative words of abuse and the public official entrusted with a discretion to initiate through arrest the criminal process, the policeman may ordinarily at least be under a necessity to preface arrest by a warning. It would appear that there is no First Amendment right to engage in deliberate and continued baiting of policemen by verbal excesses which have no apparent purpose other than to provoke a violent reaction.[18]

• In the 1975 case of *Garvey v. State,* the Tennessee Court of Criminal Appeals stated that "a police officer trained to exercise a higher degree of restraint than the average citizen would not be expected to cause a breach of the peace."[19] The one word addressed to the officer in the *Garvey* case was "sooey," and the court held that there was "no direct face-to-face conduct." The defendant was driving by the police station; the officer was on the sidewalk.

• In the 1976 case of *Stewart v. Federal Protective Services,*[20] Stewart called an officer who was issuing him a traffic ticket a "jive-ass cop" and a "motherfucker." Stewart was then arrested for disorderly conduct. Later, he sued for false arrest. The federal court in Washington, D.C., awarded Stewart $1,000, holding that Stewart's remarks were "nothing more than everyday street language." The court held that to arrest for disorderly conduct ("fighting words") required that the words "create a substantial risk of violence."

Possible Fatal Flaws in Attempting to Prove "Fighting Word" Cases

"Fighting word" violation cases are difficult to prove. Courts throughout the United States are requiring that the state prove all the essential elements beyond a reasonable doubt.

Some of the fatal flaws or defects that could cause a court to find a defendant not guilty are:

• failure to show that the language was addressed to a specific person (or persons) and that such person was aggravated to fight (*Downs v. State*[21] and *City of Milwaukee v. George Carlin*[22])

"Fighting Words" Addressed to Law Enforcement Officers

A "fighting word" violation has not occurred if the officer is only insulted or offended by the words addressed to him or her. To convict for a "fighting word" violation, there must be evidence of a likelihood that "the person addressed would make an immediate violent response." Some courts have held that:

- law enforcement officers are "trained to exercise a higher degree of restraint than the average citizen," or that
- officers should give persons who have used "fighting words" in anger a warning not to use such language to the officer again.

To obtain a conviction in some states (or jurisdictions), it must be shown that:
- the words "create a substantial risk of violence" (Washington, D.C.)
- the language "had no significance than to arouse [a] crowd into action against the police officer" (Florida)
- or that the language creates "the possibility of a riot erupting, resulting in injury to innocent bystanders" (Florida)

- the distance between the speaker and the offended person might have been too far for an immediate violent reaction. This was a factor in the *City of Oak Park v. Smith* [23] and also *In Re S.L.J.*,[24] where a small, 14-year-old child shouted "Fuck you pigs" to two police officers from a distance of 15 to 30 feet as she was going home after being told by the officers that it was past her curfew.

- failure to show that the language produced "or is likely to produce a clear and present danger of substantive evils" that a state may seek to prevent (*State v. Porter*[25])

- when the vulgar language is in response to improper or unlawful police conduct or speech. In the case of *Diehl v. Maryland*,[26] Diehl was a passenger in a car that was stopped for tire squealing. When the officer ordered Diehl to get back into the car, Diehl responded with obscenities and vulgarities. The Maryland Court of Appeals held that "the officer did not have any right to make this demand on Diehl. Only then did Diehl begin to address [Officer] Gavin. Diehl's communication expressed his outrage with this unlawful police conduct, it was addressed only to [Officer] Gavin."

Cases in which juveniles shout obscenities to police officers or berate officers with vulgar speech seem to be particularly difficult cases to obtain convictions. The Supreme Court of Minnesota ruled in the 1978 case of *In Re S.L.J.*

(footnote 8) that: "While it is true that no ordered society would condone the vulgar language used by this 14-year-old child, and as the court found, her words were intended to, and did arouse resentment in the officers, the constitution requires more before a person can be convicted of mere speech."

The 1982 case of *State v. Montgomery*[27] is another example[28] of a juvenile case occurring in Seattle, Washington. The officers stopped their squad car when they heard Montgomery screaming "fucking pigs, fucking pig ass hole." The Appellate Court held:

> We find the behavior and language of the defendant reprehensible and disgraceful. He deserves censure and rebuke, and his conduct has degraded him in the eyes of society. However, the law requires that the individual's right to free expression take precedence over the interests of others to be undisturbed by crude language. The defendant's offensive language did not create probable cause to arrest him for disorderly conduct. The marijuana seized incident to that arrest must be suppressed. The judgment and sentence of the juvenile court is reversed.

The Probable Cause Requirement

Probable cause is needed to make an arrest for a "fighting word" violation or any other offense. If there is a question whether probable cause exists, it would be a better practice for the officer to request or order the person to appear at the office of a prosecutor (city attorney or district attorney) to review the conduct and language in question.

The U.S. Supreme Court pointed out in the 1979 case of *Michigan v. DeFillippo* that:

> The validity of the arrest does not depend on whether the suspect actually committed a crime; the mere fact that the suspect is later acquitted of the offense for which he is arrested is irrelevant to the validity of the arrest. We have made clear that the kinds and degree of proof and the procedural requirements necessary for a conviction are not prerequisites to a valid arrest.[29]

The July 1976 *FBI Bulletin* article entitled "Probable Cause: The Officer's Shield to Suits Under the Federal Civil Rights Act" states that: "The civil liability of the police officer does not turn on whether the arrest was in fact legal, but whether he reasonably believed the arrest to be legal, an obviously lesser standard."

Handling Abusive Language

Some officers are assigned to duty that subjects them to more abusive language than the ordinary officer would be subjected to. Officers assigned to a radar traffic unit might find themselves subjected to occasional verbal abuse from motorists receiving traffic tickets. A Wisconsin officer who wrote out a good number of speeding tickets found an effective response to abusive language. He carried a small tape recorder in his pocket, and when a speeder's language became profane or abuse, he would say, "Hold it a minute sir (or ma'am) until I have my tape recorder going. I want to get all of this down." He would then hold the tape recorder close to the person. Even when there were no batteries in the recorder, this would usually have the desired effect.

Another officer reported an equally effective tactic. He would say to his partner in a loud voice, "Get the names of the witnesses." Then, as his partner took out his pad and pencil and began taking down the names of the witnesses, the officer would turn to the person who had used the foul language and would ask, "Now do you want to repeat that again?" This officer reported that he had used this tactic successfully a number of times, with no one taking him up on the request to repeat the abusive language. Other officers have attempted to resort to humor

through such retorts as, "Do you eat with that dirty mouth?" However, this might well trigger an additional outburst, and the officer could be accused in court of taunting and thus encouraging such responses.

The Supreme Court of Minnesota recommended in the case of *In Re S.L.J.* that "the arrest of this child [14-year-old girl who shouted obscenities at officers] under these circumstances appears to have been an overreaction by criminality; a preferable approach would have been to march her home to her parents for parental discipline."

Does Abusive Language Ever Justify a Battery?

The question is sometimes raised in criminal law classes as to whether the person called vile and abusive names may respond with physical retaliation against the name-caller. The answer is no. The child's singsong phrase, "Sticks and stones may break my bones but names will never hurt me," reflects a correct principle of the law. There is no doctrine of American law that states that words or gestures are sufficient provocation to justify an intentional battery. Nor are words or gestures justification for an intentional homicide, regardless of how insulting and abusive they are (see Chapter 13).

However, whether the person would be charged with a battery would depend on (a) the type of battery committed, (b) the injury inflicted, (c) the words and gestures used, and (d) the degree of provocation. The following actual case is used to illustrate.

Example: When a 65-year-old man reprimanded an eight-year-old boy for the foul language the boy was using on a public street, the boy directed a vulgar gesture with the middle finger of his right hand to the man. The man chased the boy and, when he caught him, shook the boy by the shoulders and spanked him a few times on the seat of his pants. When the police would not order the man into the prosecutor's office, the boy's mother took the matter to the prosecutor. The prosecutor refused to issue a battery complaint against the man. Had a complaint been issued, it undoubtedly would have been thrown out of court.

In a few situations reported during the Vietnam War, antiwar activists taunted the survivors of men killed in Vietnam. Such taunts could be highly provocative and could produce violent reactions. The question of whether the person who committed a battery in such a situation would be charged would depend on what was done and the injury inflicted.

Can an Officer Provoke Abusive Language and Then Arrest for Disorderly Conduct?

If the officer is the one who provoked the abusive language, he or she may not then make an arrest, nor would the officer be justified in ordering the person into a prosecutor's office. Situations like this have been brought before courts:

LANE v. COLLINS
Supreme Court of Wisconsin (1965)
29 Wis.2d 66, 138 N.W.2d 264

A police officer had been dating a divorced woman and the former husband objected. While on duty and in uniform, the officer stopped the former husband on the street and asked the man not to telephone him. The officer then taunted the ex-husband about the fact that the man had been convicted of nonsupport. The ex-husband called the officer a son-of-a-bitch and repeated the expression when the officer asked him to do so. The officer arrested the man and held him in custody for an hour and a half before releasing him on bail. When the city attorney refused to prosecute for disorderly conduct, the former husband began a civil suit against the officer and received a jury award of $1,500 for false imprisonment. In affirming the judgment, the Supreme Court of Wisconsin stated: "A police officer cannot provoke a person into a breach of the peace, such as directing abusive language to the police officer, and then arrest him without a warrant." [30]

Distinguishing Vulgarity and/or Profanity from "Fighting Words"

Cohen v. California has affected hundreds of cases every year. Before the *Cohen* case, it was not uncommon for vulgar or profane expressions to form the basis of a criminal prosecution. Vulgarity and profanity are concepts different than "fighting words." Communications may be vulgar and profane and not be "fighting words." [31]

Speakers before crowds who are not leveling their remarks at specific individuals in the audience now have more latitude in what they say than ever before. However, the chairperson of a meeting continues to have the power to rule a vulgar person out of order. The manager or owner of a restaurant, tavern, or other private or public place continues to have the authority and responsibility to silence vulgar or profane persons. In the following case, the speaker used the following language:

STATE v. OLIVEIRA
Supreme Court of New Hampshire (1975)
115 N.H. 559, 347 A.2d 165

The defendant addressed a crowd during an intermission at a dance in the gymnasium of a community club. In talking about the club's need for additional funds and in urging persons to attend an upcoming city council meeting, the defendant used the words "fuck" and "fucking" a number of times. Police officers were present. After the dance was over and the hall nearly empty, the defendant was arrested and convicted of rude and disorderly conduct in a public place. In dismissing the complaint, the Supreme Court of New Hampshire held:

This is not a case involving "fighting words" admittedly subject to greater regulation by the State because of their inherent capacity to occasion a breach of the peace. Chaplinsky v. New Hampshire, *315 U.S. 568, 62 S. Ct. 766, 86 L.Ed. 1031 (1942).* *The defendant's references were not to persons present at the time.* Chaplinsky *and subsequent cases clearly indicate that the term "fighting words" is meant to apply to "face-to-face words plainly likely to cause a breach of the peace by the addressee."*

* * *

The case does not involve words which, though not personally abusive, nevertheless occasion a "clear and present danger of riot, disorder . . . or other immediate threat to public safety, peace or order." Cantwell v. Connecticut, *310 U.S. 296, 308, 60 S. Ct. 900, 84 L.Ed. 1213 (1940).*

* * *

However distasteful the language used by this defendant is to the average person, this case is controlled by Rosenfeld v. New Jersey, *408 U.S. 901, 92 S. Ct. 2479, 33 L.Ed.2d 321 (1972) and* Cohen v. California, *403 U.S. 15, 91 S. Ct. 1780, 29 L.Ed.2d 284 (1971) which require dismissal of this complaint.*

D. COMMUNICATIONS THAT ARE OBSCENE

Obscenity and "Fighting Words" Are Separate and Distinct Concepts That Are Not Constitutionally Protected

In the 1975 case of *City of Columbus v. Fraley,*[32] the defendant was arrested, tried and convicted for using obscene language. The defendant had become "boisterous and loud" and called police officers "motherfuckers" and "pigs." The Ohio Court of Appeals affirmed the defendant's conviction, not because the words were obscene, but rather because they constituted "fighting words." The Ohio Supreme Court held that the words used by the defendant were not legally obscene, and that the process used denied the defendant of due process of law, holding:

Obscene expression and fighting words are separate and distinct exceptions to the freedom of speech protected by the First Amendment. Obscene expression, as indicated herein, must involve an appeal to a prurient interest in sex. Fighting words, on the other hand, are those words which "by their very utterance inflict injury or are likely to provoke the average person to an immediate retaliatory breach of the peace." Cincinnati v. Karlan, *supra,* 39 Ohio St. 2d at 110, 314 N.E.2d at 164. In making a determination whether specific language constitutes fighting words, it is irrelevant that such words may also be legally obscene.

Legal Definition of Obscenity

Obscenity is not protected by the First Amendment and may be forbidden and regulated by government. Defining obscenity, however, has been the subject of many debates and court rulings. The U.S. Supreme Court established the following tests and standards to define obscenity in the 1973 case of *Miller v. California:*[33]

• whether "the average person applying contemporary community standards" would find that the work, taken as a whole, appeals to the pruri-

"Fighting Word" Violations

Words (or other communication) may be offensive, profane, and vulgar . . .	but not be "fighting words" (see *Cohen v. California,* in which the words "Fuck the draft" were offensive but not "fighting words").
Words may make a person or an audience angry . . .	and may be protected by the First Amendment and thus not be forbidden by government.
Words may be rude, impolite, and insulting . . .	but may fall short of the "fighting word" violation.
If the person to whom the words are addressed is not angered by the words, . . .	there is no "fighting word" violation.
If the person to whom the words are addressed is not likely to make an immediate violent response, . . .	there is no "fighting word" violation.
Obscenity is a different concept than "fighting words." . . .	To be obscene, the state must show as a matter of law that (a) the work taken as a whole appeals to the prurient (lustful) interest in sex; (b) "portrays sexual conduct in a patently offensive way"; (c) the work "taken as a whole does not have a serious literary, artistic, political or scientific value." *Miller v. California,* 413 U.S. 15, 93 S. Ct. 2607 (1973)
Nudity in itself is not obscene or lewd, . . .	but a state or community may regulate (a) when nudity is in a place where liquor is sold (see *California v. La Rue,* 409 U.S. 109, 93 S. Ct. 390 [1972]) and (b) when public nudity is forbidden by a specific ordinance or law.

ent interest (prurient interest would be appealing to the sexual interest, causing a person to become sexually aroused)

• whether the work or communication depicts or describes, in a patently offensive way, sexual conduct specifically defined by the applicable state law

• whether the work or communication, taken as a whole, lacks serious literary, artistic, political, or scientific value.

Communications That Are Not Obscene

Communications may be held to be obscene if they violate all the standards established by the U.S. Supreme Court in *Miller v. California* (or standards established by a state in conformity with *Miller*). Under these standards, courts in the following cases held that the following communications were not legally obscene and therefore could not be forbidden or punished as obscene:

PAPISH v. UNIVERSITY OF MISSOURI

Supreme Court of the United States (1973)

410 U.S. 667, 93 S. Ct. 1197

The following phrases used in a campus newspaper were held not to be constitutionally obscene: "Motherfucker Acquitted," "Up Against the Wall, Motherfucker," "The Motherfuckers."

COHEN v. CALIFORNIA
Supreme Court of the United States (1971)
403 U.S. 15, 91 S. Ct. 1780

"Fuck the Draft" was held not to be constitutionally obscene.

STATE v. ANONYMOUS
Superior Court of Connecticut (1977)
34 Conn. Sup. '575, 377 A.2d 1342

The defendant, a high school student, was being transported from the school to his home in a school bus. When the bus stopped at an intersection, a police cruiser driven by a state trooper pulled up to the rear of the bus. The defendant wiped the condensation off the rear window of the bus and, on seeing the trooper, waved a school chum over to him and then proceeded to make a gesture toward the trooper in which the middle finger of the defendant's right hand was held in an upright position with the palm of the hand toward the defendant. The trooper waited for the bus driver to turn off the flashing red lights, whereupon the officer turned on his siren, pulled the bus over to the side of the road, boarded the bus, and arrested the defendant. The defendant was found guilty of being a youthful offender for having made an obscene gesture. In vacating this judgment and finding the defendant not guilty, the Superior Court of Connecticut held:

It should be noted that the allegedly obscene gesture under discussion is not offensive nonverbal conduct but offensive expression. Without its opprobrious connotation, extending one's middle finger is a neutral act. It is unlike the type of nonverbal conduct, such as tearing up a draft card, which may be subject to governmental regulation. . . . It gains its significance only from the idea it expresses. As an expression it might be a vulgar epithet. When addressed to an ordinary citizen in a face-to-face confrontation it might be inherently likely to provoke violence. As an expression directed against a particular individual or group it might be beyond the pale of constitutionally protected speech. . . . It is not obscene however. . . . To be obscene the expression must be, in a significant way, erotic. . . . It must appeal to the prurient interest in sex or portray sex in a patently offensive way. . . . It can hardly be said that the finger gesture is likely to arouse sexual desire. The more likely response is anger. Because the charge and the proof were limited to making an obscene gesture the defendant's conviction cannot stand.

Nudity and Obscenity

In the 1981 case of *Schad v. Borough of Mount Ephraim,* the U.S. Supreme Court held:

Entertainment, as well as political and ideological speech, is protected; motion pictures, programs broadcast by radio and television and live entertainment, such as musical and dramatic works, fall within the

First Amendment guarantee. . . . Nor may an entertainment program be prohibited solely because it displays the nude human figure. "Nudity alone" does not place otherwise protected material outside the mantle of the First Amendment. . . . Furthermore, as the state courts in this case recognized, nude dancing is not without its First Amendment protections from official regulation.[34]

Although "nudity alone" is not obscenity and cannot be punished as obscenity, nudity may be regulated by a state or municipality:

• in places in which alcohol is sold. Nudity may be totally forbidden or regulated as to the extent of the nudity. In *California v. LaRue,*[35] the U.S. Supreme Court pointed out that the Twenty-first Amendment gives states "broad sweep" of authority to regulate places in which alcohol is sold.[36]

• in public places in which nudity may be forbidden by specific statutes or ordinances.[37]

E. COMMUNICATIONS THAT URGE UNLAWFUL ACTION (INCITING)

Inciting (urging) other persons to commit a crime or perform an unlawful act was a misdemeanor at common law. The offense of inciting is committed even though the other person does not commit the suggested crime. Speech or other forms of communication that urge unlawful conduct are not protected by the U.S. Constitution and may be forbidden by government. To be unlawful, however, the speech or other communication must be "directed to inciting or producing *imminent* lawless action and [must be] likely to incite or produce such action."[38] The following cases came before the U.S. Supreme Court:[39]

TERMINIELLO v. CHICAGO
Supreme Court of the United States (1949)
337 U.S. 1, 69 S. Ct. 894

The defendant was a suspended Catholic priest associated with the Gerald L.K. Smith organization. He addressed a friendly audience of more than 800 persons in an auditorium in Chicago, while more than a thousand people gathered outside to protest the meeting. Disruptions occurred after the meeting, and the defendant was charged with and convicted of disorderly conduct for statements that he had made in his address. The jury was allowed to convict if it found that Terminiello's speech either stirred the public to anger or constituted "fighting words." Because only the latter may be constitutionally prohibited, the Supreme Court reversed in a 5/4 decision because it was "possible that the jury found that Terminiello's speech merely stirred the public to anger and yet had convicted him."

BRANDENBURG v. OHIO
Supreme Court of the United States (1969)
395 U.S. 444, 89 S. Ct. 1827

The defendant was a Ku Klux Klan leader who spoke at a KKK organizer's meeting to which the press and TV cameras were invited. At the meeting, on an Ohio farm, he said that "if our president, our Congress, our Supreme Court continue to suppress the white Caucasian race, it's possible that there might have to be some revengeance taken." Some of the persons attending the meeting were hooded and some carried firearms. They gathered around a large wooden cross, which they burned. The defendant was convicted under the Ohio Criminal Syndicalism statute for "advocating . . . violence or unlawful methods of terrorism as a means of accomplishing industrial or political reform" and for "assembly[ing] with . . . persons . . . to teach or advocate the doctrine of criminal syndicalism." In reversing the conviction, the Court pointed out that 20 states had enacted this statute or a statute similar to it. The Court held that the Ohio statute was unconstitutional in that the:

constitutional guarantees of free speech and free press do not permit a State to forbid or proscribe advocacy of the use of force or of law violation except where such advocacy is directed to inciting or producing imminent lawless action and is likely to incite or produce such action. As we said in Noto v. United States, 367 U.S. 290, 297–298, 6 L.Ed.2d 836, 841, 81 S. Ct. 1517 (1961), "the mere abstract teaching . . . of the moral propriety or even moral necessity for a resort to force and violence, is not the same as preparing a group for violent action and steeling it to such action." A statute which fails to draw this distinction impermissibly intrudes upon the freedoms guaranteed by the First and Fourteenth Amendments. It sweeps within its condemnation speech which our Constitution has immunized from governmental control.

* * *

Accordingly, we are here confronted with a statute which, by its own words and as applied, purports to punish mere advocacy and to forbid, on pain of criminal punishment, assembly with others merely to advocate the described type of action. Such a statute falls within the condemnation of the First and Fourteenth Amendments. The contrary teaching of Whitney v. California, supra, *cannot be supported, and that decision is therefore overruled.*

Reversed.

HESS v. INDIANA
Supreme Court of the United States (1973)
414 U.S. 105, 94 S. Ct. 326

During an antiwar demonstration on the campus of Indiana University, 100 to 150 demonstrators moved onto a public street and blocked the passage of vehicles. When the demonstrators did not respond to verbal directions to clear the street, the sheriff and his deputies began walking up the street, moving the demonstrators to the curbs on either side, where a large number of spectators had gathered. Hess was standing off the street with his back to the street as the sheriff passed him. The sheriff heard Hess say, "We'll take the fucking street later" or "We'll take the fucking street again." Hess was immediately arrested and charged with disorderly conduct.

The Indiana Supreme Court placed primary reliance on the trial court's finding that Hess' statement "was intended to incite further lawless action on the part of the crowd in the vicinity of the defendant and was likely to produce such action." In reversing the conviction, the U.S. Supreme Court held:

1. That Hess' words could not be punished as obscene.

2. That Hess' words did not amount to "fighting words" under *Chaplinsky v. New Hampshire.*

Even if under other circumstances this language could be regarded as a personal insult, the evidence is undisputed that Hess' statement was not directed to any person or group in particular. Although the sheriff testified that he was offended by the language, he also stated that he did not interpret the expression as being directed personally at him, and the evidence is clear that appellant had his back to the sheriff at the time. Thus, under our decisions, the State could not punish this speech as "fighting words."

3. That there was no evidence to show that Hess' speech amounted to a public nuisance.

In addition, there was no evidence to indicate that Hess' speech amounted to a public nuisance in that privacy interests were being invaded. "The ability of government, consonant with the Constitution, to shut off discourse solely to protect others from hearing it is . . . dependent upon a showing that substantial privacy interests are being invaded in an essentially intolerable manner." Cohen v. California, 29 L.Ed.2d 284. The prosecution made no such showing in this case.

4. That Hess' words did not incite further lawless action on the part of the crowd in the vicinity and were not likely to produce such action.

At best, however, the statement could be taken as counsel for present moderation: at worst, it amounted to nothing more than advocacy of illegal action at some indefinite future time. This is not sufficient to permit the State to punish Hess' speech. Under our decisions, "the constitutional guarantees of free speech and free press do not permit a State to forbid or proscribe advocacy of the use of force or of law violation except where such advocacy is directed to inciting or producing imminent *lawless action and is likely to incite or produce such action." [Emphasis added.] Brandenburg v. Ohio, 395 U.S. 444, 447, 23 L.Ed.2d 430, 89 S. Ct. 1827 (1969). See also Terminiello v. Chicago, 93 L.Ed. 1131. Since the uncontroverted evidence showed that Hess' statement was not directed to any person or group of persons, it cannot be said that he was advocating, in the normal sense, any action. And since there was no evidence, or rational inference from the import of the language, that his words were intended to produce, and likely to produce,* imminent *disorder, those words could not be punished by the State on the ground that they had "a tendency to lead to violence." 36 Ind. Dec., at 529, 297 N.E.2d, at 415.*

Accordingly, the judgment of the Supreme Court of Indiana is reversed.

F. VERBAL OBSTRUCTION

Obstructing an officer in the performance of his public duties was an offense at common law, punishable as a misdemeanor. Most (if not all) states have now statutorized this offense. However, state statutes vary considerably in defining the crime of obstruction. A few states limit the crime to "resisting." Other states use the words resist, obstruct, or oppose, and still other states use resist, obstruct, or abuse.[40]

Some states hold that verbal acts alone cannot constitute obstruction and that physical acts are also required. However, other states hold that verbal communication can amount to obstruction. The following cases illustrate some of the obstruction issues that have come before courts:

STATE v. TAGES

Court of Appeals of Arizona (1969)

10 Ariz. App. 127, 457 P.2d 289

The defendant stated to officers who wanted to talk to her husband, "That is my husband. . . . If you want to talk to him, talk to him right here." And to her husband, "We don't even know they are cops. . . . Don't go anywhere, Honey, until he shows you a warrant for your arrest." The defendant was arrested for obstructing and interfering with the officer.

The Court of Appeals of Arizona reversed the conviction, holding that merely remonstrating with a police officer on behalf of another or criticizing the officer while he was performing a duty does not amount to obstruction or interference with the officer. The Court stated:

While the word "obstruct" has been defined in this context as meaning ". . . to be or come in the way of," and has been said to imply ". . . some physical act or exertion," Landry v. Daley, 280 F. Supp. 938, 959 (N.D.Ill.1968), there are a number of authorities holding that resistance or obstruction may be committed without the employment of actual violence or direct force, and we are unwilling to hold that non-threatening speech, alone, without force, can never in any circumstances constitute a violation of our statute. See People v. Cooks, 58 Cal. Rptr. 550 (App. Dep't Sup. Ct. 1967) (where the defendant persistently counseled an unjustified resistance by another to a lawful police request to furnish identification). Conceivably, too, a verbal harangue may be so staged and be of such length and disconcerting in its character as to materially impair an officer's ability to carry out his duties. Cf. State v. Harris, supra, 236 A.2d 479, decided under the statute proscribing "abuse" of an officer.

* * *

Under these circumstances, we think that speech which is non-threatening, and which is not accompanied by physical force, is punishable only when it is substantially equivalent to force, that is, when it is intended to and does incite an unlawful resistance by another to the discharge of official duty or when the speech itself by its very volume and intensity interferes substantially with the carrying out of an official duty.

STATE v. HARRIS

Circuit Court of Connecticut (1967)

4 Conn. Cir. Ct. 534, 236 A.2d 479

Police officers were arresting an intoxicated man when the defendant approached them. In response to her question about what they were doing, they stated that the man was intoxicated and would be released at six o'clock in the morning. The defendant did not know the man but kept arguing with the policemen in a voice louder than conversational tone. She was warned to leave on six separate occasions over a period of 15 minutes but continued to use vile and profane language directed at the officers. When a vehicle arrived to transport the intoxicated man, the woman was arrested for obstructing, as she had made the officers' task more difficult. The conviction was affirmed.

PEOPLE v. COOKS
Superior Court, Appellate Department (1967)
58 Cal. Rptr. 550

The defendant was a bartender in a tavern. A uniformed police officer came into the bar searching for a suspect in a robbery that had occurred a short time before and saw a man who resembled the suspect sitting at the bar. When the officer asked the man for identification, the defendant continued to tell the man not to show identification until the officer "tells us what he wants in here." When the officer explained his purpose, the defendant continued to tell the customer not to show identification. The defendant was arrested for obstructing. In affirming the conviction, the Court held:

Defendant . . . deliberately and wilfully set about to delay and obstruct the police officer in his rightful attempt to question the suspect; and, defendant pointedly succeeded in his purpose. Such speech-conduct with respect to this front-line function of the law is even less tolerable than a focused attempt to influence a particular court decision.

STATE v. MANNING
Superior Court of New Jersey (1977)
146 N.J. Super. 589, 370 A.2d 499

After a vehicle passed his squad car at a high rate of speed, a New Jersey trooper stopped the car. When the trooper detected an odor of alcohol, he asked the driver to step out so he could conduct some tests to determine the driver's condition. When the driver and the trooper went to the rear of the car, the car's passenger (the defendant) also got out and joined them at the rear of the car. "Despite the fact that the trooper three times requested defendant to get back into the car, defendant refused and said 'Lock me up.'" The defendant was convicted of interfering with a state trooper's performance of his duties. In affirming the conviction, the Superior Court of New Jersey held:

The trooper testified that he would have conducted a more formal and thorough investigation of the driver's condition had he been left alone by defendant and that defendant's actions interfered with his further investigation. The Municipal Court judge found as a fact that the trooper had to cut short his investigation because of defendant's actions. In affirming the conviction, the County Court judge found as a fact that defendant interfered with the lawful exercise of police duty by the trooper.

On appeal it is defendant's contention that the investigation of the driver's condition had actually been concluded inasmuch as the trooper had already determined that the driver was not intoxicated. For that reason, defendant argues, there was no interference with the investigation. We disagree. The trooper was following routine procedures in attempting to interview the driver to determine whether he was under the influence of intoxicating liquors. It was perfectly reasonable for him to require that he be able to interrogate and observe the driver without any distraction from defendant. It was also in the interest of safety for defendant to remain in the car.

CITY OF WARRENS-VILLE HTS. v. WASON

The defendant was convicted of an ordinance violation for interfering with a police officer in performance of his duties. The defendant flashed the headlights of his car "at oncoming automobiles to warn them that they

Court of Appeals of Ohio
(1976)
50 Ohio App. 2d 21, 361
N.E.2d 546, 4 Ohio Op.3d 12

were approaching a radar speed trap." The defendant was annoyed because he had just received a speeding ticket. None of the oncoming cars were speeding, but they did slow down. The officer was asked whether the defendant was doing "anything to interfere or slow down your only duty of being there that day (sic)." The officer answered "probably not" to the question. In reversing the defendant's conviction, the Court held:

It follows that one of the elements of obstruction is the presence of an illegal act which generates the policeman's duty to enforce the law. An additional element is interference with intent to impede the performance of that duty. In the present case it is conceded that the defendant did not warn persons who were violating the law. The drivers whom he signalled were not shown to be speeding. The officer was not proceeding, did not intend to proceed and did not have a basis for proceeding, against the persons warned. Though the intent to warn was clear, the warning was not directed to persons whom the evidence revealed to have been either acting illegally or to have begun activity intended to culminate in illegality. Thus, only one of the two elements necessary to establish an offense was present and the offense was not proved.

Judgment reversed.

STATE v. TAYLOR
District Court, Bergen County,
Criminal Division (1972)
121 N.J. Super. 395, 297 A.2d
216

The defendant was charged with disorderly conduct when he was seen standing off a highway with a large cardboard sign on which was written "Radar Ahead." In finding the defendant not guilty, the Court held:

This court finds no merit in the allegation that defendant did "obstruct" or "interfere" with motorists who were driving on Shaler Boulevard. The motorists who were driving on Shaler Boulevard at the time defendant was holding the sign in question were not inconvenienced in any way. Their driving was not "obstructed" by defendant, since he was standing on the side of the road, and the legend on defendant's sign certainly did not "interfere" with their driving. Upon observing the sign motorists had the election to either disregard it or to release the pressure on the gas pedal in attention to defendant's purported warning. It is true that defendant could be construed to "interfere" with the police officers because the message on defendant's sign intermeddled with the concern of the police to discover and apprehend violators of the traffic speed limit. Practical considerations, however, indicate that a conviction resting squarely on a literal definition is not only unsound but also capable of bizarre ramifications. Could we not then conclude that the act of a citizen in alerting the police to a speeding violator is also an "interference"? Should any act which frustrates the performance of a police officer's duties be considered an "interference"?

* * *

We conclude that defendant's act of displaying a sign stating "RADAR AHEAD" is not a disorderly act within the meaning of N.J.S.A. 2A:170-29(2)(b). To hold such conduct as "disorderly" would be neither harmonious with the clear meaning of the statutory language nor with the object and intent of the Legislature, as gathered from the whole context of the statute.

PEOPLE v. CASE

Court of Appeals of New York
(1977)
42 N.Y. 2d 98, 396 N.Y.S.2d
841, 365 N.E.2d 872

The defendant used a CB radio to warn another motorist of a radar speed checkpoint and was charged with and convicted of obstructing. The New York Court of Appeals held that in New York, a physical act was necessary to commit the crime of obstructing. In reversing the defendant's conviction, the Court held:

A CB radio message from one motor vehicle operator to another as to the highway location of a radar speed checkpoint does not constitute the crime of obstructing governmental administration. To say that there is a Smokey takin' pictures up the road does not subject the speaker to a year's imprisonment.

* * *

Under the express provisions of the statute, the interference would have to be, in part at least, physical in nature. The line is so drawn. To interpret and apply section 195.05, as suggested by the prosecution, would mean that there would be no outer limits to the statute. Under such a notion, the imparting of information as to location of the radar speed checkpoint would be penally condemned without physical interference and irrespective of whether the recipients of the messages were violating or were about to violate the law. A casual meeting of two travelers at a rest stop along a thoroughfare followed by a casual remark by one that a radar setup had been seen, with nothing more, would be enough to mark the author of the remark as a criminal.

G. DEFAMATION (LIBEL AND SLANDER)

As early as 1275, the English Parliament enacted a libel statute that forbade false news and tales. The colonies and the original 13 states undoubtedly all had laws concerning libel and slander. Over the years, the laws of England and America developed into the libel, slander, and defamation laws of today.

Defamation is the offense of injuring the character or reputation of another by oral or written communication of false and untrue statements. Defamation consists of the twin offenses of libel and slander. Libel is generally a written offense, whereas slander is generally an oral offense. Although most states probably have one or more criminal defamation statutes, charges under these statutes are infrequent. Most victims choose to rely primarily on the civil actions of libel and slander that are available to them. Money awards can be obtained through the civil suits to both compensate and punish. The burdens of proof are also lower in civil actions.

The *Chaplinsky* doctrine of "fighting words" is limited to words and gestures and requires that there be a face-to-face confrontation involving words that are one step away from violence and likely to provoke a public disorder. The law of defamation requires that the communication be made to persons other than the victim and that the victim's reputation be lowered in the esteem of any substantial and respectable group. It is possible that words spoken could not only be "fighting words," but also the basis for civil libel and slander suits.

Immunity from Criminal and Civil Liability for Defamation

The doctrine of privilege in the law of defamation developed long ago, based on the premise that if a person is acting in furtherance of a socially important function, he or she should be encouraged and allowed to speak freely without the fear of a civil or criminal defamation action. Absolute immunity from criminal and civil liability for defamation is granted to the following:

1. Judges, jurors, and witnesses in civil and criminal actions for statements relevant and pertinent to the case. The statement could be made before or during the trial in any of the pleadings or affidavits or in open court. Perjury and contempt actions may be brought against witnesses if the need arises, but neither civil nor criminal defamation actions may be brought (see Chapter 21 for the law of contempt).

2. Members of legislative bodies and witnesses before legislative committees that are performing a legislative function. A graphic example of the privilege as applied to witnesses can be found in the 1947 confrontation between Whitaker Chambers and Alger Hiss. Chambers, in testifying before the congressional committee on which Congressman Richard Nixon served, stated that Alger Hiss was a courier for the Communists. Hiss, who had held high governmental offices, challenged Chambers before the committee and told Chambers that if he made the statements out and away from the committee room, Hiss would sue him for libel and slander. Chambers repeated the statements outside of the committee rooms and Hiss did commence a libel and slander suit against him. The matter was resolved with Hiss ending up in jail on a perjury charge.[41]

3. Writers state that absolute immunity to civil and criminal defamation actions is enjoyed by high officers of the executive branches of government (the president, governors, and heads of important governmental agencies) who are acting within the scope of their authority. Lesser officials may enjoy a limited privilege. The extent of these privileges is uncertain because of the lack of modern cases testing the law in this area.

4. In 1884, the case of *Vogel v. Gruaz,*[42] was heard before the U.S. Supreme Court. An Illinois State attorney had testified concerning what the defendant had told him in regard to the plaintiff committing a crime. The statements were made in the State attorney's office and contributed to a judgment against the defendant for libel and slander. In reversing the judgment, the Court held:

> The free and unembarrassed administration of justice in respect to the criminal law, in which the public is concerned, is involved in a case like the present, in addition to the considerations which ordinarily apply in communication from client to counsel in matters of purely private concern. . . . Therefore, statements made within the scope of privileged communication [to one's attorney, doctor, minister, or spouse] may not be the basis for a criminal or civil defamation action.

U.S. Supreme Court cases dealing with the power of the state to regulate and punish (either criminally or civilly) defamation are:

NEW YORK TIMES CO. v. SULLIVAN
Supreme Court of the United States (1964)
376 U.S. 254, 84 S. Ct. 710

The plaintiff was a public official (police commissioner) who was awarded a judgment and money damages in a civil libel suit against the defendant newspaper for the false statements made by the newspaper in criticizing the official conduct of the plaintiff. The U.S. Supreme Court stated:

In New York Times Co. v. Sullivan, we hold that the Constitution limits state power, in a civil action brought by a public official for criticism of his official conduct, to an award of damages for a false statement made with "actual malice"—that is, with knowledge that it was false or with reckless disregard of whether it was false or not. The Court reversed the judgment against the defendant.[43]

GARRISON v.
LOUISIANA

Supreme Court of the United
States (1964)
379 U.S. 64, 85 S. Ct. 209

The defendant, who was the district attorney of New Orleans, was convicted of criminal defamation when he criticized the judicial conduct of eight judges in New Orleans. He attributed the large backlog of pending criminal cases to their inefficiency, laziness, and excessive vacations. The Supreme Court reversed, stating:

We held in New York Times *that a public official might be allowed the civil remedy only if he establishes that the utterance was false and that it was made with knowledge of its falsity or in reckless disregard of whether it was false or true. The reasons which led us to hold in* New York Times *apply with no less force merely because the remedy is criminal. The constitutional guarantees of freedom of expression compel application of the same standard to the criminal remedy. Truth may not be the subject of either civil or criminal sanctions where discussion of public affairs is concerned.*

The February 1974 issue of the *FBI Law Enforcement Bulletin* contains an article entitled "A Law Enforcement Officer Sues for Defamation".[44] After reviewing cases on defamation nationwide, the article concludes:

Under the current state of the law, a public official faces a far more difficult situation than a private citizen with regard to obtaining recompense for defamatory publications. A law enforcement officer has been defined by case law as a public official. To succeed as a party plaintiff in a defamation proceeding he must therefore plead and move that the person publishing the defamation did so with a reckless disregard as to the truth or falsity of his statements.

H. ABUSIVE AND OBSCENE TELEPHONE CALLS

Before 1966, few states had criminal laws dealing with abusive and obscene telephone calls. However, because of the increased volume of complaints received during the 1960s, all the states and the federal government have now enacted statutes making such telephone calls a criminal offense.[45]

Abusive phone calls include the deliberate obscene call, threats, the cruel hoax, bomb scares and threats of bombs, and the "silent" call, in which the person answering the telephone hears nothing or hears breathing on the other end of the line. Criminal charges may be issued in all the above cases if it is apparent that the call was deliberate and made with intent to harass, frighten, or abuse another person. However, charges should not be issued if it appears that the person has dialed the wrong number and simply does not explain the error. Other criminal uses of the telephone include situations in which the telephone is used to "case" the residence by persons planning a burglary (in this way, they are able to determine whether anyone is in the residence).

Apprehending persons making abusive and obscene telephone calls has been a difficult task in the past, but the job is now made easier by the development of devices by telephone companies. Some of these are:

• *The pen register,* which does not eavesdrop but does record the number called on the suspected line and the time of all calls. Neither the suspect nor the complaining party know that the pen register is being used, but it is commonly believed that a court order is necessary to use such a device under present federal law. It is also necessary to have sufficient information to reasonably suspect a particular person or telephone as the source of such calls.

• *The polarity trap,* which locks in the two telephones until the telephone company chooses to release the phones. This procedure is used when a person has been receiving regular abusive calls.

Although one-shot nuisance calls are virtually untraceable, the repeat caller stands a good chance of being apprehended by teams of police and telephone company employees. The full cooperation of the victim is also required.

I. LOUD NOISE AND LOUD SPEECH

Probably all cities in the United States have ordinances forbidding loud noises and loud speech that (a) are meant and used to disturb other persons or that (b) creates a clear and present danger of violence. States and cities may reasonably regulate the volume of speech, but they may not prohibit all loud speech.[46] The Supreme Court of California, in construing the terminology of a statute regarding "loud and unusual noise," held in *In Re Brown* that:

> The statute, however, cannot be interpreted consistent with the First Amendment and traditional views as making criminal all loud shouting or cheering which disturbs and is intended to disturb persons. When the word noise in the statute is properly construed consistent with the First Amendment and traditional views, it encompasses communications made in a loud manner only when there is *a clear and present danger of violence or when the communication is not intended as such but is merely a guise to disturb persons.* [*Id.* 108 Cal. Rptr. at 469, 510 P.2d at 1021.] [Emphasis supplied.] [47]

Loud party noises in an apartment house or in a neighborhood could cause telephone calls to the police or could cause a fight among neighbors if it were the middle of the night. Such "noise" calls are common on weekends in the summer in all large cities. The noises under such circumstances are interfering with the rights of other persons. Notice and cautions are generally given before a citation is issued by the police.

The U.S. Supreme Court ruled as follows on street noises in the case of *Kovacs v. Cooper:*

> City streets are recognized as a normal place for the exchange of ideas by speech or paper. But this does not mean the freedom is beyond all control. We think it is a permissible exercise of legislative discretion to bar sound trucks with broadcasts of public interest, amplified to a loud and raucous volume, from the public ways of municipalities. On the business streets of cities like Trenton, with its more than 125,000 people, such distractions would be dangerous to traffic at all hours useful for the dissemination of informa-

tion, and in the residential thoroughfares the quiet and tranquility so desirable for city dwellers would likewise be at the mercy of advocates of particular religious, social or political persuasions. We cannot believe that rights of free speech compel a municipality to allow such mechanical voice amplification on any of its streets.

> The right of free speech is guaranteed every citizen that he may reach the minds of willing listeners and to do so there must be opportunity to win their attention. This is the phase of freedom of speech that is involved here. We do not think the Trenton ordinance abridges that freedom. It is an extravagant extension of due process to say that because of it a city cannot forbid talking on the streets through a loud speaker in a loud and raucous tone. Surely such an ordinance does not violate our people's "concept of ordered liberty" so as to require federal intervention to protect a citizen from the action of his own local government.[48]

J. SYMBOLIC SPEECH AND THE FIRST AMENDMENT

Symbols, along with gestures, conduct, and speech, have always been used to communicate between human beings. The symbol, although almost always used with other forms of communication, can be used alone. American courts have wrestled for years with the problem of which symbols should receive First Amendment protection as forms of nonverbal communication. For example, during World War II, the Nazi swastika would not have received First Amendment protection; today, it generally would, depending, of course, on the way in which it was used.

Uniforms and the manner in which people dress are forms of symbols. People communicate by their dress who they are, what their lifestyles are, and, to some extent, what they think and believe. Suppose that a police officer on duty in a squad car sees three men in Nazi uniforms walking down the street or sees a number of men dressed in the robes of the Ku Klux Klan. Is there any violation of the law by the manner in which these people are dressed? But suppose the men in Nazi uniforms are picketing with signs expressing anti-Jewish sentiments in front of a Jewish synagogue. Or suppose the Ku Kluxers are walking through a black neighborhood. Do these actions fall within the insulting

Verbal Offenses

Type of Verbal Offense	To Constitute the Verbal Offense, There Must Be:
"fighting words"	1. insulting or abusive language 2. addressed to a person on a face-to-face basis 3. causing a likelihood that "the person addressed will make an immediate violent response"
obscenity	1. a communication that, taken as a whole, appeals to the prurient (lustful) interest in sex, 2. and portrays sexual conduct in a patently offensive way, 3. and the communication, taken as a whole, does not have serious literary, artistic, political, or scientific value.
urging unlawful conduct (inciting)	1. language or communication directed to inciting, producing, or urging 2. *imminent* lawless action or conduct, or 3. language or communication likely to incite or produce such unlawful conduct
obstruction of a law enforcement officer (or of justice)	1. deliberate and intentional language (or communication) that hinders, obstructs, delays, or makes more difficult 2. a law enforcement officer's effort to perform his official duties (the scienter element of knowledge by the defendant that he or she knew the person obstructed was a law enforcement officer is required) 3. some states require that the "interference would have to be, in part at least, physical in nature" (see the New York case of *People v. Case*)
defamation (libel and slander)	1. words or communication that are false and untrue 2. and injure the character and reputation of another person 3. defamation must be communicated to a third person *When a public official is the victim, it must also be shown* that the words or communications were uttered or published with a reckless disregard as to the truth or falsity of the statements.
abusive or obscene telephone calls	1. evidence showing that the telephone call was deliberate, 2. and made with intent to harass, frighten, or abuse another person, 3. and any other requirement of the particular statute or ordinance
loud speech and loud noise	*Cities and States May:* 1. forbid speech and noises meant by the volume to disturb others 2. and forbid noise and loud speech that create a clear and present danger of violence

or "fighting words" doctrine? Suppose the Ku Kluxers have hoods covering their faces as they walk down the street. Is this within their First Amendment rights? In all the examples given, would officers be authorized to stop the men and obtain their names, addresses, and an explanation of what they were doing?

Major symbol cases that have come before the U.S. Supreme Court are:

WEST VIRGINIA BD. OF EDUC. v. BARNETTE
Supreme Court of the United

The defendants were Jehovah's Witnesses who were prosecuted because their children would not salute the American flag while in school. The Court held that the compulsory flag salute and pledge of allegiance could not be enforced against Jehovah's Witnesses because to "sustain the

States (1943)
319 U.S. 624, 63 S. Ct. 1198

compulsory flag salute, we are required to say that a Bill of Rights which guards the individual's right to speak his own mind, left open to public authorities to compel him to utter what is not in his mind." In recognizing that the flag is a symbol and that saluting the flag is a form of communication, the Court stated:

There is no doubt that, in connection with the pledges, the flag salute is a form of utterance. Symbolism is a primitive but effective way of communicating ideas. The use of an emblem or flag to symbolize some system, idea, institution, or personality, is a short cut from mind to mind. Causes and nations, political parties, lodges and ecclesiastical groups seek to knit the loyalty of their followings to a flag or banner, a color or design. The State announces rank, function and authority through crowns and maces, uniforms and black robes; the church speaks through the Cross, the Crucifix, the alter and shrine and clerical raiment. Symbols of State often convey political ideas just as religious symbols come to convey theological ones. Associated with many of these symbols are appropriate gestures of acceptance or respect; a salute, a bowed or bared head, a bended knee. A person gets from a symbol the meaning he puts into it, and what is one man's comfort and inspiration is another's jest and scorn.

STROMBERG v. CALIFORNIA

Supreme Court of the United States (1931)
283 U.S. 359, 51 S. Ct. 532

The Supreme Court reversed a conviction for the display of a red flag in a public place under a statute that punished such display of a red flag if it was used "as a sign, symbol or emblem of opposition to organized government." The Court, in holding that advocating violent overthrow of government may be punished but that advocating peaceful change within the law may not be, stated:

The right is not an absolute one (free speech) and the State in the exercise of its police power may punish the abuse of this freedom. There is no question but that the State may thus provide for the punishment of those who indulge in utterances which incite to violence and crime and threaten the overthrow of organized government by unlawful means. There is no constitutional immunity for such conduct abhorrent to our institutions. . . .

The maintenance of the opportunity for free political discussion to the end that government may be responsive to the will of the people and changes may be obtained by lawful means, an opportunity essential to the security of the Republic, is a fundamental principle of our constitutional system.

Other flag cases can be found in Chapter 11.

TINKER v. DES MOINES SCHOOL DIST.

Supreme Court of the United States (1969)
393 U.S. 503, 89 S. Ct. 733

The principal of a high school forbade the wearing of black armbands as an expression of objection to the Vietnam War. The U.S. Supreme Court held that: The wearing of an armband . . . was closely akin to "pure speech" which, we have repeatedly held, is entitled to comprehensive protection under the First Amendment. . . . Students or teachers [do not] shed their constitutional rights to freedom of speech or expression at the schoolhouse gate.

O'BRIEN v. UNITED STATES

Supreme Court of the United States (1968)
391 U.S. 367, 88 S. Ct. 1673

The Supreme Court sustained the federal law that made it an offense to destroy or burn a draft card, stating:

A government regulation is sufficiently justified if it is within the constitutional power of the government; if it furthers an important or substantial governmental interest; if the governmental interest is unrelated to the suppression of free expression; and if the incidental restriction on alleged First Amendment freedoms is no greater than is essential to the furtherance of that interest.

K. BALANCING THE NEED FOR A FREE PRESS WITH THE RIGHT TO A FAIR TRIAL

Can Newspaper and TV Publicity Jeopardize a Defendant's Right to a Fair Trial?

A free and unfettered press that seeks out and publishes the news is necessary to the functioning of a democracy. The people must be fully and adequately informed in order that they may intelligently discharge their responsibilities as citizens. On the other hand, we as a nation have long cherished the fundamental principles that a defendant in a criminal case shall be afforded all the safeguards of due process of law and shall be given a fair and impartial trial. These two principles come into conflict when newspapers and other communication media publish detailed information before a defendant has been tried.

In 1966, the case of *Sheppard v. Maxwell* [49] came before the U.S. Supreme Court. The defendant in that case, Sam Sheppard, was tried and convicted of the brutal murder of his pregnant wife, which occurred in their suburban Cleveland home. The question before the Court was whether the trial judge failed "to protect Sheppard sufficiently from the massive, pervasive and prejudicial publicity that attended his prosecution." In holding that the state trial judge "did not fulfill his duty to protect Sheppard from the inherently prejudicial publicity which saturated the community and (failed) to control disruptive influences in the courtroom," the Court quoted the Ohio Supreme Court as follows:

> Murder and mystery, society, sex and suspense were combined in this case in such a manner as to intrigue and captivate the public fancy to a degree perhaps unparalleled in recent annals. Throughout the preindictment investigation, the subsequent legal skirmishes and the nine-week trial, circulation-conscious editors catered to the insatiable interest of the American public in the bizarre. . . . In this atmosphere of a "Roman holiday" for the news media, Sam Sheppard stood trial for his life.

QUESTIONS AND PROBLEMS FOR CHAPTER 10

Choose from the following available answers the one that best describes the exercise of speech in questions 1–10.

The speech is:

a. *a "fighting word" violation.*

b. *obscene.*

c. *urging unlawful conduct (inciting) or constitutes obstruction of an officer in the performance of his or her duty.*

d. *violating a disorderly conduct or disorderly persons statute or ordinance in your jurisdiction in a manner other than listed above.*

e. *no violation.*

1. A large group of demonstrators was ordered by the police to leave an air force recruiting office located in a large office building. The demonstrators proceeded to leave peacefully, using elevators and

stairs. However, just as an elevator door was closing a young woman demonstrator yelled, "Fuck the air force." (*City of Milwaukee v. Rosnick*, Case # 1–253981 [1972])

2. The defendant called "sooey" once as an officer was walking toward the police station and the defendant was driving past in a car. (*Garvey v. State*, 537 S.W.2d 709 [Tenn. App. 1975])

3. The defendant stated to a friend in a loud voice in a crowded restaurant that he "didn't want to play the fucking pin ball machine because they beat us for too much money last week." This language was offensive to an older couple, who complained to the police. (*Reese v. State*, 17 Md. App. 73, 299 A.2d 848 [1973])

4. Strikers called employees entering a strike-bound plant "scab" and other offensive and insulting names. After they were warned and cautioned by police officers, the strikers continued their name-calling. (*Youngdahl v. Rainfair, Inc.*, 355 U.S. 131, 78 S. Ct. 206 [1957])

5. A protestor demonstrating at a political convention had the word fuck written on his forehead while he appeared in public. (*People v. Abbie Hoffman*, 45 Ill. 2d 221, 258 N.E.2d 326 [1970])

6. The defendant (an adult man) asked an 11-year-old girl, "Have you ever been laid?" The girl immediately walked away but wrote down the license number of the defendant's car. The girl's parent reported the incident to the police. (*Breau v. State*, 230 Ga. 506, 197 S.E.2d 695 [1973])

7. A Wisconsin attorney was upsetting mental patients by his statements and would not leave a mental ward when requested to do so by attendants and police officers. The attorney was arrested when he stated that he would not leave unless arrested. (*State v. Elson*, 60 Wis. 2d 54, 208 N.W.2d 363 [1973])

8. As the defendant was about to board a plane, he was asked by a security guard what was in a small sealed paper box. The defendant answered, "Nitroglycerine." A deputy sheriff was called and when the box was opened, it was found to contain food items. (See the article "His Little Joke Bombs Out," in the *Milwaukee Journal*, 27 May 1979.)

9. "On June 2, 1982, Larry Rodgers telephoned the Kansas City, Missouri, office of the FBI and reported that his wife had been kidnapped. The FBI spent over 100 agent hours investigating the alleged kidnapping only to determine that Rodgers' wife had left him voluntarily. Two weeks later, Rodgers contacted the Kansas City office of the Secret Service and reported that his "estranged girlfriend" (actually his wife) was involved in a plot to assassinate the president. The Secret Service spent over 150 hours of agent and clerical time investigating this threat and eventually located Rodgers' wife in Arizona. She stated that she left Kansas City to get away from her husband. Rodgers later confessed that he made the false reports to induce the federal agencies to locate his wife." (*United States v. Rodgers*, ___ U.S. ___, 104 S. Ct. 1942 [U.S. Sup. Ct., 1984]) If Rodgers had made such false reports to law enforcement agencies in your state, would he be charged with one or more criminal offenses? If so, indicate the offense.

10. At about 10:45 P.M. on Christmas night, 1971, the defendant was walking home from work in a high-crime neighborhood. A police officer approached the defendant because he had been notified of a "suspicious man" in the neighborhood. The defendant was 69 years old and had lived in the United States 20 years. When the officer asked him if he lived in the area, the defendant looked at him and walked away. The officer then stopped the defendant twice, but each

time the defendant threw off the officer's arm and protested, "I don't tell you people anything." The defendant would not stay in the officer's presence and he would not answer any of the officer's questions. (*Norwell v. City of Cincinnati,* 414 U.S. 14, 94 S. Ct. 187 [1973])

11. A city attorney refused to issue an ordinance citation against two juveniles who repeatedly shouted, "Fuck you, pig," "Get fucked, pig," "Fucking pig," "Oink, oink," and "Sooey" to a police officer in a squad car. Ten or fifteen people in and about an apartment complex for the elderly heard and observed the conduct of the young men. The officer took the juveniles into custody and after the city attorney refused to issue a citation, wrote the following in a report:

During recruit training, the undersigned was taught that a police officer must tolerate verbal abuse and name-calling without legal recourse during the course of an arrest or when no one other than the officer is present and takes offense to such verbal treatment. However, he was also taught that when such conduct disturbs and offends other citizens, disorderly conduct charges can be brought against offender. Further, no signed complaint from a citizen is necessary, nor would identities be disclosed. Reasonable testimony as to circumstances and time of day, etc. is sufficient.

Is the city attorney right, or is the officer correct? Could a citation be issued under these circumstances? What type of testimony would be necessary to support a citation for disorderly conduct?

Chapter 11

Maintaining Public Order in Public and Private Places

A. REGULATING THE USE OF PUBLIC AND PRIVATE PLACES

Most private property (and some public property) is closed to the public. Private homes and apartments, for example, are not open to the public nor are offices of many governmental officials.

On the other hand, private property like shopping centers and retail stores is open to the public. In determining the regulations and controls that may be used in public places and in private places open to the public, courts have pointed out that the following must be considered: (a) the character and the normal use of the property, (b) the extent to which it is open to the public, and (c) the number and type of persons who use the facilities.[1] Applying these factors, it can be seen that the waiting room of a mayor's or governor's office could ordinarily accommodate a small number of protesters but could not accommodate hundreds of protesters. Nor could sidewalks used by many people accommodate large numbers of protesters without hindering and interfering with pedestrian traffic.

Balancing of Conflicting Rights and Needs

The U.S. Supreme Court has held that when private property is not generally open to the public, access to the property for the purposes of exercising First Amendment rights may be absolutely denied.[2]

Nor is there a general right to exercise First Amendment rights on public property and private property open to the public if this interferes with the normal use of the property. As the U.S. Supreme Court pointed out (see note 1), making a speech in the reading room of a public library would interfere with the normal use of such a facility. However, students silently protesting the Vietnam War were held not to disrupt and disturb their high school classes by wearing black armbands.[3]

Therefore, both public and private places may be regulated for the normal use of the property.[4] Libraries, hospitals, and schools would have different regulations than basketball arenas, taverns, and gyms because of the different uses of such facilities.

Public and private places must be regulated by the persons in charge of such facilities because

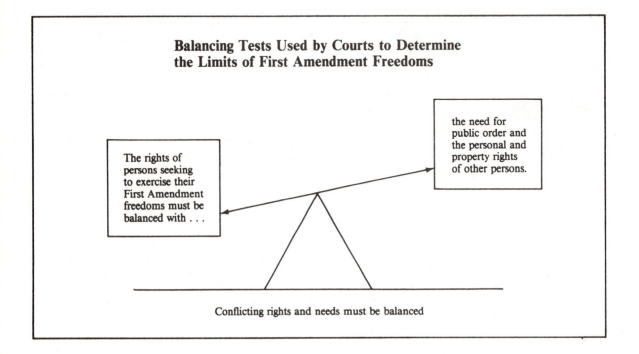

Balancing Tests Used by Courts to Determine the Limits of First Amendment Freedoms

The rights of persons seeking to exercise their First Amendment freedoms must be balanced with . . .

the need for public order and the personal and property rights of other persons.

Conflicting rights and needs must be balanced

Types of Public and "Quasi-Public" Property

	Extent of Use by the Public and Social Protesters	*Restrictions That May Be Placed on Use*
Publicly owned streets, sidewalks, and parks	Are used extensively by the public and ordinarily will accommodate the exercise of most First Amendment rights.	Reasonable regulations may be imposed to assure public safety and order (for example, traffic regulations).
Government buildings, such as courthouses, and city halls	Are used for the business of government on working days and during business hours. Open to the public at these times so that the public may ordinarily come and go as they wish.	Greater restrictions may be imposed to assure the functioning of government or the regular use of the facilities by the public. Can accommodate only limited expressions of social protest.
Public hospitals, schools, libraries, etc.	Use of these public facilities is ordinarily limited to the specific function for which they are designed.	As these facilities need more order and tranquility than do other public buildings, there are generally more restrictions concerning use by the public.
Quasi-public facilities, such as shopping centers, stores, and other privately owned buildings or property to which the public has access	Many quasi-public facilities are as extensively used by the public as are public streets, sidewalks, and parks.	Private owners of quasi-public facilities have greater authority to regulate their property than does the government of public streets and parks (see the material in this chapter).
Public property whose access by the public is limited and restricted	Government may limit and restrict in a reasonable manner the access by the public to jails, executive offices (mayor, police chief, etc.), and other facilities that must be restricted to permit government to function effectively.	Such restrictions must be made in a reasonable and nondiscriminating manner.

failure to provide ordinary care in protecting employees, customers, and other persons lawfully on their premises makes such businesses or public places liable for accidental negligence or intentional acts of third persons.

Cases Establishing Broad Rights of Access to Public Places

In 1972, the U.S. Supreme Court held:

> The right to use a public place for expressive activity may be restricted only for weighty reasons. Clearly, government has no power to restrict such activity because of its message. Our cases make equally clear, however, that reasonable "time, place and manner" regulations may be necessary to further significant governmental interests, and are permitted. For example, two parades cannot march on the same street simultaneously, and government may allow only one. A demonstration or parade on a large street during rush hour might put an intolerable burden on the essential flow of traffic, and for that reason could be prohibited. If overamplified loudspeakers assault the citizenry, government may turn them down. Subject to such reasonable regulation, however, peaceful demonstrations in public places are protected by the First Amendment. Of course, where demonstrations turn violent, they lose their protected quality as expression under the first Amendment.[5]

The importance of access to public places for freedom of expression has long been recognized by the courts. The Supreme Court of the United States held in 1951 that:

> Wherever the title of streets and parks may rest, they have immemorially been held in trust for use of the public and, time out of mind, have been used for purposes of assembly, communicating thoughts between citizens, and discussing public questions. Such use of the streets and public places has, from ancient times, been a part of the privileges, immunities, rights, and liberties of citizens.[6]

Some of the cases establishing this broad right of access to public places are:

EDWARDS v. SOUTH CAROLINA
Supreme Court of the United States (1963)
372 U.S. 229, 83 S. Ct. 680

The U.S. Supreme Court reversed the convictions of 187 students for breach of the peace. The students were conducting an orderly demonstration on the South Carolina State House grounds, carrying placards with such messages as "I am proud to be a Negro" and "Down with segregation."

BROWN v. LOUISIANA
Supreme Court of the United States (1966)
383 U.S. 131, 86 S. Ct. 719

TINKER v. DES MOINES SCHOOL DIST.
Supreme Court of the United States (1969)
393 U.S. 503, 89 S. Ct. 733

In the *Brown* case, the Supreme Court vacated convictions of five blacks for breach of the peace. The blacks sat or stood silently in a branch library that served only white persons. In the *Tinker* case, the Court held that a school could not discipline students for wearing black armbands in school in protest against the Vietnam War. In both cases, the defendants communicated political messages without disrupting the functions of either the library or the school.

GRACE v. BURGER
Court of Appeals for the District of Columbia (1981)
665 F.2d 1193

The petitioners challenged a federal statute forbidding all expressive conduct on the grounds of the U.S. Supreme Court. Mary Grace stood alone on the sidewalk in front of the Court with a sign containing the words of the First Amendment. Earlier, Mr. Zywicki had been passing out leaflets on the sidewalk in front of the Court. Both were told to discontinue their conduct and leave or that they would be arrested. Both peacefully left the grounds, but Mr. Zywicki first protested that newspapers were permitted to be sold while he was denied the right to distribute printed matter of his choosing. The Court held the federal statute 40 U.S. C.A. 13k unconstitutional and void, stating:

> *An interest in the "peace" and "decorum" of the Supreme Court cannot alone justify the absolute abridgement of expressive conduct of section 13k. Indeed, the Government cannot fairly assert that all expressive conduct outside the Supreme Court will adversely affect the peace and decorum of the Court. Thus, even if the asserted interest is legitimate by itself, it cannot justify the total ban at issue here.*
>
> *We simply do not believe that all expressive conduct "interferes with the operation of [this] vital governmental facilit[y]."*

Cases Restricting First Amendment Activity

The U.S. Supreme Court has also held that the rights of expression on public property are not absolute. Government must show, however, that the interest and reason for the restriction is sufficiently weighty to justify a limitation on First Amendment expressions.

COX v. LOUISIANA
Supreme Court of the United States (1965)
379 U.S. 559, 85 S. Ct. 476

(This case is also presented in Chapter 7.) The Supreme Court held that "there can be no question that a State has a legitimate interest in protecting its judicial system from the pressures which picketing near a courthouse might create" and concluded, holding:

A State may adopt safeguards necessary and appropriate to assure that the administration of justice at all stages is free from outside control and influence. A narrowly drawn statute such as the one under review is obviously a safeguard both necessary and appropriate to vindicate the State's interest in assuring justice under law.

ADDERLEY v. FLORIDA
Supreme Court of the United States (1966)
385 U.S. 39, 87 S. Ct. 242

The Supreme Court affirmed the convictions of 32 persons found to have violated a state trespass statute by conducting a demonstration on jailhouse grounds. The demonstrators entered the jail grounds through a driveway used only for purposes related to jail business. The court noted that jails are built for security and are not traditionally open to the public. In sustaining the convictions, the Court held:

The sheriff, as jail custodian, had power, as the state courts have here held, to direct that this large crowd of people get off the grounds. There is not a shred of evidence in this record that this power was exercised, or that its exercise was sanctioned by the lower courts, because the sheriff objected to what was being sung or said by the demonstrators or because he disagreed with the objectives of thier protest. The record reveals that he objected only to their presence on that part of the jail grounds reserved for jail uses. There is no evidence at all that on any other occasion had similarly large groups of the public been permitted to gather on this portion of the jail grounds for any purpose. Nothing in the Constitution of the United States prevents Florida from even-handed enforcement of its general trespass statute against those refusing to obey the sheriff's order to remove themselves from what amounted to the curtilage of the jailhouse. The State, no less than a private owner of property, has power to preserve the property under its control for the use to which it is lawfully dedicated. For this reason there is no merit to the petitioners' argument that they had a constitutional right to stay on the property, over the jail custodian's objections, because this "area chosen for the peaceful civil rights demonstration was not only 'reasonable' but also particularly appropriate." . . . Such an argument has as its major unarticulated premise the assumption that people who want to propagandize protests or views have a constitutional right to do so whenever and however and wherever they please.

LEHMAN v. CITY OF SHAKER HEIGHTS
Supreme Court of the United States (1974)
418 U.S. 298, 94 S. Ct. 2714

The Court upheld the city's decision not to accept paid political advertising for its transit system advertising space, noting that the decision was made "in order to minimize chances of abuse, the appearance of favoritism, and the risk of imposing upon a captive audience."

GREER v. SPOCK
Supreme Court of the United States (1976)
424 U.S. 828, 96 S. Ct. 1211

The Supreme Court upheld a regulation prohibiting all political speeches on a federal military base relying on both (a) "the historically unquestioned power . . . to exclude civilians . . ." and

(b) "the tradition of a politically neutral military establishment under civilian control."

JONES v. NORTH CAROLINA PRISONERS' LABOR UNION, INC.
Supreme Court of the United States (1977)
433 U.S. 119, 97 S. Ct. 2532

In the "interest in preserving order and authority in the prisons," the Supreme Court upheld North Carolina regulations forbidding all meetings of a prisoners' union and solicitation of prisoners to join a union and denied bulk mailing privileges to union publications.

Freedom of Expression on Property Open to the Public

Freedom of expression on property generally open to the public may be denied if:
- there is a significant governmental interest derived either from the nature of the property or from some other source;
- but the restriction on freedoms can be no greater "than is essential to the furtherance of that [significant] interest." *United States v. O'Brien,* 391 U.S. 367, 88 S. Ct. 1673 (1968)
- "the State, no less than a private owner of property, has power to preserve the property under its control for the use to which it is lawfully dedicated." *Adderley v. Florida, supra.*
- the "crucial question is whether the manner of expression is basically incompatible with the normal activity of a particular place at a particular time." *Grayned v. City of Rockford,* 408 U.S. 104, 92 S. Ct. 2294 (1972)

Such restrictions on freedom of expression:
- cannot be made because of its message (political, religious, etc.) and
- must be evenhanded enforcements applied to all persons and groups.

The Case of *Gregory v. City of Chicago*

GREGORY v. CITY OF CHICAGO

Supreme Court of the United States (1969)
394 U.S. 111, 89 S. Ct. 946

In 1968, 44 Chicago police officers accompanied civil rights marchers led by comedian Dick Gregory in a peaceful and orderly march from downtown Chicago to the home of Chicago mayor Richard Daley. The demonstrators numbered almost 85 when they reached the mayor's home, at about 8:00 P.M. They marched in the vicinity of the mayor's home for some time and, at the request of a Chicago assistant city attorney who accompanied the police, ceased singing at 8:30 P.M.

A hundred or so spectators had followed the demonstrators to the scene, but by 9:20 P.M., there were 1,000 to 1,200 people in the crowd watching the demonstration. The language and conduct of the spectators became rougher and tougher. Rocks and eggs were thrown at the demonstrators by persons in the crowd of onlookers. About 9:30 P.M. the senior police officer requested Gregory to lead the demonstrators out of the area, as the situation was dangerous and becoming riotous. Gregory would not cooperate, and after the request to leave was made five times, Gregory and other demonstrators were arrested for disorderly conduct. On conviction, Gregory was fined $200. In affirming the conviction, the Illinois Supreme Court held that "residential picketing" was, as a matter of law, disorderly conduct. The U.S. Supreme Court reversed the conviction, holding that:

The opinion of the Supreme Court of Illinois suggests that petitioners were convicted not for the manner in which they conducted their march but rather for their refusal to disperse when requested to do so by Chicago police. However reasonable the police request may have been and however laudable the police motives, petitioners were charged and convicted for holding a demonstration, not for a refusal to obey a police officer. As we said in Garner v. Louisiana, 368 U.S 157, 164, 82 S. Ct. 248 (1961): "[I]t is as much a denial of due process to send an accused to prison following conviction for a charge that was never made as it is to convict him upon a charge for which there is no evidence to support that conviction."

The Uniform Public Assembly Act and Statutes and Ordinances Prohibiting Residential Picketing

The Uniform Public Assembly Act, approved and recommended for enactment in all states by the National Conference of Commissioners on Uniform State Laws in 1972, proposes standards for the issuing of permits for public assemblies. Some states and municipalities have enacted statutes and ordinances prohibiting residential picketing because such picketing infringes on the right of privacy of the family of the person being picketed and also of persons living in the neighborhood. In the 1970 case of *City of Wauwatosa v. King,*[7] the Supreme Court of Wisconsin sustained an ordinance prohibiting the picketing of residences in that city. The Court stated that a municipality may "protect the tranquility and privacy . . . of the homes in which its people live." In affirming the conviction of the defendants who violated the ordinance in a labor dispute, the Supreme Court of Wisconsin quoted Justice Hugo Black in *Gregory v. Chicago:*

> Were the authority of government so trifling as to permit anyone with a complaint to have the vast power to do anything he pleased, wherever he pleased, and whenever he pleased, our customs and our habits of conduct, social, political, economic, ethical, and religious would all be wiped out. . . . And perhaps worse than all other changes, homes, the sacred retreat to which families repair for their privacy and their daily way of living, would have to have their doors thrown open to all who desired to convert the occupants to new views, new morals, and a new way of life. Men and women who hold public office would be compelled, simply because they did hold public office, to lose the comforts and privacy of an unpicketed home. I believe that our constitution, written for the ages, to endure except as changed in the manner it provides, did not create a government with such monumental weaknesses.

Regulation by Municipalities of Parades, Demonstrations, and Assemblies

Many municipalities require that groups obtain permits in advance for use of streets or parks. In this manner, municipalities can minimize those inconveniences that a parade or demonstration might cause other persons. Parades and demon-

strations can be scheduled at times other than rush-hour traffic periods and so that sufficient law enforcement officers are in the area to handle traffic and other problems. The following cases illustrate situations that have come before courts:

Governments may regulate parades, demonstrations, and large meetings of groups of people in public places:

1. by requiring permits that state time, place, etc. (parade permits to use public park, etc.)

2. by enforcing existing ordinances and laws that deal with:
- walking against traffic signals
- jaywalking
- blocking sidewalks, entrances to buildings, streets, etc.
- disorderly conduct, loitering, unlawful assembly, etc.

3. by ordinances and laws forbidding picketing and demonstrations:
- in or near federal courthouses
- on school grounds
- in public buildings, etc.

WE'VE CARRIED THE RICH, ETC. v. CITY OF PHILADELPHIA
United States District Court (1976)
414 F. Supp. 611, 19 CrL 2273

The plaintiff coalition wanted to conduct a July 4th parade near the official bicentennial activities in Philadelphia. The Federal District Court affirmed the city's refusal to issue a permit because contact between the two groups might lead not only to confusion, but also to violence. The Federal Court held: "If anything is clear in the area of freedom of expression, it is that two parades cannot march on the same street simultaneously and the city may allow only one."

VIETNAM VETERANS AGAINST WAR v. MORTON
United States Court of Appeals, Dist. of Columbia (1974)
164 U.S. App. D.C. 391, 506 F.2d 53

The Court held that the protest group had no constitutional right to camp and cook food on the capital mall in Washington, D.C., and that they were properly denied a permit.

NATIONAL
SOCIALIST PARTY OF
AMERICA v.
VILLAGE OF SKOKIE
Supreme Court of the United
States (1977)
434 U.S. 1327, 98 S. Ct. 14,
21 CrL 4088

(The 1978 decision of the Illinois Supreme Court of this case is presented in Chapter 10). As a result of hearings in a series of courts, it was held that the Nazis might be issued a permit to parade in the largely Jewish suburb of Skokie, Illinois. The Nazis would be permitted to march in their storm trooper uniforms and to display swastikas.

Presence in Government Buildings or Offices as a Form of Protest

Municipalities, states, and the federal government may regulate the use of their buildings in a reasonable manner. The following cases illustrate such regulations:

ALONSO v. STATE
Supreme Court of Georgia
(1973)
231 Ga. 441, 202 S.E.2d 37

The defendant and some 40 other students and faculty representatives went to the office of the president of the University of Georgia. After being informed that the president would not be in his office that day, they presented their petition on housing disputes to the president's assistant. After an hour, during which time they were milling around the offices, they were asked to leave. After they refused, the University Director of Public Safety asked secretaries in the office whether their work was being interrupted. When the secretaries stated that their work was being interrupted, the defendant and others were told that they must leave. After the defendants again refused, they were arrested for criminal trespass. In affirming the convictions, the Supreme Court of Georgia held:

The fact that appellants were on public property at the time they were requested to leave is immaterial. See Adderley v. Florida, 385 U.S. 39, 87 S. Ct. 242, 17 L.Ed.2d 149. It has been held many times, both here and in the United States Supreme Court, that the rights protected by the First Amendment to the United States Constitution, though fundamental, are not absolute, and must be tempered to a degree by the concepts of order and a healthy respect for the rights of other citizens. The constitutional attacks here made are without merit.

STATE v. WERSTEIN
Supreme Court of Wisconsin
(1973)
60 Wis. 2d 668, 211 N.W.2d
437

The four defendants (one male and three females) were arrested when they refused to leave an induction area for the Armed Forces Entrances and Examination Station (AFEES) located in Milwaukee. There was no testimony that they interfered with or disrupted the functioning of the center other than the commanding officer's testimony that he believed his staff feared for their safety because of the presence of the group. The defendants were charged with disorderly conduct, as Wisconsin has no trespass to buildings statute. In reversing the convictions of the defendants, the Supreme Court of Wisconsin held:

The defendants were merely present.   Mere presence absent any conduct which tends to cause or provoke a disturbance does not constitute disorderly conduct.

* * *

In the present action, the defendants were legally present within the AFEES.   Though we do not agree with their motives, we see no difference between their presence in support of an individual who planned to refuse induction and relatives' presence in support of an individual who planned to be inducted.   The commanding officer of AFEES determined that the mere presence of the one male and three female defendants caused his personnel to fear for their safety and ordered the defendants to leave.   No basis was shown for such apprehension.   The record doesn't indicate that like action was taken against the remaining relatives and visitors.

The defendants were legally exercising their First Amendment rights and any order in contravention of the reasonable exercise of those rights is unlawful.   The arrest made here was not based on any disorderly conduct. It was based on the defendants purporting views which were offfensive to the commanding officer.   We cannot hold that the mere exercise of one's rights to freedom of speech in communicating those views constitutes disorderly conduct.

We conclude that under the stipulated facts of this case the defendants were not guilty of disorderly conduct and the judgment must be reversed.

STATE v. JARAMILLO
Supreme Court of New Mexico
(1972)
83 N.M. 800, 498 P.2d 687

The defendants sat and lay on the floor in the governor's waiting room. They refused to leave when the office closed at 5:00 P.M. and refused to leave when the building closed at 6:00 P.M.   They were convicted under the New Mexico "wrongful use of public property" statute.   The convictions were affirmed and the statute was held to be constitutional.   The court stated: "There is no question but that a State may regulate the use and occupancy of public buildings."

When an Officer May Order a Person (or Persons) in Public Places to "Move On"

The First Amendment gives all persons the constitutional right "peaceably to assemble."   Therefore, an officer may not without good and sufficient reasons having to do with public order or keeping the streets open for public use order a person to "move on" and then arrest him or her for failure to comply with the order.   In the three previous cases, the defendants were arrested when they refused to leave government offices or buildings.   In the following cases, the defendants were in public places when ordered to "move on" by a law enforcement officer:

SHUTTLESWORTH v. BIRMINGHAM
Supreme Court of the United States (1965)
382 U.S. 87, 86 S. Ct. 211

The defendant, who was a civil rights leader, and 10 or 12 companions were standing on a sidewalk outside a department store when Patrolman Byars of the Birmingham Police Department observed the group.   After a minute or so, Byars walked up and told them they would have to move on and clear the sidewalk.   Some, but not all, of the group began to disperse, and Byars repeated this request twice. In response to the second request, Shuttlesworth said, "You mean to say we can't stand here on the sidewalk?" After the third request he asked, "Do you mean to tell me we can't stand here in front of this store?" By this time everybody in the group but Shuttlesworth had begun to walk away, and Patrolman Byars told him that he was under arrest. Shuttlesworth then responded, "Well, I will go into the store," and walked into the entrance of the adjacent department store. Byars followed and took him into custody just inside the store's entrance.

Noting the lack of any evidence showing that Defendant Shuttlesworth actually did block or obstruct the sidewalk for the use of other persons and pedestrian traffic, the Supreme Court reversed the conviction, quoting the Alabama Court of Appeals on another case regarding the same ordinance as follows:

The ordinance, that court has ruled, "is directed at obstructing the free passage over, on or along a street or sidewalk by the manner in which a person accused stands, loiters or walks thereupon. Our decisions make it clear that the mere refusal to move on after a police officer's requesting that a person standing or loitering should do so is not enough to support the offense. . . . [T]here must also be a showing of the accused's blocking free passage." Middlebrooks v. City of Birmingham, 42 Ala. App. 525, 527, 170 So.2d 424, 426.

There was thus no evidence whatever in the record to support the petitioner's conviction under this ordinance as it has been authoritatively construed by the Alabama Court of Appeals. It was a violation of due process to convict and punish him without evidence of his guilt.

BROWN v. LOUISIANA

Supreme Court of the United States (1966)

383 U.S. 131, 86 S. Ct. 719

Five black members of CORE were arrested when they refused to "move on" and leave a segregated reading room of a public library on the order of a sheriff. At the time of their arrest, the defendants were conducting themselves in a quiet and orderly manner. In reversing the convictions, the Supreme Court stated:

Petitioners cannot constitutionally be convicted merely because they did not comply with an order to leave the library. See Shuttlesworth v. City of Birmingham. . . . The statute itself reads in the conjunctive; it requires both the defined breach of peace and an order to move on. Without reference to the statute, it must be noted that petitioners' presence in the library was unquestionably lawful. It was a public facility, open to the public. Negroes could not be denied access since white persons were welcome. . . .

Petitioners' deportment while in the library was unexceptionable. They were neither loud, boisterous, obstreperous, indecorous nor impolite. There is no claim that, apart from the continuation—for ten or fifteen minutes—of their presence itself, their conduct provided a basis for the order to leave, or for a charge of breach of the peace. . . .

Here, there was no disturbance of others, no disruption of library activities, and no violation of any library regulations.

A State or its instrumentality may, of course, regulate the use of its libraries or other public facilities. But it must do so in a reasonable and nondiscriminatory manner, equally applicable to all and administered with equality to all. It may not do so as to some and not as to all. It may not provide certain facilities for whites and others for Negroes. And it may not invoke regulations as to use—whether they are ad hoc or general—as a pretext for pursuing those engaged in lawful, constitutionally protected exercise of their fundamental rights.

COLTEN v. COMMON-WEALTH

Supreme Court of the United States (1972)

407 U.S. 104, 92 S. Ct. 1953

Law enforcement officers stopped a vehicle on a highway to issue a traffic ticket. The defendant also stopped his car and identified himself as a friend of the person receiving the ticket. When the defendant began to argue, he was asked to leave four or five times by one officer and three times by another officer. When he called the officers "pigs," he was arrested for disorderly conduct. (This case is also cited in Chapter 10, as one of the officers called Colten a "loudmouth" in response to being called a "pig.") Colten appealed his disorderly conduct conviction to the U.S. Supreme Court, arguing that he had a right to remain at the scene when his friend was receiving a traffic ticket. In rejecting this argument, the Supreme Court held: [8]

Nor can we believe that Colten, although he was not trespassing or disobeying any traffic regulation himself, could not be required to move on. He had no constitutional right to observe the issuance of a traffic ticket or to engage the issuing officer in conversation at that time. The State has a legitimate interest in enforcing its traffic laws and its officers were entitled to enforce them free from possible interference or interruption from bystanders, even those claiming a third-party interest in the transaction. Here the police had cause for apprehension that a roadside strip, crowded with persons and automobiles, might expose the entourage, passing motorists, and police to the risk of accident. We cannot disagree with the finding below that the order to disperse was suited to the occasion. We thus see nothing unconstitutional in the manner in which the statute was applied.

Unlawful Assemblies and Riots

Under the old common law, an unlawful assembly was a gathering of three or more persons for any unlawful purpose or under such circumstances as to endanger the public peace or cause alarm and apprehension.[9]

An unlawful assembly became a riot under the old common law when those assembled began to execute their enterprise by a breach of the peace. A riot was a tumultuous disturbance of the peace by three or more persons assembled with a common purpose to do an unlawful act. Riot was a misdemeanor at common law, with all persons who encouraged, promoted, or took part in it being criminally liable.

Many states have statutorized one or both of these common law crimes. The state of New York, for example, has enacted the following offenses:[10]

Section 240.10 Unlawful assembly (class B misdemeanor)

Section 240.08 Inciting to riot (class A misdemeanor)

Section 240.06 Riot in the first degree (class E felony)

Section 240.05 Riot in the second degree (class A misdemeanor)

The present Federal Riot Control Statute, Section 2102, Title 18, United States Code Annotated is as follows:

> (a) As used in this chapter, the term "riot" means a public disturbance involving (1) an act or acts of violence by one, or more persons part of an assemblage, of three or more persons, which act or acts shall constitute a clear and present danger of, or shall result in, damage or injury to the property of any other person or to the person of any other individual or (2) a threat or threats of the commission of an act or acts of violence by one or more persons part of an assemblage of three or more persons having, individually or collectively, the ability of immediate execution of such threat or threats, where the performance of the threatened act or acts of violence would constitute a clear and present danger of, or would result in, damage or injury to the property of any other person or to, the person of any other individual.

Disruption of Religious Services, Public and Private Meetings

Many types of meetings and religious services are conducted daily and weekly throughout the United States. Audiences have a right to hear a speaker, and persons attending religious services have a right not to be disturbed. The Supreme Court of the United States has stated: "Hecklers may be expelled from assemblies and religious worship may not be disturbed by those anxious to preach a doctrine of atheism. The right to speak one's mind would often be an empty privilege in a place and at a time beyond the protecting hand of the guardians of public order." [11]

In the 1966 case of *State v. Smith*, [12] the defendant was ordered to leave a city council meeting on urban redevelopment because of his disruptive conduct. When the defendant resisted a police officer's efforts to remove him, he was arrested for disorderly conduct. In affirming the defendant's conviction, the Supreme Court of New Jersey held:

> Government could not govern if its vital processes could thus be brought to a halt. . . . The chair must have the power to suppress a disturbance or the threat of one, and the power to quell a disturbance would be empty if its exercise could be met by still another disturbance designed to test the officer's judgment. 46 N.J. at 517, 218 A.2d at 150.

Other meeting and religious services cases include:

GIGLER v. CITY OF KLAMATH FALLS

Court of Appeals of Oregon (1975)

21 Or. App. 753, 537 P.2d 121

Mr. Gigler, an off-duty police officer, and a Mr. Anklin were found to be out of order and ordered to leave a city council meeting. The Court held that when it was obvious that Gigler could be expected to continue disruptive conduct, it was reasonable for the mayor to order him removed. In affirming the dismissal of the civil suit against the mayor and the two police officers who removed Gigler by force, the Court held:

> *Under the circumstances existing, the mayor was not acting unreasonably in ordering the officers to remove plaintiff from the meeting. If he had gone peacefully, as Mr. Anklin did (and Mr. Anklin urged plaintiff to do the same) it is obvious that no scuffle would have ensued. The officers needed no probable cause for plaintiff's arrest at that point. They were merely following the mayor's orders given in his effort to preside over an orderly meeting while not giving way to wilful obstruction.*
>
> *When the plaintiff chose to violently give physical resistance, he brought about the eventual arrest and prosecution, regardless of the exact time an arrest was made. And that arrest and prosecution was with probable cause.*

REYNOLDS v. TENNESSEE

Supreme Court of the United States (1974)

414 U.S. 1163, 94 S. Ct. 928

The U.S. Supreme Court refused certiorari, thus permitting the defendant's conviction in the lower court to stand. Part of Justice William O. Douglas' dissent is as follows:

This case involves a demonstration occasioned by the appearance of President Nixon at the week-long Billy Graham East Tennessee Crusade being held at a football stadium in Knoxville. The petitioner, an ordained Methodist minister and a professor of religious studies, was convicted under a Tennessee statute which in relevant part proscribes "willfully disturb[ing] or disquiet[ing] any assemblage of persons met for religious worship . . . by noise, profane discourse, rude or indecent behavior, or any other acts." Disruption of the meeting is not an element of the crime under the statute, and the jury was instructed that "if you find from the evidence that the defendants indulged in any indecent or improper conduct, so near the worshipping assembly, if you find there was a worshipping assembly present on this occasion, as to attract the notice and attention of persons who were present as a part of the assembly—then, under such a state of facts, if they exist, the defendants would be guilty, and this would be so, whether witnesses say they were disturbed or not." . . . No evidence was introduced at trial that the meeting was disrupted, in the sense that speakers were shouted down, or that petitioner's group prevented, or sought to prevent, the meeting from proceeding as planned. Nor did the state appellate courts make any such findings in affirming the conviction. Although there were findings that some members of the protest group engaged in obscene chants,[13] it is uncontested that petitioner did not. The undisturbed findings of the state court of criminal appeals were that petitioner "did not chant obscenities and that his intent was for a peaceful demonstration." Petitioner's contentions that the statute was unconstitutionally vague and overbroad were rejected by the state courts.

Disruption of Political Meetings

Some courts have held that more latitude and a greater opportunity to respond should be permitted at political meetings and demonstrations than would be allowed at religious services or other types of meetings. In the case of *City of Spokane v. McDonough,* the defendant shouted "Warmonger" once to the vice-president of the United States during a political speech by the vice-president. In reversing the defendant's conviction for disorderly conduct, the Court held:

Shouting "Warmonger" but once—without more to indicate a further purpose or intention of breaking up the meeting or to deprive the speaker of his audience or to interfere with the rights of others to hear or the speaker to speak—did not amount to a disturbance of the peace, in fact or in law.[14]

The Supreme Court of California set aside the defendants' convictions for disturbing a lawful meeting in the 1970 case of *In re Kay.* The defendants clapped, shouted slogans and waived a flag bearing the emblem of farm workers at an open-air meeting in a public park at which a congressman spoke. The Court held:

After Congressman Tunney had given a portion of his speech, a comparatively small part of the total crowd, between 25 and 250 persons, engaged in rhythmical clapping and some shouting for about five or ten minutes. This demonstration did not affect the program. Congressman Tunney, who had been using a microphone, finished his speech despite the protest, pausing to assure those protesting that they had a right to do so and to urge them to be grateful that they live in a country whose Constitution protects their right to demonstrate in that manner. At no time did either the speaker or the police ask the protestors to be silent or to leave. Following the end of the protest and of the congressman's speech, the fireworks were shown. The police made no arrests during or immediately following the protest; the prosecution filed charges only some two weeks later.

* * *

Audience activities, such as heckling, interrupting, harsh questioning, and booing, even though they may be impolite and discourteous, can nonetheless advance the goals of the First Amendment. For many citizens such participation in public meetings, whether supportive or critical of the speaker, may constitute the only manner in which they can express their views to a large number of people; the Constitution does not require that the effective expression of ideas be restricted to rigid and predetermined patterns. . . .

In the instant case, the questioned conduct continued for only a few minutes, Congressman Tunney was able to complete his speech, and it does not appear that a large part of the audience could not hear his remarks. We conclude that the state failed to meet its burden of establishing a substantial impairment of the conduct of the meeting.

Finally, we do not believe that there was a sufficient showing that the defendants disturbed the meeting within the constitutionally permissible limits of the statutory term "disturb." Generally, if disturbances are occasioned by nonviolent exercise of free expression, section 403 will require that defendants be shown to have engaged in such conduct with knowledge, or under circumstances in which they should have known, that they were violating an applicable custom, usage, or rule of the meeting. In instances in which the appropriate standard of conduct lies in doubt, a warning and a request that defendants curtail their conduct, either by officials or law enforcement agents, should precede arrest or citation. If section 403 were not so interpreted, individuals would be forced to speculate as to what conduct might entail criminal sanctions and would "necessarily . . . 'steer far wider of the unlawful zone.' " [15]

Public Order in Restaurants, Taverns, and Other Business or Public Places

Such private places as restaurants, theaters, sporting facilities, and taverns are regulated to a large extent by the managers and owners of such facilities. A person using coarse and indecent language in a loud voice in a restaurant, for example, might be asked to leave by the manager or the owner. If he or she failed to leave and continued the disruptive conduct, it is likely that the police would be called. In most instances,

the police would order the person to leave if he or she could drive. The person's disruptive language would not fall within the "fighting words" doctrine unless it were addressed to a specific person.

In 1977, the case of *Griego v. Wilson* [16] came before the Court of Appeals of New Mexico. Evidence showed that Griego became angry, abusive, and profane and used obscene gestures toward John Wilson and other employees of a lumber store. The employees cautioned Griego to stop and offered to refund his money. When the employees became fearful that Griego was about to attack an employee, they restrained him. In holding that the employees used reasonable force under the circumstances, the Court held: [17]

> We hold that the proprietor of a business has the right to expel or restrain a person who by virtue of abusive conduct refuses to leave or persists in this abusive conduct after being cautioned, though that person was initially on the premises by express or implied invitation, so long as the expulsion or restraint is by reasonable force. See *Ramirez v. Chavez,* 71 Ariz. 239, 226 P.2d 143 (1951); *Penn v. Henderson,* 174 Or. 1, 146 P.2d 760 (1944); *Crouch v. Ringer,* 110 Wash. 612, 188 P. 782 (1920); *Austin v. Metropolitan Life Insurance Co. of New York,* 106 Wash. 371, 180 P. 134, 6 A.L.R. 1061 (1919); *Johanson v. Huntsman,* 60 Utah 402, 209 P. 197 (1922). Annot. Right to Eject Customer from Store, 9 A.L.R. 379.

Civil Liability for Crimes Committed on Premises

Business firms and public organizations do not have an absolute obligation to prevent crimes on their premises, but they do have a duty to provide persons lawfully on their premises with adequate security and safeguards against foreseeable risks.

The Restatement of Torts (2nd) states that civil liability should be imposed:

> for physical harm caused by the accidental, negligent, or intentionally harmful acts of third persons . . . and by the failure of the possessor (of premises or land) to exercise reasonable care to a) discover that such acts are being done or are likely to be done, or b) give (an adequate) warning.

In the 1982 case of *Butler v. Acme Markets Inc.,* [18] the Supreme Court of New Jersey upheld a jury finding of $3,600 for the 60-year-old woman plaintiff. Ms. Butler (the plaintiff) was a customer in the defendant's store and was mugged as she was putting her purchases in her car parked in the store parking lot. Plaintiff was the eighth person to be mugged in a year in the parking lot. The store posted no warnings and hired one guard who primarily remained inside the store. The court held that it was reasonable for a jury to conclude that "absent warnings, hiring one guard who primarily remained inside the store was an insufficient response in light of the known repeated history of attacks on the premises."

In December of 1979, 11 young persons died in a stampede to get seats in a first-come, open seating concert of The Who in Cincinnati's Riverfront Coliseum. Although no criminal charges were filed, many wrongful death and negligent injury lawsuits were filed. The tragedy caused the city and state to enact stricter crowd-control laws. The lawsuits caused the promoters to abandon the open-seating system and the practice of opening only one or two gates to huge crowds of persons seeking to get good seats.

B. HANDBILLS AS A FORM OF COMMUNICATION

By standing on a sidewalk of a busy street, a person may communicate with a large number of people by passing out handbills or leaflets. Handbills are an inexpensive means of communication used for many years; their message may be political, religious, social, or commercial.[19] Like pure speech, written communications, such as handbills, cannot urge violence or unlawful acts. They may not contain libel or use clearly obscene communications. They may not direct insulting or "fighting words" to the persons receiving the handbills.

The U.S. Supreme Court observed that "the unwilling listener is not like the passer-by who may be offered a pamphlet in the street but cannot be made to take it."[20] Many of the persons who do accept handbills will only glance at them and then dispose of the material. This, of course, creates a litter problem.

In the 1976 case of *People v. Remeny,* the New York Court of Appeals held:

It is settled that an ordinance which prohibits the distribution of leaflets or handbills in all public places, at all times and under all circumstances cannot be considered a reasonable regulation of constitutionally protected speech. . . .

If an ordinance absolutely prohibiting all distribution of handbills containing constitutionally protected statements on political, social and religious topics is invalid, then this ordinance relating to commercial speech, now also constitutionally protected, suffers from the same infirmity.

The City of course has a legitimate interest in seeing that the exercise of the right does not contribute to the litter on the streets or otherwise violate the law. Thus they may enact reasonable regulations governing the time, place and circumstances of the distribution. But in our view they cannot enact an ordinance absolutely prohibiting all distribution of commercial handbills on city streets and call it a reasonable regulation of the activity. Although we sympathize with the City's desire to eliminate litter from the streets, we have concluded that the ordinance, as presently worded, is unconstitutional.[21]

C. DOOR–TO–DOOR CANVASSING AS A FORM OF COMMUNICATION

Persons running for a political office or persons with a religious message are among those who frequently go from door to door. Door-to-door communication is also used by salespersons selling a product or a service. Door-to-door calls may be limited to verbal communication alone, or they may be combined (as they are in most instances) with the use of handbills.

Many ordinances and statutes have been passed regulating door-to-door canvassing. These ordinances have been designed to prevent crime, to reduce resident's fears about strangers wandering door to door, and to avoid harassment of dwellers who find it annoying to answer such calls. The U.S. Supreme Court stated in *Martin v. City of Struthers* that:

Ordinances of the sort now before us may be aimed at the protection of the householders from annoyance, including intrusion upon the hours of rest, and at the prevention of crime. Constant callers, whether selling pots or distributing leaflets, may lessen the peaceful enjoyment of a home as much as a neighborhood glue factory or railroad yard which zoning ordinances may prohibit. . . . In addition, burglars frequently pose as canvassers, either in order that they may have a pretense to discover whether a house is empty and hence ripe for burglary, or for the purpose of spying out the premises in order that they may return later. Crime prevention may thus be the purpose of regulatory ordinances.[22]

In the *City of Struthers* case, the U.S. Supreme Court struck down a municipal ordinance that made it a crime for a solicitor or canvasser to knock on the front door of a resident's home or to ring the doorbell. The Court held that the manner in which the ordinance was written conflicted "with the freedoms of speech and press."

States and municipalities, however, do have the authority to regulate door-to-door canvassing. As door-to-door canvassing falls under the First Amendment, "government may regulate . . . only with narrow specificity." [23] The U.S. Supreme Court affirmed the right to regulate door-to-door canvassing in the 1976 case of *Hynes v. Mayor and Council of Borough of Oradel,* holding:

There is, of course, no absolute right under the Federal Constitution to enter on the private premises of another and knock on a door for any purpose, and the police power permits reasonable regulation for public safety. We cannot say, and indeed appellants do not argue, that door-to-door canvassing and solicitation are immune from regulation under the State's police power, whether the purpose of the regulation is to protect from danger or to protect the peaceful enjoyment of the home.[24]

D. EXERCISING FIRST AMENDMENT FREEDOMS ON PRIVATE PROPERTY THAT IS OPEN FOR PUBLIC USE

Many shopping centers, supermarkets, and other privately owned property open for public use forbid demonstrations and the distribution of handbills on their property. The question whether private-property owners who open their property to public use may restrict such activities came before the U.S. Supreme Court in the following case:

LLOYD CORP., LTD. v. TANNER
Supreme Court of the United States (1972)
407 U.S. 551, 92 S. Ct. 2219

Tanner sought to distribute antiwar handbills in the mall area of a 50-acre privately owned shopping center. The center's management had a strict no-handbill policy that was conspicuously posted and rigorously enforced. Tanner's attorney argued that the center was equivalent to a public business district, as it had public streets running through it and was open to the general public. In holding that the center could lawfully enforce its no-handbill policy, the Court stated:

Nor does property lose its private character merely because the public is generally invited to use it for designated purposes. Few would argue that a freestanding store, with abutting parking space for customers, assumes significant public attributes merely because the public is invited to shop there. Nor is size alone the controlling factor. The essentially private character of a store and its privately owned abutting property does not change by virtue of being large or clustered with other stores in a modern shopping center. This is not to say that no differences may exist with respect to government regulation or rights of citizens arising by virtue of the size and diversity of activities carried on within a privately owned facility serving the public. There will be, for example, problems with respect to public health and safety which vary in degree and in the appropriate government response, depending upon the size and character of a shopping center, an office building, a sports arena, or other large facility serving the public for commercial purposes. We do say that the Fifth and Fourteenth Amendment rights of private property owners, as well as the First Amendment rights of all citizens, must be respected and protected. The Framers of the Constitution certainly did not think these fundamental rights of a free society are incompatible with each other. There may be situations where accommodations between them, and the drawing of lines to assure due protection of both, are not easy. But on the facts presented in this case, the answer is clear.

We hold that there has been no such dedication of Lloyd's privately owned and operated shopping center to public use as to entitle respondents to exercise therein the asserted First Amendment rights. Accordingly, we reverse the judgment and remand the case to the Court of Appeals with directions to vacate the injunction.

It is so ordered.

The Court distinguished this case from the cases of *Amalgamated Food Employees Union v. Logan Valley Plaza,*[25] and *Marsh v. Alabama.*[26] In the *Logan Valley Plaza* case, employees involved in a labor dispute sought to picket a store in the shopping center. The labor dispute was related to the center's activities and the picketers had a right to convey a message to the patrons of the store. In the *Tanner* case, the handbills were unrelated to any activity within the center and Tanner had alternative means of communication available to him.

Marsh v. Alabama concerned the distribution of religious literature in a company-owned town with "all that attributes" of a municipality. The town had its own business district, with merchants renting their store facilities, as well as a U.S. post office with six mail carriers working out of the post office. The Supreme Court held that there was a First Amendment right to distribute handbills in the *Marsh* case as there was a right to picket in the *Logan Valley Plaza* case.

E. FLAG MUTILATION AND DESECRATION CASES

Probably all states have statutes that make it a criminal offense to publicly mutilate, deface, de-

file, or cast contempt on the American flag. There were many flag cases in the early 1970s because, as a means of social protest, defendants chose the nation's flag as a means of communicating their messages, whatever they might be. Many of the flag statutes and ordinances were written years ago and have been found to be unconstitutional when courts apply today's "void-for-vagueness" and "overbreadth" tests.

There is no question that it is within the police power of the states to regulate the use and the treatment given to flags, but in doing so:

1. The statute or ordinance must be clearly and specifically written so as to give proper notice as to what conduct is forbidden (or required).

2. The conduct that is forbidden must be outside the conduct and speech protected by the First Amendment.

3. The statute or ordinance must not be so overly broad as to be possibly applicable to conduct or speech protected by the First Amendment.

In addition, the government must show that:

1. The object subjected to the alleged violation was in fact a flag (this may be difficult to do in some cases).

if regulations are reasonable.

2. The defendant did in fact mutilate, deface, defile, or cast contempt on the flag, as was forbidden by the statute or ordinance of that jurisdiction.

3. It was the defendant's intention to mutilate, deface, defile, and cast contempt on the flag. (For example, many old flags are burned on Memorial Day in ceremonies without any intent to cast contempt on or insult the flag.)

Recent U.S. Supreme Court flag cases that have caused much controversy and confusion with respect to flag regulation statutes and ordinances are:

STREET v. NEW YORK

Supreme Court of the United States (1969)
394 U.S. 576, 89 S. Ct. 1354

After hearing that civil rights leader James Meredith was killed by a sniper in Mississippi in 1966, the defendant left his apartment in New York City with an American flag. He went to a street corner, lit the flag with a match, and dropped it to the pavement, saying as he did, "We don't need no damn flag." Defendant was a black man who testified that he was provoked by a belief that Meredith had not been adequately protected. He stated at the scene, "Yes, that is my flag; I burned it. If they let that happen to Meredith, we don't need an American flag."

In a 5/4 decision, the majority reversed the defendant's conviction, concluding that the law was unconstitutionally applied in this case because it permitted the defendant "to be punished merely for speaking defiant or contemptuous words about the American flag." Justice Fortas dissented, stating:

I agree with the dissenting opinion filed by THE CHIEF JUSTICE, but I believe that it is necessary briefly to set forth the reasons why the States and the Federal Government have the power to protect the flag from acts of desecration committed in public.

If the national flag were nothing more than a chattel, subject only to the rules governing the use of private personalty, its use would nevertheless be subject to certain types of state regulation. For example, regulations concerning the use of chattels which are reasonably designed to avoid danger to life or property, or impingement upon the rights of others to the quiet use of their property and of public facilities, would unquestionably be a valid exercise of police power. They would not necessarily be defeated by a claim that they conflicted with the rights of the owner of the regulated property.

If a state statute provided that it is a misdemeanor to burn one's shirt or trousers or shoes on the public thoroughfare, it could hardly be asserted that the citizen's constitutional right is violated. If the arsonist asserted that he was burning his shirt or trousers or shoes as a protest against the Government's fiscal policies, for example, it is hardly possible that his claim to First Amendment shelter would prevail against the State's claim of a right to avert danger to the public and to avoid obstruction to traffic as a result of the fire. This is because action, even if clearly for serious protest purposes, is not entitled to the pervasive protection that is given to speech alone. It may be subjected to reasonable regulation that appropriately takes into account the competing interests involved.

The test that is applicable in every case where conduct is restricted or prohibited is whether the regulation or prohibition is reasonable, due account being taken of the paramountcy of First Amendment values. If, as I submit, it is permissible to prohibit the burning of personal property on the public sidewalk, there is no basis for applying a different rule to flag burning. And the fact that the law is violated for purposes of protest does not immunize the violator.

Beyond this, however, the flag is a special kind of personalty. Its use is traditionally and universally subject to special rules and regulation. As early as 1907, this Court affirmed the constitutionality of a state statute making it a crime to use a representation of the United States flag for purposes of advertising. Halter v. Nebraska, 205 U.S. 34, 27 S. Ct. 419, 51 L.Ed. 696 (1907). Statutes prescribe how the flag may be displayed; how it may lawfully be disposed of; when, how, and for what purposes it may and may not be used. A person may "own" a flag, but ownership is subject to special burdens and responsibilities. A flag may be property, in a sense; but it is property burdened with peculiar obligations and restrictions. Certainly, as Halter v. Nebraska, supra, held, these special conditions are not per se arbitrary or beyond governmental power under our Constitution.

One may not justify burning a house, even if it is his own, on the ground, however sincere, that he does so as a protest. One may not justify breaking the windows of a government building on that basis. Protest does not exonerate lawlessness. And the prohibition against flag burning on the public thoroughfare being valid, the misdemeanor is not excused merely because it is an act of flamboyant protest.

SPENCE v. STATE OF WASHINGTON

Supreme Court of the United States (1974)
418 U.S. 405, 94 S. Ct. 2727, 15 CrL 3263

The defendant displayed a U.S. flag from the window of his apartment. He had affixed a large peace symbol fashioned of removable tape to both surfaces of the flag, in protest against the invasion of Cambodia and the killings at Kent State University. The defendant was convicted under a Washington State statute forbidding the exhibition of a U.S. flag to which is attached or superimposed figures, symbols, or other extraneous material. In reversing the defendant's conviction, the Supreme Court held:

The statute is . . . unconstitutional as applied to appellant's activity. There was no risk that appellant's acts would mislead viewers into assuming that the Government endorsed his viewpoint. To the contrary, he was plainly and peacefully protesting the fact that it did not. Appellant was not charged under the desecration statute . . . nor did he permanently disfigure the flag or destroy it. He displayed it as a flag of his country in a way closely analogous to the manner in which flags have always been used to convey ideas. Moreover, his message was direct, likely to be understood, and within the contours of the First Amendment. Given the protected character of his expression and in light of the fact that no interest the State may have in preserving the physical integrity of a privately-owned flag was significantly impaired on these facts, the conviction must be invalidated.

F. SEDITIOUS SPEECH AND SUBVERSIVE CONDUCT

All democratic governments have had to assert their rights to protect their very existence against foreign tyrants and from conspiracies within their countries. The first national sedition law was enacted by the Congress in 1798. Over the years, various sedition statutes have been enacted. The harsh sedition law enacted by Congress in 1918 made it a crime to write, print, or publish any "disloyal, profane, scurrilous, or abusive language about the form of government of the United States . . . or any language intended to bring the form of government of the United States . . . or the flag . . . into contempt, scorn, contumely, or disrepute."

The sedition law of 1918 not only made it a crime to advocate illegal conduct, but also made criticism of government punishable. In 1919, a young woman was sentenced to 15 years in prison for distributing literature criticizing the use of American forces in Russia by President Woodrow Wilson.[27]

The sedition law in effect today is the Smith Act of 1940. It forbids advocating the forceful overthrow of the American government, the distributing with disloyal intent of material teaching and advising the overthrow of government by violence, and organizing or helping to organize any group having such purpose. In the following cases, the U.S. Supreme Court reviewed the convictions of persons convicted under the Smith Act:

DENNIS v. UNITED STATES

Supreme Court of the United States (1951)
341 U.S. 494, 71 S. Ct. 857

In this case, the first test of the Smith Act, the Court affirmed the conviction of the defendant, who was an officer in the Communist party, for conspiring to advocate the violent overthrow of the government.

YATES v. UNITED STATES

Supreme Court of the United States (1957)
354 U.S. 298 at 318, 77 S. Ct. 1064 at 1076

The Court in this case ordered the acquittal of several Yates defendants for the following reasons, which are summarized as follows in the 1961 case of *Scales v. United States:*

First, Yates makes clear what type of evidence is not in itself *sufficient to show illegal advocacy. This category includes evidence of the following: the teaching of Marxism-Leninism and the connected use of Marxist "classics" as textbooks; the official general resolutions and pronouncements of the Party at past conventions; dissemination of the Party's general literature, including the standard outlines on Marxism; the Party's history and organizational structure; the secrecy of meetings and the clandestine nature of the Party generally; statements by officials evidencing sympathy for and alliance with U.S.S.R. It was the predominance of evidence of this type which led the Court to order the acquittal of several Yates defendants, with the comment that they had not themselves "made a single remark or been present when someone else made a remark which would tend to prove the charges against them." However, this kind of evidence, while insufficient in itself to sustain a conviction, is not irrelevant. Such evidence, in the context of other evidence, may be of value in showing illegal advocacy.*

Second, the Yates opinion also indicates what kind of evidence is sufficient. There the Court pointed to two series of events which justified the denial of directed acquittals as to nine of the Yates defendants. The Court noted that with respect to seven of the defendants, meetings in San Francisco which were described by the witness Foard might be considered to be "the systematic teaching and advocacy of illegal action which is condemned by the statute." 354 U.S. at 331. In those meetings, a small group of members were not only taught that violent revolution was inevitable, but they were also taught techniques for achieving that end. For example, the Yates record reveals that members were directed to be prepared to convert a general strike into a revolution and to deal with Negroes so as to prepare them specifically for revolution. In addition to the San Francisco meetings, the Court referred to certain activities in the Los Angeles area "which might be considered to amount to 'advocacy of action'" and with which two Yates defendants were linked. Id. 354 U.S. 331, 332. Here again, the participants did not stop with teaching of the inevitability of eventual revolution, but went on to explain techniques, both legal and illegal, to be employed in preparation for or in connection with the revolution. Thus, one member was "surreptitiously indoctrinated in methods . . . of moving 'masses of people in time of crisis'"; others were told to adopt such Russian prerevolutionary techniques as the development of a special communication system through a newspaper similar to Pravda. *Id. 354 U.S. 332. Viewed together, these events described in Yates indicate at least two patterns of evidence sufficient to show illegal advocacy: (a) the teaching of forceful overthrow, accompanied by directions as to the type of illegal action which must be taken when the time for the revolution is reached; and (b) the teaching of forceful overthrow, accompanied by a contemporary, though legal, course of conduct clearly undertaken for the specific purpose of rendering effective the later illegal activity which is advocated.*

Finally, Yates is also relevant here in indicating, at least by implication, the type and quantum of evidence necessary to attach liability for illegal advocacy to the Party. In discussing the Government's "conspiratorial-nexus theory" the Court found that the evidence there was insufficient because the incidents of illegal advocacy were infrequent, sporadic, and not fairly related to the period covered by the indictment. In addition, the Court indicated that the illegal advocacy was not sufficiently tied to officials who spoke for the Party as such.

Thus, in short, Yates imposes a strict standard of proof, and indicates the kind of evidence that is insufficient to show illegal advocacy under that standard, the kind of evidence that is sufficient, and what pattern of evidence is necessary to hold the Party responsible for such advocacy. With these criteria in mind, we now proceed to an examination of the evidence in this case.

SCALES v. UNITED STATES

Supreme Court of the United States (1961)
367 U.S. 203, 81 S. Ct. 1469

The defendant was convicted under the so-called membership clause of the Smith Act (18 U.S.C.A. Section 2385), which, among other offenses, makes a felony of the acquisition or holding of knowing membership in any organization that advocates the overthrow of the government of the United States by force or violence. In affirming the conviction of the defendant and holding that the membership clause was constitutional, the Court stated:

Little remains to be said concerning the claim that the statute infringes First Amendment freedoms. It was settled in Dennis *that the advocacy with which we are here concerned is not constitutionally protected speech, and it was further established that a combination to promote such advocacy, albeit under the aegis of what purports to be a political party, is not such association as is protected by the First Amendment. We can discern no reason why membership, when it constitutes a purposeful form of complicity in a group engaging in this same forbidden advocacy, should receive any greater degree of protection from the guarantees of that Amendment.*

The Internal Security Act of 1950 and the Communist Control Act of 1954

The United States was caught unprepared in 1941 by the attack on Pearl Harbor and again, in 1950, by the outbreak of the Korean War. Because of this and the subversive activities of Communists within the United States, the Congress of the United States passed the Internal Security Act of 1950. This act was meant to disable the Communists by forcing their activities into the open. A number of sections of this act were declared unconstitutional by the U.S. Supreme Court in the 1960s, a number of sections were repealed, and what remains of the act is probably meaningless today.

The Communist Control Act of 1954 outlawed the Communist party in the United States. This was the first time in the history of the United States that a political party had been stripped of its First Amendment rights. The reasons Congress gave for taking this action are stated in Section 2 of the act:

Sec. 2. The Congress hereby finds and declares that the Communist Party of the United States, although purportedly a political party, is in fact an instrumentality of a conspiracy to overthrow the Government of the United States. It constitutes an authoritarian dictatorship within a republic, demanding for itself the

rights and privileges accorded to political parties, but denying to all others the liberties guaranteed by the Constitution. Unlike political parties, which evolve their policies and programs through public means, by the reconciliation of a wide variety of individual views, and submit those policies and programs to the electorate at large for approval or disapproval, the policies and programs of the Communist Party are secretly prescribed for it by the foreign leaders of the world Communist movement. Its members have no part in determining its goals, and are not permitted to voice dissent to party objectives. Unlike members of political parties, members of the Communist Party are recruited for indoctrination with respect to its objectives and methods, and are organized, instructed, and disciplined to carry into action slavishly the assignments given them by their hierarchical chieftains. Unlike political parties, the Communist Party acknowledges no constitutional or statutory limitations upon its conduct or upon that of its members. The Communist Party is relatively small numerically, and gives scant indication of capacity ever to attain its ends by lawful political means. The peril inherent in its operation arises not from its numbers, but from its failure to acknowledge any limitation as to the nature of its activities, and its dedication to the proposition that the present constitutional Government of the United States ultimately must be brought to ruin by any available means, including resort to force and violence. Holding that doctrine, its role as the agency of a hostile foreign power renders its existence a clear present and continuing danger to the security of the United States. It is the means whereby individuals are seduced into the service of the world Communist movement, trained to do its bidding, and directed and controlled in the conspiratorial performance of their revolutionary services. Therefore, the Communist Party should be outlawed.

In the few court cases that have tested the act, the act has been declared unconstitutional. However, the issue has never been taken to the U.S. Supreme Court.

QUESTIONS AND PROBLEMS FOR CHAPTER 11

1. Compare the case of *Maryland v. Diehl* (note 8) with *Colten v. Commonwealth* (earlier in this chapter). The *Colten* case was heard by the U.S. Supreme Court and the *Diehl* case was refused review by the U.S. Supreme Court in 1983. Are the rulings in the two cases inconsistent with each other? Under what circumstances can a person be ordered to "move on" or to get in or out of a vehicle? *if violating an ordinance*

2. Cantwell stopped two men on the street. He received permission from them and played a phonograph record that attacked their religion and church. Both men became angry and threatened to strike Cantwell unless he went away. Cantwell immediately left. He was charged with and convicted of violating the breach of the peace statute. Did the U.S. Supreme Court affirm the conviction? (*Cantwell v. Connecticut*, 310 U.S. 296, 60 S. Ct. 900 [1940]) *No because he left.*

3. The defendant addressed a group of blacks who had assembled to protest alleged police brutality. The defendant commended the crowd for their good conduct and restraint and stated that he believed in nonviolent behavior. He then stated to the crowd, "Do your own thing." Was this sufficient to justify a conviction for the offense of inciting to riot? (*State v. Douglas*, 278 So. 2d 485 [La. 1973]) *No*

4. Were the following regulations of premises lawful and reasonable? (all are true situations)
   - In Denver, Colorado, a husband and wife brought their own popcorn, hidden under their coats, into a movie theater. They would not leave when discovered and asked to leave. The police were called and the husband told a police officer he would have to be dragged out "kicking and screaming." The husband was taken to jail in handcuffs and both parties were charged with creating a disturbance.
   - Trustees in a half-way house would take detainees staying at the house for long walks in the area. The detainees were men from a maximum security prison who were to be released in the coming months. One group of eight detainees and two trustees entered a fashionable shopping mall as part of their daily walk. The presence of the group was noted immediately by the mall security force. A number of mall security persons and a city police officer approached the group of men (most were black). After inquiring as to their identity, the police officer told them that they *must* leave the mall, as their presence made the security persons nervous. Was this a proper "move-on" order by the officer? *No*
   - Was the procedure used by the corporate board in note 4 a lawful and reasonable regulation of the premises of that corporation?

Chapter 12

The Limits
of Other Freedoms

A. THE SECOND AMENDMENT RIGHT TO BEAR ARMS

"A well-regulated Militia, being necessary to the security of a free State, the right of the people to keep and bear Arms, shall not be infringed."
—Second Amendment of the U.S. Constitution

When the Second Amendment to the U.S. Constitution was ratified in 1791 as part of the Bill of Rights, the newly formed United States was a frontier nation with its 3 million or so people isolated from one another to a degree that is hard for us to imagine. There were no telephones, radios, or motor vehicles by which public officials and law enforcement officers could be summoned in an emergency. The few law enforcement officers could be found only in the towns and cities that were hours and sometimes days away from the farms and homes of many of the settlers.

Firearms were essential for survival, since most of the families depended on wild game as part of their subsistence. Guns were also needed for self-defense because organized law enforcement agencies were not within immediate call of most of the population. The American colonies were fearful of standing armies, since they had just thrown off the military control of Great Britain. The American Revolution had been fought by citizen part-time soldiers. Under the new Republic, the country had no need for a big army and looked on all able-bodied men as militia members who would be available in time of need, just as they had been in the 1770s. The "well-regulated Militia" to which the Second Amendment refers comprised the farmers and townspeople who had taken up arms against the British. Under those circumstances, the logic and meaning of the Second Amendment was apparent, since it stated a national need as basic as free speech and free religion to the newly formed democracy.

The Second Amendment Today

Today, the United States is made up of 50 states with more than 200 million people living primarily in crowded metropolitan areas. Instead of a militia made up principally of part-time citizen soldiers who bring their own weapons, we maintain huge federal military forces and National Guard units. As the country no longer needs the private arms of its citizens for defense, what is the meaning of the Second Amendment today?

Nations like England [1] and Japan strictly forbid the private possession and ownership of weapons. Other European countries have strict gun control laws. Compared with these nations, the United States exerts little control over the private ownership and possession of weapons. The United States has the highest per capita ownership of handguns in the world today. This private arsenal is estimated as high as 40 million, with an estimated 2 million or more handguns being added each year in recent years. The United States is also the most lawless of the industrial nations of the world, with the highest homicide rate of that group.

The handgun has become not only the number one tool of serious crime in the United States, but a common instrument in suicide. Although some other countries have higher overall suicide rates than does the United States, our firearm suicide death rate is the highest in the world. There are more suicides by firearms in the United States than in all the other countries combined. It also follows that because of the presence of large numbers of firearms, the United States has the highest number of accidental shootings in the world.

The National and Individualist Interpretations of the Second Amendment

Unless the Second Amendment were to be changed by constitutional amendment, the power of the states to prohibit the private ownership and possession of handguns rests on the interpretation of the Second Amendment by the U.S. Supreme Court. There are currently two interpretations of the Second Amendment, the "individualist view" and the "national view." The individualist view interprets the Second Amendment broadly and is urged by those who oppose laws forbidding the possession of handguns or registration requirements. They argue that the maintenance of a militia was only one of the purposes of the Second Amendment, and that the amendment ensures the right of individuals to bear arms to protect themselves not only from dangerous intruders against their homes and property, but also against possible oppression by government itself. They point out that when the Second Amendment was ratified, Americans had just created a strong central government and that the citizens of those days feared a repetition of the many abuses that strong centralized governments had imposed.

The national view interprets the Second Amendment strictly and holds that this amendment was meant to provide for strong militias of private citizens. Persons who advocate the national view argue that as the need for the militia no longer exists, the right of individuals to keep and bear arms no longer exists because private weapons are no longer needed either for the national defense or for emergencies.

Continuing Controversy over Handguns

In 1982, Morton Grove, Illinois (a suburb of Chicago), passed an ordinance forbidding the sale or possession of handguns in that community. At the same time, little Kennesaw, Georgia, also received national headlines by considering an ordinance requiring all heads of households to maintain a firearm and ammunition. It was also reported that more than 15 other small communities throughout the United States were considering pro-gun ordinances or resolutions.

National public opinion polls show that Americans generally favor stronger controls on handguns. However, the political battle over handguns will be fought in the big cities, the states and maybe the U.S. Congress. The police chief in Morton Grove was quoted as saying that handgun control in "one little town like Morton Grove by itself doesn't mean spit."

California attempted to pass the toughest handgun control law in the United States in Proposition 15. Despite public opinion polls indicating that the handgun control law would pass, Proposition 15 lost by a vote of 60 percent to 40 percent. This example illustrates that the outlook for stronger handgun control is dim.

Court Decisions Interpreting the Second Amendment

The U.S. Supreme Court has held that there is no right on the part of individuals to own or possess arms under the Second Amendment of the U.S. Constitution:

Deals with State Militia

UNITED STATES v. MILLER

Supreme Court of the United States (1939)
307 U.S. 174, 59 S. Ct. 816

The Supreme Court upheld a federal law making it a criminal offense to ship in interstate commerce a sawed-off shotgun, holding that "most if not all of the States have adopted provision touching the right to keep and bear arms."

QUILICI v. VILLAGE OF MORTON GROVE

Court of Appeals of the United States, Seventh Circuit (1983)
695 F. 2d 261, *cert. denied* by U.S. Supreme Court, 34 CrL 4004

The courts held that the Morton Grove ordinance that bans possession of operative handguns within the village did not violate the state or federal constitution. The U.S. Supreme Court refused further review of the Federal Court of Appeals' decision, which held:

According to its plain meaning, it seems clear that the right to bear arms is inextricably connected to the preservation of a militia. Illinois municipalities therefore have a constitutional right to ban ownership or sale of items determined to be dangerous.

Present Federal Regulation of Firearms

One of the earliest federal regulation of firearms is the 1934 National Firearms Act (Public Law 73–474), which forbids the interstate shipment of special weapons used by gangsters. It forbids the interstate shipment without a license of sawed-off shotguns, machine guns, and mufflers and silencers for guns. The 1938 Federal Firearms Act requires that firearms manufacturers, dealers, importers, and other persons engaged in firearms shipments across state lines be licensed by the federal government. The act also forbids the interstate shipment of all firearms to or by convicted felons, persons under indictment, and fugitives from justice.

The Gun Control Act of 1968 (Public Law 90–618) bans the interstate and mail order shipments of firearms to individuals and provides for the licensing of dealers, manufacturers, and importers. It requires the registration of "destructive devices" (cannons, antitank guns, bazookas, etc.) It bars the importation of cheap concealable foreign handguns, such as the six-dollar "Saturday Night Special," which killed Senator Robert Kennedy.

These three pieces of federal legislation do not make it difficult to obtain firearms in the United States. Guns are plentiful and easy to obtain by almost anyone persistent enough in attempting to purchase a weapon. However, Section 1202 of the 1968 Federal Omnibus Crime Control Act (Title VII) forbids the following persons from possessing any firearms: [3]

Any person who—

(1) has been convicted by a court of the United States or of a State or any political subdivision thereof of a felony, or

(2) has been discharged from the Armed Forces under dishonorable conditions, or

(3) has been adjudged by a court of the United States or of a State or any political subdivision thereof of being mentally incompetent, or

(4) having been a citizen of the United States has renounced his citizenship, or

(5) being an alien is illegally or unlawfully in the United States, and who receives, possesses, or transports in commerce or affecting commerce, after the date of enactment of this Act, any firearm shall be fined not more than $10,000 or imprisoned for not more than two years, or both.

"Carrying a Concealed Weapon" Statutes and Ordinances

All states have criminal statutes regulating the sale, possession, and use of weapons and probably all make it a criminal offense to carry a concealed weapon. Probably all municipalities also have ordinances regulating such conduct. The reason for enacting such statutes and ordinances is stated in Illinois as follows: "The possession and use of weapons inherently dangerous to human life constitutes a sufficient hazard to society to call for prohibition unless there appears appropriate justification created by special circumstances." [4] The Illinois Committee also commented that deadly weapons statutes have been criticized "for having the effect of prohibiting the law abiding citizen from protect-

---

Are Lack of Tough Gun Laws a Factor Relating to Criminal Homicides?	
Places with Tough Gun Laws	*Places with Easy Availability of Firearms*
London (pop. 7 million): 179 criminal homicides	Los Angeles (pop. 3 million): 1,557 criminal homicides
Canada (pop. 22.7 million): 292 criminal homicides	New York (pop. 7 million): 1,733 criminal homicides
Japan (pop. 115 million): 171 crimes with use of gun	United States (pop. just over 200 million): 21,456 homicides

Note: Approximate 1981 figures

ing himself, while at the same time failing to reach the criminal who habitually uses dangerous weapons for illegal ends."

In the Illinois case of *People v. McClendon,* the court held that:

> Concealment and accessibility are essential elements of the crime of carrying a concealed weapon on or about the person and the weapon must be in such proximity of the accused as to be within his easy reach and under his control and must be sufficiently close to his person to be readily accessible for immediate use.[5]

In the California case of *People v. Prochnau,* it was held that "(t)o establish unlawful possession of a contraband object it must be shown that the defendant exercised dominion and control over the object with knowledge of its presence and contraband character, but that such matters may be established by circumstantial evidence."[6]

Therefore, in order to convict for a CCW (carrying a concealed weapon) charge, the state or city must show:

1. that the instrument was a "dangerous weapon," "deadly weapon," or "weapon," as described by the statute or ordinance, and

2. that the weapon was concealed, and

3. that the weapon was within the defendant's "easy reach and under his control."

What Is a "Dangerous Weapon" or "Deadly Weapon"?

Statutes and ordinances vary concerning the type of instrument that is forbidden in CCW charges. Probably all states and ordinances forbid the carrying of revolvers, rifles, and shotguns concealed on the person. The following cases illustrate situations in which defendants were charged with carrying other instruments. The rulings only interpret the statutes or ordinances of those states.

STATE v. LASSLEY
Supreme Court of Kansas
(1976)
218 Kan. 752, 545 P.2d 379

After a complaint that the defendant was following a 15-year-old girl, the police found a knife with a six-inch blade concealed on the defendant's person. The Supreme Court of Kansas affirmed the conviction, despite testimony by the defendant and a fellow worker that the defendant used the knife in his job as a construction worker for an electrical power line company.

COMMONWEALTH v. ADAMS
Supreme Court of Pennsylvania
(1976)
369 A.2d 479

STATE v. MULIUFI
Supreme Court of Hawaii
(1982)
643 P.2d 546

These courts adopted the majority position, holding that nunchaku sticks are not, by themselves, deadly or dangerous weapons. The courts held that "given the present day uses of nunchaku sticks, we cannot say that the sole purpose of this instrumentality is to inflict death or bodily injury." The courts held in these cases that the sticks were not "diverted from [their] normal use and prepared and modified for combat purposes." However, in *State v. Tucker,*[7] the Oregon Court of Appeals held that concealed nunchaku sticks violated Oregon Statutes 166.240(1).

STATE v. RACKLE
Supreme Court of Hawaii
(1974)
523 P.2d 299

The court held that a flare gun was not a "deadly or dangerous weapon" within the meaning of that state's statute, as a flare gun is "not designed as an offensive weapon." However, in the 1983 case of *State v. Medeiros,*[8] the defendant fired a flare gun loaded with a shotgun shell at the victim's skull. The Hawaii Intermediate Court of Appeals held the defendant used a "firearm" within the meaning of state law to commit a homicide. The court held that the flare gun was used "as an instrument of offensive combat."

STATE v. LUCKEY
Supreme Court of Ohio (1974)
322 N.E.2d 354

FANN v. STATE
Court of Appeals of Georgia
(1980)
266 S.E.2d 307

In reversing convictions for armed robbery, the courts held that as starter pistols were incapable of firing bullets, they could not be deemed as offensive weapons when the pistols were displayed to victims to intimidate them. The Georgia court held that "we do not hold that a starter pistol could not under other circumstances be used in an offensive, deadly, or dangerous way. However, there is no evidence to indicate such a use in this case."

PEOPLE v. MALIK
Court of Appeals of Michigan
(1976)
70 Mich. App. 133, 245
N.W.2d 434

Karate sticks were not included as dangerous weapons under a "bludgeon" category.

HOWELL v. STATE
Court of Appeals of Maryland
(1976)
278 Md. 389, 364 A.2d 797

Under a Maryland statute, it was held that a tear gas pistol was not a "handgun" within the meaning of the handgun statute.

MOSLEY v. STATE
Court of Criminal Appeals of
Texas (1977)
545 S.W.2d 144

It was held that a B.B. gun was not a "deadly weapon."

PEOPLE v. GUEVARA
Criminal Court of the City of
New York (1976)
86 Misc. 2d 1044, 384
N.Y.S.2d 681

A 12-inch long, round, hollow pipe, wrapped in black tape and substantially thicker at one end, was held not to be a "blackjack" within the meaning of the applicable New York statute.

Is a Defective or Broken Weapon a Firearm?

A firearm has been defined as "any weapon from which a shot is discharged by force of an explosive or a weapon which acts by force of gunpowder." Under this definition, a New York court held that a Very pistol, designed to fire warning flares, is a firearm within the meaning of the New York Penal Code.[9]

It has been held that when a broken spring does not totally impair the use of a revolver, and the hammer can be operated manually, the instrument is a firearm within the meaning of the New York Penal Code.[10]

In the 1983 case of *York v. State*,[11] the Maryland Court of Appeals affirmed the conviction of defendant for using a handgun in the commission of a crime of violence (robbery). The gun had been damaged and could not be fired unless the person firing the gun was strong or used two hands. At the trial, a police firearms expert testifed that the gun could be made operable in about a minute's time by using a hammer and a screwdriver or a fingernail file. Not only was York convicted of the above crime, but he was also convicted of robbery with a dangerous and deadly weapon and battery.

In the 1968 California case of *People v. Jackson*,[12] the defendant had previously been convicted of a felony and was convicted of violating a California statute making it unlawful for ex-convicts to possess concealable firearms. The court reversed the conviction on the grounds that the pistol was not in operating condition, and could not have been made operable without the procurement of a replacement part. The court stated:

> We do not question the rule that "a deadly weapon does not cease to be such by becoming temporarily inefficient, nor is its essential character changed by dismemberment if the parts may be easily assembled so as to be effective." (People v. Guyette, 231 Cal. App. 2d 460, 467, 41 Cal. Rptr. 875, 880). As far as the meager evidence in the case at bar shows, the gun could not be made operable without he procurement of a replacement part.
>
> The only evidence before the court was that the pistol was not in operating condition. It is true that the judge as trier of the facts came to the opposite conclusion, but upon what evidence he based this conclusion is not known. There is nothing in the record to substantiate it.
>
> It is not a violation to carry a pistol that is so broken or out of repair that it cannot be used to shoot with or cannot be fired. (Farris v. State, 64 Tex. Cr. R. 524, 144 S.W. 249; People v. Simons, 124 Misc. 28, 207 N.Y.S. 56, 58).
>
> A pistol which was incapable of being fired because it had a broken firing pin is not a pistol within the statute (People v. Grillo [1962] 11 N.Y. 2d 841, 227 N.Y.S.2d 668, 182 N.E.2d 278) in the absence of a showing that a workable firing pin was also in the possession of defendant and that a simple substitution of pins would have made the weapon operable. (People v. Guyette, supra, 231 Cal. App. 2d 460, 41 Cal. Rptr. 875).

The Defense That the Concealed Gun Was Not Loaded

According to the majority rule in the United States, it is no defense to a charge of carrying a concealed weapon to show that it was not loaded. Some of the courts following this rule have pointed out that a gun frightens a victim whether it is loaded or unloaded, because the victim and other persons do not know whether the weapon contains live ammunition. The Supreme Court of Missouri followed the majority rule in the 1973 case of *State v. Dorsey,* stating:

> Defendant recognizes that the State is not required to prove that the gun was loaded but contends, in effect, that proof that it was not loaded is a valid affirmative defense. In our research we find that "under statutes prohibiting the carrying of pistols concealed, carrying pistols as weapons, exhibiting pistols, carrying pistols with intent to go armed, etc., the majority of courts recognize that it makes no difference, in relation to the offense charged, that the pistol was unloaded." Anno. 79 A.L.R.2d 1430. See also the following cases from other states which follow the majority rule: State v. Quail, 5 Boyce 310, 92 A. 859 (Del. 1914); Caldwell v. State, 106 S.W. 343 (Tex. Cr. App. 1907); Brooks v. State, 187 Tenn. 361, 215 S.W.2d 785 (1948); Cittadino v. State, 199 Miss. 235, 24 So.2d 93 (1945); People v. Halley, 131 Ill. App. 2d 1070, 268 N.E.2d 449 (1971); and Reed v. State, 199 So.2d 803[6] (Miss. 1967).
>
> We agree with the majority rule. The statute contains no requirement that the gun be loaded and a pistol is universally classified as a dangerous and deadly weapon even though not loaded. We accordingly rule that it is no defense to a charge of carrying a concealed weapon to show that it was not loaded.[13]

What Is Within a Defendant's "Easy Reach and Under His Control"?

STATE v. MOLINS
District Court of Appeal of Florida (1982)
424 So. 2d 29

The defendant placed a zippered canvas bag on a conveyor belt at an airport security checkpoint. A pistol was in the bag covered with other items. In affirming the defendant's conviction for carrying a concealed weapon, the court held:

For an accused to be found guilty of the offense of carrying a concealed firearm, the firearm must not only be hidden from the ordinary sight of another person, as here but must as well be "on or about the person," Ensor v. State, 403 So.2d 349, 354, 29 CrL 2304 (Fla. 1981). A firearm is considered "about the person" if it is "readily accessible" to him. . . . While it is true that in order for the defendant to gain access to the firearm in the present case, he would have had to unzip two containers, in our view the firearm was not any less accessible than one in a locked glove compartment of a vehicle which, according, to Ensor, may abe considered, in the words of the statute, "about the person."

PEOPLE v. DUNN
Court of Appeal of California (1976)
61 Cal. App. 3d Supp. 12, 132 Cal. Rptr. 921

In affirming the defendant's conviction for carrying a concealed weapon (handgun) in a suitcase, the court held:

We hold that the Legislature intended to proscribe the carrying of concealed weapons by both men and women and that a handgun concealed in a suitcase and carried by appellant is sufficiently "upon his person" to constitute a violation of section 12025.

PEOPLE v. PUGACH
Court of Appeals of New York (1964)
15 N.Y.2d 65, 255 N.Y.S.2d 833, 204 N.E.2d 176

In affirming the defendant's conviction, the New York court saw no significance in "the fact that the loaded gun was found concealed in the brief case, rather than in a pocket of the defendant's clothing." The court held that a "loaded firearm concealed in the brief case carried in the hands of the defendant was in the language of the statute 'concealed upon his person.' "

STATE v. WILLIAMS
Supreme Court of Utah (1981)
636 P.2d 1092

In holding that the defendant was "carrying" the gun that was next to him in a partially unzipped satchel on the seat of his car, the Court stated:

The danger to others is just as great where the weapon is readily accessible as where carried on the person of the individual.

STATE v. MORRISON
Court of Appeals of Oregon (1976)
25 Or. App. 609, 549 P.2d 1295

When a law enforcement officer stopped the defendant's car for a traffic violation, he saw and seized a stiletto that was partially showing on the vehicle floor by the side of the defendant's foot. The Court held that the defendant was "carrying" the stiletto, stating:

We think it obvious that the legislature intended to prohibit only such carrying as by its nature makes the instrument readily available for use as a weapon by a person who has its constructive possession. That ingredient of the offense is fulfilled by the circumstances of the case at bar.
    Affirmed.

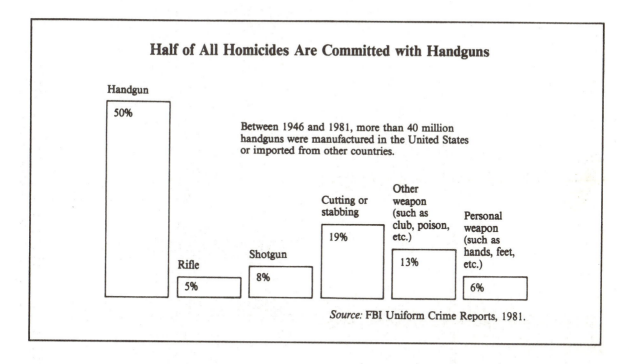

Half of All Homicides Are Committed with Handguns

Handgun

50%

Between 1946 and 1981, more than 40 million handguns were manufactured in the United States or imported from other countries.

Cutting or stabbing

19%

Other weapon (such as club, poison, etc.)

13%

Personal weapon (such as hands, feet, etc.)

6%

Rifle

5%

Shotgun

8%

Source: FBI Uniform Crime Reports, 1981.

When Is a Weapon Concealed?

The question of when a weapon is concealed has come before many courts in CCW cases. Does a weapon have to be so concealed that it gives absolutely no notice of its presence, or is a weapon concealed when it cannot be seen in ordinary observation? In the following 1981 decision, the Florida Supreme Court adopted the majority position in the United States that "a weapon need not be totally hidden from view to be 'concealed'":

ENSOR v. STATE
Supreme Court of Florida
(1981)
403 So.2d 349, 29 CrL 2304

After police officers made a lawful traffic stop, a derringer was observed protruding from a floormat in the car. The gun was held to be "concealed" within the meaning of the state law and the defendant was convicted of CCW. The court affirmed the conviction, holding:

The majority of courts in other jurisdictions that have considered the issue have concluded that a weapon need not be totally hidden from view to be "concealed." See, e.g., Mularkey v. State, 230 N.W. 76 (Wis.1930), People v. Williams, 39 Ill.App.3d 129, 350 N.E.2d 81 (1976), and Driggers v. State, 26 So. 512 (Ala.1899).

We agree with the majority view and find that absolute invisibility is not a necessary element to a finding of concealment under section 790.001. The operative language of that section establishes a two-fold test. For a firearm to be concealed, it must be (1) on or about the person and (2) hidden from the ordinary sight of another person. The term "on or about the person" means physically on the person or readily accessible to him. This generally includes the interior of an automobile and the vehicle's glove compartment, whether or not locked. The term "ordinary sight of another person" means that casual and ordinary observation of another in the normal associations of life. Ordinary observation by a person other than a police officer does not generally include the floorboard of a vehicle, whether or not the weapon is wholly or partially visible. Further, the fact that a firearm is encased in a holster does not remove it from the application of section 790.001. A firearm encased in a holster and hidden under an automobile seat is no different than a traditionally concealed firearm in a shoulder holster under one's coat. Both appear to be outside the "ordinary sight of another person."

Except for Homicide, Most Violent Crimes do not Involve the Use of Weapons

Weapon Use	Homicide	Rape	Robbery	Assault †
Firearm	62%	7%	18%	9%
Knife	19	15	21	9
Other	13	1*	9	14
Type unknown	0	2*	2	1
None used	6	77	54	68
Total	100%	100%	100%	100%

Note: Because some victimizations involve more than one type of weapon, detail may add to more than 100%.

* Estimate is based on 10 or fewer samples and is therefore statistically unreliable.

† Includes simple assaults, which by definition do not involve the use of a weapon.

Source: National Crime Survey, 1981; Uniform Crime Reports, 1981.

B. THE FREE EXERCISE OF RELIGION

The Right to Believe or Not to Believe

The First Amendment was intended to allow every one under the jurisdiction of the United States to entertain such notions respecting his relations to his Maker and the duties they impose as may be approved by his judgment and conscience, and to exhibit his sentiments in such form of worship, as he may think

proper, not injurious to the equal rights of others, and to prohibit legislation for the support of any religious tenets, or the modes of worship of any sect. The oppressive measures adopted, and the cruelties and punishments inflicted, by the governments of Europe for many ages, to compel parties to conform, in their religious beliefs and modes of worship, to the views of the most numerous sect, and the folly of attempting in that way to control the mental operations of persons, and enforce an outward conformity to a prescribed standard, led to the adoption of [this] amendment.[14]

Freedom to believe is absolute; freedom to act is not. The U.S. Supreme Court held in *Cantwell v. Connecticut* that:

Freedom of conscience and freedom to adhere to such religious organization or form of worship as the individual may choose cannot be restricted by law. On the other hand, it safeguards the free exercise of the chosen form of religion. Thus the Amendment embraces two concepts,—freedom to believe and freedom to act. The first is absolute but, in the nature of things, the second cannot be. Conduct remains subject to regulation for the protection of society. The freedom to act must have appropriate definition to preserve the enforcement of that protection. In every case the power to regulate must be so exercised as not, in attaining a permissible end, unduly to infringe the protected freedom.

* * *

Nothing we have said is intended even remotely to imply that, under the cloak of religion, persons may, with impunity, commit frauds upon the public. Certainly penal laws are available to punish such conduct. Even the exercise of religion may be at some slight inconvenience in order that the state may protect its citizens from injury. Without doubt a state may protect its citizens from fraudulent solicitation by requiring a stranger in the community before permitting him publicly to solicit funds for any purpose, to establish his identity and his authority to act for the cause which he purports to represent. The state is likewise free to regulate the time and manner of solicitation generally, in the interest of public safety, peace, comfort or convenience. But to condition the solicitation of aid for the perpetuation of religious views or systems upon a license, the grant of which rests in the exercise of a determination by state authority as to what is a religious cause, is to lay a forbidden burden upon the exercise of liberty protected by the Constitution.

* * *

In the realm of religious faith, and in that of political belief, sharp differences arise. In both fields the tenets of one man may seem the rankest error to his neighbor. To persuade others to his own point of view, the pleader, as we know, at times, resorts to exaggeration, to vilification of men who have been, or are, prominent in church or state, and even to false statement. But the people of this nation have ordained in the light of history, that, in spite of the probability of excesses and abuses, these liberties are, in the long view, essential to enlightened opinion and right conduct on the part of the citizens of a democracy.

The essential characteristic of these liberties, is, that under their shield many types of life, character, opinion and belief can develop unmolested and unobstructed. Nowhere is this shield more necesssary than in our own country for a people composed of many races and of many creeds. There are limits to the exercise of these liberties. The danger in these times from the coercive activities of those who in the delusion of racial or religious conceit would incite violence and breaches of the peace in order to deprive others of their equal right to the exercise of their liberties, is emphasized by events familiar to all. These and other transgressions of those limits the states appropriately may punish.[15]

Cases Illustrating the Limits of Religious Freedom

REYNOLDS v. UNITED STATES
Supreme Court of the United States (1879)
98 U.S. 145, 25 L.Ed. 244

Many states make polygamy a crime. However, criminal charges for polygamy have rarely been issued in recent years. The religious practice of polygamy (having more than one spouse at one time and being married to more than one person at the same time) continues to be used in other parts of the world. In 1879, the U.S. Supreme Court affirmed the conviction of the defendant, holding that the Mormon Church could not continue the religious practice of polygamy in violation of federal and state criminal codes.

PEOPLE v. WOODY
Supreme Court of California (1964)
61 Cal. 2d 716, 40 Cal. Rptr. 69, 394 P.2d 813

Because the use of peyote by Navajo Indians goes back as far as 1560, the California Supreme Court held that peyotism as a religious practice could continue in that state as a bona fide religious practice. However, the Supreme Court of North Carolina found to the contrary in the 1966 case of *State v. Bullard*,[16] in which the court held that the First Amendment could not protect the defendant.

The *People v. Woody* exemption applies in California and in other states that accept the exemption.[17] It applies to the Native American Church and their members, who must be of at least one-quarter Indian blood. In *Kennedy v. Bureau of Narcotics and Dangerous Drugs* (see 11 CrL 2090, 5/3/72), a new church (The Church of the Awakening), based on the mystical value of psychedelic experience, also sought an exemption (along with the mescaline-eating Native American Church) from laws forbidding the use of the "magic cactus" buttons. The U.S. Court of Appeals for the

Ninth Circuit refused to extend the exemption and held that the exemption was an arbitrary classification that denied equal protection of the law and violated the Fourteenth Amendment.

STATE v. MASSEY
Supreme Court of North Carolina (1949)
229 N.C. 734, 51 S.E.2d 179

According to the New Testament in Mark 16:16–18, "He that believeth and is baptized shall be saved; . . . they shall speak with new tongues; they shall take up serpents; and if they drink any deadly thing, it shall not hurt them." In *State v. Massey,* the defendant was convicted of handling poisonous snakes in a religious ceremony, taking literally these words from the New Testament. The court ruled that the state law forbidding the handling of poisonous snakes was a valid use of the police power of the state of North Carolina and held that the public safety factor outweighed the right to religious freedom.

However, the practice of handling poisonous snakes continues to a limited extent in some southern Appalachian churches. In 1972, two young men who had successfully handled such snakes as copperheads further testified to their belief in Mark 16:16–18 by drinking a mixture of strychnine and water at an evening service. Both were dead by the next morning.

HEFFRON v. INTERNATIONAL SOCIETY FOR KRISHNA CONSCIOUSNESS
Supreme Court of the United States (1981)
452 U.S. 640, 101 S. Ct. 2559

The Minnesota State Fair made distribution or sale of literature or merchandise away from a booth rented on the fairgrounds a misdemeanor, subject to arrest and expulsion from the fairgrounds. Booths were rented on a nondiscriminatory first-come, first-served basis. The Krishna religion argued that this regulation suppresses their religious practice of Sankirtan, which requires its members to go into public places to distribute or sell religious literature and to solicit donations for the support of their sect.

The U.S. Supreme Court held that the rule of the Minnesota State Fair did not violate First Amendment rights of the Hare Krishna sect. The fairgrounds consist of a relatively small area in view of the massive crowds of people and the enormous variety of goods, services, entertainment, etc. that is exhibited. The Court held that the state's interest in maintaining the orderly movement of the crowd is sufficient to impose the time, place, and manner restriction not only on the Hare Krishna sect, but also on the many other groups seeking to exercise their First Amendment rights.

U.S. POSTAL SERVICE v. COUNCIL OF GREENBURG CIVIC ASSN.
Supreme Court of the United States (1981)
453 U.S. 917, 101 S. Ct. 3150

The Federal postal statute 18 U.S.C. 1725 forbids putting unstamped "mailable matter" into letter boxes used to receive mail. Groups wishing to use mail boxes to deposit material argued that this seldom-used statute violated their First Amendment rights. The Supreme Court held that a letter box is not a "soap box" and upheld the statute that punishes misuse with a fine up to $300 for each offense.

WISCONSIN v. YODER
Supreme Court of the United
States (1972)
406 U.S. 205, 92 S. Ct. 1526

The defendants were convicted of a misdemeanor for violating the Wisconsin compulsory school attendance law, which requires parents to have their children attend school until age 16. The defendants, who were of the Amish faith, took their children out of school after they had finished the eighth grade because they believed that secondary schooling exposed their children to worldly influences in terms of attitudes, goals, and values that were contrary to the religious development of an Amish child. The U.S. Supreme Court sustained the Wisconsin Supreme Court in reversing the convictions and holding that the compulsory school attendance law violated the rights of the Amish to practice their religion freely. Justice William O. Douglas, in dissenting, stated in part that "on this important and vital matter of education, I think the children should be entitled to be heard."

Cults, Sects, and Nontraditional Churches in the United States

Estimates of the membership in cults and sects in the United States range from 3 million to 8 million persons belonging to more than 3,000 groups. Some cults are small, whereas others have memberships in the hundreds of thousands.

Recently, there has been increased concern over cults. In November 1978 the public was shocked when Congressman Leo Ryan was killed by members of the California-based People's Temple. The ambush killing was followed by murders and mass suicide of approximately 900 cult members in Jonestown, Guyana (South America).

Although some cults and sects are ordinary religious groups, others have given rise to reports concerning some of the following:

- strange religious practices
- brainwashing
- questionable practices used to detain members [18]
- incredible devotion to a cult leader
- cult leaders who live in extreme luxury and acquire considerable wealth from their followers
- in few instances, bizarre sexual acts, torture, and killings

Such behavior has caused an increased number of persons to view cults as the dark side of religion.

The *FBI Law Enforcement Bulletin* presented a three-part article entitled "Cults: A Conflict Between Religious Liberty and Involuntary Servitude?" commencing in the April 1982 issue. The June article concludes:

With the increase in cult membership over the last 10 years, law enforcement investigations involving cult members is increasing. Whether these investigations will be routine, such as proselytizing activities on the street, or criminal, such as shoplifting or drug use, the cult member should be treated the same as any other person. A more serious problem arises when an officer encounters a "kidnapping" for deprogramming or receives a complaint involving cult coercion by a parent of a cult member.

Clearly, the officer cannot proceed to release the deprogrammer after observing him with a hostage or let him retain a person kidnapped against his or her will. Nor can they invade the property of a cult to release a victim, unless there is evidence of imminent harm to the cult member.

Practical considerations would come into play at every stage, which would require close coordination with the prosecution. Who should be charged with a crime? What type of charges could be filed? What if the "kidnappers" include a close relative? What jury is going to convict a 50-year-old father for kidnapping his 20-year-old son! And if the state cannot prosecute the father, is it just to charge the deprogrammer who was hired by the father to perform the actual kidnapping? What defenses does the law allow in the jurisdiction, and what charges should be given to the jury? Law enforcement officers may wish to consult with their local prosecutors to determine whether any guidelines are in place or being contemplated in their jurisdictions to answer these questions.

The article recommends that the following conduct be made crimes: "misrepresentation in recruitment and in proselytizing activities, preventing a [cult] member from contacting individuals outside the organization, or preventing members from leaving the cult." Such legislation must be drafted so as to not interfere with individuals' rights to enter and participate in cults. But new legislation is needed, as the article points out, "to resolve the problem facing parents and law enforcement. The coercive acts of some cults in recruitment and proselytizing activities should not go unchallenged. Nor should some cults be allowed to hide behind the first amendment, while at the same time denying constitutional rights to some of their followers."

Court Cases Involving Cults

UNIVERSAL LIFE CHURCH, INC. v. **UNITED STATES** U.S. District Court, Eastern District California (1974) 372 F. Supp. 770	The creed of the Universal Life Church was "do your own thing." For $20 the church mailed credentials of ministry to anyone requesting them and ordained millions of ministers in this way. Tax exemptions could then be claimed by the new "ministers." The government challenged the church's tax exempt status, but the court held the ordinations were a traditional religious activity.
UNITED STATES v. **HUBBARD** U.S. District Court, District of Columbia (1979) 493 F. Supp. 209	Nine members of the Church of Scientology were convicted of various offenses ranging from conspiracy to obstructing justice, stealing government property, burglary, bugging, harboring fugitives from justice, and perjury.
UNITED STATES v. **MOON** U.S. Court of Appeals, Second Circuit 718 F.2d 1210 *review denied* by U.S. Supreme Court 35 CrL 4042	The Rev. Sun Myung Moon, founder of the Unification Church, was convicted of failing to pay $162,000 in federal taxes. His conviction and sentence of 18 months in prison with a $25,000 fine was affirmed by the federal appeals court and review denied by the U.S. Supreme Court. Nine major religious and civil liberties groups filed friend-of-the-court briefs on Moon's behalf.[19]

C. THE RIGHT OF PRIVACY

The Use and Distribution of Contraceptives

GRISWOLD v. **CONNECTICUT** Supreme Court of the United States (1965) 381 U.S. 479, 85 S. Ct. 1678	In the *Griswold* case, the Court struck down a Connecticut criminal law forbidding the use of contraceptives to prevent conception. The law was held to be an unconstitutional infringement of the right of marital privacy. In *Eisenstadt v. Baird,* the Court, citing the equal protection of the laws clause, held unconstitutional a Massachusetts statute prohibiting the distri-

EISENSTADT v. BAIRD

Supreme Court of the United States (1972)

405 U.S. 438, 92 S. Ct. 1029

bution of contraceptives to an unmarried person except to prevent disease. The Court stated:

If under Griswold *the distribution of contraceptives to married persons cannot be prohibited, a ban on distribution to unmarried persons would be equally impermissible. It is true that in* Griswold *the right of privacy in question inhered in the marital relationship. Yet the marital couple is not an independent entity with a mind and heart of its own, but an association of two individuals each with a separate intellectual and emotional make-up. If the right of privacy means anything, it is the right of the* individual, *married or single, to be free from unwarranted governmental intrusion into matters so fundamentally affecting a person as the decision whether to bear or beget a child.*

CAREY v. POPULA- TION SERVICES INTERN.

Supreme Court of the United States (1977)

431 U.S. 678, 97 S. Ct. 2010

The U.S. Supreme Court voided a New York law that: (a) required that nonprescription contraceptives be sold by pharmacists only to persons age 16 and over, (b) mandated that persons 15 years and younger obtain contraceptives from doctors only, and (c) prohibited advertisements for contraceptives from display in drugstores.

Quoting *Eisenstadt v. Baird,* the Court held that "if the right of privacy means anything, it is the right of the individual, married or single, to be free from unwarranted governmental intrusion into matters so fundamentally affecting a person as the decision whether to bear or beget a child."

Holding that the New York law served no compelling state interest in denying minors a right of privacy enjoyed by adults, the Court held:

Although we take judicial notice, as did the District Court, 398 F. Supp., at 331–333, that with or without access to contraceptives, the incidence of sexual activity among minors is high, and the consequences of such activity are frequently devastating, the studies cited by appellees play no part in our decision. It is enough that we again confirm the principle that when a State, as here, burdens the exercise of a fundamental right, its attempt to justify that burden as a rational means for the accomplishment of some significant State policy requires more than a bare assertion, based on a conceded complete absence of supporting evidence, that the burden is connected to such a policy.

The Abortion Question

Until 1973, abortion was a crime in most states, with only four states permitting abortion on demand by women. In 1973, the following cases of *Roe v. Wade* and *Doe v. Bolton* came before the U.S. Supreme Court. The rulings in these cases caused the abortion laws in 31 states to be unconstitutional and made revisions necessary in the abortion statutes of 15 other states.

ROE v. WADE

Supreme Court of the United States (1973)
410 U.S. 113, 93 S. Ct. 705

DOE v. BOLTON

Supreme Court of the United States (1973)
410 U.S. 179, 93 S. Ct. 739

The women in both these cases ("Jane Roe" and "Mary Doe") had requested abortions when they were pregnant and, like thousands of other women, were turned down. Both women went to court to attack their state statutes on abortion. Before the Court was the question of the power of government to enact criminal laws forbidding and regulating abortion. When does the fetus have legal rights that obligate the state to protect its existence? In a long, complicated decision, the Court held that:

• In the first three-month period, abortion "although not without risks, is now relatively safe" and "any interest of the state in protecting the woman from an inherently hazardous procedure . . . has largely disappeared." During this period, "the abortion decision and its effectuation must be left to the medical judgment of the pregnant woman's attending physician."

• After the first trimester, a state may "regulate the abortion procedure in ways that are reasonably related to maternal health."

• Only during the last 10 weeks of pregnancy, when the fetus has developed enough to have a chance of survival on its own, does the state's "important and legitimate interest in potential life" actually outweigh the mother's individual rights. It is when the fetus becomes "viable," usually during the seventh month of pregnancy, that a state "may go so far as to proscribe (forbid) abortion . . . except when it is necessary to preserve the life or health of the mother." Justice Harry A. Blackmun, writing for the majority, held that a fetus is not a person under the Constitution and thus has no legal right to life. Antiabortionists strongly object to this last point, as they maintain that there is a "right to life."

Abortion Practices in the United States Today

Approximately 6 million pregnancies occur in the United States each year; it is estimated that more than half these pregnancies are unintended. Of these unintended pregnancies, it is estimated that nearly half are terminated by abortion.

Almost 90 percent of abortions occur in the first trimester; approximately 10 percent of abortions occur in the second trimester; only a small fraction of 1 percent of abortions occur in the third trimester.

States may regulate abortions to protect the life of a "viable" fetus [20] and in doing so "may proscribe [forbid] abortion except where it is necessary, in appropriate medical judgment,' for the preservation of the life or health of the mother." [21] Abortion, however, is controversial [22] and many states have not enacted new abortion laws to replace the old statutes. Abor-

tion practices in the United States are therefore generally governed by the following:

1. As only a licensed physician may perform an abortion, any other person who engages in such acts may be charged with practicing medicine without a license. [23]

2. Licensed physicians should limit abortions to early in the pregnancy, because of the increased possibilities of:
   a. a civil malpractice suit
   b. criminal charges if the fetus is "born alive" and then destroyed
   c. loss of license as a disciplinary measure taken by the medical licensing board
   d. loss of hospital privileges for violating hospital rules and thereby making the hospital vulnerable to civil suit
   e. increased malpractice insurance premiums because of increased liability.

D. THE EQUAL PROTECTION OF THE LAWS

The "equal protection of the laws" clause of the Fourteenth Amendment requires that states must treat all persons alike, not only in enacting legislation, but also in enforcing rules. A state may enact laws forbidding marriages between persons of close blood relationships. Marriages between a brother and a sister, for example, are forbidden in all states because of the increased likelihood of deformed offspring. Such consanguinity laws apply to all persons, regardless of status, race, or religion, and represent a valid exercise of the police power of the state.

However, criminal statutes that forbid marriages between members of different races (miscegenation laws) violate the "equal protection of the laws" clause of the Constitution. This issue was brought before the U.S. Supreme Court in the 1964 case of *McLaughlin v. Florida.*[24] A criminal law that punished a white person who lived with a black person was declared invalid, as it was a denial of the equal protection of the laws guaranteed by the Fourteenth Amendment.[25]

E. THE PRIVILEGE AGAINST SELF-INCRIMINATION

The Fifth Amendment states that "no person . . . shall be required in any criminal case to be a witness against himself." This constitutional right to remain silent is usually thought of as pertaining only to the law of criminal procedure and investigation in which, for example, the *Miranda* requirement imposes a duty on law enforcement officers to warn persons being questioned while in custody. However, this constitutional provision also limits the creation of criminal laws that compel communications. The following exaggerated example is used to illustrate:

Example: A state passes a criminal law requiring bank robbers to register before committing the offense of robbery. Failure to register would permit the state not only to charge the offender with the crime of robbery, but also with the offense of failing to register. If the offender registers as required, the state is then alerted to the criminal conduct that is contemplated.

In the example, the proposed criminal law compels the disclosure of information that could assist the state in bringing charges against persons. The laws would require offenders, in effect, to be witnesses against themselves. In the following cases, the issue of the extent of the Fifth Amendment privilege against incrimination came before appellate courts:

MARCHETTI v. UNITED STATES
Supreme Court of the United States (1968)
390 U.S. 39, 88 S. Ct. 697

GROSSO v. UNITED STATES
Supreme Court of the United States (1968)
390 U.S. 62, 88 S. Ct. 709

All states, except Nevada, have criminal laws regulating gambling, wagering, and associated activities. Congress passed a law requiring that all gamblers in the United States register and pay an annual occupational tax. The defendants were convicted of violating the federal wagering tax statutes. The defendants argued that their statutory obligation to register and pay the occupational tax violated their Fifth Amendment privilege against self-incrimination. In reversing the convictions and holding that such laws "may not be employed to punish criminally those persons who have defended a failure to comply with their requirements with a proper assertion of the privilege against self-incrimination," the Court stated:

The issue before us is not *whether the United States may tax activities which a State or Congress has declared unlawful. The Court has repeatedly indicated that the unlawfulness of an activity does not prevent its taxation, and nothing that follows is intended to limit or diminish the vitality of those cases.* . . .

The issue is instead whether the methods employed by Congress in the federal wagering tax statutes are, in this situation, consistent with the limitations created by the privilege against self-incrimination guaranteed by the Fifth Amendment. We must for this purpose first examine the implications of these statutory provisions.

* * *

The terms of the wagering tax system make quite plain that Congress intended information obtained as a consequence of registration and payment of the occupational tax to be provided to interested prosecuting authorities.

* * *

(W)e can only conclude, under the wagering tax system as presently written, that petitioner properly asserted the privilege against self-incrimination, and that his assertion should have provided a complete defense to this prosecution. This defense should have reached both the substantive counts for failure to register and to pay the occupational tax, and the count for conspiracy to evade payment of the tax. We emphasize that we do not hold that these wagering tax provisions are as such constitutionally impermissible; we hold only that those who properly assert the constitutional privilege as to these provisions may not be criminally punished for failure to comply with their requirements. If, in different circumstances, a taxpayer is not confronted by substantial hazards of self-incrimination, or if he is otherwise outside the privilege's protection, nothing we decide today would shield him from the various penalties prescribed by the wagering tax statutes.

CALIFORNIA v. BEYERS

Supreme Court of the United States (1971)
402 U.S. 424, 91 S. Ct. 1535

All states have statutes that require drivers of motor vehicles who are involved in an accident to stop at the scene and give their names and addresses. These "hit and run" or "stop and report" statutes impose criminal penalties on motorists who fail to comply with the requirements of the statute. The defendant argued that the California "hit and run" statute violated his privilege against compulsory self-incrimination. In holding that "disclosure of name and address is an essentially neutral act," and that "there is no constitutional right to refuse to file an income tax return or to flee the scene of an accident in order to avoid the possibility of legal involvement," the Court sustained the legality of the California requirement, stating:

Driving an automobile, unlike gambling, is a lawful activity. Moreover, it is not a criminal offense under California law to be a driver "involved in an accident." An accident may be the fault of others; it may occur without any driver having been at fault. No empirical data are suggested in support of the conclusion that there is a relevant correlation between being a driver and criminal prosecution of drivers. So far as any available information instructs us, most accidents occur without creating criminal liability even if one or both of the drivers are guilty of negligence as a matter of tort law.

The disclosure of inherently illegal activity is inherently risky. Our decisions in Albertson and the cases following illustrate that truism. But disclosures with respect to automobile accidents simply do not entail the kind of substantial risk of self-incrimination involved in Marchetti, Grosso, *and* Haynes. *Furthermore, the statutory purpose is noncriminal and self-reporting is indispensable to its fulfillment.*

UNITED STATES v. LAUCHLI

Court of Appeals of the United States, Seventh Circuit (1971)
444 F.2d 1037

The defendant was convicted of 15 violations of the National Firearms Act and the Gun Control Act. On one occasion, he illegally sold two Thompson submachine guns and 10 silencers to an undercover officer. On another occasion, he sold 10 Thompson submachine guns and 15 barrels to the officer. When officers searched his home and business place under the authority of a search warrant, they found 461 submachine guns and two white phosphorus rifle grenades. In the case of *Haynes v. United States,*[26] the Supreme Court held in 1968 that the National Firearms Act violated the Fifth Amendment privilege against self-incrimination. Defendant Lauchli was convicted in 1971 under the amended National Firearms Act, which the court held did not violate the Fifth Amendment privilege against self-incrimination because (a) it is no longer directed to a selective group inherently suspect of criminal activities but applies to all possessors of firearms and (b) the government does not disclose the information that is provided by the person who is required to register.

QUESTIONS AND PROBLEMS FOR CHAPTER 12

Select the correct answer for the questions from the following available answers:

a. *This is a reasonable and proper use of the police power of the state*

b. *Violates First Amendment (freedom of religion, speech, press, right of assembly, and right to petition the government in redress of grievance)*

c. *Violates Fourth Amendment (unreasonable search and seizure or right of privacy violation)*

d. *Violates Fifth Amendment (privilege against self-incrimination, due process of law, etc.)*

e. *Violates right to bear arms, cruel and unusual punishment, equal protection of laws requirement*

1. A state law makes abortion a crime regardless of the stage of pregnancy at the time of abortion.

2. A municipality takes away the liquor license from a night club that featured nude entertainment.

3. A state statute permits the death penalty to be imposed in first-degree murder convictions at the discretion of the jury or judge.

4. A state law forbids the criticism of any public official in that state.

5. Citations and arrests were made when demonstrators violated red traffic lights as a means of social protest.

6. A state statute forbids the possession of a loaded revolver whether the gun is carried concealed or in open view.

7. A state statute forbids the sale of obscene material.

8. A state statute forbids the use or sale of contraceptives to anyone (married or unmarried).

9. A state law requires a motorist involved in an accident to stop and leave his or her name and address.

10. A statute forbids loitering in a public school building by persons who have no legitimate business in the building.

11. A state statute forbids the carrying or possession of a loaded rifle or shotgun in a motor vehicle on the public highways. (See *State v. Duranleau,* 128 Vt. 206, 260 A.2d 383 [1969].)

12. A state statute forbids the sale of firearms to anyone without an identification card issued by the local police department. (See *Burton v. Sills,* 53 N.J. 86, 248 A.2d 521 [1968].)

13. A chronic alcoholic was arrested when he was disorderly and broke a store window while intoxicated.

Part Three

Crimes Against the Person

Chapter 13

Homicide

A. HOMICIDE IN GENERAL

Homicide, the killing of one human being by another, is not always criminal. Sir William Blackstone, a famous English lawyer, wrote in the 18th century that there were three kinds of homicide—justifiable, excusable, and felonious. He stated that the first involved no guilt, the second involved little guilt, and the third was the highest crime that man was capable of committing against the law of nature.

Justifiable homicide is defined in the common law as an intentional homicide committed under circumstances of necessity or duty without any evil intent and without any fault or blame on the person who commits the homicide. Justifiable homicide includes state executions, homicides by police officers in the performance of their legal duty, and self-defense when the person committing the homicide is not at fault.

Excusable homicide is the killing of a human being, either by misadventure or in self-defense, when there is some fault, error, or omission on the part of the person who commits the homicide. The degree of fault, however, is not enough to constitute a felonious homicide.

Criminal (or *felonious*) *homicide* occurs when a person unlawfully and knowingly, recklessly, or negligently causes the death of another human being. The common law and the states have divided criminal homicide into the crimes of murder, manslaughter, and negligent homicide.

This chapter deals with criminal homicide and the circumstances that give rise to specific charges. Criminal homicide encompasses a wide variety of acts. The acts and the intent with which they were committed determine whether the homicide is intentional or unintentional. Such determination is relevant because penalties are severer when the killing was intentional rather than a result of recklessness, negligence, or carelessness.

B. THE REQUIREMENT OF PROVING *CORPUS DELICTI*

Corpus delicti means the body or substance of the crime. *Corpus delicti* must be proved in all criminal charges. The state must show that a crime has actually been committed before it may charge a person with committing the crime. If the state cannot show that a crime was committed, it may not then charge a person with a criminal offense.

Corpus delicti cannot be presumed and must be established by legal evidence. Mere hearsay or the showing that the defendant had a motive to commit a crime is not sufficient to prove *corpus delicti*. As a general rule, *corpus delicti* must be established beyond a reasonable doubt.[1] It may be established not only by direct and positive evidence, but also by circumstantial evidence. When *corpus delicti* is established by circumstantial evidence, the general rule is that the evidence must be so conclusive as to eliminate all reasonable doubt in showing that a crime was actually committed. If there is no evidence of the *corpus delicti,* the court may so properly hold. But whether the *corpus delicti* has been proven is a question of fact for a jury.[2]

The Supreme Court of Pennsylvania stated in the 1967 case of *Commonwealth v. Leslie* that in order to prove *corpus delicti* in a criminal homicide case, the state must show "that the person for whose death the prosecution was instituted is in fact dead and that the death occurred under circumstances indicating that it was criminally caused by someone."[3]

In the *Leslie* case, the state police officer who investigated a fire that destroyed a summer cottage found no evidence that the fire was a deliberate burning. However, he had a hunch that it was not accidental. Because Leslie's description was similar to the description of a person seen in the area at the time of the fire, the officer interviewed Leslie in prison when he heard that Leslie had been arrested on other charges. Leslie confessed that he had started the fire and the officer went back to the scene of the fire but could not uncover any evidence that the fire was not started accidentally. As there was no corroborating evidence supporting the confession, the Supreme Court of Pennsylvania reversed Leslie's conviction for arson.

Proving *Corpus Delicti* in "No Body" Cases

Thousands of persons disappear every year in the United States and cannot be accounted for.

Most of these persons are living elsewhere and are not communicating with their families and friends. Some, however, are victims of murders and other crimes. A California Court of Appeal stated in the *Charles Manson* case that the "fact that a murderer may successfully dispose of the body of the victim does not entitle him to an acquittal. That is one form of success for which society has no reward." [4]

However, in cases in which a body is never found, the state must carry the burden of showing *corpus delicti* (that the crime alleged by the state has been committed). *Corpus delicti* can be proved by circumstantial evidence or by confessions that have been corroborated and affirmed by other evidence. The following two cases illustrate these rules:

PEOPLE v. LIPSKY
Court of Appeals of New York (1982)
443 N.E.2d 925, 457 N.Y.S.2d 451

While the defendant was in custody on an assault charge in Utah, he confessed that he murdered a prostitute in Rochester, New York. The victim, Mary Robinson, had been reported missing, but her body had not been found. To corroborate the confession, the state showed that the victim's purse, sandals, wallet, glasses, identification card, and other personal effects were found in an apartment that the defendant had rented in New York within a week of her disappearance. Although the defendant had registered to go to college in New York, he left the state a week after the victim's disappearance and appeared emotionally overwrought. Then, while he was in prison in Utah, he wrote a poem indicating that he had killed another person. In affirming the defendant's conviction and holding that there was sufficient evidence to justify the jury's verdict of guilty, the Court held:

The evidence reviewed above, when read with defendant's confession, the poem he composed and his admissions to his two Provo co-workers, sufficiently establishes both Mary Robinson's death and defendant's strangulation of her as the cause of it to take the issues to the jury. More is not required.

EPPERLY v. COMMONWEALTH
Supreme Court of Virginia (1982)
294 S.E.2d 882

An 18-year-old college girl was last seen leaving a dance with the defendant. Her body was never found, but her blood-soaked clothes were. Her car was found, and there was evidence of a violent struggle at a house on Claytor Lake, where the defendant was seen after the dance. Dog-tracking evidence corroborating some of the allegations made by the state was permitted to be used at the defendant's trial. The defendant also made incriminating statements. In affirming the defendant's convictions, the court held:

We think the evidence was sufficient to warrant the jury in finding, to the full assurance of moral certainty, that Gina Hall was dead as the result of the criminal act of another person. The jury was entitled to take into account, in this connection, her sudden disappearance, her character and personal relationships, her physical and mental health, the evidence of a violent struggle at the house on Claytor Lake, her hidden, blood-soaked clothing, and the defendant's incriminating statements—particularly his reference to "the body" before it was generally thought she was dead.

"Body Without Proof of the Cause of Death" Cases

The body of the deceased is available in most criminal homicide cases. But if doctors are not able to testify specifically that the cause of death was due to an unlawful act, *corpus delicti* has not been proved. Unexplained deaths are unusual but not rare in medical history. If the doctors are unable to determine the cause of death, or if they are uncertain and unable to state whether the death resulted from criminal acts or from natural causes, then a reasonable doubt may have been created.

A doctor's testimony that he or she "suspected" or had a "hunch" that the criminal act was the cause of death is not sufficient to prove *corpus delicti.* The following cases illustrate the *corpus delicti* requirement that proof of the cause of death must be established:

PEOPLE v. ARCHERD
Supreme Court of California
(1970)
3 Cal. 3d 615, 91 Cal. Rptr. 397, 477 P.2d 421

In the early 1940s, the defendant learned that insulin is a natural body hormone that (at that time) could not be traced or identified in the blood and tissues of the human body. He made the statement that death by insulin could be the "perfect" murder. He was suspected of six deaths that had occurred from 1947 through 1966 and from which he benefited financially. All the victims died after being in a coma for a number of hours. Massive injections of insulin were suspected, but it was not until 1967 that doctors were able to testify with certainty that the brain tissue of the victims (the defendant was charged with three deaths) showed that massive doses of insulin had been administered. A movie was made of the trial and conviction of the defendant, and a detailed account of the investigation can be found in the January 1969 *FBI Law Enforcement Bulletin,* in an article by Sheriff Pitchess, "Proof of Murder by Insulin—A Medico-Legal First."

IN RE FLODSTROM
Supreme Court of California
(1955)
134 Cal. 2d 871, 277 P.2d 101, *proceeding dismissed* 45 Cal. 2d 307, 288 P.2d 859

The court ordered the release of a mother despite the fact that she had confessed to smothering her baby. However, doctors could not determine whether the baby died of the mother's alleged criminal act or of natural causes. As there was no corroborating evidence to support the confession, the charges against the mother were dropped.

The "Born Alive" Requirement

Under the common law, the killing of a fetus (unborn baby) was not a homicide. A fetus is not a "person" or a "human being," and as most criminal homicide statutes forbid only the killing of a "person" or "human being," these statutes do not include the killing of a fetus.

Most states follow the common law, which requires that if the state is charging the homicide of a newborn baby, it must show that the child was "born alive" and was living at the time it was killed. The testimony of a competent witness that he or she saw the living child or heard the baby cry would ordinarily be sufficient to prove "born alive."

California statutes now define murder as the "unlawful killing of a human being, or a fetus, with malice aforethought" (Title 8, Sec. 187). This statute makes the killing of a fetus in California "with malice aforethought," murder and changes the common law. This statute, however, does not make abortion murder in California, as Section 187 does not apply when the "act was solicited, aided, abetted, or consented to by the mother of the fetus."

However, most American courts and states have not made the changes made by California. For example, in 1983, the Kentucky Supreme Court held that a man who killed a 28 to 30-week-old fetus cannot be charged with "criminal homicide" in Kentucky.[5] The court followed the common law rule limiting criminal homicide to the killing of one who has been "born alive." A New Jersey court also followed this ruling, holding in 1982 that a "viable fetus, wounded while in the mother's womb and then dying within the womb so as to be stillborn, could not cause one to be answerable under the . . . homicide statute."[6] Persons in such cases could, however, be charged with other offenses.

Before effective birth control and legal abortion, there were many more infant homicide cases than there are today. Because of the difficulty of obtaining proof that the child was born alive and then killed, many states long ago enacted statutes making the concealing of the death of an infant a crime. These cases usually came to the attention of the police when the corpse of an infant was found in a garbage pail or elsewhere. Probably most prosecutions in cases of this type were based on statutes making it an offense to conceal the death of a child, rather than on criminal homicide.

Proof That the Victim Was Still Alive at the Time of the Defendant's Unlawful Act

Because homicide is the unlawful killing of a living human being, the state has the burden of showing that the victim was alive at the time of the unlawful act. All persons have a right to life, and whether they have 10 minutes or 10 years left to live makes no difference in the eyes of the law.

However, if the victim had already died of illness or other injuries at the time of the defendant's unlawful act, the crime of criminal homicide was not committed. In the 1973 murder trial of a New York doctor, the doctor was charged with causing the death of a dying cancer patient by injecting a lethal dose of potassium chloride. The patient was in a coma and was not expected to live longer than two days. During the 12-day trial in New York City, the defense attorney argued that the deceased was already dead of natural causes when the injection was made. The state failed to show conclusively that the deceased was still alive at the time of the injection, and the jury acquitted the doctor of homicide.

Motive is no defense in a murder charge. Nor is it a defense to show that the victim wanted to die. The crime of murder has been committed if it is shown that the unlawful act that caused the death was done deliberately and with premeditation. Motive and consent by the victim may be considered by the judge in sentencing the defendant in those states in which the sentence is not mandatory.

There have been many euthanasia (mercy-killing) cases in the United States and in Europe over the years. The author of an article entitled "Euthanasia: None Dare Call it Murder"[7] points out that the victims of this type of homicide fall into three groups: (1) persons with painful and terminal diseases, such as cancer, who have only a short time to live; (2) mentally defective or retarded persons and old people suffering from senility (some of whom are kept alive by artificial medical means); and (3) infants and young children with gross mental or physical defects. The author relates the 1967 Chicago trial of a 23-year-old college student who was charged with shooting his mother in the head three times. His mother had terminal leukemia and wanted to die. She begged her son to kill her and three days before the shooting had tried to commit suicide by taking an overdose of sleeping pills. After 40 minutes of deliberation, a Chicago jury found the defendant not guilty by reason of insanity. The jury also found that he was no longer insane, and the defendant was released.

When Is a Person Legally Dead?

Historically, death has been defined in terms of cessation of heart and respiratory function.[8] Until recently, the heart was considered the body's most vital organ. However, medical technology is now able to keep the heart and other organs alive for transplantation to other persons. Medical science now recognizes that the body's real seat of "life" is the brain.

As the medical profession now defines death in terms of "brain death," courts and state legislative bodies have followed with changes in the legal definition of death. In 1981, the Supreme Court of Indiana pointed out that 28 states have followed the "virtually universal acceptance [of 'brain death'] in the medical profession." [9] In defining death as the "permanent cessation of all brain functions," the Supreme Court of Indiana joined the other states in holding "that for purposes of the law of homicide proof of the death of the victim may be established by proof of the irreversible cessation of the victim's total brain functions. The trial court did not err in so instructing the jury." Massachusetts had also adopted this definition of death in the case of *Commonwealth v. Golston*. [10] The defendant had struck the 34-year-old victim on the head with a baseball bat. Surgeons were required to remove a portion of the victim's skull to relieve pressure on his brain in an attempt to save his life. In affirming the defendant's conviction of first-degree murder, the Court stated:

> There was medical testimony that on August 25 only the part of the victim's brain responsible for the most primitive responses, the brain stem, was still to some degree working. On August 26, the remaining brain stem functions, such as responding to painful stimuli and gasping for air, had disappeared; the victim never again exhibited any signs that his brain stem or cortex was functioning. In the opinion of the responsible physician, the victim was then dead, having reached the stage of irreversible "brain death." This opinion was confirmed by an electroencephalogram on August 26 and by another on August 28. The removal of the respirator on August 31 was in accordance with good medical practice. An autopsy the next day revealed a brain without architecture, a decomposed, jelly-like mass, consistent with a brain dead for substantially more than two days. The medical examiner concluded that the victim had been dead since August 28.

In 1983, two California doctors were charged with murder and conspiracy to commit murder. After one of their patients had undergone major surgery, the patient had a serious heart attack.

The patient was revived and immediately was placed on life-support equipment. However, the patient had suffered severe brain damage and was in a deep comatose state from which he was not likely to recover. The patient was not "dead" by either statutory or historic standards, as there was some "minimal brain activity."

When the family members were informed, they requested that all life-support equipment be removed from the patient. In holding that no crime was committed by the two doctors who ordered removal of the life-support system, the California Court of Appeal held in *Barber v. Superior Court* that:

> In summary we conclude that the petitioners' omission to continue treatment under the circumstances, though intentional and with knowledge that the patient would die, was not an unlawful failure to perform a legal duty. In view of our decision on that issue, it becomes unnecessary to deal with the further issue of whether petitioners' conduct was in fact the proximate cause of Mr. Herbert's ultimate death. [11]

C. THE CAUSATION REQUIREMENT

Causation and Proximate Cause

Causation and proximate cause are discussed in Chapter 3 of this text. Causation is an essential element of all crimes. The state must show that what the defendant did (or failed to do) was the direct and proximate cause of the harm that occurred. The following two examples illustrate the law of causation:

Example 1: After loading a gun with live ammunition, X points the gun at Y and pulls the trigger. The firing pin comes down hard on the back of the live cartridge that X has placed in the chamber of the gun. The blow of the hammer detonates the primer in the cartridge and the primer detonates the powder in the cartridge. The powder burns so rapidly that hot gases immediately build up tremendous pressure in the chamber of the gun. This pressure forces the propellant (the bullet) out of the muzzle of the gun at a high rate of speed. Because of rifling in the barrel of the gun and the direction in which X is pointing the gun, the bullet travels through the air and strikes Y in the head, killing him immediately.

Example 2: X goes into a bank with a handgun and points the gun at a bank clerk, declaring in a loud voice his intention to rob the bank. X does not know that the bank clerk has a bad heart and that the robbery will be too great a strain for him. The bank clerk has an immediate heart attack and dies before X leaves the bank.

As a jury can easily conclude in Example 1 that X intended the natural and probable consequences of his deliberate act, it would then find that X intended to kill Y. In Example 1, X's acts were the direct and proximate cause of Y's death. The chain of events that occurred after X pulled the trigger was expected and desired by X. Therefore, X can be held criminally responsible for Y's death. In Example 2, the death of the bank clerk was not the normal and expected result of pointing a gun at another person. Therefore, X could not be charged successfully with homicide unless it could be shown that he knew that the bank clerk had a bad heart and might not be able to take such a frightening experience. The following case further illustrates the requirement to show causation:

PEOPLE v. STEWART
Court of Appeals of New York
(1976)
389 N.Y.S.2d 804, 358 N.E.2d
487

In a dispute over a former girlfriend, the defendant stabbed another man in the stomach with a knife. The victim was taken to a hospital, where surgery was performed. After the doctor had successfully closed the stomach wound that was inflicted by the defendant, the doctor then commenced correcting a hernia that was discovered. The hernia was not related to the stab wound. While the doctor was working on the hernia, the patient went into a cardiac arrest (heart attack) and died. A doctor testified that the patient probably would have survived the stab wound if the hernia surgery had not been performed. Defendant was convicted of first-degree manslaughter and appealed. The Court of Appeals noted that although causation is frequently an issue in civil cases, it is rarely encountered in appellate criminal cases.[12] In reducing the manslaughter conviction to assault in the first degree, the Court held:

> *The requirement . . . is that "the defendant's actions must be a sufficiently direct cause of the ensuing death before there can be any imposition of criminal liability." . . . Thus an "obscure or merely probable connection between an assault and death will, as in every case of alleged crime, require acquittal of the charge of any degree of homicide." . . . We have held that "direct" does not mean "immediate." The defendant may be held to have caused the death even though it does not immediately follow the injury. . . . Neither does "direct" mean "unaided" for the defendant will be held liable for the death although other factors, entering after the injury, have contributed to the fatal result. Thus if "felonious assault is operative as a cause of death, the causal co-operation of erroneous surgical or medical treatment does not relieve the assailant from liability for homicide."*

The "Year-and-a-Day" Rule

More than 200 years ago, Sir William Blackstone stated the "year-and-a-day" rule as follows: "In order also to make the killing murder, it is requisite that the party die within a year and a day after the stroke received, or cause of death administered; in the computation of which the whole day upon which the hurt was done shall be reckoned the first." [13]

The Supreme Court of Michigan pointed out in 1982 that the "year-and-a-day" rule dates back to 1278 and that the "original rationale for the rule was probably tied to the inability of 13th Century medicine to prove the cause of death beyond a reasonable doubt after a prolonged period of time." [14]

Noting that most courts that consider the "year-and-a-day" rule have abolished it, the Michigan Supreme Court also abolished the rule, holding that "the advances of modern medical science, by extending life and by providing strong evidence of the cause of death, have undermined the wisdom of the irrebuttable presumption that the death of one who expires more than a year and a day after receiving an injury was not caused by the injury."

D. MURDER

The first murder to be reported in the American colonies occurred 10 years after the Pilgrims landed at Plymouth Rock. In 1630, John Billington, one of the original band of 102 Pilgrims to come over on the *Mayflower,* fired his blunderbuss at a neighbor and killed the man at close range. John Billington was charged with the

---

The Right to Die

The common law recognized that a competent adult has a right to control his own body. Therefore, an adult who had all his mental facilities could refuse medical treatment, medication, or an operation, knowing that the refusal would cause his death. The decision to refuse medical assistance could be made at the time of the crisis or it could be stated in a document, such as a will.

Although a competent adult can make such a decision, a child (minor) or an incompetent adult cannot. The following incidents have received considerable attention:

Karen Ann Quinlan was 22 years old when she lapsed into an irreversible coma, which doctors now recognize as distinct from brain death. Brain death includes the destruction of all portions of the brain. With Karen's vegetative state, some brain function continued (heartbeat and respiration). When doctors refused to withdraw life-support systems for fear of being charged criminally, her father went into court. The Supreme Court of New Jersey granted his request to be appointed her guardian so that he might exercise, on her behalf, her right to die under her right of privacy. *In the Matter of Quinlan,* 355 A.2d 647, *cert. denied,* 429 U.S. 922, 97 S. Ct. 319.

Elizabeth Bouvia, 26 and a quadriplegic cerebral palsy victim, who in 1983 checked into a California hospital, telling persons that she wanted to be allowed to die. As she could not physically kill herself, she requested that she not be fed but did ask for painkillers for her arthritis. The hospital, stating that they did not want to be a party to a suicide, took the matter into court. The court held that a severely handicapped but otherwise healthy person who is not terminally ill cannot be aided by society in seeking to end her own life.

Pamela Hamilton the 12-year-old daughter of a preacher with the Church of God, a sect that does not allow members to take medicine and believes that only God can cure. Pamela's parents refused to take her for medical treatment for a cancerous tumor in her leg. When a Tennessee court ordered treatment, the matter was appealed to the Court of Appeals. Pamela's father argued that his religious beliefs should outweigh the state's medical beliefs. Doctors said Pamela would not survive without the court-ordered treatment. The Court of Appeals affirmed the ordered treatment in 1984.

"Baby Doe" cases. Baby Jane Doe was born in October 1983 with an open spine, water on the brain, and an abnormally small head. With repeated surgery, she would always be severely retarded, paralyzed, in constant pain, yet might live to age 20. Her parents decided against surgery, which would mean that she would probably die by age 2. The U.S. Justice Department demanded that the baby's medical records be turned over so it could be determined if the baby's civil rights were being violated. A New York court upheld the parents' and hospital's refusal to turn over the records.

- Homicide is the least frequent violent crime.
- 93 percent of the victims were slain in single-victim situations.
- At least 55 percent of the murderers were relatives or acquaintances of the victim.
- 24 percent of all murders occurred or were suspected to have occurred as the result of some felonious activity.

The chance of being a violent crime victim, with or without injury, is greater than that of being hurt in a traffic accident.

The rates of some violent crimes are higher than those of some other serious life events. For example, the risk of being the victim of a violent crime is higher than the risk of being affected by divorce, or death from cancer, or injury or death from a fire. Still, a person is much more likely to die from natural causes than as a result of a criminal victimization.

Source: 1983 U.S. Department of Justice Report to the Nation on Crime

---

common law offense of murder under the English law and, after a prompt trial and conviction, was hanged.[15]

Under the common law there was only one degree of murder, and that was punishable by death. After the American Revolution, some state legislative bodies began creating other degrees of murder. They were probably motivated by a desire to separate murder to be punished by death from murder that they did not want to be punished by death.

By the year 1900, probably all the states had more than one degree of murder, with most states having two degrees and some having three degrees. At that time, the degree system was a useful and meaningful method of distinguishing between murder that was punished by capital punishment and that which was not. With the decline in the use of the death penalty in this century and its virtual nonuse in the 1960s, the usefulness of the degree system declined considerably. With the blurring of the distinction in the wording of state statutes and the shift in the philosophy of punishment in recent years, the value of the degree system has declined even further.

The degree system is still meaningful today when first-degree murder carries a mandatory life imprisonment sentence or is punished by the death penalty. The degree system is also used as part of plea bargaining when, if it is of advantage to the state, the defendant may be allowed to plead guilty to second-degree murder or to some other lesser offense if a reduction is appropriate.

Intent-to-Kill Murder

The unlawful, intentional killing of another human being is considered the most serious criminal offense. Unlawful intentional killings range from those that are coldly and carefully made by a paid assassin to those that are the culmination of one spouse's rage and frustration toward the other. The weapon used to implement the murder can be anything from a firearm to one's bare hands. The type of weapon used or the manner in which the fatal blow is delivered is not necessarily significant. It is the specific intent to take the life of another human being that separates this crime from all other degrees of homicide. The type of weapon and the manner in which it is used, however, may give rise to the legal inference that a person intends the natural and probable consequences of his or her deliberate acts.

Murder at common law and as enacted by the statutes of many states at first-degree murder is defined as unlawful homicide with malice aforethought. The phrase "malice aforethought" signifies the mental state of a person who voluntarily, without legal excuse or justification, does an act that ordinarily will cause death or serious injury to another. Although the word malice ordinarily conveys the meaning of hatred, ill-will, or malevolence, it is not limited to those meanings in "malice aforethought" and can include such motives as a mercy killing, in which the homicide is committed to end the suffering of a loved one. "Aforethought" has been interpreted

Types of Killings

Passionate (Rage) Killings

- committed ordinarily by friends, acquaintances, or relatives of the deceased

- often committed in a terrible rage, in the heat of passion, or in an emotionally disturbed condition

- often committed with no effort made to commit the crime secretly; therefore, in many situations, witnesses observe the commission of the crime.

The offender is often under the influence of alcohol or a drug at the time the crime is committed.

Witnesses are often cooperative and can usually give the name or an accurate description of the offender.

The offender is apt to make incriminating statements and is likely to be remorseful for what he or she has done. Because of the remorse or because of the evidence, the offender will sometimes confess.

This type of offense has a high clearance rate and accounts for more than half the murders in the United States.

Gangland Killings

- committed ordinarily by professional or organized criminals

- seldom committed impulsively and often deliberately and carefully planned

Great care is often used to commit the crime secretly or in such a manner that the offender cannot be identified and can escape the scene.

The offender is seldom under the influence of alcohol or drugs at the time of the commission of the crime.

Witnesses are sometimes fearful and uncooperative and often are unable to provide helpful information.

As there is no sorrow or remorse and the offender is likely to be knowledgeable about crime, there are seldom incriminating statements or confessions.

Clearance rates for gangland killings are probably the lowest for any type of crime.

Serial and Random Murders

The number and brutality of serial and random murders increased dramatically in the United States in the 1970s and 1980s. In 1984, the U.S. Justice Department estimated that 35 serial killers may be on the loose. A computer-based tracking system is being used to apprehend the murderers who strike again and again, sometimes moving from city to city, choosing strangers as victims, then moving on to kill again.

Motiveless and Random

Many of the killings are without apparent motive and leave few clues. Because of these factors and criminal cunning, some of the killers are extremely difficult to catch. Law enforcement officers from 20 states gathered in Louisiana in 1984 to compare notes on two drifters, Otis Toole and Henry L. Lucas, who admitted killing more than 300 persons (mostly women and children) during the 1970s and early 1980s. A major reason given for such killers remaining at large for years is the lack of a centralized information and tracking system. It is hoped that the new computer-based system will prove to be effective.

Sex as a Motive

Sex is the apparent motive of some random killings. Although many of the victims are women and children, an increasing number of homosexual males are committing multiple murders of male victims. In the United States, more than 4,000 bodies are found each year that are never identified. Some of these murders are motiveless, whereas others appear to be brutal sexual attacks. Almost 20,000 murder victims are identified each year in the United States.

Prison Murders

Another form of murder increasing rapidly in the United States is prison murder by inmates against guards and other inmates. Federal inmates who commit murder while in prison are sent to the federal penitentiary in Marion, Illinois. Marion is the successor to Alcatraz and is the maximum security prison to which the most violent and escape-prone prisoners are sent. On one day in October 1983, two guards were killed in separate incidents by different prisoners. Both prisoners had murdered three times before with homemade knives. Both killers were cheered by other prisoners for their bloody deeds. One of the killers raised his hands in a gesture of triumph as he was led away from his victim. As the federal government has no death penalty for such offenses, the killers received additional terms of life imprisonment.

to mean that the malice must exist at the time of the homicidal act. Courts have held that if the design and intent to kill precede the killing for even a moment, the person can be convicted of first-degree murder.[16]

Other states have defined first-degree murder as causing "the death of another human being with intent to kill that person." The American Law Institute Model Penal Code uses the words purposely and knowingly, whereas the proposed Federal Criminal Code uses the wording "intentionally or knowingly causes the death of another human being."

The Deadly-Weapon Doctrine

Although intentional killings are the most common of all murders, there is rarely direct evidence of the intent. The evidence most often available to the state is objective observations of the cause of death, for example, the defendant pointed a gun at the deceased and pulled the trigger, or the defendant plunged a knife into the body of the deceased. Witnesses who have heard the defendant express intention to kill the deceased are seldom available. The questions that then arise are whether such evidence is sufficient to support a finding that malice existed and whether there was an intent to kill.

The deadly-weapon doctrine is related to and is part of the inference that a person intends the natural and probable consequences of his or her deliberate acts. A loaded revolver is certainly a deadly weapon when aimed and fired at close range. Under such circumstances, a jury can easily infer an intent to kill, as the natural and probable consequences of this act would be death or serious bodily harm.

Determining what is a deadly weapon would depend on the object used and the circumstances that existed at the time of the homicide. A strong man who struck a year-old infant in the head several times with his fists could easily be found to have an intent to kill, and his fists, under these circumstances, would be considered deadly weapons. However, a man who was in a fistfight with another man just as strong and agile as he would not ordinarily be considered to have used a deadly weapon when he used his fists.

Therefore, in determining what a deadly weapon is, a jury would consider the instrument used, who used it, and how it was used. Some items are almost per se deadly weapons because of the potential harm they can cause. Other instruments, such as automobiles, would have to be viewed in light of their uses. The U.S. Supreme Court ruled in the 1895 case of *Allen v. United States*[17] that a lower court erred when it withdrew the question of self-defense from a jury on the ground that sticks and clubs were not deadly weapons. Sticks and clubs can be deadly weapons, depending on their size, who is using them, and how they are used.

The deadly-weapon doctrine is used in cases in which a killing occurred and in assault, battery, and attempt cases. The following case illustrates:

PEOPLE v. CARTER
Court of Appeals of New York (1981)
53 N.Y.2d 113, 423 N.E.2d 30

While driving in the defendant's car, the defendant and his girlfriend began to quarrel. The defendant became angry when his girlfriend got out of the car and walked away. The defendant caught her and viciously assaulted her, knocking her to the ground. While she lay helpless on the pavement, the defendant kicked and "stomped" on her head and face. The woman lapsed into a coma, and at the time of trial, a medical expert testified that, in his opinion, the victim would never come out of the coma. Defendant was charged with attempted murder and assault with a deadly weapon or dangerous instrument. The jury acquitted the defendant of attempted murder and convicted him of the felony assault. The Court of Appeals affirmed the conviction, holding that a jury could find that the pair of rubber boots that the defendant was wearing could be a "dangerous instrument." Citing New York cases and cases from other states, the Court held:

> *The object itself need not be inherently dangerous. It is the temporary use rather than the inherent vice of the object which brings it within the purview of the statute.*
>
> *The courts of this State have consistently adopted this use-oriented approach. In* People v. Cwikla, *. . . for example, we noted our agreement with the Appellate Division that a common handkerchief with which a victim was gagged and which led to his asphyxiation was a "dangerous instrument" within the meaning of the Penal Law. In a like manner, leather boots used to kick a victim in the face . . . and a spatula used to inflict a cut . . . have been found to satisfy the statutory standard. Thus, although the rubber boots in issue are not inherently dangerous, we must determine whether the evidence in this case is sufficient to support the jury's conclusion that they were readily capable of causing serious physical injury in the way in which they were used.*
>
> *Here, there is evidence that the defendant used the rubber boots to stomp upon the head and face of his victim, causing her head to contact the pavement below with tremendous force. The jury apparently concluded that the pair of boots, when used in this fashion, was readily capable of causing serious physical injury and, thus, was a "dangerous instrument" within the meaning of subdivision 13 of section 10 of the Penal Law. On this record, we cannot say that such a conclusion was erroneous as a matter of law.*

"Transferred Intent"

If X intends to kill Y but shoots and kills W instead, can X be charged and convicted of "intent-to-kill" murder? Courts have never found it difficult to convict X of the intentional death of W. The two elements of the crime are present: (1) the criminal act and (2) the criminal intent to kill. To rule otherwise would allow X to escape culpability because he was a bad shot.

The reasoning for justifying such a result varies. One explanation is that the requisite intent to kill a human being was present and that a human being was killed. In another explanation, the intent to kill Y is transferred (by legal construction, if not in fact) to an intent to kill W.

In 1974, the Maryland Court of Special Appeals adopted the common law doctrine of "transferred intent" in the case of *Gladden v. Maryland,*[18] commenting that the doctrine, strangely, had never been before the appellate courts of that state. Gladden was convicted of first-degree murder because, in a dispute over a bad batch of heroin, he emptied a revolver, firing wildly at another heroin user but killing an innocent 12-year-old boy instead. In affirming Gladden's murder conviction, the Court of Appeal ruled:

> The doctrine of "transferred intent" has long been recognized at common law. Sir Matthew Hale, in 1 History of the Pleas of the Crown (published posthumously in 1736), said, at 466: "To these may be added the cases abovementioned, *viz.* if A. by malice forethought strikes at B. and missing him strikes C. whereof he dies, tho he never bore any malice to C. yet it is murder, and the law transfers the malice to the party slain; the like of poisoning."
>
> Forty years later, Sir William Blackstone, in 4 Commentaries on the Laws of England, reiterated the common law rule according to Hale; at 200–201: "Thus if one shoots at A. and misses *him,* but kills B., this is murder; because of the previous felonious intent, which the law transfers from one to the other. The same is the case where one lays poison for A.; and B., against whom the prisoner had no malicious

intent, takes it, and it kills him; this is likewise murder."

* * *

The appellant contends that he should not have been convicted of murder, since he bore no malice toward the victim. He urges upon us that the common law doctrine of "transferred intent" should not be received into Maryland, although he acknowledges that this is the law in the overwhelming majority of common law jurisdictions. We have no difficulty in deciding that "transferred intent" is, and should be, a part of the common law of this State.

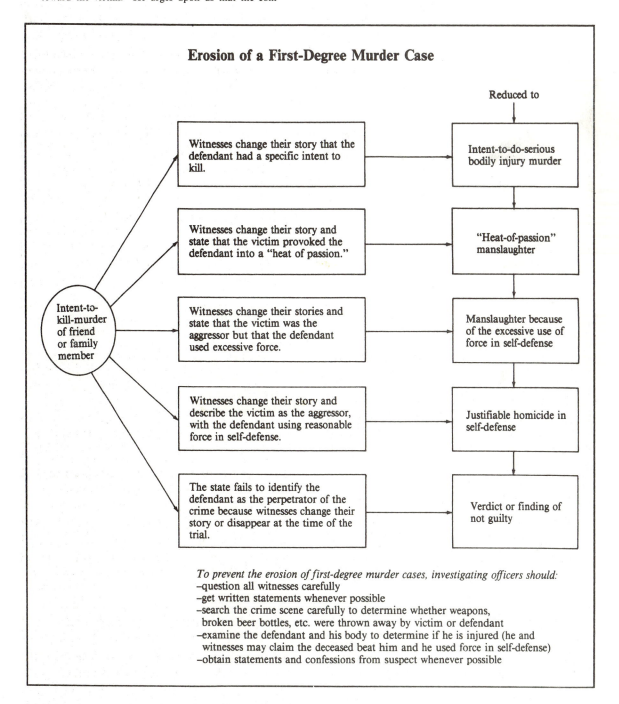

Erosion of a First-Degree Murder Case

Reduced to

Intent-to-kill-murder of friend or family member

Witnesses change their story that the defendant had a specific intent to kill. → Intent-to-do-serious bodily injury murder

Witnesses change their story and state that the victim provoked the defendant into a "heat of passion." → "Heat-of-passion" manslaughter

Witnesses change their stories and state that the victim was the aggressor but that the defendant used excessive force. → Manslaughter because of the excessive use of force in self-defense

Witnesses change their story and describe the victim as the aggressor, with the defendant using reasonable force in self-defense. → Justifiable homicide in self-defense

The state fails to identify the defendant as the perpetrator of the crime because witnesses change their story or disappear at the time of the trial. → Verdict or finding of not guilty

To prevent the erosion of first-degree murder cases, investigating officers should:
–question all witnesses carefully
–get written statements whenever possible
–search the crime scene carefully to determine whether weapons, broken beer bottles, etc. were thrown away by victim or defendant
–examine the defendant and his body to determine if he is injured (he and witnesses may claim the deceased beat him and he used force in self-defense)
–obtain statements and confessions from suspect whenever possible

Intent-to-Do-Serious-Bodily-Harm Murder

The courts long ago decided that a death at the hands of one who intended to do only serious bodily harm was nevertheless murder. Under modern homicide statutes, such killing is not "intent-to-kill" murder but is usually considered a lesser degree of murder. The following old English cases illustrate this type of offense:

REX v. ERRINGTON
2 Lew. C.C. 148, 217 (1838)

The defendants covered a drunken man, who was sleeping, with straw on which they threw a shovel of hot cinders. The man was burned to death in the fire that resulted. The court instructed the jury that if it found that the defendants intended to do any serious harm to the deceased, the crime was murder under the common law; if the defendants' only intent was to play a joke or frighten the deceased, the crime was manslaughter.

HOLLOWAY CASE
79 Eng. Rep. 715 (K.B. 1628)

The defendant tied a boy to a horse's tail and hit the horse to make it run. The boy was killed. The defendant was convicted of murder even though it was found that there was no intent to kill.

Depraved-Mind or Depraved-Heart Murder

This classification, in some states called second-degree murder, is similar in some aspects to the "intent-to-do-serious-bodily-harm" murder. The primary difference is that in the "depraved-mind" murder, there is no specific intent to injure or harm. However, if the conduct of the defendant was so reckless as to create a high degree of risk of death, he or she would, in many instances, be found guilty of "depraved-heart" or "reckless conduct" murder.

The Supreme Court of California pointed out in the following case that "malice" may be implied where a person, knowing that his conduct endangers the life of another, deliberately continues to act in a manner that shows a conscious disregard for life: [19]

PEOPLE v. WATSON
Supreme Court of California (1981)
637 P.2d 279, 179 Cal. Rptr. 43

After drinking a large volume of beer in a bar, the defendant drove through a red light and avoided a collision with another car, late at night, only by skidding to a halt in the middle of the intersection. After the near collision, the defendant drove off at a high rate of speed (twice the 35 mph speed limit). On approaching another intersection, the defendant again applied his brakes, but he struck a Toyota sedan, killing the driver and her six-year-old daughter. Defendant's blood alcohol content one-half hour after the collision was .23 percent, which is twice the .10 percent necessary to find a person legally intoxicated.

The issue before the Supreme Court of California was whether the defendant can be charged and forced to go to trial on two counts of second-degree murder instead of the usual charges of homicide by intoxicant use of a vehicle or of vehicular manslaughter. In holding that the conduct of the defendant was sufficient to support probable cause finding of implied malice to justify charging and trying the defendant for second-degree murder, the court stated:

We have said that second degree murder based on implied malice has been committed when a person does "an act, the natural consequences of which are dangerous to life, which act was deliberately performed by a person who knows that his conduct endangers the life of another and who acts with conscious disregard for life." People v. Sedeno . . . *Phrased in a different way, malice may be implied when defendant does an act with a high probability that it will result in death and does it with a base antisocial motive and with a wanton disregard for human life. . . .*

Based upon our independent review of the record, we believe that there exists a rational ground for concluding that defendant's conduct was sufficiently wanton to hold him on a second degree murder charge.

Felony Murder

The felony murder rule came into existence in England many years ago. The rule states that if a death occurs while a defendant is committing or attempting to commit a felony, the defendant could be convicted not only of the felony (or attempt to commit the felony), but also of felony murder, even if the death were unintended.

The Supreme Judicial Court of Massachusetts and the drafters of the Model Penal Code point out that American courts have narrowed the scope of the felony murder rule by imposing one or more of the following limitations:

1. The felony that was attempted or committed must be one that is dangerous to life.
2. There must be a direct causal connection between the felony and the death that occurred.
3. The act that caused the death must have occurred while the felony was in progress.
4. The felony must be *malum in se.*
5. The act must be a common law felony.

England abolished the felony murder rule in 1957. The Supreme Judicial Court of Massachusetts pointed out in the 1982 case of *Commonwealth v. Matchett* [20] that some American courts have also abolished the rule.

WHITMAN v. PEOPLE
Supreme Court of Colorado
(1966)
161 Colo. 110, 420 P.2d 416

PEOPLE v. FULLER
California Court of Appeals
(1978)
86 Cal. App. 3d 618, 150 Cal. Rptr. 515

In both of the above cases, the defendants were fleeing in vehicles after committing felonies (armed robbery and burglary). Both were traveling at high rates of speed in cities, to avoid apprehension. Whitman ran six stop signs and several red lights. Fuller almost collided head-on with another car while driving on the wrong side of the street. Both hit other vehicles, killing the drivers. The courts in both states held that the felony murder doctrine was applicable and the California court pointed out that Fuller "may also be prosecuted for ordinary second-degree murder." The Colorado Supreme Court held:

In the Andrews *case, in commenting upon the statute which is the predecessor of the particular statute with which we are here concerned, we said: "There is no question, from the testimony, but that the defendants committed the homicide in an attempt to perpetrate the crime of robbery. That fact is undisputed. The element of malice does not enter into the crime of murder committed in such circumstances. The purpose of the statute was to make* every homicide committed in the perpetration or attempt to perpetrate certain felonies murder, *which may be punished by death, if the jury so determine, without regard to malice, deliberation, or premeditation. When, therefore, the proof was undisputed that the homicide was committed in an attempt to perpetrate a robbery which the defendants had conspired to commit,* it was not necessary to prove any facts from which malice, deliberation, or premeditation could be inferred." *(Emphasis added.)*

* * *

The "perpetration of a robbery" does not come to an end the split second the victim surrenders his money to the gunman, and most certainly the "robbery" continues where, as in the instant case, the robbers are trying desperately to avoid arrest by police officers who are in extremely hot pursuit. In support of this, see Bizup v. People, *150 Colo. 214, 371 P.2d 786, where we stated that a robber's "escape with his ill-gotten gains was as important to the execution of the robbery as gaining possession of the property." Suffice it to say, in this regard, the facts and circumstances of the instant case clearly discloses that this was a murder committed in the perpetration of a robbery.*

STATE v. AMARO,
et al.
Florida Court of Appeals
(1983)
436 So.2d 1056

All four defendants were involved in a felony drug transaction. Just moments after three of the defendants were arrested and held in custody, the fourth defendant shot and killed a law enforcement officer. Instead of charging defendants as parties to the crime of first-degree murder, the prosecutor charged the three defendants with felony murder. The Court of Appeals pointed out that the situation was of the defendants' own making and that the time frame was "extremely short." In holding that the three defendants were accountable under Florida's felony murder statute, the Court stated:

In the felony murder context, the intent of the appellees need not be an intent to commit a homicide. The intent which would support a conviction of third degree murder is the intent to participate in the underlying felony.

* * *

It is well settled that a felon is liable for the acts of his co-felons. Likewise, there is liability for the acts of a felon on the part of one who aids and abets the commission of a felony. The result is not changed by the fact that prior to the perpetration of the underlying felony, there was no premeditated design on the part of any of the felons to commit a homicide. Campbell v. State, *227 So.2d 873 (Fla. 1969),* cert. dismissed, *400 U.S. 801, 91 S. Ct. 7, 27 L.Ed. 33 (1970) . . . It is not even necessary that the accused be present at the time of the killing perpetrated by a cohort. . . . Of course, the homicide must have been committed in furtherance of the common criminal scheme, or as a probable, predictable, reasonably foreseeable, or causally connected result of the underlying felony.* Bryant v. State, *412 So.2d 347 (Fla. 1982); . . .* See Christian v. United States, *394*

A.2d 1 (D.C.1978), cert. denied, 442 U.S. 944, 99 S. Ct. 2889, 61 L.Ed.2d (1979); Haskell v. Commonwealth, 218 Va. 1033, 243 S.E.2d 477 (Va. 1978); State v. Hokenson, 96 Idaho 283, 527 P.2d 487 (1974); People v. Mitchell, 61 Cal. 2d 353, 392 P.2d 526, 38 Cal. Rptr. 726 (1964), cert. denied, 384 U.S. 1007, 86 S. Ct. 1985, 16 L.Ed.2d 1021 (1966); Commonwealth v. Doris, 287 Pa. 547, 135 A. 313 (1926).

Case law has also made clear that a felon is liable for a homicide committed by a co-felon during the latter's attempt to escape from the scene of the underlying felony. Such a killing is considered to be a part of, and in furtherance of, the felony. Campbell, supra; Hornbeck, supra; People v. Salas, 7 Cal. 3d 812, 500 P.2d 7, 103 Cal. Rptr. 431 (1972), cert. denied, 410 U.S. 939, 93 S. Ct. 1401, 35 L.Ed.2d 605 (1973); People v. Goree, supra; People v. Jackson, 20 N.Y.2d 440, 231 N.E.2d 722, 285 N.Y.S.2d 8 (1967), cert. denied, 391 U.S. 928, 88 S. Ct. 1815, 20 L.Ed.2d 668 (1968).

STATE v. CANOLA
Supreme Court of New Jersey
(1977)
374 A.2d 20

Over the years, there have been many robbery cases in which one of the robbers is killed during the robbery. In this case, the victim of the robbery shot and killed one of the robbers. May the defendant, who was a co-felon in the robbery, be liable for felony murder? In reviewing the case law, the Supreme Court of New Jersey could not find any American court that would hold such a defendant liable for felony murder. In reversing the felony murder conviction and affirming the robbery conviction, the Court held:

It is clearly the majority view throughout the country that, at least in theory, the doctrine of felony murder does not extend to a killing, although growing out of the commission of the felony, if directly attributable to the act of one other than the defendant or those associated with him in the unlawful enterprise. Commonwealth ex rel. Smith v. Myers, 438 Pa. 218, 261 A. 2d 550 (Sup. Ct. 1970); People v. Washington, 62 Cal. 2d 777, 44 Cal. Rptr. 442, 402 P.2d 130 (Sup. Ct. 1965); Commonwealth v. Balliro, 349 Mass. 505, 209 N.E.2d 308 (Sup. Jud. Ct. 1965); People v. Wood, 8 N.Y.2d 48, 201 N.Y.S.2d 328, 167 N.E.2d 736 (Ct. App. 1960); People v. Warren, 44 Mich.App. 567, 205 N.W.2d 599 (Ct. App. 1973); Alvarez v. District Ct. In and For City & Cty. of Denver, 186 Colo. 37, 525 P.2d 1131 (Sup. Ct. 1974); State v. Garner, 238 La. 563, 115 So.2d 855 (Sup. Ct. 1959); State v. Majors, 237 S.W. 486 (Mo. Sup. Ct. 1922); Commonwealth v. Moore, 121 Ky. 97, 88 S.W. 1085 (Ct. App. 1905); Sheriff, Clark County v. Hicks, 89 Nev. 78, 506 P.2d 766 (Sup. Ct. 1973); State v. Oxendine, 187 N.C. 658, 122 S.E. 568 (Sup. Ct. 1924). See Annot. 56 A.L.R.3d 239 (1974). This rule is sometimes rationalized on the "agency" theory of felony murder.

A contrary view, which would attach liability under the felony murder rule for any *death proximately resulting from the unlawful activity—even the death of a co-felon—notwithstanding the killing was by one resisting the crime, does not seem to have the present allegiance of any court.*

Classifications of Common Law Murder

Intent-to-kill Murder   The most common of the criminal homicides, the intentional unlawful killing of another human being is considered the most serious criminal offense.

Intent-to-do-serious-bodily-harm Murder   In this type of murder, it is found that the defendant intended to do serious bodily injury short of death, but his or her acts resulted in a killing.

Depraved-mind or Depraved-heart Murder   When a death results from conduct that shows a wanton disregard for human life and when there is a high probability that the conduct will result in death, the homicide can be classified as this type of murder.

Felony Murder   At common law, one who caused another's death while committing or attempting to commit a felony was guilty of felony murder. However, when the felony murder doctrine was created, there were only eight felonies and all were punishable by death. Because all states have many felonies, they generally limit the felony murder doctrine to felonies of violence.

E. MANSLAUGHTER

Definition

Manslaughter was defined by common law as a classification of criminal homicide that is less than murder. The common law divided manslaughter into the two categories: voluntary and involuntary. Most American jurisdictions have followed the common law classifications, but a few states have created three categories. For example, Section 192 of the California Penal Code creates the three classifications of voluntary, involuntary, and manslaughter in the driving of a vehicle. A few states have only one degree of manslaughter.[21] A form of classification other than voluntary and involuntary manslaughter is that of identifying manslaughter by degrees (first, second, etc.).[22]

Manslaughter is a criminal homicide, but the penalties for manslaughter are less than the penalties that can be imposed for murder. Two of the reasons given for the lesser penalties are:

1. The victim provoked the killing and by his (or her) unlawful conduct set into motion a chain of events that resulted in his (or her) death.
2. The killings are not bad enough to be charged and punished as murder but are bad enough to be criminal.

Manslaughter is a crime that is generally considered to be separate and distinct from murder.

Because the penalties are less severe than for murder, defense lawyers who are unable to obtain an acquittal for clients would seek a conviction of manslaughter rather than murder.

Voluntary Manslaughter

The following 1984 example is used to illustrate voluntary manslaughter:

Example: When Robert Lee Moody was 18 years old, he killed his father with a shotgun and then went to a California police station to turn himself in, stating what he had done. The prosecutor charged Moody with voluntary manslaughter because of the reported conduct of the father: he had seduced his two teenage daughters, had begun fondling his 11-year-old daughter, had forced his wife into prostitution to help pay for a pleasure boat, was a child-and wife-beater, had opened his older son's head with a screwdriver (son was committed to a mental hospital). After the trial court convicted Moody of voluntary manslaughter, the court received more than 700 letters, most of which urged a lenient sentence for Moody. The sentence handed down in 1984 was five years of probation, with two of the years served in "Peace Corps-like" missionary work.[23]

In such cases as the *Moody* case, spouse beating, and other cases of shocking conduct, judges and juries have used manslaughter as an alternative to the severer penalties of murder. Al-

---

Homicide Investigations in 1980s Receiving National Attention

Tylenol Killings In September 1982, seven persons in the Chicago area died from cyanide-laced Extra-Strength Tylenol capsules. The killer has not been apprehended. James W. Lewis was convicted in 1983 in a federal court for attempting to capitalize on the Tylenol killings and extort $1 million from the manufacturer of Tylenol.

"Twilight Zone" Concerning a helicopter accident in which actor Vic Morrow and two children were killed in July 1982, the National Transportation Safety Board held that debris from a special-effect explosion used in the film caused the crash. The board blamed film director John Landis and the helicopter pilot. These two men and three others were indicted of involuntary manslaughter.

Collapse of Skywalks In the Kansas City, Missouri, Hyatt Regency Hotel, 114 persons were killed and more than 300 were injured in July 1981. After a two-year investigation, a joint statement was made by the federal and state prosecutors that there was insufficient evidence to charge any person criminally. Manslaughter by culpable negligence was one of the possible charges.

Slaying of Vincent Chin Vincent Chin, who was Chinese, was mistaken for Japanese and was blamed for unemployment in the Detroit area. The men who clubbed Vincent to death with a baseball bat were charged with second-degree murder. After plea bargaining, they plead guilty to manslaughter and received three years probation and $3,780 in fines and court costs. Federal charges were filed by the U.S. Justice Department against the men for violation of Vincent's civil rights.

"Jilted Lovers" Killings Jean Harris (head mistress of a fashionable school) killed the author of the Scarsdale Diet books, Dr. Herman Tarnower, after being jilted for other women. Richard Harrin bludgeoned to death his college sweetheart, Bonnie Garland. Her killing and his conviction of manslaughter caused some division in the Yale University community, where they were both students.

Miami Police Killing Officer Luis Alvarez used self-defense against the charge of manslaughter for the shooting of Nevell Johnson. The state alleged that the killing, which sparked a three-day riot, was the result of "gross negligence" by Alvarez. When a jury acquitted Officer Alvarez in 1984, additional rioting occurred, with more than 300 persons arrested in Miami.

"Battered Spouse" Killings In 1983, Leslie Ann Emick went to trial in Belmont, New York, charged with manslaughter for the killing of her common law husband. The 1983 book *Manslaughter* (Doubleday & Co.) tells the story of Jennifer Patri who was convicted of manslaughter for the killing of her husband. These women and other women told of beatings, choking, suffocating, and other physical, psychological, and sexual abuses.

Midwest Crime Spree Alton Coleman and Debra Brown were apprehended in July 1984 after a seven-week crime spree in six Midwest states. It was decided that the state of Ohio would have the first crack at prosecuting the alleged slayers as prosecution for murder in Ohio "is the most likely to result in the swiftest imposition of the death penalty."

---

though state criminal codes permit 6 to 15 years' imprisonment for voluntary manslaughter, the judge in the *Moody* case imposed a lenient sentence because of the facts in the case.[24]

Heat-of-Passion Voluntary Manslaughter

The usual type of voluntary manslaughter involves the intentional killing of another while the defendant has temporarily lost his normal self-control because of the conduct of the victim. To lower and reduce murder to manslaughter, courts

hold that the following four requirements must exist: [25]

1. There must be adequate provocation.

2. The killing must have been in a heat of passion (anger, rage, emotional disturbance).

3. There must have been no opportunity to cool off.

4. There must be a causal connection between the provocation, the rage, anger, and the fatal act.

What Is Sufficient and Adequate Provocation?

Sufficient provocation is the provocation that naturally and instantly produces in the mind of an ordinary person the highest degree of exasperation, rage, anger, sudden resentment, or terror. The provocation must be of such a nature and so great as to overcome or suspend an ordinary person's exercise of judgment. The provocation must be such as to cause the person to act uncontrollably. The killing must occur immediately on the provocation and during the intense heat of passion. Only a few categories of provocation have been recognized by the law as producing legally sufficient and adequate provocation to justify reduction of a murder charge to that of manslaughter.

In the United States, there is an almost uniform rule that words and gestures are never sufficient provocation to reduce a charge of murder to that of manslaughter. The U.S. Supreme Court stated in the 1895 case of *Allen v. United States* that "mere words alone do not excuse even a simple assault. Any words offered at the time [of the killing] do not reduce the grade of the killing from murder to manslaughter." [26]

Just as insulting words are not sufficient provocation, neither is failure to pay a debt. In the California case of *Morse v. People,* [27] the fact that the deceased victim welched on a gambling debt to the defendant and then had the audacity to try to "bum" cigarettes from him was held to be insufficient provocation.

The American rule that words and gestures are never sufficient provocation has been criticized as bringing about harsh results in some cases. However, if other provocation, such as a battery, accompanies the verbal provocation, then it might be held to be sufficient. In *People v. Rice* [28] the deceased slapped the defendant's child and a quarrel resulted. This was held to be sufficient provocation. A minor and technical battery accompanied with words was held in the 1928 Georgia case of *Lamp v. State* [29] to amount to a sufficient provocation to justify reducing the conviction from murder to manslaughter. But in *Commonwealth v. Cisneros,* [30] the Pennsylvania Supreme Court arrived at an opposite conclusion.

A violent, unjustified, and unreasonable battery that caused pain and anger to the defendant could be determined by a jury to be sufficient provocation. In *State v. Kizer,* [31] the deceased was pounding on the back door of the defendant's house with an axe and threatening to kill him. When the deceased broke the door, the defendant shot and killed him. The trial court held that as there was no actual battery, the defendant had no right to a jury instruction on voluntary manslaughter. The jury convicted him of murder. The appellate court ruled that the evidence warranted an instruction of the defense of habitation and reversed and remanded the case for a new trial.

The Illinois court in *People v. Williams* held that "it is the defendant's state of mind at the time of the incident that is the critical element." [32] The following batteries were held to be sufficient provocations: a severe beating with a nightstick that fractured the defendant's jaw (*People v. Sain,* 384 Ill. 394, 51 N.E.2d 557 [1943]); throwing hot water into the defendant's face and partially blinding him (*People v. Rice,* 351 Ill. 604, 184 N.E. 894 [1933]); an attack with a knife in a fight in which several people were involved (*People v. Oritz,* 320 Ill. 205, 150 N.E. 708 [1926]); shoving and knocking the defendant into a rock pile (*State v. Ponce,* 124 W.Va. 126, 19 S.E.2d 221 [1942]).

There have been many American cases holding that when a married person finds his or her spouse in an act of adultery, this amounts to sufficient provocation if it causes a genuine heat of passion. [33] However, this rule does not apply if a girlfriend is caught "cheating" on her boyfriend (or vice versa).

Trespass, like battery, depends on the facts and circumstances in each particular case. A homeowner certainly would not have sufficient and adequate provocation to kill someone who walked across a lawn, yard, farm, or field in the middle of an afternoon. But snowmobilers who broke onto a farmer's land in Wisconsin and were circling the farmhouse at midnight caused a Wisconsin prosecutor to charge manslaughter when the farmer, in a terrible anger and rage, shot and killed one of the trespassers.

Heat of Passion and the Test of the Reasonable Person

The test of sufficiency or adequacy of

Most crimes are not cleared by arrest.

	Reported crimes cleared by arrest
Murder	72%
Aggravated assault	58
Forcible rape	48
Robbery	24
Larceny-theft	19
Burglary	14
Motor vehicle theft	14
All UCR Index crimes	19

Serious violent crimes are more likely to be cleared than serious property crimes.

The rate of clearance for crimes of violence (murder, forcible rape, aggravated assault, and robbery) is nearly 43 percent, as compared with the 17 percent clearance rate for property crimes (burglary, larceny, motor vehicle theft). This wide variation is largely due to the fact that—

● Victims often confront perpetrators in violent crime incidents.

● Witnesses are more frequently available in connection with violent crimes than with property crimes.

● Intensive investigative efforts are employed more frequently with crimes of violence, resulting in a greater number of arrests.

Source: 1983 U.S. Justice Department Report to the Nation on Crime

---

provocation must be made in view of how the average or reasonable person would react to such provocation. Some persons have extraordinary self-control and could endure much provocation before an uncontrollable rage would cause them to use deadly force. Others have short tempers and fly into a rage with little provocation.

A jury cannot give any special consideration to a defendant who has an extraordinarily bad temper. If the provocation is such that it would not cause the average reasonable person to explode in a sudden outburst of rage, it is not adequate or sufficient provocation to reduce murder to manslaughter. California courts have quoted the 1917 California case of *People v. Logan* as follows:

> The fundamental . . . inquiry is whether or not the defendant's reason was, at the time of his act, so disturbed or obscured by some passion—not necessarily fear and never of course the passion for revenge—to such an extent as would render *ordinary men of average disposition* liable to act rashly or without due deliberation and reflection, and from this passion rather than from judgment.[34] [Emphasis added.]

The defendant in the 1971 case of *Bateman v. State*[35] was convicted of two counts of murder in the second degree. He had found his wife being warmly hugged by a man whom the defendant had told to stay away from his wife. This occurred at a party of 10 adults to which the

defendant had not been invited. The Maryland Court of Special Appeals affirmed the trial court's refusal to give the "heat of passion" instruction to the jury. With respect to the question of the use of intoxicants, the court stated:

> Furthermore, it is still the well-settled law in Maryland that "voluntary intoxication will not reduce murder to manslaughter," Chisley v. State, 202 Md. 87, 106, 95 A.2d 577, but will be considered simply for purposes of lowering first-degree murder to second-degree murder.

The case of *Bedder v. Director of Public Prosecutions*[36] received considerable attention throughout the English-speaking world. The defendant, who knew that he was impotent, attempted to have sexual intercourse with a London prostitute in a quiet courtyard. She jeered when he was unsuccessful and attempted to get away from him. He tried to hold her, and she slapped him in the face and punched him in the stomach. When he grabbed her shoulders, she kicked him in the groin. He took a knife from his pocket and stabbed her twice, killing her. The House of Lords affirmed both the finding of the jury that there was not sufficient or adequate provocation and the following jury instruction given by the trial court:

> The reasonable person, the ordinary person, is the person you must consider when you are considering

the effect which any acts, any conduct, any words, might have to justify the steps which were taken in response thereto, so that an unusually excitable or pugnacious individual, or a drunken one or a man who is sexually impotent is not entitled to rely on provocation which would not have led an ordinary person to have acted in the way which was in fact carried out.

Cooling of the Blood "Cooling of the blood," also known as "cooling time" or "reasonable time to cool off," is a factor that must be considered when there is a time interval between the provocation and the killing. Assume that after Y provokes X into a "heat of passion," X, who has lost his self-control, runs to get his gun. If it took X two minutes to get his gun, was this sufficient time for X to cool off? If it took X a half hour or an hour to obtain his gun, was this sufficient time for the heat of passion to cool off? These questions would have to be answered by a court and jury that would consider the type and degree of the provocation that caused the heat of passion.

"Imperfect" (Unlawful) Force in Self-defense Charged as Manslaughter

Homicide in "perfect" self-defense is either justifiable or excusable, and there is no criminal liability. "Perfect" self-defense requires that the killer not only subjectively believes that his conduct was necessary and reasonable, but also that, by objective standards, it was lawful and complied with the requirements of the law.

In "imperfect" self-defense, the killer subjectively believes that his conduct was necessary. But if the killing was done with excessive or unnecessary force in self-defense, it is therefore unlawful. An unnecessary killing in self-defense, in defense of another, or to prevent or terminate a felony could be "imperfect".

The fact that a killing was "imperfect" would cause it to be reduced from murder to manslaughter because:

1. The deceased victim provoked the killing by his conduct (however, the killing was not legally justified).

Example: Two men are in the process of stealing an expensive boat on a trailer when the owner sees the felony being committed. In a frantic effort to terminate the felony and prevent the loss of the boat, the owner shoots and kills one of the men. As deadly force cannot be used to defend property, the killing is "imperfect" in the defense of property and to prevent a felony.

2. As the killer believed that his (or her) conduct was lawful, there is no "malice."

In the 1983 case of *Faulkner v. State,* the Maryland Court of Special Appeals held that:

> Homicide in "perfect" self-defense is either justifiable or excusable and when established the killer is not culpable. . . . Perfect self-defense requires not only that the killer subjectively believed that his actions were necessary for his safety but, objectively, that a reasonable man would so consider them. Imperfect self-defense, however, requires no more than a subjective honest belief on the part of the killer that his actions were necessary for his safety, even though, on an objective appraisal by a reasonable man, they would not be found to be so. If established, the killer remains culpable and his actions are excused only to the extent that mitigation is invoked.
>
> The mitigating effect of imperfect self-defense is to negate malice. It therefore serves not only to reduce murder to manslaughter in the case of a felonious homicide but applies also to the felony of assault with intent to murder. It fatally erodes an assault with intent to murder charge. Since there is no crime of assault with intent to manslaughter, when malice is negated with respect to assault with intent to murder, the accused, if so charged, may be found guilty of simple assault and battery.[37]

Involuntary Manslaughter

Involuntary manslaughter consists of two types: (1) criminal negligence manslaughter and (2) unlawful act manslaughter. An example of the criminal negligence manslaughter is the *Twilight Zone* helicopter accident case in which actor Vic Morrow and two children were killed in July 1982.

A California prosecutor issued involuntary manslaughter charges against film director John Landis and four other workers, charging that they did not take all the required and necessary precautions, which resulted in the death of the three persons. However after a long preliminary hearing in 1984, charges against two of the workers were dropped. John Landis and two associ-

The *most frequent* criminal homicide in the United States is caused by drunk driving. In a front page story of 4/20/82, the *Wall Street Journal* reported that drunk driving causes 70 fatalities a day in the United States. The article stated that federal officials estimated that the use of other drugs is involved in as many as 20% of fatal traffic accidents, and that in about half of these crashes, the driver is also drunk.

Feticide has been made a crime in some states. For example, Georgia statute section 16–5–80(a) provides that a "person commits the offense of feticide if he willfully kills an unborn child so far developed as to be ordinarily called 'quick' by any injury to the mother of such child which would be murder if it resulted in the death of such mother." The Georgia Supreme Court defined "quick" as that ". . . time when the fetus is able to move in its mother's womb." *State v. Brinkley,* 36 CrL 2163 (1984). See also *State v. Willis,* 36 CrL 2163 (1984) where the Mississippi Supreme Court held that if an unborn 'quick' child and the mother both die as the result of an assault, the defendant may be convicted of the separate crimes of murder and feticide (which is manslaughter in Mississippi).

ates were ordered to face trial on the involuntary manslaughter charges.

The following case illustrates unlawful act manslaughter:[38]

COMMONWEALTH v. KONZ

Superior Court of Pennsylvania (1979)
265 Pa. Super. 570, 402 A.2d 692

The Rev. David Konz was a diabetic and decided to withdraw from insulin and rely on his faith that God would heal him. However, he assured others that if his condition required it, he would resume taking insulin. When he arrived at the point where he needed insulin immediately, he went to the refrigerator but discovered his wife (the defendant) had hidden it. His attempt to leave the house was blocked. Mr. Konz was physically forced into the bedroom, where his wife and a friend talked to him. When he attempted to make a telephone call, his wife and the friend disconnected the telephone. In reinstating the conviction for involuntary manslaughter for the death of Mr. Konz, the Court held:

We hold that appellee Dorothy Konz, as wife of decedent, was under a duty to obtain medical aid for her diabetic husband when it became readily apparent that he was suffering the effects of lack of insulin, and in serious need of medical attention.

The state of the law as to the duty owed by one spouse to obtain medical assistance for the other is not well-settled, with only a handful of cases addressing the issue. Indeed, our research uncovered no recent Pennsylvania case of import to the instant appeal. Nevertheless, a review of the case law from other jurisdictions discloses a duty of care, vague though it may be, arising from the spousal relationship.

F. SUICIDE[39]

At common law, suicide was considered to be self-murder and was a felony. Because the person who committed such a crime was beyond the reach of the law, the punishment was forfeiture of property and burial off the highway.

Insanity, Self-Defense, and Manslaugher as Defenses

	Degree of Liability	Tests Used to Determine Liability	Disposition of Person
Finding of not guilty because of mental disease or defect (insanity)	No criminal liability	(1) M'Naghten "right or wrong" test or (2) Model Penal Code "substantial capacity" test (see Chapter 5)	Confined to state institution until released under the statutes or procedures of that state
Finding that the killing was lawful in self-defense or in defense of another (or in some states, to prevent or to terminate a felony of violence)	No criminal liability	Was the killing necessary to avoid death or serious bodily harm? Was it lawful under the laws of that state or jurisdiction?	Person is not charged, or if charged may use the defense before a jury or judge. If defense is proven, the defendant would be acquitted.
Manslaughter • Voluntary manslaughter • Heat-of-passion manslaughter • "Imperfect" use of force manslaughter • Criminal negligence manslaughter • Unlawful act manslaughter	Defendant is convicted of manslaughter instead of murder (partial forgiveness).	(1) The victims provoked the killings by their unlawful conduct; or (2) the killings are not bad enough to be charged and punished as murder, but bad enough to be criminal; or (3) the killings violated a section of the manslaughter statute of that state (manslaughter is often the catch-all category of criminal homicide)	Defendant is sentenced for the crime of manslaughter.

If the attempt to commit suicide failed, the person who made the attempt was guilty under common law of the misdemeanor of attempted suicide. If in the course of the attempt, the person killed another (for example, in a struggle for the gun), the person was guilty of murder under the doctrine of transferred intent or malice.

In only a few states today is attempted suicide an offense. Probably all states make aiding and assisting another to commit suicide a crime. The following "mutual suicide pact" case came before the California Supreme Court in 1983.

Changes (1970s–early 1980s) in the Pattern and Method of Suicide in the United States

• There has been a 40 percent increase in the suicide rate among young people (particularly white males) aged 15 to 24, and suicide is now the third leading cause of death in this age-group.

• Young adults aged 20 to 24 have approximately twice the number and rate of suicides as do adolescents aged 15 to 19.

• The ratio of male to female suicides in the age-group 15 to 24 is now 4 to 1.

• Dramatic changes in the method of suicide occurred by increased use of firearms and explosives instead of poisoning.

Source: Centers for Disease Control

FORDEN v.
JOSEPH G.

Supreme Court of California
(1983)
194 Cal. Rptr. 163, 667 P.2d
1176

Joseph G. (the minor defendant) drove a car containing himself and a friend over a 350-foot cliff in an attempt to carry out a mutual suicide pact. Joseph G. survived but his passenger was killed. The lower court held that the defendant should be charged with murder in the first degree. The Supreme Court of California ruled that he should be charged with aiding and abetting the deceased friend's suicide, holding:

Traditionally under the common law the survivor of a suicide pact was held to be guilty of murder.

*   *   *

Most states provide, either by statute or case law, criminal sanctions for aiding suicide, but few adopt the extreme common law position that such conduct is murder. Some jurisdictions instead classify aiding suicide as a unique type of manslaughter. But the predominant statutory scheme, and the one adopted in California, is to create a sui generis crime of aiding and abetting suicide.

*   *   *

In essence, it is actually a double attempted suicide, and therefore the rationale for not punishing those who attempt suicide would seem to apply.

QUESTIONS AND PROBLEMS FOR CHAPTER 13

1. The defendant, James Jackson, admitted that he had shot and killed his friend, Mrs. Cole. Jackson testified that he was not drunk at the time of the shooting but that he had been "pretty high." He testified that Mrs. Cole had taken off some of her clothes and then attacked him with a knife when he had resisted her sexual advances. Jackson testified that he had fired warning shots and then reloaded the gun and killed her. Without seeking help for the victim, he drove her car to another state. No other person was at the scene of the shooting and defendant argues not only self-defense, but also that he was too intoxicated to form the specific intent necessary for conviction of first-degree murder.

   A deputy sheriff also testified at the trial. He knew the defendant and Mrs. Cole and had seen them in a restaurant just before the shooting. Because Jackson appeared intoxicated, the sheriff offered to hold Jackson's revolver until Jackson sobered up. Jackson said that this was unnecessary because he and Mrs. Cole were about to engage in sexual activity. Jackson waived his right to a jury trial and was tried before a judge. The judge found him guilty of first-degree murder. (*Jackson v. Virginia,* 443 U.S. 307, 99 S. Ct. 2781 [U.S. Sup. Ct. 1979])

   Which of Jackson's arguments would justify the U.S. Supreme Court reversal of Jackson's conviction of intent-to-kill murder:

   a. That there was insufficient evidence to support the conviction
   b. That the evidence shows he should be found not guilty, as the shooting was in self-defense

c. That the evidence showed that he was too intoxicated to form the specific intent necessary to convict of intent-to-kill murder

2. A young married woman, Pamela Robbins, suffered from epilepsy and diabetes for many years. She required two daily injections of insulin along with other medication. Pamela and her husband, Robert, became deeply religious, "born again" Christians. They joined a group led by a minister who believed that if one had sufficient faith, God would cure all illnesses. During a religious meeting, Pamela had a revelation and she believed that she was healed and resolved to stop taking all medication. She discontinued all medication and she and her husband prayed. He did all he could to ease her discomfort and attended to her every need. After her death, Robert Robbins was charged with criminal negligent homicide and the minister was charged with "counseling, urging, suggesting and directing" that Pamela refrain from taking insulin or seeking medical assistance. Is there criminal liability for one or both of the defendants? (*People v. Robbins,* 83 A.D.2d 271, 443 N.Y.S.2d 1016 [1981])

3. During the robbery of a liquor store, the storeowner obtained a gun and fired at a 21-year-old robber. Witnesses state that the robber ran out of the store and fell in the store's parking lot. The storeowner, Ray Verbanic, ran out and fired 13 shots from two guns into the motionless body lying face down in the lot. A medical pathologist stated that it was unlikely that the robber moved once he was on the ground. In 1984, a Kansas City, Kansas, prosecutor charged the liquor store owner with attempted second-degree murder for the shots fired into the robber outside the store, while the robber was lying face down. What possible defenses would the liquor store owner have to the charge? State reasons for defenses and state arguments a prosecutor might use.

4. An elderly woman resisted a purse snatching near her home and was knocked to the pavement. The two purse-snatchers escaped with $15 to $20 in the purse. The woman was taken to a hospital with a cut on the back of her head. Because a blood clot developed in her brain, surgery was performed. The woman remained in a coma into which she had lapsed within hours of the purse-snatching and died six weeks after the incident. What criminal charges should be issued against the two men and what defenses to these charges would be used by a defense lawyer?

5. In 1984, a St. Paul, Minnesota man admitted to police that he murdered his wife and buried her body in the snow. His defense attorney then advised him not to provide any further information. The man was arrested, and for weeks the police attempted to find the body of the woman. In order to obtain information as to the location of the body, the district attorney agreed to accept a plea to second-degree murder. Based on the plea bargain, the man disclosed the location of the body. The court, upon receiving the guilty plea, imposed a sentence of 25 years in prison, with parole eligibility in 17 years.

• What are the factors that would cause a prosecuting attorney to make a plea bargain offer of second-degree murder instead of going for a conviction of first-degree murder in this case?

• What bargaining leverage does a defense attorney have in a situation such as this?

• Are the interests of the public and justice served by the outcome in this case?

Chapter 14

Assault, Battery, and Other Crimes Against the Person

A. THE CRIME OF ASSAULT

Under common law, assault and battery were two separate crimes. Today, however, the term assault and battery is sometimes used to indicate one offense. As an assault is often an attempt to commit a battery, the California courts point out that an assault is an attempt to strike, whereas a battery is the successful attempt. A battery cannot be committed without assaulting a victim, but an assault can occur without committing a battery.

Most states have statutorized the old common law crime of assault. Included in the crime of assault are (a) an attempt to commit a battery in which no actual battery or physical injury resulted and (b) an intentional frightening (such as pointing a loaded gun at a person or menacing with a fist or knife). Generally, in an assault, the state must show apprehension or fear on the part of the victim if no blow, touching, or injury occurred.

In many states, the crime of assault also includes batteries. The state of New York does not have a crime of battery.[1] Therefore, in New York, a person who swings a knife at another with intent to cause serious physical injury is guilty of first-degree assault if he succeeds but is guilty only of attempted assault if he fails. (See New York Commentaries, Art. 120, p. 331.)

Section 240 of the California Penal Code (enacted in 1872) defines assault as "an unlawful attempt, coupled with a present ability, to commit a violent injury on the person of another."[2] Chapter 38, Section 12–1 of the Illinois Statutes provides that "a person commits an assault when, without lawful authority, he engages in conduct which places another in reasonable apprehension of receiving a battery."

In some states (including California), the lack of "present ability" to commit the injury (or battery) is a defense to an assault charge.[3] The defendant in the 1983 case of *People v. Fain*[4] used this defense. He argued that the rifle he pointed at three men was not loaded. However, one of the victims (Steen) testified that the defendant fired a shot from the gun during the incident and that the defendant struck two of the victims with the gun. In affirming the defendant's convictions, the Supreme Court of California held:

> Defendant testified that the gun was unloaded. The threat to shoot with an unloaded gun is not an assault, since the defendant lacks the present ability to commit violent injury. . . . The jury, however, may not have believed defendant's testimony in this regard, as Steen had testified that at one point defendant had fired a round from the rifle.
>
> In any case, even an unloaded gun can be used as a club or bludgeon. . . . Defendant struck both Maestas and Steen with the gun, and approached sufficiently near Watkins to have the present ability to injure Watkins in the same manner.

Assault Under the Present Federal Criminal Code

Under the present Federal Criminal Code, the crime of assault also includes an actual battery; 18 U.S.C. Section 113(c) forbids "assault by striking, beating, or wounding." Therefore, the two common law aspects of assault are used, as well as a third aspect in which the crime of assault is committed by inflicting injury on another person. The following federal case illustrates:

UNITED STATES v. MASEL[5]

United States Circuit Court of Appeals, Seventh Circuit (1977)
563 F.2d 322, 22 Cr.L. 2065

After the defendant spat in the face of U.S. Senator Henry Jackson, he was charged and convicted of assaulting a member of Congress. In affirming the defendant's conviction, the Court held:

Defendant would read the assault offense as confined to an attempt to commit a battery or an act putting another in reasonable apprehension of bodily harm. . . . The district court concluded that assault, in this statute, had a broader meaning. "Because the statute contemplates that personal injury may result from the 'assault,' it is clear that Congress intended to include 'battery' within the term 'assault.'" Accordingly, the district court instructed, in effect, that if the jury found a battery had been committed, defendant should be convicted of the charge of assault. . . . We find the reasoning of the district court persuasive. Moreover, comments in Senate debate suggest that battery as well as an unsuccessful attempt was thought of as constituting assault. . . . We also note that every battery must include or be the culmination of an assault (in the sense of attempt), U.S. v. Bell, 505 F.2d 539, 540 (7th Cir. 1974), citing Hawkins, Pleas of the Crown, c. 62, § 1 (6th ed. 1788). That being true, defendant, charged with assault, could not complain of an instruction which required proof that he had committed the battery which culminated it. Moreover, the court says, the instructions required the government to prove that the defendant willfully caused, by spitting, an offensive touching. "We think this is an adequate statement. . . . It is ancient doctrine that intentional spitting upon another is battery. . . . No more severe injury need be intended."

Hands as "Dangerous Weapons"

As pointed out in Chapter 13, the issue of what is a dangerous or deadly weapon is a question of fact for the fact finder (jury or judge). Just as it was held in New York that a common handkerchief can, under certain circumstances, be a deadly weapon, many courts have also held that hands can be dangerous or deadly weapons, even if the assailant has no training in martial arts or boxing.

The relative size and strength of the assailant as compared with the victim, the manner and duration of the assault, and the severity of the injuries are all facts that must be taken into consideration in determining whether hands are dangerous or deadly weapons.

The defendant in the 1982 case of *State v. Zangrilli* [6] broke his ex-wife's jaw in two places, grabbed her by the throat and strangled her until she could feel her "eyes bulge," dragged her through several rooms in her house, punched her several times in the face and neck, and shoved her into a bathtub. The Supreme Court of Rhode Island affirmed his conviction of assault with a dangerous weapon, quoting the trial judge's holdings:

> The manner in which he used his hands on her throat constituted use of his hands in such a way that it could easily have led to her death.
>
> For that reason, I have concluded that his assault upon her was done with a dangerous weapon. As I

say, hands are not per se dangerous weapons, but they are a means to produce death. And they were used, even though briefly, they were used in a manner and in such circumstances as could be reasonably calculated to produce death.

B. BATTERY

In order for an offense to constitute assault, the victim must ordinarily be apprehensive of the impending harm or danger. This is not necessary in a battery. A blow from behind is a battery whether the victim is aware that it is coming or not. Battery is a crime that, like murder and manslaughter, is defined in terms of the conduct of the offender and also in terms of the harm done.

A battery is an unlawful striking; in many states, even a touching could be charged as a battery. Batteries can be committed with fists, feet, sticks, stones, or other objects used to inflict injury. Under some circumstances, dogs or other animals could be used to commit a battery if they are used to injure another person.

All states that make battery a crime require that the act to commit a battery must be intentional (or must be done knowingly), as an accidental physical contact or injury is not a battery.

Street Fights and Public Brawls

Under the old common law, an affray was the offense of two or more persons fighting in a public place. In such street fights and public brawls, assaults and batteries occurred. Today, an affray could be charged as disorderly conduct (or either assault or battery).

Affrays differ from assaults and batteries in that the old offense of affray had to be committed in a public place. Assaults and batteries can be committed in either a private or a public place. Affrays also required two or more persons engaged in mutual combat, whereas an assault or a battery may be committed by one person on another.

A victim of an assault or battery can claim the privilege of self-defense, as necessary and reasonable force may be used to defend against an unlawful attack (see Chapter 6 on defenses to the use of force). In an affray (fight in a public place), the combat generally is mutual, which would make it more difficult to assert self-defense or the defense of another.

Sexual Assault—Sexual Battery

More than 20 states have enacted sexual assault statutes to replace their old rape statutes. These statutes generally provide for three or four degrees of sexual assault. In addition to defining "sexual intercourse" broadly, these statutes also forbid and punish "offensive touching."

Before the enactment of the sexual assault statutes, offensive touching was ordinarily charged under the general assault statute, or as a battery, or as disorderly conduct. Although offensive touching may continue to be charged under the old statutes, the sexual assault statute is now available. However, under the sexual assault statutes, the offensive touching generally must be of an "intimate part" or "private part" of the body and for the purpose "of arousing or gratifying sexual desire of either party" (Section 213.4 Model Penal Code).

Most sexual assault or sexual abuse statutes include the buttocks as an "intimate part" or "private part." However the New York statute did not when the case of People v. Thomas [7] came before the Criminal Court of New York City in 1977. Thomas was charged with the offensive touching of the buttocks of a woman on a rush-

hour train. On the complaint of the woman, the defendant had been arrested by a transit patrolman. The court affirmed the defendant's conviction, holding that the buttocks are an "intimate part" and that the defendant's intentional touching without consent violated the statute.

Sexual battery is charged in Illinois under a 1979 statute that provides that "a person commits battery if he intentionally or knowingly without legal justification and by any means . . . makes physical contact by an insulting or provoking nature with an individual." [8]

The rape charge in the 1983 case of People v. Margiolas was dropped because of lack of evidence of resistance. However, the defendant admitted that he unbuttoned the victim's blouse, despite her verbal as well as physical objections. The defendant was convicted of sexual battery in forcibly unbuttoning the blouse. [9] Under such a statute, a prosecutor with a weak case might also issue a sexual battery charge when it is apparent that the rape charge has defects that might be fatal. [10]

Defenses to Assault or Battery Charges [11]

Defenses to an assault or battery charge could be as follows:

1. Self-defense
   - "perfect"—the force used was necessary and reasonable in self-defense, defense of another, or in the defense of property
   - "imperfect"—some force was necessary because of unlawful conduct but an excessive or unnecessary amount of force was used (defendant would be liable only for the amount of excessive or unnecessary force)
2. That the discipline of a child was reasonable in view of (a) the type of punishment inflicted and the manner in which it was inflicted, (b) the conduct of the child that brought about the punishment, and (c) the age, health, size, and sex of the child. This defense could not be used by persons other than:
   - parents, guardians, and those who act in the place of the parents who have the duty and obligation to educate, discipline, and train the child

• teachers and school administrators as governed by state law, which was summarized by the U.S. Supreme Court as follows:

Of the 23 States that have addressed the problem through legislation, 21 have authorized the moderate use of corporal punishment in public schools. Of these States only a few have elaborated on the common law test of reasonableness, typically providing for approval or notification of the child's parents, or for infliction of punishment only by the principal or in the presence of an adult witness. Only two States, Massachusetts and New Jersey, have prohibited all corporal punishment in their public schools. Where the legislatures have not acted, the state courts have uniformly preserved the common law rule permitting teachers to use reasonable force in disciplining children in their charge.[12]

3. That the conduct is within the rules of the sport being played. A bone-jarring tackle in football or a hard right to the jaw in boxing is within the rules of those sports and would be consented to by persons engaged in those contests. Prosecutors have warned that violence outside of the rules of a sport is subject to criminal or civil prosecution.

4. Consent is a defense to "offensive touching" batteries and also "intent-to-injure" contacts if done within the rules of such body contact sports as boxing, ice hockey, and football.[13]

5. Where the conduct is necessary and lawful:
 • in the accomplishment of a lawful arrest
 • when necessary to lawfully detain or hold a person in custody
 • when necessary to prevent an escape of a person lawfully in custody
 • when necessary to prevent a suicide
 • for any other reason when the conduct is privileged by the statutory or common law of that state

C. FELONIOUS AND AGGRAVATED ASSAULTS AND BATTERIES

Misdemeanor assault and misdemeanor batteries are probably classified as class A or B misdemeanors in most states. The degree of these crimes and the penalties are increased with aggravating factors used by state legislatures. The Supreme Court of Oregon pointed out that the three factors used in Oregon are (1) the severity of the injury, (2) the use of a deadly or dangerous weapon, and (3) culpable mental state.[14] The presence of one or more of these aggravating factors could result in a felonious assault or battery. For example, when only minor injury

---

Factors Used In Charging and Proving Attempted Murder

	"Intent to Kill" and "Attempt to Kill" Are More Likely to Be Charged:	A Lesser Offense is Likely to Be Charged:
when the conduct of the defendant:	almost caused death or serious bodily harm to the victim	did not seriously threaten the safety of the victim
when the weapon or instrument used:	was dangerous	is not ordinarily dangerous
when the disposition and attitude of defendant:	showed extreme hostility, malice, and disregard for life	did not show an intent to kill or intent to cause serious harm
when the defendant:	came within "dangerous proximity" of causing death or serious bodily harm	did not come within "dangerous proximity" of killing or causing serious harm
when the evidence showed that the defendant:	had a strong intent (or motive) to kill the victim	had little reason (or intent) to kill the victim

occurred where hands were used, a misdemeanor assault or battery could be charged. However, in the 1982 *Zangrilli* case, the defendant almost caused the death of his ex-wife by strangling her with his hands. The Supreme Court of Rhode Island held that hands in the *Zangrilli* case were dangerous weapons and affirmed the felony conviction.

Mayhem

The common law offense of mayhem was the unlawful and violent depriving of the victim of full use of any functional member of the body (hand, arms, feet, eyes, legs, etc.) that would make the victim less able to defend himself or herself. State statutes have incorporated this concept in the form of maiming or mayhem statutes. Article 1166 of the Texas Penal Code provides that "whoever shall wilfully and maliciously cut off or otherwise deprive a person of the hand, arm, finger, toe, foot, leg, nose, or ear, or put out an eye or in any way deprive a person of any other member of his body shall be confined in the penitentiary not less than two nor more than ten years." [15]

Mental Culpability Increasing the Degree of the Crime

Probably all states have statutes making assaults and batteries felonies because of the seriousness of injuries or because dangerous or deadly weapons were used to commit the offense. Some statutes increase penalties and degree of crimes because of mental culpability.

The Oregon assault statute raises the offense from third- to second-degree assault if the crime is committed "under circumstances manifesting extreme indifference to the value of human life." [16] In holding that a jury must find not only recklessness, but also conduct that shows extreme indifference, the Oregon Supreme Court affirmed the defendant's conviction of assault in the second degree in the 1983 case of *State v. Boone*, holding:

Witnesses testified that prior to the accident defendant was swerving across the road, tailgating so closely he almost hit the car in front of him and passing on a curve. The overwhelming weight of the evidence indicated that the accident occurred because defendant was across the center line in the oncoming lane of traffic. He sideswiped the first oncoming vehicle, bounced or swerved into his own lane and then swerved back across the center line into the second oncoming vehicle, causing serious injury to the passenger. Defendant had a blood alcohol content of .24 percent two hours after the accident. He was belligerent at the scene of the accident, threatening to hit the passenger of the first car he sideswiped. Because of his intoxication he was not only unable to assist the victim, but at one point interfered with the assistance. The degree of intoxication, defendant's erratic driving and his conduct at the scene of the accident are circumstances the jury could properly consider in determining whether defendant was extremely indifferent to the value of human life.

We hold that the circumstances which exist in this case suffice to establish defendant's extreme indifference to the value of human life. From the facts before it the jury in this case could infer, and thus find, such indifference on the part of defendant. [17]

D. CHILD ABUSE AND NEGLECT

Child abuse, child neglect, and sexual abuse are serious problems throughout the United States. Hundreds of children are killed every year either by their parents or persons who are responsible for caring for them. Thousands of children in the United States suffer head injuries; broken bones from beatings; burns from cigarettes, stoves, hot liquids; ruptured internal organs (such as liver, spleen, kidney, and bowels) from blows to the abdomen; missing teeth; multiple scars; knife and gunshot wounds; and bruises and lacerations.

Persons who inflict such injuries on children may be charged with assault, battery, assault with a dangerous weapon, aggravated battery, and other offenses in the criminal code of the state in which the offense occurred. Criminal codes also have child abuse statutes and statutes forbidding the neglect of children. These statutes seek to protect children from injury and trauma inflicted on them by parents, stepfathers, paramours, relatives, baby-sitters, and other adults.

Parents and persons responsible for children have a duty to protect children and provide food, clothing, shelter, medical care, education, and a reasonable physical and moral environment for them. Child neglect is the failure to provide adequate food, clothing, shelter, sanitation, medical care, or supervision for a child.

The child abuse that generally appears in courts is often physical abuse, such as deliberate injuries inflicted on children. Such injuries could result from excessive and unreasonable force used in disciplining children. The U.S. Supreme Court pointed out in *Ingraham v. Wright* that parents and persons taking the place of parents may use force "reasonably believed to be necessary for [the child's] proper control, training, or education." [18] What is reasonable is determined in view of the child's age and sex; the physical, emotional, and mental health of the child; and the conduct that prompted the punishment. Unfortunately, most children who are victims of abuse are under age five and are helpless in protecting themselves.

To protect children against child abuse and neglect, information has to be provided to government officials who can take protective measures. An increasing number of states have passed statutes requiring doctors, nurses, dentists, teachers, law enforcement officers, and other specifically designated persons to report suspected cases of child abuse or neglect. Such statutes require reporting of "suspected" child abuse or neglect and may punish willful failure to report as a misdemeanor. Other persons (such as neighbors, relatives, friends, etc.) are encouraged to provide what information they may have to assist in necessary investigations.

Sexual abuse and exploitation of children is discussed in Chapter 19. Sexual abuse may be combined with physical abuse or child neglect. Abuse or neglect in any form may have a severe emotional and psychological effect on a child, causing behavioral problems that could impact greatly on the child's life.

E. OFFENSES AGAINST THE LIBERTY OF A PERSON

Kidnapping

Kidnapping was a crime at old common law punishable by life imprisonment. All states and the federal government have enacted statutes making kidnapping a crime. The usual elements of the modern kidnap statutes are:

1. The defendant must have seized or confined another by force or threat of imminent force.
2. Such acts must have been unlawful and without authority.

The Child Abuse and Child Neglect Problem *

The Dimensions of the Problem

- More than 900,000 child abuse or neglect cases were *reported* in 1983.
- About half the reported abused children came from families headed by young, poor, single women.
- Every year about a million teenage girls become pregnant, with about 600,000 delivering babies.
- About 1.8 million children are reported missing every year. Some of these children of "run-away" age are victims of abuse and neglect.
- Characteristics of high-risk adults who may become abusers are economic deprivation, abuse of alcohol or drugs, social isolation, lack of parenting skills, abuse in their own childhood.

Myths of Suspected Abuse and Neglect

- That the child claiming abuse is fantasizing. Most children making such disclosures are so fearful that they are probably telling the truth.
- That lack of actual physical evidence means no abuse has occurred. It was reported that in more than half the abuse cases, there is no actual physical evidence.
- That a child with a sexually transmitted disease could have easily obtained it by means other than sexual contact. Sexual contact is the chief transmitter.
- That abused children exhibit characteristic behavorial patterns, such as emotional disturbance. It was reported that some do, but other children do not.

* As identified at the First National Conference on Child Abuse and Neglect, American Medical Association, 1984

3. Such acts could be done by fraud, deceit, and enticing with intent to kidnap.

4. Such acts were done without consent and against the will of the victim.

5. There must be a forcible movement of the victim against his or her will.

Motive or reason for kidnapping could be to obtain ransom or other valuables (such as in the kidnapping of 26 children from a school bus in Chowchilla, California, in 1976); to obtain a hostage for escape or other reasons; for the purposes of robbery, rape, murder, or other felony; to terrorize or blackmail; or for political reasons.

The question that has come before many courts is whether movements incident to the commission of such crimes as rape or robbery constitute kidnapping. According to California jury instruction # 652:

> To constitute the crime of simple kidnapping . . . there must be a carrying, or otherwise forcibly moving, for some distance of the person who, against his will, is stolen or taken into custody or control of another person, but the law does not require that the one thus stolen or taken be carried or moved a long distance or any particular distance.

In interpreting "some distance," the California courts have held that "movement across a room or from one room to another" is not sufficient movement to justify a kidnapping conviction.[19] The general rule seems to be that movement "merely incident to the commission of the robbery [or rape]" is not kidnapping.[20]

In 1982, the Supreme Court of Florida stated that there is a "definite trend" toward allowing a kidnapping conviction "where the purpose in confining or moving another person is to use that person as a hostage." In *Mobley v. State,*[21] the defendants were inmates in a jail. They took two guards and an attorney captive in the course of an escape attempt. In affirming the convictions of the defendants for kidnapping and other offenses, the Supreme Court held that the "confinement was not incidental to the attempted escape once [defendants] began using [the victims] as hostages and threatening physical harm."

In the 1983 case of *State v. Masino,* the defendant dragged his victim from her car and down an embankment, out of sight from passersby, before sexually assaulting her. The Supreme Court of New Jersey affirmed the convictions of sexual assault and kidnapping, holding:

> One is transported a "substantial distance" if that asportation is criminally significant in the sense of being more than merely incidental to the underlying crime. That determination is made with reference not only to the distance travelled but also to the enhanced risk of harm resulting from the asportation and isolation of the victim. That enhanced risk must not be trivial.[22]

However, the Supreme Court of New Jersey also added in the *Masino* case that its decision "is not to be read as a crack in the door against overzealous or creative prosecution for kidnapping nor as encouragement for use of a kidnapping charge as some sort of 'bonus' count in an indictment."

The New Crime of "Taking Hostage"

Because kidnapping requires a forcible movement of the victim "some distance" or a "substantial distance," some states have created the new crime of "taking hostage." A movement of the victim is not required to prove this offense. In creating this new offense, the state legislature can require all the elements of the serious felony of kidnapping, except movement of the victim. They can require the state to prove "intent to use the person as a hostage."[23] As "taking hostage" is a serious offense, it can be made a class A or B felony. To encourage offenders to release victims unharmed, the offense can be reduced to a class B or C felony under such conditions.

False Imprisonment

Under the old common law, false imprisonment was also a crime that, like kidnapping, was punishable by life imprisonment. Many states have enacted statutes making false imprisonment a crime within those states. The usual elements of this crime are:

1. The defendant must have confined or restrained the liberty or freedom of movement of another.

2. Such act must have been intentional and without the consent of the victim.

3. The defendant had no lawful authority to confine or restrain the movement of the victim.

False imprisonment differs from kidnapping in that in kidnapping, the victim must be moved to another place. In false imprisonment, the confinement or restraint may be at the place of the false arrest or unlawful detention of the victim. Under the old common law, it was also required that kidnapping be done secretly; this was not required for false imprisonment. However, the requirement of secretness for kidnapping has probably been eliminated by most state statutes.

Today, false imprisonment is seldom charged as a crime. Most false imprisonment actions are civil actions, in which it is alleged that there was a false arrest or an improper restraint of the freedom of movement of the plaintiff. Many such civil suits originate from shoplifting incidents. To avoid such civil suits, it should be remembered that the freedom of movement of a person should not be restrained unless authority exists to make such a detention or arrest.

Parental Kidnapping, or Child Snatching

"Child Snatching" is the abduction of a child by one parent without the consent of the other parent. It could occur before the parents had commenced a divorce action, during the time in which a divorce action was pending, or after divorce judgment had been granted. Child snatching is also known as parental kidnapping, child abduction, or child stealing.

Thousands of children disappear each year as a result of parental kidnapping.[24] Although the offending parent may state that he (or she) seeks to protect the child's welfare, other motives for child snatching are:

• retaliation against and harassment of the other spouse

• as a means to bargain for reduced child support or reduced division of property in the divorce settlement

• an attempt to bring about a reconciliation of the marriage

Children who are kidnapped by a parent experience changes that may lead to emotional damage. First, the child will probably be told that the parent who had custody is either dead or no longer loves the child. Second, in most instances, the child begins a life-style in which they grow up with only one parent. Third, the child is frequently exposed to life "on the run," as parental kidnapping is a felony in most states. The pain, fear, guilt, anger, and anxiety from these experiences can cause severe, irreparable psychological harm.

As most states make child snatching a felony, they are generally prepared to extradite the offending parent back to the state in which the offense was committed, if he (or she) can be located.[25] Before the passage of the Uniform Child Custody Jurisdiction Act (UCCJA), a fleeing child-snatcher could run to another state, where residence would be established and a custody order would be sought from the courts of the new state. Under UCCJA, the home or resident state would continue to have jurisdiction.

Because the federal kidnapping statute (the "Lindberg Act")[26] specifically excludes parents from its scope, a federal Parental Kidnapping Prevention Act was passed by Congress in 1981. This act facilitates interstate enforcement of custody and visitation determinations. The act also declares that the Fugitive Felon Act[27] applies in state felony parental kidnapping cases, giving the FBI jurisdiction when the child-snatcher crosses state lines.

The Missing Children Act[28]

Because of increasing concern of child kidnapping by strangers or parents, voluntary programs to fingerprint children for identification have commenced throughout the nation. The parents or legal guardians retain the fingerprint cards for use if the child, at a later date, gets lost or is missing.

In 1982, the Missing Children Act became law. The act requires the Attorney General to "acquire, collect and preserve any information which would assist in the location of any missing person (including children, unemancipated persons as defined by the laws of the place of residence) and provide confirmation as to any entry [into FBI records] for such a person to the parent, legal guardian or next of kin." The act thus gives parents, legal guardians, or next of kin access to the information in the FBI National Crime Information Center's (NCIC) missing person file.

Offenses Against the Liberty of a Person

	Usual Definition	Usual Motivation	Use of the Offense
False imprisonment	False imprisonment is the unlawful restraint of another and is committed when a person is detained unlawfully.	False imprisonment most often occurs today when employees of a retail store make an improper detention for shoplifting, or a law enforcement officer makes an illegal arrest.	False imprisonment charges are most often brought in civil suits in civil courts.
Kidnapping	Kidnapping is a false imprisonment that is aggravated by the movement or conveyance of the victim to another place.	• to obtain a hostage • to obtain ransom • for the purposes of rape • robbery, murder, etc. • to terrorize, blackmail, etc.	Kidnapping is one of the most serious crimes against a person's liberty and is punished severely.
"Taking hostage"	The criminal act of "taking hostage" is used to gain an advantage and compel others to comply with demands.	"Taking hostage" is a tactic often used as part of an escape attempt.	The crime of "taking hostage" does not require forcible movement of the victim "some distance."
Parental kidnapping or child snatching	This crime is a kidnapping by a parent who has lost (or will lose) custody of the kidnapped child.	To harass; to retaliate against other spouse or use as a leverage in determining support payments, etc.; or to maintain custody and control of the child.	This problem is serious in the United States. It is estimated that 60% to 70% of the abducted children are never seen again by the other parent.
Abduction	The English enacted the first abduction statute in 1488. For many years, the crime forbade taking a female for any sexual purposes. Today, states have limited abduction to taking a child from the person having lawful custody of the child.	If the taking were by force, kidnapping would probably be charged. Abduction could be charged when a natural parent took a child in violation of a court order or when a victim was old enough to cooperate in the taking.	States using abduction as a crime have generally limited it to taking a child from a person having lawful custody.
Slavery and involuntary servitude	The Fourteenth Amendment forbids "slavery . . . [and] involuntary servitude, except as a punishment for crime."	Two Michigan residents were convicted in 1984 of violations of civil rights and involuntary servitude of two mentally retarded men, who the federal prosecutor stated were held as slaves for at least 11 years.	Slavery, serfage, peonage, debt bondage, exploitation of children still exist in parts of the world.

The individual making the request is notified of the results of the check. If a record has not been entered, the person is instructed to contact local law enforcement authorities to determine whether the disappearance of the missing person meets the criteria for entry into the NCIC computer. Missing unemancipated minors is one of the four categories of records entered into the NCIC computer. Should a child of that description be found by another department, this information would be exchanged.

The act does not confer on the FBI any new investigative jurisdiction. The FBI can enter parental kidnapping cases through the Fugitive Felony Act if the following conditions exist:

1. A state arrest warrant has been issued charging the parent with a felony violation.

2. There must be evidence of interstate flight.

3. A specific request for FBI assistance must be made by state authorities who agree to extradite and prosecute.

4. A U.S. attorney must authorize issuance of an unlawful flight warrant.

The National Center for Missing and Exploited Children coordinates efforts to recover missing children. A telephone hot line and other new facilities were established in 1984 to aid in these efforts.

Missing Children In America

The U.S. Department of Health and Human Services estimates that 1.5 million children disappear from their homes each year. Unfortunately, no governmental agency or any other group has specific information as to what happens to many thousands of these children. Following is a breakdown generally presenting the problem:

Runaways The majority of missing children are runaways (runaway age generally does not commence until 9 or 10). Most of these children return home, but while they are on the street, they are frequent victims of street crime or exploitation. As many as 60 percent report some type of sexual abuse during their time away from home.

Parental Kidnapping Estimates of the number of children who are the victims of parental snatching vary from 25,000 to 100,000 per year. Unfortunately, when a parent kidnaps his or her own child, the parent is frequently acting out of revenge, not love. Child Find, Inc., of New Paltz, New York, estimates that as many as 60 percent of the abducting parents have some type of a criminal record.

Killed or Died Two to five thousand bodies are buried each year in the United States in John or Jane Doe graves, unidentified. It is estimated that approximately half the unidentified dead are children.

Abducted by Strangers and the Victims of Crimes Strangers who steal children are broadly categorized by the Behavioral Science Department of the FBI Academy as follows:

• *The pedophile.* The pedophile abducts a child primarily for sexual purposes. The Center for Child Advocacy and Protection states that such persons are generally young and middle-aged men who seek to control children rather than injure them. They will, however, murder children and perhaps make up the largest group in this category.

• *The "Serial" Killer* (see Chapter 13). The killings of 29 young blacks in Atlanta, after abduction, shocked the nation. Wayne Williams was convicted for the murders of two of the older victims.

• *The Psychotic.* The psychotic is usually a woman who has lost a baby or cannot conceive. To solve her problem, she abducts another family's child.

• *The Profiteer.* This person seeks to make money by stealing children. The child may be used by a baby adoption ring, pornographers, or, in rare instances, as a kidnapping for ransom.

A survey conducted by the U.S. Senate Subcommittee on Investigations showed that more than 85,000 children were missing in 25 of the largest American cities in 1981. Tragically, at the end of the year at least 7,000 of the cases remained unsolved. Law enforcement officers report that few stranger-abducted children are recovered alive. (See "Plight of the Children," *The Prosecutor Magazine* Vol. 16, No. 5 (1983). The entire issue is devoted to this subject.)

F. FAMILY VIOLENCE AND DISTURBANCES

A study conducted for the National Institute of Mental Health concluded that "physical violence occurs between family members more often than it occurs between other individuals or in any other setting except wars and riots."

The disturbance is often a quarrel between family members. It may have started with a few angry words, or it could have been a simmering dispute that exploded into violence. Destruction or damaging or taking of property may have occurred. One or both (or all) the parties may have been under the influence of alcohol or drugs. Job stress or unemployment may contribute to the situation.

Hitting, pushing, choking, wrestling combined with other abusive behavior may have occurred. Insulting and offending language is almost always used. Injuries range in severity from minor to critical and life threatening.

Both parties could be at fault or one party could be the agitator and the offender. The offender may have a prior record of violence and may be under a court order (divorce) or restraining order (criminal) forbidding such conduct. Or the offender may be on probation or parole and his domestic conduct may violate the terms of his probation or parole. The offender's presence on the premises may be in violation of a court order or a condition of probation or parole. In addition to these violations, the offender may also be a trespasser.

Family units include not only the traditional family-type relationships, but also homosexuals and unwed heterosexual couples. The disturbance or violence could include not only adults, but also children within the family unit.

Past experience has demonstrated that "family trouble" calls can be dangerous for law enforcement officers. Approximately one-fifth of police deaths and almost one-third of assaults on officers occur in responding to family quarrels and domestic disputes in which a weapon is used.

In past years, unless serious injury occurred, or unless a clear violation of a court order or probation (or parole) existed, an arrest would ordinarily not be made. Police officers would attempt to mediate the dispute. In counseling women, officers would sometimes ask: "Who will support you if he's locked up? Do you realize he could lose his job? Do you want to spend days in court? Why don't you kiss and make up? Why did you get him so worked up that he slugged you? Why do you want to make trouble? Think of what he'll do to you the next time."

Recent studies by the Police Foundation have shown that police arrests sharply reduce violence

---

Appraising Domestic Disturbances

Injury Inflicted
- No injury inflicted (but does the potential for violence exist?)
- Moderate violence—simple assaults or batteries that did not cause severe or life-threatening injuries
- Severe violence occurred—was a weapon used?

Emotional and Physical Condition of Aggressor Was the aggressor intoxicated or under the influence of drugs? Was the aggressor repentant, apologetic, and calm, or was he (or she) enraged, revengeful, and likely to retaliate?

Previous Incidents Have there been previous problems or previous police calls? Have the parties recently moved to their present address? Have the parties recently commenced living together?

Status of Parties A 1983 Police Foundation study shows that in a high percentage of domestic problem cases:
- one or both of the persons were unemployed
- many suspects were unmarried to their victims
- many had criminal records

Family Violence

Domestic violence is common, yet is one of the most unreported crimes in the United States. Among the offenses committed are:

- *homicides.* One-quarter to one-third of all homicides are domestic murders in which one family member kills another.

- *battered spouses* (wife beating and occasional husband beating)

- *crimes against children* (child beating, child neglect, child abuse—physical and sexual—incest)

- *crimes against other members of the family* (abuse of parents by children, abuse of the elderly [the British refer to this as "granny bashing" or "gram slamming"])

- *crimes against law enforcement officers.* The FBI estimates that about 20 percent of police deaths and 28 percent of assaults on officers occur while police officers are responding to a "family trouble" call.

---

in the home. The police commissioner of New York City stated that because of this study and because of his own experience as a "cop on the street," he concluded that past police efforts to mediate have done little to stop what has been a growing problem. The commissioner stated that arresting violent members of a household would be more effective in protecting other family members and would help to safeguard police officers who are called to intervene in situations in which violence could occur.

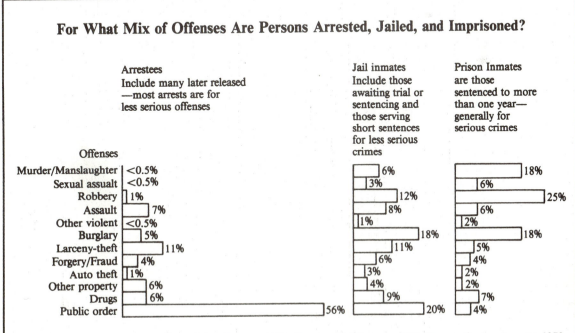

For What Mix of Offenses Are Persons Arrested, Jailed, and Imprisoned?

Arrestees
Include many later released —most arrests are for less serious offenses

Jail inmates
Include those awaiting trial or sentencing and those serving short sentences for less serious crimes

Prison Inmates
are those sentenced to more than one year— generally for serious crimes

Offenses	Arrestees	Jail inmates	Prison Inmates
Murder/Manslaughter	<0.5%	6%	18%
Sexual assualt	<0.5%	3%	6%
Robbery	1%	12%	25%
Assault	7%	8%	6%
Other violent	<0.5%	1%	2%
Burglary	5%	18%	18%
Larceny-theft	11%	11%	5%
Forgery/Fraud	4%	6%	4%
Auto theft	1%	3%	2%
Other property	6%	4%	2%
Drugs	6%	9%	7%
Public order	56%	20%	4%

Sources: FBI Uniform Crime Reports, 1980. *Survey of jail inmates 1978. Survey of prison inmates 1979.*

Responses to Domestic Violence

The following are some of the responses available to violent family situations:

- arrest of the offending person (or persons)

  —under the state criminal code

  —under a municipal or county ordinance
- obtain a protective court order under the statutes of that state
- seeking shelter for the victim (spouse, children, parent, etc.) under the shelter program available in that community
- divorce action and obtaining immediate (and also permanent) court orders that could:
  - protect
  - remove offending spouse from premise
  - forbid communication or contact by offending spouse
  - restrict visitation rights with children and other restrictions
- issuing (or threatening to issue) a civil citation with a substantial money fine
- use of the emergency detention section of the state mental health act (if applicable) to place the offending party into custody for observation
- revocation of probation or parole if the offender has violated terms of a probation or parole agreement

---

Criminal charges could be, for example, assault, battery, disorderly conduct, trespass, criminal damage to property (if another person's property was damaged or destroyed), reckless use of a weapon. In addition to spending time in jail, the offender could be placed under a restraining order or injunction in an attempt to prevent repeated violence or disturbances.

In past years, it was not uncommon for police departments to receive calls from women asking for protection from men who had threatened them or from wives who expected to be beaten by their husbands when they came home from a tavern. Threats to injure can be the basis of a criminal charge. If the threat was made over a telephone, the charge of unlawful use of a telephone may be made.

The battered woman problem has caused crisis counseling centers and shelters to be established throughout the United States to assist victims and their families. These centers provide shelter when needed, counseling, support, and emergency food and clothing. Location of the shelters are generally not disclosed to the public to avoid further confrontation by the victim with the offender.

Complaints of domestic violence are increasing in number throughout the United States. However, experts are uncertain whether there has been an actual increase in family violence. The violence may have existed for many years but for the most part had gone unreported until recently, when victims have been encouraged to report such abuse.

Part Four

Crimes Against Property

Chapter 15

Theft, Robbery and Burglary

A. GENERAL PROPERTY LAW CONCEPTS

A law student taking criminal law would also probably be taking courses in personal property law and real property law that would provide the necessary background for understanding criminal property law more thoroughly. The following concepts and principles are presented to acquaint the student who has not had courses in business law or property law with a few elementary property principles:

• Two important rights to property are (1) the right of ownership and (2) the right of possession of the property. A person may have the lawful possession of property but may not necessarily be the owner of the property. Possession of personal property is presumptive evidence of ownership if there is no evidence to the contrary. Possession accompanied by the exercise of the complete acts of ownership for a considerable period is strong evidence of the ownership of property.[1]

• Property ownership may be in the form of sole ownership. It may be in the form of joint ownership that can be between husband and wife, between business partners, or between friends or relatives. The property may be owned by a corporation or a business partnership. Property ownership may be vested in a governmental unit, such as a city, a state, a county, or the national government.

• There are many forms of lawful possession of property. The owner may have the possession of property or may permit another person to have lawful possession and use of the property. An employee or agent of the owner of the property may have possession. Bailees and pledgees also have the lawful possession of property that belongs to other persons. A bailment would exist, for example, when a man takes his car into a garage for repairs. The owner of the car retains title and ownership to the vehicle but gives possession to the garage so that the repair work may be done on the vehicle. State statutes give the garage a lien on the vehicle in the amount of the work that was done on the car. The garage then has a superior right of possession of the vehicle until the owner satisfies the amount lawfully due

to the garage. In many states, the owner of the property could be charged with theft if he intentionally and unlawfully took possession of such property from a pledgee or bailee who had a superior right of possession.

• A thief wrongfully deprives the true owner of the property of his lawful possession of the property. The unexplained or falsely explained possession of recently stolen property might give rise to an inference that the person had received the stolen property.[2] To prove theft, burglary, or robbery, there must be "other facts or circumstances indicating guilt."

• A thief cannot deprive the owner of property of the right of ownership and lawful possession of the property. For example, if X steals Y's $500 watch and sells the watch to A for $50, Y may demand from A the return of his watch and may go into a civil court in a replevin action to assert his right to the lawful ownership and possession of the watch.

• In most instances, an innocent purchaser of stolen goods takes only those ownership rights that the seller had. If the seller was a thief, then the buyer has only unlawful possession of the property. The ancient concept of *caveat emptor* (let the buyer beware) puts a buyer on notice that if he or she purchases items from a seller whose reputation is questionable, the lawful owner of the property may assert his or her right to possession and ownership of the property. Under the old common law, with its severe penalties, it was dangerous to purchase anything from a stranger.

• If stolen money or negotiable securities have been passed by a thief to persons who receive the money in good faith and for valuable consideration, the money and the negotiable instruments cannot be recovered by the victims. In 1967, a man named Hanzl robbed a bank in Pennsylvania and obtained $18,500. Two days later, he paid the Internal Revenue Service $4,500 in back taxes. When Hanzl was arrested a week later, he disclosed what he had done with the money. A federal judge ruled that the $4,500 could not be recovered by the insurance company that covered the bank loss in the robbery. The court stated:

It is a rule of law that title to currency passes with delivery to the person who receives it in good faith and for valuable consideration. It seems clear that an obligation to pay income taxes constitutes a valid preexisting debt, and the transfer of currency in payment of that debt is for value. Thus, we hold that Hanzl's [the robber] obligation to pay income taxes constituted a valid debt, and his transfer of currency in payment of those taxes was for value.

* * *

It is absolutely necessary for commerce and business to continue that one who receives money, cashier's checks or money orders is not put on inquiry as to the source from which the funds have been derived. It is generally impossible or impractical to discover the source of money, and for this reason one who receives money in good faith for valuable consideration prevails over the victim.[3]

B. LARCENY/THEFT

A Modern Definition of the Crime of Stealing

Today, all states have defined the crime of stealing in terms of larceny or theft. The federal government alone has "well over 100 separate statutes now in Title 18 that deal with theft or some other theft-related activity."[4]

1. THE TAKING

Direct Taking

There are many types of direct taking. Some of those listed in the Uniform Crime Report are purse snatching, pocket picking, shoplifting, theft of bicycles, theft of motor vehicles, and theft of vehicle accessories. The Uniform Crime Report states that "the nature of larceny [theft] makes it an extremely difficult offense for law enforcement officers to solve. A lack of witnesses and the

tremendous volume of these crimes work in the offender's favor."[5]

The state must show that there was a "taking" at least for a brief time and the defendant had control over the property "of another." The "taking" must be deliberate, with "intent to steal" (intent to permanently deprive the owner of possession).

The Taking of Lost and Mislaid Goods or Goods That Are Delivered by Mistake

Are finders keepers? Does a man who has lost his wallet containing $200 abandon his ownership and right of possession to the money and other valuables within the wallet? The answer is no. Finders may have possession of lost or mislaid property, but they do not have lawful ownership. Probably all states have statutes establishing the procedures to be used in handling lost and mislaid property. Persons who find valuables are obligated to comply with these statutes. Failure to comply with such statutes and ordinances would constitute a taking.

Example: Chambermaids in a midwest Playboy Club found $107,690 stashed in two flight bags in a hotel room they were cleaning. Law enforcement officers questioned six men about the money, but no one claimed it. It is believed that the money was unclaimed because it was earnings from gambling or some other illegal activity. A jury held that the money was legally abandoned, and after legal fees, costs, etc., the balance was given to the finders.

Example: While Joey Coyle was driving on a Philadelphia street in 1981, he found two sacks of money in a metal case that had just fallen

Theft and larceny can be defined as:	
a taking and carrying away	But many states expand these requirements to include "uses, transfers, conceals or retains possession of."
of personal property	All states have broadened this element to include "anything of value," "movable property," etc.
of another	See your state statutes with respect to what is property "of another."
with intent to steal.	Which is the intent to permanently deprive the owner of the possession of property.

from an armored truck that hit a pothole. Joey and his friends took the money and left the metal case in the street. The $1.2 million in unmarked $100 bills was soon missed and the metal case

---

Forms of Taking and Types of Theft

Shoplifting (retail theft) or price altering
- shoplifting—the most common form of theft in retail stores—is the taking by concealment to avoid payment for goods
- price altering avoids payment of the full price of an object by altering the price to a lower price

Taking by employee, bailee, or trustee
- employee theft of money and other objects causes large losses in business places
- embezzlement of funds or negotiable securities that are in the custody of employees, bailees, or trustees

Snatch and run—where the taking is observed and the offender flees to avoid apprehension

Till tap
- thief opens cash register unobserved and takes cash and coins
- while store employee has cash drawer open, money is grabbed and the thief flees (snatch and run)

Taking by trick, deception, or fraud (stings and scams)
- con games and operations
- deceptions and tricks to obtain property illegally
- obtaining property by false pretense

Taking by force, or the threat of the use of force (robbery)

Taking during a burglary (trespass with intent to steal or commit a felony)

Taking from a person
- purse snatching (a form of snatch and run)
- pickpocketing
- rolling a drunk (taking from person incapacitated by alcohol, drugs, or other means)
- taking from a deceased person or corpse

Taking of lost or mislaid goods or money

Taking of objects or money delivered by mistake (Example: check for too much money is mailed to a person by mistake)

Looting—taking property from or near a building damaged, destroyed or left, unoccupied by tornado, fire, physical disaster, riot, bombing, etc.

Taking by failure to return a leased or rented object (Example: failure to return a rented car within the time specified by state statutes)

Taking by illegal entry into locked coin box (vending machine, pay telephone, parking meter, etc.)

Smash and run—a store or other window is broken, and after snatching objects, the thief runs to avoid apprehension.

Taking by illegal use of a credit card or credit card number

Taking from a person with a superior right of possession—persons may acquire a superior right of possession over the owner of property because of a bailment, pledge, or contract. State criminal codes may make taking from a person with a superior right of possession a crime.

Ordinary theft
- taking occurs observed or unobserved by owner or other persons

---

Sing-Song Phrases of Children

An inaccurate statement of law: *"Finders keepers, losers weepers."*

An accurate statement of law: *"Sticks and stones will break my bones but names will never hurt me."* (Neither battery nor homicide is ever justified because of name calling or insulting language.)

---

was found. The incident was extensively covered in newspapers, radio, and TV stories. Purolator Armored, Inc. offered $50,000 reward for the return of the money. Joey and his friends did not return the money to claim the reward. Under the statutes and case law of your state, is there criminal and civil liability?

Example: In the 1982 U.S. Supreme Court case of *United States v. Johnson,*[6] the U.S. postal service delivered a check for $4,681.41 to the wrong address. Secret Service agents obtained arrest warrants for the defendants on information that they were attempting to negotiate the misdelivered U.S. Treasury check. Johnson was acquitted by a jury, but his codefendant, Dodd, was convicted of aiding and abetting the receipt of stolen property.

Taking by Trick, Deception, or Fraud

Taking has been achieved by the use of many tricks, frauds, and deceptions. The owner of the property may be deceived by false representations that cause the owner to give up possession of the property. Con games would fall into this category. Modern theft and larceny statutes specifically define these forms of taking as elements of the crimes of theft and larceny.

Cases involving theft by fraud, false pretense, or deception include:

ARKANSAS v. HIXSON

Court of Appeals of Arkansas (1980)

587 S.W.2d 70, *review denied,* United States Supreme Court 26 CrL 4201

Members of various churches made the mistake of paying the defendant in advance for church directories containing their pictures. A jury found that the defendant's promises were not "mere puffing" and when the defendant received the monies, he did not intend to carry out his promise to deliver the church directories in return for the money. The jury also found that the defendant knew that the promises were false and were made for the purposes of depriving the owners of their money. The appellate court found there was sufficient evidence to sustain the jury findings.

LAMBERT v. STATE

Supreme Court of Wisconsin (1976)

73 Wis. 2d 590, 243 N.W.2d 524

The defendant obtained substantial amounts of money from different women by promising to marry them. The Supreme Court of Wisconsin affirmed the convictions of the defendant for six charges of theft by fraud. (Broken promises are only punished in a minority of the states as theft by fraud. In the *Hixson* case, the defendant did not break a promise that he originally planned to keep. The jury found that when the defendant in the *Hixson* case made the statements, he knew that they were false and he made the "promises" with intent to deceive and to commit fraud.)

Theft and Larceny by a Bailee or Trustee

Because of their employment, businesses, or positions of trust, bailees, trustees, and other persons have possession and custody of valuable property belonging to others. The unauthorized use, concealment, transfer, or wrongful retaining of property that is in the possession of a bailee or trustee could amount to a taking and a theft or larceny under the laws of the jurisdiction in which the incident occurred.

2. THE CARRYING AWAY

Under the common law, there had to be a "carrying away" (asportation). This requirement was fulfilled by some movement of the property. The distance that the property had to be moved or "carried away" could be slight under the law.

The carrying away, in most cases, is done by the thief, although it can be done by an innocent third person, such as the one who purchased the property. Most states have included the requirement of carrying away in their theft or larceny statutes. A few do not include the requirement in their definitions of theft or larceny. Section 206.1 of the Model Penal Code uses the words "taking or exercising of unauthorized control." The following case illustrates the requirement of carrying away:

BERRY v. STATE
Supreme Court of Wisconsin
(1979)
90 Wis. 2d 316, 280 N.W.2d 204

An employee of a men's clothing store observed the defendant facing a wall in the lower level of the store and trying to force something under his coat and into his pants. When the employee approached the defendant, he saw a bulge under the parka and the trousers. When the defendant stated that there was nothing under the parka, the employee opened the parka and saw a brown leather coat that belonged to the store. In a tug of war, the employee pulled the leather coat out and away from the defendant. The defendant then pushed the employee and walked away quickly. A jury found the defendant guilty of attempted theft. The issue of whether there was a carrying away (asportation) was before the Supreme Court of Wisconsin. The court affirmed the conviction for attempted theft, holding:

The court of appeals determined that the defendant "took" the leather coat within the meaning of the statute when he moved the jacket from wherever he got it to his trousers. The court further determined that that movement and the acts of stuffing the jacket into his trousers and turning to face the clerk fulfilled the statutory requirement of "carrying away."

*   *   *

The question is whether a jury could properly be convinced that the evidence did not support a finding that the defendant was guilty of "taking" and "carrying away" the leather jacket. We conclude that it could. It is clear that "asportation is a separate and necessary element of the crime of theft."

*   *   *

The court of appeals, noting that any movement however slight has been held to satisfy this requirement, was of the opinion that there was sufficient proof of asportation in the present case.

The asportation requirement should be considered in light of the statute's general purpose to proscribe the exercise of unauthorized control over the movable property of another. "Carrying away" must be given a practical, common-sense construction. While the asportation requirement may be satisfied by proof of the slightest movement, it is implicit in the statute that the movement must be a movement away from the area where the product was intended to be. A retail store owner selling clothing consents to having a potential purchaser, during business hours, take an item of clothing from a rack and into a nearby room for the purpose of trying it on. The part of the store in which Radtke first noticed the defendant was not restricted to authorized personnel; it was clearly accessible to customers. The defendant, when he had possession of the leather coat, did not evade the final point of purchase which, according to Radtke's testimony, was located at the opposite end of the lower level of the store. The test is not whether the court of appeals or this court is convinced that the defendant did not consummate the crime of theft by "taking away" the coat as charged in the information, but whether the jury acting reasonably could be convinced that the defendant did not consummate the crime of theft. While it is unnecessary to decide the issue in view of the disposition of the first issue, we conclude that under the circumstances of the present case the jury could have been so convinced.

3. PERSONAL PROPERTY

Under the old common law, only tangible personal property could be stolen. Real estate and items attached to the land could not be stolen. Such documents as stocks, bonds, checks, or promissory notes were not subject to theft, as they are intangible personal property.

All states and the federal government have broadened the original common law definition of property that can be stolen. Some modern criminal codes include any sort of property of value that can be moved. Illinois defines property subject to theft as "anything of value," including real estate, money, commercial instruments, tickets, written documents, etc.[7] Minnesota defines "property" to include documents and things growing on or affixed to land.[8] Section 223.2 of the Model Penal Code defines "Theft by Unlawful Taking or Disposition" as:

1. *Movable Property.* A person is guilty of theft if he takes, or exercises unlawful control over, movable property of another with purpose to deprive him thereof.

2. *Immovable Property.* A person is guilty of theft if he unlawfully transfers immovable property of another or any interest therein with purpose to benefit himself or another not entitled thereto.

Under modern statutes, not only personal property can be stolen, but also real estate and fixtures. Trees, crops, minerals, electricity, gas, and documents are all subject to theft. In the 1966 case of *United States v. Bottone,*[9] the Court pointed out that the content of a document is often much more important and valuable than the paper on which it is written.

In this age of computers, courts must now consider the questions of whether information itself can be stolen. Situations occur when information is taken from the owner and used or sold to someone else. In the 1976 case of *United States v. DiGilio,*[10] the defendant copied FBI investigative records and sold them to persons who were subjects of the investigations. As the copies were made during office time, with a government machine and on government paper, the copies themselves were government property. However, the Third Circuit Court stated that it would not rest its decision on the "narrower ground that a technical larceny has been proved," but held that contents of the documents also had been stolen.[11]

In the 1982 case of *Moser v. State,*[12] the defendant was convicted of theft for tapping into a cable television line. In the 1984 case of *State v. McGraw,*[13] the defendant, who was a municipal employee, was convicted of using the city's computer to conduct his private business. The Indiana Court of Appeals held that "computer services, leased or owned, are a part of our market economy in huge dollar amounts. Like cable television, computer services are 'anything of value.' . . . Thus computer services are property within the meaning of the definition of property subject to theft." However, in a similar case in Kings County, New York, the New York Criminal Court held that the New York statute was not intended to protect equipment used (computer) internally by an employee.[14]

Value of Property

If the property had no intrinsic value, it would be hard to sustain a prosecution for theft or larceny. A single sheet of paper worth a penny or less would have little intrinsic value. But if a signed promissory note for $1,000 were on the sheet of paper, the value of the paper would increase considerably. In charging theft or larceny, the state must introduce evidence showing the value of the property alleged to have been stolen.

The value of the property sto'   in most instances, determines whether the charge is a misdemeanor or felony. The value of the property must be determined by the court or jury. Statements by the owner concerning what he or she paid for the property, how long it was possessed, and its condition are admissible in determining value. Evidence of the value of comparable property in comparable condition is admissible to show the value of the property in issue. Experts and appraisers may, in some instances, be called into court to testify as to value.

In the New York case of *People v. Harold,* the defendant was convicted of grand larceny for the theft of a water pump that had been purchased five days before the theft. However, the pump had been damaged before the theft by two men, Crego and Terpening, who had attempted to install the pump. In ordering a new trial, the court stated:

> The question presented by this appeal pertains to the value of the stolen pump. . . . Section 1305 of the former Penal Law, as first interpreted by this court in People v. Irrizari (5 N.Y.2d 142 p. 146, 182 N.Y.S.2d 361, 364, 156 N.E.2d 69, 71), states that the market value of a stolen item is to be measured by what the thief would have had to pay had he purchased the item instead of stealing it. Since we stated in *Irrizari* that the price for which an item is sold in a particular store is some evidence but not conclusive proof of its

value when stolen from that store, it necessarily follows that the original cost of an item is not proof of its value some five days after the goods have left the store. In the instant case, the value of the pump must also be reduced to reflect the mechanical prowess of Crego and Terpening. Additionally, an allowance must be made for the fact that the pump, when taken, was no longer new.

Many state statutes provide that "value" means the market value at the time of the theft or the cost to the victim of replacing the property within a reasonable time after the theft. The replacement value to a retail store would be the replacement cost to the store, and not the retail price of the item.[15]

4. PROPERTY OF ANOTHER

Difficulties in Identifying Property

In order to prove theft or larceny, the state must show that the property belonged to another. A showing that the property belonged to the city, a school, a corporation, or an individual would suffice. Since the consent of the owner would constitute a total defense in a theft or larceny charge, the owner (or a representative of the owner) must testify that the taking was without his or her consent. A showing that the owner did not consent to the conduct of the defendant is also necessary in criminal damage to property, in trespass, and in arson of either real property or personal property.

Some property is difficult for owners to identify. Diamonds and other valuable stones provide an example. Valuable stones may be easily identified by their settings, but once they are removed, it is difficult to distinguish them. The four "Cs" of the diamond business—cut, clarity, carat, and color—provide only the roughest means of identification. An owner's testimony, "That looks like my property, but I am not sure," is not sufficient identification. Because of the difficulty of identification, there have been situations in which police have been forced to return property to a known thief because of lack of evidence that the property was stolen.

The stolen property must be identified by the introduction of evidence showing that there is no reasonable doubt as to its identity. For this reason, law enforcement agencies urge the marking of property in such ways that the identification marks cannot be easily removed or obliterated.

Abandoned Property and Other Problems in Proving "Property of Another"

If the property has been abandoned or if the owner of the property cannot be located, then theft or larceny cannot be proved.

Abandonment has been defined as the relinquishment or surrender of property or the rights to property. In 1952, the U.S. Supreme Court considered the case of *Morissette v. United States*.[16] Morissette was charged with the theft of scrap metal from an old bombing range. His defense was that he honestly thought that the property had been abandoned. Because the trial court would not allow the jury to determine whether the property had been abandoned or whether Morissette honestly, but mistakenly, believed that the property was abandoned, the conviction was reversed.

Wild animals, while in a wild state, are not the property of any person, even though they may be on the property of some person. A person who shoots and takes a wild deer could not be charged with theft, because the deer is not the property of another. However, the hunter could be charged with trespass or a firearms violation if he killed a wild animal on the land of another.

Many people hold property jointly with other persons. Suppose a business partner takes $1,000 out of the partnership checking account and uses it for his personal needs. Or suppose a wife runs off with another man and takes $500 out of a savings and loan account that is in the name of her husband and herself. Is this stealing the property "of another"? Whether this constitutes theft or larceny would be determined by the statutes of that jurisdiction in defining the property "of another."

The question of property "of another" came up in the Michigan case of *People v. Newsom and Young*. In that case, the defendants took back from prostitutes the $10 they had paid the women for their sexual services. In affirming the convictions for the crime of larceny from the person, the court stated:

On appeal defendant Young's only argument is that his actions did not constitute a crime since the agreement he made to purchase sexual services was illegal and so his forcefully taking back the $10 was not a crime.

We are not persuaded by that argument. The trial court did not enforce any contract legal or otherwise. The agreement had been completed and both parties had received the agreed-upon consideration. Defendant Young then forcefully took back the $10 which by that time belonged to the woman. Such action constituted the crime of larceny from a person. "Public policy requires that courts should lend active aid in punishing persons who obtain money or property from others by criminal means, and it is no defense that the complaining witness was himself engaged in an illegal transaction." 1 Gillespie, Michigan Criminal Law and Procedure (2d Ed.), § 29, p. 49.[17]

5. WITH INTENT TO STEAL (OR TO DEPRIVE THE OWNER PERMANENTLY OF POSSESSION)

To establish *corpus delicti* for a theft or larceny, there must be a showing that the property was taken and carried (or a showing of other conduct forbidden by the state's theft or larceny statute). There must also be a showing that the defendant was not given permission to take or use the property. If the property was taken from a business place, there could also be an additional showing that the property was not sold to a customer.[18] However, "proof of the corpus delicti does not require proof of the identity of the perpetrators of the crime, nor proof that the crime was committed by the defendant."[19]

"Borrowing" is not stealing. If A borrows B's book for a few hours, he would not be guilty of theft or larceny unless a jury or court found that there was an intent to deprive B of permanent possession of his book. If W loans Z his lawn mower and Z does not return the mower, this would not be a theft or a larceny. The original taking was with W's consent. W's recourse would be to go to a civil court in a replevin action to recover the possession of his lawn mower.

If W saw his lawn mower sitting in Z's backyard and recovered possession of the mower, W would not have committed the crime of theft or larceny. However, if W took other items belonging to Z to compensate for money that Z owed him, this would be considered stealing in most jurisdictions.

Is It Lawful to Collect a Debt at Gunpoint?

Is it a theft to collect a debt at gunpoint? Can the person who does so be charged with robbery? These questions come before the courts from time to time. The general rule in the United States is that if the taker in good faith believes that he or she owns or is entitled to the possession of the property, a charge of robbery (or theft) will fail even if the money or property is taken at gunpoint.[20]

However, many courts today refuse to use the old rule. In the 1970 case of *Edwards v. State,*[21] the Wisconsin Supreme Court refused to follow the old rule and held that a person who collected a debt at gunpoint could be convicted of robbery in Wisconsin.

In the 1979 case of *People v. Robinson,*[22] the Illinois Appellate Court held that the minority view "simply makes more sense." The defendant in the *Robinson* case retook a gambling loss by use of the threat of deadly force. The Illinois court refused to substitute the "rule of the gun" for the "rule of reason" and, like the Wisconsin Supreme Court, refused to sanction an interpretation that permitted individuals to take the law into their own hands.

Proving Intent to Steal

Theft or larceny requires a specific intent to deprive the owner of permanent possession of the property. The intent to steal may be proved by direct evidence or by circumstantial evidence. Generally, the fact finder (jury or judge) concludes and infers an intent to steal from the conduct and acts of the defendant. The following cases illustrate the issue of intent to steal:

MULLEN v. SIBLEY & COMPANY
Court of Appeals of New York (1980)
415 N.E.2d 971, 434 N.Y.S.2d 982

Mr. Mullen was leaving a store with a shopping bag in which he had a tie rack that he had not paid for. He was stopped by a security guard at the door of the store and immediately admitted that he had not paid for the tie rack. He stated that he was about to pay for it and proceeded immediately to a checkout counter, where he tendered a $20 bill. While at the counter he was arrested and taken to a security office for questioning. He was then taken to a state police barracks, where he was photographed and fingerprinted. A jury found him not guilty of the petit larceny charge. The New York Court of Appeals held that probable cause to arrest by the security guard did not exist as a matter of law, and that this issue would have to be determined by a jury in this civil suit against the store.

PEOPLE v. JASO
Court of Appeals of California (1970)
4 Cal. App. 3d 767, 84 Cal. Rptr. 567

The defendant was walking toward the parking lot and his car when he was stopped with unpaid merchandise in a shopping bag from a Sears store. The defendant stated that he left his wallet in the glove compartment of his car because he was wearing tight Levis. He stated that he was going to get his wallet and would pay for the merchandise but when the security officer held him and would not let him go, he struggled with the security officer. Defendant was subdued and placed in handcuffs. A new trial was ordered after the defendant was convicted at the first trial. The Court of Appeals held that the trial court had failed to give the following California jury instruction:

In the crime of [theft], there must exist in the mind of the perpetrator the specific intent to [take the property of another], and unless such intent so exists that crime is not committed. (CALJIC Instruction # 71.11.)

The specific intent with which an act is done may be manifested by the circumstances surrounding its commission. But you may not find the defendant guilty of the offense charged in Count [II] unless the proved circumstances not only are consistent with the hypothesis that he had the specific intent to [take the property of another] but are irreconcilable with any other rational conclusion. (CALJIC Instruction # 27–A.)

6. OTHER LARCENY/THEFT OFFENSES

"Breaking Bulk"

The crime of "breaking bulk" is committed when a person takes a portion of goods that have been temporarily placed in his or her custody by the owner. This could be done by a warehouseman or a common carrier in charge of transporting a shipment of goods.

Example: Dock workers loading cases of beer into a railroad car remove many bottles from cases for their own consumption.

Some states have statutorized the common law crime of "breaking bulk" (or "breaking bale"). Other states have made the offense that of larceny or embezzlement; still others include it as "larceny by bailee."

Embezzlement

Embezzlement is another form of theft and larceny. In this offense, the thief has legal possession of property or negotiable instruments of another but uses, converts, or retains the property fraudulently, usually to his or her own use or to the use of someone other than the owner. Some states list the various types of persons who might have lawful possession of property of another. The following examples illustrate:

• A cashier who occasionally takes a portion of the day's receipts and uses the money for his or her own use
• A bank teller who falsifies accounts and takes money from the bank to finance a vacation
• A stockbroker who sells stock belonging to a client and uses the money to invest in speculative stock. The stockbroker intends to return the stock to his client's portfolio before the client is aware that the stock is missing

The statutes of many states provide that the crime of embezzlement can also be committed by state or local officials who have public funds in their possession. It is also common to divide embezzlement into grand embezzlement (a felony) and petit embezzlement (a misdemeanor). As with larceny and theft, a series of small fraudulent conversions over a period of time that are part of a single scheme may be charged as one large embezzlement.

C. ROBBERY

Robbery is forcible stealing. It is one of the most frequent crimes of violence in the United States. The common law crime of robbery was defined before the early English courts had defined larceny. The usual elements incorporated into the modern statutory definition of robbery are:

• a taking and carrying away (only a slight movement of the property is needed)
• of the property of another
• with intent to steal
• from the person or from the presence of the victim
• by the use of force against the person or
• with the threat of the use of imminent force with the intent to compel the victim to acquiesce in the taking and carrying away of the property.

Strong-armed robbery, such as mugging and yoking (or simple robbery), is distinguished in probably all state statutes from the aggravated form of robbery, commonly called "armed robbery." Armed robbery carries penalties that are

Car Theft:
The Crime Causing the Largest Monetary Loss
of All Property Crimes

What happens to stolen cars and vehicles?

More than one million vehicles per year are stolen in the United States with values in the billions of dollars.

Chop-shop operations, in which professionals cut up the vehicle for parts. As nothing is left of the vehicle, the criminals are called "buzzards." Chop-shop operations are generally believed to be under the control of organized criminal groups.

Strippers who "strip" cars for some of the easily resalable parts: tires, wheels, doors, fenders, hoods, radios, batteries, spark plugs. Strippers are considered semiprofessionals; some are dope addicts who sell car parts to finance their habits. Stripped cars are generally recovered by owners.

Exported from the United States — The National Automobile Theft Bureau estimates that between 25,000 and 200,000 vehicles are exported to other countries, where the vehicle or the parts sell at prices much higher than in the United States.

Abandoned or Returned or Recovered
- after use by a "joy-rider" (once the biggest offender but now estimated to be responsible for 10 percent of missing cars)
- after being used for a crime
- after being abandoned by strippers
- after a breakdown or being damaged

Phony car thefts — Car owners hide or abandon their vehicles and then falsely report them stolen in hopes of collecting insurance. Estimates range from 15 percent to as high as 30 percent of reported car thefts are phony.

Used on Streets and Highways of United States
- with original VIN numbers and different plates
- with identification numbers salvaged from similar model cars in junkyards ("salvage and switch" operations)

more severe than those for simple robbery. Some of the statutory distinctions used by various states in distinguishing between "armed robbery" and "simple robbery" are:

1. that the perpetrator was armed with a "dangerous" or "deadly" weapon

2. that the perpetrator intended to kill or wound if the victim resisted

3. that the perpetrator did actually inflict a bodily injury.[23]

Robbery, then, is the taking of property from a person or from the presence of a victim by the use of force or the threat of the use of force. The crime of robbery creates a great deal of anxiety, because the victim is threatened not only with the use of force and violence, but also with the loss of property.

The Chicago Police Department Training Bulletin [24] lists the following factors that favor a robber:

- He can carry out his crime swiftly.
- He will usually leave few clues that would lead to his arrest.
- The robbery is committed in such a short period that the victim and witnesses sometimes do not have sufficient time and composure to view the offender so as to furnish an accurate description to the police.
- The probability of interruption is limited because of the short time needed to successfully commit a robbery.

Distinguishing Robbery from Theft/Larceny

Robbery differs from theft/larceny because in charging the crime of robbery, it must be also be shown that:

- property was taken from the victim or taken from the presence of the victim
- the use of force or the threat of the use of force was used in the taking.

If there is no force or fear of the use of force, the crime of robbery has not been committed. The majority of American states and courts now hold that when an offender steals property without force or the threat of force but uses force (or the threat of force) to escape or to keep the property, the crime of robbery has been committed. The Florida Court of Appeals stated this position in the 1983 case of *Stufflebean v. State:*

> Our view of this case is supported by considerable authority. See *People v. Anderson,* 64 Cal. 2d 633, 51 Cal. Rptr. 238, 414 P.2d 366 (1966) (if one who has stolen property from the person of another uses force or fear in removing the property from the owner's immediate presence, the crime of robbery has been

committed); *People v. Kennedy,* 10 Ill. App. 3d 519, 294 N.E.2d 788 (App. Ct. 1973) (while the taking may be without force the offense is robbery if the departure with the property is accomplished by use of force); *People v. Sanders,* 28 Mich. App. 274, 184 N.W.2d 269 (Ct. App. 1970) (woman who saw defendant run from her house with her purse and bag of money called for help; her grandson, who pursued defendant, gave up chase when defendant fired a gun); *Hermann v. State,* 239 Miss. 523, 123 So.2d 846 (1960) (defendant asked service station to fill up gas tank, then displayed a rifle in a threatening manner and drove away without paying); *State v. Bell,* 194 Neb. 554, 233 N.W.2d 920 (1975) (defendant took cash register from service station while attendant's back was turned, threw it into automobile and attempted to drive off; pursuing attendant stuck his hand through automobile window and was struck and pushed from moving vehicle). Three other states, Oregon, Maine and New York, have enacted statutes similar to the Florida statute which define as an act of robbery, the use of force to unlawfully retain property after a taking.

> We hold that where an offender gains possession of property of another without force and with intent to deprive the true owner of its use, but the victim gives instant and uninterrupted protest or pursuit in an effort to thwart a taking, and the offender then assaults the victim in order to complete a taking of the property and make good an escape, the offense is robbery.[25]

The minority view was stated in 1983, by the Kansas Court of Appeals in *State v. Long.* In the *Long* case, the defendant took $40 from an "honor system" cash box. When he was observed, the defendant shoved and pushed his way out of the building and got into his car and left. The court reversed the conviction:

> Robbery is not committed where possession is obtained without the use of force. Neither is there a robbery where there is no use of force except to resist arrest or escape. To constitute the crime of robbery, it is necessary that the use of force precede or be contemporaneous with the act of obtaining physical possession of the property. . . . The "taking," if it occurred, was accomplished and completed before Mrs. Wolf observed defendant. It neither was preceded by nor occurred contemporaneously with defendant's use of force. Defendant's conviction for robbery must be reversed.[26]

The Requirement That Fear or Apprehension Exists If Actual Force Is Not Used

If actual force is not used on the victim, there then must exist a genuine fear or apprehension by the victim that force or violence will be used. There also must be a fear or apprehension that the perpetrator is capable of inflicting injury or violence. In the following case, the Supreme Court of Louisiana stressed the reaction of the victim when he saw a toy pistol held up "in the air":

STATE v. BYRD
Supreme Court of Louisiana
(1980)
385 So.2d 248

The Supreme Court of Louisiana reversed the attempted armed robbery conviction, holding that the toy pistol was not a "dangerous weapon" under the facts of this case. The court held:

Defendant ordered a single piece of fried chicken at the side window of a restaurant. When the employee rang up the sale on the cash register and asked for 57 cents, defendant produced a toy pistol from his pocket and held it up in the air, demanding all of the money in the register. The employee stated there was no money, and defendant grabbed the piece of chicken and began to walk away. However, the employee grabbed the chicken back and closed the window on defendant, who then left the window. . . . Numerous cases have developed the theory that the victim's potential reaction to an instrumentality not inherently dangerous can be considered by the jury in determining whether the instrumentality "in the manner used" is likely to produce great bodily harm and is therefore a "dangerous weapon." Under that theory the pertinent inquiry here is whether defendant's use of the toy pistol created a life endangering situation. . . . The undisputed facts in this record simply do not provide reasonable support for the apparent conclusion that the toy pistol in the manner used was likely to produce bodily harm. The actions of the victim and of the defendant refute the State's contention that the manner of use created the "highly charged" atmosphere described by the Court in State v. Levi, 250 So.2d 751 (La. 1971). While defendant admitted he intended to rob the restaurant, he asserted he used the toy pistol so as not to hurt anyone. He did not threaten to harm, nor did he even refer to the toy pistol as a weapon. The victim testified that defendant did not point the toy pistol at him. Indeed, the victim's subjective reaction indicates he did not perceive any likelihood of great bodily harm. This is not to say that a toy pistol can under no circumstances be used as to create a life endangering situation which supports a guilty verdict of armed robbery.

Sudden Taking or Snatching

If a man snatches an item off a counter in a store and runs off with the item, the crime is stealing and not robbery. Purse snatching is ordinarily charged as theft from the person. The general rule in the United States is that purse snatching does not ordinarily involve sufficient force to constitute robbery. However, if the victim resists and a struggle occurs, or if the victim is knocked down or assaulted, a jury or a court could find that the crime of robbery had occurred.

A few courts, however, have adopted the rule that the snatching of a purse without the use of any other force is sufficient to permit a jury verdict on the charge of robbery. The Supreme Judicial Court of Massachusetts adopted this rule in the 1972 case of *Commonwealth v. Jones.*[27] In affirming the defendant's conviction of unarmed robbery for a purse snatching, the court stated:

> The question whether the snatching or sudden taking of property constitutes robbery has arisen in other jurisdictions although not in Massachusetts. In Kentucky, the rule is that snatching, without more, involves the requisite element of force to permit a jury verdict on a charge of robbery. See Jones v. Commonwealth, 112 Ky. 689, 692–695, 66 S.W. 633; Brown v. Commonwealth, 135 Ky. 635, 640, 117 S.W. 281. According to the rule prevailing in most jurisdictions, however, snatching does not involve sufficient force to constitute robbery, unless the victim resists the taking or sustains physical injury, or unless the article taken is so attached to the victim's clothing as to afford resistance. . . .
>
> We prefer the Kentucky rule on purse snatching. The majority jurisdiction rule, in looking to whether or not the victim resists, we think, wrongly emphasizes the victim's opportunity to defend himself over the willingness of the purse snatcher to use violence if necessary.

Convictions for More Than One Robbery Offense

Most (if not all) states will permit convictions for more than one robbery offense if property belonging to two or more victims is taken by the threat of force. For example, in *Ashe v. Swenson,*[28] the defendant was charged with six counts of armed robbery when six men playing poker were robbed of their wallets. As each man lost personal property, the six charges were justified.

Robbery as an Aggravated Form of Theft　In the 1982 case of *State v. Faatea,*[29] the defendant robbed a Ramada Inn and took hotel money from five hotel employees. The Supreme Court of Hawaii held that the defendant could be convicted of only one robbery, as the court held that "robbery is merely an aggravated form of theft" and that "there was but one act of theft here, from one owner" and "each of the five employees named were simply custodians of the property for the benefit of their employer." Other courts have reached the same results.[30]

Robbery as an "Offense" Against the Person Assaulted　Some courts, however, view robbery as an "offense" against the person assaulted. In the 1982 case of *Commonwealth v. Levia,*[31] the Supreme Judicial Court of Massachusetts affirmed the defendant's convictions for two counts of masked armed robbery. The defendant robbed a Cumberland Farms store, taking money belonging to the store from two employees. In holding that the emphasis should be placed "on the assault element of the crime of robbery," the court concluded:

> The "offense" is against the person assaulted, and not against the entity that owns or possesses the property taken. See *Barringer v. United States,* 399 F.2d 557 (D.C. Cir. 1968), cert. denied, 393 U.S. 1057, 89 S. Ct. 697, 21 L.Ed.2d 698 (1969); *State v. Shoemake,* 228 Kan. 572, 576–577, 618 P.2d 1201 (1980). So long as

---

Can Words Be "Robbed" of Their Meaning?

In the parable of the good Samaritan, the King James version of the Bible (Luke 10:25–37) tells of the man who "fell among thieves, which stripped him of his raiment, wounded him . . . leaving him half dead."

Some newspaper stories also mistakenly report that "thieves beat the victim." However, other newspapers and other modern English Bibles correctly use words such as "robbers," "bandits," or "assailants" to describe criminals who use force to obtain valuables.

Another common misuse occurs when a person reports that "My apartment was robbed" when they mean to say, "My apartment was burglarized." A person could be robbed in his apartment if he is confronted with a person with a gun who takes valuables by the threat of the use of force. Most apartments, however, are burglarized when the occupants are not present.

A thief steals either secretly or by snatching and running. A robber uses (or threatens to use) force and takes from the presence of the victim, whereas a burglar trespasses with intent to steal or with intent to commit a felony. The thief and burglar ordinarily do not want to confront the victim face to face. The robber does confront face to face.

the victim of the assault has some protective concern with respect to the property taken, and the property is taken from his person or presence, then the defendant may be convicted and sentenced for a separate and distinct robbery as to that person.

The court rejected the "double jeopardy" argument made by the defense, holding that the "appropriate inquiry, then, is whether the Legislature intended that the putting in fear and taking from two individuals money belonging to a single entity would constitute one robbery or two, where the taking occurred during the course of a single episode."

Distinguishing Robbery from Extortion

Robbery and extortion (blackmail) are methods used to obtain money or property illegally. Extortion differs from robbery in that:

• There is a threat to inflict a future harm (extortion) rather than an immediate harm (robbery).

• The victim must comply immediately with the demands or the harm will result (robbery), rather than future compliance with demands or harm that could be threatened against third persons (extortion).

The harm that is threatened differs also. In robbery, immediate force is threatened or used against the owner or victim to compel the victim to acquiesce in the taking of the property. In extortion, the victim might agree to the taking to prevent and avoid:

• destruction of property. Bombing a restaurant or business place has been a standard practice of organized crime that could result in a serious loss of life and injuries if the restaurant or business place were open for business.

• kidnapping or injuries to the victim or his family or friends

• accusations of crime, etc.

• damaging the good name or business reputation of the victim or his family

• exposing a secret or failing of the victim or family

English textbooks point out that the term blackmail originated to describe the tribute paid Scottish chieftains by landowners to secure immunity from raids on their lands. In the early days of common law, blackmail seems to have been an offense included within the crime of robbery. Cases illustrating the crime of extortion are:

MOORE v. NEWELL
United States, Court of Appeals (Sixth Circuit, 1977)
548 F.2d 671

The defendant was convicted of extortion because he attempted to coerce a store to contribute to a charitable fund. Defendant threatened to close the store by picketing if a donation was not made.

UNITED STATES v. BALISTRIERI
———— (1984)
577 F. Supp. 1532

A witness testified that the defendant bragged that no one got into the vending business in Milwaukee without his permission. When an undercover FBI agent ("Conte") went into the vending business, the defendant declared that Conte was slated to be "hit." Conte made a deal with the defendant after which the defendant and his two lawyer sons were charged with attempted extortion and conspiracy to extort. All were convicted and also face charges in Kansas City, Missouri, in 1985, of skimming about $2 million of unreported profits from Las Vegas casinos. Defendant was also convicted in 1983 of five felony gambling and tax charges.

PEOPLE v. DISCALA
Supreme Court of New York
(1978)
407 N.Y.S. 2d 660, 379 N.E.2d
187

When a hospital administrator refused to use his influence to have criminal indictments dismissed (for offenses committed in the hospital), the defendant threatened the administrator in a telephone conversation, telling him that he could kill him or have him killed. The defendant's conviction of attempted coercion in the first degree was affirmed.

When Does the Crime of Attempted Robbery Become the Crime of Robbery?

The crime of robbery has occurred when there has been a completed theft with the use of force or threat of the use of force. Therefore, if there has been a "taking" (caption) and "carrying away" (asportation) of property with intent to deprive the owner permanently of possession, there has been a theft. The following cases illustrate "takings" and "carrying away" in cases where it was held that the completed crimes of robbery had occurred:

PEOPLE v. MARTINEZ
Court of Appeals of California
(1969)
274 Cal. App. 2d 170, 79 Cal.
Rptr. 18

The defendant argued that he should have been convicted of attempted robbery and not of the completed offense of robbery, because there was no showing of asportation or taking by the defendant. In affirming the defendant's conviction for the completed crime of the robbery, the court stated: "The evidence provided a reasonable inference that Currin [the victim] at gunpoint, had been forced to take the money from the cash box and place it in a paper sack." The court held that this act of the victim constituted asportation, stating: "Robbery does not necessarily entail the robber's manual possession of the loot. It is sufficient if he acquired dominion over it, though the distance of movement is very small and the property is moved by a person acting under the robber's control, including the victim."

Examples of Different Theft Crimes

Theft	A man lays down his ring on the edge of a sink while washing his hands. Another man takes the ring and runs off while the owner is not looking. (Felony if value is more than amount determined by state statute)
Theft from person	A ring is taken from a pocket by a pickpocket or taken in a purse by a purse snatcher. (Felony in most or all states)
Simple robbery (Mugging)	A woman is accosted in an alley by a menacing thief who threatens to beat her if she does not give the thief the ring on her finger. (Felony)
Armed robbery	A woman is held at gunpoint by a thief who demands that she give him the ring on her finger. (Higher felony than "mugging")

PEOPLE v. ALEXANDER Court of Appeals of Michigan (1969) 17 Mich. App. 30, 169 N.W.2d 190	The defendant, after ordering a gas station attendant to place money in a bag, was apprehended before he took physical possession of the money. The court held that the function of asportation was to demonstrate that the offense had passed the attempt stage and was a completed crime, and it affirmed the defendant's conviction for the completed crime of robbery.
PEOPLE v. SMITH Court of Appeals of Illinois (1971) 132 Ill. App. 2d 657, 270 N.E.2d 136	The defendant, while armed, forced a bartender to place money and whiskey on the bar. The defendant chose to leave the items on the bar for a time and was arrested before he touched the property. The defendant's conviction for the completed crime of robbery was affirmed, with the court holding that the defendant had constructive possession of the property and that actual possession was not necessary to satisfy the requirement of the robbery statute.

D. BURGLARY

Burglary is the most frequently committed major crime in the United States, with more than 3.5 million burglaries committed every year. Because burglary is a crime of stealth and opportunity, the national clearance rate, as reported by the Uniform Crime Report, is low at approximately 15 percent (that is, arrests are made in only approximately 15 percent of the burglaries reported).

Burglary is a crime committed by both amateurs and professionals. It is committed against residences (homes and apartments) and nonresidences (offices, business places, etc.). It is committed not only at nighttime, but also during the day.

Under the old common law, burglary was punished by death. Because of the severe penalty, burglary required a breaking under the common law. It was also limited to the dwelling house of another, in the nighttime, and with intent to commit a felony.

All states have modified and changed the definition of burglary in their jurisdiction, with the result that there are many different definitions of burglary in the United States.[32] The Uniform Crime Reporting Program defines burglary "as the unlawful entry of a structure to commit a felony or theft. The use of force to gain entry is not required to classify an offense as burglary."

Breaking

At common law, a "breaking" or a "breach" was required to constitute the crime of burglary. An entry through an open door or window without the consent of the person living in or controlling the building was not a "breaking." Many states have abolished the common law concept of "breaking," but it is used in a minority of jurisdictions.

Unlawful Entry into Premises

Because burglary is a form of trespass, there must be an unlawful entry into the premises. An entry could be made by inserting a hand or an arm into the premises. For example, suppose X threw a brick through a jewelry store window and then inserted his hand and arm through the broken window to obtain watches and rings that were in the window display. This would be an unlawful entry that would justify a conviction of X for burglary of the jewelry store.

Suppose that instead of using his arm, X inserted a cane into the window and began removing watches and rings by hooking them with the cane. Would this be an entry so as to justify a conviction of burglary? Most courts would

	Essential Elements of the Crime of Burglary	
Burglary at Old Common Law	*Burglary as Defined by Most States Today*	*Burglary in Your State Today*
Breaking	(not required)	_____
Entry	same	_____
Dwelling of another	any building or dwelling	_____
Without consent of person in lawful possession	same	_____
In the nighttime	at any time	_____
With intent to commit a felony	with intent to steal or commit a felony	_____

probably hold that this was an entry, since the cane was an extension of X's body inserted into the store to carry out his criminal purpose.[33]

In the 1983 case of *People v. Tingue,*[34] the defendant entered a New York church that was open at all hours so that the public could pray and meditate. However, instead of praying, the defendant stole the amplifier system from behind the altar rail and entered a room of the church not open to the public, where he attempted to force the lock of a safe. The defendant was charged with burglary. In his first trial, the state failed to "muster sufficient evidence" to prove unlawful entry and the case was dismissed. The state tried again and in the second trial obtained a conviction for burglary, but the appellate court reversed the conviction, as double jeopardy forbade the second trial and conviction.

Any element of a crime may be proved by circumstantial evidence. In the U.S. Supreme Court case of *United States v. Edwards,*[35] someone had burglarized a U.S. post office by using a pry bar on a window. The defendant had stolen property taken from the post office in his possession. Direct evidence of the break-in was not available, as there were no witnesses. However, crime lab tests showed paint and wood fragments on the defendant's clothing similar to the paint and wood on the post office window. As a jury

held this evidence proved unlawful entry, the defendant's conviction was affirmed.

In the 1976 case of *State v. Tixier,*[36] police officers responded to a triggered burglary alarm within a minute. They found a small hole near the door-opening mechanism of a garage. The defendant was found hiding among tires stacked near the door. The piece of the door that had been removed was found near the defendant. It was concluded that the defendant had used an instrument to penetrate the building. In affirming the defendant's burglary conviction, the court held:

> Evidence of a break-in by use of an instrument which penetrates into the building is, in our opinion, evidence of entry into the building. The sufficiency of this evidence is not destroyed by a failure to prove that the instrument was used to steal something from the building or to commit another felony. Such proof is unnecessary because burglary does not depend upon actions after the entry; the crime is complete when there is an unauthorized entry with the requisite intent.

In the 1978 case of *Champlin v. State,*[37] the defendant entered a hotel lobby open to the general public 24 hours a day and removed a television set and a cash register. Instead of charging the defendant with theft, a prosecutor charged the defendant with burglary. In reversing the conviction for burglary, the court pointed out that the defendant's conduct, although illegal, was not burglary, as the premises were open to the general public.

The Dwelling House of Another

A "dwelling house" is a place where people live and sleep. Under the old common law, unlawful entry and theft from a business place would not be a burglary, as a business place is not a "dwelling house." Hotel rooms and apartments are "dwelling houses," since people live and sleep in such places. A new building into which no one had yet moved has been held not to be a "dwelling house." [38]

All the states and the federal government have changed the old common law restricting burglary to only "dwelling houses." Today, virtually all buildings are contained within the scope of the crime of burglary. Many states punish the burglary of an inhabited building more severely than that of an uninhabited building. In the case of *People v. Lewis,* [39] the court held that the question of "inhabited" or "uninhabited" turns not on the immediate presence or absence of people in the building, but rather on the character of the use of the building.

Are outdoor telephone booths "buildings" within the meaning of burglary statutes? What about a telephone booth within a building? In past years, some courts have held that outdoor telephone booths are "buildings," so persons entering a booth with intent to steal from the coin container could be convicted of burglary. However, other courts have held otherwise. Today, most such cases would involve a charge of one or more of the following:

- theft/larceny
- entry into a locked coin box (or vending machine)
- criminal damage to property
- possession of a burglarious tool

In 1975, the California Supreme Court held that a defendant could not be convicted of burglarizing his own home. [40] But sons or daughters who live away from home and do not have permission to enter the home of their parents

may be convicted of burglary if all the other elements of burglary are proved. In the 1974 Indiana case of *Farno v. State,* [41] the Court of Appeals of Indiana affirmed the conviction of the defendant for the burglary of his mother's home. A restraining order had been issued prohibiting the defendant from visiting the home.

Nighttime

The old common law required that burglary be committed at night, which was defined as the time between sunset and sunrise. An entry into a dwelling house with an accompanying theft during the day could not be charged as a burglary under this definition. The defendant, however, could be charged with the separate crimes of trespass, stealing, and, depending on the circumstances, criminal damage to property. Today, about half the burglaries in the United States are committed during the day, and all jurisdictions recognize daylight burglaries. Some states impose severer penalties for nighttime burglaries.

With Intent to Commit a Felony

The common law element of burglary with "intent to commit a felony" has been broadened in all American jurisdictions. State laws vary in their intent requirement. Some provide that the intent necessary to convict for burglary must be that of intent to steal or to commit a felony. Others provide that the intent must be to commit a crime (which would include both misdemeanors and felonies). Other state statutes specify crimes, whereas still others require that an intent to commit a larceny or theft or other felony be shown.

Robbery and stealing are property crimes in which the state must show that there was a taking and carrying away. In theft and larceny, the state must show the value of the property taken, since this determines the classification of the crime. The value of the property taken in a robbery does not affect the classification of the robbery. A robbery is committed whether $2 or $2,000 are taken. If property is taken in a burglary or a felony is committed, such evidence is used to show the intent of the defendant to commit the crime of burglary. However, a person may be convicted of burglary even if there has been no theft or other felony committed. The state must show an intent to commit theft, or crime, or felony as required by the statute of the jurisdiction.

Proving Intent for Burglary When There Is No Evidence of Stealing or Any Other Crime

If a defendant is apprehended in a warehouse in the middle of the night with his arms filled with merchandise, there is usually no question concerning his intent in that particular situation. With respect to proving intent for burglary when there is no evidence of stealing or of any other crime, the Supreme Court of Illinois stated in the case of *People v. Johnson* that:

> Intent must ordinarily be proved circumstantially, by inferences drawn from conduct appraised in its factual environment. We are of the opinion that in the absence of inconsistent circumstances, proof of unlawful breaking and entry into a building which contains personal property that could be the subject of larceny gives rise to an inference that will sustain a conviction of burglary. Like other inferences, this one is grounded in human experience, which justifies the assumption that the unlawful entry was not purposeless, and, in the absence of other proof, indicates theft as the most likely purpose. This conclusion is supported by the decisions of other courts. (Commonwealth v. Eppich (1961), 342 Mass. 487, 174 N.E.2d 31; State v. Hopkins (1961), 11 Utah 2d 363, 359 P.2d 486; Behel v. State (1960), 40 Ala. App. 689, 122 So.

2d 537; Ex parte Seyfried (1953), 74 Idaho 467, 264 P.2d 685; People v. Les (1939), 267 Mich. 648, 255 N.W. 407; State v. Woodruff (1929), 208 Iowa 236, 225 N.W. 254; Bloch v. State (1903), 161 Ind. 276, 68 N.E. 287; People v. Soto (1879), 53 Cal. 415; cf. State v. Kennedy (1962), 15 Wis. 2d 600, 113 N.W.2d 372.[42]

In the 1973 Pennsylvania case of *Commonwealth v. Muniem*,[43] the defendant, who had been found in an empty warehouse about noon, was convicted of burglary. The door was half open and the defendant was walking out when the police arrived. He was cooperative, did not run, and had nothing in possession. The owner testified that nothing was missing. The defendant stated that he had to go to the toilet and had looked for a lavatory in the empty building. The defendant was 33 years old, employed, married, and had no prior record. In reversing the conviction and ordering the defendant discharged, the court stated:

> In the instant case, the only evidence produced against the appellant is his presence, perhaps as a trespasser, in a vacant building in daylight at about noontime. When found by the police, he was walking to the open door by which he testified he entered the building. The owner of the building testified that nothing was missing and there was no evidence of a forceable entry, or possession of any burglary tools, other tools or anything else.
>
> Each case must stand on its own facts in determining whether the Commonwealth has sustained its bur-

In order to charge:	*a. that there was a stealing (taking and carrying away)?*	*b. the value of the property taken?*	*c. elements other than the crime of stealing?*
Theft/Larceny	Yes	Yes	No
Robbery	Yes	Not necessary as long as the property was something of value	Yes, *a.* that the taking was by force or the threat of use of force and *b.* that the taking was from the victim's person or presence.
Burglary	No, only that there was an intent to steal or an intent to commit a felony as required by the statutes of that state	Not necessary as long as the property was something of value (or there was an intent to steal).	Yes, there must be a showing of an unlawful entry (in some states a breaking) into a dwelling or building.

Is the State Obligated to Show:

den of proof. At best, the evidence of the Commonwealth may give rise to suspicion and conjecture of
guilt but most certainly does not have such volume
and quality capable of reasonably and naturally justifying an inference of a willful and malicious entry into
a building with the intent to commit a felony so as to
overcome the presumption of innocence and establish
guilt beyond a reasonable doubt of the crime of
burglary.

Defendants often have explanations for why
they entered the property of another. For example, the defendant in the case of *Commonwealth
v. Muniem* stated that he made the entry into the
warehouse because he had to go to the toilet.
The trial court did not believe the defendant's
explanation and convicted him on evidence that
the Superior Court of Pennsylvania held to be
insufficient. The Supreme Court of Illinois made
the following statement concerning the testimony
of defendants explaining their conduct:

> A person accused of a crime is not required to prove
> his innocence or even to testify in his defense. When
> he does so, however, his testimony must be considered
> and weighed according to the same rules which are
> applicable to the testimony of any other witness.[44]

The following cases illustrate some of the reasons
put forward by defendants to explain why they
were in buildings belonging to other persons:

• In the 1972 Nevada case of *Harris v. State,*[45]
the defendant stated that he had been in the
parking lot outside the pharmacy when the officers arrived, and that one of the officers forcibly
dragged him into the building. When he tried to
run out of the store, one of the police dogs butted
him from the rear, knocking him into the box in
which he was found hiding.

• In the 1971 Wisconsin case of *Strait v. State,*[46]
the defendant stated that he broke a window in a
restaurant building at 4:00 A.M. and hid in the
building because he was afraid of some teenagers
he had seen in a car out on the street.

• In the 1966 Illinois case of *People v. Schnell-
er,*[47] the defendant explained his presence in the
Chicago Historical Museum after the museum
was closed as follows: While he was visiting the
museum in the afternoon, he observed a man and
woman arguing. When he went to the aid of the
woman, the man hit him and knocked him out.
He did not remember anything until after the
police placed him in custody (the defendant had
a pistol, tools, and flashlight in his possession).

The trier of fact (judge or jury) in all the above
cases did not believe the stories of the defendants,
in view of other evidence presented in each case.
In all the cases, it was held that the defendant
intended to steal and could therefore be convicted of the crime of burglary.

Proof of Burglary When There Is Stealing or Other Crimes Are Committed

As a trespass offense, burglary is most often
committed by a defendant who steals or who has
an intent to steal. Criminals, however, enter
private premises for criminal purposes other than
to steal. Offenders have entered the premises of
others with intent to commit rape, arson, or
other serious felonies. The charge of burglary is
sometimes one of multiple serious charges against
a defendant who went on a criminal rampage in a
private home or business place. The charge of

The general rule of law is that intent to steal cannot be inferred from the single fact of an unlawful
entry into a building. Additional circumstances must be considered, such as:

• type of entry—was it forcible?
• manner of entry—was there a breaking or splintering?
• place of entry—was it the rear or side of the building?
• type of building—did the building contain items that a thief would be interested in stealing?
• time of entry—was it the middle of the night or the middle of the day?
• conduct of the defendant when interrupted—did he or she attempt to hide or escape?

Source: This material is adapted from a chart originated by the Supreme Court of Wisconsin in the case of *State
v. Barclay,* 54 Wis. 2d 651, 196 N.W.2d 745 (1971).

Forms of Theft

Theft/Larceny	Theft from the Person	Robbery (Theft by Force or Threat of Force)	Burglary (Trespass with Intent to Steal or to Commit a Felony)
• ordinary theft (usually done secretly) • snatch and run theft • shoplifting • theft from autos • theft from buildings • theft by fraud (con game) • embezzlement • theft by bailee • fraud on innkeeper, restaurant • "looting"—taking property from building that has been destroyed by disaster, riot, bombing, fire, tornado, etc.	• purse snatching • pickpocketing • "rolling a drunk" (taking valuables from an intoxicated person or person in stupor) • taking valuables from injured, dead, or disabled persons	• mugging or yoking (strong-armed robbery) • armed robbery • robbery in which the victim is placed in apprehension that the criminal is armed with a dangerous weapon • masked robbery (identity is concealed) • purse snatching and pickpocketing in which such force is used against the person that it constitutes strong-armed robbery	• ordinary burglary (some states punish burglary committed at night more severely) • armed burglary • burglary in which an occupant of the building is injured • "break and run" burglary (breaking store window and running off with property)

---

burglary also offers prosecutors an alternative charge when there is doubt as to whether the state can prove attempted rape, murder, arson, etc. If X broke into W's apartment with the intent to rape her but found that she was not home, X could be charged with burglary if the state could prove his intent to commit a felony. The following cases illustrate various kinds of proof-supported convictions for burglary:

MITCHELL v. STATE
Court of Criminal Appeals of Oklahoma (1971)
489 P.2d 499

Evidence showed that at approximately 1:30 A.M. the defendant drove his fist through the screen door of a house and unlatched it after he tore the screen door off the facing. After gaining entry, he choked the 79-year-old woman who lived in the house. He demanded $25 from her and struck her in the face. He then discharged a firearm into the floor of the house. He left after an hour, demanding that the woman give him $100 by the following morning or he would come back and kill her. He received no money from the woman, who called the sheriff as soon as the defendant left. The conviction for first-degree burglary and the sentence of 15 years of imprisonment were affirmed by the Court of Criminal Appeals of Oklahoma.

STATE v. HANSON
Supreme Court of South Dakota (1974)
215 N.W.2d 130

The defendant was employed as an undercover narcotics agent by the Division of Criminal Investigation of the state of South Dakota. He admitted to participating in a burglary in which whiskey, cigarettes, and cash were taken but contended that he committed the crime to avoid "blowing his cover" as an undercover agent for the state. After the following jury instruction was given, the jury found him guilty of third-degree burglary. The Supreme Court of South Dakota affirmed the conviction.

In this case, the Defendant, David Hanson, has introduced evidence that he was acting as an undercover agent for the Division of Criminal Investigation and Law Enforcement Agency of Bon Homme County, State of South Dakota, thereby justifying his presence and participation in the alleged crime. Because of the introduction of such evidence, the State has the burden of proving beyond a reasonable doubt that the Defendant, David Hanson, was not acting within the scope of his legal authority as an undercover agent. If the State fails to prove beyond a reasonable doubt that the Defendant, David Hanson, was not acting within the scope of his duties as an undercover agent, you shall find the Defendant not guilty.

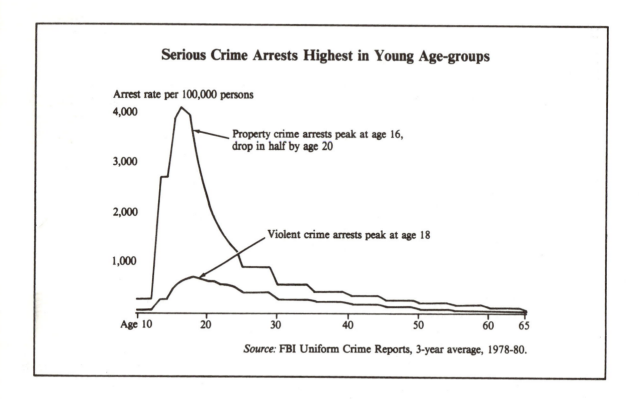

Serious Crime Arrests Highest in Young Age-groups

Arrest rate per 100,000 persons

Property crime arrests peak at age 16, drop in half by age 20

Violent crime arrests peak at age 18

Source: FBI Uniform Crime Reports, 3-year average, 1978-80.

In most states, the following are the essential elements of:

Larceny/Theft	*Burglary*	*Robbery*
a taking and carrying away	illegal entry or remaining (trespass)	a taking and carrying away
of the personal (or movable) property of another	in a building or structure	of the property of another
with intent to steal (or permanently deprive the owner of possession).	with intent to steal, or intent to commit a felony (as specified by statute).	with intent to steal from the person or the presence of the victim by the use of force or the threat of the use of imminent force.

QUESTIONS AND PROBLEMS FOR CHAPTER 15

After reviewing the criminal property statutes of your state, select the correct answer for the questions from the following choices:

The offense committed is:

a. *Stealing (theft or larceny)* Taking with intent to deprive

b. *Robbery (indicate whether armed or* Forceful *unarmed)*

c. *Burglary* B+E

d. *Attempt to commit one of the above (specify)*

e. *None of the above (specify if another offense was committed)*

1. X and Y, who are big men, tell a small clerk who is alone in a store that they b, unarmed will take what they want and she had better not interfere. They take merchandise and walk out of the store. Because of fear of injury, the woman clerk does nothing while the men are in the store.

2. An officer of a savings and loan association embezzles money from the association. A?

3. X obtains $500 from Y by threatening to reveal to Y's boss and wife that Y has a criminal record. extortion

4. X breaks into a heroin pusher's car and takes $2,000 worth (street value) of heroin.

5. X breaks the window of a private club at night and steals $125 from an illegal slot machine that the club has for gambling purposes.

6. X takes Y's automobile and uses it for two days. On the third day, he abandons the car on the city street, where it is found by the police on the fourth day.

7. X tells Y that he has an order for a certain type and color of car. Y steals the car and sells it to X, who also sells the car. What is the maximum charge that X can be charged with?

8. X purchases an automobile for $700 and pays for the car with a check on a bank in which he knowingly has no account.

9. X and Y ring the doorbell of a home at night. When the occupant answers, they demand money at gunpoint and take valuables from the persons in the house.

10. A married woman takes $400 from the joint checking account that she and her

husband have and runs off with another man.

11. In a pigeon-drop scheme, X tricks an old man into giving X his life savings of $2,000.

12. X drives off from a filling station without paying for the $10 worth of gas that the attendant put in his car.

13. At gunpoint, X takes $4,000 worth of heroin from a heroin pusher.

14. X goes into a drug store and pretends that he has a gun in his pocket. The frightened clerk gives X money from the cash register on demand. X has no gun.

15. A housewife makes a bad mistake in the family checking account and writes checks in excess of the money in the account. The additional funds are deposited as soon as the family is notified.

16. X breaks into a restaurant building at 3:00 A.M. but is apprehended before he moved, disturbed, or stole anything in the restaurant.

17. X is apprehended attempting to fish money out of a bank night depository box with a fishline and hook. The incident occured at midnight, when the streets were empty of people and traffic.

18. X took the wallet of a drunk when the man was too intoxicated to know what happened ("rolling a drunk").

19. The police are called to a tavern where X has bought a round of drinks for the whole house but does not have the $18 to pay for the drinks.

20. While a bank clerk was not watching, X reached his hand into the bank cage and took a bundle of $5 bills. A guard saw X putting the money into his pocket.

21. X took an old bike that was placed in an alley for trash pick-up.

22. A business partner took $1,000 out of the business checking account without his partner's consent or knowledge and used the money for gambling.

23. X snatched a bag of money off a counter in a store and ran out.

24. X threw a brick through a jewelry store and with a long stick was able to hook watches and rings worth more than $500.

25. A $10,000 check endorsed for deposit to a Miami bank disappeared in the mail. The defendant obtained possession of the check and deposited it to an account that he had opened at the bank. To make the deposit, the defendant had to alter the account number on the check to show the defendant's new account number at the bank. After the 20-day hold on the funds in his account, the defendant withdrew all the funds and closed the account. Has the defendant committed a crime? If so, what should he be charged with? Are there any defenses to the charge? *Bell v. United States,* ___ U.S. ___, 103 S. Ct. 2398 (1983).

Chapter 16

Shoplifting and Other Crimes Against Businesses and Corporations

A. SHOPLIFTING (RETAIL THEFT)

Theft is generally the single biggest crime problem of any retail business. Shoplifting is the form of theft that occurs most frequently and probably causes the greatest losses. In 1982, the *Economic Crime Digest* reported that shoplifting losses amounted to at least $16 billion a year nationwide. On the basis of this figure, shoplifting costs consumers more than a nickel on every dollar they spend in retail stores.

The crime of shoplifting, or retail theft, is a form of theft and larceny. Shoplifting has the same essential elements as theft and larceny: (a) a taking and carrying away (b) of the property of another (c) with intent to steal and permanently deprive the owner of possession of the property.

Taking and Carrying Away in Shoplifting

In modern self-service stores, customers are invited to examine merchandise on display. Garments may be taken to dressing rooms and tried on. Customers carry about merchandise either in their hands or in shopping carts provided by the store. The Court of Appeals of New York pointed out in the 1981 case of *People v. Olivo* [1] that stores therefore consent "to the customer's possession of the goods" for limited purposes.

Stores do not consent, however, to concealment of their merchandise by customers. The merchandise is offered for sale, and if the customer is not going to purchase an object, he (or she) is obligated to return the merchandise to the display counter in good condition. If the customer is going to take the merchandise, there is a legal obligation to pay the purchase price. The New York Court of Appeals stated in the *Olivo* case:

> If the customer exercises dominion and control wholly inconsistent with the continued rights of the owner, and the other elements of the crime are present, a larceny has occurred. Such conduct on the part of a customer satisfies the "taking" element of the crime.
>
> * * *
>
> A taking of property in the self-service store context can be established by evidence that a customer

exercised control over merchandise wholly inconsistent with the store's continued rights. Quite simply, a customer who crosses the line between the limited right he or she has to deal with merchandise and the store owner's rights may be subject to prosecution for larceny. Such a rule should foster the legitimate interests and continued operation of self-service shops, a convenience which most members of the society enjoy.

In affirming the convictions of the three different defendants whose shoplifting cases had been consolidated on appeal, the New York Court of Appeals held:

> In *People v. Olivo,* defendant not only concealed goods in his clothing, but he did so in a particularly suspicious manner. And, when defendant was stopped, he was moving towards the door, just three feet short of exiting the store. It cannot be said as a matter of law that these circumstances failed to establish a taking.
>
> In *People v. Gasparik,* defendant removed the price tag and sensor device from a jacket, abandoned his own garment, put the jacket on and ultimately headed for the main floor of the store. Removal of the price tag and sensor device, and careful concealment of those items, is highly unusual and suspicious conduct for a shopper. Coupled with defendant's abandonment of his own coat and his attempt to leave the floor, those factors were sufficient to make out a prima facie case of a taking.
>
> In *People v. Spatzier,* defendant concealed a book in an attaché case. Unaware that he was being observed in an overhead mirror, defendant looked furtively up and down an aisle before secreting the book. In these circumstances, given the manner in which defendant concealed the book and his suspicious behavior, the evidence was not insufficient as a matter of law.

Must a Shoplifter Leave a Store to Be Guilty of the Offense? *No*

The question of whether it is necessary to allow a shoplifter to leave a store in order to detain the person for shoplifting has been before many courts. The Criminal Court of the City of New York held in *People v. Britto:*

> There are a number of myths about the criminal law, comfortably shared and nourished by those in the street, the business community and sometimes, the courts. One of these is the belief that an observed shoplifter acts with impunity unless and until he or she leaves the store with the goods. So strong is this

belief that the majority of store detectives are instructed to refrain from stopping the suspect anywhere inside the premises; although the likelihood of apprehension is thus enormously decreased.[2]

In the 1981 case of *People v. Olivo,* the New York Court of Appeals held:

> Case law from other jurisdictions seems unanimous in holding that a shoplifter need not leave the store to be guilty of larceny (e.g., *State v. Grant,* 135 Vt. 222, 373 A.2d 847; *Groomes v. United States,* 155 A.2d 73 [D.C. Mun. App.], *supra; People v. Baker,* 365 Ill. 328, 6 N.E.2d 665; *People v. Bradovich,* 305 Mich. 329, 9 N.W.2d 560; accord *People v. Britto,* 93 Misc. 2d 151, 402 N.Y.S.2d 546, *supra*). This is because a shopper may treat merchandise in a manner inconsistent with the owner's continued rights—and in a manner not in accord with that of prospective purchaser—without actually walking out of the store. Indeed, depending upon the circumstances of each case, a variety of conduct may be sufficient to allow the trier of fact to find a taking. It would be well-nigh impossible, and unwise, to attempt to delineate all the situations which would establish a taking. But it is possible to identify some of the factors used in determining whether the evidence is sufficient to be submitted to the fact finder.
>
> In many cases, it will be particularly relevant that defendant concealed the goods under clothing or in a container (see, e.g., *People v. Baker,* 365 Ill. 328, 6 N.E.2d 665, *supra; People v. Bradovich,* 305 Mich. 329, 9 N.W.2d 560, *supra*). Such conduct is not generally expected in a self-service store and may in a proper case be deemed an exercise of dominion and control inconsistent with the store's continued rights. Other furtive or unusual behavior on the part of the defendant should also be weighed. Thus, if the defendant surveys the area while secreting the merchandise or abandoned his or her own property in exchange for the concealed goods, this may evince larcenous rather than innocent behavior. Relevant too is the customer's proximity to or movement towards one of the store's exits. Certainly it is highly probative of guilt that the customer was in possession of secreted goods just a few short steps from the door or moving in that direction. Finally, possession of a known shoplifting device actually used to conceal merchandise, such as a specially designed outer garment or false bottom carrying case, would be all but decisive.
>
> Of course, in a particular case, any one or any combination of these factors may take on special significance. And there may be other considerations, not now identified, which should be examined. So long as it bears upon the principal issue—whether the shopper exercised control wholly inconsistent with the

owner's continued rights—any attending circumstance is relevant and may be taken into account.[3]

The Requirement of Probable Cause Based on Personal Knowledge

Private security persons and retail store employees are often told, "If you have not seen it, it has not happened." Customers are not to be treated as shoplifters until there is hard, firsthand information demonstrating that a shoplifting has occurred. The Criminal Court of New York emphasized the probable cause requirement in *People v. Britto:*

> It must be emphasized that this court's holding in no way lessens the burden of proof on the People in shoplifting cases. On the contrary, there is, and should be, a higher standard of proof upon the People in self-service situations than in other larceny cases, because the mere fact of possession may not be used to demonstrate larceny. This remains true even when such possession is accompanied by suspicious or equivocal actions, such as placing unpaid goods directly into the defendant's shopping bag (see, *Durphy v. United States,* 235 A.2d 326 [D.C. App. 1967]). It is only when the trier of fact concludes, beyond a reasonable doubt, that defendant's actions were totally inconsistent with and clearly adverse to the owner's interests that a conviction may lie. If the facts are sufficient to support such a conclusion *before* the defendant leaves the store, the fact that he has not left is wholly irrelevant and should not absolve him from the consequences of his acts.[4]

The U.S. Supreme Court defined probable cause as "facts and circumstances within their knowledge and of which they had reasonable trustworthy information [that] were sufficient in themselves to warrant a man of reasonable caution in the belief"[5] that the suspect had committed a crime. The Supreme Judicial Court of Massachusetts held:

> Historically, the words "reasonable grounds" and "probable cause" have been given the same meaning by the courts.
>
> * * *
>
> The Oregon Supreme Court construed the meaning of the words "reasonable grounds" in its "shoplifting statute" as having the same meaning as they have in a statute authorizing arrest without a warrant and ap-

plied the probable cause standard to the facts before it.[6]

The following incident (and the problems at the end of this chapter) further illustrates the probable cause requirement:

Example: On a hot July day, a woman customer stated to a clerk in a large food store that "I suspect that young man of shoplifting." She pointed at a young black man wearing a jogging suit. The clerk relayed the statement to the assistant manager of the store, who confronted the young man, accusing him in a voice overheard by other persons of shoplifting. The young man was detained and the police were called. Did probable cause exist to justify this action?

This incident resulted in a civil lawsuit, with a jury awarding the young man money damages for false imprisonment and defamation (slander). When the police arrived, they immediately realized probable cause did not exist from the facts known to the store employees. The woman customer was questioned by the police, but she had not seen a shoplifting occur and only "suspected" the offense.

Proving Intent to Steal in Shoplifting Cases

As pointed out in Chapter 15, intent to steal and permanently deprive the owner of possession can be inferred and concluded by the fact finder (jury or judge) based on the facts and evidence presented. The following case illustrates:

PEOPLE v. BRITTO
Criminal Court of the City of New York (1978)
402 N.Y.S.2d 546

A security supervisor in a supermarket observed the defendant placing paper towels and other items in a brown paper bag. Defendant then put six or seven ham steaks under his belt and walked past the checkout counter and registers without paying. The defendant was stopped while still in the store and asked for a receipt. Instead, the defendant handed the security officer the paper bag, stating "You got me—have the meat." Defendant was detained and the meat was recovered. The court held:

It seems clear that the People have presented enough evidence to permit a trier of fact to conclude that the defendant had exercised sufficient control over the goods to constitute a completed larceny. When one considers the realities of modern shopping, the wisdom of the Court of Appeals' decision to avoid slavish "adhere[nce] to the auxiliary common-law element of asportation" . . . is evident. In self-service stores, shoppers have a right to pick up, and often to move, merchandise for periods of time clearly long enough to satisfy asportation as required at common law. Yet no one would consider such possession felonious, for the self-service shopper is deemed to have conditional, or implied, possession until the merchandise is paid for. . . . However, when a defendant's actions are wholly inconsistent with that of a prospective purchaser, it is up to the trier of fact to decide whether at the time of acquiring possession and thereafter, the defendant possessed the requisite felonious intent.

Thus when the instant defendant placed six or seven ham steaks under his belt and walked by the place where goods are paid for, his actions were not consistent with those of a prospective purchaser, and he was not acting within the implied invitation to conditional possession tendered by the supermarket owner. Accordingly, the People have presented a prima facie case, and the defendant's motion to dismiss at the end of the People's case is denied.

Handling A Shoplifting Case

1. Make sure you have probable cause and a good solid case before you restrain the freedom of movement of a person for shoplifting. Probable cause (or "reasonable grounds to believe") must be based on personal knowledge (firsthand information) by you or another reliable adult employee. Remember: If you did not see it, it did not happen. When in doubt, let him go.

2. Observing a person concealing "something" or putting "something" in their pocket or purse is not sufficient to establish probable cause. You must have "reasonable grounds to believe" (probable cause) that the object is unpaid merchandise and that the item belongs to the store. If you do not have probable cause, you may:
• keep the person under observation
• engage in voluntary conversation ("May I help you?" "Are you looking for something?" etc.)
• ask the person what they put in their pocket, or whether they have a receipt for merchandise in their possession under circumstances in which there is no restraint of their freedom of movement

3. After a person is observed shoplifting, the following options are available to store employees or a security officer:
• Confront the person immediately and ask that they produce the item. *Always* ask if they have a receipt showing that they paid for the item. Under these circumstances, you may seek only recovery of the item and deterrence, rather than prosecution in court
• You may be under instructions to allow the person to go beyond the last pay station (or in some cases, even out of the store). Under these circumstances, the person should be kept under surveillance. If the person becomes aware of your surveillance, he or she may attempt to discard the shoplifted item or pass it onto another person. If you fail to observe the "discard" or "pass-on," you may then be unable to explain why the stolen property was not recovered. If it appears that the person may out run you and other store employees, it may be wise to position yourself between the exit door and the person.

4. Shoplifting cases are handled by your local law enforcement agency (police or sheriff), prosecutor, and judge. It is advisable to consult a knowledgeable official to determine whether any specific standards are required, such as:
• whether the local judge requires that the person observed shoplifting be allowed beyond the pay station (or out of the store) before they are detained. (A young man in gym shoes who gets near a door or out of the store is going to outrun most store security people.)
• whether cases will be prosecuted when:
   —the value of the merchandise stolen is small (what is the minimum for prosecution?)
   —the merchandise or item stolen has not been recovered
   —the offender is very young or very old
   —whether other factors are considered

5. Absolute defenses to civil suits are:
• that the person either voluntarily stayed in the area, or that the restraint of movement was made in good faith on probable cause based on personal knowledge
• that if any force was used, it was necessary either
   —in self-defense, or
   —to detain the person, and/or
   —to prevent the unlawful theft of the property and that the amount of force was reasonable under the circumstances

B. FRAUDULENT USE OF CREDIT CARDS (OR NUMBERS)

Credit cards are a means of extending short-term credit. The three parties ordinarily involved in a credit card transaction are (1) the issuer of the credit card, which could be a bank or an organization, such as Diner's Club, American Express, or Master Charge; (2) the credit card user, who is the holder of the card and the person purchasing the merchandise or service; and (3) the merchant, department store, or restaurant providing and selling the merchandise or the service.

A person holding a valid credit card signs for the receipt of the goods and commits himself or herself to pay for the service or the property that has been received. The merchant or business organization supplying the goods or services is then reimbursed for the amount of the billing by the issuer of the credit card. The credit card issuer then bills the credit card holder monthly for the cost of the property and services that have been extended to the credit card holder.

Obtaining Credit Cards (or Numbers) for Fraudulent Use

The methods of obtaining credit cards for fraudulent use are many and varied. Burglars, robbers, and thieves seek credit cards because of the potential fraudulent use of such cards. Cards are stolen by pickpockets and purse snatchers. A prostitute might decide that stealing credit cards is more profitable than "turning tricks."

Personnel in a restaurant, retail store, or gas station might retain a card after a credit card transaction. Cards can be stolen from the mail or through the break in of an automobile or truck. Cards can be counterfeited or altered. They can be obtained through the corruption of employees of companies making cards or of postal employees.

Credit card numbers are also easy to obtain. A woman walked into a drugstore in Arlington, Virginia, and asked if she could have the used carbons from credit card transactions for a children's school project. The store set aside bundles of used carbon for her, but when complaints began coming in from customers as to unauthorized charges to their bills, the purpose of obtaining the carbons became apparent.

Credit Card Violations and Fraud

In addition to the many forms of theft of credit cards, knowingly receiving stolen credit cards is also a common illegal practice. Other violations are:

- use of a credit card without the cardholder's consent

- use of a revoked or cancelled credit card
- knowing use of a counterfeit or altered card
- illegal use of a credit card number (or use of pretended number of a fictitious card)
- use of an expired credit card
- use of an illegally possessed card to negotiate a check
- receiving or possession of an illegally obtained card with intent to defraud
- delivery or sale of an illegally obtained credit card

Misusing a Credit Card Number

One of the most common illegal uses of credit card numbers is in fraudulent use of telephones. A labor union in Michigan received an excessive telephone bill for about $321,000. A woman in Bedford, New York, received a bill for $109,500. Similar situations are reported throughout the United States. As the long distance calls include global calls and the practice is persistent, it is believed that much fraud is committed by narcotic and organized criminal groups that do not want law enforcement and tax officials to trace such calls.

Is misuse of a credit card number, as opposed to the misuse of the card itself, a credit card fraud under federal statute 15 U.S.C. 1644(a)? In the 1982 case of *United States v. Callihan*,[7] the Ninth Circuit Court of Appeals held that it was not. However, in the 1983 case of *United States v. Bice-Bey*,[8] the Fourth Circuit Court of Appeals held that a defendant can be convicted of credit card fraud by misusing a credit card number. The court held that "the core element of a 'credit card' is the account number, not the piece of plastic."

The Increasing Problem of Credit Card Fraud

The average adult in the United States carries five to six credit cards. It is reported that almost 550 million cards are in use. With the increased use of credit cards as part of everyday life, the possibilities for fraud will continue to exist.

To reduce the opportunity for fraud, increased precautions are being taken. More investigators are being hired. Checks are being made before

---

Credit Card and Debit Card Frauds

The rate of credit card and debit card crimes is increasing each year because:
- they are easy to carry out
- they are difficult, in some instances, to prosecute
- most offenders have little remorse, as the victim is generally a bank or large corporation (cardholder is generally liable for only the first $50 of the loss)

To Protect Against Unauthorized Credit or Debit Card Use

The following precautions should be taken:
- Make copies of each card you own (or have the card number and data), with the toll-free numbers of the firm issuing the card.
- Report lost and stolen cards immediately. By reporting the lost card within two days, or reporting an unauthorized withdrawal within two days of the finding, your penalty and loss cannot exceed $50 (no penalty or loss if bank decides not to charge you).
- Do not delay reporting a lost or stolen credit or debit card because of a telephone call from a stranger stating that your cards have been found and will be returned promptly. The call may be a ruse and trick to give thieves time to run up charges on your cards.
- If you delay longer than two days in reporting a theft or fraud of cards, you can be charged up to $500 of the loss for each card.
- Debit cards are used on automatic-teller machines and authorize automatic withdrawals from your account (in some cities, debit cards may also be used as credit cards). *With debit cards:*
   —Do not carry your PIN number (personal identification number) with your debit card, as the loss of both provides immediate access to your account and funds.
   —Do not disclose to any person what your PIN number is, as this may be a scam that will allow a thief to steal every cent in your account. It is never necessary to identify yourself by your PIN.
- Failure to report an unauthorized withdrawal within 60 days of the mailing of your statement could make you liable for the entire loss. With debit cards, this loss could be the amount in your account plus the total loan that can be charged automatically to your card.

---

credit is extended, and verifications are made before shipments are sent out to determine whether the true cardholder placed the order. While losses are only a small fraction of a percent of total credit card sales, yearly losses in the United States are estimated between $100 and $300 million in credit card fraud.

C. CHECK VIOLATIONS

Nonsufficient (Insufficient) Fund Checks

The NSF (nonsufficient fund) or ISF (insufficient fund) check is a common business problem, with probably every state having statutes imposing a criminal penalty for failure to provide funds to make good these bad checks.

Generally, the person who issues an NSF or ISF check unintentionally overdrew their checking account owing to an error or carelessness.

Persons with joint accounts can have difficulty unless accurate record keeping is maintained.

No-Such-Account Checks

No-such-account checks are those checks that are written against an account that either never existed or has been closed. Writing a check on a nonexisting account reflects an intent to defraud. This type of bad check is generally passed by a professional fraudulent check passer.

The Crime of "Uttering"

The Supreme Court of Virginia defined the crime of uttering as:

> Under our bad-check statute, the gravamen of the offense is the intent to defraud, and the offense is complete when, with the requisite intent, a person utters a check he knows to be worthless. . . . A check is uttered when it is put into circulation; for

example, when it is presented for payment. . . . The presentment is more than a request for payment; it constitutes an implied representation that the check is good. The statute itself dispenses with proof of an extrinsic representation.

* * *

It need not be shown that the implied representation was relied upon or that anything was received in return for the check; indeed, the discovery by a payee that a check is worthless before a purchase transaction is completed does not preclude a conviction under the statute. . . . And, while we have stated that the statute is "specifically aimed to discourage the giving of bad checks for what purports to be a cash purchase," . . . such a purchase is not the only transaction proscribed; the statute clearly encompasses a worthless check given to obtain cash.[9]

The crime of uttering a forged instrument is most often committed when a person presents a forged instrument for payment. In the 1968 case of *England v. State,*[10] the defendant handed a forged check to a bank teller without saying anything. In affirming the defendant's conviction for uttering a forged instrument, the Supreme Court of Indiana held: "We conclude the offering of the check to the teller with no instructions, when this act is generally construed in the banking industry as a request to exchange said check for cash, is sufficient conduct to warrant the jury to believe that the appellant intended to cash a forged instrument."

The Crime of Forgery

Documents and writing are important in the functioning of a modern society. The crimes of forgery and uttering are offenses created primarily to safeguard confidence in the genuineness of documents and writing. Forgery is committed when a person with an intent to defraud falsely makes or alters a writing or document. Forgery may be committed by:

• creating a wholly new false writing or document
• altering an existing writing or document (raising the amount of a check would be an example)
• endorsing a check or other instrument with another person's name (example, X steals Y's

---

Safeguards in Handling Checks

Do not endorse checks in blank (with just your name), as the instrument then becomes a bearer instrument that can be cashed by any person obtaining possession.

Do not sign blank checks, as any person obtaining possession of the checks could fill in the amount and cash the checks.

In sending checks through the mail, make the checks payable to a specific person or corporation. Make bank deposits payable to "deposit only" or "for deposit to your account number."

---

check and cashes the check by endorsing Y's name on the back of the check)
• filling in blanks over a signature of another, either without authority or with unauthorized terms.

When a check is presented either for cash or in payment for goods, there is an implied representation that the check is good. A common business practice is to request a person presenting a check to either endorse or sign the check in the presence of the person who is about to honor the document. If the presenter of the check (the bearer) knows that the check is forged, he has committed the crime of uttering in presenting the forged document. If he (or she) signs a false name to the check, he (or she) has then committed the crime of forgery in the presence of the person who is about to honor the check.

Operation of Check-forging Rings

Check-forging rings operate in all large cities in the United States. In many instances, these rings obtain checks from business and industrial firms as a result of burglaries. By means of check-writing machines and typewriters, the stolen checks are then forged to appear as payroll checks.

The checks are often forged using names found on stolen identification cards and papers. Such identification can be obtained by purse snatching and pickpocketing. The thief looks for a victim with the same general appearance as the person who will utter (pass) the check. With a good set of identification cards and with checks that have all the appearances of payroll checks, the check-forging ring goes to work.

To minimize the possibilities of being apprehended, professional criminals will often recruit other persons to commit the actual uttering and passing of the checks. This can be done by selling the checks made out in whatever amount and name the person wishes. Or, the criminal transaction can be done under an agreement to share the criminal loot.

If a criminal is apprehended while attempting to pass a forged check, he or she is likely to attempt to destroy the evidence of the crime. This might be done by eating the check or destroying it in some other way. Should the offender be successful, he or she could then be charged with the offense of destroying (or attempting to destroy) evidence of a crime.

Check "Kiting"

Check "kiting" can be compared to a "shell game" at a carnival, in that manipulations are used in both to deceive. The most common reason for the deception in check kiting is to create a false bank balance from which to draw and run off with money that does not belong to the person. The U.S. Supreme Court used the following example to explain a check kiting scheme in the 1982 case of *Williams v. United States*:

> The check kiter opens an account at Bank A with a nominal deposit. He then writes a check on that account for a large sum, such as $50,000. The check kiter then opens an account at Bank B and deposits the $50,000 check from Bank A in that account. At the time of deposit, the check is not supported by sufficient funds in the account at Bank A. However, Bank B, unaware of this fact, gives the check kiter immediate credit on his account at Bank B. During the several-day period that the check on Bank A is being processed for collection from that bank, the check kiter writes a $50,000 check on his account at Bank B and deposits it into his account at Bank A. At the time of the deposit of that check, Bank A gives the check kiter immediate credit on his account there,

and on the basis of that grant of credit pays the original $50,000 check when it is presented for collection.

> By repeating this scheme, or some variation of it, the check kiter can use the $50,000 credit originally given by Bank B as an interest-free loan for an extended period of time. In effect, the check kiter can take advantage of the several-day period required for the transmittal, processing, and payment of checks from accounts in different banks.[11]

Another variety of check kiting is presented in *United States v. Payne*,[12] in which used-car dealers exchanged checks for fictitious sales of automobiles between themselves. They then used the immediate credit that they received to operate their businesses. The same nonexistent automobile was sold seven or eight times a week for a four-month period. The court concluded that:

> Payne and Fountain successfully managed a kite for four months with a float that rose to $178,000. They obtained that credit, advance, loan, only by falsely representing the worthless checks as worth their face value. 18 U.S.C. § 1014 makes their misrepresentation a federal offense when the injured bank is insured by the FDIC.

D. COMPUTER CRIMES

In the 1950s, a reformed bank robber named Willie Sutton was sometimes asked on talk shows why he robbed banks. His response was, "That's where the money is."

Today, computers are where the money is. It is estimated that over $400 billion is transferred every day through commercial and governmental computers. Our society is becoming an increasingly cashless society through credit cards and a paperless society through computers.

In 1977, a governmental committee[13] estimated the average loss in a computer crime at $430,000, compared with a $19,000 average where accounting was done manually. Computer crime is reported to be at a "staggering level."[14] There is much concern as to computer crime that has been committed and remains undetected. Estimates as to the risk of detection and risk of prosecution were given as only 1 in 22,000.[15] Computer crime has been called the "crime of the future" and home computers, the "burglar tool of the electronic age." These accusations may be exaggerations, but they do reflect the concern for the rising rate of computer crime in the United States.

Crimes that may be committed with computers are:

1. Theft of funds [16]

   a. By an outsider (or insider) who, by using a telephone and the necessary passwords from a remote terminal, could make the unauthorized transfer of millions of dollars to a designated account

   b. By an insider who would falsify claims in an insurance company (such as medical insurance) and the computer would process and mail out checks paying such claims

2. Theft of information or data. Computer data banks hold many different types of information worth billions of dollars (lists of customers, employees, banking information, consumer records, business plans, etc.). Two examples cited in Chapter 15 are theft of FBI investigative records [17] and the theft of the names of Drug Enforcement Administration informants and status of drug investigation cases.[18]

3. Theft of services. If an authorized person uses a computer for unauthorized purposes, or an unauthorized user uses a system for unauthorized purposes, such misuse could be charged as theft in many states (see Chapter 15 for examples).

4. Electronic break-ins. In 1983, a group of young "hackers" (ages 15 to 22) from Milwaukee, with nothing more than personal home computers and a modem (a device that links a computer to a telephone), were able to "call up" computers connected by a giant network known as GTE Telenet. They were able to guess at some passwords and learned others by intercepting the calls of legitimate computer users. In this manner, they penetrated dozens of computer systems, including Los Alamos and the New York Sloan-Kettering Cancer Center. In the cancer center, computer memory containing accounting information was erased in part and new user accounts were installed. In some of the states that have created "computer crime" statutes, such unauthorized access and destruction of data could be charged as a felony. As the federal government did not have a "computer crime" statute, wire fraud and theft of government property were considered as charges.

Not only may trade secrets be stolen from computers; secrets regarding the manufacturing of computers are also valuable and subject to theft. In a 1983 sting operation, FBI agents arrested employees of the Japanese firm of

---

Crimes That Concern Businesses and Corporations

Theft of company assets: theft, fraud, embezzlement, shoplifting

Worksite crimes: burglary, robbery, damaging or destroying equipment, arson

Crimes against employees, customers, etc.: rape, assault, battery, robbery, kidnapping, etc. (Corporations are obligated under civil law to provide reasonable security to prevent crime on company premises.)

Street crimes not on company premises: robbery, battery, assault, rape, criminal homicide, etc., as these offenses could seriously affect the lives and abilities of employees to work effectively

Crimes By Corporations

Under the old common law, corporations were not capable of committing any crime. Corporations are not persons, only legal entities, and the law found it sufficient to charge the corporate employee or officer with criminal conduct when necessary. Today, because the increased number of corporations and corporate-related crimes, corporations may be charged with many, but not all, crimes. (See Chapter 5 for a discussion of the criminal liability of corporations.)

Hitachi, Ltd. who were attempting to buy computer secrets of IBM. Two Hitachi employees pleaded guilty to conspiracy to commit theft, and Hitachi pleaded guilty and was fined $10,000 on federal charges of conspiring to transport secrets across state lines.

The outcome was an out-of-court cash settlement of an IBM civil suit against Hitachi reported to be $300 million plus attorney fees.

QUESTIONS AND PROBLEMS FOR CHAPTER 16

In view of the information (evidence) available in problems # 1 through # 11, indicate which of the following courses of action may be taken by a store employee or a security person:

1. As the store employee has probable cause, a detention may be made of the person until the police arrive.

2. As less than probable cause exists, the store should not restrain the freedom of movement of the person but may:
  a. engage in a voluntary conversation with the person, or
  b. keep the person under observation (surveillance)

3. There is no legal authority or justification to do either of the above.

1. A well-dressed woman was looking at merchandise in a drugstore. After she left the store without purchasing anything, a clerk observed that only six items were on the shelf of the seven previously observed on the shelf. (*Crase v. Highland Village Value Plus Pharmacy,* 374 N.E.2d 58 [Ind. Ct. App. 1978])

2. Would it make any difference in Problem # 1 if the woman were poorly dressed, or very young, or very old?

3. A man was leaving a department store with a shopping bag. In the bag was a tie rack that he had not paid for. He was stopped at the door of the store by a security guard. The man immediately admitted that he had not paid for the tie rack. Stating that he would pay for it, he went to a check-out counter and tendered a $20 bill. (*Mullen v. Sibley &*

Company, 415 N.E.2d 971, 434 N.Y.S.2d 982 [1980])

4. A man was observed walking briskly up and down the aisles of a Sears store. The man was then observed backing his car up to a portable building used to display merchandise. The man took a lawn mower from the building and put it in the trunk of his car. The man would not produce a sales receipt for the mower. When the man was asked to get out of his car, he broke and ran away. (*Tinsley v. State,* 461 S.W.2d 605 [Texas Ct. App. 1971])

5. A woman was waiting in a check-out line in a drugstore. The cashier saw a wrapping bow on the counter in front of the woman. The bow had all the appearances of bows that were on sale in the store. A few minutes later, the bow was not on the counter. When the woman paid for other items, the cashier asked if she had anything else to pay for at the cash register stand. The woman did not pay for the bow and as she walked away from the store, she was asked if she had anything in her purse for which payment had not been made. The woman answered no. (*Kon v. Skaggs Drug Centers, Inc.,* 563 P.2d 920 [Ariz. Ct. App. 1977])

6. A man was seen leaving a men's clothing store with a bulge under his overcoat. A security officer who had arrested the man for shoplifting on two prior occasions, followed the man to a barber shop. When the man sat down in the

barber shop, the security officer returned to the clothing store, where he determined that a man's leather coat was missing. The security officer started back to the barber shop and saw the man on the street. The officer identified himself and asked for the coat. The man gave the officer the coat and then ran away. When the officer followed, the man threatened him with a knife. (*State v. Gonzales,* 604 P.2d 168 [Wash. Ct. App. 1979])

7. Police warned the manager of a Woolworth store to be on the lookout for three teenage girls believed to be shoplifting (two dark haired and one blonde). When girls matching this description were observed in the store, it was determined that two hair pieces were missing. A clerk stated that the girls were near the hair piece counter. (*Meadows v. F. W. Woolworth Co.,* 254 F. Supp. 907 [1966])

8. A store clerk saw a woman place a lower-priced sticker on a tube of suntan lotion, reducing the price from $1.99 to $1.12. The woman then paid the lower price at the check-out counter and commenced to leave the store. (*Duhe v. Schwegmann Bros. Giant Super Market,* 384 So. 2d 1019 [La. Ct. App. 1980])

9. An assistant security manager identified herself to a woman leaving a K-Mart store and asked the woman to show her a receipt for the scarf in the loop of the handle of the woman's purse. The woman stated, "Oh, I must have forgot to pay for it." The woman was then asked to go to the store office, where she was asked to show identification. When the guard asked, "You come all the way from North Riverside to steal at K-Mart?" the woman responded, "Sure, why not?" The woman signed a report stating that she "was wandering around in the store, took the price [tag] off the scarf and put the scarf on her purse." (*People v. Raitano,* 401 N.E.2d 278 [Ill. Ct. App. 1980])

10. A woman was leaving a department store when an antishoplifting device sounded. (*Sears, Roebuck v. Young,* 384 So.2d 69 [Sup. Ct. Miss. 1980], and *Clark v. Rubenstein, Inc.,* 326 So. 2d 497 [Sup. Ct. La. 1976])

11. A security guard observed two women stuffing a pantsuit into a shopping bag. The women were not in the pantsuit department at the time. The women were then seen leaving the store. When the guard attempted to place the younger woman under arrest, a skirmish broke out. (*Jones v. Montgomery Ward,* 619 P.2d 907 [Ore. Ct. App. 1980])

Chapter 17

Fraud and
Other Property Crimes

A. FRAUD AND FRAUDULENT PRACTICES

Fraud consists of deceitful means or acts used to cheat a person, corporation, or governmental agency. Theft by fraud or larceny by fraud is often the criminal charge used, as fraud can be a form of theft and larceny. Fraud is always intentional, as distinguished from negligence. The following material illustrates the wide range of deception, fraud, and corruption that occurs at all levels of society.

Fraud and Corruption in Government

Fraud against government is as old as government itself. Reports of fraud and corruption date back to biblical times and throughout early civilizations. As the U.S. government today is spending more than $600 billion per year in its total budget, it is not surprising that it has serious fraud and corruption problems. The General Accounting Office reported in 1978:

> Opportunity for defrauding the government is virtually limitless because of the number, variety, and value of federal programs. . . . The involvement of so much money, and so many people and institutions makes the federal programs vulnerable to fraud.

Losses through fraud and corruption occur in many ways, but the following three areas account for most fraud losses in the federal government:

- *program fraud:* "ghost eligibles" in the many programs funded by the federal government, such as Medicaid, Medicare, food stamps, small business loans, subsidy programs, aid programs, etc.

- *contract fraud:* when the federal government contracts for billions of dollars of supplies and services yearly. Fraudulent procedures in contract fraud include "bid-rigging," "bribes," and "kickbacks." An article in *The Wall Street Journal* (17 January 1983) quoted an expert on fraud and waste in the military, who estimated that "criminal activity costs the military $1 billion a year." The expert also commented that the "varieties of theft and fraud seem endless."

- *fraud by public officials:* includes "bribes," "kickbacks," and other types of fraud. Fraud and corruption by public officials could be charged as theft or larceny, misconduct in public office, bribery, etc. Abscam and other sting operations have uncovered such dishonesty.

Consumer Fraud

Consumer fraud consists of fraudulent promotions, dishonest business practices, and fraudulent schemes directed at buyers of products and services. Consumer frauds range from small money losses to losses of hundreds and thousands of dollars. The elderly are often targets of consumer frauds because of their vulnerability and trust in statements made by persons seeking to defraud them.

Among the most frequent consumer complaints are complaints of fraud in home improvement and repair, auto repairs, door-to-door sales, fraudulent insurance pitches, health and medical aids, land sales schemes, unlawful and deceptive charitable solicitations, and unsolicited merchandise.

Door-to-door selling can be deceptive if deceptive contract terms are used, if poor-quality merchandise is used deliberately, if nondelivery of goods ordered occurs, or if pressure selling and scare tactics are used. Generally, such victimizing occurs with uninvited sellers.

Deceptive selling practices include the "bait and switch" practice of deceptive advertising and sales.[1] The technique of "bushing" occurs when the selling price of an item is increased above that originally quoted to the purchaser. The increase occurs after the purchaser, in good faith, makes a down payment with money or a trade-in and before acceptance of a purchase order by the seller.

Charitable solicitations are fraudulent if the collectors plan to use the money for their own use or if there is no cause or organization. Fraud to obtain money also occurs if the collector falsely asserts that he (or she) is associated with a charity or religious group. Misrepresentation as to the use of the contribution could also be fraudulent, depending on the representations.

Phony billing schemes include sending out invoices and billings for merchandise, supplies, or services that were never ordered or supplied. Substantial amounts of money have been lost through carelessness and failure to recognize the scheme. Other phony billing schemes include selling "phony" advertisement or directory advertising; the publication may not exist or the ad is not run.

Fraudulent Insurance Claims

Fraudulent insurance claims can occur with any type of insurance. The claim could be for a burglary loss of property when no burglary occurred, or for property that was not stolen. It could be for a fraudulent damage claim or for the loss of property in a robbery that is a false claim. Arson for profit is the crime of arson committed to present a false insurance claim.

Medical and health insurance fraud occurs when a person uses someone else's ID card for medical care. It can occur when medical records or receipts are falsified and used to receive insurance payment. Billing for service that has not been rendered is also a fraud.

Insurance claims for damages to automobiles or injuries in phony car accidents are common forms of fraud. Insurance companies believe that they pay out millions of dollars every year in false claims.

Although motor vehicle insurance fraud occurs in every major city in the United States, California is identified as the crime capital of the country for this type of offense. Common forms of this type of fraud in California include the following:

• the "squat": a bump from behind involving two vehicles participating in the fraud

• the "swoop and squat": one vehicle swerves into another lane and strikes a vehicle from the rear

• the "rideout": a perpetrator seeks out an expensive car driven by a person of apparent wealth and rams the vehicle

Both personal injury and damages to vehicles are ordinarily claimed in this type of fraud. With the assistance of crooked lawyers and doctors, the claims can be for considerable amounts of money. Insurance executives estimate that if this type of fraud could be eliminated, insurance premiums could be lowered by up to 8 percent.

The "Con Game" as a Form of Fraud

"Con games," or confidence games, obtain their names because the swindle depends on gaining

---

Famous Cases of Fraud and Forgery

The "Hitler Diaries" In 1983, Konrad Kujau received almost $4 million from a West Germany magazine for 62 "Adolf Hitler" diaries. Kujau later admitted that he spent two years studying and practicing Hitler's handwriting before writing the forgeries.

The "Howard Hughes" Forgery In 1971, Clifford Irving received more than a million dollars from McGraw-Hill and Time, Inc. for a transcript that he represented to be a biography of the then living billionaire Howard Hughes. The fraud was discovered when Hughes broke 15 years of silence to denounce the book. Irving was convicted and received a prison term of two and a half years.

The "Mussolini Diaries" In 1968 these diaries were sold to the *London Times* for $100,000. When the forgery was discovered, experts stated that the two Italian women who had forged the papers had virtually perfected Mussolini's handwriting.

The Hoax of the "Eight-Year-Old Heroin Addict" A 26-year-old newspaper reporter won an award in 1981 for an article entitled "Jimmy's World." The article described an eight-year-old heroin addict named Jimmy. The award caused the author to admit that the writing was fictional and that Jimmy did not exist.

Other hoaxing, fraud, and forgery include letters falsely represented to be written by Abraham Lincoln and Mary Magdalene and works of William Shakespeare. Obtaining money by means of such false representations is fraud and criminal.

the victim's confidence. Most con men (or women) believe that there is a little bit of larceny in everyone. By selecting the right victim and applying the right techniques to gain the confidence of the victim, the con man goes to work.

The "short con" operation generally is limited to the money that the victim has with him at the time. Examples of "short con" games are card games where fraud is used, handkerchief switch, and dropped pocketbook or wallet. The famous "pigeon drop" is a "short con" game that usually involves all or a good portion of someone's life savings.

The "big con" operation usually takes a considerable length of time to accomplish. The confidence of the intended victim must be gained. The stage must be set and the victim lured into believing that he (or she) can make a quick profit. The "take" in the "big con" operation is generally larger than the "take" in a "small con" operation.

The *Chicago Police Department Training Bulletin* makes the following observations of con games:

> Confidence men are successful in their operations because many people are eager for the opportunity to make some "easy" money. When people have the opportunity to realize a quick profit, they fail to inquire too diligently into the legality of the transaction.
>
> Victims are often reluctant to report the crime to police due to the publicity or embarrassment that may

follow. The confidence man knows that his victim or "mark" may complain to the police. In most cases, however, he firmly believes that the victim will not complain. The fact that the victim can be "conned" out of making a complaint is an integral part of all confidence schemes. The con man usually feels he is safe, because the victim has entered into collusion with him to obtain money from someone else. The embarrassment of having to admit he was taken usually precludes a victim from notifying police authorities. Another part of the operation in favor of the con man is that the victim and the con man are friends up to the "break-away." The lapse of time that passes before the victim realizes that he has been "taken" usually gives the con man ample time to make good his disappearance.

In many instances, the intended victim is permitted to profit by dishonest means (this operation is known as the "convincer"). Then, he is induced to make a large investment and is "fleeced." The victim in these swindles is usually referred to as the "mark," "egg," "sucker," "boob," "chump" and other similar names.[2]

B. COUNTERFEITING OF MONEY AND COMMERCIAL PRODUCTS

Counterfeiting of Currency and Coins

Counterfeiting of currency and coins is a serious federal offense because it could have a severe economic impact on society. The history of counterfeiting in the United States can be summarized as follows:

● *Until and during the Civil War,* counterfeiting was a serious problem, as thousands of different

---

Big Thefts, Robberies, and Frauds

In 1984, two former officers of Drysdale Government Securities, Inc. pleaded guilty to stealing more than $270 million by computer fraud and other schemes.

In 1984, $2.7 million was missing from a vault in the Las Vegas Nevada National Bank.

In 1983, five men were charged in the nation's biggest tax scam of $130 million in phony write-offs. Victims included Sidney Poitier, Henry Mancini, Norman Lear, and others.

In 1978, robbers obtained $5.4 million from a Lufthansa airport warehouse in New York City.

In 1977, the First National Bank of Chicago lost $1 million in 50- and 100-dollar bills that were probably smuggled out of the bank in a trash bag (weight 80 lbs.)

In 1973, the Equity Funding Corporation of America lost $2 billion in a corporate fraud.

The biggest false income tax refund fraud occurred when a former IRS employee obtained refund checks totaling $560,000 before he was caught. A social security number was obtained under an alias.

legal bills were being printed by more than 1,500 state banks. It is estimated that as much as one-third of the currency used during the Civil War was counterfeit. Counterfeiting was easy during that period.

• *Establishment of a single national currency* in 1863 and creation of the U.S. Secret Service immediately made counterfeiting difficult. Counterfeiting the new currency required highly skilled persons with highly sophisticated equipment. The diligent efforts of the Secret Service made the pooling of the necessary material and equipment plus the necessary highly trained skills difficult. Counterfeiting and alteration of currency were kept at a minimum over the years.

• *Today* counterfeiting has increased as a crime because:—new printing and copying equipment and methods have made it possible for less sophisticated individuals to become counterfeiters—much of the counterfeiting of American money is done outside the United States and is either passed off to others abroad or smuggled into the United States.

Counterfeiting of Commercial Products

Designer jeans, phonograph records, videotapes of movies, electronic components, computers, books, circuit relays, and drugs are counterfeited and sold extensively in the United States. Many of the counterfeit products are manufactured in foreign countries where they are also sold under the well-known label. Usually, the counterfeit product is a cheap or inferior copy of the real thing. However, the phony label deceives many dealers and consumers who believe that they are buying the name brand product.

Importation, manufacture, or sale of a counterfeit product in the United States could result in (a) prosecution under the criminal code of a state, which would probably treat the offense as a misdemeanor; (b) civil suit and sanctions in federal or state civil courts; or (c) federal prosecution under the mail fraud statute (18 U.S.C. Section 1341), the wire fraud statute (18 U.S.C. Section 1343), the Food, Drug and Cosmetic Act (21 U.S.C. Sections 301, 321, etc.), or other federal statutes.

Counterfeiting of consumer and commercial goods and products is increasing in the United States and in other countries. American businesses and consumers who have been cheated by counterfeit products are requesting that the U.S. Congress pass additional legislation to cope with the problem.

C. THE CRIME OF TRAFFICKING IN STOLEN GOODS ("RECEIVING STOLEN PROPERTY")

The crimes of trafficking in stolen goods are defined by the statutes of each state and ordinarily include (a) receiving (a single act), (b) concealing and possessing (continuing acts), and, in some states, (c) buying and transferring. In determining the statute of limitations for these offenses, the Supreme Court of Minnesota held in the 1981 case of *State v. Lawrence:*

> The crime commonly known as "receiving stolen property," when used in a shorthand sense, is a misnomer, since it includes a number of different legal concepts in addition to and separate from receiving. The offense includes not only receiving, but concealing; . . . it includes buying; and . . . it also includes possessing and transferring. The issue here is whether any of these terms may be deemed continuing in nature. The two most likely descriptions of defendant's conduct are possession and concealment. Does either, or both, apply? In answering this question we should keep in mind that a crime is not continuing in nature if not clearly so indicated by the legislature. . . .
>
> Both possessing and concealing are distinguishable from receiving in that the latter connotes a single act. Behind possessing and concealing, however, is the notion that property is being kept from someone in violation of a duty to return and this duty to return continues. One of the reasons for including possessing and concealing as crimes is to be able to prosecute even though the time has run out on receiving. Surely this serves the purpose of the statute, which is to deter trafficking in stolen goods.
>
> *   *   *
>
> We hold, therefore, that either concealing or possessing stolen goods is a continuing offense for the purpose of the statute of limitations. We hold this defendant may not assert the statute of limitations as a bar where he kept the goods he stole in his house and garage, thereby not only possessing the goods but making their discovery more difficult for the owner.[3]

To convict of trafficking in stolen goods, it is ordinarily required that the state prove:

- that the property involved was stolen property
- that the defendant received, concealed, possessed, purchased, or transferred the property as forbidden by the statutes of that state
- that the defendant knew the property was stolen.

"Stolen" means that the property was obtained as a result of a theft, burglary, robbery, or any other form of theft crime, such as shoplifting or obtaining property by deception.

Can a Thief Be Convicted of Trafficking in Stolen Goods?

In the 1981 case of *State v. Lawrence,*[4] the defendant was convicted of possessing or concealing stolen property more than three years after the defendant took possession of the stolen property. The Supreme Court of Minnesota affirmed the conviction despite the argument that a thief cannot be convicted of possessing and concealing. The court held:

> Defendant first argues he cannot be convicted of receiving stolen property because he was the thief and he cannot receive from himself. One cannot quarrel with this logic. The statute, however, includes more than "receiving"; it applies to one who knowingly "receives, possesses, transfers, buys or conceals" any stolen property. Here both possession and concealment are present. While it may happen that one should not be convicted for stealing and concealing the same item, . . . it is acceptable to charge someone with either or both offenses and convict on only one of them. Since section 609.53 is directed at trafficking in stolen goods, it might be argued that to use the statute here against the thief is to use it for a purpose for which it was not intended. But the fact that defendant chose to keep and enjoy his stolen merchandise rather than pass it on to a fence only makes him, in a practical sense, his own fence.

The "Fence" and "Fencing" Stolen Property

A "fence" is a person who traffics in stolen property (receiving, concealing, possessing, buying, transferring, etc.). A fence acts as a middleman and pays the thief for stolen property, which the fence in turn attempts to merchandise at a profit to himself. The compensation paid by the fence to the thief is usually a small fraction of the value of the goods. The report of the President's Commission on Law Enforcement and Administration of Justice makes the following observations regarding fencing in the United States:

> Nearly all professional theft is undertaken with the aim of selling the goods thereafter. Although the thief himself may retail his stolen merchandise, he probably will prefer to sell to a fence. He thereby increases his safety by reducing the risk that he will be arrested with the goods in his possession, or that they will be stolen in turn from him. He also avoids the dangers associated with the disposal process itself. In addition, large quantities of goods which may be perishable or otherwise quickly lose their value, or for which there is a specialized demand, will require a division of labor and level of organization beyond the capacity of an individual thief operating as his own retailer. The professional thief thus needs a "middleman" in the same way and for some of the same reasons as the farmer, manufacturer, or other producer.

* * *

> Some fences engage in fencing as a supplement to their legitimate businesses, often on a more or less regular basis. The consultants learned of clothing and appliance dealers who regularly serve as outlets for stolen goods. The major outlets for stolen jewels in one of the cities studied were reported to be legitimate jewelry merchants. Other fences deal primarily or wholly in stolen goods, and are therefore professional criminals themselves.

> Some narcotics pushers act as fences, taking stolen goods instead of cash for narcotics. While dealing with addicts is generally regarded as more dangerous than dealing with nonaddicts, it is also more profitable. The addict in need of a "fix" does not bargain well.

> Little research has been done on fencing, despite its central role in professional crime. More information is needed about the nature of the market for illicit goods and the extent to which demand for various types of goods affects the incidence of theft. More should also be learned about the relationship of legitimate and illegitimate markets. Little is known about the pattern of distribution of stolen goods. When stolen automobiles are excluded, only a very small proportion of the total amount of goods stolen is returned to its owners. The redistribution of goods through theft and resale might constitute a significant subsidy to certain groups in our society; its curtailment might have significant side effects which should be explored. Finally, it would be desirable to have more information about the organization and operations of large-scale fencing operations, to aid in the development of better methods of law enforcement.[5]

Fences are hard to apprehend because they often operate behind the fronts of legitimate businesses, such as service stations, beauty salons, junkyards, jewelry stores, and taverns. Salesmen for the fence may work on factory assembly lines and in other industrial plants. People who cannot resist a bargain become an easy target for the fence and his salesmen.

Law enforcement officials are well aware that if they can put fences out of business or prevent them from operating profitably, they will minimize burglaries, shoplifting, and robberies in their jurisdictions. If there is no outlet for stolen goods, the incentive to steal is lessened considerably. One way of developing cases against fences has been through burglars who face trials with overwhelming evidence against them. Motivations that have caused burglars to testify against a fence are:

• to get even with a fence who has cheated on them

• to give up a life of crime

• to lessen the stiff prison term that they face.

When Property Loses Its Character as Stolen Goods

UNITED STATES v. MONASTERSKI
United States Court of Appeals, Sixth Circuit (1977)
567 F.2d 677, 22 CrL 2357

Three juveniles were caught attempting to steal tires from a railroad boxcar. The juveniles cooperated with FBI agents and delivered some of the tires to the defendant, whom they identified as their prospective fence. The defendant was convicted of receiving stolen property (the tires). In reversing the defendant's conviction, the Sixth Circuit held that once the thieves were caught, the tires lost their character as stolen goods and could no longer support the defendant's conviction. The court further held:

In accord with the common law rule, one cannot be convicted of receiving stolen goods when actual physical possession of the stolen goods has been recovered by their owner or his agent before delivery to the intended receiver. We further hold, also in accord with the common law rule, that the term "agent" means any person with a right to possession or control over the goods.

D. POSSESSION OF BURGLARY TOOLS

Probably all states have statutes making the possession of burglary tools a criminal offense.[6] The usual elements of this crime are:

• that the defendant had a device or implement in his possession

• that such device or implement was suitable or capable of being used in committing burglary[7]

• that the defendant intended to use such device or implement to break into a building, dwelling, or depository with the intent to steal.

Like the crime of receiving stolen property, possession of burglarious tools is also difficult to prove. The difficult element to prove in receiving stolen property is knowledge by the defendant that the property was stolen. In possession of burglarious tools, the difficult element is intent by the defendant to use such device or implement to break into a building, dwelling, or depository with the intent to steal. Possession of ordinary work tools will not ordinarily be sufficient to justify a conviction for possession of burglarious tools. There must be additional evidence of intent to use such tools for burglarious purposes.

Cases in which most convictions have been obtained can be divided into the following categories:

• The defendant was apprehended committing or attempting to commit a burglary.

• The defendant was observed under suspicious circumstances and attempted to throw away (or did rid self of) the tool.

• The defendant was in the possession of a specifically designed or adapted tool under circumstances in which a judge or jury could infer the tool's use for an illegal purpose of entry.

E. DESTROYING OR DAMAGING THE PROPERTY OF ANOTHER

No American city, town, or village escapes the physical and psychological disfigurement caused by vandalism to public and private property. Vandalism is a serious problem in most public transport systems, costing millions of dollars in large cities. Schools are often hit hard, with broken windows, break-ins, broken property, and spray paint used on walls.

Veteran law enforcement officers observe that vandalism (criminal damage to property) occurs in cycles. In the summertime, public parks are hit. Benches are piled up, debris is thrown into lagoons, and beaches are littered. If buildings are left vacant, they sometimes are vandalized to the point where they must be razed. Criminal damage to private property varies considerably and is a constant source of citizen complaint to law enforcement agencies. The types and categories of vandalism, including some of the reasons such acts are committed, are presented in the following chart.

Destroying and Damaging

Destroying and damaging can be perpetrated in many ways, depending on the physical characteristics of the property involved. Windows, glass doors, and street lights can be damaged and destroyed by rocks or hard objects. Aerosol paint can disfigure a beautiful building, wall, or landscape in a short time. A sharp object can scrape the paint on an automobile or puncture a

tire. A twist of the hand can bend or break a car antenna. Because of the terrible human danger presented by fire and the harm it can cause to property, intentional damage by fire is charged as arson in all states.

Physical Property

Persons are not ordinarily charged with theft of buildings and real property. However, criminal damage to buildings is a common criminal charge. Buildings and real estate may be easily damaged by vandalism. Grave markers, flowers, trees, shrubbery, and other property attached to the land are often also damaged deliberately. Crops, vegetables, and fruit may be the subject of theft and may also be subject to vandalism, as they may be intentionally damaged or destroyed.

Property Belonging to Another

In charging criminal damage to property, there must be a showing that the property belonged to another person and that the owner did not consent to having the property damaged or destroyed. Persons may damage or destroy their own property if they do so in a manner that does not disrupt public order or present a threat to public safety or health.

Police officers are sometimes called into a home in which the husband has destroyed an item of property, such as the television set. If the set belongs to the man and he has paid for it out of his wages, then no criminal offense ordina-

---

When Damage to Property is Not Criminal

• When the damage was not done intentionally (many states also make reckless damage to property a crime)

• When the property belongs to the defendant (the damage must be done "to the property of another" to be criminal)

• When the damage was done with the consent of the owner

• When the property was abandoned (not the property "of another") or when the owner of the property cannot be located or determined

Categories of Vandalism

Type of Vandalism	Purpose and Effects of Vandalism
Vandalism to acquire property	Damage to vending machines, telephone coin boxes, etc. to obtain money; damages to motor vehicles, homes, and other buildings to obtain parts, fixtures, or other objects.
Sign vandalism	Damaging or removing highway signs or other signs to obtain souvenirs or as a prank. As the removal or damage to highway signs has caused accidents, injuries, and deaths, statutes such as Section 86.192 of the Wisconsin Statutes specifically forbid and punish as a misdemeanor.
Tactical or protest vandalism	Property damage to call attention to a grievance or to bring about a change. This might involve damage to a jail cell or to a prison mess hall, or damage to military or construction equipment.
Ideological vandalism	Vandalism to express political and ideological ideas. This is often done through signs pasted or nailed on buildings, walls, posts, etc. Greater damage is done when spray paint is used. Such vandalism is a serious threat to public safety when arson or explosives are used.
Revenge vandalism	Vandalism as an act of revenge against a person, business, or governmental unit. Revenge could be the act of a student against a school, or the act of an employee against his or her employer.
Play vandalism	Breaking windows or street lamps as part of a play activity of a gang or group would be play vandalism. Seeing who can throw rocks the furthest or the highest might be the test of play vandalism.
Graffitti	Graffitti is also called "harmless vandalism" and consists of words or names placed on walls, bridges, sidewalks, stairs, and other objects.
Rage or frustration vandalism	Criminal damage to property done in a rage or as an expression of frustration would be referred to as malicious vandalism. This type of vandalism is often directed at an institution or some group or class.

rily has been committed. But if the man has broken a number of windows in the house deliberately, and the family is renting the house, the property of another has been damaged or destroyed.

The Requirement That the Act of Destroying or Damaging Be Intentional or Reckless

Cases often come into prosecutors' offices in which shoplifters, in their efforts to avoid being taken into custody, have broken something in a store as they were running or as they bumped into a display and knocked merchandise down. If the statute or ordinance of that jurisdiction requires that the damaging or destroying be "intentional," the shoplifter may not then be charged with criminal damage to property. However, if the statute or ordinance reads that the damaging or destroying be "recklessly" done, the shoplifter may be charged if the state can show that the conduct was "reckless." In either case, the shoplifter is civilly liable for the damage caused. Courts will sometimes, as a condition of their sentences, require that the shoplifter (or any other person damaging property) make compensation for the damage or work to repair damage caused.

F. ARSON

One of the first concerns of a fire investigator is the fire's origin. Fires can be classified by their causes as accidental fires, natural fires (caused without human intervention), arson (fires of incendiary origin), and fires of unknown origin.

Many fires are started accidentally as when children play with matches or when persons are careless with cigarettes, cigars, or pipe ashes. Some fires are of natural origin and occur without human intervention. These fires occur because of spontaneous combustion, defective heating units, faulty electrical appliances or wiring, and the like.

Arson is the deliberate, willful, and malicious burning of a building or personal property by a person. Arson is the easiest of the major crimes to commit, the most difficult to detect, and the hardest to prove in court.

It is estimated that arson kills 500 to 1,000 persons every year in the United States, in addition to injuring thousands of others. More than a billion dollars in property damages occur every year plus the loss of millions of dollars in jobs and in property taxes to local governments. Arson also causes fire insurance rates to increase significantly, passing the costs of arson on to the general public.

Motives for Arson

If it can be shown that a fire was of incendiary origin and is indeed arson, the next questions are why and who. Why a person would commit arson is important, because there usually is a motive that causes a person to burn a building or personal property deliberately. Some of the common motives for arson are:

• *For profit.* For example: (a) Persons who are in serious financial trouble will sometimes burn their own buildings or personal property in order to collect insurance money. (b) Owners of property who no longer want the property and cannot

sell it. (c) Business owners who are in financial trouble and seek to dispose of obsolete merchandise, or who want to move to a new business location.[8]

• *For revenge or out of anger.* "Spite" fires are started to retaliate against a former boss or a wife who has commenced a divorce action, or in anger over a failed love affair.

• *For political motives,* committed by political extremists or radical groups.

• *For destruction of evidence of other crimes,* such as murder, burglary, theft, or embezzlement.

Motive is important in the investigation of arson cases, because the person who might benefit from the crime is then identified as a possible suspect. When no motive for arson is apparent, the fire investigator may then suspect that the fire was set by a pyromaniac or as an act of vandalism.

The pyromaniac, or "firebug," may be a pathological fire setter who has been in trouble before. A desire for sexual excitement often motivates the pyromaniac to start a fire. Police officers should be suspicious of intoxicated persons in a crowd watching a fire. Some firebugs are able to control themselves unless they have been drinking or taking drugs. If their inhibitions are lowered, they acquire enough false courage to set a fire. Often they stay in the area to watch the fire.[9]

Arson as vandalism is often committed by juvenile thrill seekers. There is seldom a reason for this type of crime. Experienced fire investigators point out that if the fire was set in a part of a building readily accessible to the public and the "plant" was simple, the odds are great that the fire was set by a person who did not have a rational motive. A "plant" is the means of starting a fire; simple plants could be newspapers or some rubbish ignited with a match.

Essential Elements of the Crime of Arson

All states have enacted statutes that define arson. In general, most statutes require that the state prove the following elements:

• That there was a fire and that some part of the building or personal property was damaged by the fire. Mere blackening, discoloration, or blistering of the paint or parts of a building is not sufficient to prove arson of a building.[10] When the fire has not burned an actual part of a building or personal property the offense should be charged as attempted arson.

• That the fire was of incendiary origin and was willfully and intentionally set. This is the required proof of *corpus delicti* (that a crime was in fact committed). For a fire inspector to testify in court that he "suspected" arson or that the fire was of "unknown origin" is insufficient to prove *corpus delicti.*[11] An expert witness is usually required to testify specifically that arson did occur. The witness must then be able to support his or her statement with specific evidence.

• That the accused committed or was party to the crime of arson charged. Like all other crimes, the evidence required to convict a person of arson is proof beyond a reasonable doubt.

The "Torch"

If the investigation of a fire shows that it was of incendiary origin and was indeed arson, a natural suspect would be the person receiving the fire insurance, unless other motives can be shown for the crime. As arson for profit is common, further investigation must be conducted concerning the finances of the property owner. Serious financial difficulties or inability to sell the property can raise further suspicions, as these conditions could be motives for arson.

Arson for hate and spite must also be considered, along with the possibility that the crime was committed by a professional "torch" (an arsonist for hire). There are a number of professional arson rings operating throughout the United States. By hiring a "torch," the person seeking to commit arson for hate or profit would (a) have the crime of arson committed in a more "professional" manner and (b) allow himself or herself an opportunity to establish whereabouts elsewhere at the time the crime is committed. Attempting to hire a "torch" (solicitation to commit arson) is in itself a felony in most states. As arson is one of the more serious felonies of violence, such an offense is viewed as a serious threat to both property and life.

Evidence Obtained at the Scene of the Fire

Persons who are among the first to be at the scene of a fire may obtain information that could be valuable to investigating officers. Such persons should observe:

• the color of the smoke and flames, which might provide valuable information as to whether the fire is of incendiary origin and is arson. Gasoline and other chemicals burn with different colored flames and smoke.

• the size of the fire

• the speed at which it travels

• the number of separate fires

• weather conditions at the time of the fire

• persons in the area at the time and the license number (if possible) of any vehicle leaving the scene.

The U.S. Supreme Court placed restrictions on the extent of investigation that can be carried out at the scene of a fire by firefighters or law enforcement agencies. In *Michigan v. Tyler,*[12] the Court ruled that investigators may not remain on the scene of a burned building indefinitely or search indiscriminately. The rules made applicable to the firefighters and investigating officers allow them to remain on the scene without a warrant only for a reasonable time. A reasonable length of time is determined by the size of the building, the contents thereof, the extent and intensity of the fire, the time of day or night the fire occurs, and other such factors. Once the reasonable time has expired, if the fire officials wish to reenter the burned building to determine whether a code violation caused the fire, an administrative search warrant must be obtained. The Court further pointed out that even with an administrative search warrant, if probable cause that a crime has been committed is uncovered during the administrative search, the administrative search must stop and a search warrant must be obtained under the criminal procedure.

G. TRESPASS

In its broad sense, the word trespass means an unlawful act against a person, property, or right of another. For example, court decisions today continue to speak of the trespassory taking of property, meaning that the property was wrongfully taken. Murder, assault, and battery are trespassory acts because they are wrongful and unlawful acts that violate the rights of other persons.

However, in its usual and more common use, the word trespass refers to a wrongful intrusion on the land or into the premises of another person. All states have statutes that reflect this usual and common concept of the offense, and when newspapers use the word trespass, they are usually using the word in this limited sense.

A variety of trespass statutes can be found in criminal codes and municipal ordinances. The trespass to land statutes make the unlawful entry on land (when the land has been posted or the person notified to stay off) a criminal offense if the entry or the remaining on the land is without the consent of the owner or the person in lawful possession. Trespass to dwelling statutes and ordinances forbid the entry into homes and residences unless it is with the consent of an occupant.

Other trespass statutes and ordinances forbid entry into specific places, such as schools with classes in session, unless the person has legitimate business or is a parent. Trespass statutes generally have a section dealing with entry and also a section pertaining to "failure to depart." The following cases illustrate the application of trespass statutes in various jurisdictions throughout the United States.[13]

PEOPLE v. DORNER
Supreme Court (Kings County)
(1982)
458 N.Y.S. 982

During school hours, the defendant was on the fourth floor of a high school and attempted to pass himself off as a student in the school. When it was discovered that the defendant had been suspended from the high school and was unlawfully in the school, he was arrested for trespass. A search disclosed that the defendant was carrying a concealed weapon. In denying the motion to suppress the evidence obtained through the search, the court held:

A person walking through a school building under these circumstances could reasonably expect that he would be asked to account for his presence to school personnel. As recognized in People v. Scott D., *34 N.Y.2d 483, 486–487, 358 N.Y.S.2d 403: "A school is a special kind of place in which serious and dangerous wrongdoing is intolerable. Youngsters in a school, for their own sake, as well as that of their age peers in the school, may not be treated with the same circumspection required outside the school or to which self-sufficient adults are entitled."*

* * *

Since Police Officer Moore had probable cause to arrest defendant, that arrest was lawful and, therefore, the police officer had the right to search defendant as an incident to a lawful arrest.

PEOPLE v. SPENCER
Appellate Court of Illinois
(1971)
131 Ill. App. 2d 551, 268
N.E.2d 191

The defendant, a Chicago high school teacher, was given a letter of dismissal by his principal while the defendant sat at his classroom desk. The teacher was asked to leave and report to a central administrative office. The defendant refused to leave after repeated warnings that he would be arrested if he did not. He was convicted of a criminal trespass to land statute that provided that a person who remained on the land of another after receiving notice from the owner or occupant to depart is guilty of criminal trespass. The defendant argued that, as his entry into the building was lawful, he had not committed a trespass. The appellate court affirmed his conviction and $25 fine, holding that remaining on the land after he had been ordered to leave violated the statute.

STATE v. CARRIKER
Court of Appeals of Ohio (1964)
5 Ohio App. 2d 255, 214 N.E.2d 809

The defendant would not leave the premises of a business corporation when ordered to do so by officials of the firm in the presence of police officers. He was convicted of criminal trespass but argued that since his entry on the property was lawful he could not be convicted of criminal trespass. In affirming his conviction, the court stated:

In substance the defendant urges in the present case that an unlawful entry is indispensable to a conviction under the terms of the statute, and that the status of a business invitee cannot be changed to that of a trespasser. If this be so, the subject statute employs considerable unnecessary verbiage, and its practical application could lead to bizarre results. For a mild example, in comparison with the facts of the present case, is a businessman helpless against the will of a customer who refuses to leave his store after closing hours? Or for a somewhat harsher example, may a business invitee who, like the defendant in the instant case, admits that he had no intention of making a purchase, use the business premises of another for his own gain with complete immunity after his invitation has been revoked?

In our opinion, the trespass statute is not so impotent as suggested by the defendant. It not only provides that the entry upon the premises of another without lawful authority is an offense, but it also provides that remaining upon the premises of another without legal authority after being notified to leave is a misdemeanor.

OKLAHOMA v. STAHL
Supreme Court of the United States (1984)
Review denied, 34 CrL 4153, affr. Okla. Ct. App. 9 MedLRptr 1945

A nuclear power plant site had been closed to both the public and newspaper reporters. The defendants (journalists working for a newspaper) entered the grounds of the nuclear plant without consent. They were arrested and charged with criminal trespass. Their convictions were affirmed by the U.S. Supreme Court (review denied), as there was no First Amendment violation.

H. LANDLORD–TENANT DISPUTES

The police are sometimes called when disputes arise between landlords and tenants. Although some disputes between landlords and tenants should be reported to a law enforcement agency, most are not police matters. The officers responding to the calls (or the dispatcher) must therefore determine whether the complaint involves a civil or criminal matter. The parties most likely to call the police (or a sheriff department) in "civil matters" are persons who have neither the money to hire a private lawyer nor the sophistication to distinguish between civil and criminal matters. They turn to the police because they need help and cannot think of anyone else who can help them.

Landlords' Complaints

Studies show that the following reasons cause landlords to call a law enforcement agency for assistance:

• Tenant has destroyed property.

• Landlord's property or the property of another tenant stolen by a tenant.

• Tenant refuses to pay rent.

• Tenant allows garbage to accumulate.

• Tenant refuses to allow the landlord to inspect or enter the premises.

• Tenant keeps pets or animals, in violation of the lease or rental agreement.

The deliberate destruction of property is a criminal offense. But accidental destruction of property, failure to care for the property properly, and the permitting of property to deteriorate rapidly are civil matters. Theft of property, whether it be the landlord's or another tenant's, is a criminal matter. Refusal to pay rent can be aggravating to a landlord who may be hard pressed for money, but this is a civil matter.

The accumulation of garbage, or other sanitation problems, should be referred to the health or sanitation departments of the jurisdiction. Refusal to permit the landlord to enter at reasonable times is also a civil matter, as is the presence of pets or domestic animals in violation of the lease or the rental agreement.

Landlords sometimes report their suspicions that tenants are engaged in criminal activities, but unless there is sufficient evidence that amounts to probable cause, neither a search warrant nor an arrest would be justified. Such suspicions, if based on evidence, could justify referring the matter to the vice squad or to the detective bureau for further investigation.

Tenants' Complaints

Some of the complaints that tenants have made to law enforcement agencies include:

• Landlord has trespassed by entering the tenant's apartment or building without the consent of the tenant.

• Landlord has seized property of the tenant.

• Property of the tenant was stolen by the landlord.

• Landlord locked the tenant out of the premises (this is usually accompanied by a lock-in of the tenant's possessions).

• Landlord failed to provide sufficient heat (or the premises are too hot).

• Electric, water, or gas services were cut off by the landlord.

Landlords may enter the premises of a tenant if an emergency exists, such as a broken water pipe or the smell of smoke. The lease or the rental agreement may provide for entry into the tenant's premises by the landlord under specifically prescribed circumstances. However, an unauthorized entry by a landlord could possibly be charged as a trespass if it could be shown that the entry was made for an unlawful purpose or to harass the tenant. Most of the complaints by tenants, like those of landlords, are civil matters that must be settled peacefully between the parties or, if necessary, can be taken into a civil court.

I. COMPLAINTS FROM RESTAURANTS, INNKEEPERS, CAB DRIVERS, AND OTHER SERVICE SUPPLIERS

Law enforcement agencies receive a considerable number of complaints from restaurants, innkeepers, cab drivers, and other service suppliers about customers who cannot or will not pay the amount they owe for services received. Officers who handle such calls must be aware of the statutes and ordinances of their jurisdiction, because some of these matters have been made criminal offenses. Officers should be aware of the general orders of their departments, which should state departmental procedures to be used in handling such complaints.

As a general rule, officers should make reasonable efforts to settle these matters without resorting to an "order-in" or an arrest. Officers tell of situations in which a customer agreed to leave his wristwatch as a pledge with a restaurant manager until he paid the amount owed. Gasoline and other merchandise may be taken back by the merchant or service station attendants if it is not paid for, but the services of a restaurant, innkeeper, or cab driver cannot be returned.

The ability of a police officer as an adjudicator, peacemaker, and arbitrator is really put to the test in some of the street situations with which he or she is confronted in this area. If the officer cannot settle the matter between the parties, he or she may issue an ordinance citation, request that the parties appear in the city or district attorney's office, or, when necessary, make an arrest.

QUESTIONS AND PROBLEMS FOR CHAPTER 17

1. A stranger asked a well-dressed man at a shopping center if he had change for a $10 bill. The man accommodated the stranger but later found that he had accepted a $1 bill with the corners from four $10 bills pasted on it to make it appear like a $10 bill. The stranger made a profit of $9 and could have the partially mutilated $10 bills exchanged at a bank for new bills. Has a criminal violation occurred? *Larceny*

2. A California sheriff's department learned from a telephone call that a footlocker containing a large number of vials and bottles had been found in a remote area. Investigation showed that the vials and bottles had been taken in a recent burglary of a drugstore. Officers kept the footlocker under surveillance until the defendant arrived at the scene. He was heard to express relief that the "stuff" was still there and then began to bury the footlocker. Can the defendant be charged with the burglary on this information? If not, what could he be charged with? State reasons. (*People v. Schroeder*, 264 Cal. App. 2d 217, 70 Cal. Rptr. 491 [1968].) *insuficient evidence/meaning 4 Concealing Stolen property*

3. A nationally known football player was approached by a man who stated that he was a great fan of the player. The man said that he wanted to show his appreciation and offered to sell the player an expensive automobile with only a few thousand miles at less than one-fourth the retail price. The player agreed; the vehicle was delivered; cash was paid for the vehicle. The player was told that he would receive the title to the car in short time through the mail, but he never received the title. The vehicle was determined to be stolen and the true owner demanded that the vehicle be returned to him. May the owner recover the vehicle? Has the football player committed a criminal offense? How would this matter be settled?

4. A burglar apprehended in the act with burglarized goods fears a long prison sentence. He agrees to cooperate and the stolen goods are returned to him. The burglar sells the goods to his regular fence. The fence is arrested and charged with receiving stolen goods. Is the arrest and the charge of receiving stolen property valid and going to stand up in court? State your reasons. *No police must pur chase stolen items first.*

Part Five

Sex Crimes

Sex crimes occur often in the United States. The term sex crime includes a broad classification of offenses that range from serious offenses to nuisance offenses and private offenses between consenting adults.

The enforcement and definition of the more serious offenses is generally uniform throughout the United States, but the enforcement of lesser offenses varies considerably from state to state and somewhat from community to community within each state. To illustrate the wide range of sexual offenses, the following classifications are used:

1. Sexually motivated crimes in which violence is used or threatened
   - murders of lust or sexual perversion
   - forcible, violent rapes
   - sadistically motivated offenses in which sexual excitement is derived from inflicting pain or injury on other persons
   - kidnapping or abduction when violence is threatened or used
   - forceful and violent sexual attacks on children
   - pyromania (a persistent impulse to set fires, in many cases accompanied by a desire to derive sexual excitement from watching a building burn)
   - pedophilia (committed by mentally ill persons who lust for children, are capable of kidnapping them, and after using them sexually, are capable of killing them)

2. Offenses against children and mentally defective or deficient adults in which violence is not used or threatened
   - "statutory rape" or sexual intercourse with a child
   - sexual intercourse with a person known to be mentally deficient or defective
   - abduction or "enticement" when force is not used or threatened
   - incest in which force or threat of force is not used but the victim is not legally capable of consenting to act
   - child pornography (exploitation and exhibition of children for financial and sexual purposes)

3. Offenses that violate the right of privacy
   - "offensive touching" of the person of another (see the case of *People v. Thomas* in Chapter 14, in which the defendant offensively touched the buttocks of a woman on a rush-hour train in New York City)
   - window peeping (form of voyeurism)

4. Commercial offenses that are profit oriented
   - prostitution (male and female)
   - pimping and pandering
   - sexual perversion
   - sale of obscene material or presentation of obscene acts or films
   - abortion violations

5. Offenses that are not physically dangerous but are against public policy
   - forms of voyeurism

351

- public nudity forbidden by a specific statute or ordinance
- sexual acts in public places
- public nudity such as:
  - college and fraternal-type "streaking"
  - "mooning" (displaying the derriere from such places as a moving vehicle)
  - nonhumorous exposure to women and children ("flasher")
- obscenity not done for profit
- nuisances and other public indecencies

6. Private offenses between consenting adults
   - fornication
   - seduction (in states that have such statutes)
   - adultery
   - bigamy
   - incest (sexual intercourse between persons related within the degree in which marriage is prohibited)
   - homosexual relations

Chapter 18

Rape and
Related Sex Crimes

Rape is one of the most underreported crimes. The crime is one of degradation as well as violence, and fear of reprisal and embarrassment contributes to the victim's hesitation to report it. Those who do report it must confront the trauma of the encounter with the police, the investigation of the crime and the ordeal of trial.[1]

Many reasons are given for not reporting rape. If the victim knows her assailant (which is often the case in a nonreported rape), she may not report the crime because of fear of retaliation or because she does not want to get the man in trouble. The "after-the-date" rape victim may have the same feelings. The rape victim who has never seen her assailant before may believe that the police will not be able to solve the crime and therefore conclude that the trouble and embarrassment of reporting the crime would be useless. Other women may either distrust the police or dislike the prospects of having to relate their shocking experiences to male police officers. Many law enforcement agencies now have female officers available for women who find it easier to tell such matters to another woman.

A. FORCIBLE RAPE OF WOMEN AND GIRLS

Capacity to Commit Forcible Rape

Vaginal rape is the most common form of rape, with women and girls being the victims not only to rape, but also to sexual assaults and batteries. Women of any age or status may be the victims of rape, including prostitutes.[2]

Under the old common law, a husband could not rape his wife. This concept was probably adopted by all states. A husband could be charged with assault or battery if he used considerable force to compel his wife to have sexual intercourse with him against her will. However, the new sexual assault laws that almost half the states adopted in the 1970s changed this concept. State statutes in many states now permit husbands to be charged with the rape of their wives under the conditions established by the statutes of the state in which the rape is committed.

Under both the old rape laws and the new sexual assault laws, a husband can be charged as a party to the crime of rape (either as a principal or as an aider and abettor) if he assisted, hired,

encouraged, or procured another man to rape his wife. A woman cannot be charged with raping another woman, but she can be charged as a party to the crime of the rape of another woman if she hired, encouraged, assisted, or procured a man to rape another woman.[3]

In the Missouri case of *State v. Drope*,[4] the defendant and four other men tied the defendant's wife to a bed, and while the defendant held a gun to her head, each of the men had sexual intercourse with the woman. The Supreme Court of Missouri affirmed the defendant's conviction as a principal to the crime of the rape of his wife.

In the 1981 case of *State v. Thomas*,[5] the defendant was found guilty of two counts of first-degree criminal sexual conduct when he forced a woman, at gunpoint, to perform fellatio on her husband. The defendant then forced the woman to perform fellatio on himself. The Supreme Court of Tennessee affirmed the two convictions, holding that a "defendant who forces an innocent party to commit armed robbery, burglary, rape, incest, etc. is guilty as the only principal, even though the defendant does not commit the crime with his own hand." (See Chapter 4 on criminal liability.)

Essential Elements of the Crime of Forcible Rape

The usual elements of the crime of forcible rape are:

- proof that a sex act (as defined by the statute) occurred
- proof that force (actual or constructive) was used to perform the sex act
- proof that the sex act was done "without consent" and "against the will" (these terms being synonymous in the law of rape [6]).

Proving That Actual Force Was Used

Proof of actual force that will corroborate and affirm the statements of the victim could be:

- witnesses who observed (and also colored photographs of) bruises, black and blue marks, lacerations, cuts, scratches, and injuries on the victim
- scratches and injuries to the suspect

Classifications of Rape

Type of Rape		Most Common Defense Used
Forcible rape by a stranger	Because rape is the crime least often reported to law enforcement officers, statistics vary. One study shows that ⅔ of forcible rapes occur between strangers*, whereas another study reports that in ½ the offenses, the parties are strangers.†	Victim or other witnesses have identified the wrong man (mistaken identification).
Forcible rape by an acquaintance, friend or relative	Many of these offenses are not reported to law enforcement agencies. The "after-the-date" rape is particularly hard to prosecute unless substantial evidence is available.	Victim consented to the sexual act.
Nonforcible rape in which the victim is under age of consent	All states have laws that protect infants and children from sexual seduction by adults. Such statutory rape or SIWAC (sexual intercourse with a child) laws punish as a major crime such sexual intercourse (or sexual conduct) when committed with a child.	Sex act did not occur or that the defendant made an honest mistake as to the child's age (not permitted as a defense in most states).
Nonforcible rape in which the victim was mentally defective or diseased and incapable of giving consent	This type of criminal statute seeks to protect persons who are mentally incompetent and incapable of giving consent to sexual acts. The offense requires that the state show that the defendant knew of mental incapacity of the victim.	Defendant denies that he knew of the mental incapacity of the victim or that any sex act occurred.
Nonforcible rape in which the victim is unconscious	Such statutes seek to protect persons who are unconscious (the defendant is aware of this condition). Some statutes also forbid sexual intercourse with a person known to be in a stupor. Such stupor could be caused by alcohol or drugs.	Defendant asserts that the person was conscious and consented or that no sex act occurred.
Sexual intercourse by deception	Such statutes punish sexual intercourse in which the victim is deceived into thinking that the act is a marital act. For example, a phony wedding is staged by the defendant.	No deception or sexual act occurred.
Sexual intercourse obtained by threats other than threats of violence, which would be forcible rape	In the few states that have enacted a statute such as this, the threat might be to disclose information that the victim did not want disclosed. Today, job-related sexual harassment is remedied through civil proceedings or in other ways.	No threat was made or implied or no sexual act occurred.

* "Forcible Rape: A National Survey of the Response by Police," National Institute of Law Enforcement and Criminal Justice, U.S. Department of Justice.

† Criminologist Freada Klein

- blood, semen, saliva, nail scrapings taken from the victim or suspect, as well as pubic and head hair obtained at scene of crime and from the bodies of the victim and suspect
- weapons or instruments that may have been used to force the victim to submit to the assault
- buttons, torn clothing, items that victim or suspect may have lost in the struggle
- soiled or stained clothing of the suspect and victim that contains blood, seminal stains, or other evidence of the crime
- fingerprints found at the scene of the sexual assault or elsewhere that can be used to corroborate or to identify the suspect
- observations by doctors, nurses (and samples of fluids) from vagina, rectum, oral cavity showing that forcible intercourse had occurred.

The physical evidence collected and preserved by investigating officers could provide strong or conclusive evidence of guilt. On the other hand, lack of physical evidence could result in a weak case.

Proving That the Victim's Fear of Imminent Death or Serious Bodily Injury Was Genuine and Real

If little or no actual force was used, the state must then show that the victim's resistance was overcome by the threat of the use of force or that a genuine and real belief existed that imminent force would be used. The California courts have held that: "While generally the woman has the power to determine for herself the extent to which she feels she can safely resist, . . . her conduct must always be measured against the degree of force manifested and each case must be resolved on all of the circumstances present." [7]

The Maryland Court of Appeals pointed out in 1981 [8] that the "vast majority of jurisdictions have required that the victim's fear be reasonably grounded in order to obviate the need for either proof of actual force on the part of the assailant or physical resistance on the part of the victim." [9] Pointing out that the reasonableness of a victim's apprehension of fear was plainly a question of fact for a jury to determine, the Maryland Court of Appeals held:

> It was for the jury to observe the witnesses and their demeanor, and to judge their credibility and weigh their testimony. Quite obviously, the jury disbelieved Rusk [defendant] and believed Pat's [victim] testimony.

> * * *

> Just where persuasion ends and force begins in cases like the present is essentially a factual issue, to be resolved in light of the controlling legal precepts. That threats of force need not be made in any particular manner in order to put a person in fear of bodily harm is well established. . . . Indeed, conduct, rather than words, may convey the threat.

> * * *

> That a victim did not scream out for help or attempt to escape, while bearing on the question of

Why Are Rapes and Murders Frequently Combined?

The FBI Uniform Crime Reports show an almost 50 percent increase in the number of forcible rapes reported in the 10 years from the early 1970s to the early 1980s. During this period, women became more assertive and were more likely to report and cooperate in the prosecution of offenders. Plausible explanations for the association between rape and murder are:

• the rapist may have been known to the victim and the rapist may have killed the victim to avoid identification and prosecution
• resistance by the victim may have lead to confusion and panic and may have escalated and increased violence on the part of the offender.

Serial killers Christopher Wilder (rapist) and John Wayne Gacy (homosexual) and others like them would not come within these explanations.

consent, is unnecessary where she is restrained by fear of violence.

Defenses Used to the "After-the-Date" Rape Charge

Close to one-half of the forcible rapes that are reported are committed by friends, acquaintances, or relatives. The "after-the-date" rape (or "dates who rape") case can be particularly difficult to prove unless evidence of actual physical violence exists. Because of the friendly and sometimes close relationship that existed between the parties, the man can often convincingly argue:

• The woman consented to the sex acts because, after all, she came up to his apartment or she invited him up to her apartment.
• "It is a defense to a charge of forcible rape that the defendant entertained a reasonable and good faith belief that the female person voluntarily consented to engage in sexual intercourse" (*California Jury Instruction* 10.23). [10]

Acquaintance and Date Rapes

In 1983, almost 60% of the 400 plus sexual assault cases prosecuted in Milwaukee County were acquaintance and date rape charges. There was close to an 85% rate of conviction or guilty pleas to these cases. Theories attempting to explain the acquaintance and date rape problem are:

- male aggressiveness based on attitudes of:
  —stereotyping of sex roles, with males as the dominant sex and women as the weaker sex
  —callousness toward the victim and desensitivity toward the act of rape
- miscommunication between the sexes of various types but often including a male belief that the incident will not be reported

Acquaintance and date rape is the most underreported felony in the United States (petty theft is the most unreported crime). Of the reported cases, some are too weak to prosecute as felonies because of lack of convincing evidence. In others that go to trial, the defendant is acquitted.

- Therefore, "if the defendant had a bona fide reasonable belief based upon 'all of the circumstances present' that the prosecutrix [woman] voluntarily consented, the defendant must be acquitted of forcible rape."[11]

To obtain an acquittal ("not guilty") or a "hung jury," the defense has only to raise a reasonable doubt in the minds of one, some, or all the jurors that (a) the woman consented to the sex, (b) the man reasonably believed that she consented, or (c) there is a reasonable doubt as to the guilt of the defendant.

Forcible Rape Cases That Cannot Be Established by Proof Beyond a Reasonable Doubt

A rape case could be classified as a "weak" case if there is a lack of evidence of resistance by the woman, if there is insufficient testimony as to

genuine fear of injury, or if the woman became so upset that she was unable to testify effectively.

In anticipating such problems, prosecutors could file a number of charges, including lesser charges to fall back on. Examples of such charges are:

- *Sexual battery or sexual assault.* For example, see the 1983 case of *People v. Margiolas,* in which the rape charge was dropped owing to lack of evidence of resistance, and the defendant was convicted of "sexual battery," as he admitted that he forcibly unbuttoned the woman's blouse despite her verbal as well as physical objections.[12]

- *"Statutory rape",* in which the victim is underage. In the 1981 case of *Michael M., v. Superior Court of Sonoma County (California),*[13] a forcible rape of a 16½-year-old girl was committed by the defendant, who was then 17½ years old. Because the state was unable to present proof sufficient to obtain a conviction for forcible rape, the defendant was charged with and convicted of "statutory rape." The U.S. Supreme Court affirmed the conviction. The California prosecutor stated in his brief that the "statutory rape" statute "is commonly employed in situations involving force, prostitution, pornography, coercion due to status relationships, and the state's interest in these situations is apparent." Justice John Paul Stevens dissented, stating:

> I cannot accept the State's argument that the constitutionality of the discriminatory rule can be saved by an assumption that prosecutors will commonly invoke this statute only in cases that actually involve a forcible rape, but one that cannot be established by proof beyond a reasonable doubt. That assumption implies that a State has a legitimate interest in convicting a defendant on evidence that is constitutionally insufficient. Of course, the State may create a lesser-included offense that would authorize punishment of the more guilty party, but surely the interest in obtaining convictions on inadequate proof cannot justify a statute that punishes one who is equally or less guilty than his partner.[14]

- *Sodomy and/or Kidnapping.* Sodomy (or "sexual perversion" or "an abominable and detestable crime against nature") does not require a showing of the use of force for conviction. The following case illustrates:

STATE v. SANTOS
Supreme Court of Rhode Island (1980)
413 A.2d 58

The victim met the defendant at a tavern where they talked and danced for three hours until closing time. After having a cup of coffee at a nearby restaurant, the woman testified that the defendant grabbed her and would not let her go. The defendant told her to get into his car and stated that he had a knife, which he would use if he had to. The woman was driven to a secluded area, where the defendant first had sexual intercourse and then anal intercourse with her. The woman stated that she was too afraid to resist other than to push the defendant away. The defendant asked that she not complain that she had been raped, as two other women had previously done so. The jury acquitted the defendant of rape and kidnapping but convicted him of transporting for immoral purposes and committing an abominable and detestable crime against nature (anal intercourse). The Supreme Court of Rhode Island affirmed the convictions.

• *Burglary* is defined as an unlawful entry into a building or dwelling with intent to commit an offense (in some states a "felony") or intent to steal. The following case is not a forcible rape case but illustrates how the crime of burglary may be charged:

CLADD v. STATE
Supreme Court of Florida (1981)
398 So.2d 442

The defendant was separated from his wife (no legal action commenced). One morning he used a crowbar to break into her apartment, in which he had no possessory interest. He struck the woman and attempted to throw her over a second-floor stair railing. The next morning he attempted to break into the apartment again but left as the police arrived. The defendant was convicted of burglary and attempted burglary. In affirming the convictions, the Supreme Court of Florida held:

Since burglary is an invasion of the possessory property of another, where the premises are in the sole possession of the wife, the husband can be guilty of burglary if he makes a nonconsensual entry into her premises with intent to commit an offense, the same as he can be guilty of larceny of his wife's separate property.

The Effect of Delay in Reporting

After a sexual assault, the victim is many times confused and fearful of her assailant returning. This often results in a delay in the reporting of the assault to the authorities. Such delay can seriously weaken the possibilities of a conviction. Not only does the delay raise the question of credibility concerning the allegations of the victim, but it also substantially diminishes the possibility of obtaining physical evidence concerning

---

Sexual Assault Cases That Received National Attention

New Bedford, Massachusetts Six men were charged with raping a 22-year-old woman who went into a bar to buy cigarettes and stayed for a quick drink. The woman was raped on a barroom pool table while other men in the bar cheered.

Akron, Ohio A physician charged with 60 counts of raping and terrorizing women received prison terms totaling 665 years. Under Ohio law, the doctor technically will be eligible for parole in 9½ years, but it is unlikely that he will be released that soon.

Wisconsin A man who was sentenced to 60 years in prison for the rape and attempted murder of a 15-year-old girl was released after 8½ years, when semen tests showed that he was innocent. (In 80% of tests, semen shows the blood group. If the assailant in a rape case has had a vasectomy, uses a condom, or was infertile, no sperm will be found to use as evidence.) The man received $500,000 in settlement of a lawsuit against his defense attorney and $85,260 from the state to compensate for his time in prison.

New Hampshire Christopher Wilder was killed when he resisted arrest. Wilder abducted, sexually assaulted, and murdered eight young women in Florida, Texas, Oklahoma, and other states. In 1979, Wilder was charged with attempted rape and pleaded guilty to the lesser charge of attempted sexual battery, for which he received five years' probation.

Madison, Wisconsin A Wisconsin judge, in 1982, sentenced a man to three years' probation for fondling (sexual assault) the five-year-old daughter of his girlfriend. The judge commented on the record that the little girl was "an unusual, sexually promiscuous young lady." These comments caused voters to petition for the judge's recall, which resulted in his defeat in the following election.

---

the offense. Even if such physical evidence is found, the intervening period of time weakens the probative value of the evidence, since it raises the possibility that the evidence found came from a source other than the assailant.

False Charges

The FBI Uniform Crime Reports state that "a national average of 15% of all forcible rapes reported to police were determined by our investigations to be unfounded. In other words, the police established that no forcible rape offense or attempt occurred."

It should be noted, however, that sexual assault is not the only offense subject to false reporting. Burglaries and auto thefts are frequently reported falsely for the purpose of obtaining insurance money; armed robberies of single-employee businesses are falsely reported to the financial benefit of that employee; and one can only speculate about the number of homes, businesses, and other buildings that are destroyed in "accidental" fires.

Rape Shield Laws

Many states have passed rape shield laws that limit the extent to which a defense lawyer can inquire into the details of a rape victim's sex life and practice. These laws were passed to protect victims of rape and to encourage women to report rape and cooperate in prosecuting offenders.

The National Organization for Women (NOW) urges that neither specific acts of prior sexual conduct nor evidence of the previous general reputation of the victim for unchastity should be admitted.

All courts permit defense lawyers to ask the victim whether she has ever had sexual relations with the defendant. If she answers no, this would then generally close the door to further questions. However, if the woman answers yes, then further questions may be asked as to the sexual relationship.

In the 1984 case of *State v. Vaughn,*[15] the defendant was convicted of raping a 15-year-old runaway. Evidence was permitted showing that she had slept several nights in a bed with the defendant and two other women and had had sex with the defendant. The Supreme Court of Louisiana held that it was proper to forbid evidence that the girl had sex with another man after she left the defendant and before the rape.

B. THE SEXUAL ASSAULT STATUTES OF THE 1970s AND 1980s

In the early 1970s, there was much criticism of the traditional rape statutes used by most states. These statutes generally followed the old common law and presented many problems in prosecuting rape offenders. In the mid-1970s, states commenced enacting comprehensive "sexual assault" laws, which brought about some or all of the changes indicated in the following chart:

C. HOMOSEXUAL RAPE

Males may be raped by forcible anal sodomy and other forms of homosexual rape. Such offenses are not as common as rape of women except, as reports indicate, within prisons. U.S. Supreme Court Justice Harry A. Blackmun wrote in his dissenting opinion in the 1980 case of *United States v. Bailey:*

> A youthful inmate can expect to be subjected to homosexual gang rape his first night in jail, or, it has been said, even in the van on the way to jail. Weaker

---

Traditional Rape and the New Sexual Assault Laws

Old Common Law Rules Regarding Rape	*Statutory Changes Enacted in Many States*
• Only females can be the victims of rape.	• Any person (male or female) may be a victim.
• Only a male could directly commit the crime.	• Any person (male or female) can directly commit the crime.
• A husband could not rape his wife (under the common law, however, the husband could be charged with assault and battery).	• A husband can be charged with the rape of his wife under the law of states that have made this change from the old common law.
• Rape was defined in one (or at most a few) degree.	• A variety of degrees of criminal conduct are defined in more specific language.
• Rape was defined only as the insertion of the penis into a vagina by force and against the will of the female.	• "Sexual intercourse" is broadly defined not only as vaginal intercourse, but also "cunnilingus, fellatio, anal intercourse, or any other intrusion, however slight, of any part of a person's body or of any object into the genital or anal opening of another, but emission of semen is not required" (Section 940.225[5][c] of the Wisconsin Criminal Code).
• Common law rape did not include the crime of "offensive touching" (however, this could be charged either as disorderly conduct or assault and sometimes battery if there was an injury).	• Many modern sexual assault laws include the offense of "offensive touching" in that they forbid "sexual contact" (intentional touching of an intimate part of another person's body without consent).
• As consent by the victim was a total defense, the common law tended to focus on the resistance offered by the victim in determining this issue.	• The new statutes focus on the degree of force threatened or used and the degree of harm done in determining the issue of consent.
• Rape was classified as a crime against sexual morality.	• Sexual assault is more often classified as a crime against a person.

inmates become the property of stronger prisoners or gangs, who sell the sexual services of the victim. Prison officials either are disinterested in stopping abuse of prisoners by other prisoners or are incapable of doing so, given the limited resources society allocates to the prison system. Prison officials often are merely indifferent to serious health and safety needs of prisoners as well.[16]

The defendant in the 1984 case of *United States v. Boone* [17] testified that he used a razor blade in self-defense because he feared that the complainant was going to forcibly commit anal sodomy on him. As the trial judge did not believe the defendant and concluded that the issue was weak, he did not give a jury instruction on self-defense. The court of appeals reversed, holding that this issue should have gone to the jury. Pointing out that a woman who had alleged such facts after cutting up another person would be entitled to instructions on self-defense, the court held that the results should be the same "unless we are to make sexist differences."

D. "STATUTORY RAPE"

Probably all states have statutes that make sexual intercourse with a female who is not the wife of the perpetrator a criminal offense if the female is under the age stated by the state criminal code. This crime is called "statutory rape." The origin of the American statutes go back to the English statute of 1275, when the age of consent was set at 12 years. In 1576, the age was reduced to 10 years. California, for example, enacted their first statute in 1850 making the age 10. In 1913, it was fixed at 18, where it remained into the 1980s.

In 1981, the California "statutory rape" statute was challenged before the U.S. Supreme Court, when it was alleged that the statute unlawfully discriminates on the basis of gender, since men alone were criminally liable under the statute. The Court upheld the power of the states to enact such statutes in the case of *Michael M. v. Superior Court of Sonoma County,* [18] holding:

> We are satisfied not only that the prevention of illegitimate pregnancy is at least one of the "purposes" of the statute, but that the State has a strong interest in preventing such pregnancy. At the risk of stating the obvious, teenage pregnancies, which have increased dramatically over the last two decades, have significant social, medical and economic consequences for both the mother and her child, and the State. Of particular concern to the State is that approximately half of all teenage pregnancies end in abortion. And of those children who are born, their illegitimacy makes them likely candidates to become wards of the State.
>
> We need not be medical doctors to discern that young men and young women are not similarly situated with respect to the problems and the risks of sexual intercourse. Only women may become pregnant and they suffer disproportionately the profound physical, emotional, and psychological consequences of sexual activity. The statute at issue here protects women from sexual intercourse at an age when those consequences are particularly severe.
>
> The question thus boils down to whether a State may attack the problem of sexual intercourse and teenage pregnancy directly by prohibiting a male from having sexual intercourse with a minor female. We hold that such a statute is sufficiently related to the State's objectives to pass constitutional muster.
>
> Because virtually all of the significant harmful and inescapably identifiable consequences of teenage pregnancy fall on the young female, a legislature acts well within its authority when it elects to punish only the participant who, by nature, suffers few of the consequences of his conduct. It is hardly unreasonable for a legislature acting to protect minor females to exclude them from punishment. Moreover, the risk of pregnancy itself constitutes a substantial deterrence to young females. No similar natural sanctions deter males. A criminal sanction imposed solely on males thus serves to roughly "equalize" the deterrents on the sexes.

Many states have statutes that do not permit the defense of mistake as to the age of a minor. In such states, a defendant could not argue before a jury that he honestly made a mistake as to the age of a minor. However, other states do not have such statutes. The 1984 case of *State v. Elton* [19] occurred before the Utah legislature disallowed a mistake of fact as to age of a minor as a defense. In the *Elton* case, the Utah Supreme Court held the defendant could use the defense.

E. SEXUAL ABUSE AND EXPLOITATION OF CHILDREN

In 1982, the U.S. Supreme Court stated in *New York v. Ferber*: [20]

> In recent years, the exploitive use of children in the production of pornography has become a serious na-

tional problem. The federal government and forty-seven States have sought to combat the problem with statutes specifically directed at the production of child pornography. At least half of such statutes do not require that the materials produced be legally obscene. Thirty-five States and the United States Congress have also passed legislation prohibiting the distribution of such materials; twenty States prohibit the distribution of material depicting children engaged in sexual conduct without requiring that the material be legally obscene.

The defendant in the case of *New York v. Ferber* challenged the child pornography law of New York. The U.S. Supreme Court stated that:

- 19 states prohibit the dissemination of material depicting children engaged in sexual conduct, regardless of whether the material is obscene
- 15 states prohibit the dissemination of such material only if it is obscene
- 12 states prohibit only the use of minors in the production of the material.

The U.S. Supreme Court gave the following reasons for holding that state child pornography statutes do not violate the First Amendment of the U.S. Constitution:

First. It is evident beyond the need for elaboration that a state's interest in "safeguarding the physical and psychological well being of a minor" is "compelling.

Increased Public Awareness of Child Sexual Abuse

Events in 1984 that increased public awareness of sexual abuse of children:

- More than 100 counts of sexual abuse of children were filed against three teachers at a California preschool and three family members of the 76-year-old headmistress of the school.
- Investigations in Minneapolis resulted in arrests for child molesting. Among those arrested was the director of the Children Theatre Co.
- U.S. Senator Paula Hawkins of Florida disclosed at a Senate hearing that she had been sexually abused when she was five years old. The matter went to court, but the judge dismissed the matter.

. . . A democratic society rests, for its continuance, upon the healthy well-rounded growth of young people into full maturity as citizens."

* * *

Second. The distribution of photographs and films depicting sexual activity by juveniles is intrinsically related to the sexual abuse of children in at least two ways. First, the materials produced are a permanent record of the children's participation and the harm to the child is exacerbated by their circulation. Second, the distribution network for child pornography must be closed if the production of material which requires the sexual exploitation of children is to be effectively controlled. Indeed, there is no serious contention that the legislature was unjustified in believing that it is difficult, if not impossible, to halt the exploitation of children by pursuing only those who produce the photographs and movies. While the production of pornographic materials is a low-profile, clandestine industry, the need to market the resulting products requires a visible apparatus of distribution. The most expeditious if not the only practical method of law enforcement may be to dry up the market for this material by imposing severe criminal penalties on persons selling, advertising, or otherwise promoting the product.

* * *

Third. The advertising and selling of child pornography provides an economic motive for and is thus an integral part of the production of such materials, an activity illegal throughout the nation.

* * *

Fourth. The value of permitting live performances and photographic reproductions of children engaged in lewd sexual conduct is exceedingly modest, if not *de minimis.* We consider it unlikely that visual depictions of children performing sexual acts or lewdly exhibiting their genitals would often constitute an important and necessary part of a literary performance or scientific or educational work.

* * *

Fifth. Recognizing and classifying child pornography as a category of material outside the protection of the First Amendment is not incompatible with our earlier decisions.

F. THE CRIME OF INCEST

The crime of incest may be committed by adults within a family, but the public concern and prosecution are generally for cases involving children. Like "statutory rape," the crime does not require a showing that force was used (or threatened) or that the victim did not consent.

Incest was not a crime at common law, nor was it statutorized in England until 1908. Before that time, the offense was dealt with by the English ecclesiastical (religious) courts. Probably all the states have statutes making the offense a crime.

An article entitled "Incest: The Last Taboo," in the January 1984 *FBI Law Enforcement Bulletin,* states:

> One thing every State has in common is the prohibition of marriage between parents and children, between siblings, between grandparents and grandchildren, uncles and nieces, and aunts and nephews.
>
> Incest is usually defined as sexual exploitation between persons so closely related that marriage is prohibited by law. While this definition indicates that there is sexual intercourse, it is important to note that not all incestuous relationships involve intercourse. The term "intercourse" refers specifically to sexual activity between two individuals of the opposite sex. Beyond this usual definition are two other types of sexual child molestation that are closely related to incest and share some common features.
>
> The first type, psychological incest, does not require that the individuals be blood relatives. It only requires that the adult assume the role of a parent. This type of incest extends to other nonrelated family members as well, such as step-uncles and aunts and step-siblings. This type of incest often occurs in families that include a step-parent, a foster parent, or a live-in boyfriend of the mother.
>
> The second type of incest involves sexual contact between persons of the same sex, such as father/son, mother/daughter, or siblings of the same sex. Because, father/son and mother/daughter incest are basically unstudied areas, very little can be written about

their frequency of occurrence, the dynamics of the situation, the traumatic effects, or mode of treatment. It is known that in these types of incest, the parent is usually either a latent or overt homosexual.

The article also points out that it is estimated that between 60,000 and 100,000 female children are sexually abused annually and that 80 percent of sexual abuse is not reported. It is believed that incest affects more than 10 percent of all American families, with at least 5,000 cases of father/daughter incest.

Penalties for incest, the article reports, range from 90 days to life imprisonment. Enforcement, however, is practically impossible unless a member of the family cooperates. Unfortunately, the credibility of the child victim is often attacked and severely questioned.

In 90 percent of cases, the victim is female and the abuse may commence while the child is too young to realize the significance of the problem. When the child becomes knowledgeable about what has happened, or is happening, the child will probably feel guilt, betrayal, confusion, and fright.

The defendant in the case of *Hamilton v. Commonwealth* [21] was convicted of both rape and incest, resulting from a single act of sexual intercourse with his then 10-year-old daughter. The Supreme Court of Kentucky held that the two convictions for the single act violated double jeopardy and vacated the incest conviction. The conviction for rape was affirmed with the life imprisonment sentence. However, the state appealed the ruling and the matter was before the U.S. Supreme Court in 1984.

QUESTIONS AND PROBLEMS FOR CHAPTER 18

From the following choices, indicate the criminal charge, if any, in the questions:

X, who is a 24-year-old man, should be charged with:

a. rape or sexual assault (indicate which and the degree)

b. sexual perversion or deviate sexual conduct

c. indecent and improper behavior or liberties with a child

d. attempt to commit one of the above

e. none of the above (if he should be charged with an offense not listed, specify the offense as statutorized by the laws of your jurisdiction)

   1. X, by using great physical force and striking blows, forces his wife to have sexual intercourse with him.* 1st deg

2. X has nonmarital sexual intercourse with a 15-year-old girl who consented to the act.

3. X takes his 20-year-old girlfriend to a city in another state for a weekend. They share a hotel room.

4. X forces a woman to perform oral copulation on him.

5. X forces a 12-year-old boy to submit to anal copulation.

6. A 12-year-old boy consents and submits to an act of anal copulation with X.

7. X is caught stealing bras and panties from washlines.

8. X is impotent and knows that he cannot complete the sex act. He violently assaults a woman with intent to rape her and is apprehended during his assault.

9. X touches and fondles the genitals of a 12-year-old girl.

10. X touches and fondles the genitals of a 10-year-old boy.

11. X had a six-year-old neighborhood girl in his house for over an hour when no one else was in the house. The girl stated that X kissed her, but there was no evidence of any other sexual behavior.

12. Without permission from the boy's parents, X took an eight-year-old boy in his car for several hours. X bought the child candy, but there was no evidence of sexual misconduct.

13. In a one-hour assault on a woman, X rapes her and forces her to perform oral copulation with him. May X be charged with any other offense in addition to rape?

14. X encourages his girlfriend to drink a great amount of liquor at a party. Because of her intoxicated condition, he is able to have sexual intercourse with her for the first time. The next day she accuses him of rape. Should he be charged?

Chapter 19

Prostitution
and Related Crimes

A. PROSTITUTION

The offense of prostitution can be one of at least three non-marital acts:

1. engaging in sexual relations with another person for a fee or something of value
2. offering (or soliciting) to engage in sexual relations with another person for a fee or something of value
3. requests (or agrees) to pay a fee or something of value to another person for sexual services and acts

The "fee" or "something of value" is most often money. Members of either sex may now be convicted of prostitution as distinguished from the past, when only women could be convicted. Most (if not all) state prostitution statutes forbid prostitution by males selling sexual services to other males. Males who offer to pay a woman to engage in sex acts may also be charged with the crime if the statutes of that jurisdiction apply to both sexes.

Often referred to as the oldest profession, prostitution has been described in history's earliest written records. The Bible, for instance, makes many references to whores and whoremongering. Prostitution is an activity that grows and recedes, depending on the changing mores and morals of a particular civilization. Many believe that, like the poor, it will always be with us.

Throughout the world efforts have been made to suppress, control, organize, or discourage prostitution, with varying degrees of success. Prostitutes range from the common streetwalker to the privately kept woman or man. In England and France, prostitution is legal, but publicly soliciting customers is against the law. In some countries, particularly in the Orient, government-inspected houses of prostitution are allowed.

Efforts to decriminalize prostitution in the United States have met with little success. Only one state (Nevada) has legalized prostitution. In Nevada, each county has the option as to whether prostitution will be legalized. Fifteen of Nevada's seventeen counties have decided to remove the legal restraints against prostitution.

Why Do States Make Prostitution a Crime?

The Commentary to the Hawaiian prostitution statute refers to the Delaware Commentary and states: [1]

> History has proven that prostitution is not going to be abolished either by penal legislation nor the imposition of criminal sanctions through the vigorous enforcement of such legislation. Yet the trend of modern thought on prostitution in this country is that "public policy" demands that the criminal law go on record against prostitution. Defining this "public policy" is a difficult task. Perhaps it more correctly ought to be considered and termed "public demand"—a widespread community attitude which the penal law must take into account regardless of the questionable rationales upon which it is based.

*   *   *

> Our study of public attitude in this area revealed the widespread belief among those interviewed that prostitution should be suppressed entirely or that it should be so restricted as not to offend those members of society who do not wish to consort with prostitutes or to be affronted by them. Making prostitution a criminal offense is one method of controlling the scope of prostitution and thereby protecting those segments of society which are offended by its open existence. This "abolitionist" approach is not without its vociferous detractors. There are those that contend that the only honest and workable approach to the problem is to legalize prostitution and confine it to certain localities within a given community. While such a proposal may exhibit foresight and practicality, the fact remains that a large segment of society is not presently willing to accept such a liberal approach. Recognizing this fact and the need for public order, the Code makes prostitution and its associate enterprises criminal offenses. [2]

Sexual Conduct That Constitutes Prostitution

Modern prostitution statutes generally forbid not only vaginal intercourse, but also oral sex (cunnilingus and fellatio), anal intercourse, masturbation, and, in many instances, sexual contact.

As most cases that go into a court involve police decoys, solicitation to commit any of these acts are almost always the basis of the criminal charge. Defendants in such cases are women who solicit male undercover officers, men who proposition female officers, and male prostitutes offering sex for a fee.

Is a Home a Protected Zone of Privacy for Prostitution?

In the 1983 case of *State v. Mueller,*[3] the defendant offered to provide sexual services for hire in the privacy of her apartment. Neither street nor public solicitation was used. The persons involved were consenting adults. There were "no signs of advertising" anywhere in the apartment building.

The Supreme Court of Hawaii affirmed the defendant's conviction, holding that her right of privacy in her home did not give her a right to practice prostitution in her home in violation of the criminal code. The court quoted the U.S. Supreme Court, holding:

> The sum of experience, including that of the past two decades, affords an ample basis for legislatures to conclude that a sensitive, key relationship of human existence, central to family life, community welfare, and the development of human personality, can be debased and distorted by crass commercial exploitation of sex. Nothing in the Constitution prohibits a State from reaching such a conclusion and acting on it legislatively simply because there is no conclusive evidence or empirical data.

Old Offenses That Are No Longer Crimes or Are Seldom Charged

Offense	Definition	History
Bigamy (or polygamy)	Marriage to two or more spouses at the same time	Statutorized in 1604 (prior to that time was an ecclesiastical crime in England)
Adultery	Voluntary sexual intercourse in which one or both parties are married to another person (parties not married to one another)	Goes back in history to old Roman law
Fornication	Voluntary sexual intercourse between two unmarried persons	Formerly a crime in all states. Some states have removed this offense and adultery from their criminal codes.
Seduction	Enticement by a male of an unmarried woman of prior chaste character to have sexual intercourse	Was a crime in early English law and in many states
Miscegenation	Intermarriage (and in some states living together) of persons of different races (generally white and black)	Was a crime in some of the states. Such statutes were declared unconstitutional by the U.S. Supreme Court in the case of *Florida v. McLaughlin* (see Chapter 12)
Buggery (or bestiality)	Any type of sexual intercourse with an animal or, in some states, anal intercourse with a man or woman (now charged under other statutes)	A statutory offense in England until 1967. Some states also used either or both of these terms to forbid this conduct.
Blasphemy, profanity, and indecent language	Cursing or reviling God; unbecoming, not decent or impious language	Can no longer punish for language violations unless the language falls within one of the crimes listed in Chapter 10.
Abortion	Causing the expulsion of a human fetus prematurely.	Previously a crime in all states. States may not now make abortion a crime until the third trimester of pregnancy. Some states no longer have a crime of abortion (see Chapter 12).

Organized Crime and Prostitution

The National Advisory Committee on Criminal Justice Standards and Goals makes the following observations in its report on organized crime:

> Prostitution was one of organized crime's early rackets, dating from the turn of the 20th century. Unfortunately, not much has been written about how organized crime got into and ran the operations, or where illegal syndicates were most heavily involved.

*   *   *

> One form of prostitution—streetwalking—probably became too conspicuous and hard to regulate for organized crime. It is the street prostitute whom the police arrest most frequently, and she may have a bad reputation because of prostitution-related crimes (e.g., robbery of customers, assault, etc.). Also, . . . streetwalkers have pimps, who serve the practical functions of providing bail and clients. It has been said that organized crime does not want to be involved with pimps, believing that they are stupid, unreliable, and treacherous. . . . Thus it seems that organized crime, when it is involved in prostitution, has concentrated on call girls and the brothel trade, employing a variety of legal fronts such as massage parlors and "rap" and "encounter" joints.

*   *   *

> Organized crime has also invented some ingenious gimmicks involving prostitution. For one, prostitutes apply for computer dates, enabling them to obtain economic data on prospective "pigeons" who are then set up to be robbed. Others are placed in public relations companies, which they then represent at business conventions, an ideal situation for blackmailing the men they entice.[4]

Procuring, Promoting, and Pimping for the Practice of Prostitution

Many prostitutes operate without pimps or other persons procuring or promoting for them. Some prostitutes, however, have pimps who could procure customers and provide protection and bail as needed. In addition to pimps, other persons could obtain money by procuring and promoting prostitution.

Procuring, promoting, and pimping for prostitution are generally forbidden by state criminal codes. Because of financial gains, this group of persons have a motive to encourage and coerce young persons into prostitution. They increase the volume and extent to which prostitution is practiced and often gain a vicious hold over the prostitutes they work with.

The means used to profit and to advance prostitution varies from serious offenses to minor violations. These offenses can be classified generally as follows:

- Criminal coercion by force, drugs, or other means to compel persons to remain in prostitution. This offense is further aggravated when it is used against young persons.
- Advancing or profiting from prostitution by operating or owning a house of prostitution or a business or enterprise involving prostitution. Such a person could be a madam or a person involved in a call girl ring. However, the New Jersey courts held in *State v. Alveario* that the owner of a hotel who rented out rooms knowing that the rooms were being used for prostitution could not be convicted of solicitation.[5]
- Small-scale promoters and procurers, such as taxicab drivers, bartenders, hotel doormen, and clerks, who set up customers for prostitutes or provide other services.

The Offense of Loitering to Solicit Prostitution

Many cities and states have ordinances and statutes that create the offense of loitering to solicit prostitution. Such laws do not require proof of prostitution or solicitation to commit prostitution, but instead are addressed to streetwalkers who are loitering for the purposes of soliciting for prostitution. To prove this offense, the city or state must generally show:

- that the defendant was in an area used by prostitutes or from which complaints of prostitution had been made
- that the defendant was on the street and was seen waving to strangers in cars or approaching and talking to strangers on the street
- that it could reasonably be concluded from the appearance, dress, conduct, and activity of the defendant that his (or her) conduct in that area was for the purposes of soliciting prostitution

---

Prostitution

Prostitutes may operate (a) independently, (b) under the control of a pimp, (c) as part of an organized syndicate, (d) with persons other than the above.

Type of Operation	Type of Complaint Received by Law Enforcement Agencies
Streetwalkers (and prostitutes who operate out of taverns and bars)	• From business establishments (restaurants, hotels, etc.) when streetwalkers hurt business by driving customers away • From homeowners when streetwalkers are walking in their neighborhood • From women who have been mistaken for prostitutes by cruising men • From men who have been embarrassed or annoyed by prostitutes • From customers complaining of theft, robbery, etc. of their wallets, credit cards, or other personal property *This is the form of prostitution most visible to the public. Streetwalkers are also most susceptible to arrest by law enforcement officers.*
Call girls	Generally, only customer complaints *Unless call girls have developed their own customers, they must rely on others to pander for them. Pimps, bartenders, cab drivers, etc. could be used to refer customers to call girls.*
Employees of "massage parlors," "artist's studios," "model shops," etc.	Generally only customer complaints. However, legitimate businesses in the neighborhood of "massage parlors," etc. are apt to complain to their local or county government. Persons living in the neighborhood are also likely to complain.

• that the defendant was given an opportunity to explain his or her conduct and was unable to provide and show a satisfactory explanation.

In the 1981 case of *City of Portland v. Marshall*,[6] the defendant challenged the Portland loitering-for-prostitution ordinance. The defendant argued that "failure to give a satisfactory explanation or a good account of one's conduct" was an element of this crime and that it shifted the burden of proof to her and also violated her privilege against self-incrimination. The court ruled against the defendant and held that a "satisfactory explanation" was not an essential element of this offense, holding: "The defendant is not required to prove intent, or lack thereof, or that he or she was engaged in a lawful activity. Of course, if the defendant chooses to testify and his or her testimony discloses a lawful purpose,

the testimony would provide a defense for the jury's consideration." However, some state statutes and city ordinances that punish the offense of loitering to solicit prostitution have been declared unconstitutional under the void-for-vagueness doctrine.

B. SODOMY OR DEVIATE SEXUAL INTERCOURSE (CONSENTING ADULTS)

Homosexuality has received a great deal of attention in recent years in the United States. Homosexual adults living together and engaging privately in homosexual relations generally have no legal problems. The military services, however, continue to discharge persons for homosexuality.

In 1983, the U.S. Navy discharged 1,167 personnel, including 12 officers, for homosexuality.

Many states continue to have sodomy (or deviate sexual intercourse, or sexual perversion) statutes in their criminal codes. These statutes could be used, and their constitutionality have been affirmed by the U.S. Supreme Court in the 1976 case of *Doe v. Commonwealth.*[7] This case involved consenting adult males who privately engaged in homosexual relations. The Court affirmed the criminal charge, holding "that the sodomy statute, so long in force in Virginia, has a rational basis of State interest demonstrably legitimate and mirrored in the cited decisional law of the Supreme Court."

The criminal charge of sodomy (or deviate sexual intercourse) is generally used only when such acts are committed in public. However, the following cases illustrate the use of such criminal charges for acts done in private:

Crimes Against and By Homosexuals

Murders of homosexuals: Committed by (a) "pickups" or "tricks," (b) persons who hate gays, or (c) lovers or other homosexuals in an angry argument

"Fag bashing": Persons who hate homosexuals beat them and sometimes rob them (in past years, many of these incidents were not reported to the police).

"Gacy-style" murders: John Wayne Gacy slew 33 young men and boys in the Chicago area after homosexually assaulting them, in 1980. In 1983, police investigated a series of similar murders in northern Indiana.

Assaults, batteries, knifings, and disorderly conduct: Result from lovers' quarrels and fights between homosexuals

---

KELLY v. STATE
Court of Special Appeals of
Maryland (1980)
412 A.2d 1274

A woman testified that she was abducted at knifepoint from a shopping mall by the defendant and another man. She was taken to a secluded area, where she was assaulted, raped, and forced to engage in fellatio. She was then released and reported the incident. The defendant and his friend each took the witness stand and testified that the woman voluntarily had sexual relations with each of them and also performed fellatio on each of them several times. The jury found the defendant not guilty on all charges where force or threat of force was an element but found the defendant guilty of count six, "perverted sexual practices." The court affirmed the conviction, holding:

Appellant argues that inasmuch as fornication is not prohibited by Maryland law, persons indulging in private, consensual acts of sodomy are denied equal protection of the law. The argument is that there is no essential difference between vaginal intercourse and other sex acts. He also argues that any punishment for sodomy is cruel and unusual. Once again we repeat, we will not invalidate laws of such ancient vintage without clear authority from higher courts.

STATE v. POE
Court of Appeals of North
Carolina (1979)
252 S.E.2d 843, appeal dismissed by U.S. Supreme Court,
27 CrL 4023 (1980)

The defendant was charged with rape and committing a crime against nature with a woman. The Court dismissed the rape charge and the jury found the defendant guilty of sodomy. The defendant appealed, arguing that North Carolina made fellatio a crime between unmarried persons, but it was not a crime if done by married persons in North Carolina. In affirming the conviction, the court held:

In this state, fornication and adultery have been proscribed [forbidden] since at least 1805. . . . We believe the state, consistent with the Fourteenth Amendment, can classify unmarried persons so as to prohibit fellatio between males and females without forbidding the same acts between married couples. We hold that the constitutional right of privacy does not protect the defendant in this case.

C. PUBLIC SEX ACTS

Private sex acts between consenting adults are rarely charged as crimes even if they violate specific sections of criminal codes. Public sex acts, however, are charged as criminal conduct. The following cases illustrate:

UNITED STATES v. LEMONS
United States Court of Appeals, Eighth Circuit (1983)
697 F.2d 832

The defendant and another man were observed in a toilet stall in Hot Springs National Park men's room engaging in oral sex. Defendant was convicted of violating the Arkansas sodomy statute under the assimilative crimes statutes and appealed. In affirming the conviction, the court held:

Lemons contends that public sexuality is not the issue here. To the contrary, we find that Lemons' public sexual conduct is the sole issue here. We remain unconvinced that the constitutional right to privacy extends to Lemons' conduct, much less that the State of Arkansas does not have a compelling interest in limiting public sexuality, even if arguably given some constitutional protection, to prohibit oral sex in a public restroom within the confines of a national park.

CAMMACK v. STATE
Texas Court of Appeals (1982)
641 S.W.2d 906, 32 CrL 2137

The defendant was convicted of the Texas public lewdness statute when he followed a police officer into a peep show booth in a porn shop and fondled the genitals of the officer. The court held that the offense occurred in a public place, even though the defendant closed the door to the booth. In affirming the conviction, the court held:

The public nature of the booth could not be changed by the appellant, acting alone, closing and locking the door, closeting himself with a stranger. [Note: If the defendant were alone in the booth with the door closed, a right of privacy would exist.]

STATE v. BLACK
Supreme Court of Arkansas (1977)
545 S.W.2d 617

The defendant was observed engaging in oral sex while in the "drunk tank" of a jail. Other inmates could observe the two men, and families and visitors coming into the jail had to pass the "drunk tank." In holding that the "drunk tank" was a public place within the meaning of the public sexual indecency statute, the Supreme Court of Arkansas held:

Summarizing, what is a public place? Primarily, the circumstances must be considered. While the fact situation was different, the language of the

Maryland Court of Appeals in the indecent exposure case of Messina v. State, *212 Md. 602, 130 A.2d 578, we think, succinctly answers the question asked. There, the court said: "An exposure is 'public,' or in a 'public place,' if it occurs under such circumstances that it could be seen by a number of persons, if they were present and happened to look."*

D. HARASSMENT AS AN OFFENSE

Cities and states have enacted offenses entitled "harassment," "mashing," "hassling," etc., which prohibit such conduct as improper accosting, ogling, insulting, pursuing, following, molesting, touching a person of the opposite sex whom the defendant does not know. The primary purpose of such statutes and ordinances is to protect women and young persons from behavior that can be menacing and threatening. There are different types of harassment.

Sexual Harassment

Sexual harassment can be a criminal or civil offense. It is defined as unwelcome sexual advances or requests for sexual favors that may be combined with other verbal or physical conduct of a sexual nature. Ordinarily, women and girls are the victims of sexual harassment but occasional cases concern men who are the victims of unwelcome sexual advances that amount to sexual harassment. Workplace sexual harassment could occur when:

• the boss expects submission by an employee to sexual harassment as an explicit or implicit term or condition of employment
• pay raises, promotions, type of work, etc. is used as a reward for submission to sexual harassment and providing sexual favors
• such conduct interferes with work performance or creates an intimidating, hostile, or offensive working environment.

Regulation of Nudity by States or Municipalities

Place of Nudity	Manner in Which Nudity May Be Regulated
Public nudity (public beach or public place, such as street)	May be forbidden or regulated by a specific statute or ordinance
Nude entertainment or nudity in a place licensed to serve alcoholic beverages	May be forbidden or regulated under the authority given to states by the Twenty-first Amendment of the U.S. Constitution to regulate the sale and use of alcohol. The U.S. Supreme Court stated that "the broad sweep of the 21st Amendment has been recognized as conferring something more than the normal state authority over public health, welfare, and morals." (*California v. LaRue,* 409 U.S. 109, 93 S. Ct. 390 [1973])
Nudity in a private place (a nudist camp for example) or in a stage play or in a movie ("Hair" and "Oh Calcutta," for example). Such places do not sell alcoholic beverages nor are they public places in this sense.	May not be regulated unless the conduct or display is obscene. Nudity, by itself, is not obscene, lewd, or indecent.

Telephone Harassment

Before 1966, few states had criminal laws dealing with harassing, abusive, or obscene telephone calls. However, because of the increased volume of complaints received during the 1960s, all the states and the federal government have now enacted statutes making such telephone calls criminal offenses.[8]

Harassing, abusive, or obscene phone calls include the deliberate obscene call, threats, the cruel hoax, bomb scares and threat of bombs, and the "silent" call, in which the person answering the telephone hears nothing or hears breathing on the other end of the line. Criminal charges may be issued in all the above cases if it is apparent that the call was deliberate and made with intent to harass, abuse, or threaten another person. However, charges should not be issued if it appears that the person has dialed a wrong number and simply does not explain the error.

The Illinois telephone harassment statute, which outlaws "harassment by telephone," was found to be constitutional by the Illinois Supreme Court in the 1980 case of *Parkins v. Illinois.*[9] The appeal to the U.S. Supreme Court was dismissed for want of a substantial federal question.

Other Types of Harassment

In the 1979 case of *State v. Keller,*[10] the Oregon Court of Appeals held that spitting on another person could be "offensive physical contact" within the meaning of the Oregon statute forbidding harassment. Spitting on another person could also be charged as an "assault" or "disorderly conduct" if such an act violates these statutes.

QUESTIONS AND PROBLEMS FOR CHAPTER 19

1. An adult boy scout leader conducted a number of "lollipop" initiations. In this ceremony, scouts blindfolded new recruits and had them kiss another boy's hand or arm. Meanwhile, another scout drops his pants and bares his buttocks. When the blindfold is removed, the recruit thinks that he has kissed a bare rear end. The adult boy scout leader was said to have played the bottomless role himself. He did not touch or fondle any of the boys with intent to arouse sexual desire. Sexual parts of the body were not exposed or touched. The scouts and the boy scout leader viewed the whole matter as a joke. Should the boy scout leader be charged with a criminal offense? If so, what charge? (*People v. Feuling,* 411 N.E.2d 1106 [Ill. App. Ct. 1980])

2. Mr. Metzger (an adult) lived in a ground floor apartment. Another tenant saw Metzger standing nude in front of a large window one morning in his apartment, which faced the parking lot. When police officers responded to the tenant's call, they observed Metzger standing in front of the window, nude, eating a bowl of cereal. Metzger was standing near the window with his body visible from the thighs up. What action should the officers take regarding Metzger? (*State v. Metzger,* 319 N.W.2d 459 [Sup. Ct. Nebr. 1982])

Part Six

Other Criminal Conduct

Chapter 20

Organized Crime
and Gambling

A. THE DANGER OF ORGANIZED CRIME

1967 In many ways organized crime is the most sinister form of crime in America. The men who control it have become rich and powerful by encouraging the needy to gamble, by luring the troubled to destroy themselves with drugs, by extorting the profits of honest and hardworking businessmen, by collecting usury from those in financial plight, by maiming or murdering those who oppose them, by bribing those who are sworn to destroy them. Organized crime is not merely a few preying upon a few. In a very real sense it is dedicated to subverting not only American institutions, but the very decency and integrity that are the most cherished attributes of a free society.

—President's Commission on Law Enforcement and Administration of Justice in 1967

1970 Organized crime in the United States has three goals: exploitation, corruption and destruction. What it cannot directly exploit, it seeks to corrupt; what it cannot directly corrupt, it seeks to destroy. Its degrading influence can be felt in every level of American society, sometimes in insidious, subtle ways, but more often in direct acts of violence and illegality. It is a malignant growth in the body of American social and economic life that must be eliminated.

—Former President Richard Nixon on the establishment of the National Council on Organized Crime on June 4, 1970

1983 Organized crime today is a more dangerous and pervasive force than ever before. It affects virtually every aspect of our nation and its economy.

—Federal Appeals Judge Irving Kaufman, Chairman of the 1983 President's Commission on Organized Crime

B. CRIME IN AMERICA IS DOMINATED BY ORGANIZED CRIME

In outlining the duties and responsibilities of the Pennsylvania Crime Commission, Pennsylvania statutes define "organized crime" as:

The unlawful activity of an association trafficking in illegal goods or services, including but not limited to gambling, prostitution, loan-sharking, controlled substances, labor racketeering or other unlawful activities or any continuing criminal conspiracy or other unlawful practice which has as its objective large economic gain through fraudulent or coercive practices or improper governmental influence.

Organized Crime Is More Than the Mafia

FBI Director William Webster stated in testimony before the President's Commission on Organized Crime that organized crime is no longer synonymous with one group—the Mafia or Cosa Nostra—but includes many other groups that present serious growing threats to the nation. Among these groups are the relatively new phenomenon of prison and motorcycle gangs.

Webster testified that "although these criminal groups have often been glamorized in books, movies and television, they are associations of career criminals who operate with utter contempt for our laws and the rights of others. In short, they are purveyors of crime, violence, death and human misery."

The Mafia is widely known throughout the world. Many law enforcement officers call it La Cosa Nostra. The Chicago branch, which is believed to have several hundred members, is called the "Outfit."

The Mafia is a small organization when compared with the impact they have on American life and economics. The FBI estimates that the Mafia numbers about 5,000 "made men," or members. All Mafia members are of Italian ancestry, with most having roots in Sicily.

Although the Mafia is a small organization, it is the most experienced, diversified, and possibly the best disciplined. It also has the greatest financial resources of all criminal groups.[1]

Many other organized groups of mobsters and criminals exist in the United States. Some are ethnic groups, such as blacks and Hispanics. Some run rackets in a particular area, whereas others are involved in criminal activity, such as drugs. Prison and motorcycle gangs are rapidly growing threats in the United States.

Not only is the Mafia the best organized of the criminal groups in the United States, but they also have contacts with many of the other organized criminal groups. These affiliates and contacts (whether in a group or not) create a confederation that is estimated by some criminologists to number at least 50,000 criminals.

This confederation of organized and professional criminals dominates much of American crime. The Attorney General of the United States, in testifying before the Senate Judiciary Committee, stated that the "profits of organized crime are so huge that we have been outmanned and outgunned in the battle." In pointing out that more organized crime figures are going to jail, he stated that the problem of organized crime "remains a gigantic one."

Dangerous Motorcycle Gangs

During the Fourth of July weekend in 1947, the small California town of Holister was taken over by a motorcycle gang. The gang literally tore the small community apart. They intimidated everybody with their violence and their numbers. The incident drastically demonstrated the dangerous potential of motorcycle gangs. Because of their success, membership in the gang grew and they took the new name of "Hell's Angels."

Today, it is reported that there are more than 900 dangerous motorcycle gangs in the United States. Many of the gangs are large; they have acquired sufficient money to finance themselves and have developed sophisticated organizations capable of committing more than street crimes.

New mobility and flexibility have been obtained by some of the gangs using other means of transportation when committing crime. Testimony of gang members show that they have taken contracts for murder from the Mafia and have acted as "enforcers" and "muscle" to collect debts from criminal activities.

The Big Four of Motorcycle Gangs

Of the 800 motorcycle groups thought by law enforcement officers to be dangerous groups, the following are not only the largest, but also the most sophisticated, well-organized groups, with regular organization structures:

Hell's Angels The oldest and most famous of the gangs, this group concentrates on the West Coast. Its Oakland, California, chapter is considered the most important. Hell's Angels have chapters in Europe, Australia, and New Zealand. The Hamburg, West Germany, chapter was shut down in 1983 with the arrest of 28 members for extortion, white slavery, and other offenses. It is thought that the strong-arm enforcers of the U.S. gang is the "Filthy Few."

The Pagans This group is found mostly in the mid-Atlantic states. The Pagans have tangled with the Mafia in Philadelphia and have not backed down from the La Cosa Nostra, whom they consider a bunch of old men.

The Bandidos Found mostly in the Southwest, the strong-arm enforcement group for the Bandidos is thought to be the "Nomads."

The Outlaws This group is concentrated in the Midwest and on the East Coast. In a clash with the Hell's Angels in Charlotte, North Carolina, members of both groups were seriously injured and killed. T-shirts worn by some of the group say, "God Forgives, Outlaws Don't."

Other information regarding these gangs thought to be just a step below the Mafia in sophistication:

• The rank-and-file members of the gangs seem to take special efforts to appear menacing and tough. Many never clean their filthy motorcycle vests. Tattoos are common. When the tattoo "1%" is seen, it refers to the statement of the American Motorcycle Association that 99 percent of the nation's motorcyclists are decent, law-abiding citizens.

• It seems that to be a member of one of the "big four" gangs, the person must be white and must operate a U.S.-made Harley-Davidson motorcycle. Imported bikes are commonly referred to as "Jap scrap."

• The gangs are believed to be heavily involved in the illegal drug trade. Fights and disputes between gangs occur apparently over control of illegal rackets.

Some of the criminal activities motorcycle gangs have been involved in are theft, prostitution, narcotics, illegal weapon violations, extortion, burglary, forgery, counterfeiting, welfare fraud, arson, loan sharking, murder.

Violence Among Organized Criminals

Organized criminal groups are not operated on democratic principles. Power in many gangs is obtained by force. When treachery or murder is used to advance, fear and suspicion will almost always continue to exist.

The old saying that there is no honor among thieves is probably true. Terrible violence erupts periodically among criminal groups and criminals. Such murder and violence could be the result of:

• internal struggles within gangs over money, policy, or power

• warfare between gangs, attempted mob rubouts, family rivalries, or struggle for control of rackets or territories

• attempts to retaliate or revenge acts of violence

• belief that an individual has violated the code of silence and has provided information to law enforcement or to a rival gang

• an attempt to rob or prevent a robbery of money or drugs (law enforcement officers conducting drug raids have stated that criminals sometimes express relief that it is a police raid and not a raid by a rival, warring gang)

Mafia violence has been portrayed to the public through movies, books, and TV series. Similar wars were fought in the 1980s over the cocaine trade in southern Florida. When cocaine reaches the United States, it is distributed by "cocaine cowboys," who are, for the most part, Colombians and Cubans. Hundreds of murders have occurred in smuggling the drug and protecting the racket.

As the profits in the cocaine trade are gigantic, "cowboys" and rival criminals became increasingly well armed and violent. Elaborate intelligence and counterintelligence systems are used, and suspected squealers are subject to exe-cution. The "cowboys" cannot request assistance from law enforcement nor can they go to the police to report the crime if a million dollars worth of cocaine is stolen.

C. CRIMINAL PROFITS: WHERE DO THEY GO?

Who Does the Banking for Criminals?

Most narcotic and other such criminal transactions are cash transactions. The offender receiving the cash often has the problem of determining what is to be done with huge amounts of cash. As $20 bills are commonly used in the purchase of narcotics, cardboard boxes of cash can accumulate quickly.

Taking this money to a U.S. bank or other financial institution would create problems, as large cash transactions are recorded as such and are routinely scrutinized. The Internal Revenue Service may obtain such records and this information could be used to build a tax case.

Criminals do not want their governments to know where they are banking and they want their banking records kept secret. In past years, Switzerland has been a good haven for "flight money." However, under a 1977 treaty between the United States and Switzerland, access to Swiss bank-deposit information is now given to U.S. prosecutors for certain white-collar crimes. In another former haven, the high court in the Cayman Islands ruled that Cayman banks must open their records if the information is vital in the prosecution of a crime that is also a crime in the Cayman Islands.

Panama has now become a leading tax haven to which "flight capital" is attracted. In 1983, the U.S. Senate Permanent Subcommittee on Investigations warned that because of changes that have occurred in other tax havens, "in 10 years much of the European and Western world's criminal money will reside in Panama." Panama is therefore becoming a leading banking system for criminals.

To ship money out of the United States to Panama or another tax haven, the criminal also violates U.S. custom laws, which require declarations when more than $5,000 is taken out of the country. As illegal drugs are a major source of profits for criminals, law enforcement officers are not only looking for illegal narcotics coming into their countries, but they are also on the alert for large cash shipments going out of their countries.

Panama City is only two and a half hours by plane from Miami, Florida, which is the U.S. distribution center for illegal cocaine and marijuana shipped from South America. Many of the major drug traffickers in the United States are Hispanic, and they prefer doing business with banks in Spanish-speaking Panama rather than European bankers or English-speaking Cayman Islanders. Shipments of dollars to Panama are increasing in size and volume. In 1983, a Miami accountant, Ramon Milian-Rodriquez, was arrested in Florida when he attempted to take $5.4 million in cash by air from Miami to Panama.

Laundering "Dirty" Cash

Criminals and racketeers do not report to the Internal Revenue Service that they support themselves and their families by committing crimes. They need a source of reportable income for income tax purposes in reporting to federal and state tax departments. The reportable income must be large enough to justify the standard of living of the criminal and his family.

Acquiring a legitimate business is therefore a common procedure. Legitimate businesses can be profitable in themselves. "Dirty" money might be held until it can be "laundered" through a legitimate business and returned in a "clean" reportable form to the owner. The owner then reports this amount to federal and state tax departments.

Shipping cash out of the United States is necessary in illegal drug trafficking to pay for further shipments of narcotics in South America and elsewhere in the world. "Laundering" dirty money can also be done outside the United States. This service, when combined with banking criminal dollars, can be profitable. Customs agents report that in the 1980s, Panama has become the No. 1 country for laundering narcotic dollars.

Loan Sharking as a Criminal Investment and as a Criminal Banking Venture

Loan sharking has always been a profitable source of income for organized crime and racketeers. Not only is it a profitable criminal investment, but the loan sharker also often acts as another form of a banker for criminals.

The loan sharker will finance criminal ventures, such as narcotic purchases. Such loans are made at high rates of interest. Failure to repay a loan could result in brutality or death. Gamblers will borrow from loan sharks to pay gambling debts or may find that if they run up a gambling debt, the obligation has been turned over to a loan shark.

Persons who are threatened by a loan shark for failure to pay a large debt will sometimes become a police informant or will become a witness for the government as a way out of their dilemma.

D. ORGANIZED CRIME INVESTMENT IN LAWFUL BUSINESSES

An article in the November 1981 *FBI Bulletin*, "How Illicit Funds Are Acquired and Concealed," states:

Today, it is estimated that organized crime has invested more than $20 billion into between 15,000 and 50,000 business establishments in the United States. It is estimated that annually, organized crime businesses take in at least $48 billion in gross revenues, with about $25 billion in untaxed profits. If these figures are accurate, it becomes obvious that organized crime has historically been successful in concealing from law enforcement officials and legitimate businessmen the true nature and origin of funds invested in business enterprises. . . .

Alphonse Capone, the infamous gangster of the 1920's is said to have amassed a fortune of $20 million in a 10-year period through such illegal activities as bootlegging and gambling. Yet, when Capone was sentenced to 11 years in prison in 1931, it was for an income tax evasion conviction, not because he had been charged with any of these illegal activities.

The conviction of Capone taught other organized crime members an important lesson: Money not reported on an income tax return is money that cannot

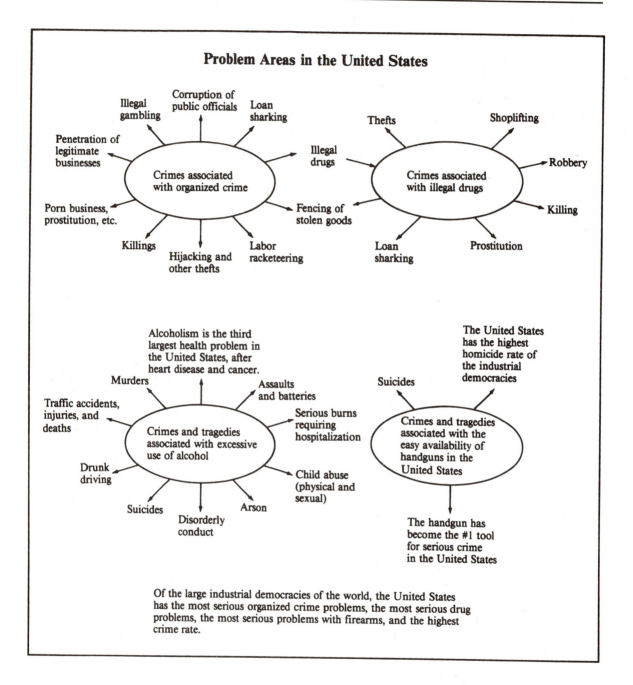

Problem Areas in the United States

Crimes associated with organized crime
- Illegal gambling
- Corruption of public officials
- Loan sharking
- Illegal drugs
- Penetration of legitimate businesses
- Porn business, prostitution, etc.
- Killings
- Hijacking and other thefts
- Labor racketeering
- Fencing of stolen goods

Crimes associated with illegal drugs
- Thefts
- Shoplifting
- Robbery
- Killing
- Loan sharking
- Prostitution

Crimes and tragedies associated with excessive use of alcohol
Alcoholism is the third largest health problem in the United States, after heart disease and cancer.
- Murders
- Assaults and batteries
- Serious burns requiring hospitalization
- Traffic accidents, injuries, and deaths
- Child abuse (physical and sexual)
- Drunk driving
- Suicides
- Disorderly conduct
- Arson

Crimes and tragedies associated with the easy availability of handguns in the United States
The United States has the highest homicide rate of the industrial democracies
- Suicides
The handgun has become the #1 tool for serious crime in the United States

Of the large industrial democracies of the world, the United States has the most serious organized crime problems, the most serious drug problems, the most serious problems with firearms, and the highest crime rate.

be spent or invested without risk of detection and prosecution.

Since most monies collected by organized crime activities are from illegal sources such as loansharking, prostitution, gambling, or narcotics, the individual racketeer is understandably reluctant to report the income and its source on his tax return. Before spending or otherwise using these funds, it is necessary

that these monies be given an image of legality so that they can be reported on a tax return without revealing the true nature of their origins. This process of conversion is known as "laundering."

*   *   *

While laundering money can be accomplished in a wide variety of legitimate businesses, it should be recognized that certain domestic businesses have characteristics which lend themselves to successful laundering operations. For example, the business selected as a "laundry" must be capable of absorbing a large volume of cash income, since most illicit income is received in the form of cash. The purpose of laundering funds is to commingle licit and illicit monies so that they cannot be separated, whole simultaneously preventing the discovery of the introduction of illegal monies into the business. Since almost all checks and credit card receipts are traceable by law enforcement officials, businesses such as restaurants, bars, and massage parlors, which normally take in a high proportion of cash, tend to be more desirable as a potential "laundry" than a business normally receiving most of its income in the form of checks or other traceable financial instruments.

Another favorable characteristic for a "laundry" is relatively fixed expenses which do not vary with sales volume. An example of such a business is a movie theater showing pornographic films. The expenses of such a business (rent, electricity, wages) are almost constant, regardless of whether the theater is full. Illicit income can be introduced and camouflaged in this type of business quite easily, since the additional sales volume does not result in a proportional increase in business expenses. Law enforcement officials who later examine the records of such a movie theater would have a difficult time proving that the actual or "legitimate" income generated by the theater was much less than that recorded on the books and reported to the taxing authorities.

Businesses that normally experience a high rate of spoilage or other loss of goods also have a high potential for being used to launder money. Groceries and restaurants are good examples, since some spoilage of goods is expected during the normal course of business. When such a business is controlled, large blocks of illicit money are introduced into the business and recorded in the general income accounts of the grocery store or restaurant as if this money were received from customers. Fraudulent invoices for produce or other perishable items are then issued to these businesses by other mob-owned or mob-controlled companies acting as suppliers. The grocery store or restaurant either issues checks to these "suppliers" or records the transaction as a cash payment and charges the expenditure to an expense account, such as cost of goods sold. The undelivered produce or perishable items listed as spoiled and discarded are written off the books.

By using this method, the grocery store or restaurant avoids substantial tax liability on large blocks of illicit monies introduced into the business, since this income is offset by corresponding expenses relating to the nondelivered goods. The funds paid to the "supplier" by the grocery or restaurant have taken on an image of legality and may be spent or invested with

very little risk of discovery. Within a week of this "transaction," it is almost impossible for law enforcement officials to disprove the story of the grocer or restaurant owner.

E. ILLEGAL PRACTICES AFTER TAKING OVER LEGITIMATE BUSINESSES

When organized criminals take over legitimate businesses, do they run the businesses in a lawful way? The National Advisory Committee answered this question in the Task Force Report on Organized Crime:

> In recent years, organized crime has acquired a large number of legitimate businesses—either by direct purchase, using funds accumulated from illegal activities, or by forfeiture because of gambling debts, or through foreclosure on usurious loans. Once acquired, such businesses may be operated legitimately, but, more often than not, illegal practices are used to increase profits. The Task Force Report describes one such practice, involving bankruptcy fraud:

> *With the criginal owners remaining in nominal management positions, extensive product orders were placed through established lines of credit, and the goods were immediately sold at low prices before the suppliers were paid. The organized criminal group made a quick profit of three-quarters of a million dollars by pocketing the receipts from sale of the products ordered and placing the firm in bankruptcy without paying the suppliers.*

> Other types of frauds sometimes perpetrated after an organized crime takeover of a business include fraudulent stock sales and arson of the business property (committed with intent to defraud the insurance company).

> When organized crime takes over a business or enters the field of labor, it brings with it a variety of criminal techniques that supplement ordinary business activity in a manner designed to extract extra profits. Bribery and illegal kickbacks are used extensively. In addition, the President's task force found that, "Strong-arm tactics are used to enforce unfair business policy and to obtain customers . . . ," and that "[I]nfiltration of labor unions . . . provides opportunities for stealing from union funds and extorting money by threats. . . ."

> The fact that organized crime is heavily involved in commercial vice and illegal activities in connection with otherwise legitimate businesses does not mean that it has abandoned traditional crimes, such as theft and receiving stolen property. Looting and pilferage frequently accompany organized crime's entry into

legitimate activities, and receiving stolen property can itself be big business.

F. CORRUPTION OF PUBLIC OFFICIALS

In 1967, the President's Commission on Law Enforcement stated:

All available data indicate that organized crime flourishes only where it has corrupted officials. As the scope and variety of organized crime's activities have expanded, its need to involve officials at every level of government has grown. And as government regulation expands into more and more areas of private and business activity, the power to corrupt likewise affords the corrupter more control over matters affecting the everyday life of each citizen.[2]

In 1983, the Attorney General of the United States, in testifying before the Senate Judiciary Committee, cited instances of huge payments to law enforcement officials to ignore organized criminal activities. He stated: "The dollar amounts involved are so great that bribery threatens the very foundations of law and law enforcement."

The Criminal Justice Standards and Goals Task Force Report on Organized Crime states:

The primary goals of organized crime, whether through enterprises such as illegal gambling or legitimate businesses such as construction, are the making of money and the maximization of profit. In order to achieve the greatest possible return, organized crime has found it expedient to invest some of its capital in government; that is, to distribute varying sums of money to carefully chosen individuals serving in strategic government and law enforcement capacities who can provide organized crime with the services it requires. If the individual happens to be a publicly elected official, a bribe may arrive in the form of a cash contribution to the campaign fund or a promise for the delivery of large blocs of votes. Sometimes, though, an individual whom organized crime has designated as desirable to be "in their hip pocket" will refuse to accept a bribe. In such cases, organized crime will seek to corrupt through threats and/or blackmail.

* * *

Failure to arrest and prosecute those whom the officer knows have violated the law is only one form police corruption can take. Herman Goldstein, in his monograph, *Police Corruption,* lists several others:

- Agreeing to drop an investigation prematruely;
- Agreeing not to inspect various locations where a violation may be occurring;
- Reducing the seriousness of a charge against an offender;
- Agreeing to alter testimony at trial;
- Influencing departmental recommendations regarding the granting of licenses, e.g., recommending for or against continuance of a liquor or amusement license by either giving or suppressing derogatory information;
- Agreeing to alter departmental records of arrested persons.

* * *

Of course, not all police corruption is rooted in organized crime. The officer who accepts a bribe from a businessman, even on a continuing basis, not to enforce certain parking regulations is guilty of corruption, but not corruption perpetrated by a syndicate. However, the Knapp Commission testimony revealed alliances between enough police officers and organized crime figures to lend credence to the belief that such relationships exist. And other instances of the phenomenon indicate that such police corruption is not limited to New York City.

Police corruption has other serious implications. In addition to eroding public confidence in the police, both intradepartmental and interdepartmental cooperation is undermined. Officers do not know whom they can trust. Says Cressey, "if a policeman in one city calls the police department of another city to report a piece of valuable information about organized crime activities in either of the two communities, he can never be sure that a corrupt policeman will not answer the telephone."[3]

G. THE INVOLVEMENT OF ORGANIZED CRIME IN VICTIMLESS CRIMES*

Advantages for Organized Crime

The nature of some victimless crimes makes them excellent targets for organized crime. Says one observer: "Organized criminal groups participate in any illegal activity that offers maximum profit at minimum risk of law enforcement interference." Generally, these activities involve something the public wants badly enough to risk criminal sanctions. Providing them requires certain skills and an organization, in return for which there is great potential for profit.

---

* This material is from the Criminal Justice Standards and Goals Report on Organized Crime, pp. 218–219.

Gambling, drugs, prostitution, and pronography all meet these conditions, and supplying them is relatively free of risk. Because the public tolerates the activity—indeed, a large segment demands it—there rarely is a complainant. Moreover, there is little incentive for strict law enforcement or tough judicial decisions. Even if there were, the laws are extremely difficult to enforce. Evidence is hard to come by, witnesses are scarce, and the organized crime masterminds are insulated from implication in the activities.

Characteristics of Involvement

Organized crime attempts to achieve monopolistic control over specific activities and geographic areas in which it operates. However, there is some dispute over the extent of this control. The Organized Crime Task Force of the President's Commission on Law Enforcement and Administration of Justice (1967) stated that few independent operators exist in cities where organized crime is present. Others agree, saying that where independents exist, they do so at the sufferance of organized crime, and last only as long as they are not a threat or major source of competition to that element. In short, "Until they become a threat to the 'big group' they are permitted to exist and to continue to grow."

It is also probable that organized crime tolerates independents only up to a point, so that "Only when profits are of sufficient consequence do the larger organizations move in to become affiliated with local groups."

* * *

The top echelons of organized crime have established a shield between themselves and the law. Actual street merchandising of illegal goods and services usually is handled by nonmembers of the organization who know little about their suppliers, and thus are unable to inform on them. For those who do know, organized crime figures combine the threat of retribution with a promise to provide a lawyer and court costs in case of arrest, and to care for an individual's family in the case of conviction.

Some observers stress the significance of this buffer, contending that as long as the higher levels of the organization are protected, the supply of goods and services will flow without interruption, because there will never be a shortage of sellers or customers. Others, however, believe this point is exaggerated. They argue that organized crime depends entirely on its market; and if that can be severely disrupted, organized crime will be crippled.

A third point to note is that the survival of organized crime does not depend on a single individual. "Like any large corporation, the organization functions regardless of personnel changes, and no individual—not even the leader—is indispensable."

The next factor to consider is control. Organized crime is able to hold sway over not just its street-level operators but, to some degree, the official forces arrayed against it. There is general agreement that organized crime's illegal activities could not be sustained without the complicity of local law officers, judges, and politicians at all levels. In effect, "The organization . . . provides a systematized method of corrupting the law enforcement process by centralizing procedures for the payment of graft." Corruption has been well documented, perhaps most elaborately by the Knapp Commission in New York City and in a study of Reading, Pennsylvania, by John Gardiner.

The method of corruption varies with the positions of the officials to be corrupted. The higher they are, the more subtle and difficult the corruption will be to trace. Politicians are offered campaign contributions, for example, and there are cases where organized crime has swung an election or affected the course of legislation.

Many authors cite the parallels between organized crime operations and large-scale, legitimate businesses. They may speak, for example, of a "large-scale, organized system, often of national scope, comprising an integration of the stages of production and distribution of the illicit product on a continuous and thoroughly business-like basis."

Thomas Schelling, author of a number of economic analyses of organized crime, adds that because organized crime must use extortion to monopolize its area of activity, the street-level suppliers are vulnerable to this tactic. These suppliers cannot complain to the police, because they are committing crimes. Also, they cannot hide, because they must be accessible to their customers, and they cannot move their businesses out of town.

As with legitimate enterprises, organized crime's "businesses" require certain conditions and characteristics in order to be profitable. Schelling believes that by analyzing the structure and operations of the businesses, a strategy can be devised to affect their profitability, a practice that occurs among competitors in the legal marketplace.

An economic approach might involve "regulation, accommodation or the restructuring of markets and business conditions." If, for example, an illicit operation is profitable because a law "protects" it from legitimate competition, then removal of the law should undercut it. However, if the operation is profitable because it is a monopoly based on extortion, removing the law would have little effect. The end of the Prohibition Period, followed by a free, though regulated, liquor trade, is an example of how competition drove organized crime out of one activity.

H. SHOULD VICTIMLESS CRIMES IN WHICH ORGANIZED CRIME IS EXTENSIVELY INVOLVED BE LEGALIZED OR DECRIMINALIZED?

The National Advisory Committee on Criminal Justice Standards and Goals offered this advice on the above question:

States and localities should exercise caution in considering the legalization or decriminalization of so-called "victimless crimes," such as gambling, drug use, prostitution, and pornography, which are known to provide income to organized crime because there is insufficient evidence that legalization or decriminalization of such crimes will materially reduce the income of organized crime and on the contrary, evidence does exist that the elimination or reduction of legal restraints can encourage the expansion of organized crime activities.

I. RACKETEER INFLUENCED AND CORRUPT ORGANIZATIONS ACT

In 1970, Congress enacted a criminal statute with such broad provisions that it has been called the "new darling of the prosecutor's nursery." The Racketeer Influenced and Corrupt Organization

---

RICO (Federal Racketeer Influenced and Corrupt Organization Act)*

RICO forbids a person or persons from:
- using income received from a pattern of "racketeering" activity to acquire an interest in an "enterprise" an "enterprise" is defined as "any individual, partnership, or corporation, association, or other legal entity, and any union or group of individuals associated in fact although not a legal entity" (18 U.S.C. Sec. 1961 [4]). The U.S. Supreme Court held that this included both legitimate and illegitimate "associations in fact" (*United States v. Turkette,* 101 S. Ct. 2524 [1981])
- acquiring or maintaining an interest in an "enterprise" through a pattern of "racketeering" activity
- conducting or participating in the affairs of an "enterprise" through a pattern of "racketeering" activity
- conspiring to commit any of the above offenses.

Criminal Penalties:	*Civil Penalties:*
fines up to $25,000 and/or imprisonment not longer than 20 years for each offense plus forfeiture of interests acquired in violation of RICO	"any person" may commence a private civil action for treble damages and attorney fees when the forbidden conduct causes injury to "business or property"

Designated Potentially Associated Statutes

Mail and Wire Fraud Statutes The two elements for these federal crimes are (a) formation of a "scheme or artifice to defraud" and (b) use of the mails or wires to further the fraudulent scheme.
Travel Act Statute This statute forbids travel in interstate commerce or use of any facility in interstate commerce with intent to (a) distribute the proceeds of unlawful activity; (b) commit any violent crime in furtherance of unlawful activity; or (c) manage, promote, or establish any unlawful activity.
Extortion (Hobbs Act, 18 U.S.C. Sec. 1951) This defines extortion as "the obtaining of property from another, with his consent, induced by wrongful use of actual or threatened force, violence, or fear, or under color of official right."
Obstruction of Justice, Criminal Investigations, and State and Local Governments
Unlawful Labor Payments (violation of the Taft-Hartley Act, 29 U.S.C. sec. 186[a][b]) The making of payments by an employer or his representative to a union official, and the receiving of payment by a union official from an employer or their representatives is forbidden. (Specific intent, such as in bribery, need not be proved and only general intent is required.)

* 18 U.S.C. Sec. 1961–68 first enacted by Congress in 1970. See Tarlow, "RICO: The New Darling of the Prosecutor's Nursery," *Fordham Law Review* 49 (1980): 164.

(RICO) Act was enacted as Title IX of the Organized Crime Control Act of 1970.

RICO has proved to be a valuable tool in the fight against organized crime in the United States. Since 1980, senior mob figures from Los Angeles, New Orleans, New York, Cleveland, and Philadelphia have been convicted. A high-ranking FBI agent stated in 1983 that "I think we've proven that the myth of the invincibility of organized crime is total fantasy. You can indict them and you can convict them, but that doesn't mean you can put them out of business." [4]

Although more crime figures are going to jail, FBI Director Webster points out that the organized crime "problem remains a gigantic one," particularly in the drug trafficking area.

Gangland executions and mobsters who turn informers also seem to be on the increase.[5] For example, after being criminally convicted and while awaiting sentencing, millionaire Allen Dorfman was gunned down gangland style in a hotel parking lot. It is speculated that Dorfman was killed to prevent him from talking and disclosing information regarding organized crime.

In October 1983, federal indictments were announced against 15 alleged mobsters, including top figures in Chicago, Kansas City, and Milwaukee. The criminal charges were skimming profits from Las Vegas casinos.[6] Shortly after the indictments were issued, the Stardust Casino in Las Vegas lost its license.

In 1983, FBI Director Webster explained that it was not until recently that law enforcement agencies, prosecutors, and courts learned how to use RICO effectively. Many states have enacted similar statutes ("little RICOs"). Webster indicated that new and extensive investigations into such areas as labor racketeering and international drug traffic would be opened up. With RICO, every transaction involving the use of the mail, telephone, or interstate wire facilities creates the potential for criminal prosecution or a civil lawsuit.

Why Organized Crime Is Successful

In 1983, FBI Director William Webster testified before the President's Commission on Organized Crime as to the "edges" organized crime has and why organized crime has been successful. He stated:

> Such organizations are involved in every conceivable type of crime, including extortion, pornography, labor racketeering, bribery and murder. Their main sources of revenue, however, are narcotics and gambling.

*   *   *

> The activities of organized crime are not limited to open acts of criminality. Today there are few businesses or industries in our communities that are not affected by organized criminal enterprises. This brand of crime is costing the American people billions of dollars every year. Those engaged in organized crime are "no-holds-barred" competitors who seek an edge. They don't face the problems of legitimate businesses. . . . Instead—and this is their hallmark—they concentrate on intimidation, extortion, fear and the corruption of public officials.

*   *   *

> Still another edge comes from the practice of putting laundered funds from illegal activities into legitimate enterprises. This allows organized crime to undercut competition by reducing the cost of doing business.

The Attorney General of the United States testified that "it is only in the past 15 years that the government has been able to make much headway against these crime cartels." He stated:

> Of the 425 cases under investigation by the Organized Crime Drug Enforcement Task Forces, only a small number involve traditional organized crime. Most involve the new cartels.

J. GAMBLING*

The history of State and local gambling legislation in this country is one of flux between permissiveness and prohibition. The legal and informal status of gambling at any given time was closely tied to the extent of abuse, the limits of public tolerance, and the State's need for revenue without taxation. When abuses got out of hand, reformers would provoke a crackdown. After a period of quiescence, the games would reemerge. Sooner or later abuses would mount again, and a new crackdown would be ordered. From time to time some games would be legalized in the interests of revenue raising, but, until the Depression [1930s], abuses of legal games usually led to renewed prohibition.

A new swing toward legalization came during the Depression. States needing revenue and unable or unwilling to raise taxes looked to gambling as an answer. A trend to legalization as a revenue measure has continued to the present day, and in some States had been expanded to include consideration of a wide range of games.

The Federal Government has always prohibited gambling and sought to restrict it by outlawing the use of mails and interstate commerce for gambling activities. Since the 1950's, when the involvement of organized crime with illegal gambling was well documented by the Kefauver committee, much of the Federal emphasis has been on combating its involvement. Various laws have been passed with that in mind.

* * *

Probably more attention has been paid to the legalization of gambling than to any other victimless crime. While much of the discussion has focused on the revenue-raising potential of legalization and on social issues, a fair amount of attention also has been paid to the impact of this action on organized crime. Obviously, if maximum revenues are to be raised, organized crime's markets must be won over.

* * *

Inevitably, attention turns to the experiences of various States with legalized gambling. Nevada, of course, has been a focal point, since this State permits all forms of gambling except numbers, subject to State regulation and Federal tax laws.

Extensive involvement of organized crime in Nevada casinos has been documented since the earliest days of legalization. Organized crime not only became involved with legal operations, but found ways to maximize its profits illegally—by skimming off the top of the profits and sending that money out of the

country to be disguised or "laundered." Thus the first lesson in Nevada was that legalization per se would not preclude the involvement of organized crime, at least not without carefully planned regulations.

To end organized crime's influence, Nevada has enacted several reforms over the years, and the State maintains that these attempts have been successful. The absence of any proof to the contrary in the literature of recent years suggests that the claim may be valid.

What is the situation elsewhere? Horseracing is the most common form of legalized gambling. Though often beset by organized crime scandals—fixing of racing dates and results, illegal communication of results from the tracks, altering of the odds—most thoroughbred racetracks now seem to be free of organized crime's influence. Whether this is also true for dogtracks is less clear, and there have been accusations recently of fixes at New York harness racing tracks.

* * *

The lottery is the game most often legalized now. Instituted primarily to raise revenue, it was also intended to cut into the numbers racket in areas where that game flourished, particularly New York and New Jersey. That does not appear to be the case, despite efforts to make lotteries competitive. New Jersey, for example, started a daily drawing and allows players to pick their own number, a popular feature of the numbers game. Still, the legal activity is unable to match the door-to-door service, quick payoff, credit, anonymity, and community satisfaction that numbers offers. Though some numbers bettors may also play the lottery, it appears that the legal market consists primarily of new bettors.

* * *

Casino-type games, bingo, and other legal charity operations are also fairly common, and organized crime is involved here too. In several New York cases, organized crime has used a charity operation as a front for high stakes gambling or has taken an overly large share of the charitable enterprise's yield as its fee for running the game.

* * *

There are almost no advocates of total decriminalization, though that alternative has been proposed for social gambling. (For example, one advocate believes that "There is no economic or political justification for interference by government in any of the common forms of private, social gambling . . . .") This caution about decriminalization results from a recognition that gambling does have some negative social consequences that should be controlled, and that the public needs to be protected from unscrupulous opera-

---

* This material is from the National Advisory Committee Report on Organized Crime.

The Federal Crime of Gambling: 18 U.S.C. Section 1955

Major gambling activities were a principal focus of congressional concern. Large-scale gambling enterprises were seen to be both a substantial evil and a source of funds for other criminal conduct.

—U.S. Supreme Court, in *Iannelli et al. v. United States*
420 U.S. 770, 16 CrL 3127 (1975)

The U.S. Supreme Court pointed out that the federal offense created by the U.S. Congress has the following requirements:

Participation of "five or more persons" as an element of the substantive offense under Sec. 1955 represents a legislative attempt to merge the conspiracy and the substantive offense into a single crime.

*   *   *

Recognizing that gambling activities normally are matters of state concern, Congress indicated a desire to extend federal criminal jurisdiction to reach only "those who are engaged in an illicit gambling business of major proportions." . . . It accordingly conditioned the application of Sec. 1955 on a finding that the gambling activities involve five or more persons and that they remain substantially in operation in excess of 30 days or attain gross revenues of $2,000 in a single day.

*   *   *

We think it evident that Congress intended to retain each offense as an "independent curb" available for use in the strategy against organized crime.

---

tors. Further, a large segment of the population opposes gaming, and its opinions cannot be totally ignored. Perhaps the main reason, though, is the desire of States to tax gambling operations.

Currently, a significant incentive for regulation is the desire to combat illegal gambling and to keep organized crime out of the legal games. By comparison, total repeal "would leave the market to large, exploitative criminal organizations that would probably use violence to protect their monopoly privileges." The experience of Nevada shows that organized crime is only too happy to participate in legitimate businesses and that carefully drawn, strictly enforced regulations are necessary. Likewise, strict prohibition of illegal games is essential.

Distinguishing Illegal Gambling From Friendly Gambling

For a game of chance or lottery to be illegal, it must violate a specific law or ordinance. Illegal gambling is often distinguished from legitimate commercial promotions in that illegal gambling or lotteries have (a) a prize, (b) consideration, and (c) chance elements.

Friendly gambling (office or factory football pool, neighborhood poker game, etc.) can be distinguished from commercial gambling by some or all of the following factors:

- where the game is played and who the players are
- size of the pot
- whether the house takes a percentage of each pot
- whether the players bet against the house, and the house acts as the banker, and whether the house acts as the dealer in such games as blackjack and craps, etc.
- other factors, such as the type of game played

Chapter 21

The Crime of Contempt and Other Crimes Against Government

A. CONTEMPT

Contempt is the willful disregard of the authority of court of justice or of a legislative body. Acts that delay, impede, or frustrate the functioning or the dignity of a court or legislative body may be held to be in contempt of that body. The deliberate, willful, and contumacious (obstinate) disobedience of a lawful order is a common reason for finding a person in contempt. The U.S. Supreme Court held in the 1975 case of *Maness v. Meyer*:

> We begin with the basic proposition that all orders and judgments of courts must be complied with promptly. If a person to whom a court directs an order believes that order is incorrect the remedy is to appeal, but, absent a stay, he must comply promptly with the order pending appeal. Persons who make private determinations of the law and refuse to obey an order generally risk criminal contempt even if the order is ultimately ruled incorrect.[1]

Contempt and contempt proceedings originated in early England, when English kings gave their judges the power to punish conduct that interfered with the functioning of the courts. Although many American states have statutes defining contempt, the offense of contempt remains today in England as a common law misdemeanor. The following example of contempt received national attention in November 1983:

Example: In a hearing before the U.S. Supreme Court, *Hustler* magazine publisher Larry Flynt became angry and shouted obscenities at the nine justices. The hearing concerned a civil libel suit by a vice-president of *Penthouse* against *Hustler*. Flynt wanted to argue the case himself, but the Court refused and appointed a lawyer to represent him. Flynt (who was in a wheelchair, paralyzed in a 1978 assassination attempt) was taken to a jail and booked on contempt charges. Flynt apologized later and the charges were dropped.

Civil and Criminal Contempt

Contempt is classified as civil or criminal. The difference between civil and criminal contempt is the purpose for which the sentence is imposed. A contempt sentence imposed to compel action (such as to compel a witness to testify) is generally held to follow from civil contempt. A sentence imposed to punish is generally held to follow from a contempt that is criminal in nature.[2]

Example: Custody of a 12-year-old boy was awarded to the father (the trial judge knew at the time that the father was a practicing homosexual). The mother, who was a Christian fundamentalist and a member of a Pentecostal church, kidnapped the child in 1982. In 1984, the mother refused to disclose the location of the child and was jailed on civil contempt in Denver. After 12 days in jail, the boy was produced and hearings to determine custody were scheduled. The boy stated publicly that he wanted to live with his mother.

Criminal contempt is designed to protect the public interest by ensuring the effective functioning of the judicial and legislative systems. In 1968, the U.S. Supreme Court stated in *Bloom v. Illinois* that "criminal contempt is a crime in the ordinary sense; it is a violation of the law, a public wrong which is punishable by fine or imprisonment or both."[3] The Court quoted Justice Oliver Wendell Holmes as stating that "these contempts are infractions of the law, visited with punishment as such. If such acts are not criminal, we are in error as to the most fundamental characteristic of crimes as that word has been understood in English speech." The defendant in the *Bloom* case was sentenced to 24 months in prison for submitting a falsely prepared will for probate. His demand for a jury trial was denied. In holding that in serious contempt cases the defendant had a right to a jury, the Court stated:

> Prosecution for contempt plays a significant role in the proper functioning of our judicial system; but despite the important values which the contempt power protects, courts and legislatures have gradually eroded the power of judges to try contempts of their own authority. In modern times, procedures in criminal contempt cases have come to mirror those used in ordinary criminal cases. Our experience teaches that convictions for criminal contempt, not infrequently resulting in extremely serious penalties are indistinguishable from those obtained under ordinary criminal laws. If the right to a jury trial is a fundamental matter in other criminal cases, which we think it is, it must also be extended to criminal contempt cases.[4]

Direct and Constructive (or Indirect) Contempt

Contempt is also classified as either direct or indirect (constructive contempt). Direct contempt is committed in the immediate presence and view or hearing of the court or legislative body. Acts of violence, insulting or abusive language, or failure to obey a proper order of the court or the legislative body are examples of conduct that have been held to be in direct contempt. Direct contempt may be punished summarily, since the person is present before the court or the legislative body at the time.

Constructive (or indirect) contempt arises from matters not occurring in or near the presence of the court or the legislative body but that nevertheless tend to obstruct or delay the functioning of the court or legislative body. Failure to appear as ordered or as required would be an example of conduct that could be found to be in constructive contempt. Constructive contempt may not be punished summarily, since the person is entitled to procedural due process. This entitles the person to an opportunity to show cause within a stated time why an order adjudging one in contempt should not be issued; to a hearing after receiving notice of its time and place; to a reasonable time for preparation of one's defense; to a statement of facts constituting the contempt charged; to service on him or her of a copy of any writing or document filed in support of the alleged contempt with such matters set out in order issued by the court determining to cite the person for contempt.

The Requirement of Intentional Wrongdoing

In the 1976 case of *Commonwealth v. Washington,* the Supreme Court of Pennsylvania quoted other courts, holding:

> There is no contempt unless there is some sort of wrongful intent. *Offutt v. United States,* 98 U.S. App. D.C. 69, 232 F.2d 69, 72 (1956), *cert. den.* 351 U.S. 988, 76 S. Ct. 1049, 100 L.Ed. 1501 (1956). ". . . [A] degree of intentional wrongdoing is an ingredient of the offense of criminal contempt." *In Re Brown,* 147 U.S. App. D.C. 156, 454 F.2d 999, 1006 (1971). "Willfulness is, of course, an element of criminal contempt and must be proved beyond a reasonable doubt." *United States v. Greyhound Corporation,* 508

F.2d 529, 531 (7th Cir.1974). In *United States v. Seale,* 461 F.2d 345, 368 (7th Cir.1972), the Court thoroughly discussed the necessity for proof of the element of intent, and concluded that the minimum intent required is a volitional act done by one who knows or should reasonably be aware that his conduct is wrongful.[5]

In the *Washington* case, the defendant overslept and failed to appear in time at his trial. In reversing his contempt conviction, the Supreme Court of Pennsylvania held:

> Were we to accept the prosecution's argument, any person, judge, attorney, witness, or party, who comes into the courtroom late can be held guilty of contempt of court, regardless of the reason for the lateness. We cannot accept such a conclusion. Unless the evidence establishes an intentional disobedience or an intentional neglect of the lawful process of the court, no contempt has been proven. Such is the case here.
>
> Judgment of sentence reversed.

In the 1976 case of *People v. Harris,*[6] the defendant failed to pay a fine imposed for a prior criminal conviction. Although the defendant showed that he had no money and was unemployed, he was found in contempt for failure to pay the fine. The Illinois Court of Appeals reversed the contempt finding, holding that there was no showing that the defendant willfully placed himself in a position to be unable to pay the fine.

When the Basis of the Contempt Is a Personal Attack on the Trial Judge

It is a well-settled law that in order to prevent a breakdown of the judicial process, courts have the power to punish persons summarily for contempt of court that consists of personal attacks on the trial judge. In *Mayberry v. Pennsylvania,*[7] the defendants and two others were tried for holding hostages in a prison break and for escaping from prison. The defendants rejected the court-appointed attorney and represented themselves, using disruptive tactics, which included verbal attacks on the trial judge. Because of Mayberry's disruptions while the judge was attempting to instruct the jury, Mayberry had to be gagged and put in a straitjacket. When this did not work, Mayberry was placed in an adjoining room, where he was able to listen to the conclu-

Contempt

Classification	Type	Procedure Used to Punish
Civil contempt is remedial and is used to force persons to do what they are lawfully required to do (answer questions, identify themselves, pay support money as ordered by a divorce court, etc.)	*Direct contempt* is committed in the immediate presence and view or hearing of the court or legislative body.	*Summary process.* Only direct contempt may be punished summarily. If the court or legislative body does not act at the time the contempt is committed, notice and an opportunity for a hearing must be given to the persons.
"Criminal contempt is a crime in the ordinary sense; it is a violation of the law, a public wrong which is punishable by fine or imprisonment or both." U.S. Supreme Court in *Bloom v. Illinois,* 391 U.S. 194, 88 S. Ct. 1477 (1968)	*Constructive (or indirect) contempt* is committed out of the presence or hearing of the court or legislative body. Although the matter or incident does not occur in or near the presence of a court or legislative body, it must tend to obstruct or delay the functioning of the court or the legislative body.	*Contempt hearings.* Notice and an opportunity for a hearing (plus other due process rights) must be given for constructive (indirect contempt) and for direct contempt when the court or legislative body does not act immediately.

sion of the trial over a public address system. Before sentencing the defendants on the basis of the jury finding of guilty, the trial judge sentenced Mayberry to not less than 11 or more than 22 years in prison on 11 contempt citations.

After the sentence for contempt was affirmed by the Supreme Court of Pennsylvania, the case was appealed to the U.S. Supreme Court in 1971. This Court based its decision to vacate and remand for a new trial on the concept that "justice must satisfy the appearance of justice." The two factors that the Court held did not meet the "appearance of justice" were the length of the sentence and the "appearance" of an angry judge seeking revenge. Justice William O. Douglas wrote:

A judge, vilified as was this Pennsylvania judge, necessarily becomes embroiled in a running, bitter controversy. No one so cruelly slandered is likely to maintain that calm detachment necessary for fair adjudication.

Justice Harland wrote in his concurring opinion: "These contempt convictions must be regarded as infected by the fact that the unprecedented long sentence of 22 years which they carried was imposed by a judge who himself had been the victim of petitioner's shocking abusive conduct. That circumstance seems to me to deprive the contempt proceeding of the appearance of even-handed justice which is the core of due process."

The Supreme Court held that "where . . . he [the trial judge] does not act the instant the contempt is committed, but waits until the end of the trial, on balance, it is generally wise where the marks of the unseemly conduct have left personal stings to ask a fellow judge to take his place."

But what of the unruly and disruptive defendant who not only attacks and vilifies the trial judge, but also personally insults the second judge who is presiding at the contempt hearing? This question was presented in the 1971 case of *Knox v. Municipal Court of Des Moines.*[8] The defendant was charged with operating a motor vehicle after his driver's license was suspended. He was openly antagonistic to the trial judge and after he was sentenced to five days in jail (maximum sentence was 30 days), he spat at the judge. The trial judge chose to transfer the contempt hearing to another judge. The defendant was so disruptive at the contempt hearing that in addition to sentencing the defendant to six months for the first contempt, the second judge summarily sentenced the defendant to six months for the second contempt. The Iowa Supreme Court affirmed the contempt sentences in a 4–3 decision. The dissenting judge argued that a third judge should have sat on the matter as the second judge himself had been vilified. If the dissenting opinion in *Knox* were followed, the question would then rise as to what course of action should be followed if the determined disruptive defendant vilifies the third and fourth judges hearing the contempt motions.

In *Illinois v. Allen,*[9] the U.S. Supreme Court held that a defendant who continues to engage in disruptive behavior, after being properly warned, can lose his right to remain in the courtroom. Although such defendants have a constitutional right to the confrontation of the witnesses against them, by engaging in disruptive conduct they may affect proceedings to the point where it may be impossible to complete the trial. In addition to summary and delayed contempt against such disruptive defendants, trial judges may have such defendants removed from the courtroom, bound and gagged, or moved to other rooms where they can hear the trial proceedings over a public address system or closed-circuit TV.

Language by a Witness or Attorney That Would Justify a Contempt Finding

While answering a question on cross examination, a witness used the expression "chicken shit." As a result, the witness was found to be in direct contempt for the use of this term in a courtroom. The U.S. Supreme Court reversed the defendant's conviction in the case of *Eaton v. City of Tulsa,*[10] holding: [11]

This single isolated usage of street vernacular, not directed at the judge or any officer of the court, cannot constitutionally support the conviction of criminal contempt. "The vehemence of language used is not alone the measure of the power to punish for contempt. The fires which it kindles must constitute an imminent, not merely a likely, threat to the administration of justice." *Craig v. Harney*, 331 U.S. 367, 376 (1947). In using the expletive in answering the question on cross-examination "it is not charged that [petitioner] here disobeyed any valid court order, talked loudly, acted boisterously, or attempted to prevent the judge or any other officer of the court from carrying on his court duties." *Holt v. Virginia*, 381 U.S. 131, 136 (1965); see also *In re Little*, 404 U.S. 553 (1972). In the circumstances, the use of the expletive thus cannot be held to "constitute an imminent . . . threat to the administration of justice."

The Power of Legislative Bodies to Punish for Contempt

Constitutions grant legislative bodies the power to legislate. In order to inform themselves as to what laws and measure should be enacted, legislative bodies must gather necessary information on which to base their decisions. They therefore have the power to hold hearings and make investigations into matters relevant to their jurisdiction to legislate. Neither Congress nor the state legislatures possess the general power to make inquiries into the private affairs of citizens that are not relevant to measures they may be considering. Legislatures possess inherent power to protect their existence and their power to proceed in their legislative functions. The following case came before the U.S. Supreme Court in 1972:

GROPPI v. LESLIE
Supreme Court of the United States (1972)
404 U.S. 496, 92 S. Ct. 582

A former Catholic priest, Father Groppi, lead a group who seized the Wisconsin Assembly chamber and held it for a short time. Father Groppi was arrested and held in jail. Two days after the incident, the Wisconsin Assembly voted to hold Groppi in contempt and gave him six months in jail as punishment. The U.S. Supreme Court unanimously held that the action violated Groppi's due process rights, as he received a jail sentence without any notice of the hearing and there was no opportunity for him to appear and defend himself.

B. CRIMES BY PUBLIC OFFICIALS

If all people were angels and were to live in peace and harmony with one another, then, as James Madison observed in *The Federalist Papers,* there would be no need for governments. But people are not angels, nor are they governed by angels (as Madison also pointed out almost 200 years ago). The sad fact that in recent years many high public officials have had to resign, or have been convicted of offenses, illustrates this. The Supreme Court of the United States observed that "nothing can destroy a government more quickly than its failure to observe its own laws, or worse, its disregard of the charter of its own existence." [12] In 1928, Justice Louis D. Brandeis stated in his dissenting opinion in *Olmstead v. United States:* "Our Government is the potent, the omnipresent teacher. For good or ill, it teaches the whole people by its example. . . . If the Government becomes a lawbreaker, it breeds contempt for law; it invites every man to become a law unto himself; it invites anarchy." [13]

Cicero wrote long ago in *Pro Cluentio 53* that "we are in bondage to the law in order that we may free." Calvin Coolidge observed, while he was the president of the United States: "Wherever the law goes, there civilization goes and stays. When the law fails, barbarism flourishes. Whoever scouts the law, whoever brings it into disrespect, whoever connives at its evasion, is an enemy of civilization. Change it if you will . . . but observe it always. That is government."

Categories of Offenses Committed by Public Officials

All public officials, whether they be judges, governors, legislators, or law enforcement officers, are subject to the law and must obey the law of their jurisdictions. Civil and criminal offenses that are applicable to public officials have been categorized as follows:

● *Nonfeasance*—the omission or failure to perform a duty or undertaking that the public official is obligated to perform as part of his or her public office. Failure to execute a writ and failure to obey a court order are examples of nonfeasance.

● *Malfeasance*—the commission of an act that the public official has no right to do and that may be a criminal violation.

● *Misfeasance*—the improper performance of an act that the public official may perform but should not perform in the manner in which he or she has performed it. Misfeasance is the failure to do a lawful act in a proper manner.

The state of New York has statutorized nonfeasance and misfeasance in Section 195.00 of the New York Criminal Code as follows:

> A public servant is guilty of official misconduct when, with intent to obtain a benefit or to injure or deprive another person of a benefit:
>
> 1. He commits an act relating to his office but constituting an unauthorized exercise of his official functions, knowing that such act is unauthorized; or
>
> 2. He knowingly refrains from performing a duty which is imposed upon him by law or is clearly inherent in the nature of his office.
>
> Official misconduct is a class A misdemeanor.

Malfeasance would include many offenses that are statutorized in every criminal code. The following offenses could be committed not only by public officials, but also by ordinary persons:

● Unauthorized (or excessive) use of force (assault and battery)

● False imprisonment

● Extortion or accepting a bribe (accepting unlawful fees)

● Unauthorized wiretapping (federal felony) or bugging (state offense)

● Perjury [14] and subornation of perjury. [15] (The crime of perjury consists of knowingly testifying falsely while under oath; the crime of subornation of perjury is committed when another person is induced or knowingly permitted to testify falsely.)

● Official misconduct and misconduct in public office (using the powers of one's office to obtain a dishonest advantage for oneself or falsifying an entry in a record or report)

● Aiding, assisting, or permitting the escape of a prisoner

- Intimidating witnesses, prisoners, or other persons

- Misprision of felony—"to sustain a conviction . . . for misprision of felony it was incumbent upon the government to prove beyond a reasonable doubt (1) that . . . the principal had committed and completed the felony alleged . . .; (2) that the defendant had full knowledge of that fact; (3) that he failed to notify the authorities; and (4) that he took . . . affirmative steps to conceal the crime of the principal." [16]

- Bribery.[17] This offense was described by the Court in the 1976 case of *United States v. Arthur,* as follows:

> Not every gift, favor or contribution to a government or political official constitutes bribery. It is universally recognized that bribery occurs only if the gift is coupled with a particular criminal intent. . . . That intent is not supplied merely by the fact that the gift was motivated by some generalized hope or expectation of ultimate benefit on the part of the donor. . . . "Bribery" imports the notion of some more or less specific quid pro quo for which the gift or contribution is offered or accepted. . . .
>
> This requirement of criminal intent would, of course, be satisfied if the jury were to find a "course of conduct of favors and gifts flowing" to a public official in exchange for a pattern of official actions favorable to the donor even though no particular gift or favor is directly connected to any particular official act. *U.S. v. Baggett* (4th Cir.1973) 481 F.2d 114, cert. denied 414 U.S. 1116 (1973) (Travel Act prosecution involving alleged bribery of Maryland County Commissioner). Moreover, as the Seventh Circuit has held, it is sufficient that the gift is made on the condition "that

the offeree act favorably to the offeror when necessary." *U.S. v. Isaacs* (7th Cir.1974) 493 F.2d 1124, 1145, 15 Cr.L. 2002, cert. denied 417 U.S. 976 (1974) (construing Illinois statute in a Travel Act prosecution). It does not follow, however, that the traditional business practice of promoting a favorable business climate by entertaining and doing favors for potential customers becomes bribery merely because the potential customer is the government. Such expenditures, although inspired by the hope of greater government business, are not intended as a quid pro quo for that business: they are in no way conditioned upon the performance of an official act or pattern of acts or upon the recipient's express or implied agreement to act favorably to the donor when necessary.[18]

C. CRIMES AGAINST GOVERNMENT

Environmental laws—The article entitled "Enforcing Environmental Laws—A Modern Day Challenge" in the November 1983 *Law Enforcement Bulletin* concludes:

> The philosophy still quite prevalent in the criminal justice system, business community, political arena, and engineering and scientific circles is that environmental laws should not be enforced in the same manner as "regular" criminal law classifications. We are discovering however, after decades of nonenforcement that the price for this inaction is much too high. The temptation is always great to quote the all-too-true horror stories which have resulted because of this program of nonenforcement which was the policy until the 1970's. Suffice it to say that the destruction of the air we breathe, the poisoning of the water we drink, and the contamination of our land and food with toxins is much too serious a crime to overlook.

Appendix

Slang and Colloquial Criminal Law Terms

bagman (bagwoman) Person who picks up illegal money payments for bribes, blackmail payments, etc.

bait and switch Tactic of offering bargains for retail sale at low prices **(bait)** to get customers into a store and then using other tactics to get the customer to buy other merchandise instead **(switch)** (see Chapter 17)

blackmail (extortion) Demanding money (or valuables) by threats of violence or threats to reveal accusations or information

black market Market in which illegal products are sold (or in which objects are sold in a manner that is illegal or improper)

blind pig (blind tiger or **after hours house)** Place that sells intoxicants illegally. The Detroit riot of 1966 commenced after a police raid on a blind pig.

booster box (booster coat, skirt, bloomers, pants, etc.) Devices used in shoplifting to receive and conceal shoplifted items. (Pregnancy baskets are similar devices.) Such devices can be used as evidence in court to show the intent and means to shoplift.

brainwashing Systematic indoctrination and pressuring to undermine or change political, religious or other beliefs, and views. Drugs or physical coercion and duress are sometimes used and the victim is often prevented from moving about freely and contacting friends and family members. Some religious cults have used brainwashing (see Chapter 12). Patty Hearst used brainwashing as a defense against the charge of bank robbery (see Chapter 7).

bushwack Criminal ambush to waylay for a criminal attack

buzzards Criminals who steal cars to cut up for parts

canary Informant; derogatory term

casing a place Viewing and looking at a business place or home to plan a crime that is to be committed on the premises (or in the area)

CCW Offense of carrrying a concealed weapon

chop shop Operation that steals cars to cut up for parts. As nothing is left of the vehicles, these criminals are often called buzzards.

chump Victim of a con game

clearance rate A crime is generally considered cleared when a suspect is taken into custody for the crime. Crimes have different clearance rates. For example, passionate (rage) killings have a very high clearance rate, while gangland killings have a very low clearance rate.

clipper Person who cuts the corners off of a large bill and pastes them on a $1 bill to pass and cheat the receiver of the bill

collar An arrest. For example persons commenting on an arrest might say, "It was a good collar."

con games Confidence games, such as the pigeon drop, dropped wallet, card games, envelope switch, used to obtain money or property from a victim by a swindle, trick, or device (see Chapter 17)

cooking the books (book cooking or **fudging)** Fraudulent changing and alteration of business or organizational books or records in order to benefit someone in some way (see Chapter 17)

cop a plea Negotiate or accept a plea or sentence bargain to a criminal charge (or charges). Pleas of guilty are entered in 70% to 80% of criminal charges. Many (but not all) of these guilty pleas are part of a plea or sentence bargain.

counterfeiting Imitating and making to pass for something else. Criminal counterfeiting of money, coins, and commercial products, such as designer jeans, videotapes, phonograph records, electronic components, etc. is a constant problem (see Chapter 17).

decoys Plainclothes officers who pose as potential victims in high-crime or trouble areas. Decoys are used when victims could be the elderly, disabled, women, drunks, etc. Decoys are also used to apprehend men who solicit for prostitution or homosexual relations. The use of decoys differ from "blending" where police officers in plainclothes mingle in large crowds to watch for purse snatchers, pick pockets and other offenders.

embezzlement Fraudulent appropriation (theft) of property or money entrusted to such a person as an employee, trustee, or public official or to another person (see Chapter 15).

fencing Crime of trafficking in stolen goods (see Chapter 17)

fink Informant or informer; derogatory term for person who provides information regarding criminal activity

frame-up Making it appear that a person has committed a crime when he has not; set-up (see Chapter 7)

good time laws Reduction in jail and prison sentences for good behavior of a prisoner. For example, under Section 53.43 of the Wisconsin Statutes, an inmate may earn a reduction of one-fourth of his or her term for good conduct.

harassment Offensive and improper accosting, hassling, molesting of another person. Harassment can be sexual (of the opposite sex) or by use of a telephone (see Chapter 19).

heist Most often used to indicate an armed robbery; however, sometimes used for a burglary or a theft

hijacking Taking or seizing an aircraft or semitruck for profit or political reasons. The CB radio now provides the means by which truck hijackers can be spotted quickly as they flee. Shippers now clearly mark their trucks for identification both on the ground and from the air.

hit and run Motor vehicle accident in which driver does not stop and report identity (or render assistance) (see Chapter 12)

hit man Professional killer

hold up Halt and rob

hooker Prostitute (The term is believed to have originated from the American Civil War, when female camp followers of General Hooker's army were called hookers.)

hot When referring to an object, could be used to indicate that the object is stolen; also used to indicate that merchandise is selling rapidly.

hung jury A jury which is deadlocked and unable to arrive at a verdict. When it is determined that a jury is deadlocked, the trial judge would declare a mistrial and dismiss the jury. The prosecutor could re-issue criminal charges and retry the case or could drop the matter by not taking any further action.

john Customer of a prostitute

juice Illegal interest from loan sharking

kingpin statute The only federal criminal statute (21 USC 848) that does not allow parole and requires that heavy penalties be imposed on a person who commits a felony narcotic violation that "is part of a continuing series of violations . . . which are undertaken by such person (the kingpin) in concert with five or more other persons . . . and from which such person (the kingpin) obtains substantial income or resources."

kiting Illegal manipulation of checks (see Chapter 16)

laundering Converting illegal (dirty) money into money that appears to be clean and can be reported for tax purposes (see Chapter 20)

loan sharking Money lending with illegal rates of interest. Collection can be by brutality and murder. The illegal interest is sometimes called juice (see Chapter 20).

long-arm statute State law permitting a state to claim jurisdiction over a person outside the state. For example, a person who has never been in state A hires another person to go into state A and kill a man. State A would have jurisdiction over the out-of-state conspirator under the long-arm statute (see Chapter 9).

looting Offense of stealing from a building or area that has been damaged by a physical disaster (tornado, hurricane, etc.), riot, bombing, fire, etc.

MADD Mothers Against Drunk Drivers. Drunk drivers kill more than 70 persons a day in the United States. This is the most frequent form of criminal homicide.

mark Victim of a con game

mole Person who penetrates an organization or group. For example, in the Chicago Greylord operation, an undercover FBI agent posed as a corrupt lawyer and engaged in conversations with Chicago court personnel while wearing a body recorder. Newspapers referred to the undercover agent as an FBI mole.

mugging (strong-arm robbery) Unarmed robbery. Conviction for armed robbery requires proof that a weapon was used (or in many states, proof that the victim was reasonably lead to believe that a deadly weapon was threatened).

Murphy man Person who pretends to be a pimp and on the pretense of leading Johns (customers) to girls, instead cheats them of their money or leads them to a trap for a mugging or a heist

nudity Forms of public nudity are streaking, flashing, mooning (see Introduction to Part V).

numbers game (policy, bolita, the figures, the digits) Popular form of gambling among the poor and in central cities. Layoff persons, pickup men, and runners are persons involved in the functioning of the game.

Oklahoma credit card Siphon hose and pail used to steal gasoline from motor vehicles and other sources

OWI Operating a vehicle while under the influence

paper hanger Person who passes bad checks

pay-off As an illegal transaction, a bribe. Pay-offs can be picked up by bagmen (or women).

payola Payment (usually secret) in return for a favor, such as paying a disc jockey to promote a record

pen man (pen woman) Forger

piece Handgun; from military reference to a battery of cannon or guns as having six pieces (artillery pieces)

pimping (procuring) Offense related to prostitution (see Chapter 19)

pirating Originally, crime of seizing a ship or boat and the persons on the ship. Now includes the offense of unlawful reproduction of copyrighted tapes, records, movies, etc. Sometimes used to refer to counterfeiting of name brand products, such as jeans, sweaters, shirts.

pistol whip Strike a person with the barrel of a pistol

price fixing Along with conspiracy to restrain trade, this is a criminal violation of the federal Sherman Anti-trust Act. Other business violations are bid rigging, bribes, kickbacks (see Chapter 17).

protection money Money paid as part of an extortion or blackmail scheme, to avoid personal injury or property damage; also money paid to a law enforcement officer or government official in a bribery scheme. Could be picked up by a bagman or woman (see Chapters 15 and 17).

pusher (drug peddling) Salesperson to the 10 million Americans who use cocaine, the 500,000 who use heroin, and the millions who use marijuana. The director of the Federal Drug Enforcement Administration quoted a study showing that the average heroin addict committed 175 to 250 crimes to support his or her habit.

quick-change artist Person who will short change another in changing money.

rabbit punch Short, choping blow delivered to the back of the neck or the base of the skull

racketeer Person engaging in a dishonest or illegal racket. The federal RICO statute and the little RICO statutes of many states are specifically aimed at racketeering (see Chapter 20).

reading the riot act In order to avoid a riot, the statutes of many states authorize public officials to read the riot act when specific conditions exist. Under these unlawful assembly statutes, persons can be ordered to leave an area or face arrest (see Chapter 11).

ringing short Ringing up a sale short and pocketing the difference

rip-off Fraud, theft, loss (usually criminal)

rolling a drunk Taking valuables from an intoxicated person or person in a stupor. Generally classified as a theft from a person and ordinarily a felony (see Chapter 15)

Russian roulette Suicidal game or contest in which a gun with one bullet in the cylinder is placed against the head and the trigger is pulled after the cylinder is spun

Saturday night special Cheap handgun of such poor construction that sportsmen and collectors would not generally purchase them. As such guns are of low caliber with short barrels, they are not practical to use for sport. Persons purchase such guns to commit crimes or to protect themselves.

scam (sting) Operation meant to deceive. For example, Abscam began as an attempt to catch art thieves. FBI Director Webster pointed out, however, that members of Congress walked into the net. Webster stated that "Abscam was purposely sleazy so that no one would stick around it, except someone who wanted to deal with sleazy people" (see Chapter 7).

shakedown A form of extortion or blackmail. Shakedowns have been made by government officials, police officers, or persons such as a prostitute. A city inspector could threaten enforcement of an ordinance, or threaten to issue a citation for a building code violation unless payment were to be made. The term shakedown is also used to describe a prison or jail search by officials for weapons contraband, or means of escape.

shoo-fly cops Law enforcement officers who investigate complaints against other officers in their department. Large law enforcement departments and agencies have separate offices of internal affairs to handle such complaints.

shrinkage Losses in merchandise for unknown reasons but believed to be from theft, pilferage, and shoplifting

SIWAC Sexual intercourse with a child

skid row Street or section of a city where alcoholics and other persons who are down and out frequent. Said to have originated in Seattle, Washington, when loggers used a street (Yesler Way) to skid logs down a hillside to the water. This area and parts of the Bowery in New York, and sections of Madison Street in Chicago became known as skid row because of the persons who frequent those areas.

skimming Taking money off the top of funds, such as the proceeds from a gambling casino. As the exact amount of the fund is not known, stockholders are cheated and taxes are not paid on the skimmed money.

smash and grab Smashing a store window and grabbing merchandise. Usually charged as a burglarly if offender is apprehended.

snatch and run Theft in which the object (or money) is snatched and the offender flees the scene. Shoplifting differs from snatch and run in that the taking in shoplifting is attempted to be done unobserved and in most instances the object is concealed.

snitch Informant; derogatory term

stable Group of prostitutes or a house of prostitution

stonewall To stand mute and not talk, or to engage in delaying or distracting tactics

stoolie Informant; derogatory term

strippers Criminals who steal parts that are easily removed, such as batteries, radios, tires, wheels, leaving the car to be recovered by the owner (see Chapter 15)

sucker Victim of a con game

SWAT team Special weapons and tactical squad such as the SWAT team which responded in San Diego to the shooting in a McDonald's restaurant resulting in the death of eleven persons. The SWAT team had to kill the offender.

throwaway An unregistered gun (or sometimes a knife) that could be carried by a police officer. In addition to having an extra weapon, the throwaway is available in the event of an illegal or accidental shooting. The throwaway could then be placed on the victim and self-defense claimed.

till tap Theft from a cash register. Till taps can occur when the cash register is open, while change is being made (a form of snatch and run), or while store employees are away from the cash register.

tinsel passer Person who passes bad checks

torch Person who will burn and commit arson for profit

TPF (tac squad) Tactical patrol force. A police or sheriff squad on alert or patrol for dangerous situations such as an armed robbery.

vigorish House advantage in gambling. In some games, the house takes a cut of the pot. However, when players are playing against the house, vigorish gives the house an advantage.

yoking Unarmed robbery

Notes

Chapter 1: Criminal Law Generally

1. Governor Thompson's remarks appear in the *Journal of Criminal Law and Criminology,* 73 (1982): 867.

2. Only about one-third of the world's population enjoy civil and political liberties. The other two-thirds do not have such civil and political freedoms to be classified as living in a free society.

3. See James Q. Wilson's book, *Thinking About Crime* (New York: Basic Books 1983), in which he states that "the average citizen thinks it obvious that one major reason why crime has increased is that people have discovered they can get away with it." This reflects a belief that the criminal justice system is neither efficient nor effective.

4. See Report of the National Advisory Commission on Criminal Justice Standards and Goals, 1976.

5. The word forensic means belonging to courts of law or to public discussion and debate. Therefore, forensic science is that science used by expert witnesses who testify in both criminal and civil courts. See H.J. Walls, *Forensic Science: An Introduction to Scientific Crime Detection,* 2d ed. (New York: Praeger Publishers, 1974).

6. 410 U.S. 113, 93 S. Ct. 705 (1973).

7. See 65 C.J.S. Negligence, sec. 63 (106) (1966), and Restatement (2d) of Torts, sec. 314 (1965).

8. See Restatement (2d) of Torts, sec. 314A, "Special Relations Giving Rise to a Duty to Aid or Protect."

9. When good reasons are given, state governors are likely to grant a pardon for a felony or misdemeanor conviction. The pardon will wipe the slate clean for the person.

10. Fifth Amendment to the U.S. Constitution.

11. 432 U.S. 282, 97 S. Ct. 2290, 21 CrL 3159.

12. 381 U.S. 437, 85 S. Ct. 1707 (1965).

13. *Connally v. General Construction Co.,* 269 U.S. 385, 46 S. Ct. 126 (1926).

14. See *Papachristou v. City of Jacksonville,* 405 U.S. 156, 162, 92 S. Ct. 839, 843 (1972), and *United States v. Harriss,* 347 U.S. 612, 617, 74 S. Ct. 808, 811 (1954).

15. See *Coates v. City of Cincinnati,* 402 U.S. 611, 614, 91 S. Ct. 1686, 1688 (1971), and *Shuttlesworth v. Birmingham,* 382 U.S. 87, 90–91, 86 S. Ct. 211, 213–214 (1965).

16. *Grayned v. City of Rockford,* 408 U.S. 104, 109, 92 S. Ct. 2294, 2299 (1972).

17. *Zwickler v. Koota,* 389 U.S. 241, 250, 88 S. Ct. 391, 396 (1967).

18. See *Grayned v. City of Rockford,* 408 U.S. 104, at 109, 92 S. Ct. 2294, at 2299 (1972), and *Dombrowski v. Pfister,* 380 U.S. 479, 486, 85 S. Ct. 1116, 1120 (1965).

19. 370 U.S. 660, 82 S. Ct. 1417 (1962).

20. 392 U.S. 514, 88 S. Ct. 2145 (1968).

21. 261 Ind. 471, 306 N.E.2d 95.

Chapter 2: Purposes, Scope and Sources of Criminal Law

1. *Lanzetta v. New Jersey,* 306 U.S. 451, 455, 59 S. Ct. 618 (1939).

2. 146 F. Supp. 258, 262 (1956).

3. *Katz v. United States,* 389 U.S. 347, 88 S. Ct. 507 (1967).

4. 336 U.S. 77, 69 S. Ct. 448 (1949).

5. 416 U.S. 1, 94 S. Ct. 1536 (1974).

6. 152 U.S. 133, 14 S. Ct. 499.

7. 42 Wis. 2d 42, 165 N.W.2d 377, and appeal dismissed 395 U.S. 709 (1969). Other majority-rule decisions are *Commonwealth v. Coffman,* 453 S.W.2d 759 (Ky. 1970); *Penney v. City of North Little Rock,* 455 S.W.2d 132 (Ark. 1970); *State v. Albertson,* 93 Idaho 640, 470 P.2d 300 (1970); *Love v. Bell,* 465 P.2d 118 (Colo. 1970); *State v. Lee,* 51 Hawaii 516, 465 P.2d 573 (1970); *State v. Cushman,* 451 S.W.2d 17 (Mo. 1970); *State v. Laitinen,* 77 Wash. 2d 130, 459 P.2d 789 (1969); *State v. Eitel,* 227 So.2d 489 (Fla. 1969). *City of Albuquerque v. Jones,* 87 N.M. 486, 535 P.2d 1337 (1975). In 1977, the Wisconsin legislature repealed the law requiring that adult operators and passengers of motorcycles wear protective head gear. This was in response to political lobbying and large demonstrations against this requirement.

8. 42 Ill. 2d 446, 250 N.E.2d 149 (1969).

9. *State v. Betts,* 21 Ohio Misc. 175, 252 N.E.2d 866, (Franklin Mun. Ct., Ohio, 1969).

10. 356 U.S. 165, 78 S. Ct. 632 (1958).

11. 11 U.S. (7 Cranch) 32, 3 L.Ed. 259 (1812).

12. *Krulewitch v. United States,* 336 U.S. 440, 69 S. Ct. 716 (1949).

13. Blackstone defines a common scold as a troublesome and angry woman who by her brawling and wrangling among her neighbors, breaks the peace, increases discord and becomes a nuisance to the neighborhood. Depending on the situation, such conduct might be a violation of a state disorderly conduct statute, but the statute cannot be addressed only to a woman.

14. 220 U.S. 506, 31 S. Ct. 480 (1911).

15. *M. Kraus & Bros., Inc. v. United States,* 327 U.S. 614, 66 S. Ct. 705 (1946).

16. American Bar Association's Special Committee on Administrative Law, 59 A.B.A. Rep., pp. 552–555 (1934).

17. Vernon's Penal Code of the State of Texas, Art. 1.26.

18. McKinney's Consolidated Laws of New York, Annotated, Sec. 5.00.

Chapter 3: Essential Elements of a Crime

1. *Powell v. Texas,* 392 U.S. 514, 535, 88 S. Ct. 2145 (1969).
2. *Morissette v. United States,* 342 U.S. at 251 (see Chapter 7).
3. 444 U.S. 394, 26 CrL ·3065.
4. 438 U.S. at 445, 98 S. Ct. at 2877 (1978).
5. 444 U.S. 394, 26 Cr.L. 3065.
6. See 22 Corpus Juris Secundum Criminal Law, Sec. 30–36.
7. 512 F.2d 1281.
8. See *State v. Ward,* 512 S.W.2d 245 (Mo. App. 1974).
9. 362 U.S. 199, 80 S. Ct. 624.
10. Smith and Hogan, *Criminal Law,* 3d. ed. (London: Buttersworth, 1973).
11. *United States v. Bailey,* 444 U.S. 394, 406, 100 S. Ct. 624, 632.
12. See the section on causation and intervening causes (pp. 246–267) in *Criminal Law,* by LaFave and Scott (St. Paul: West Pub. Co., 1972).
13. *United States v. Hamilton,* 182 F.Supp. 548 (D.D.C. 1960) is a similar case.
14. Blackstone Comm. 197.
15. See *Ker v. California,* 374 U.S. 23, 83 S. Ct. 1623 (1963), for an example of joint possession.
16. See Gardner and Manian, *Principle and Cases of the Law of Arrest, Search and Seizure* (New York: McGraw-Hill Book Co., 1974).
17. *Commonwealth v. Vogel,* 440 Pa. 1, 17, 268 A.2d 89, 102 (1970).
18. *Sumpter v. State,* 261 Ind. 471, 306 N.E.2d 95 (1974).
19. 442 U.S. 510.
20. 32 CrL 3053.
21. *Chapman v. California,* 386 U.S. at 23.
22. 343 U.S. 790 (1952).
23. See *New York v. Belton,* 453 U.S. 454, 101 S. Ct. 2860 (1981).
24. *State v. Marques,* 135 Ariz. 316, 660 P.2d 1243 (1983).
25. See *People v. Marshall,* 362 Mich. 170, 106 N.W.2d 842 (1961).

Chapter 4: Criminal Liability

1. 336 U.S. 440, 445, 69 S. Ct. 716, 719 (1949).
2. *Commonwealth v. Hunt,* 45 Mass. (4 Metc.) 111, 123 (1842).
3. Judge Learned Hand, in the 1925 case of *Harrison v. United States,* 7 F.2d 259, 263 (2d Cir. 1925).
4. 1961 Committee Comments to Section 8–2 Conspiracy, Smith-Hurd Illinois Annotated Statutes.
5. 33 CrL 2404.
6. 364 U.S. 51, 80 S. Ct. 1589 (1960).
7. 14 Pa. 226, 227 (1850).
8. Named after the author who stated the rule in 2 F. Wharton, Criminal Law, sec. 1604 (12th ed., 1932).

9. 287 U.S. 112, 53 S. Ct. 35 (1935). Prosecution under the Mann Act is now limited to the commercial transportation and exploitation for prostitution and other immoral purposes in which women can be used. The Mann Act was formerly known as the "White Slave Act."
10. Committee Comment to Section 8–2 of the Illinois Criminal Code, p. 460. Smith-Hurd Illinois Annotated Statutes, Chapter 38.
11. *Iannelli* et al. *v. United States,* 420 U.S. 770, 16 CrL 3127 (1975).
12. Sec. 1004.
13. Sec. 110.00, McKinney's Consolidated Laws of New York, Annotated, Book 39.
14. *People v. Ditchik,* 228 N.Y. 95, 41 N.E.2d 905 (1942).
15. 16 N.Y.2d 719, 262 N.Y.S.2d 104, 209 N.E.2d 722 (1965).
16. Sec. 663 of Title 16 of the California Penal Code also permits conviction of attempt when the evidence shows that the crime was completed. This section was enacted in 1872.
17. 671 P.2d 653, 33 CrL 2531.
18. 185 N.Y. 497, 78 N.E. 169 (1906).
19. 345 Mo. 325, 133 S.W.2d 336 (1939).
20. 32 Ind. 220 (1869).
21. 385 U.S. 323, 87 S. Ct. 429 (1966).
22. See also *United States v. Roman,* 356 F. Supp. 434, *aff'd,* CA 2 1973, 484 F.2d 1271, in which the defendants were transporting a suitcase containing heroin. Through the aid of an informer and unknown to the defendants, the contents of the suitcase were replaced with soap powder. The defendants were arrested when they attempted to sell the contents of the suitcase and were subsequently charged with attempted possession with intent to distribute. The court concluded that since the objective acts of the defendants were criminal, factual impossibility would not be recognized as a defense. In *United States v. Berrigan,* 482 F.2d 171, 13 CrL 2361 (CA 3 1973), the defendants were charged with attempting to violate 18 U.S.C. 1791, which prohibits the smuggling of objects into or out of a federal prison. Since the evidence established that the warden had knowledge of the smuggling plan, and since lack of knowledge was a necessary element of the offense, the court held that the warden's knowledge precluded any conviction for attempt, since attempting to do that which is not a crime is not attempting to commit a crime.

In the 1976 case of *United States v. Oviedo,* 525 F.2d 881, 18 CrL 2411, the defendant sold undercover agents a substance he thought was heroin but that was not heroin or a controlled substance. The U.S. Court of Appeals for the Fifth Circuit reversed the attempt conviction, holding that it could not conclude that the defendant's objective acts, apart from any direct or indirect evidence of his intent, indicated the defendant's conduct was criminal.

In the 1977 case of *People v. Dlugash,* 41 N.Y.2d 725, 395 N.Y.S.2d 419, 363 N.E.2d 1155, and in the case of *United States* ex rel. *Rangel v. Brierton,* 437 F. Supp. 908 (D. Ill. 1977), the courts held that the defendants could be found guilty of attempt to murder an intended victim already dead.
23. Committee Comments, p. 513, Chapter 38, Smith-Hurd Illinois Annotated Statutes.

24. Sec. 5.05(2) Model Penal Code.

25. Stephens, *A History of the Criminal Law of England,* vol. 2, pp. 226–227 (1883).

26. 85 Cal. Rptr. 589, 6 Cal. App. 3d 61 (1970).

27. In the 1980 case of *Standefer v. United States,* 27 CrL 3143, the U.S. Supreme Court stated in footnote 9 that "four states—Maryland, North Carolina, Rhode Island and Tennessee—clearly retain the common-law bar."

28. See the 1978 case of *State v. Williamson,* 282 Md. 100, 382 A.2d 588, in which the Maryland court observes that Maryland is the only state that has not abolished the old common law doctrine of accessoryship. The court also notes that all of the English-speaking countries of the world have also made statutory changes. England changed the old common law doctrine as early as 1861.

29. In the 1980 case of *Standefer v. United States,* 447 U.S. 10, 27 CrL 3143, the U.S. Supreme Court held that a defendant may be convicted of aiding and abetting the commission of a federal crime, even though the person who actually committed the crime had been acquitted of the offense.

30. *United States v. Sannicandro,* 434 F.2d 321 (9th Cir. 1970).

31. *Gradsky v. United States,* 376 F.2d 993 (5th Cir. 1967), *cert. denied,* 389 U.S. 908.

32. In 1980, a well-known physician, Dr. Halberstam, returned to his Washington, D.C. home one evening and came upon a burglar. The burglar, Bernard Welch, shot the doctor twice in the chest. The doctor tried driving himself to the hospital and on the way saw Welch. The doctor swerved the car and ran Welch down. The doctor died and Welch was taken into custody. A search of Welch's home by the police revealed $4 million worth of loot, which Welch said "was just peanuts." Over a five-year period, Welch and the woman he lived with, Linda Hamilton, had acquired a fortune from the many burglaries that Welch committed. Hamilton did not participate in the burglaries and was not charged criminally for any of the many crimes. However, the doctor's estate commenced a civil suit against both Welch and Hamilton and received a judgment of $5,715,188.05 (*Halberstam v. Welch,* 705 F.2d 472, D.C. Cir. 1983). The basis of liability was civil conspiracy and aiding and abetting.

It now seems that Hamilton could have also been charged criminally but was not because of the following reasons given by police officers at the civil trial (ftnt. 4, p. 476): (1) the police "did not realize the full extent of Hamilton's involvement with Welch's operations"; (2) "might have had difficulty charging Hamilton because of jurisdictional restrictions"; (3) "noted that all papers on transactions were in Hamilton's name and so concluded she helped sell the goods (gold, silver, furs, jewelry, antiques, etc.)."

33. *People v. Bracey,* 110 Ill. App. 2d 329, 249 N.E.2d 224 (1969).

34. 29 P.2d 902, 136 Cal. App. 722 (1934).

35. 313 A.2d 563, 19 Md. App. 640.

36. 102 Ala. 25, 15 So. 722 (1894).

37. 24 Wis. 2d 527, 129 N.W.2d 155 (1964).

38. N.H. Rev. Stat. Ann. Sec. 169.32.

Chapter 5: Criminal Responsibility and the Capacity to Commit a Crime

1. Sir James FitzJames Stephen, *A History of the Criminal Law of England* (MacMillan & Co., 1883), vol. 1, p. 73. See also the historical accounts of Joan of Arc. Joan was charged by the English as being a witch and was condemned to death. She was burnt at a stake in France, in 1431. England was at that time at war with France and Joan was a French national heroine leading French armed forces.

2. In *Lynch v. Overholser,* 369 U.S. 705, 82 S. Ct. 1063 (1962) a municipal court refused to accept a former mental patient's plea of guilty to a minor check forgery charge. Instead, the court found the defendant not guilty by reason of insanity. As the defendant was a first offender, he would probably have not received a jail sentence. After the defendant served two years in a mental institution, the U.S. Supreme Court reversed the trial court, holding that the trial court was not justified in committing the defendant to a mental institution on bare reasonable doubt concerning past sanity.

3. 406 U.S. 715, 92 S. Ct. 1845 (1972).

4. Justice Thurgood Marshall pointed out in his 1983 dissent in *White v. Estelle,* 459 U.S. 1118, 32 CrL 4149, that: "This Court has approved a test of incompetence which seeks to determine whether the defendant 'has sufficient present ability to consult with his lawyer with a reasonable degree of rational understanding—and whether he has a rational as well as factual understanding of the proceedings against him.' *Dusky v. United States,* 362 U.S. 402 (1960)." Many state statutes have adopted this standard as part of their code of criminal procedure.

5. 357 U.S. 549, 551, 78 S. Ct. 1263 (1958).

6. 10 Cl. & F. 200, 8 Eng. Rep. 718.

7. For a discussion of the "New Hampshire test," see pp. 286–287 of *Criminal Law* by LaFave and Scott (St Paul: West Pub. Co., 1972).

8. 81 Ala. 577, 2 So. 854 (1887).

9. It is unethical for either a prosecutor or a defense lawyer to fabricate a situation in which a defendant appears to be insane and suffering from a mental disease or defect. In the novel *Anatomy of a Murder,* the defense lawyer delivers the famous "lecture" that lets his client (the defendant) become aware that the only way that he could avoid a murder conviction would be by faking "irresistible impulse," which defense was permitted in Michigan at that time. The defense laywer (played by James Stewart in the movie) won his case by manipulating the system but lost his legal fee. In the movie and book, loss of the legal fee seems to have been a just punishment for the improper conduct of the defense lawyer.

10. 94 U.S. App. D.C. 228, 214 F.2d 862 (1954).

11. *Sauver v. United States,* 241 F.2d 640 at p. 648 (1957).

12. In 1981, Connecticut enacted a statute (P.A. 81–301) creating the verdict of "guilty but not criminally responsible."

13. *The Journal of Criminal Law and Criminology* 73 (1982): 867–874 contains the entire text of Governor Thompson's remarks as cochairman of the National Violent Crime Task Force. Governor Thompson stated that "the insanity

defense has been described as the chronic scandal of American criminal law."

14. "The Insanity Defense: Ready for Reform?" *Wisconsin Bar Bulletin,* December 1982.

15. *People v. McLeod,* 288 N.W.2d 909 (1980).

16. *Taylor v. State,* 32 CrL 2150 (1982).

17. 32 CrL 2089.

18. *People v. White,* 117 Cal. App. 3d 270, 172 Cal. Rptr. 612.

19. Los Angeles Deputy District Attorney Dinko Bozanich was quoted as stating that "it (defense of "diminished capacity") works very, very often. All they have to do is paint the picture of a poor bastard, a social misfit, who could not possibly have premeditated." See "Insanity on Trial," *Newsweek,* May 8, 1978.

20. See p. 6 of the Law Enforcement Assistance Administration book entitled *The Mentally Retarded Offender and Corrections.*

21. 32 CrL 2215.

22. 364 So.2d 687, *review denied,* 25 CrL 4018 (Ala. 1978).

23. 406 U.S. 715, 92 S. Ct. 1845 (1972). See also the book *Dummy* and the 1979 television movie. The book and the movie tell the story of Donald Lang, an 18-year-old black, totally illiterate, deaf mute. Lang could not talk, write, read lips, or understand sign language. In 1965, he was charged with the murder of a Chicago prostitute (Cook County criminal case #65–3421). Because he could not hear, speak, read, or write, he was declared incompetent to stand trial and was placed in a state mental hospital. After Lang was held for five years, the Illinois Supreme Court ordered him tried or released. Because witnesses were no longer available, he was released. In 1973, Lang was charged with killing another woman. After a conviction for the second murder, he was held to be incompetent and the conviction was reversed. He was found to be incompetent to stand trial but also not in need of hospitalization. Lang, however, continues to be held in Illinois institutions.

24. C. 18, sec. 12.

25. Section 2.07 of the Model Penal Code on "Liability of Corporations, Unincorporated Associations and Persons Acting, or Under a Duty to Act, in Their Behalf."

26. 24 CrL 2454 (Ind. 1979).

Chapter 6: Defenses that Seek to Justify the Use of Force

1. 11 N.Y.2d 274, 229 N.Y.S.2d 1, 183 N.E.2d 319 (1962).

2. Two dissenting judges urged that the case be sent back to the trial court for a determination as to whether the degree of force used by Young was reasonable under the circumstances.

3. 447 A.2d 880, 31 CrL 2371 (1982).

4. Although there is no legal duty to retreat (flee) from a person who is larger and stronger, in most instances, retreat (if possible) would be practical and sensible.

5. Florida holds that a spouse must retreat (if practical) before using deadly force, but this rule does not apply to a paramour who is held to be "an invitee on the premises," as distinguished from a "legal co-occupant."

6. 415 So.2d 724, 31 CrL 2371 (1982). See also *Rippie v. State,* 404 So.2d 160, in which the Florida District Court of Appeal pointed out that "often when one party to an argument or fight leaves the room, the other party tends to calm down, become more rational and escalation of the dispute is avoided."

7. *Florida Standard Jury Instruction* (Crim.), 2d ed., p. 64.

8. 455 N.E.2d 209, 34 CrL 2168.

9. 183 N.W.2d 657.

10. After a boy scout leader's home in Miami had been burglarized three times within a few months, the leader rigged a booby trap intended to injure the burglars. A 14-year-old neighborhood boy who was a member of the leader's troop smashed a window and entered the house. The youth was killed when he opened the door to which a .22-caliber rifle had been rigged.

11. 120 So.2d 23 (Fla. App. 1960).

12. *Wirsing v. Krzeminski,* 61 Wis. 2d 513, 213 N.W.2d 37.

13. *Sauls v. Hutto and Ruppert,* 304 F. Supp. 124 (E.D. La. 1969).

14. 697 F.2d 18 (1st Cir. 1983).

15. 103 S. Ct. 1660, 33 CrL 3038 (1983).

16. *Diehl v. State,* 451 A.2d 115, *review denied* by U.S. Sup. Ct., 33 CrL 4018 (1983).

17. *Commonwealth v. Moreira,* 447 N.E.2d 1224, 33 CrL 2078.

18. 649 S.W.2d 916.

19. 605 P.2d 46 (1980).

20. *People v. Weeams,* 665 P.2d 619.

21. 430 U.S. 651, 97 S. Ct. 1401.

22. *State v. Kinney,* 34 Minn. 311, 25 N.W. 705 (1885).

Chapter 7: Other Criminal Offenses

1. The fact that a law enforcement officer made an "honest mistake" as to an important fact in making an arrest would not necessarily invalidate the arrest. In the 1971 Supreme Court case of *Hill v. California,* 401 U.S. 797, police made an "honest mistake" in arresting the wrong man. In the 1980 case of *United States v. Allen,* 629 F.2d 51, 27 CrL 2307, the appellate court held that "the case law establishes that an arrest based on actual assumptions later found erroneous may be valid if there is adequate basis in the record to determine the reasonableness of the officer's conduct in making the arrest."

2. The three examples were prepared by Richard G. Denzer and Peter McQuillan in McKinney's Consolidated Laws of New York Annotated. Permission to use the examples was granted by the West Publishing Company.

3. *United States v. Freed,* 401 U.S. 601, 91 S. Ct. 1112 (1971).

4. 79 Wis. 2d 473, 255 N.W.2d 581 (1977).

5. Other cases in which courts have recognized that a state of intoxication at the time of a killing may properly be considered in determining whether the accused acted with

"premeditation" are *State v. Stasio,* 396 A.2d 1129, 24 CrL 2438 (1979); *People v. Garcia,* 398 Mich. 250, 247 N.W.2d 547 (1976); *Harris v. U.S.,* 375 A.2d 505 (D.C. Ct. App. 1977); *Commonwealth v. Sires,* 350 N.E.2d 460 (1976); *People v. Horn,* 12 Cal. 3d 290, 115 Cal. Rptr. 516, P.2d 1300 (1974); *Commonwealth v. Reid,* 432 Pa. 319, 247 A.2d 783 (1968); *State v. Tansimore,* 3 N.J. 516, 71 A.2d 169 (1950).

6. For cases following this majority rule, see *State v. Rice,* 379 A.2d 140, 22 CrL 2194 (Me., 1977); *Commonwealth v. McAlister,* 365 Mass. 454, 313 N.E.2d 113 (1974); *City of Minneapolis v. Altimus,* Minn., 238 N.W.2d 851, 855 (1976); see also 21 Am. Jur. 2d, Criminal Law sec. 108, and relevant cases cited therein.

7. 383 N.E.2d 1115.

8. 82 Cal. App. 778, at 785, 256 P. 251, at 254 (1953).

9. *Johnson v. State,* Del., 379 A.2d 1129.

10. 43 Cal. App. 3d 823, 118 Cal. Rptr. 110 (1975).

11. 444 U.S. 394, 100 S. Ct. 624.

12. Blackstone Commentaries, iv, 30.

13. See Wisconsin Statute 939.46.

14. In the 1980 case of *United States v. Bailey,* 444 U.S. 394, 100 S. Ct. 624, the U.S. Supreme Court pointed out the distinctions between the defenses of duress and necessity as follows: "Common law historically distinguished between the defenses of duress and necessity. Duress was said to excuse criminal conduct where the actor was under an unlawful threat of imminent death or serious bodily injury, which threat caused the actor to engage in conduct violating the literal terms of the criminal law. While the defense of duress covered the situation where the coercion had its source in the actions of other human beings, the defense of necessity, or choice of evils, traditionally covered the situation where physical forces beyond the actor's control rendered illegal conduct the lesser of two evils. Thus, where A destroyed a dike because B threatened to kill him if he did not, A would argue that he acted under duress, whereas if A destroyed the dike in order to protect more valuable property from flooding, A could claim a defense of necessity. See generally LaFave & Scott 374–384.

"Modern cases have tended to blur the distinction between duress and necessity. In the court below, the majority discarded the labels 'duress' and 'necessity,' choosing instead to examine the policies underlying the traditional defenses. See 190 U.S.App.D.C., at 152, 585 F.2d, at 1097. In particular, the majority felt that the defenses were designed to spare a person from punishment if he acted 'under threats or conditions that a person of ordinary firmness would have been unable to resist,' or if he reasonably believed that criminal action 'was necessary to avoid a harm more serious than that sought to be prevented by the statute defining the offense.' *Id.,* at 152, 585 F.2d, at 1097–1098. The Model Penal Code redefines the defenses along similar lines. See Model Penal Code § 2.09 (duress) and § 3.02 (choice of evils)."

15. Model Penal Code, Sec. 3.02 (Justification Generally).

16. Would "disorderly conduct" or "disorderly person" be the proper charge in your state? Did the defendants create a disorder by their nonviolent conduct? Or did their conduct tend to create an immediate public disorder? Would obstructing, hindering, and failure to obey an order of a law enforcement officer be a better charge?

17. Selected Writings of Justice Cardozo, 390.

18. 2 All E.R. at p. 181 (1971).

19. A suspect who has a witness who can testify that the suspect could not have committed the crime would ordinarily provide this information to the police and the prosecutor before being charged. Such information could cause the police and the prosecutor to conclude that the suspect is innocent of the crime. Notice-of-alibi statutes are enacted to protect the government against surprise witnesses brought on at the last minute. Such statutes were held by the U.S. Supreme Court as to not violate the privilege against self-incrimination in 1970 case of *Williams v. Florida,* 399 U.S. 78, 90 S. Ct. 1893.

20. 412 U.S. 470, 93 S. Ct. 2208.

21. *Williamson v. United States,* 207 U.S. 425, 453, 28 S. Ct. 163, 173 (1908).

22. 311 So. 678 (Fla. App. 1975).

23. See Criminal Law by LaFave and Scott (West Publishing Co., 1972), p. 368 for a discussion of the defense.

24. 437 U.S. 82, 98 S. Ct. 2187.

25. In the case of *North Carolina v. Pearce,* 395 U.S. 711, 717 (1969), the U.S. Supreme Court pointed out that the double jeopardy clause affords three distinct constitutional protections: (1) protection against a second prosecution for the same offense after acquittal; (2) protection against a second prosecution for the same offense after conviction; (3) protection against multiple punishments for the same offense.

26. ___ U.S. ___, 34 CrL 3019.

27. *Downum v. United States,* 372 U.S. 734 (1963).

28. *Wade v. Hunter,* 366 U.S. 684 (1949).

29. *Westfall v. United States,* 274 U.S. 256, 47 S. Ct. 629, 71 L.Ed. 1036.

30. 359 U.S. 121, 79 S. Ct. 676 (1959).

31. 397 U.S. 387, 90 S. Ct. 1184 (1970).

32. 432 U.S. 161, at 165, 97 S. Ct. 2221, at 2225.

33. 397 U.S. at 451–452, 90 S. Ct. at 1198.

34. 83 Wis. 2d 150, 256 N.W.2d 274.

35. See *United States v. Oppenheimer,* 242 U.S. 85, 37 S. Ct. 68 (1916).

36. 287 U.S. 435, 53 S. Ct. 210 at 217 (1932), separate opinion.

37. The Supreme Court of California established a new test for the defense of entrapment in the 1979 case of *California v. Barraza,* 23 Cal. 3d 675, 153 Cal. Rptr. 459, 591 P.2d 947. Pointing out that the federal courts and all but seven states use the "origin-of-intent" (subjective) standard and test, the California Supreme Court established a test that focuses on the guilt of the particular defendant and asks whether he or she was predisposed to commit the crime charged.

38. Footnote 4 of *Russell v. United States.*

39. 692 F.2d at 835.

40. *United States v. Williams,* 705 F.2d at 619.

41. 705 F.2d at 619.

42. 692 F.2d at 836.

43. 425 U.S. at 495, n. 7.

44. 692 F.2d at 837.

45. 705 F.2d 621.

46. *Id.* at 621.

47. 692 F.2d at 860. Because of the criticism of the Abscam tactics, FBI Director Webster held a 90-minute interview to answer charges. He pointed out that Abscam began as an attempt to catch art thieves, not members of Congress. However, the Congressmen walked into the net. Director Webster said that "they found their way to us." He stated that "Abscam was purposely sleazy so that no one would stick around it, except someone who wanted to deal with sleazy people." When asked if the FBI would ever conduct another undercover investigation of Congressmen, Webster said, "The answer is, we will always follow our leads."

48. *Id.* at 836.

49. *Id.* at 836.

50. *Id.* at 837.

51. 468 A.2d 1342, 34 CrL 2283.

52. 404 U.S. 307 (1971).

53. *Id.* at 320.

54. 30 CrL 3111.

55. "The Statute of Limitations in Criminal Law," 102 *U. Pa. L. Rev.* 630.

56. See *Toussie v. United States,* 397 U.S. 112, 114–115, 90 S. Ct. 858, 859–860 (1970).

57. *United States v. Levine,* 658 F.2d 1113 (3rd Cir. 1981).

58. 124 Kan. 340, 259 P. 802 (1927).

Chapter 8: Criminal Punishment

1. *A History of the Criminal Law of England* (3 volumes) by Sir James FitzJames Stephens, Judge of High Court of Justice, Queen's Bench Division, (England, 1883), I: 477.

2. Blackstone's *Commentaries,* 4 Comm. 18.

3. *A History of the Criminal Law of England,* chapt. 13, pp. 491–492.

4. *A History of English Criminal Law and Its Administration,* Radzinowicz (London: Stevens Publications, 1948) and *Crime, Courts, and Probation,* Chute and Bell (New York: MacMillan, 1956).

5. It is interesting to note that "transportation" was used by a number of countries. The Roman Empire transported prisoners to Rumania; Russia transported hundreds of thousands of political prisoners to Siberia. In addition, the frontiers of the world have always been used as a refuge by people fleeing from the law or in political trouble.

6. *Furman v. Georgia,* 408 U.S. 238, 92 S. Ct. 2726 (1972).

7. I Annals of Congress, 782 (1789).

8. *Furman v. Georgia,* 408 U.S. at 258, 92 S. Ct. at 2736.

9. ___ U.S. ___, 34 CrL 3027.

10. 404 F.2d 571. The Court gave the following reasons for holding whipping to be unconstitutional: "Our reasons for this conclusion include the following: (1) We are not convinced that any rule or regulation as to the use of the strap, however seriously or sincerely conceived and drawn, will successfully prevent abuse. The present record discloses

misinterpretation and obvious overnarrow interpretation even of the newly adopted January 1966 rules. (2) Rules in this area seem often to go unobserved. Despite the January 1966 requirement that no inmate was to inflict punishment on another, the record is replete with instances where this very thing took place. (3) Regulations are easily circumvented. Although it was a long-standing requirement that a whipping was to be administered only when the prisoner was fully clothed, this record discloses instances of whippings upon the bare buttocks, and with consequent injury. (4) Corporal punishment is easily subject to abuse in the hands of the sadistic and the unscrupulous. (5) Where power to punish is granted to persons in lower levels of administrative authority, there is an inherent and natural difficulty in enforcing the limitations of that power. (6) There can be no argument that excessive whipping or an inappropriate manner of whipping or too great frequency of whipping or the use of studded or overlong straps all constitute cruel and unusual punishment. But if whipping were to be authorized, how does one, or any court, ascertain the point which would distinguish the permissible from that which is cruel and unusual? (7) Corporal punishment generates hate toward the keepers who punish and toward the system which permits it. It is degrading to the punisher and to the punished alike. It frustrates correctional and rehabilitative goals. This record cries out with testimony to this effect from the expert penologists, from the inmates and from their keepers. (8) Whipping creates other penological problems and makes adjustment to society more difficult. (9) Public opinion is obviously adverse. Counsel concede that only two states still permit the use of the strap. Thus almost uniformly has it been abolished. It has been expressly outlawed by statute in a number of states. See for example, N.D.Cent. Code § 12–47–26 (1960); S.D.Code § 13.4715 (1939). And 48 states, including Arkansas, have constitutional provisions against cruel or unusual punishment. Ark.Const. art. 2, § 9.

We are not convinced contrarily by any suggestion that the State needs this tool for disciplinary purposes and is too poor to provide other accepted means of prisoner regulation. Humane considerations and constitutional requirements are not, in this day, to be measured or limited by dollar considerations or by the thickness of the prisoner's clothing."

11. 430 U.S. 651, 97 S. Ct. 1401 (1977).

12. 408 U.S. 238, 92 S. Ct. 2726 (1972).

13. 408 U.S., at 366, 92 S. Ct. at 2791.

14. In the 1984 case of *Pulley v. Harris,* the Supreme Court defined and explained the use of "proportionality."

15. 428 U.S. 153.

16. 428 U.S. 242.

17. *Jurek v. Texas,* 428 U.S. 262.

18. ___ U.S. ___, 34 CrL 3027.

19. 408 U.S. 238, 92 S. Ct. 2726.

20. 428 U.S. 153.

21. The Court summarizes California's "special circumstances" as follows: "Briefly, the statutory special circumstances are: 1) the murder was for profit; 2) the murder was perpetrated by an explosive; 3) the victim was a police officer killed in the line of duty; 4) the victim was a witness to a crime, killed to prevent his testifying in a criminal proceed-

ing; 5) the murder was committed during the commission of robbery, kidnapping, rape, performance of a lewd or lascivious act on someone under 14, or burglary; 6) the murder involved torture; 7) the defendant had been previously convicted of first or second degree murder, or was convicted of more than one murder in the first or second degree in this proceeding. Cal. Penal Code Ann. § 190.2 (West 1977). These are greatly expanded in the current statute. See Cal. Penal Code Ann. § 190.2 (West Supp. 1983)."

22. California's statute Sec. 190.3 does not separate aggravating and mitigating circumstances. The statute provides: "In determining the penalty the trier of fact shall take into account any of the following factors if relevant:

(a) The circumstances of the crime of which the defendant was convicted in the present proceeding and the existence of any special circumstances found to be true pursuant to § 190.1.

(b) The presence or absence of criminal activity by the defendant which involved the use or attempted use of force or violence or the expressed or implied threat to use force or violence.

(c) Whether or not the offense was committed while the defendant was under the influence of extreme mental or emotional disturbance.

(d) Whether or not the victim was a participant in the defendant's homicidal conduct or consented to the homicidal act.

(e) Whether or not the offense was committed under circumstances which the defendant reasonably believed to be a moral justification or extenuation for his conduct.

(f) Whether or not the defendant acted under extreme duress or under the substantial domination of another person.

(g) Whether or not at the time of the offense the capacity of the defendant to appreciate the criminality of his conduct or to conform his conduct to the requirements of law was impaired as a result of mental disease or the effects of intoxication.

(h) The age of the defendant at the time of the crime.

(i) Whether or not the defendant was an accomplice to the offense and his participation in the commission of the offense was relatively minor.

(j) Any other circumstance which extenuates the gravity of the crime even though it is not a legal excuse for the crime."

23. The Law of Criminal Corrections, Rubin (St. Paul, Minn.: West Pub. Co., 1963).

24. England also had debtors' prisons in which persons who owed civil debts could be imprisoned until the civil debt was paid. England abolished the practice of debtors' prison in 1869. Such imprisonment would not be lawful under the U.S. Constitution and some state constitutions specifically forbid this form of imprisonment. Although most of the democratic world has abolished the practice, Hong Kong continues to allow creditors to put their debtors behind bars.

25. Williams v. Illinois, 399 U.S. 235, 90 S. Ct. 2018 (1971).

26. See the two volume Prisoner's Rights by Haft and Hermann, published by the Practising Law Institute (1972).

27. 445 U.S. 263.

Chapter 9: Criminal Jurisdiction

1. See Ford v. State, 184 Tenn. 443, 201 S.W.2d (1945) in which it was held that a presumption arises that the homicide occurred in the county in which the body was found.

2. If the accused were arrested while he was a witness extradited from another state to testify, or on a speedy trial conveyance, or while he was in court in response to a subpoena, he would then have grounds to challenge the court's jurisdiction over his person. See your legal adviser for the law in your state in regard to these exceptions.

3. 414 U.S. 17, 94 S. Ct. 194.

4. Ordinarily jurisdiction is obtained over a fugitive who has fled from a jurisdiction by means of extradition. The United States presently has over eighty extradition treaties in force with foreign countries. A compilation of these treaties can be found in 18 U.S.C.A. section 3181.

5. Gerstein v. Pugh, 420 U.S. 103, 119, 95 S. Ct. 854, 865 (1975); United States v. Crews, 445 U.S. 463, 474 (1980); also see Akins v. Hamlin, 327 So. 2d 59 (Fla. App., 1976).

6. 109 Wis. 2d 138, 325 N.W.2d 695. In a case such as the Monje case, the officer should have taken Monje before an Illinois judge, who would determine whether probable cause existed to hold Monje. Extradition proceedings would then be commenced to return Monje to Wisconsin, where he had committed an armed robbery.

7. Article 19 of the Geneva Convention on the High Seas, 1958 states: "On the high seas, or in any other place outside the jurisdiction of any State, every State may seize a pirate ship or aircraft, or a ship taken by piracy and under pirates, and arrest the persons and seize the property on board. The courts of the State which carried out the seize may decide upon the penalties to be imposed, and may also determine the action to be taken with regard to the ships, aircraft or property, subject to the rights of third parties acting in good faith."

8. 679 F.2d 1373 (Eleventh Cir).

9. If federal property is intentionally damaged or destroyed, the federal government ordinarily has jurisdiction over the matter. When state property is intentionally damaged or destroyed within that state, the state government has jurisdiction. What about a situation in which the property is internationally owned, such as the United Nations building in New York City? In the 1976 case of People v. Weiner, 85 Misc. 2d 161, 378 N.Y.S.2d 966, the defendant was charged with criminal mischief for having sprayed red paint on the outside wall of the United Nations headquarters. The New York Criminal Court held that the court had jurisdiction over the person of the defendant and the offense.

10. This material was presented in the Working Papers of the National Commission on Reform of Federal Criminal Laws, Vol. II, p. 832.

11. At the time of the assassination of President Kennedy, only the state of Texas had jurisdiction to try the homicide charges.

12. 355 U.S. 286, 78 S. Ct. 291 (1958).

13. 31 U.S. (6 Pet.) 515, 8 L.Ed. 483 (1832).

14. 118 U.S. 375, 6 S. Ct. 1109 (1886).

15. 241 U.S. 602, 36 S. Ct. 699 (1916).

16. 430 U.S. 641, 97 S. Ct. 1395, 21 CrL 3007 (1977). In the 1965 case of *Colliflower v. Garland,* 342 F.2d 369 (9th Cir.) an Indian woman was found guilty by an Indian tribal court in the Fort Belknap Indian Community (Montana) of failing to remove her cattle from another Indian's land. She was fined $25 or five days in jail for failing to obey the tribal court's order to remove her cattle. She elected to take the jail sentence, stating that she could not pay the fine. She sought a writ of habeas corpus in a federal district court, alleging that the tribal court had denied her Fifth Amendment rights under the U.S. Constitution. The federal court concluded that it was "without jurisdiction to issue a writ of habeas corpus" in her case. This ruling was appealed to the Circuit Court of Appeals. After reviewing some of the decisions cited above, the Court of Appeals held that the district court did have the jurisdiction to issue a writ of habeas corpus and hear the matter.

The Court held: "We do not pass upon the merits of Mrs. Colliflower's claims, because the district court did not reach them. It does not follow from our decision that the tribal court must comply with every constitutional restriction that is applicable to federal or state courts. Nor does it follow that the Fourteenth Amendment applies to tribal courts at all; some of the cases cited above indicate that it does not."

17. Supra., see footnote #14.

18. Title 18 U.S.C. Sec. 1153 provides in pertinent part: "Any Indian who commits against the person or property of another Indian or other person any of the following offenses, namely, murder, manslaughter, rape, carnal knowledge of any female, not his wife, who has not attained the age of sixteen years, assault with intent to commit rape, incest, assault with intent to kill, assault with a dangerous weapon, assault resulting in serious bodily injury, arson, burglary, robbery, and larceny within the Indian country, shall be subject to the same laws and penalties as all other persons committing any of the above offenses, within the exclusive jurisdiction of the United States."

19. 412 U.S. 205, 93 S. Ct. 1993 (1973).

20. In the 1978 case of *Oliphant v. Suquamish Indian Tribe,* 435 U.S. 191, 98 S. Ct. 1011, 22 CrL 3055, the U.S. Supreme Court held that an Indian tribal court could not try non-Indians unless it had been granted specific authority by the Congress of the United States.

21. 10 U.S.C.A. Sec. 801–940 (Supp. V, 1970) amending 10 U.S.C.A. Sec. 801–940 (1964).

22. 420 U.S. 738, 16 CrL 3136.

23. In the *Relford* case, Relford was convicted of raping two civilian women in separate attacks on a military base. The U.S. Supreme Court unanimously held that the military could properly try offenses committed by a person in the military against a person or property that occurred on a military base.

24. 32 CrL 2464.

25. The best known SOFA (status of forces agreement) is that with the NATO countries. The largest American military commitment has existed in these European countries since 1945 in a continuous effort to keep the peace.

26. 34 CrL 2154.

27. 14 CrL 2387.

28. 437 F.2d 200 (4th Cir. 1971).

29. 327 U.S. 304, 66 S. Ct. 606 (1946).

30. From the testimony of Major General Wilson, Chief of the National Guard Bureau, before the President's Commission on Campus Unrest, 116 Cong. Rec. 27,339.

31. 10 U.S.C.A. Sec. 331 also provides: "Whenever there is an insurrection in any State against its government, the President may, upon the request of its legislature or of its governor if the legislature cannot be convened, call into federal service such of the militia of the other States, in the number requested by that State, and use such of the armed forces, as he considers necessary to suppress the insurrections."

32. 100 U.S. 158, 25 L.Ed. 632 (1880).

33. See *Abel v. United States,* 362 U.S. 217, 80 S. Ct. 683 (1960). The *Abel* case illustrates the fact that all persons, including spies and persons illegally in the United States, have all the rights under the U.S. Constitution. The Bill of Rights uses the terms persons and people. Officers must therefore give all persons *Miranda* warnings and receive a waiver if they seek to use any statements in evidence against such persons.

34. See Justice Frankfurter's concurring opinion in *Korematsu v. United States.*

35. 320 U.S. 81, 63 S. Ct. 1375 (1943).

Chapter 9: Supplemental Reading

1. The White Slave Act or "Mann Act" prohibits the interstate transportation of a woman for immoral purposes. 18 U.S.C.A. § 2421 et seq.

2. *United States v. Hill,* 248 U.S. 420, 425 (1919).

3. 18 U.S.C.A. §§ 111, 1114.

4. 18 U.S.C.A. §§ 471 et seq.

5. 18 U.S.C.A. §§ 641, 2112.

6. 18 U.S.C.A. § 1708.

7. 18 U.S.C.A. §§ 286, 287, 371 & 1001.

8. Tax evasion and similar offenses. See 26 U.S.C.A. § 7201 et seq.

9. 18 U.S.C.A. § 201.

10. 18 U.S.C.A. §§ 205, 207, 208, 209.

11. 18 U.S.C.A. §§ 1503, 1504.

12. 18 U.S.C.A. §§ 1621, 1622, 1623.

13. 18 U.S.C.A. § 1341.

14. 18 U.S.C.A. § 876.

15. 18 U.S.C.A. § 1952.

16. 18 U.S.C.A. §§ 1005, 1006, 2113.

17. 18 U.S.C.A. §§ 407, 411; 42 U.S.C.A. § 1857 et seq.

18. 18 U.S.C.A. § 13.

19. *United States v. Hyde,* 448 F.2d 815, 836–837 (5th Cir. 1971), cert. denied 404 U.S. 1058 (1972).

20. 18 U.S.C.A. § 2312.

21. 21 U.S.C.A. § 811 et seq.

22. 18 U.S.C.A. ch. 44, § 921 et seq., 18 U.S.C.A. Appendix, §§ 1201, 1202.

23. 18 U.S.C.A. § 659.

24. 18 U.S.C.A. § 1073.

25. 49 U.S.C.A. § 1422(I) & (J).

26. 18 U.S.C.A. § 1462.

27. 18 U.S.C.A. § 1951.

28. 18 U.S.C.A. § 241.

29. 18 U.S.C.A. § 242.

30. 18 U.S.C.A. § 1074.

31. *Bartkus v. Illinois,* 359 U.S. 121 (1959); *Abbate v. United States,* 359 U.S. 187 (1959).

32. *Harris v. Superior Court of Sacramento County,* 196 P. 895 (1921); *Goulis v. Judge of District Court,* 246 Mass. 1, 140 N.E. 294 (1923).

33. *Marsh v. United States,* 29 F.2d 172 (2d Cir. 1928); other cases have found such authority without detailed consideration. *Theriault v. United States,* 401 F.2d 79 (8th Cir. 1969); *Davida v. United States,* 422 F.2d 528 (10th Cir. 1970).

34. *Henderson v. United States,* 237 F.2d 169, 175 (5th Cir. 1956).

35. *United States v. Montos,* 421 F.2d 215 (5th Cir. 1970).

36. *Weeks v. United States,* 232 U.S. 383 (1914).

37. *Bram v. United States,* 168 U.S. 532 (1897).

38. *Harrison v. United States,* 392 U.S. 219, 221 (1968); See also: *Wong Sun v. United States,* 371 U.S. 471, 488 (1963).

39. *McNabb v. United States,* 318 U.S. 322 (1943); *Mallory v. United States,* 354 U.S. 449 (1957); *Westover v. United States,* 384 U.S. 436, 494–497 (1966).

40. *Sharp v. United States,* 280 F. 86 (5th Cir. 1922).

41. 18 U.S.C.A. §§ 1701, 1702, 1709.

42. 18 U.S.C.A. § 2511.

43. 18 U.S.C.A. § 2511.

44. 18 U.S.C.A. § 2511.

45. 18 U.S.C.A. § 2512.

46. 18 U.S.C.A. § 2511.

47. 18 U.S.C.A. § 2511.

48. 18 U.S.C.A. § 2511.

49. 26 U.S.C.A. §§ 5861 & 5871.

Chapter 10: The Limits of Free Speech

1. *Cox v. New Hampshire,* 312 U.S. 569, 61 S. Ct. 762 (1941).

2. *Speiser v. Randall,* 357 U.S. 513, 78 S. Ct. 1332 (1958).

3. See *Watts v. United States,* 394 U.S. 705, 89 S. Ct. 1399 (1969).

4. 268 U.S. 652, 45 S. Ct. 625 (1925).

5. 249 U.S. 47, 39 S. Ct. 247 (1919).

6. 301 U.S. 242, 258, 57 S. Ct. 732 (1936).

7. 413 U.S. 15, 93 S. Ct. 2607 (1973).

8. 315 U.S. 568, at 571, 62 S. Ct. 766, 769.

9. 405 U.S. 518, at 521, 92 S. Ct. 1103, 1105.

10. 403 U.S. 15, 91 S. Ct. 1780.

11. *Id.* at 25, 91 S. Ct. at 1788.

12. 422 U.S. 205, 95 S. Ct. 2268.

13. 405 U.S. 518, 92 S. Ct. 1103.

14. This case demonstrates that it is the owner or manager of the business place who is obligated to maintain order. If he or she fails to take action after becoming aware of the type

of provocative language Downs was using, and a fight erupts, causing injury to bystanders, civil liability would exist that might give rise to a lawsuit.

15. 29 Wis.2d 66, 138 N.W.2d 264 (1965).

16. *City of St. Petersburg v. Waller,* 261 So. 2d 151 (Fla. 1972) in which the Florida Court of Appeals states the "defendant as a police car approached a group gathered at a corner, stepped into the street, thrust his amplified megaphone close to the window of the police car, and yelled 'pig.' This Court held that under the circumstances the language had no significance than to arouse the crowd into action against the police officer."

17. *Bradshaw v. State,* 286 So. 2d 4 (Fla. 1973) in which the defendant used abusive and insulting language in the presence of 100 to 150 people when the possibility of a riot existed. See also *Phillips v. State,* 314 So. 2d 619 (Fla. App. 1975) in which the defendant told the arresting officer "fuck you" twice before he was arrested. As none of the Florida extenuating circumstances existed, the Florida Court reversed holding: "It is our view that the use of the expletive was not such as to afford the arresting officer with substantial reason to believe the defendant was committing the misdemeanor of a breach of the peace in violation of F.S. 877.03, *supra.* . . . Thus, we reverse."

18. 136 U.S. App. D.C. 56, 419 F.2d 638 (1969).

19. 537 S.W.2d 709.

20. ___ F. Supp. ___.

21. 278 Md. 610, 366 A.2d 41.

22. Milwaukee County Case #1–264020. In 1972, George Carlin was arrested for disorderly conduct when he included in an hour-long show before thousands of young people and adults the seven words not allowed on television or radio. Carlin was acquitted in a trial when the city failed to show either (a) that Carlin caused a disturbance or breach of the peace or (b) that he angered his audience to the point that persons in the audience were "aggravated to fight." Most of the audience was amused by the presentation, which Carlin presented as humorous and not meant as "fighting words." However, several complaints were made to police officers because of the language.

23. 79 Mich. App. 757, 262 N.W.2d 900.

24. 263 N.W.2d 412 (1978). The Supreme Court of Minnesota held that "with the words spoken in retreat from more than 15 feet away rather than eye to eye, there was no reasonable likelihood that they would tend to incite an immediate breach of the peace or to provoke violent reaction by an ordinary, reasonable person."

25. 384 A.2d 429 (Me. 1978).

26. 451 A.2d 115, *review denied* United States Supreme Court 1983 (33 CrL 4018). Officer Gavin testified that Diehl said, "Fuck you, Gavin"; "I know my rights"; "You can't tell me what to do." After the arrest, he was alleged to have told Gavin he was "full of shit" and "a crazy son-of-a-bitch."

27. 644 P.2d 747.

28. Juvenile cases similar to *State v. Montgomery* are *State v. John W.,* 418 A.2d 1097 (Me. 1980), and *White v. State,* 330 So.2d 3 (Fla. 1976).

29. 99 S. Ct. 2627.

30. In the 1971 case of *Colten v. Commonwealth,* 467 S.W. 2d 374, the defendant complained that the arresting officer had called him a "loudmouth." However, the defendant argued in his brief that he had the right to call policemen and their wives "pigs" as he had done. The Kentucky Court held that "the evidence warrants the conclusion that Colten was in fact a 'loudmouth.'"

31. The Supreme Court of Rhode Island reviewed "profanity" cases as follows in the 1978 case of *State v. Authelet,* 385 A.2d 642:

"Several courts have . . . determined that profanity may only be prohibited if it is considered within the category of fighting words. In *Tallman v. United States,* 465 F.2d 282 (7th Cir. 1972), the court held that unless the *Chaplinsky* test of fighting words was read into a statutory proscription against profanity, the statute would be unconstitutionally overbroad. Likewise, in *Williams v. District of Columbia,* 136 U.S. App. D.C. 56, 419 F.2d 638 (1969), the court reversed a conviction for the use of 'profane language, indecent and obscene words.' The court held that the only interests which the state could assert in forbidding profane or indecent language were those delineated in *Chaplinsky.* A third case, *Conchito v. City of Tulsa,* 521 P.2d 1384 (Okla. Crim. 1974), ruled that a city ordinance proscribing 'profane or obscene language' was unconstitutionally broad on the ground that it was not limited in accordance with the Supreme Court's previous rulings. The court implicitly found that profanity could only be constitutionally punished if the penal statute was restricted to the proscription of fighting words. Finally, in *Reese v. State,* 17 Md. App. 73, 299 A.2d 848 (1973), the court held that the statutory phrase 'profanely cursing, [or] swearing' was meant to restrict only such language as came within the category of fighting words.

We subscribe to the position taken by courts in *Tallman, Williams, Conchito,* and *Reese,* all *supra.* Although the Supreme Court has not specifically decided whether profanity may be independently proscribed, we feel that choosing to analyze profanity under the fighting words approach strikes the proper balance between the state's interest in maintaining order and an individual's right to free speech. While we do not condone the use of profanity in any context, neither can we countenance unwarranted state intrusions upon how a person comports or expresses himself. Of course, we would all perhaps wish that each person would conduct himself or herself in the most exemplary way possible, but failure to measure up to what society considers to be in good taste is not, and has never been, grounds for the imposition of criminal sanctions."

32. 41 Ohio St. 2d 173, 324 N.E.2d 735 (1975).

33. 413 U.S. 15, 93 S. Ct. 2607 (1973).

34. 452 U.S. 61, 101 S. Ct. 2176.

35. 409 U.S. 109.

36. See *New York State Liquor Authority v. Bellanca,* 29 CrL 4104 (1981).

37. *Doe v. Indiana,* 28 CrL 4021 (1981).

38. The U.S. Supreme Court in *Brandenburg v. Ohio,* 395 U.S. 444, 89 S. Ct. 1827 (1969).

39. See also the section on "Seditious Speech and Subversive Conduct" in Chapter 11.

40. The Wisconsin Criminal Code defines obstructs as follows in Sec. 946.41(2)(b) *Resisting or Obstructing Officer:* (b) "Obstructs" includes without limitation knowingly giving false information to the officer with intent to mislead him in the performance of his duty including the service of any summons or civil process.

41. Books written by Whitaker Chambers, Alger Hiss and Richard Nixon relating this incident in greater detail from the point of view of each of the writers are available in public libraries.

42. 110 U.S. 311.

43. The quotation used is from the ruling by the U.S. Supreme Court in *Garrison v. Louisiana,* 379 U.S. 64, 85 S. Ct. 209 (1964).

44. For other defamation cases see *Gertz v. Robert Welch, Inc.,* 418 U.S. 323, 94 S. Ct. 2997 (1974); *Munn v. Burks,* 19 Or. App. 144, 526 P.2d 104 (1974); and *Kerpelman v. Bricker,* 23 Md. App. 628, 329 A.2d 423 (1974).

45. The Consumer Credit Protection Act (Pub. Law 95–109 Stat. 877) prohibits debt collectors from "placing telephone calls without meaningful disclosure of the caller's identity"; from "engaging any person in telephone conversation repeatedly or continuously with intent to annoy, abuse, or harass any person at the called number"; and from "us[ing] obscene or profane language or language the natural consequence of which is to abuse the hearer or reader."

46. *Saja v. New York,* 334 U.S. 558, 560–562 (1948).

47. 108 Cal. Rptr. 465, 510 P.2d 1017, *cert. denied,* 416 U.S. 950 (1974).

48. 336 U.S. 77, 69 S. Ct. 448 (1948).

49. 384 U.S. 333, 86 S. Ct. 1507 (1966).

Chapter 11: Maintaining Public Order in Public and Private Places

1. In the case of *Grayned v. City of Rockford,* 408 U.S. 104, 92 S. Ct. 2294 (1972), the U.S. Supreme Court held that: "The nature of a place, 'the pattern of its normal activities, dictates the kinds of regulations of time, place, and manner that are reasonable.' Although a silent vigil may not unduly interfere with a public library, making a speech in the reading room almost certainly would. That same speech should be perfectly appropriate in a park. The crucial question is whether the manner of expression is basically incompatible with the normal activity of a particular place at a particular time. Our cases make clear that in assessing the reasonableness of regulation, we must weigh heavily the fact that communication is involved; the regulation must be narrowly tailored to further the State's legitimate interest. 'Access to [the streets, sidewalks, parks, and other similar public places] for the purpose of exercising [First Amendment rights] cannot constitutionally be denied broadly.' Free expression 'must not, in the guise of regulation, be abridged or denied.'"

2. See *Breard v. Alexandria,* 341 U.S. 622, 71 S. Ct. 920 (1951); *Hall v. Commonwealth,* 188 Va. 72, 49 S.E.2d 369 (1948), *appeal dismissed,* 335 U.S. 875, 69 S. Ct. 240.

3. *Tinker v. Des Moines School Dist.,* 393 U.S. 503, 89 S. Ct. 733 (1969). See this case in Chapter 10.

4. An example of controlling premises that startled the business world occurred in Milwaukee in 1983. Mr. Checota, the founder of a large corporation, had been the president and chairman of the board. Mr. Checota had hired retired Admiral Elmo Zumwalt (former U.S. Chief of Naval Operations) as president, but in 1979, Admiral Zumwalt quit his job as president because of a dispute but stayed on the board. While Mr. Checota was vacationing in Italy in 1983, the board voted him out of office. On Mr. Checota's return to work, he was informed that he had been "fired" and was told to leave the premises immediately "or be physically carried out by security guards." As numerous guards were nearby, Mr. Checota was not permitted to go to his office and obtain his personal belongings. Mr. Checota then enlisted former Secretary of State Alexander Haig and a proxy fight and lawsuit was commenced. Retired General Haig (and former NATO commander) was heading the attacking forces and retired Admiral Zumwalt was defending.

5. *Grayned v. City of Rockford,* 408 U.S. 104, 92 S. Ct. 2294 (1972).

6. *Kunz v. New York,* 340 U.S. 290, 71 S. Ct. 312 (1951).

7. 49 Wis. 2d 398, 182 N.W.2d 530 (1972).

8. See *Diehl v. Maryland,* 451 A.2d 115, *review denied,* 33 CrL 4018 (1983), in which an officer made a traffic stop in an A&P parking lot for "tire squealing." Diehl was a passenger and got out of the car. The officer ordered Diehl to get back into the car. The Maryland Court of Appeals held "the officer did not have any right to make this demand on Diehl." To order a person to get into a car (or to get out of a car) on a traffic stop (civil violation), the officer must show a good and sufficient reason, such as concern for safety of the person, or of the officer, or the public. This requirement was not shown in the *Diehl* case. See also *Delaware v. Prouse,* 440 U.S. 648, 99 S. Ct. 1391 (1979).

9. Under the old common law, if a number of persons met together and suddenly quarreled and fought among themselves, this would constitute an "affray." An "affray" differs from a riot in that an "affray" is not premeditated. Under the old common law, a riot required three or more persons, while an "affray" could consist of two or more.

10. Under New York statutes, four or more persons plus the person charged are needed for the crime of "unlawful assembly." To convict of any of the riot offenses, it must be shown that there were 10 or more persons plus the person charged.

11. *Kovacs v. Cooper,* 336 U.S. 77, 69 S. Ct. 448 (1948).

12. 46 N.J. 510, 218 A.2d 147 (1966).

13. Among the chants that petitioner did *not* engage in were "Bullshit, bullshit," during the president's speech, and "one, two, three, four, we don't want your fucking war." One isolated member of the group rose during a minister's prayer and screamed an obscenity.

14. 79 Wash. 2d 351, 485 P.2d 449 (1971).

15. 1 Cal. 3d 930, 83 Cal. Rptr. 686, 464 P.2d 142 (1970).

16. 91 N.M. 74, 570 P.2d 612 (1977).

17. *Griego v. Wilson* was a civil action for damages for injuries which the plaintiff alleged that he received at the hands of the store employees. The dismissal of the case by the trial court was affirmed by the Court of Appeals.

18. 31 CrL 2222.

19. Commercial messages include commercial advertising by firms or persons seeking to promote sales of their products or services. In the 1942 case of *Valentine v. Chrestensen,* 316 U.S. 52, 62 S. Ct. 920, the U.S. Supreme Court held that cities and states could absolutely forbid the distribution of commercial handbills in public places. However, in 1976 the U.S. Supreme Court reversed itself in *Virginia State Board of Pharmacy v. Virginia Citizens Consumer Counsel, Inc.,* 425 U.S. 748, 96 S. Ct. 1817, 44 U.S.L.W. 4686, in which the Court held that "commercial speech, like other varieties, is protected."

20. 336 U.S. 77, 69 S. Ct. 448 (1949).

21. 40 N.Y. 2d 527, 387 N.Y.S.2d 415, 355 N.E.2d 375, 19 CrL 2366 (1976).

22. 319 U.S. 141, 63 S. Ct. 862 (1943).

23. *NAACP v. Button,* 371 U.S. 415, 433, 83 S. Ct. 328, 338 (1963).

24. 425 U.S. 610, 96 S. Ct. 1755 (1976).

25. 391 U.S. 308, 88 S. Ct. 1601 (1968).

26. 326 U.S. 501, 66 S. Ct. 276 (1946).

27. *Abrams v. United States,* 250 U.S. 616, 40 S. Ct. 17 (1919).

Chapter 12: The Limits of Other Freedoms

1. The right to carry arms was regulated in England as early as 1328 in the Statute of Northampton. The English Bill of Rights of 1688 denounced the discriminatory arming of persons and seemed to acknowledge the legislature's power to regulate. Carrying weapons was not an absolute right under the old common law. See *Burton v. Sills,* 53 N.J. 86, 248 A.2d 521 (1968).

2. See also the 1976 case of *Commonwealth v. Davis,* 369 Mass. 886, 343 N.E.2d 847, in which the defendant argued that he had a constitutional right to possess a sawed-off shotgun. The Supreme Judicial Court of Massachusetts held: "The Second Amendment to the Constitution of the United States declares: 'A well regulated Militia, being necessary to the security of a free State, the right of the people to keep and bear Arms, shall not be infringed.' This was adopted to quiet the fears of those who thought that the Congressional powers under article I, § 8, clauses 15 and 16, with regard to the State militias might have the effect of enervating or destroying those forces. The amendment is to be read as an assurance that the national government shall not so reduce the militias."

3. See the 1980 U.S. Supreme Court case of *Lewis v. United States,* 445 U.S. 55, 26 CrL 3095, in which Lewis was convicted of possessing a firearm shipped in interstate commerce after being convicted of a Florida felony.

4. Committee Comments (1961) to Article 24, Deadly Weapons, Smith-Hurd Illinois Annotated Statutes, Chap. 38, p. 565.

5. 23 Ill. App. 2d 10, 161 N.E.2d 584 (1959).

6. 59 Cal. Rptr. 265, 251 Cal. App. 2d 22 (1967). California is also one of the states that makes it an offense for an ex-felon to possess a concealable firearm. California Penal Code Section 12021(a), which was originally enacted in 1923, cur-

rently provides in part that: "Any person who has been convicted of a felony under the laws of the United States, of the State of California, or any other state, government, or country, or who is addicted to the use of any narcotic drug, who owns or has in his possession or under his custody or control any pistol, revolver, or other firearm capable of being concealed upon the person, is guilty of a public offense."

A 1975 study shows that the inexpensive, poorly made "Saturday Night Special" continues to be a serious problem in the United States. Of the 219 guns picked up by the Milwaukee Police in a 60-day period in 1975, one-third of them could not be traced, indicating that they may have been purchased illegally or stolen. Almost 70 percent of the guns had barrels so short that they could not be used practically for sport. At least 43 percent were of such low caliber and poor construction that they probably would not be purchased by a sportsman or a collector. Forty percent of the guns were imported and 74 percent of the guns were revolvers. The study was conducted by federal agents with the cooperation of the Milwaukee Police Department.

7. 558 P.2d 1244.

8. 665 P.2d 181.

9. People on Complaint of *Altomari v. Evergood*, 74 N.Y.S.2d 12 (Mag. Ct. 1947).

10. *People v. Tardibuono*, 174 Misc. 305, 20 N.Y.S.2d 633 (1940).

11. 467 A.2d 552, 34 CrL 2163 (Md. App. 1983).

12. 266 Cal. App. 2d 341, 72 Cal. Rptr. 162 (1968).

13. 491 S.W.2d 301.

14. *Davis v. Beason*, 133 U.S. 333, 10 S. Ct. 299, 33 L.Ed. 637 (1890).

15. 310 U.S. 296, 60 S. Ct. 900, 84 L.Ed. 1213 (1940).

16. 267 N.C. 599, 148 S.E.2d 565 (1966).

17. States adopting Sec. 115 of the Uniform Controlled Substance Act could include a provision permitting the exception. See also *United States v. Kuch*, 288 F. Supp. 439 (D.D.C. 1968), in which the Court held that the Neo-American Church was not a religion so as to qualify for the exception. Their solemn motto was "Victory over Horseshit" and their church "catechism" stated: "We have the right to practice our religion, even if we are a bunch of filthy drunken bums."

18. Many civil lawsuits involving cults and sects have occurred throughout the United States. In Santa Ana, California, Robin George, a 23-year-old woman, was awarded $32 million in 1983 against the Hare Krishna sect and their leaders for false imprisonment, intentional emotional distress, libel, and wrongful death of George's father, who died during the search for his daughter. Robin George and her mother alleged that she was kidnapped and brainwashed by the Krishnas. In 1982, a 25-year-old man (Bill Eilers) and his wife were abducted from a parking lot in Minnesota by five religious deprogrammers. His wife was successfully deprogrammed, but Eilers escaped and went back to the Disciples of the Lord Jesus Christ. His wife divorced him and has custody of their child. Eilers sued the deprogrammers for nearly $6 million. The jury awarded Eilers $10,000

in 1984 for his false imprisonment. Both sides claimed victory for the relatively small damage award.

19. Most criminal cases have to do with members of cults, sects, and nontraditional churches. In 1981, a federal grand jury began investigations to determine whether the late John Cardinal Cody of the Chicago Catholic Archdiocese had illegally diverted as much as $1 million in tax-exempt church funds to an old friend.

20. A "viable" fetus is defined by the U.S. Supreme Court in *Colautti v. Franklin*, 439 U.S. 379, 99 S. Ct. 675 (1979) as follows: "In *Roe v. Wade*, the Court defined the term "viability" to signify the stage at which a fetus is "potentially able to live outside the mother's womb, albeit with artificial aid." This is the point at which the State's interest in protecting fetal life becomes sufficiently strong to permit it to "go so far as to proscribe abortion during that period, except when it is necessary to preserve the life or health of the mother." 410 U.S., at 163–164, 93 S. Ct. at 732."

21. The U.S. Supreme Court in *Planned Parenthood of Central Missouri v. Danforth*, 428 U.S. 52, 96 S. Ct. 2831 (1976).

22. An example of an abortion controversy is a U.S. Supreme Court ruling that any state law requiring parental consent for minors to have an abortion must ensure that parents do not have absolute (and possibly arbitrary) veto (443 U.S. 622, 99 S. Ct. 3035 [1979]).

23. In the case of *Connecticut v. Menillo*, 423 U.S. 9, 96 S. Ct. 170 (1975), the U.S. Supreme Court held that a state may prohibit abortions by nonphysicians.

24. 379 U.S. 184, 85 S. Ct. 283 (1964).

25. There are many equal protection of the laws cases in the areas of discrimination that is racial, sexual, employment, educational, etc. Another example in the criminal area is the case of *Jackson v. Indiana*, 406 U.S. 715, 92 S. Ct. 1845 (1972). The Supreme Court held that Jackson, a mentally defective deaf mute who was charged with robbery, was committed to a institution under a more lenient commitment standard but was a more stringent release standard than persons not charged with crimes. This was held to deprive Jackson of equal protection of the laws.

26. 390 U.S. 85, 88 S. Ct. 722 (1968).

Chapter 13: Homicide

1. 23 Corpus Juris Secundum Criminal Law 917.

2. 23A Corpus Juris Secundum Criminal Law 1124.

3. 424 Pa. 331, 227 A.2d 900 (1967).

4. *People v. Manson*, 71 Cal. App. 3d 1, 42, 139 Cal. Rptr. 275, *cert. denied*, 98 S. Ct. 1582 (1978).

5. 33 CrL 1005.

6. In re A.W.S., 182 N.J.Super. 334, 30 CrL 2478.

7. *The Journal of Criminal Law, Criminology and Police Science*, (1974) 60:351.

8. *Matter of Quinlan*, 355 A.2d 647, 656, *cert. denied* 429 U.S. 922.

9. *Swafford v. State*, 421 N.E.2d 596.

10. 366 N.E.2d 744, *cert. denied* 434 U.S. 1039, 98 S. Ct. 777.

11. 195 Cal. Rptr. 484.

12. The "speedy trial" requirement is one reason there are few causation cases. When a suspect is taken into custody for causing serious injury to another person, he (or she) must be taken before a court and charged. This causes the "speedy trial" time to commence running and the person must be tried within that time (100 days in federal courts). If a victim is in critical condition, a knowledgeable defense lawyer is not going to waive "speedy trial" in an effort to get his client to trial on a lesser charge. Criminal homicide can be changed if the victim dies before the case goes to trial. Once the case goes to trial on the lesser charge (or charges), double jeopardy would apply and the defendant cannot be charged with criminal homicide. (See Chapter 7 for "speedy trial" and "double jeopardy" defenses.) Could such a condition be a factor in causing a family to "pull the plug" on a terminal case so that the suspect could be charged with murder?

13. 4 Blackstone Comm. 197 (California Statutes Title 8, Sec. 194 makes the time three years and a day.)

14. *People v. Stevenson,* 331 N.W.2d 143 (Mich. 1982). See also *State v. Hefler,* 299 S.E.2d 456, *affirmed* 34 CrL 2374 (1984), in which the North Carolina court stated: "For the courts to remain judicially oblivious of these advances [in medical science] when considering whether to extend an ancient common law rule would be folly."

15. See *Bloodletters and Badmen: A Narrative Encyclopedia of American Criminals from the Pilgrims to the Present* by Jay Robert Nash (New York: M. Evans & Co., 1974).

16. In a case in which the defendant shot a 15-year-old gasoline service station attendant in the head, neck, and back six times, the Supreme Court of Minnesota held: "Extensive planning and calculated deliberation need not be shown by the prosecution. The requisite 'plan' to commit a first-degree murder can be formulated virtually instantaneously by a killer. . . . Moreover . . . premeditation can be inferred from either the number of gunshots fired into the victim, . . . or the fact that a killer arms himself with a loaded gun in preparation for the commission of a lesser crime." *(State v. Neumann,* 262 N.W.2d 426, 22 CrL 2465 [1978]).

17. 157 U.S. 657, 15 S. Ct. 720.

18. 20 Md. App. 492, 316 A.2d 319.

19. The Supreme Court of Oregon pointed out in *State v. Boone,* 661 P.2d 917 (1983) that "other cases have inferred implied malice, often defined as depravity of mind and reckless and wanton disregard of human life, from the act of driving while intoxicated which causes death. *Jolly v. State,* 395 So.2d 1135 (Ala. Cr. App. 1981); *Hamilton v. Commonwealth,* 560 S.W.2d 539 (Ky. 1978); *Commonwealth v. Taylor,* 461 Pa. 557, 337 A.2d 545 (1975); *Edwards v. State,* 202 Tenn. 393, 304 S.W.2d 500 (1957); *Cockrell v. State,* 135 Tex. Cr. R. 218, 117 S.W.2d 1105 (1938); *State v. Trott,* 190 N.C. 674, 130 S.E. 627 (1925). These cases share many facts in common. While driving under the influence of intoxi-

cants, the defendants drove erratically—speeding, swerving, running red lights, driving on the wrong side of the road. Such erratic driving, coupled with impairment of driving ability caused by intoxication, sufficed to indicate the implied malice necessary for second degree murder convictions."

20. 436 N.E.2d 400.

21. Wisconsin has only one degree of manslaughter, Sec. 940.05 Wisconsin Criminal Code.

22. See the New York Penal Code Sec. 125.20.

23. See "Sentence by Public Opinion?" *Newsweek,* March 5, 1984.

24. For an example of a controversial finding of voluntary manslaughter, see *People v. White,* 172 Cal. Rptr. 612 in Chapter 5. In 1978 Dan White shot San Francisco Mayor George Moscone four times. After killing the mayor, White also killed Supervisor Harvey Milk by shooting him six times. The defense of "diminished capacity" ("Twinkie" defense) was used. Instead of convicting White of two counts of murder, the jury convicted him of voluntary manslaughter, setting off a riot by gays in downtown San Francisco in protest of the finding. In California, voluntary manslaughter was, at that time, a maximum term of four years. After this incident, the maximum term was increased to six years for each count and the defense of "diminished capacity" was abolished in California.

25. See *Whitehead v. State,* 9 Md. App. 7, 262 A.2d 316 (Md. Ct. of App.)

26. 157 U.S. 675, 15 S. Ct. 720 (1895).

27. 76 Cal. Rptr. 391, 452 P.2d 607.

28. 351 Ill. 604, 184 N.E. 894 (1933).

29. 38 Ga. App. 36, 142 S.E. 202 (1928). In this case the deceased used profane and insulting language, with threats to cut the defendant's throat.

30. 381 Pa. 447, 113 A.2d 293 (1955).

31. 360 Mo. 744, 230 S.W.2d 690 (1950).

32. 56 Ill. App. 2d 159, 205 N.E.2d 749 (1965).

33. Texas, New Mexico, and Utah changed this common law ruling by statutes that provided that killings by husbands under these circumstances were justified homicides. Critics of these statutes argued that this permitted an "open shooting season" on paramours if they were caught by husbands in the act of adultery. Women's groups in these states angrily demanded that the statutes either be repealed or amended so as to give wives the same rights. It is reported that all three states have repealed these statutes and probably have gone back to the common law rule.

34. 175 Cal. 45, 164 P. 1121 (1917).

35. 10 Md. App. 630, 272 A.2d 64 (1971).

36. House of Lords, 2 All Eng.R. 801 (1954).

37. 458 A.2d 81.

38. A man was killed playing "Russian roulette" with two other men. The survivors were charged with and convicted of involuntary manslaughter. The court held that the game involved an unreasonable and high degree of risk of death. *Commonwealth v. Atencio,* 345 Mass. 627, 189 N.E.2d 223 (1963).

39. Suicide is now the 10th leading cause of death in the United States, ranking just ahead of criminal homicide. Suicide is recognized as a rising and devastating public health problem. There are hundreds of suicide prevention centers and hot lines in the United States that have been helpful to troubled persons. It is estimated that close to a quarter of a million persons spend some time every year in hospitals and institutions under emergency detention statutes of state mental health laws after attempting suicide or threatening violence.

Chapter 14: Assault, Battery, and Other Crimes Against the Person

1. A few states (including Wisconsin) have not statutorized the common law crime of assault. Disorderly conduct and attempt to commit a battery are substituted for assault in charging.

2. See West's Annotated California Codes, Chap. 9, Sec. 240.

3. Probably all states gave passed statutes that criminalize the conduct of pointing an unloaded gun at a victim who does not know that the gun is unloaded and becomes apprehensive and frightened. The New York crime of "menacing" (Sec. 120.15) by placing "or attempting to place another in fear of imminent serious physical injury" is an example of such criminal statutes.

4. 193 Cal. Rptr. 890, 667 P.2d 694 (1983).

5. See also *United States v. Frizzi*, 491 F.2d 1231 (1st Cir., 1974), in which the defendant spat in the face of a mail carrier and then hit the carrier in the face when he demanded an apology. The Court affirmed the defendant's conviction of assaulting a federal officer in the performance of his duties.

6. 440 A.2d 710 (1982). Other courts cited that have held that, depending on the circumstances, hands alone may be found to be a deadly weapon are *People v. Zankich*, 189 Cal. App. 2d 54, 69–70, 11 Cal. Rptr. 115, 124–25 (1961); *Thomas v. State*, 237 Ga. 690, 691–92, 229 S.E.2d 458, 460 (1976); *State v. Heinz*, 223 Iowa 1241, 1259, 275 N.W. 10, 21 (1937); *Vogg v. Commonwealth*, 308 Ky. 212, 214 S.W.2d 86 (1948); *State v. Born*, 280 Minn. 306, 307–08, 159 N.W.2d 283, 284–85 (1968); *Pulliam v. State*, 298 So.2d 711 (Miss. 1974); *State v. Gardner*, 522 S.W.2d 323 (Mo. Ct. App. 1975); *Pettigrew v. State*, 430 P.2d 808, 812–13 (Okla. 1967); see generally, 33 A.L.R.3d 922 (1970); note, *The Fist or Teeth as a Dangerous Weapon*, 7 La. L. Rev. 584 (1947).

7. 91 Misc. 2d 724, 398 N.Y.S.2d 821.

8. Chap. 38, para. 12–3(a)(2).

9. 453 N.E.2d 842. The Illinois Appellate Court cited the following: "Other instances of conduct held to be simple battery based solely on insulting or provoking physical contact [include]: *People v. Hamilton*, . . . 401 N.E.2d 318 . . . (where defendant reached around the female complainant and placed his hand over her mouth); *People v. Siler*, . . . 406 N.E.2d 891 . . . (where defendant lifted up complainant's dress during a confrontation having sexual overtones).

10. See Chapter 18 for further material on sexual assault and rape.

11. Also see Chapter 6 on defenses to the use of force.

12. *Ingraham v. Wright*, 430 U.S. 651, 97 S. Ct. 1401 (1977). See also *People v. Donn Decaro*, 17 Ill. App. 3d 553, 308 N.E.2d 196.

13. Until recently all battery statutes in Wisconsin required a showing that the "bodily harm" was done without the consent of the victim. Because battered spouses and other victims would sometimes testify that beatings were done with their consent, it became necessary to take the consent element out of the aggravated battery statute in Wisconsin. The "consent" requirement in the Wisconsin misdemeanor battery (sec. 940.19[1]) continues to cause occasional cases to be dropped.

14. *State v. Boone*, 661 P.2d 917 (1983).

15. Vernon's Penal Code of the State of Texas Annotated.

16. Oregon Stat. 163.175(1)(c).

17. 661 P.2d 917 (1983).

18. 97 S. Ct. 481 (1977).

19. See *People v. Daniels*, 71 Cal. 2d 1119, 80 Cal. Rptr. 897, 459 P.2d 225 (1969).

20. See *People v. Williams*, 2 Cal. 3d 894, 88 Cal. Rptr. 208, 471 P.2d 1008 (1970).

21. 409 So.2d 1031.

22. 466 A.2d 955.

23. Sec. 940.305 Wisconsin "taking hostage" felony.

24. Estimates vary that from 25,000 to 100,000 children are victims of child snatching. See the article on parental kidnapping in *The Journal of Criminal Law & Criminology* 73 (1982) 1176.

25. Four months after her husband kidnapped her child, a Colorado woman learned that her husband had appeared on TV on the *Phil Donahue Show*. The show provided baby-sitting service and when the mother of the child requested information and help from the show, the TV company stood on their pledge of confidentiality to a news source. In a civil lawsuit against the TV company for aiding and abetting parental kidnapping, the mother of the child was awarded $5.9 million. The father was arrested in Tulsa, Oklahoma, on a fugitive warrant in 1983, and the child was returned to the mother.

26. 18 U.S.C. Sec. 1201.

27. 18 U.S.C. Sec. 1073.

28. In October, 1984, the President of the United States signed the "Missing Children's Assistance Act" (36 CrL 3063), which provides for the operation of a national toll-free telephone line for exchanging information on missing children through the national resource center and clearing house. The administrator of the program will "facilitate effective coordination among all federally funded programs relating to missing children." Section 406(a) of the Act provides that: "The Administrator is authorized to make grants to and enter into contracts with public agencies or nonprofit private organizations, or combinations thereof, for research, demonstration projects, or service programs designed—

"(1) to educate parents, children, and community agencies and organizations in ways to prevent the abduction and sexual exploitation of children;

"(2) to provide information to assist in the locating and return of missing children;

"(3) to aid communities in the collection of materials which would be useful to parents in assisting others in the identification of missing children;

"(4) to increase knowledge of and develop effective treatment pertaining to the psychological consequences, on both parents and children . . ."

Chapter 15: Theft, Robbery, and Burglary

1. 22A Corpus Juris Secundum (Criminal Law) section 597.

2. 22A Corpus Juris Secundum (Criminal Law) section 597.

3. *Transmerica Ins. Co. v. Long,* 318 F. Supp. 156 (D.C. Pa.1970).

4. "Working Papers of the National Commission on Reform of Federal Criminal Laws," 2:913.

5. 499 S.W.2d 236 (Mo. App. 1973).

6. 457 U.S. 537, 102 S. Ct. 2579.

7. Illinois Rev. Stat. Ch. 38 Sec. 15–1.

8. Minnesota Statut. Ann. Sec. 609.25.

9. 365 F.2d 389 (2nd Cir. 1966).

10. 538 F.2d 972 (3rd Cir. 1976).

11. Also see the 1978 case of *United States v. Lambert,* 466 F. Supp. 890, 22 CrL 2478, in which the defendant was convicted of the theft of computer-stored information that listed the names of informants and the status of government drug investigations conducted by the Drug Enforcement Administration.

12. 433 N.E.2d 68.

13. 459 N.E.2d 61, 34 CrL 2390.

14. *People v. Weg,* 450 NYS2d 957, 31 CrL 2266 (1982).

15. 22 N.Y.2d 443, 293 N.Y.S.2d 96, 239 N.E.2d 727 (1968).

16. 342 U.S. 246, 72 S. Ct. 240 (1952). This case is also discussed in Chapter 7.

17. 25 Mich. App. 371, 181 N.W.2d 551 (1970). In the 1983 case of *United States v. Perez,* 707 F.2d 359, (8th Cir. 1983) the defendant stole an exhibit of the government that was being used in a criminal case against him and others for the distribution of cocaine. The exhibit consisted of 15 hundred-dollar bills. The Court of Appeals affirmed the conviction, holding: "We have little difficulty holding that here the United States had sufficient possession and control, if not actual title, to the property." The property had been seized when the defendants were arrested.

18. *People v. Brooks,* 154 Cal. App. 2d 631, 316 P.2d 435 (1957).

19. *People v. Cobb,* 45 Cal. 2d 158, 287 P.2d 752 (1955).

20. See 77 C.J.S., Robbery, P. 464, Sec. 22 and the American Law Reports. In the 1980 case of *People v. Fain,* 193 Cal. Rptr. 890, 667 P.2d 694, the defendant recovered $35

that he had lost in a poker game by pointing a gun at the other players. Instead of being convicted of three counts of armed robbery, the defendant was convicted of assault with a deadly weapon. The California Supreme Court ordered the six-year sentence to run consecutively with a Nevada life sentence for second-degree murder.

21. 49 Wis. 2d 105, 181 N.W.2d 383 (1970).

22. 25 CrL 2037.

23. Many states also make "concealing identity" while committing a crime such as robbery conduct for which the degree of the crime and the penalty may be increased. The Supreme Court of Wisconsin has held that where one robber concealed his identity and the other did not, the second robber could be a party to the crime of "concealing identity". *Vogel v. State,* 96 Wis. 2d 372, 291 N.W.2d 850 [1980]).

24. Volume IX, No. 27, July 1, 1968.

25. 436 So.2d 244. See also *State v. Mirault,* 457 A.2d 455 (1983), in which a homeowner came home to find her house being burglarized. When a police officer arrived the defendant jumped on the officer and fought with him until other officers arrived. The New Jersey Supreme Court affirmed the convictions of burglary and robbery but merged the aggravated assault conviction into the robbery conviction.

26. 667 P.2d 890.

27. 283 N.E. 840 (Mass. 1972).

28. 397 U.S. 436, 90 S. Ct. 1189 (1970).

29. 648 P.2d 197.

30. See *State v. Canty,* 469 F.2d 114 (D.C. Cir. 1972) (holding that the robbery of each of four bank tellers did not constitute a separate "taking" within the meaning of the federal bank robbery statute and therefore defendant could not be convicted on four counts of robbery based on a single incident); *People v. Nicks,* 23 Ill. App. 3d 435, 319 N.E.2d 531 (1974) (holding that where the defendant robbed a store owner and two cashiers, separately, but all in one transaction, he could only be convicted of one count of armed robbery); *Rogers v. State,* 396 N.E.2d 348 (Ind. 1979) (holding that the defendant was improperly convicted on two counts of robbery of a grocery store despite the fact that money was taken from two employees); *Williams v. State,* 395 N.E.2d 239 (Ind. 1979) (holding that an individual who robs a business establishment, taking that business's money from four employees, can be convicted of only one count of armed robbery); *State v. Potter,* 285 N.C. 238, 204 S.E.2d 649 (1974) (holding that when the lives of all employees in a store are threatened and endangered by the use or threatened use of a firearm incident to the theft of their employer's money or property, a single robbery is committed); *State v. Whipple,* 156 N.J.Super. 46, 383 A.2d 445 (1978) (holding that the defendant's robbery of a liquor store and its owner constituted but a single transaction, which could not be fractionalized to enhance the defendant's punishment for a single crime). See also the 1980 case of *State v. Perkins,* 45 Ore. App. 91, 607 P.2d 1202.

31. 431 N.E.2d 928.

32. Florida's burglary statutes, adopted in 1975, provide that "burglary means entering or remaining in a structure or conveyance with the intent to commit an offense therein,

unless the premises are at the time open to the public or the defendant is licensed or invited to enter or remain."

33. The New Mexico Court of Appeals held in the 1976 case of *State v. Tixier,* 89 N.M. 297, 551 P.2d 987, that: "A one-half inch penetration into the building is sufficient. Any penetration, however slight of the interior space is sufficient. The fact that the penetration is by an instrument is also sufficient. 2 Wharton's Criminal Law and Procedure (1957) § 421; Clark and Marshall, Crimes, 6th ed., § 13.04."

34. 458 N.Y.S.2d 429.

35. 94 S. Ct. 1234 (1974).

36. See note 33.

37. 84 Wis. 2d 621, 267 N.W.2d 295 (1978).

38. *Woods v. State,* 186 Miss. 463, 191 So. 283 (1939).

39. 274 Cal. App. 2d 912, 79 Cal. Rptr. 650 (1969).

40. *People v. Gauze,* 15 Cal. 3d 709, 125 Cal. Rptr. 773, 542 P.2d 1365 (1975).

41. 308 N.E.2d 724 (Ind. App. 1974).

42. 28 Ill. 2d 441, 192 N.E.2d 864 (1963).

43. 225 Pa. Super. 311, 303 A.2d 528 (1973).

44. *People v. Urbana,* 18 Ill. 2d 81, 163 N.E.2d 511 (1959).

45. 88 Nev. 385, 498 P.2d 373 (1972).

46. 41 Wis. 2d 552, 164 N.W.2d 505 (1971).

47. 69 Ill. App. 2d 50, 216 N.E.2d 510 (1966).

Chapter 16: Shoplifting and Other Crimes Against Businesses and Organizations

1. 438 N.Y.S.2d 242.

2. 402 N.Y.S.2d 546 (1978).

3. 438 N.Y.S. at 246. See also the case of *Berry v. State,* in Chapter 15, in which the Supreme Court of Wisconsin affirmed the conviction of the defendant for attempted theft when the defendant was apprehended for shoplifting before he left a men's clothing store.

4. 402 N.Y.S.2d at 548.

5. *Carroll v. United States,* 267 U.S. 132, 45 S. Ct. 280 (1925).

6. *Cobylyn v. Kennedy's Inc.,* 268 N.E.2d 860 (1971).

7. 666 F.2d 422 (9th Cir. 1982).

8. 701 F.2d 1086 (4th Cir. 1983).

9. *Warren v. Commonwealth,* 247 S.E.2d 692 (1978).

10. 249 Ind. 446, 233 N.E.2d 168.

11. 458 U.S. 279, 102 S. Ct. 3088 (1982).

12. 602 F.2d 1215, (5th Cir. 1979) *review denied,* 26 CrL 4209 (1980).

13. Committee on Government Operations, "Staff Study of Computer Security in Federal Programs" (Washington, D.C.: Government Printing Office, 1977).

14. Committee Report, note 13 and LEAA Newsletter, January 1980.

15. Committee Report, note 13.

16. The Equity Funding fraud of the late 1970s, which resulted in losses of over $100 million, was done with the use of computers. Also in a computer fraud, Jack Benny, Liza Minnelli and another man lost $925,000.

17. 538 F.2d 972.

18. 22 CrL 2478.

Chapter 17: Fraud and Other Property Crimes

1. "Bait and switch" schemes usually consist of an attractive bargain that is offered at an eye-catching low price. The bargain is the "bait" to lure customers into the store. The "switch" to get the customer to buy a higher-priced item is done by knocking the quality of the advertised item, or stating that it has been sold out or that it is not available on the premises.

2. Vol. 10, no. 39 (1969).

3. 312 N.W.2d 251 (1981).

4. See note 3. In the 1961 case of *Milanovich v. United States,* 365 U.S. 551, 81 S. Ct. 728, the U.S. Supreme Court held that a person could not be convicted of both stealing and receiving the same property. However a thief can be punished for either stealing or receiving (see *United States v. Trzcinski,* 553 F.2d 851 (3d Cir. 1976), *cert. denied,* 431 U.S. 919 [1977]).

5. Task Force Report, "Crime and Its Impact—An Assessment," p. 99.

6. The English refer to this offense as "Going Equipped for Stealing." See *Moriarty's Police Law,* 21st ed. (London: Butterworths).

7. See 33 A.L.R.3d 798 (1970).

8. Arson for "indirect" profit is a more difficult crime to solve, as there is often no apparent connection between the fire setter and the target. The "indirect" profit could be (a) a business person who burns out a competitor to increase his own business; (b) tenants seeking to break a lease, or landlords seeking to get the tenant out, collect insurance, and use the property for other or more profitable use; (c) neighbors who burn a property to prevent an occupancy that might decrease property value; (d) prospsective buyers who want the land but not the buildings.

9. In some instances, pyromanics are detected by studying photos of crowds who go to fires. If the same face shows up repeatedly at a series of fires, this might indicate a person committing arson because of emotional or mental problems. The pyromaniac sometimes remains at the scene after starting a fire, and there have been situations in which pyromaniacs have been hailed as heroes for saving lives at fires they started.

10. If the completed crime of arson cannot be proved beyond a reasonable doubt, the state may then consider charging attempt to commit arson (or in an appropriate situation, conspiracy to commit arson).

11. See the case of *Hughes v. State,* 6 Md. App. 389, 251 A.2d 373 (1969) in which the court pointed out that mere presence of the accused at the scene of a fire is not proof beyond reasonable doubt that the fire was willfully and maliciously set. In *Hughes v. State,* a fire chief testified that he could not determine the cause of the fire. The court reversed the defendant's conviction, holding that the evidence was legally insufficient to establish the *corpus delicti* of the crime of arson.

12. 436 U.S. 499, 98 S. Ct. 1942 (1978).

13. See Chapter 11 for additional trespass cases and problems.

Chapter 18: Rape and Related Sex Crimes

1. Supreme Court of Oregon in *State v. Bashaw,* 672 P.2d 48 (1983).

2. An admitted prostitute may be the victim of a rape. In the case of *People v. Gonzales,* 24 CrL 2194 (N.Y. Crim. Ct. 1978), the defendant did not pay the agreed fee for sexual services but obtained them at the point of a revolver. In affirming the conviction of the defendant, the court held: "It is the conclusion of this court that sexual intercourse with an admitted prostitute accomplished, if proven, by evidence establishing guilt beyond a reasonable doubt, by the coercive force of the weapon described constitutes rape in the third degree."

3. See 131 A.L.R. 1322, 84 A.L.R.2d 1017.

4. 462 S.W.2d 677 (Mo. 1971).

5. 619 S.W.2d 513 (1981).

6. See e.g., *McDonald v. State,* 225 Ark. 38, 279 S.W.2d 44 (1955); *Wilson v. State,* 10 Terry 37, 49 Del. 37, 109 A.2d 381 (1954), *cert. denied,* 348 U.S. 983, 75 S. Ct. 574, 99 L.Ed. 765 (1955); *Commonwealth v. Goldenberg,* 338 Mass. 377, 155 N.E.2d 187, *cert. denied,* 359 U.S. 1001, 79 S. Ct. 1143, 3 L.Ed.2d 1032 (1959); *State v. Catron,* 317 Mo. 894, 296 S.W. 141 (1927); *State v. Carter,* 265 N.C. 626, 144 S.E.2d 826 (1965); *Commonwealth v. Stephens,* 143 Pa. Super. 394, 17 A.2d 919 (1941); R. Perkins, *Perkins on Criminal Law,* 160–161 (2d ed., 1969).

7. *People v. Hunt,* 72 Cal. App. 3d at 194, 139 Cal. Rptr. at 676.

8. *State v. Rusk,* 424 A.2d 720 (1981).

9. See *State v. Reinhold,* 123 Ariz. 50, 597 P.2d 532 (1979); *People v. Hunt,* 72 Cal. App. 3d 190, 139 Cal. Rptr. 675 (1977); *State v. Dill,* 3 Terry 533, 42 Del. 533, 40 A.2d 443 (1944); *Arnold v. United States,* 358 A.2d 335 (D.C. App. 1976); *Doyle v. State,* 39 Fla. 155, 22 So. 272 (1897); *Curtis v. State,* 236 Ga. 362, 223 S.E.2d 721 (1976); *People v. Murphy,* 124 Ill. App. 2d 71, 260 N.E.2d 386 (1970); *Carroll v. State,* 263 Ind. 86, 324 N.E.2d 809 (1975); *Fields v. State,* 293 So.2d 430 (Miss. 1974); *State v. Beck,* 368 S.W.2d 490 (Mo. 1963); *Cascio v. State,* 147 Neb. 1075, 25 N.W.2d 897 (1947); *State v. Burns,* 287 N.C. 102, 214 S.E.2d 56, *cert. denied,* 423 U.S. 933, 96 S. Ct. 288, 46 L.Ed.2d 264 (1975); *State v. Verdone,* 114 R.I. 613, 337 A.2d 804 (1975); *Brown v. State,* 576 S.W.2d 820 (Tex. Cr. App. 1979); *Jones v. Com.,* 219 Va. 983, 252 S.E.2d 370 (1979); *State v. Baker,* 30 Wash. 2d 601, 192 P.2d 839 (1948); *Brown v. State,* 581 P.2d 189 (Wyo. 1978).

Some jurisdictions do not require that the victim's fear be reasonably grounded. See *Struggs v. State,* 372 So.2d 49 (Ala. Cr. App.), *cert. denied,* 444 U.S. 936, 100 S. Ct. 285, 62 L.Ed.2d 195 (1979); *Kirby v. State,* 5 Ala. App. 128, 59 So. 374 (1912); *Dinkens v. State,* 92 Nev. 74, 546 P.2d 228 (1976); *citing Hazel v. State, supra; State v. Herfel,* 49 Wis. 2d 513, 182 N.W.2d 232 (1971). See also *Salsman v. Com.,* 565 S.W.2d 638 (Ky. App. 1978); *State v. Havens,* 264 N.W.2d 918 (S.D. 1978).

10. However, "if as a result of self-induced intoxication, the defendant believed that the female was consenting, that belief would not thereby become either reasonable or in good faith." (*California Jury Instruction* 4.20).

11. *People v. Guthreau,* 162 Cal. Rptr. 376 (Cal. Ct. App. 1980).

12. 453 N.E.2d 842. See also the case of *Florida v. Meyers,* 35 CrL 4022 (1984), in which the defendant was convicted of sexual battery. The conviction was affirmed by the U.S. Supreme Court.

13. 450 U.S. 464, 101 S. Ct. 1200.

14. See Section D in this Chapter on "Statutory Rape" where there is further material on the U.S. Supreme Court, case of *Michael M. v. Superior Court of Sonoma County (California).*

15. 35 CrL 2064.

16. 444 U.S. 394, 100 S. Ct. 624 (1980).

17. ___ A.2d ___, 35 CrL 2070 (D.C. Ct. App. 1984).

18. 450 U.S. 464, 101 S. Ct. 1200.

19. 35 CrL 2071.

20. 458 U.S. 747, 102 S. Ct. 3348.

21. 659 S.W.2d 201.

Chapter 19: Prostitution and Related Crimes

1. HRS Commentary Sec. 721–1200.

2. The National Advisory Committee on Criminal Justice Standards and Goals states, on p. 242 of its report on Organized Crime: "Decriminalization is offered as a serious alternative to prostitution. . . . Proponents of decriminalizing all aspects of the trade believe that prostitution should be looked on as just another occupation or business, and that any laws or regulations deprive women of their fundamental constitutional rights. Legalization proposals would perpetuate their deprivation, because they generally restrict the women to certain areas and otherwise regulate them. Another argument is that legalization proposals requiring prostitutes to work in licensed brothels simply substitute slavery to a pimp with slavery to the State government, legislators, vice profiteers, and the managers of the house."

3. 671 P.2d 1351.

4. See pp. 225–226.

5. 381 A.2d 38 (1977).

Although the defendant in the *Alveario* case was not convicted of solicitation for prostitution, he could be charged with other offenses for which the likelihood of conviction would be greater. Take, for example, Sec. 712–1204, promoting prostitution in the third degree of the Hawaiian Penal Code. The statute prohibits "knowingly advanc[ing] or profit[ing] from prostitution."

6. 622 P.2d 764.

7. 425 U.S. 901, 96 S. Ct. 1489, *aff'g,* 403 F. Supp. 1199.

8. In addition to statutes forbidding abusive, harassing, or obscene telephone calls, federal statutes also forbid other abusive use of the telephone, such as the Consumer Credit Protection Act (Pub. Law 95—109 Stat. 877), which prohibits debt collectors from "placing telephone calls without meaningful disclosure of the caller's identity"; from "engaging any person in telephone conversation repeatedly or continuously with intent, to annoy, abuse, or harass any person at the called number"; and from "us[ing] obscene or profane language or language the natural consequence of which is to abuse the hearer or reader."

9. 396 N.E.2d 22, 27 CrL 4055.

10. 594 P.2d 1250.

Chapter 20: Organized Crime and Gambling

1. See Report of the Task Force on Organized Crime, p. 8.

2. Ibid., p. 6.

3. Criminal Justice Standards and Goals Task Force Report, p. 23.

4. "The Mob Taps Out in Vegas," *Newsweek,* 24 October 1983.

5. See the article entitled "Chicago's Mob Figures Run Scared—To Death," *Chicago Tribune,* 7 August 1983.

6. Skimming is the illegal practice of taking some of the proceeds from casino gambling before it is counted for state and federal tax purposes.

Chapter 21: The Crime of Contempt and Other Crimes Against Government

1. 419 U.S. 449, 95 S. Ct. 584 (1975). However, in the *Maness* case, the U.S. Supreme Court held that a lawyer is not subject to the penalty of contempt for advising his client, during a civil trial, to refuse to produce material that would incriminate him. The Court held: "The privilege against compelled self-incrimination would be drained of its meaning if counsel, being lawfully present, as here, could be penalized for advising his client in good faith to assert it."

2. See *United States v. North,* 27 CrL 2303 (1980), and *Shillitani v. United States,* 384 U.S. 364 (1966).

3. U.S. 194, 88 S. Ct. 1477 (1968).

4. New Jersey courts have held that "before a judge makes a contempt determination the accused should be permitted to speak." 357 A.2d at 276. In the case of *In re Logan Jr.,* 52 N.J. 475, 246 A.2d 441 (1968), the Court held:

"The pronouncement of guilt before according that opportunity places the defendant at the disadvantage of trying to persuade a mind apparently already made up, and also puts the judge in the possibly embarrassing position of reversing himself if such persuasion results."

5. 466 Pa. 506, 353 A.2d 806 (1976).

6. 41 Ill. App. 3d 690, 354 N.E.2d 648 (1976).

7. 400 U.S. 455, 91 S. Ct. 499 (1971).

8. 185 N.W.2d 705 (Iowa 1971).

9. 397 U.S. 337, 90 S. Ct. 1057 (1970).

10. 415 U.S. 697, 94 S. Ct. 1228, 14 CrL 4237 (1974).

11. In a dissenting opinion, Justice William H. Rehnquist suggests "a flat rule, analogous to the hoary doctrine of the law of torts that every dog is entitled to one bite, to the effect that every witness is entitled to one free contumacious or other impermissible remark.

12. *Mapp v. Ohio,* 367 U.S. 643, 81 S. Ct. 1684 (1961).

13. 277 U.S. 438, 48 S. Ct. 564 (1928).

14. In 1968, the President's Commission on Crime noted that perjury has always been widespread and that there must be more effective deterrents against perjury to ensure the integrity of trials. Another writer commented that few crimes "except fornication are more prevalent or carried off with greater impunity." See "Perjury: The Forgotten Offense," *The Journal of Criminal Law & Criminology* 65 (1974).

15. Some of the Watergate defendants were charged with and convicted of subornation of perjury.

16. Court in *United States v. Stuard,* 566 F.2d 1, 22 CrL 2337 (6th Cir. 1977), quoting *Neal v. United States,* 102 F.2d 643 (8th Cir. 1939).

17. The bribery investigation of the Chicago courts (Operation Greylord) in 1984 resulted in 17 persons (including judges) being charged with bribery, mail fraud, racketeering, obstruction of justice, etc.

18. 544 F.2d 730, 20 CrL 2173.

Table of Cases

Index